Pathways to Successful Transition for Youth with Disabilities

A Developmental Process

Second Edition

Carol A. Kochhar-Bryant
The George Washington University
Washington, DC

Gary Greene
California State University, Long Beach

Merrill
is an imprint of

PEARSON

Upper Saddle River, New Jersey
Columbus, Ohio

D1361787

Library of Congress Cataloging-in-Publication Data

Kochhar-Bryant, Carol A.
  Pathways to successful transition for youth with disabilities : a developmental process / Carol A.
Kochhar-Bryant, Gary Greene.—2nd ed.
      p. cm.
  Earlier ed. entered under Gary Greene.
  Includes bibliographical references and index.
  ISBN-13: 978-0-13-205086-9
  ISBN-10:   0-13-205086-2
  1. Youth with disabilities—Education—United States.   2. Youth with disabilities—Services
for—United States.   I. Greene, Gary.   II. Greene, Gary. Pathways to successful transition for
youth with disabilities.   III. Title.
  LC4031.G68 2009
  371.904—dc22   2008011823

Vice President and Executive Publisher: Jeffery W. Johnston
Executive Editor: Ann Castel Davis
Senior Managing Editor: Pamela D. Bennett
Editorial Assistant: Penny Burleson
Production Editor: Sheryl Glicker Langner
Production Coordination: Satishna Gokuldas
Design Coordinator: Diane C. Lorenzo

Cover Designer: Aaron Dixon
Cover Art: Super Stock
Photo Coordinator: Sandy Schaefer
Production Manager: Laura Messerly
Director of Marketing: Quinn Perkson
Marketing Manager: Erica DeLuca
Marketing Coordinator: Brian Mounts

This book was set in Garamond Book by TexTech International. It was printed and bound by R. R. Donnelley & Sons
Company. The cover was printed by R. R. Donnelley & Sons Company.

Chapter Opening Photo Credits: Laima Druskis/PH College, pp. 2, 196; Anthony Magnacca/Merrill, pp. 28, 264,
294; Martial Colomb/Getty Images, Inc.–Photodisc, p. 66; Stan Wakefield/PH College, p. 106; Scott Cunningham/
Merrill, pp. 162, 236; Robert Pham/PH College, p. 326; Anne Vega/Merrill, p. 372; Amy Etra/Jupiter Images/Picture-
Quest, p. 394; ©Bob Daemmrich/PhotoEdit, p. 426; Barbara Schwartz/Merrill, p. 460.

Pearson Education Ltd., London
Pearson Education Singapore, Pte. Ltd.
Pearson Education Canada, Inc.
Pearson Education—Japan
Pearson Education Australia PTY, Limited

Pearson Education North Asia, Ltd., Hong Kong
Pearson Educación de Mexico, S.A. de C.V.
Pearson Education Malaysia, Pte. Ltd.
Pearson Education Upper Saddle River, New Jersey

Merrill
is an imprint of

**This book is not for sale or
distribution in the U.S.A. or Canada**

10 9 8 7 6 5 4 3 2 1
ISBN 13: 978-0-13-205086-9
ISBN 10:   0-13-205086-2

Dedication

This book is dedicated to my students who have graduated with masters and doctoral degrees and who are exercising their leadership every day to build capacity for transition services for youth at local, state, and national levels. Their impact on the field and on youth with disabilities is the true measure of our work. To my husband John, my anchor and inspiration, this work would not have been possible without his extraordinary patience, encouragement and humor. To my daughter Anjali, becoming a powerful teacher in her own right, this book is dedicated to her maturity, discipline, wisdom beyond her years, and her dedication to her young students. And finally, to my son, Shawn, who is navigating the difficult transition passage, gradually gaining independence, I dedicate this work to his long-fought achievements.

—Carol A. Kochhar-Bryant

This book is dedicated to the numerous individuals whom I have had the honor and privilege to train as special educators. I hope I have had an impact upon you, the students you teach, the schools in which they learn, and the families you serve. I also wish to dedicate this book to my best friends, Skipper Arthur Carillo "The Ballplayer" and Paul Snyder. These two individuals, more than anyone I know, possess the spirit to inspire persons with disabilities to achieve a quality adult life. This book is further dedicated to my late wife Corinne who, in the most trying of life's circumstances, continued giving to others, rarely taking for herself. Finally, this book is dedicated to my children, Charise and Nathan, and my new bride, Linda, and stepdaughter, Serah, all of whom have given me enthusiasm for life again and hope for a wonderful future!

—Gary Greene

Preface

Transition is not just a fad. It is not a program or a project that has a beginning and an end. It is a vision and a goal that is linked to a greater effort to advance a democratic and civilized society. Like the idea of "democracy" it embodies ideals and goals that are continually reached for, though possibly never perfectly achieved.

Career development and transition services have become not only a respected field of study, but also a field that is rapidly gaining national attention. The concept and processes of "transition" are still emerging, and states struggle to balance the requirements of law, the needs of students for long-range planning, and the constraints of local resources. Despite the tensions, transition has come to be understood and defined as a systematic set of interventions that can make the difference in successfully moving from secondary schooling to the postsecondary world or long-term struggle to adjust to adult life. Educators and policy makers have come to view the success of an individual's transition from school to postsecondary life as a measure of the effectiveness of our educational system and of the investment this nation is making in it. A great deal more research and development must be conducted by creative professionals to continue to advance our knowledge and our practice in the field of career development and transition.

As we approach the second decade of the 21st century, the journey toward achieving improved transition outcomes for our nation's youth is just beginning. This is an era of great experimentation in education and transition planning that will profoundly affect the lives of youth with disabilities. Continuing challenges remain in the nation's efforts to improve outcomes for youth with disabilities as they transition from schooling to adult independence. Under the Individuals with Disabilities Education Improvement Act (referred to as IDEA) of 2004, states are required to have in effect policies and procedures that demonstrate that they have established a goal of providing full educational opportunity to all children with disabilities, aged birth through 21. The Individuals with Disabilities Education Act protects both a student's right to access to the general education curriculum *and* to individualized education services, including transition. Transition services are essential for providing full educational opportunity.

➡ WHY WAS THIS BOOK WRITTEN?

Numerous publications in the form of books, pamphlets, reports, and articles exist on the topic of transition processes and services for youth and adults with disabilities. What would motivate anyone to write another textbook on this subject? We have developed and taught graduate level courses on transition for over 25 years, using countless textbooks and journal articles, and discussed textbook content needs with students and colleagues from a variety of disciplines. We concluded that several emerging issues and content areas have not been addressed adequately in primary texts on the subject.

First, in implementing transition services for special learners, the general education teacher is moving to center stage. Though there are special education consultants, team teachers, and teacher aides, the responsibility for successful transition for students with disabilities also falls upon the shoulders of the general education teacher. As teachers restructure their classrooms to include special learner populations, the successful transition of each student depends increasingly upon what happens in middle and secondary general education classrooms and in community-based experiences.

Second, the transition of youth from schooling to postsecondary and adult life requires much more than cooperation among school and community agencies. Rather, a comprehensive reenvisioning of our educational and employment preparation systems is needed to better support youth with disabilities in the crucial transition stages.

Third, in schools everywhere, growing populations of students with academic and social learning needs are adding to the challenge of teaching and helping youth with disabilities prepare for responsible adulthood. Educators today are expected to develop educational programs that can serve a diverse population of learners, including those with disabilities, those at risk for school failure, former school dropouts, students with limited English proficiency, teen parents, and many others. In some school systems today, these "special" populations represent a majority of the student population.

Fourth, professionals who desire to contribute to improved career development and transition outcomes for youth with disabilities must acquire a higher level of sensitivity to and knowledge about the needs of diverse ethnic and cultural groups and to the needs of various disability populations. There is a growing recognition that transition services are shaped by the needs and context of different cultural and socio-economic realities and goals. There is a need for sensitivity to and conceptual understanding of how cultural orientation affects attitudes toward work and careers.

Fifth, in an inclusive educational system, practitioners hold as a highest principle the belief in options, choices, and the self-determination of youth to participate in charting their own life courses and choosing the pathways to their destination. Self-determined individuals are those who are actively engaged in the personal and career decision-making process, connecting present educational experiences with future goals and visions. For practitioners involved in assisting youth with transition, there is a need to clearly link self-determination concepts, career assessment, and individual transition planning.

Sixth, teachers and transition practitioners require an understanding of the history of transition services and the federal and state laws that provide authority and guidance to practice. They know that special education laws are rooted in civil rights legislation designed to protect access, participation, and progress in education and can apply these principles to transition services. Furthermore, they are aware of significant court decisions that eliminate discrimination and bias and entitle all students to a free, appropriate public education in the least restrictive environment.

Finally, we have conducted research in the field of special education and transition services for more than 25 years. During this period we have seen great advances among educators and policy makers toward understanding the important role of career development and transition in the development of youths with disabilities. The chapters included in this book have been shaped by our direct experiences in public schools, collaboration with a variety of community agencies, lectures and writing over the past two decades, as well as the constant flow of questions posed by students and practitioners.

We believe that educators and researchers have an obligation to effectively translate research into practice and that this can be accomplished in a readable text that provides useful material for practitioners and policy makers. In any research endeavor, however, facts are collected, hypotheses formed, preconceptions challenged, and new theories constructed and tested. Because the field of transition is relatively new, facts are scarce and conclusions are often more speculative than those in more established fields of study.

Our goal is to provide the reader with an understanding of the possibilities and potential of transition practices, as well as their philosophical and legal foundations. This book is based on the assumption that the goals of public education are most likely to be achieved for youth with disabilities (and indeed for all youth) when

1. all students learn, play, and grow together, learning from each other as well as from teachers;
2. students are intentionally supported in preparing for transition from middle school, to secondary, and to postsecondary services and adult independence;
3. schools integrate transition goals and activities into each student's curriculum and individualized education program; and,
4. students are actively engaged in planning for their postsecondary future.

This book includes models for transition services for populations of students with mild, moderate, and severe disabilities, with a proportional focus on promising and best practices for the largest group of students with disabilities, those who have mild disabilities. It will discuss the transition process as well as new frontiers for successful practices today.

➡ A PATHWAYS APPROACH

The 21st century heralds an era of great experimentation in education and employment preparation that will profoundly affect the lives of youth with disabilities. Although federal law promotes access to the general education curriculum, it also preserves schools' obligation to individualize education programming and supports. This means options for students with different levels of needs. Therefore, transition services are clustered into *pathways or service patterns* that are arranged to meet the needs of students with different long-term goals and which vary by level of support, type and emphasis of curriculum, type of assessments, and expected postschool placement and service needs. *Such patterns or pathways provide an organized way for schools, families, and students to make decisions about the kinds of transition services needed in relation to the student's individual disability, abilities, and expected graduation goal. A pathways approach also provides a framework for examining student needs and goals early in their educational program, long before graduation is upon them, and developing a course of preparation to achieve those goals.*

This book examines the processes of career development and transition, synthesizing what we know about effective practices to assist youth with disabilities in their passage. We hope that it provides useful and practical information and tools for professionals and advocates, seeking to improve upon current transition practices. This book is written for our college and university colleagues and their students at the undergraduate and graduate levels who are studying the topic of transition.

This book is also designed to directly aid college level instruction and student conceptual learning by including case examples and activities for discussion, ideas for field-based internships, and activities for leadership and action research. The book relies heavily on case examples to convey ideas and concepts and to provide concrete illustrations of transition practices that serve as a window on real world situations. Case examples help make the unfamiliar familiar and give readers a common language about transition services and planning. They provide narratives that serve as a basis for class discussion and challenge students to apply the concepts they have learned in the chapters and in real-life situations. Case examples are also designed to engage students and to assess whether they have mastered the material in the chapters well enough to apply it. Each case example begins with and is focused on the child or youth and his or her family.

➡ INTRODUCTION TO THE CHAPTERS

Chapters 1 through 5 comprise the Philosophical and Policy Foundations for Transition section of the book. Chapter 1 defines transition services within the framework of youth development and introduces the pathways model. It discusses the benefits of transition planning and services for youth and for society. Finally, the chapter explores how transition services can be aligned with the general education curriculum, while preserving individualized education planning. Chapter 2 examines various populations of special learners and their transition needs, explores the transition choices and challenges that they face, and examines the needs of families in the dynamic interaction with their children along the developmental path of transition to adulthood.

Chapter 3 traces the historical, political, and social forces that have shaped the evolution of career development and transition as a field. It presents philosophical foundations for transition and for the "pathways" approach that forms the organizing framework for this book. Chapter 3 also presents a framework of positive youth development and provides a synthesis of research on promising and best practices that promote student self-determination. Chapter 4 reviews current laws and policy initiatives that give states and local educational agencies and community agencies the mandate and authority to implement transition service systems. It also introduces recent case law, or legal challenges, that has helped interpret the intent of Congress in mandating transition services under IDEA and set important new precedents. Finally, the chapter presents provisions in the No Child Left Behind Act (NCLB) that support transition services for youth. Chapter 5 defines interagency service coordination and its functions and introduces a framework for a "systematic" approach to transition services for coordinating school-linked and community-based agencies that share responsibility for positive youth outcomes.

Chapters 6 through 12 comprise the second section of the book, Implementing Transition in Local Systems. Chapter 6 defines research-based practices in transition and reviews the historical and contemporary literature to identify a set of recommendations for practices. Chapter 7 provides an overview of career assessment and its essential role in transition planning, and Chapter 8 examines the framework for transition pathways to postsecondary life in detail. Chapter 9 explores how special education and transition personnel effectively complete the transition planning process and write the transition portion of an IEP for high-school-age youth with disabilities. It explains the decision making process for developing coordinated services and educational programs that address state educational standards, both academic and career, and meet the student's postsecondary goals. Information on transition planning for middle-school-age youth with disabilities is also discussed.

Chapter 10 draws on the framework introduced in Chapter 5 to describe the steps for developing and implementing interagency agreements for transition at both the individual student and interagency (system) levels. Chapter 11 examines the final phase of transition, the culmination and hand-off process, transition follow-up, and transition service evaluation. Chapter 12 explores transition strategies for students as they move from the secondary to postsecondary (post–high school) settings. It also discusses laws that provide supports for young people and protect them from discrimination in postsecondary institutions and employment settings.

Chapters 13 and 14 close the final section of the book, Cultural Issues and Leadership for Transition. The transition status of culturally and linguistically diverse (CLD) youth with disabilities is explored in Chapter 13 as well as the barriers faced by CLD families when interacting with schools and with transition service agencies and personnel. Chapter 14 explores the challenges and promise of leadership for promoting transition services and facilitating organizational change. It also explores leadership skills, professional standards for the field, and the role of teachers as transition leaders.

ACKNOWLEDGMENTS

We wish to thank the many colleagues whose comments on the draft of sections of this book have helped to improve its accuracy, clarity, and coherence. We are indebted to the following colleagues whose frank and honest recommendations for various parts of the book have greatly added to its balance, fairness, accuracy, and overall quality: Brian Berry, Holy Family University; Larry Kotering, Appalachian State University; Karen Lietzow, National-Louis University and University of Wisconsin, Milwaukee;

Caron Mellblom-Nishioka, California State University, Dominguez Hills; and John Palladino, Eastern Michigan University.

We also want to thank our editor, Ann Davis, for her intelligent and patient guidance and support throughout the process. We also thank Penny Burleson for her editorial skills. We have learned once again how important it is to have a superior editing team and supportive and savvy publication support. We have enjoyed the journey.

Brief Contents

Contents

CHAPTER 3   **History and Philosophy of Transition   66**

Carol A. Kochhar-Bryant

CHAPTER 4   **Federal Legislation, Research, and State Initiatives Advance
Transition Services   106**

Carol A. Kochhar-Bryant

CHAPTER 5   **Coordinating Systems and Agencies for Successful
               Transition   162**

Carol A. Kochhar-Bryant

PART II   IMPLEMENTING TRANSITION IN LOCAL SYSTEMS

CHAPTER 11　　**The Final Phases of Transition: Follow-Up and Evaluation　372**

Gary Greene

CHAPTER 12　　**Planning for Postsecondary Transition　394**

Carol A. Kochhar-Bryant

PART III   CULTURAL ISSUES AND LEADERSHIP FOR TRANSITION

Note: Every effort has been made to provide accurate and current Internet information in this book. However, the Internet and information posted on it are constantly changing, so it is inevitable that some of the Internet addresses listed in this textbook will change.

Chapter 1

Introduction to Transition

Carol A. Kochhar-Bryant

Life is about change, and about movement,
and about becoming something other than
what you are at this very moment.

—Kochhar-Bryant & Bassett, 2002

Chapter Questions

- How is transition defined?
- What is the pathways approach? A developmental framework for transition
- Why is transition important for youth with disabilities, and what are the benefits?
- How does transition fit within the general education curriculum?

INTRODUCTION

During the past 20 years, major transformations have occurred in educational, social, political, and economic areas that continue to affect the education and development of youth with disabilities and the institutions that support them. Youth with disabilities are now typically educated with their nondisabled peers. Antidiscrimination laws have improved access to postsecondary education and employment for youth and young adults with disabilities in a variety of occupations. A greater national investment is being made to improve all individuals' access to education and employment preparation programs and to increase their social and economic independence. Interest in youth development, career preparation, and transition is greater than it has ever been, both in the United States and around the globe. Successful transition from secondary school is becoming recognized as a chief indicator of the effectiveness of our educational system for preparing youth and young adults for adult independence.

This chapter defines transition services within the framework of youth development and introduces the pathways model. It discusses the benefits of transition planning and services for youth and for society. Finally, the chapter explores how transition services can be aligned with the general education curriculum, while preserving individualized educational planning. The following case illustration demonstrates transition planning for Joel, who plans to continue education beyond high school.

Joel's Plan for College

Joel, a 16-year-old junior in high school with a significant learning disability, plans to attend community college upon graduation. Joel loves working with computers and demonstrates skill and interest in using computers for graphic design. Over the past 2 years, his Individualized Education Program (IEP) has linked standards-based academic objectives with Joel's career goals, allowing him to explore computer-related careers within his assignments in English classes, social studies, and government. Joel's IEP team includes him and his family, a guidance counselor, an independent living center representative, a postsecondary education support services provider, and a student with a learning disability who had graduated 2 years ago and is currently attending college.

Because Joel is interested in pursuing a career involving computers, but is still undecided about what he would like to major in, the guidance counselor provided a list of colleges that offer a variety of computer-related degrees, including graphic design, programming, and management information systems. Joel agreed to attend the local college fair, and his family agreed to take him to visit campuses and observe and inquire regarding the support Joel may need. The team agreed that, to be successful in college, Joel would need a college that offered small classes, student-mentoring services, and note-taking services. The team agreed that Joel had depended on others to advocate for him. They recommended that Joel improve his self-advocacy skills. The representative from the Center for Independent Living invited Joel to participate in their next self-advocacy program as a means of meeting this transition service need, and the school division agreed to pay for the cost of this service.

The postsecondary service provider told Joel, his family, and the other professionals that a local college was offering an orientation for new students that would give Joel a flavor of the demands of the college setting. Funding for this was possibly available from the local advocacy group representing individuals with learning disabilities. The special educator reported that the advocacy group was looking for individuals to apply to their program. The guidance counselor set up an appointment with the family to discuss options for college financial assistance.

Joel's Plan for Education after High School: What Does This Student Need?

Joel requires an *assessment* that identifies strengths, needs, interests, preferences for postsecondary education; development of postsecondary education options; matching of student and postsecondary education setting; *preparation* for postsecondary education; and *placement and follow-along*. The following actions during the secondary years would help prepare Joel for successful transition into the postsecondary setting.

Assessment Actions: Assess Joel's self-advocacy skills, academic preparation, and college bound test scores; assess technical skills, social skills, and independent living skills; conduct interviews about preferences for educational settings—size, location, and programs; identify long-term career goals; identify accommodations that have been successful during schooling and could be recommended for the next setting; identify support needs to achieve postsecondary education goals; and discuss health care issues that may impact Joel in the postsecondary setting.

Development Actions: Visit campuses; participate in college night; talk with current college students with and without disabilities; conduct research on colleges and universities that offer special services to students with disabilities; and discuss financial issues.

Matching Actions: Analyze the demands and expectations of the postsecondary education setting—accessibility, support services availability, academic rigor, social culture, and independent living setting; and match student's assessment and list of needed supports to the demands of the postsecondary education setting.

Preparation Actions: Provide developmental academic support and coursework needed to prepare for postsecondary education goals; assist youth with applications, interviews, and test preparation; identify potential service providers; develop natural supports; and provide self-advocacy training.

Placement and Follow-along Actions: Monitor progress in the postsecondary setting and changing need for services, advocating for adjustments.

➡ HOW IS TRANSITION DEFINED?

The case of Joel discussed earlier demonstrates the multidimensional nature of transition. *It is not an "event" but rather a process* that is comprised of a set of activities including assessment, development of postsecondary goals, matching the student with the appropriate postsecondary setting, preparation for postsecondary education, and placement and follow-along. The transition process is viewed as a broad framework for preparing youth to successfully navigate the passages through schooling and into the spectrum of adult life roles—continued learning, career, social, and civic.

Although career development for children, youth, and adults of all exceptionalities has been evolving for centuries, the concept of transition has emerged relatively recently, since the 1950s. For decades, educators and policy makers have recognized the importance of career–technical education within the overall framework of adolescent development. Many have sought to identify effective interventions that are positively associated with improved transition of youth with disabilities from school to employment and adult life roles. Historically, transition practices have lacked empirical evidence of their effectiveness. One of the early studies to generate empirical evidence to support "best practices" in transition services was conducted by Kohler (1995). Her four-phase study resulted in the Taxonomy for Transition Programming, a conceptual framework of transition practices that has served as a model for planning, organizing, and evaluating transition education, services, and programs. Her five clusters of best practices, still widely used today, are summarized in Table 1–1.

Before 1997, the Individuals with Disabilities Education Act (IDEA) had basically one purpose—to ensure equality of opportunities for children with disabilities. In other words, it was a civil rights statute that ensured access to a free, appropriate public education. In 1997, however, IDEA was amended to clarify that the purpose of IDEA is not only to provide equal access but also to improve two outcomes for students: independent living and economic self-sufficiency or employment. **Transition planning** was identified as a core strategy to achieve these outcomes.

Recent emphasis on accountability for students' academic progress has created new challenges for the delivery of career-technical (vocational) education and sparked new initiatives for linking academic and career content across secondary and

Table 1–1   A Taxonomy for Transition Programming

Student-focused planning	**Program structure**
IEP development	Program philosophy
Student participation	Program policy
Planning strategies	Strategic planning
	Program evaluation
Student development	Resource allocation
Life skills instruction	Human resource
Career and vocational curricula	
Structured work experience	**Interagency collaboration**
Assessment	Collaborative framework
Support services	Collaborative service delivery
Family involvement	
Family training	
Family involvement	
Family empowerment	

Source: From *Taxonomy for Transition Programming* (p. 3) by P. D. Kohler, 1996, Champaign: University of Illinois.

postsecondary settings. On this new frontier many are asking: How can we align the goals of academic and career education with transition and postsecondary planning? When is the appropriate time to implement transition planning for postsecondary goals? There are conflicts in our laws as to when such planning should begin, which will be explored in chapter 4.

Societal interest in career awareness, career choice, and adjustment to the roles of adult, worker, and productive citizen has emerged as a new subfield within education. Transition from school to adult life involves changes in the self-concept, motivation, and development of the individual and is a fragile passage for the adolescent seeking to make difficult life choices (Akos & Galassi, 2004b; German, Martin, Marshall, & Sale, 2000; Michaels, 1994). This passage is even more delicate for youth with disabilities who need additional support and preparation to make the journey. For professionals seeking to help students on this journey, the process involves linking education and human service agencies, employment and training agencies, rehabilitation services, business and industry, and postsecondary institutions.

Transition is not a linear process, for it must take into account the wide variation in the development of adolescents and their particular needs for long-range planning and services. Today, the definition of transition is rooted both in federal legislation and in the broad efforts by practitioners to interpret that legislation and develop effective field-based practices. Interpretation of laws in our federal system is subject to wide variation among the states, and therefore transition services look very different in communities across the nation.

What Does IDEA 2004 Require?

Transition refers to a change in status from behaving primarily as a student to assuming adult roles in the community. As mentioned earlier, these roles include employment, participating in postsecondary education, maintaining a home, becoming appropriately involved in the community, and experiencing satisfactory personal and social relationships. The process of enhancing transition involves the participation and coordination of school programs, adult agency services, and natural supports within the community.

On December 3, 2004, the IDEA 2004 (Pub. L. No. 108-446) was signed into law effective from July 1, 2005, and introduced important changes in transition-related provisions. Appendix 1 compares language in IDEA 1997 and IDEA 2004 related to transition services for youth. Appendix 2, discussed later, describes important provisions in the No Child Left Behind Act of 2001 (NCLB, Pub. L. No. 107-110) that support transition for all youth, particularly those who are disadvantaged and placed at risk for failure in public education. The term *transition services* means a **coordinated set of activities** for students that

1. is designed within a **results-oriented process** that promotes movement from school to postschool activities, including postsecondary education, vocational training, integrated employment (including supported employment), continuing and adult education, adult services, independent living, or community participation;
2. is based on the individual student's strengths, taking into account the student's preferences and interests; and
3. includes instruction, related services, community experiences, the development of employment and other postschool adult living objectives, and, when appropriate, acquisition of daily living skills and functional vocational evaluation (IDEA, 2004, §602).

The IEP, beginning not later than the first IEP in effect when the student is aged 16 (or younger if determined appropriate by the IEP team) and updated annually, must include "appropriate measurable postsecondary goals based on age-appropriate transition assessments related to training, education, employment and, where appropriate, independent living skills." Transition services (including courses of study) are needed to assist the child in reaching those goals (Code of Federal Regulations [CFR] 300.320 (b) and (c); [20 U.S.C. 1414 (d) (1)(A)(i)(viii)]). Students' success depends on their active participation in setting postsecondary goals and planning a coordinated set of services to achieve those goals.

Understanding a "Coordinated Set of Activities" Under IDEA

The systematic, cumulative, and long-range nature of transition planning and decision-making process has not been made explicit in IDEA statutory language, and therefore states have worked hard to interpret this provision in the best interest of the individual student. The word *coordinated* was the first reference—and an oblique one—to a *systematic approach* to transition. The term was first defined in the 1990 IDEA (Pub. L. No. 101-476) regulations to mean both "(1) the linkage between each of the component activities that comprise transition services, and (2) the interrelationship between the various agencies that are involved in the provision of transition services to a student" (U.S. Department of Education, 1992). IDEA 1997 amendments redefined transition services as a "coordinated set of activities aimed at a specific student outcome" (e.g., employment, referral to rehabilitation services, and enrollment in college (§602(34)(A)). Transition services must be coordinated, and the different agencies responsible for providing the services must do the same, making sure that the services they provide to the student meet, in a coordinated, nonduplicating fashion, his or her transition needs. Because the transition process relies on the involvement of many individuals and many service providers, coordination is essential. Transition viewed as a systematic, individualized process that incorporates a coordinated set of activities

1. is a continuous process that begins with transition from middle school and through high school;
2. is a long-range planning and decision-making framework for students and families, which addresses a variety of domains of education and life preparation;
3. considers students' anticipated postsecondary goal;
4. addresses curriculum options, including participation in the general education curriculum, career–technical, community-based learning, and nonacademic learning activities;
5. provides continuity of planning and links each student with a transition coordinator, counselor, or ombudsman (advocate);
6. incorporates related and supportive services identified by students, parents, and professionals;
7. engages appropriate community-based and adult service agencies, vocational rehabilitation, health and mental health agencies, postsecondary institutions, and employment development services.

Transition planning is foundational for the IEP planning process. Long-term transition planning provides an overarching framework that guides the development of the IEP and provides continuity in the process for the immediate and long-term future of the student (Kochhar-Bryant & Bassett, 2002). It is a blueprint for direction setting and for constructing a plan that is aimed at high school exit goals most appropriate for the individual.

Transition Is a Comprehensive Planning Process with Options and Choices: Applying Universal Design

Universal design for learning (UDL), a concept that emerged from the field of architecture, is an approach to designing products and environments for maximum usability by a diverse population. Ramped entrances and automatic doors are architectural examples of universal design (Center for Applied Special Technology, 2004; Smith & Leconte, 2004). In educational settings, **universal design** means that environments and curricula are designed to be flexible and usable by students of widely varying abilities and developmental and learning needs. Students with widely varying abilities all have the opportunity to access the general curriculum and achieve the academic content standards that have been established for all students in the school (Casper & Leuchovius, 2005; Wehmeyer & Agran, 2006).

In the past, providing "access" to general education meant enabling physical access to the classroom and, for some students, providing adaptive equipment to facilitate sensory and motor access to the curriculum. Providing students with disabilities with meaningful access to the general secondary curriculum through universal design requires the integration of transition planning and services. It is the course of study requirement in IDEA that connects transition with curriculum standards and assessment for all students. To meet the criteria of "flexible and widely useable curricula and environments," the UDL framework at the secondary level (a) offers choices in pathways to graduation for students, (b) incorporates transition planning and participation in a general education course of study, and (c) provides for flexible combinations of academic and career–vocational classes and community-based work experiences to achieve alternative pathways to graduation.

For some students with disabilities, the typical planning and preparation for 2- or 4-year college or employment proceeds much the same way as it does for students without disabilities. For many students, however, decisions about postsecondary choices can be complex and require long-term advanced planning. Transition services, therefore, are tailored to the individual needs of the student and their postsecondary goals. Transition, as required by IDEA 2004, represents an individualized, flexible planning process, offering a spectrum of services and choices for youth who have separate and individual needs. Transition is fully consistent with the concept of UDL environments.

IDEA 2004 and Beyond: Multiple Domains of Transition

Implementing transition involves much more than accessing and progressing in the secondary education curriculum. The transition process represents a broad framework for preparing youth to successfully navigate the passages through schooling and into the adult life roles—academic, vocational, social–psychological, and civic.

The case of Joel discussed earlier demonstrated that transition is not an "event" but rather a process that embraces several *activity domains*: assessment, development of postsecondary goals, matching of student with the postsecondary setting; preparation for postsecondary education; and placement and follow-along. Neither is transition a linear process, for it must take into account the *wide variation in the development of adolescents* and young adults and their particular needs for long-range planning and services before age 16, the current age of initiation of transition services under IDEA 2004.

Several facilitative implementation processes are key to achieving effective transition and ensuring adequate planning for students to get them ready for the final stage of transition—the exit from high school and entry into a postsecondary setting. *Facilitative processes* mean practices that state and local educational agencies have developed over the years as a result of professionals' and their students' experiences with transition under IDEA and their own evaluation of services. These practices are longer-term, comprehensive processes of decision making that

1. begin as the student prepares to exit middle school and to make decisions and choices about the high school course of study (Balfanz & Herzog, 2006; National High School Center, 2007c);

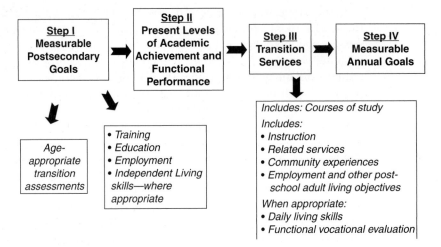

Figure 1–1   Backward Planning
Source: From conference presentation by Ed O'Leary, Council for Exceptional Children International Conference, Transition Policy and the Public Agenda: Today, Tomorrow and the Future, April 20, 2007. By Permission.

2. involve support and assistance with the adjustment to high school;

3. involve IEP planning that defines a postsecondary goal and designs a course of study, supportive and supplemental services, and a variety of transition-related activities that support the postsecondary goal (§614);

4. prepare the student and family to take an active role in planning during high school and for the student to take responsibility for his or her own life (self-determination and self-advocacy) upon exit from high school.

As Steven Covey (2004) advised, "begin with the end in mind." Interpreting Covey for transition, the student and the IEP team conducts a careful backward planning process with a clear eye to the final outcome—the postsecondary goal. Figure 1–1 depicts the long-range transition planning process that many local districts are developing.

WHAT IS A PATHWAYS APPROACH? THE DEVELOPMENTAL FRAMEWORK FOR TRANSITION

Transition as a Developmental Process

It is important to place the discussion of transition within the broader framework of youth development. The **youth development** approach is a process that prepares young people to meet the challenges of adolescence and adulthood through a coordinated, progressive series of activities and experiences that help them to become socially, emotionally, physically, and cognitively competent. The youth development approach calls for a dialogue about youth that is centered on their strengths, capabilities, and unique developmental needs rather than on their problems, risks, and vulnerabilities. It is an appreciative, health-based approach that assumes that young people can make successful transitions to adulthood and can gain lifelong resilience if they have appropriate and positive supports from adults and peers and are engaged in planning for their future.

Positive youth development addresses the broader developmental needs of youth, in contrast to "adultist" or deficit-based models that focus solely on youth problems (Hall, Yohalem, Tolman, & Wilson, 2002; National Collaboration for Youth, 1998). The word adultism refers to behaviors and attitudes that are based on the assumption that adults are "better" than young people and entitled to act upon young people without their agreement or participation (Checkoway, 2005). These assumptions are reinforced by social institutions, laws, customs, and attitudes. As Lofquist (1989) observed 20 years ago, our reliance on a deficit-focused, diagnostic label–centered model to frame youth behavior has fostered an overly negative perspective and a limited vision.

Interest in positive youth development has grown because of studies that show the same individual, family, school, and community factors often predict both positive (e.g., success in school and social relationships) and negative (e.g., delinquency and truancy) **outcomes for youth** (Catalano, Berglund, Ryan, Lonczak, & Hawkins, 2002). Such factors as developing strong bonds with healthy adults and maintaining regular involvement in positive activities not only create a positive developmental pathway but can prevent the occurrence of problems. Much recent attention has been given to the task of distinguishing a "set of personal and social assets that increase the healthy development and well-being of adolescents and facilitate a successful transition from childhood, through adolescence, and into adulthood" (National Research Council and Institute of Medicine, 2002, p. 6). Individuals have various combinations and ranges of assets, or strengths, and continued exposure to positive experiences, people, and settings increases the growth and acquisition of these assets. Strengths-based principles involve a deliberate focus on strengths, assets, existing capacities, and competencies of youth. Such principles promote the engagement of existing natural supports, the development of plans that build on the full range of people's assets and strengths, and the matching of strengths to workplace or role functions (Cooperrider & Whitney, 1998).

Programming for youth, therefore, becomes part of a larger *developmental space* and should be intentionally linked to other settings in which young people grow and develop, particularly postsecondary settings. Youth development means purposefully seeking to address youth supports and build youth abilities to become successful adults. Rather than seeing young people as problems, this positive development approach views them instead as capable of building on their strengths and talents and contributing to their own community. Meaningful participation of young people in their own educational and future planning is considered a key youth development practice and promotes healthy development and learning (Roth & Brooks-Gunn, 2003; Sagawa, 2003). Meaningful participation means activities through which young people have opportunities to make meaningful decisions, develop and practice leadership skills, and experience a sense that they belong or matter to others. The youth development framework is based on the following assumptions for effective programs:

1. Focus on strengths, capabilities, and developmental needs rather than on problems, risks, and vulnerabilities
2. Appreciative, health-based approaches
3. Belief that young people can make successful transitions to adulthood and gain lifelong resilience
4. Appropriate and positive supports from adults and peers
5. Building self-determination skills is developmental

Effective youth development programs are characterized by the following:

1. Promoting comprehensive and flexible youth development
2. Engaging youth in planning for the future
3. Integrating multiple developmental domains: academic, social–psychological, and career
4. Including a curriculum that blends school-based and community-based approaches
5. Designing programming as part of a larger developmental space linked to other settings
6. Designing programs to be intensive during middle to high school transition years, in grades 9–12 and through age 21 if needed
7. Accounting for variation in the development of adolescents and their needs for long-range planning and services before age 16
8. Focusing the IEP postsecondary goals to help students move away from home, establish a social life, become lifelong learners, and work a part- or full-time job
9. Designing individual programming around a coordinated set of activities and systematic approach as required by IDEA 2004

Youth Development and Self-Determination

The concept of self-determination is an important element in the youth development framework. The student is viewed as a central participant in educational planning and postschool goal-setting. Many youth and young adults with disabilities have difficulty assuming control of their lives and participating in the educational decisions that are made each year about their educational programs and their future life goals. In 1993, the U.S. Office of Special Education developed and adopted the following working definition of **self-determination**:"choosing and enacting choices to control one's own life to the maximum extent possible, based on knowing oneself, and in pursuit of one's own needs, interests and values" (Campeau & Wolman, 1993, p. 2). Self-determination theory is based on the assumption that people have inborn tendencies to grow and develop psychologically, to strive to master challenges in their environment, and to integrate experience into their self-concepts (Deci & Ryan, 1985, 2000; National Research and Training Center, 2002; Ryan & Deci, 2000). According to self-determination theory, these human tendencies are fully expressed only within a supportive social context. Self-determination will be discussed in greater detail in chapter 3.

Transition—a coordinated planning process and a set of objectives—is, of course, fundamentally about children and youth and their development and preparation for adult life. Children make multiple transitions from elementary to middle to high school and into the adult world. At each stage, transition planning and supports can play a crucial role in facilitating adjustment to the next developmental stage. Transition at the high school level involves structuring educational services and supports that are appropriate to the developmental needs of adolescents as they plan and prepare for the adult world. The remaining chapters in this book emphasize a **developmental framework** that reflects adolescent development and youth development principles.

The Pathways Model

Throughout this book, transition is viewed within the context of several choices or **pathways** that provide different service models and sets of long-term goals for students. These pathways move beyond the somewhat arbitrary categories of "mild," "moderate," and "severe" disabilities and are concerned with decision making based on distinctly different sets of postsecondary goals. Transition services, therefore, can be clustered into service patterns (pathways) that can provide an organized way for schools, families, and students to make decisions about the kinds of transition services needed in relation to the student's individual disability, developmental needs, abilities, and expected postsecondary goal. These pathways are aligned with the required transition services under IDEA 2004.

Transition planning involves a variety of decisions and can be quite confusing for students and families. There are decisions about

1. the appropriate postsecondary goal;
2. appropriate secondary curriculum choices to support the goals;
3. appropriate assessments to inform the decisions;
4. kinds of support services and accommodations that will be needed during and beyond high school;
5. specific planning and services required at the point of transition; and
6. community agency services needed to support the postsecondary goal.

A pathways approach also provides a framework for matching planning strategies with students' postsecondary goals early in their educational program, long before graduation is upon them, and for developing a course of preparation to achieve those goals. The pathways framework builds upon several transition models that have evolved over the past two decades and these models are described in greater detail later in this book.

Although some students may need time-limited transition supports and some may need ongoing services, the transition planning process for students with disabilities should begin early as they enter secondary education or even in the middle school years if needed. For students without disabilities, such long-range vision and secondary planning to achieve postsecondary goals is the typical model that begins as the student exits from middle school and makes choices for a high school course of study. Table 1-2 presents four pathways and the postsecondary goals and coordinated services associated with each.

Table 1–2 Transition Pathways and Levels of Support

Path/ Postsecondary Goal	Domains Emphasized	Coordinated Set of Activities (aligned with IDEA 2004 requirements)	Focus for Assessments	Expected Outcome or Exit Goal
1. Academic/ postsecondary education	Academic	IEP/transition planning based on postsecondary goals Academic course of study designed to achieve postsecondary goals Self-determination and self-advocacy skill development Support services accommodations Vocational rehabilitation (VR) and agency services as needed	Academic/ standardized	Two-or four-year college enrollment
2. Career–technical training	Career and social	IEP/transition planning based on postsecondary goals Blended academic and career–vocational courses (career pathway) designed to achieve postsecondary goals Self-determination and self-advocacy skill development Vocational evaluation Support services and accommodations VR and agency services as needed	Academic assessments and vocational and community-based "authentic" assessments	Vocational-technical school or career apprenticeship
3. Employment	Career–vocational and independent living	IEP/transition planning based on postsecondary goals Blended academic and career–vocational courses designed to achieve postsecondary goals Community-based employment experiences Self-determination and self-advocacy skill development Vocational evaluation Support services and accommodations VR and agency services as needed	Academic assessments and vocational assessments in authentic or simulated settings	Competitive employment
4. Supported setting	Social and independent living	IEP/transition planning based on postsecondary goals Functional academics, social and life skills designed to achieve postsecondary goals Community-based competitive or supported employment experiences Self-determination and self-advocacy skill development Vocational evaluation Support services and accommodations in the workplace VR and agency services as needed	Social, adaptive behavior, and independent living skills assessments	Competitive or supported employment and independent or supported living

The pathway is determined by the postsecondary goal established jointly among the student, the parents, and the IEP team. Transition planning is the coordination of the postsecondary goal with the curriculum, assessment, and related services that the student needs to achieve that goal. It is a process of backward design or *backward planning* that begins with the postsecondary goals. Transition, therefore, becomes the *unifying concept* for the process of decision making throughout the secondary years.

Transition services must be structured to facilitate each student's potential for personal, social, and economic fulfillment and participation in family and community. The structure of transition services must be both flexible and rational. A transition service system, therefore, cannot be "one size fits all." Rather, it must be *flexible* to provide a spectrum of service options, choices, or pathways for students with a variety of learning needs, fill a range of support needs, and respond to individualized postsecondary goals. *Rational* refers to the degree to which the transition services match and are appropriate to the unique needs and goals of the individual student preparing to enter the adult world. A transition service system is *rational* when it aligns the individual education plan and student graduation goals with the basic principles embodied in IDEA: (1) student's right to the least restrictive environment; (2) student's right to differentiated services and accommodations determined by appropriate assessments; (3) the expectation that students will gain educational benefit from the setting and services; and (4) the student's right to social benefits from interaction with nondisabled peers. Chapter 4 will examine these principles and the legal basis of transition services.

➡ WHY IS TRANSITION IMPORTANT?

Continuing Need for Individualized Transition Planning: What Does Research Tell Us?

Many youth with disabilities face significant challenges both in the school environment and as they transition to adult life. For decades, state and federal initiatives have been aimed at improving postschool outcomes for youth. Implementing transition services across the states has required a complex systemic change process that involves coordination across schools and agencies and can take decades. Federal and state leaders continue to explore new strategies in the face of persistent challenges for youth with disabilities. National studies have shown that, compared to their nondisabled peers, students with disabilities are still less likely to receive a regular high school diploma, drop out twice as often, and enroll in and complete postsecondary education programs at half the rate; and, up to 2 years after leaving high school, about 4 in 10 youths with disabilities are employed as compared with 6 in 10 same-age out-of-school youth in the general population (National Center for Education Statistics, 2000a; National Longitudinal Transition Study-2 [NLTS2], 2005). These and related findings on the secondary and postsecondary outcomes of youth with disabilities have prompted federal and state efforts to improve transition policies and practices.

Federal and state efforts to improve the postschool outcomes of youth with disabilities have resulted in some important gains over the past decade, including increases in graduation rates, enrollment in postsecondary education, and the number of youth entering the workforce (Cameto & Levine, 2005; Newman, 2005; U.S. Office of Special Education Programs, 2006). Despite these gains, far too many youth with disabilities continue to experience difficulties in achieving successful postschool outcomes (NLTS2, 2005 U.S. General Accountability Office, 2004; U.S. Government Accountability Office, 2005). The transition needs of young people with disabilities require individualized services based on the unique needs of the student. Research studies reveal, however, that such "customized" services are elusive:

1. A direct assessment of students' language arts, mathematics abilities, and content knowledge in science and social studies suggests that from 77% to 86% of youth with disabilities have standard scores below the mean for the general population. Youth with disabilities from low income households (i.e., $25,000 in annual income or less) have lower average scores in all domains relative to youth from moderate income households, independent of racial or ethnic and other differences between them (U.S. Department of Education, 2006a; Wagner, Newman, Cameto, & Levine, 2006).

2. There is emerging evidence of the link between the socioeconomic status of school districts and the rate of inclusion of students with disabilities in general education (Ralabate, 2007).

3. About 3 in 10 out-of-school youth with disabilities have been enrolled in some kind of postsecondary school since leaving high school, with 1 in 5 attending a postsecondary school at the time of the Wave 2 interview. This rate of current enrollment is less than half that of their peers in the general population (41%) (Wagner et al., 2006).

4. Average standard scores for youth with disabilities on functional skills measures, assessed on four clusters of functional skills (motor skills, social interaction and communication, personal living skills, and community living skills), range from 43 to 57, compared with a mean of 100 for the general population. From 22% to 38% of youth with disabilities across subtests have scores more than six standard deviations below the mean (Wagner et al., 2006).

5. Youth with disabilities drop out of high school at twice the rate of their peers without disabilities (National Organization on Disability, 2004); the dropout rate for all disabilities is currently 37.6% in 2001–2002, down from 45.1% in 1993–2004 (U.S. Department of Education, 2004b). For students with emotional disturbance, the rate is 61.2% (U.S. Department of Education, 2004a).

6. Data on students aged 14 and older with disabilities who graduated or dropped out, by race or ethnicity, showed that in 2001–2002 dropout rates for Native Americans was 52.2%; for African Americans, 44.5%; for Hispanics, 43.5% (U.S. Department of Education, 2004).

7. Only one fourth of young people who need life skills training, tutoring, interpreting, or person counseling services receive them (National Alliance for Secondary Education and Transition, 2005).

8. Less than one in four students participates in organized extracurricular activities, and 2% have no interactions with friends. Autism and multiple disabilities, including deaf-blindness, are disabilities that appear to present significant obstacles to these kinds of interaction (Wagner et al., 2003).

9. Compared to nondisabled persons of working age, individuals with disabilities are less likely to achieve a high school education, and even less likely to pursue postsecondary educational opportunities (Berry, Conway, & Chang, 2004; Stodden, Dowrick, Gilmore, & Galloway, 2003; Wagner, Newman, Cameto, Garza, & Lavine, 2005).

10. Educators are inadequately prepared to provide transition services required under IDEA, and state departments of education often indicate that primary training takes place *on the job* rather than through professional development (Anderson et al., 2003; Kochhar-Bryant, 2003).

11. Teachers often view the completion of the transition component of the IEP as paperwork, not as a document intended to reflect a transition team's postschool plan and vision for a student (Cameto, Marder, Wagner, & Cardoso, 2003; DeStefano, Heck, Hasazi, & Furney, 1999; National Council on Disability, 2000b; O'Leary, Lehman, & Doty, 2001; Storms, O'Leary, & Williams, 2000; Thompson, Fulk, & Piercy, 2000).

The continuing discrepancies in secondary education performance and postsecondary outcomes between youth with and without disabilities underscore the need for more intense planning and support for students preparing for transition to adulthood. It is vital to move beyond the technical requirements of IDEA and view transition planning as a thoughtful, unified set of goals and plans that will lead to an *individualized course of action* for each student (Thompson et al., 2000). Systematic linkages are needed among professionals, families, schools, community agencies, the business community, and higher education.

Who Benefits from Transition Services?

Research has attested to the benefits of transition services for students with disabilities. As practitioners, policy makers, and consumers have realized these benefits, the development of transition policies and practices has accelerated in the past 5 years. Such development can be observed in many local school districts in which there are strong interagency agreements among schools and community agencies that **share responsibility** for transition services to youth with disabilities.

Benefits to Students. When students receive comprehensive transition services and participate in transition planning, their preparation for postsecondary education and employment improves. Research has demonstrated a relationship between students' involvement in their own individualized educational planning and transition goal-setting and improved postsecondary outcomes (Bremer, Kachgal, & Schoeller, 2003; Martin, 2002; Repetto, Webb, Neubert, & Curran, 2006). Such involvement in personal goal-setting and exercise of decision making is referred to as *self-determination* or *self-advocacy*. Students experience higher self-esteem and personal success as a result of interaction with nondisabled peers and others in the community. A wider "circle of support" and social support system that includes nondisabled classmates is correlated with improved social skills development, positive behaviors, and improved academic progress. Learning is improved from working in community-based learning teams and social interaction is increased in community-based employment and training settings. Overall, youth experience a greater adjustment to adult roles as a result of their participation in a supportive transition planning process.

Benefits to Youth Placed At Risk.   Individualized transition programs provide strategies to motivate students with disabilities, and those placed at risk of school dropout, to remain in school to complete their degrees. Transition programs often employ creative and integrated academic–vocational-technical curricula and alternative student performance assessments such as exhibitions, demonstrations, and work projects.

Benefits to Parents and Guardians.   The transition planning processes link parents with teachers, counselors, and related services personnel; include parents in the school-to-work transition planning process; prepare professionals to help parents strengthen personal decision making, goal-setting, and self-advocacy in their children (Akos & Galassi, 2004a; Furney & Salembrier, 2000).

Benefits to 2- and 4-Year Colleges and Technical Schools.   Colleges and universities benefit from students' preparation for transition to postsecondary education. When students understand their strengths, abilities, and needs and the change in their status as they leave secondary education, then they can better advocate for themselves and for appropriate services in the postsecondary setting. When they are better prepared to make decisions and choices about their future, then they are more likely to enroll in and complete advanced education and to enter and sustain employment (Benz, Lindstrom, & Yovanoff, 2000; National Center on Secondary Education and Transition, 2004b; U.S. Government Accountability Office, 2003a; Wehmeyer, Abery, Mithaug, Powers, & Stancliffe, 2003).

Benefits to Community Agencies.   **Systematic transition services** promote collaboration among related services agencies and personnel to better support youth with disabilities who are participating in general secondary education or **career–vocational education** classes. Interagency coordination for transition stimulates resource sharing among schools and community service agencies and promotes systematic assessment of services and evaluation (Dunst & Bruder, 2002; Kochhar-Bryant, 2008 Research and Training Center on Service Coordination, 2001).

Benefits to Businesses and the Community at Large.   Transition services promote innovative linkages between schools and the business community to provide career-related work experiences in real-world work settings (Luecking & Fabian, 2000; Plank, DeLuca, & Estacion, 2005). Transition programs transform the role of the business and community agency partners from that of donors and philanthropists to active partners in school restructuring to better connect career–vocational education programs with the expectations and environments of today's industries.

Benefits to the Nation.   Transition services help expand the pool of qualified and skilled workers, which ultimately reduces young adults' dependence on family or public support. Successful transitions lead to increased participation of youth and young adults with disabilities in civic activities and the political process. National investment in youth transition demonstrates to the nation and the world a national commitment to the welfare, self-determination, and full participation of all residents in communities across the United States.

HOW DO TRANSITION SERVICES FIT WITHIN THE GENERAL EDUCATION CURRICULUM?

The challenge to expand transition services has become even more complex as general education reforms place increasing emphasis on academic performance for students and reduced emphasis on career–vocational development and community-based learning. **Standards-based** educational systems with **high-stakes testing** present challenges to both the individualized education and individualized transition planning models required by IDEA. Educators seek creative approaches to blending the standards-based and individualized education approaches that differ in important ways. It is important to understand the differences in the principles and assumptions that undergird both transition services and standards-based education to appreciate the challenges in aligning the two educational models.

How can the standards-based curriculum be reconciled or aligned with the individualized education process required for students with disabilities? How should students with disabilities be included in standardized assessments? The standards-based educational model is grounded in the assumption that all students should meet common standards for what should be taught and learned. The individualized education process, however, is grounded in the principle of "appropriate" education that meets individual needs of each student who requires specialized educational services. As a result, professional collaboration to align these systems has taken center stage in IDEA 2004 and NCLB.

How Do NCLB and IDEA Differ in Principles and Policies?

In considering the twin goals of *equity* (access for all) and *excellence* (high standards) in education, it is important to understand the differences between the principles that underlie NCLB and IDEA. For more than two decades, the primary policy tool for improving outcomes for students with disabilities has been the IDEA and its equity provisions—free and appropriate education and protection of individual rights. Education under NCLB has introduced a fundamentally different set of policies and practices that are based on uniform learning standards within a *standards-based curriculum*. The students' mastery of the curriculum content is measured by standardized tests or assessments. Standards-based education is grounded in the assumption that *common standards for all students* are a catalyst for improved educational results and serve as a basis for what should be taught and for measuring what students should be expected to know (Kochhar-Bryant & Bassett, 2002; McDonnell, McLaughlin, & Morison, 1997). SBE is also based on the assumptions that content and performance standards can be clearly and precisely defined, student performance can be measured validly and reliably, and accountability can be strengthened through public reporting of aggregate data on student performance.

In contrast to the assumption of common performance standards, special education services are guided by the special education framework that defines the rights of students with disabilities to a free and appropriate education and specifies the responsibilities of school systems to accommodate their individual needs (IDEA, 2004).

Individualized education relies on a *private process*—the IEP and transition plans are centered on the *needs of the individual student,* and *students' individual rights* are enforced through a set of procedural safeguards (McDonnel et al., 1997). Also, in contrast to the focus on academic outcomes that are the hallmark of standards-based education, the special education framework for students with disabilities encompasses a broader range of educational outcomes for students with disabilities (e.g., career related, social–behavioral, and health related).

As mentioned earlier, the transition service framework for students with disabilities also addresses a broad range of educational outcomes for students with disabilities. For example, Ysseldyke and Erickson (1997) and Ysseldyke, Thurlow, Kozleski, and Reschly (1998) clustered outcomes into eight domains, including presence and participation, accommodation and adaptation, physical health, responsibility and independence, contribution and citizenship, academic and functional literacy, personal and social adjustment, and satisfaction.

Critics of highly standardized education for all students claim that states have crafted standards that are too narrow and do not allow educators to include nonacademic learning objectives such as those that are focused on social and behavioral skills, career–vocational development, physical and health development, and functional skills (Izzo, Hertzfeld, Simmons-Reed, & Aaron, 2001). To address the broader life domains of the student, the foundation for transition planning must be laid during the elementary and middle school years, guided by the broad concept of career development and preparation of the whole person for postsecondary life (Clark, 2007; Clark & Kolstoe, 1995). Table 1–3 compares the assumptions of individualized transition services (IDEA) and standards-based (NCLB) education.

IDEA 1997 and 2004 emphasized the importance of an equitable accountability system and required states to include students with disabilities in general state- and district-wide assessments and school improvement efforts. States are now required to establish goals for the performance of children with disabilities and to assess their progress toward achieving those goals. They must establish indicators such as student participation in assessments, dropout rates, graduation rates, and guidelines for alternate assessment of children with disabilities. IDEA, however, also protects the child's right to "appropriate" and "individualized" methods for achieving common standards and goals, including nonacademic goals. The challenge for educators is to align standards-based education policies with those under IDEA that are based on individual rights and individualized educational processes. Transition, therefore, must be viewed as a comprehensive framework (a) to ensure effective alignment between secondary education and transition services and (b) to guide planning and decision making among students, families, and professionals.

Alignment of Transition and Standards-Based Education

Challenges to implementing the federal transition requirements have been fraught with uncertainty about what is expected of states and local educational agencies, families, and students. As a result, progress in implementing transition in many states has not resulted in adequate improvement in postsecondary outcomes for youth.

Table 1–3   Comparing the Assumptions of Transition Planning and Standards-Based Education

Transition Principles Based on an Individualized Process	Standards-Based Education Principles
1. The foundations for transition should be laid during the elementary and middle school years, guided by the broad concept of career development.	1. Common standards that apply to all students are a catalyst for improved educational outcomes— serving as a basis for what should be taught and measuring what students should be expected to know (McDonnel et al., 1997).
2. A broad range of educational outcomes for students with disabilities includes eight domains: presence and participation, accommodation and adaptation, physical health, responsibility and independence, contribution and citizenship, academic and functional literacy, personal and social adjustment, and satisfaction (Ysseldyke, Olsen, & Thurlow, 1997).	2. Academic and basic literacy outcomes are central, and there are shared curricular values.
3. Special education framework defines the rights of students with disabilities to a free and appropriate education and specifies the responsibilities of school systems to accommodate their individual needs.	3. Accountability is ensured through public reporting of aggregate data on student performance.
4. Student's individual rights are enforced through a set of procedural safeguards. Transition planning should begin no later than age 14, and students should be encouraged to the full extent of their capabilities, to assume a maximum amount of responsibility for such planning (Halpern, 1994, p. 117).	4. Content and performance standards can be clearly and precisely defined.
5. Transition means a coordinated set of activities aimed at a specific student outcome or result (e.g., employment, referral to rehabilitation services, and enrollment in college). The coordinated set of activities must be (a) based on the individual student's strengths, (b) take into account the student's preferences and interests, and (c) include needed activities in the areas of instruction, related services, community experiences, the development of employment and other postschool adult living objectives, and when appropriate, daily living skills and functional vocational evaluation (IDEA, 2004).	5. Student performance can be measured validly and reliably.
6. Transition means a coordinated set of activities that promotes the movement of a student from school to postschool activities including postsecondary education, vocational training, integrated employment (including supported employment), continuing and adult education, adult services, independent living, or community participation.	6. Instruction consistent with the standards can be implemented in individual schools and classrooms.

Table 1–3 *Continued*

Transition Principles Based on an Individualized Process	Standards-Based Education Principles
7. The IEP, beginning no later than the first IEP in effect when the student is 16 and updated annually, must include a statement of "appropriate measurable post-secondary goals based on age appropriate transition assessments related to training, education, employment and independent living skills" (IDEA 2004, §614).	7. Increased standards will yield several results for students with disabilities: a. The number of "low-track" English, math, and science classes would decrease b. More students would enroll in college preparatory classes c. Tracking will be eliminated d. Inclusion into general education would be promoted e. There would be broader options and improved transition outcomes for youth (Jorgensen, 1998)
8. The IEPs of students with disabilities attending high school reflect the general education curriculum and standards.	8. Creating rigorous learning standards within the curriculum will refocus teaching and learning on a common understanding of what schools expect students to know and be able to do.
9. The individual's status changes from student to adult roles in the community, including employment, participating in postsecondary education, maintaining a home, becoming appropriately involved in the community, and experiencing satisfactory personal and social relationships.	
10. The process of enhancing transition involves the participation and coordination of school programs, adult agency services, and natural supports within the community.	
11. For students whose primary option is to enter the workforce after school, the curriculum is focused on vocational and functional skills and includes community-based instruction and vocational assessment.	

Source: Adapted from *Aligning Transition and Standards-Based Education: Issues and Strategies* (pp. 15–16), by C. A. Kochhar-Bryant and D. S. Bassett, 2002, Arlington, VA: Council for Exceptional Children.

Many educators have called for a unified vision of middle and secondary education and transition planning (Balfanz & Herzog, 2006; Clark, Sitlington, & Kolstoe, 2000; National Council on Disability, 2000b; Plank et al., 2005; Thompson et al., 2000). New questions have arisen about the relationship between transition and standards-based education:

1. How do standards-based educational practices fit within the broader, individualized career development and transition framework for students with disabilities?

2. To what extent do schools have the responsibility for preparing youth for careers if they are not bound for postsecondary education after graduation?
3. How can transition be implemented for students who are in inclusive middle and secondary classrooms?

Until recently, the concept of *transition* has implied a separate postschool planning process in which students with disabilities work with special educators to develop transition components of the IEP, whereas students without disabilities work with guidance counselors to develop graduation plans. The perception of transition as a separate planning process makes it difficult to integrate needed transition services when students are participating in the general education curriculum. For most students with disabilities, transition planning should not conflict with participation in the regular education curriculum or meeting high academic standards and graduating with a regular high school diploma. In other words, students who need transition services should not be forced to choose between transition services and the general education curriculum.

The potential benefits of aligning transition and standards-based (general) educational systems are enormous. First, transition research has demonstrated that students in successful transition and school-to-work programs are highly integrated with their nondisabled peers in both school and community activities. Second, transition personnel are now more likely to be teachers, counselors, or coordinators who serve students both with and without disabilities. Third, the IDEA and NCLB transition requirements emphasize transition practices that maximize students' integration with nondisabled peers. A core principle for secondary students with disabilities is that the IEPs must reflect the general education curriculum and standards, participation in standardized assessments, and the needed transition services (Levine, Marder, & Wagner, 2004). Misperceptions about the relationship of transition planning to the general education curriculum illustrate the tensions that arise between the goals of individualized educational planning and the standards-based education model (common standards for all). As one parent put it, "I don't want to have to choose between general education advantages or transition services. My son should have both" (personal communication, October 10, 2006).

Transition as a Unifying Framework

Implementation of transition programs within a standards-based education framework presents a conceptual and practical challenge for educators, many of whom see the principles and goals as mutually exclusive. To align special education programs with general education reforms to improve postsecondary outcomes, IDEA 1997 and 2004 added new requirements that were designed to ensure that youth have greater access to the secondary education curriculum. IDEA emphasized both transition services and access to the general education curriculum. This emphasis, therefore, placed expectations on state and local educational agencies to seek practical solutions for aligning secondary education and transition systems. The requirement logically holds educational agencies responsible for (a) providing appropriate transition planning through the IEP; (b) secondary education curriculum accommodations and redesign; and (c) interagency coordination to help students and families achieve postsecondary goals.

Although designing education that is based on both common standards and the right of students with disabilities to an individualized education and transition planning is a challenging task, many school districts across the United States are proceeding with such an approach. The transition planning framework can be instrumental as a comprehensive, foundational framework for

1. incorporating the concept of integrated transition planning and participation in a general education course of study;
2. recognizing different pathways to graduation for different students;
3. guiding decision-making among students, families, and professionals for postsecondary planning;
4. meeting universal design criteria of flexible combinations of academic, career–vocational classes, and community-based work experiences to achieve different pathways to graduation.

Building on traditional career development frameworks, Kohler (1998) characterized the high school years as requiring a *transition perspective* for education of youth with disabilities. Based on this vision, transition can be viewed as a *unifying framework* for aligning standards-based education and transition services (Kochhar-Bryant & Bassett, 2002) (Figure 1–2).

Transition planning, therefore, is the foundational concept and integrates the **four building blocks of individualized education**—curriculum standards, outcomes in

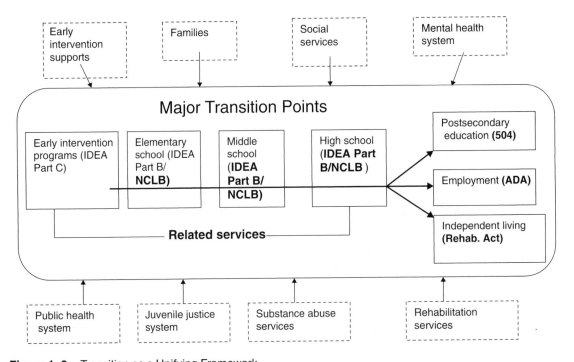

Figure 1–2   Transition as a Unifying Framework
Source: Adapted from *Successful Inclusion: Practical Strategies for a Shared Responsibility,* by C. A. Kochhar, L. L. West, and J. M. Taymans, (2002). Upper Saddle River, NJ: Merrill/Prentice Hall. Reprinted with permission.

multiple life domains, opportunities to learn (accommodations and supports), and curriculum choices.

Opportunity standards are an important element in a framework for aligning standards-based education and the provision of individualized and appropriate transition planning. Glatthorn and Craft-Tripp (2000) synthesized the various opportunities that a local school needs to provide for helping students achieve the performance standards now required of all students. Examples of opportunities that are needed by students with disabilities to participate in the general education classroom include the following:

1. A planned program of study, built around postsecondary transition goals
2. Individualized education program
3. Individualized instruction
4. Grouping that does not stigmatize students
5. A responsive curriculum
6. Adequate time for learning
7. Extended school year programming
8. Positive behavioral supports
9. Responsiveness to native language
10. Valid assessment

Glatthorn and Craft-Tripp (2000) concluded that setting educational goals for many students with disabilities means looking beyond academic goals to a broader set of outcomes. As others have previously suggested, a focus on a broad set of outcomes means that curricula for some students with disabilities, particularly at the secondary level, include nonacademic components and emphasis on the transition to work and other aspects of adult life (Halpern, 1994; Patton & Dunn, 1998; Polloway, Patton, Smith, & Rodrique, 1991; Tashie & Jorgenson, 1998).

Blending Multiple Standards

Transition planning to achieve postsecondary goals includes a variety of standards: (1) academic curriculum standards, (2) occupational skill standards, and (3) opportunity standards to assist students to progress in their educational program (supports and accommodations). Transition planning, the foundational concept, integrates the four building blocks of individualized education—standards, outcomes in **multiple domains,** opportunities, and curriculum options (Figure 1–3).

In summary, a transition planning process that blends standards and opportunities

1. is a process of continuous and systematic planning, coordination, and decision making to define and achieve postsecondary goals;
2. provides curriculum options or pathways to accommodate students' needs and different postsecondary goals;
3. blends academic, career–technical, and community-based learning;
4. addresses multiple outcome domains and measures; and
5. integrates appropriate aids and supports (opportunities).

Transition planning provides the passage or "bridge" between school and adult life for students with disabilities.

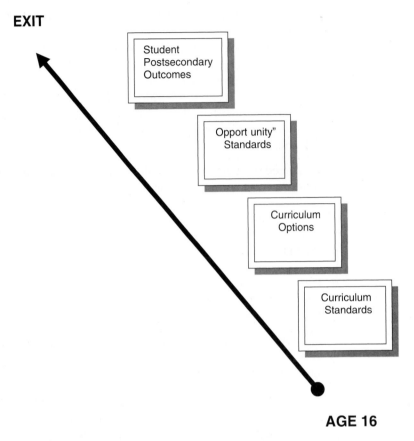

EXIT

Student
Postsecondary
Outcomes

Opport unity"
Standards

Curriculum
Options

Curriculum
Standards

AGE 16

Figure 1–3   Blending Standards: Four Building Blocks

SUMMARY

This chapter defined transition services and provided an overview of conditions for youth with disabilities that make transition services essential for improving post-secondary outcomes. It reviewed educational reforms that are affecting transition services and summarized the many benefits of transition services and community-based education for students. New national and regional research initiatives on effective practices to promote successful transition are underway and are providing new insights into barriers and strategies for strengthening transition services. The positioning of transition services within the framework of youth development for all students adds a new imperative to national efforts.

Students with disabilities can be full and contributing members of a community through the dedicated collaboration among schools, families, community agencies, postsecondary systems, and employers. Transition is not just a fad. It is not a program or a project that has a beginning and an end. It is a vision and a goal that is linked to a greater effort to advance a democratic and civilized society for all youth. An investment in effective transition services for youth demonstrates this nation's commitment to the full participation of all its citizens and residents in the work and progress of the nation.

KEY TERMS AND PHRASES

career–vocational education
coordinated set of activities
developmental framework
four building blocks of individualized
   education
high-stakes testing
multiple domains
pathways model
results-oriented process

self-determination
shared responsibility
standards-based reforms
systematic transition services
transition planning
universal design
youth development
youth outcomes

QUESTIONS FOR REFLECTION, THINKING, AND SKILL BUILDING

1. In what ways has the concept of transition changed during the past 20 years? Why were these changes important, and how did they advance transition services?

2. What is meant by the idea that transition involves many "domains" that are interrelated?

3. What is meant by *systematic transition services* or *coordinated set of services,* and why is it an important concept for youth and families?

4. What does it mean to "align" transition and standards-based education?

5. How do the assumptions of "standards-based reform" and "individualized education" for students with disabilities differ? What strategies can be used to align the frameworks and reduce the conflicts?

6. Discuss the benefits of transition services and community-based education for students with disabilities.

7. Examine your school district's and state's documents related to transition, including planning documents, guidelines for implementation, or personnel training materials. How is *transition* defined? How consistent is that definition with the legal definition and requirements?

8. Research youth outcomes in your school district. How do they differ from youth outcomes in your state? Are conditions better or worse for students in your district in comparison with state data?

9. What are the trends for career–technical (vocational) education in your district? Are programs and services expanding or diminishing? Gather evidence and develop a profile on the status of vocational–technical education using several methods: (a) interview several vocational–technical education teachers and administrators, (b) locate new articles, and (c) review local school planning documents or annual plans over time. Synthesize the changes you observe and reach a conclusion about the trend.

10. Examine your state's Special Education State Improvement Plan, and discuss the transition goals and initiatives that it addresses. In your judgment, do they satisfactorily address the priority needs of your local educational agency?

Chapter 2

Student Populations and Their Transition Needs

Carol A. Kochhar-Bryant

Come to the edge, you won't fall.

Come to the edge, you won't fall.

I came to the edge, they pushed me,

and I flew.

—Guillaume Apollinaire

Chapter Questions

- What is diversity?
- Who are special learners and what are their transition needs?
- What other risk factors affect successful transition to adult life?
- Who are culturally and linguistically diverse students?
- Who are middle school students and what are their transition needs?
- How do families' needs change along the developmental path to transition?

INTRODUCTION

In the past two decades, students with disabilities have made significant progress in gaining access to postsecondary education. Individuals with disabilities, including those with significant disabilities, are successful in careers as teachers, doctors, lawyers, politicians, business leaders, computer specialists, and technical workers in a variety of industries. What has led to this progress? It is our belief that this trend has resulted from the combined efforts of students themselves to set high goals and work to achieve them, of parents believing in and supporting those goals, of teachers and counselors and other professionals who appreciate students' abilities and are willing to collaborate to assist youth in the transition process. It is the advocacy of postsecondary support personnel and employers dedicated to opening doors for such students and willing to provide a range of supports. More broadly, it is the result of a larger societal shift in values and beliefs that (a) all individuals should be supported in reaching their greatest potential and (b) humans are capable of rising above extraordinary challenges. Together, these shifts in attitudes and practices are increasing the likelihood that young people will pursue advanced education and pursue their career possibilities. This chapter explores the concept of diversity, defines the heterogeneous population of special learners, explores the transition choices and challenges that they face, and examines the needs of families in the dynamic interaction with their children along the developmental path of transition to adulthood.

The number of students exiting schools has increased over the past 20 years due to improvements in special education identification, accommodations, intervention strategies in mainstream settings, and greater access to technology. Although there has been progress among many youth with disabilities, there is a continuing cause for concern when comparing outcomes with their nondisabled peers, including higher absenteeism, lower grade point averages, high dropout rates (National Dropout Prevention Center for students with Disabilities, 2006), lower rates of enrollment in postsecondary education, lower employment rates, and poor adult adjustment (National Dropout Prevention Center for students with Disabilities, 2006; Osgood, Foster, Flanagan, & Ruth, 2005). According to the U.S. Department of Education's Office of Special Education Programs (2007), only 51% of students with disabilities exited school with a standard diploma in the 2001–2002 academic school year. Of those students who do not complete high school 61.2% are students with emotional disabilities and about 35% are students with learning disabilities (National High School Center, 2007b). Only 14.6% of all students with disabilities transition into 2-year or 4-year colleges. In other words, too few students with disabilities (a) are encouraged by their teachers and parents to consider postsecondary education as a viable goal, (b) are academically prepared for college, (c) have appropriate transition goals and planning, and (d) receive appropriate accommodations and support services that are easily identified and readily available at both the secondary and postsecondary level (Ward & Berry, 2005).

The National Longitudinal Transition Study-2 (NLTS2) studied the issue of problem behavior among students with disabilities that resulted in negative consequences, by assessing the extent to which youth had ever been suspended or expelled from school, fired from a job, or arrested. For youth with learning disabilities (LD), those experiencing any of these negative consequences increased from 13% in 1987 to 19% in 2001. Arrest rates are relatively high, about one third of students with disabilities who drop out of high school have spent a night in jail, a rate three times that of students who complete high school (National High School Center, 2007a). These disabilities are not just "school-related" disabilities but life disabilities. Lack of basic academic skills, career guidance, and preparation affect all other areas of life. Teenage high school dropouts, specifically from low-income families, and those with disabilities face the most difficult challenges in finding employment opportunities and are more likely to generate other social costs including incarceration and welfare (Benz, Lindstrom, & Yovanoff, 2000; Blum, 2005; Checkoway, 2005; Izzo, Cartledge, Miller, Growick, & Rutkowski, 2000; Madson-Ankeny, 2000; Riccomini, Bost, Katsiyannis, & Zhang, 2005; Sitlington, Clark, & Kolstoe, 2000; Sum et al., 2003).

Responding to sustained national concerns about the preparation of youth for employment and independence, congressional leaders have called for studies of outcomes of youth-centered programs, including special education, career-vocational education, job training, and rehabilitation. Results of congressional studies over the past decade have highlighted a lack of coordination among education and training agencies in addressing the complexities of youth unemployment (U.S. Government Accountability Office, 1998, 2001, 2003). National and state experts conclude that a more aggressive and comprehensive effort must be made to improve outcomes for America's youth with disabilities and indeed for all youth.

⇒ WHAT IS DIVERSITY?

Diversity as Human Variation

All of us are bound by our cultural and experiential lenses through which we see the world. It is difficult to step outside these boundaries, but it is essential for professionals in the educational field to do so. For teachers, counselors, and administrators to make meaning of their worlds, they must expand their abilities to interpret the world from multiple perspectives. The greater our ability to appreciate perspectives that are rooted in variations among people—different cultures, ethnic backgrounds, disabilities, and gender differences—the greater our ability to reflect on our practices and establish collaborative relationships with a wider group of colleagues. Such collaborative practice is essential in the development of coordinated transition services for youth with disabilities.

Although diversity in the educational field has typically meant cultural and linguistic differences, more recently, the concept of diversity embraces the broader notion of human variability or *human variation*. **Human variation** refers to the range of possible values for any measurable characteristic, physical or mental, that constitute differences among us (Schriner, 2001). Common human variations include gender, race or ethnicity, language, physical and cognitive disabilities, and cultural background. Variation also encompasses aspects of human physical appearance such as body shape and size, intellectual abilities, temperament and personality traits, special talents, and sexual orientation. Akin to human variation is the term *neurodiversity*, which means that differences among us in neurological "wiring" is a normal human difference that is to be as respected as any other human difference. Differences can be trivial or important, transient or permanent, voluntary or involuntary, congenital or acquired, genetic or environmental. What is important for education and transition planning for students with disabilities is the social value that is placed on these differences by society and how those values affect every aspect of a person's life.

There is considerable controversy about certain human differences and the degree to which a difference is part of a person's "essential" nature or is partly a socially constructed attribute. For example, in the United States there are several continuing debates that connect the human difference of "disability" with social values and public policies:

1. Is Down syndrome a disability or is it a "difference" that is part of the natural variation among humans?
2. Are there genetic differences in the way males and females learn?
3. Are there systematic differences in the way different ethnic groups learn?
4. Should individuals with emotional and behavioral disabilities be permitted to own guns?
5. Should individuals who are linguistically different be immersed in the mainstream language or taught in their native language?
6. Should children with severe cognitive disabilities be integrated into mainstream classrooms in schools or colleges?
7. Should surgery be used to alter physical differences and appearance on demand?
8. Is sexual orientation biological or discretionary (a social choice)?
9. Are psychiatric illnesses "real" illnesses when their causes still unknown?
10. Is intelligence a reflection of general cognitive ability as currently measured by available psychometric tests, or are there multiple factors or components to intelligence?

The boundaries between "wellness" and "normal are also surrounded with controversy." In some cultures, physical imperfections and disabilities can fully exclude children from social participation. In some societies today (and in the United States until the 20th century) being female is considered a negatively valued human difference. The way a society or group views, values, or devalues a difference has implications for social patterns of prejudice or acceptance.

Many children and adults try various ways to *socially renegotiate* the negative values assigned to certain differences. For example, people have developed communities of individuals with disabilities (e.g., community of the deaf on Martha's Vineyard in the 19th century), struggled politically for recognition and social justice, changed physical differences through surgery or other means, and acquired the mainstream language and culture. The concept of *differently abled* has been advanced by individuals seeking to persuade society to view incapacities as a human difference with a less negative value. In Western culture, there has been large-scale renegotiation of the social significance of human variations in the schools and workplace. Various civil rights laws have been passed to increase the social opportunities available to children and adults with disabilities.

How does diversity relate to democratic values and to transition? Many diverse groups of individuals in U.S. history—women, people with disabilities, and cultural and language minorities—have initiated social movements to fight for civil rights for social recognition and access to the benefits of society. Such social movements are born from and result in a broader fundamental change in thinking and beliefs about human differences and the values we place upon them. The American way of life, grounded in the U.S. Constitution, means protecting and strengthening the rights of all American people, both citizens and newcomers, to share equally in the benefits and bounty and responsibilities of a democratic society. On a philosophical level of discussion, a fundamental interesting question has been posed for contemporary Western discourse on **disability**: Is equality, sameness, or similarity always desired by those in society (Stiker & Sayers, 2000)? Stiker and Sayers highlight the consequences of such a mindset, illustrating that when great importance is placed on equality and sameness, then intolerance of diversity and individualism arises. Difference is not only acceptable, but it is desirable and necessary. This notion can serve as an analogy for transition services because transition planning and implementation need to be highly individualized for each student, based on their unique needs and postsecondary goals. Transition services are not efficient or effective when they are *generic* or delivered to each individual in the same manner.

WHO ARE SPECIAL LEARNERS AND WHAT ARE THEIR TRANSITION NEEDS?

Today, general education teachers, in collaboration with special educators and related service specialists, share responsibility to develop educational programs for a highly diverse population of students. The population includes those with disabilities, students with disabilities who are gifted and talented, students placed at risk for failure in the general education setting, returning school dropouts, students with limited

English proficiency, teen parents, and many others. Each of these groups may be considered a *special population* of students that possesses unique needs that require specialized educational services and supports.

Special learners refers to a broad group of students, including those with disabilities who are receiving special education, those at risk of being identified as needing special education, and those who are placed at risk of failure in the educational system for reasons other than disability. Such reasons may include lack of motivation, pressure to leave school to work and support a family, substance abuse, or lack of availability of needed academic or support services. A *student with a disability* refers to a child with any of the following disorders, who needs special education and related services, identified under IDEA: mental retardation, hearing impairments (including deafness), speech or language impairments, visual impairments (including blindness), emotional disturbance, orthopedic impairments, autism, traumatic brain injury (TBI), other health impairments, or specific learning disabilities.

IDEA 2004 has added new definitions of individuals with special learning needs who are at risk of failure in the educational system. This category includes students in preschool through grade 12 (K-12) who are suspected of having a disability, who need additional academic and behavioral supports to succeed in a general education environment, and who require *early intervening services* to prevent referral to special education. This group also includes those with limited English proficiency and those who are economically disadvantaged, migrant, and homeless [§613(a)(2)(C)]. The 2004 IDEA also emphasized the goal of engagement and progress of students in the general education curriculum. In the development of the IEP, the IEP team is also required to consider special factors for children. There are several special factors that must also be considered when developing the IEP, including the following:

1. *Behavior That Impedes Learning.* In the case of a child whose behavior interferes with his or her learning or that of others, consider appropriate strategies and supports, including positive behavioral interventions, to address that behavior.
2. *Limited English Proficiency.* In the case of a child with limited English proficiency, consider the language needs of the child in relation to the child's IEP.
3. *Braille Needs.* In the case of a child who is blind or visually impaired, provide for instruction in Braille unless the IEP team determines that it is not appropriate.
4. *Communication Needs.* Consider the communication needs of the child, and in the case of a child who is deaf or hard of hearing, consider the child's language and communication needs and opportunities for communication with others, along with the full range of needs.
5. *Assistive Technology.* Consider whether the child requires assistive technology services [§300.346(a)(2)].

Teachers are expected to work together in a climate of shared responsibility to ensure full participation of all children and youth.

According to income data from the U.S. Department of Commerce (2007), **economically disadvantaged** students live in families with very low incomes. Such learners are likely to have circumstances in their life experience that may predispose them to learning difficulties. The households where youth grow up, the resources available in them, and the characteristics of the parents who head them can have implications for students' economic security and emotional support (Jerald, 2006; Wagner, Cameto, & Guzmán, 2003). There are higher rates of dropout and wider gaps in academic achievement between students from low and high socioeconomic communities.

How does poverty contribute to risk of failure in transition to responsible and productive adult life? The child poverty rate is perhaps the most widely used measure to identify the health and well being of children. According to Smith, Polloway, Patton, and Dowdy (2001), "Poverty is a social condition associated with many different kinds of problems. Poverty has been related to crime, physical abuse, learning problems, behavior problems, and emotional problems" (p. 355). Whereas the number of poor children living in families totally dependent on welfare has actually fallen in the past two decades, the number living in families earning an income (no income from public assistance) increased from 4.4 million in 1976 to 6.9 million in 2000 (Kidscount, 2003). Despite the wealth in the United States, the rate of poverty among children in the United States is higher than any other developed country. Elders (2002) observes that children of the "Five H Club"—hungry, healthless, homeless, hugless, and hopeless—have difficulty concentrating on schoolwork, which often leads them to "mask" learning difficulties by exhibiting acting-out behaviors (White & Gallay, 2005).

Today, these **special populations** represent a majority of students in many school systems across the United States. The percentage of the total school population with disabilities who are receiving special education services ranges from 9.1% nationally (U.S. Office of Special Education, 2005) to over 20% as reported by some individual states. The percentage of total school population of all of special learner groups can range from 25% to 80% in some urban areas (Blechman, Fishman, & Fishman, 2004). Teachers and related services professionals are expected to work to improve the achievement and development of each of these groups of students.

Defining Students with Disabilities and Their Transition Needs

IDEA 2004 identified specific categories of disabilities under which children may be eligible for special education and related services. A student with a disability refers to a child who needs special education and related services (IDEA, 2004, §1401). The NLTS2 provides information on the characteristics of youth who received special education. Almost 13% of all youth, age 13 through 16, who were enrolled in school in the 2000–2001 school year received special education (Wagner, Cameto, & Guzmán, 2003). More than 6 in 10 students (62%) in this age group who were receiving special education were classified as having a learning disability. Those with intellectual disabilities (mental retardation) comprised 12% of students receiving special education and those with emotional disturbances comprised 11%. Youth with other health impairments comprised 5% and those with speech or language impairments comprised 4% of the total group of students receiving special education. More than half (55%) of all youth with disabilities were reported to have more than one kind of disability. Besides those classified as having multiple disabilities or deaf-blindness, secondary disabilities were particularly common for youth with mental retardation (81%) or emotional disturbances (76%) and least common for those with hearing or visual impairments (38%) (Wagner, Cameto, & Guzmán, 2003). The following sections define the major disability categories recognized by IDEA 2004 and present key transition issues for these populations of youth.

Learning Disability. A **learning disability** is a disorder of one or more of the basic psychological processes involved in understanding or using language, spoken or written. Such a disability may manifest itself in the imperfect ability to listen, think, speak, read, write, spell, or do mathematical calculations. The U.S. Department of Education, 2004a examined the most prevalent disability types reported by students in postsecondary education in the year 2003–2004. Learning disabilities represented less than 7.4% (15% as reported by NLTS2), whereas they represent over 60% of the total population of students with disabilities in high school.

Under IDEA 2004, a local educational agency is no longer required to take into consideration whether a child has a severe discrepancy between intellectual ability and achievement in oral expression, listening comprehension, written expression, basic reading skill, reading comprehension, mathematical calculation, or mathematical reasoning (IDEA, 2004, §1414). Instead, a local educational agency (LEA) may use a *response to intervention* (RTI) evaluation process—usually implemented by a collaborative team—to determine if a child would respond to educational interventions.

Career Development and Transition Issues. Career counseling in secondary schools is important for all students, but it is especially critical for students with learning disabilities. This group comprises about half of the identified exceptional students. Although they are similar to their nondisabled peers in intellectual characteristics, their learning problems in the acquisition and use of listening, speaking, reading, writing, reasoning, or mathematical abilities (Deshler, Ellis, & Lenz, 1996; Kovaleski & Prasse, 2004) can prevent them from acquiring knowledge when they are taught in large groups or counseled with unstructured approaches.

Characteristics of youth with learning disability (LD) that can contribute to their difficulties in career development and planning include the following: lack of awareness of their own abilities and talents; underdeveloped planning, organization, and problem-solving skills; delayed social skills and social awareness; low academic achievement, particularly in literacy (Blum, 2005; Brinckerhoff, McGuire, & Shaw, 2002).

Because youth with LD have a higher dropout rate than their nondisabled peers, they have a greater need for transition services that focus on career assessment counseling and obtaining and maintaining employment. Instructional career counseling using cognitive approaches has been recommended for youth with LD while they are still enrolled in secondary school (Biller, 1987; Riccomini, Bost, Katsiyamis, & Zhang, 2005; Silverberg, Warner, Rong, & Goodwin, 2004). Cognitive approaches have been used to enhance learning in a number of curriculum areas, to increase self-control in students with LD (Blum, 2005; Englert, Tarrant, & Mariage, 1992; Riccomini et al., 2005).

For young people with disabilities, mentoring can impact many of the goals that are part of the transition process: succeeding academically, understanding the adult world, developing career awareness, accepting support while taking responsibility, communicating effectively, overcoming barriers, and developing social skills (Rhodes Grossman, & Resch, 2000). Mentors can assist greatly by providing connections for youth within the world of work and opening possibilities for employment. Mentoring can be a dynamic catalyst for the achievement of transition goals (Sword & Hill, 2002).

Students with LD need to be aware of the postsecondary options available to them. There are many postsecondary options for youth with disabilities in the United States. Four-year colleges and universities offer Bachelor of Arts or Bachelor of Science degrees. Some also offer graduate and professional degrees. Community colleges are public, 2-year colleges that typically serve people in the surrounding communities and offer academic, technical, and continuing education courses. These programs typically lead to a license, a certificate, or associate of arts or science degrees. Some community colleges offer programs specifically for individuals with learning disabilities, to help them with organizational and study skills (Burgstahler, Crawford, & Acosta, 2001).

Vocational and technical colleges offer a variety of options, including associate degrees, certificates, and work apprenticeships. Associate degree programs prepare students for technical occupations (e.g., accounting, dental hygienist, computer programmer). Technical diploma programs meet the needs of businesses and industry and provide employees with required certification for employment (e.g., automotive maintenance, accounting assistant, pharmacy technician). Apprenticeships are geared toward those interested in working in industrial or service trades (e.g., carpentry, plumbing, machining). Military service can also help young people achieve their career goals; the military branches, however, are not required to accommodate individuals on the basis of disability (Brown 2000; HEATH Resource Center, 2005). Finally, employment in competitive jobs or supported work settings is available to many youth who need extended support in transitioning to employment. Students with LD can benefit from guidance in considering appropriate career choices and often need additional instruction and support to develop independent living skills.

Emotional and Behavioral Disabilities. **Emotional and behavioral disabilities** involve one or more of the following characteristics, displayed over a long period of time and to a marked degree that adversely affects a child's educational performance: (a) an inability to learn that cannot be explained by intellectual, sensory, or health factors; (b) an inability to build or maintain satisfactory interpersonal relationships with peers or teachers; (c) inappropriate behavior and feelings under normal circumstances; (d) a general pervasive mood of unhappiness or depression; and (e) a tendency to develop physical symptoms or fears associated with personal or school problems. The term does not apply to children who are identified as *socially maladjusted* or have a *conduct disorder,* unless they also have an emotional disability. The 2004 National Postsecondary Student Aid Study examined the most prevalent disability types reported by students in postsecondary education in the year 2003–2004 and found that emotional or psychological conditions represented 21.9% of students (U.S. Department of Education, 2004b).

Adolescents with emotional and behavioral disabilities (EBD) have only a 32.1% graduation rate and the highest dropout rate (61.2%) of any disability category (U.S. Department of Education, Office of Special education, 2005b, 2001–2002 data). Relatively, a small number of students with EBD go on to a postsecondary degree (Rogers & Rogers, 2001). Three years after graduating from high school, 52.7% of youth and young adults with disabilities are working full time or 35 hours per week or more (Cameto, 2005; Cameto & Levine, 2005, NLTS2, 2005 data). Following a decision to leave school, 10% of youth with EBD live in a correctional facility, halfway house, drug treatment center, or "on the street"—twice as many as students with other disabilities (Leone, Quinn, & Osher, 2002). Overall, parents report that about one third of students aged 13–17 with disabilities have been suspended or expelled, and 18.9% of students aged 10–12 years (U.S. Department of Education, Office of Special Education, 2005b data 2004). The suspension and expulsion rate is 27% for those with learning disabilities, 73% for those with emotional disturbances, and 41% for those with other health impairments (including ADHD when it is the primary disability) (SRI International, 2006).

Secondary school youth with EBD differ from the general population of youth in many ways other than their disability—differences that can help in understanding their outcomes. For example,

1. More than three fourths of youth with EBD are male (Snyder, 2000), and therefore, conditions that are more common among young men (such as criminal justice system involvement) are likely to be more common among youth with EBD than the general population, apart from any effects of their disabilities (Wagner, Newman, Cameto, & Levine, 2006).

2. Almost two thirds of youth with EBD are reported by their parents to also have attention deficit or attention deficit/hyperactivity disorder (ADHD), with its associated impacts on behavior.

3. One fourth of youth with EBD are rated low by parents on a scale of social skills, which could be expected to influence relationships both in and out of school.

4. Of youth with EBD, 38% have been held back a grade at least once in their school careers, according to parents.

5. A history of social adjustment concerns also accompanies many youth with EBD to high school—almost three-fourths of them have been suspended or expelled at least once, a rate more than twice that of youth with disabilities as a whole.

6. According to school staff, 55% of youth with EBD have a behavior management plan or participate in a behavior management program, half receive behavioral interventions, and a similar percentage receives mental health services.

7. Substance abuse education or services are provided to 45% of youth with emotional disability (ED) and 43% take part in a conflict resolution or anger management program (Wagner, Cameto, & Newman, 2003; Wagner, Newman, Cameto, & Levine, 2005, 2006).

This population of students has among the highest need for early academic, social, and career-transition support to prevent long-term postschool dependence.

Career Development and Transition Issues.   Some research reports are projecting that depression among young people will increase rapidly between now and 2010 and that it will frequently develop right at the point when youth are transitioning to adulthood and taking on more responsibility for their lives. It is critical, therefore, to consider both physical and mental health issues facing youth as they transition into the community (HSC Foundation, 2006).

The educational programs for students with serious emotional disabilities need to include attention to mastering academics; developing social skills and life skills; and increasing self-awareness, self-esteem, and self-control. Peer support for youth with emotional disabilities is also an important element of a transition program. Additional life skills programs include independent living skills training for 14–21 year-olds, life mapping workshops, and consultation with adult case coordinators to ensure the smooth transition to needed services for youth reaching age 18 (Morningstar & Benitez, 2004; Smink & Schargel, 2004). Service coordination that is centered on the individual needs of the youth is aimed at decreasing the rate of hospitalization and incarceration for these youth and developing resilience and coping skills.

Career education is also a central part of secondary education for these students and should be a part of every adolescent's transition plan within his or her IEP. Services offered to youth include social skills training, individual and group psychosocial educational services, structured recreation, community service, and exploration and development of educational and career interests and opportunities. Transition planning should also include health and mental health coverage as a key element in postsecondary settings.

Intellectual Disabilities.   Previous definitions of **intellectual disability**, or *mental retardation,* included substantial limitations in levels of functioning that adversely affect an individual's educational performance and adaptive behavior. *Adaptive behavior* means an ability to cope with the demands of the environment, self-help, communication, and social skills that are manifested during the early developmental period. In the last few years, the definition that was previously centered on deficits has shifted to reflect significant success of people with intellectual disabilities based on increased support in their homes, communities, and work places (Getzel & Wehman, 2005; Wehman, 2006). The American Association of Mental Retardation (AAMR) defines mental retardation as a particular state of functioning that begins in childhood and is characterized by limitation in both intelligence and adaptive skills. AAMR places limitations of adaptive skills within cultural, linguistic, and community environmental contexts and recognizes that such limitations coexist with strengths in other adaptive skills (AAMR, 2002).

Career Development and Transition Issues.   Although NLTS2 reports approximately 13% of students with disabilities have intellectual disabilities in high school, they comprise only 3.7% of the disabled population at the postsecondary level, mostly at 2-year colleges. Beginning career assessment and planning in middle school and early postsecondary planning is also essential for these students. Assessments should be modified to include authentic and portfolio-based assessments rather than standardized assessment.

Guidance with developing appropriate postsecondary goals and curriculum choices to meet those goals is essential. Students also need orientation to careers or types of jobs, assistance to develop realistic goals for their future, and opportunities to explore their communities and career interests (Wehman, 2006). Community-based skills training and a functional curriculum is essential to promote community integration (McGlashing-Johnson, Agran, Sitlington, Cavin, & Wehmeyer, 2003; White & Weiner, 2004). In other words, curriculum content should be structured to promote students' independent living and functional life skills. Postsecondary opportunities should also be explored because a growing number of community colleges are establishing campus-based programs for students with intellectual disabilities.

Social skills is an important part of the transition planning process along with community support services to promote continued social adjustment in the post-secondary setting (Crites & Dunn, 2004; Getzel & Wehman, 2005). Students should be expected to participate in their transition planning and encouraged to express their career interests and desires. Furthermore, students should be assisted to access vocational rehabilitation services, social security benefits, medical benefits, and employment incentives to which they may be entitled.

Autism. **Autism** is a developmental disability that significantly affects verbal and non-verbal communication and social interaction, is generally evident before age three, and adversely affects educational performance. Other characteristics include repetitive activities and stereotyped movements, resistance to change in the environment or in daily routines, and unusual responses to sensory experiences. Autism is also referred to as autism spectrum disorder and includes pervasive developmental disorder not otherwise specified (PDD-NOS) and Asperger's syndrome. A 2007 report by Centers for Disease Control found that 1 in 150 children in America today have an autism spectrum disorder (ASD). The Autism Society of America (ASA, 2007) estimates that 1.5 million Americans and their families are now affected. Although most funding for autism research is focused on early intervention, many of these children are entering transition years and services will be needed (Gabriels & Hill, 2007; Muller, 2004).

Career Development and Transition Issues. Secondary transition poses unique challenges for students with autism. The NLTS2 compared transition experiences of students from all 13 federal disability categories and found that students with autism differ from students with other types of disability in a number of significant ways. For example, students with autism experience greater difficulty with social adjustment and are the least likely of all students with disabilities to socialize with their peers, engage in extracurricular activities (e.g., sports or special interest groups), participate in transition planning, and assume high levels of responsibility within their households (Wagner et al., 2003; Wagner, Marder, & Cardoso, 2002). Furthermore, although students with autism are among the most likely to be engaged in work–study employment, they are the least likely to hold regular paid jobs (Wagner et al., 2003.).

Postschool outcomes for adults with autism and other autism spectrum disorders are often discouraging (Howlin, 2000; Muller, 2004; Müller, Schuler, Burton, & Yates, 2003). Despite the transition requirements of IDEA and a growing body of research in support of effective transition planning for middle and high school students with autism spectrum disorders (ASD) (e.g., Schall, Cortijo-Doval, Targett, & Wehman, 2006), adults on the spectrum remain without employment in large numbers (e.g., Howlin, 2000). Even those generally regarded as most capable often live lives of social isolation, dependence, and few opportunities to improve their quality of life (Howlin, Goode, Hutton, & Rutter, 2004).

One study, for example, found that despite having the potential to work, few individuals with Asperger's syndrome were in regular employment and that even among those with formal qualifications, employment levels were disappointing and occupational status was low (Howlin, 2000; Howlin, Goode, Hutton, & Rutter). A second study found that adults with autism often experienced high levels of unemployment and underemployment and that lack of social skills frequently led to poor outcomes including being fired from jobs (Müller et al., 2003).

There is a critical need to revisit the ways in which such learners are prepared for adult life beyond the classroom, in the community, and on the job. National trends toward noncategorical educational and transition services has sometimes resulted in a generic or one-size-fits-all approach to transition programming, often making it difficult to meet the unique needs of students with autism in an individualized manner. Direct and sustained social skills training has been demonstrated to be very effective with students with autism and such training needs to be integrated as part of transition planning (Cohen, 2005; Gabriels & Hill, 2007; Gerhardt & Holmes, 2005).

Sensory Impairments (Hearing, Including Deafness, and Visual, Including Blindness). About 1.5 out of every 1,000 school age children in the United States have a visual impairment, a hearing impairment, or both. Hearing impairment means an impairment in hearing, permanent or fluctuating, which adversely affects a child's educational performance. Visual impairment means impairment in vision, including both partial sight and blindness, that even with correction, adversely affects a child's educational performance. There have been significant improvements in the enrollment of deaf students to postsecondary education, increasing from 250 in 1950 to over 23,800 enrolled in 2- and 4-year colleges (Lewis, 1999). However, transition challenges persist.

Career Development and Transition Issues.   Programs and services for deaf and blind students are well established across the United States, but students continue to have problems with persistence while in postsecondary institutions. There is a continuing need for postsecondary institutions to take responsibility for the quality and effectiveness of support services for deaf and blind students. Many students, however, are not well prepared for the academic and social challenges that confront them in postsecondary settings. Transition preparation and planning for secondary students and first-year college students are crucial to support student persistence and completion of a postsecondary program.

Transition needs for students with hearing and visual impairments must be individualized and may be highly variable. (National Longitudinal Transition Study 2, 2005). Transition services must be part of a visually impaired student's IEP by age 16. Transition services can be provided by schools in cooperation with vocational rehabilitation (VR) under memoranda of understanding between state education and VR agencies.

Under these cooperative relationships, visually impaired teens can also receive skills training; participate in after school, weekend, and summer programs; and gain work-experience training from private or public agencies for the blind and visually impaired.

There are many agencies and organizations within each state that can provide transition supports and services for students with visual impairments. These include national and state agencies such as the American Council for the Blind, National Federation for the Blind, National Association for Visually Handicapped, National Braille Association, Developmental Disabilities Service Offices, State Transition Technical Assistance projects, Parent Training and Information Centers, Private Agencies for the Blind, Independent Living Centers, and Braille, Tape and Large Print Services. Students with sensory impairments, however, continue to indicate a lack of assistive and adaptive equipment (Burgstahler et al., 2001).

For individuals with visual impairment, availability of transportation is not the only impediment to independent travel. They must also know what systems of transport are available, how to access these, how to plan their travel, and how to execute their travel plans safely. For many individuals, learning how to travel on public transportation requires systematic training. Travel training, then, is often a crucial element in empowering people with disabilities to use the newly accessible transportation systems to attend postsecondary institutions, or for employment.

Speech or Language Impairment. Speech and language impairments refer to problems in communication and related areas such as oral motor function, stuttering, impaired articulation, language impairments, or a voice impairment that adversely affects a child's educational performance (Hamaguchi, 2001). Language impairment often coexists with speech impairment. By age 14, few students have a lone identification of speech impairment; in most cases, the speech impairment is associated with a language impairment or another exceptionality including autism/pervasive developmental disorder or developmental or physical disability (Ehren & Nelson, 2005). Some causes of speech and language disorders include hearing loss, neurological disorders, brain injury, mental retardation, drug abuse, physical impairments such as cleft lip or palate, and vocal abuse or misuse. Students with language impairments will typically have difficulty with reading and writing, listening and learning demands of the classroom or workplace, using oral expressive language to communicate and interact in academic and social situations, organizing and formulating oral and written information, using oral language to problem solve and reflect on behavior, and may be frustrated with communication difficulties.

A student with a severe speech impairment (e.g., articulation, apraxia, dysarthria, dysfluency or stuttering), or who may be almost nonspeaking, may exhibit poor communication skills with strangers or in new situations, may require extensive accommodations in the classroom or workplace (e.g., visual supports, communication devices), may use an alternative or augmentative communication system, or may demonstrate frustration and social isolation (Ehran & Nelson, 2005).

More than 1 million of the students served in the public schools' special education programs in the 2000–2001 school year were categorized as having a speech or language impairment. This estimate does not include children who have speech or language problems secondary to other conditions such as deafness. Language disorders may be related to other disabilities such as mental retardation, autism, or cerebral palsy. It is estimated that communication disorders (including speech, language, and hearing disorders) affect 1 of every 10 people in the United States.

Career Development and Transition Issues.   Language impairment may also be associated with other exceptionalities such as learning disability, mild intellectual disability, behavior, autism/pervasive developmental disorder, and developmental disability. It is likely that transition planning for students with these exceptionalities will need to consider the student's speech and language skills. Speech impairments that may require specialized transition planning include stuttering, dysarthria, and apraxia. Students with severe difficulty in speech, such that it may be nonfunctional, require accommodations such as communication boards, voice output devices and may require the services of a speech-language pathologist.

The transition planning team for students with speech or language impairments should include special education teachers familiar with the student's strengths and needs and a speech-language pathologist who has been closely involved in the assessment of the student's strengths and needs and the provision of services. For some students, specialists in the areas of augmentative and alternative communication may need to be involved, particularly in regard to equipment recommendations. For some students with physically or neurologically based speech disorders, medical input may be beneficial.

Transition planning for these students will require the team to consider the listening, speaking, reading, and writing demands of postsecondary or workplace settings. The team will need to identify the student's strengths as well as the compensatory strategies that the student will need to function in the workplace or in a postsecondary institution. Strategies to consider include the following:

1. Identification of the student's personal learning style and accommodations necessary for successful learning and working
2. For students who stutter, modifications and accommodations may include support for class participation, intervention by a speech-language pathologist, and alternative oral presentation options (e.g., in writing, audio- or videotaping, or one-on-one with teacher)
3. Investigation of assistive technology tools that can increase community involvement, postsecondary, and employment opportunities
4. Training in the use of assistive technology, communication devices, and/or computers in a variety of settings
5. Development of student's study skills including strategies for improved listening skills, note taking, test performance, and small group or class participation
6. Development of appropriate interpersonal communication and social skills for different settings (e.g., school, recreation, employment)
7. Development of self-advocacy skills to obtain support and necessary accommodations for postsecondary or work environments
8. Identification and development of specific employment skills for targeted workplace (e.g., competence in latest versions of computer software and hardware,

woodworking, metal working or technical knowledge, fine art or performance portfolio)

9. Development of positive work habits, including punctuality, responsibility, timely task completion, and appropriate appearance
10. Participation in a coop program, possibly with the assistance of a peer mentor or a job coach (paid or volunteer)
11. Ongoing monitoring of courses, with program modifications and accommodations of required secondary school programs (Ontario Association for Families of Children with Communication Disorders, 2001).

Orthopedic Impairments.   Severe orthopedic impairments that adversely affect children's educational performance include impairments caused by congenital anomaly (i.e., clubfoot, absence of an extremity), impairments caused by disease (i.e., poliomyelitis, bone tuberculosis), and impairments from other causes (i.e., cerebral palsy, amputations, and fractures or burns that cause muscle contractures). The 2004 National Postsecondary Student Aid Study was a nationally representative survey of students who attended postsecondary education institutions during the 2003–2004 academic year (U.S. Department of Education, 2004b). The NPSAS study of disabling conditions in post secondary education revealed that 25% of students identified orthopedic or mobility impairment as the main disabling condition (U.S. Department of Education).

Career Development and Transition Issues.   Medical advances have greatly prolonged the lives of youth with severe orthopedic impairments. Therefore, for youth with disabilities or serious medical conditions, transition planning represents a critical component of their lives. Such planning should start early, involve the young person in decision making, include career development programming, and build a strong support system for the youth, which includes the medical community, family, friends, peers, and the larger community in which they live (Blum, 2005; Blum, White, & Gallay, 2005).

In the postsecondary environment, many students with orthopedic and other health impairments may not require additional accommodations and services but do rely on accessibility features on campuses (Ward & Berry, 2005). Students with physical disabilities listed physical barriers on campus and difficulty accessing the health care system as major challenges to participation in postsecondary education. The school district plays a large role in providing health services or connecting the student to health services (Thoma, 1999), but once the student exits special education, the school district is no longer responsible for providing such services (Morningstar, Kleinhammer-Tranill & Lattin 1999). Health insurance, therefore, is vital for youth entering postsecondary settings; however, many youth in the age group 18–24 who are from low income families and who do not work lack such insurance (Anderson, 1995; Brindis, Driscoll, Biggs, & Valderrama, 2002). Transition planning should address health and mental health coverage as a key element in postsecondary settings. Specialized support programs are also essential for some students with significant physical disabilities. For example, "transitional disability management programs" that are emerging on college campuses are highly individualized programs designed to improve the student's disability management and knowledge and skills for independent residential living. Students and a disability specialist collaborates with students to create customized individual goals and a work plan (Collins, Hedrick, & Stumbo, 2007; Gallagher & Hedrick, 2004).

TBI.   **TBI** refers to an injury to the brain caused by an external physical force, resulting in total or partial functional disability or psychosocial impairment, or both. TBI adversely affects a child's educational performance. The term applies to open or closed head injuries resulting in impairments in one or more areas: cognition; language; memory; attention; reasoning; abstract thinking; judgment; problem solving; sensory, perceptual, and motor abilities; psychosocial behavior; physical functions; information processing; and speech. National Association of Protection and Advocacy Systems (2004) reports that 4.2% of students with disabilities who attend college have TBI, whereas there is only a statistically insignificant percentage identified at the secondary level.

TBI can cause significant changes in an individual's cognitive, behavioral, and physical functioning. Students who return to their schools from hospital are often tested and diagnosed with learning disability (LD), emotional disability (ED), or behavior disorder (BD). Misdiagnosis and inappropriate placement may result in educational interventions that only partially address the educational needs of the student (Hibbard, Gordon, Martin, Raskin, & Brown, 2001; Savage 1991).

Career Development and Transition Issues.   Research on transition from rehabilitation center or hospital to the home school and family shows transition support is rare or poorly coordinated (Tepas, 2004). About 85% of families of children with TBI, ages 14 to17, report that they did not receive guidance and support with transition from secondary to postsecondary (Hood, Todis, & Glang, 2005; Ylvisaker, Adelson, & Braga, 2005). Furthermore, families and professionals have limited knowledge of how to assist an individual with brain injury in the transition process.

On reentry from a hospital or rehabilitation center after a brain injury, the individual may need an IEP or a 504 plan. Students transitioning from acute care facilities and reentering the community benefit from the expertise of a comprehensive team working on their behalf. Mental health professionals should also be involved because of the frequent co-occurrence of emotional disabilities in youth with traumatic brain injuries. Communication among medical and school personnel can optimize student's success during the reentry period and beyond. A student with TBI typically needs a brain injury team or expert to assist with the reentry transition. A caseworker may visit the student's school to train the staff and help establish an appropriate IEP or 504. Transition support from middle to high school and from high school to postsecondary is essential for the student whether he or she was injured in middle school or elementary years. It is important to ensure that medical documentation and a summary of functional performance (SOP) is obtained for the student as documentation of the disability, to enable him or her to access accommodations in the postsecondary setting (chapter 4 will discuss the SOP in greater detail). Each year the student's needs and services must be reassessed because the stages of functioning in the recovery process can change very rapidly.

Other Health Impairments.   IDEA defines students with health impairments as having limited strength, vitality, or alertness, including a heightened alertness to environmental stimuli (*sensory integration dysfunction*), which results in limited alertness with respect to the educational environment and affects educational performance (IDEA, 2004). Sensory integration is the ability to take in information through the senses and integrate and organize this information in the brain. Children with sensory integration dysfunction may be hyperreactive to stimuli in the environment, impulsive, distractible, and have difficulty in planning tasks and adjusting to new situations. Others may react with frustration, anger, aggression, or withdrawal when they encounter failure (DiMatties & Sammons, 2003).

Such impairments may be due to chronic or acute health problems such as asthma, attention deficit disorder or attention deficit hyperactivity disorder (ADD/ADHD), diabetes, epilepsy, heart conditions, hemophilia, lead poisoning, leukemia, nephritis, rheumatic fever, and sickle-cell anemia. Asthma is by far the biggest reason for hospitalization in this population, with 375,000 youth under the age of 20 being hospitalized for asthma each year. Just over 85,000 (roughly 23%) of these hospitalizations involve adolescents between the age of 14 and 20 (HSC Foundation, 2006).

Career Development and Transition Issues.   Adolescents who are hospitalized with chronic illnesses miss time from school and work or are unable to work at all. Roughly one in five (19%) of those with diabetes report missing school or work, whereas those with asthma are five times more likely than the general population to report an inability to work (HSC Foundation, 2006). This jeopardizes their employment positions or college work. In fact, between 45% and 52% of adolescents with cystic fibrosis are unemployed, as are 32% to 38% of adolescents with inflammatory bowel disease.

Another challenge for these students relates to the readiness of the adult health care system to provide services once the student ages out of the pediatric system at age 21. Adult health care providers lack sufficient knowledge about the needs of this population and compounding this is a reimbursement system that does not provide adequate additional payments to compensate providers for the additional effort that is required. A recent survey of 28 physicians (primarily pediatricians) by the Healthy & Ready to Work (HRTW) National Resource Center found that more than half reported that reimbursement issues (e.g., lack of understanding of eligibility requirements, limited coverage by private insurers and Medicaid, and low reimbursement rates) were a major barrier to accessing needed health services after age 21 (HSC Foundation, 2006).

Finally, a major challenge facing youth in transition is the fragmentation of the service system. Individuals with other health impairments often interact with many different agencies and organizations (e.g., hospitals, physicians' offices, mental health providers, schools, career-vocational training and rehabilitation, social services, the juvenile justice system), each of which is concerned with one aspect of that individual's life. No single agency has the authority to require another agency to coordinate with it. There is a need to improve interagency coordination and provide the services of a coach or coordinator who can help the youth and family plan for and access needed services throughout the transition process.

Youth in Alternative Education Programs

This section provides a picture of students—both with and without disabilities—who are placed into alternative education settings because they (a) are *at risk* of failure in the traditional school setting and need an alternative learning environment; (b) are disruptive, violent, or have been involved in juvenile crime; or (c) have violated school discipline codes. In the United States, an increasing number of students without disabilities, as well as those with IEPs or §504 plans, are being placed in alternative settings because of stricter discipline policies in schools that affect all students (Kauffman & Brigham, 2000).

Second, many students with hidden disabilities that affect learning go undiagnosed, and they do not get the special educational services and supports they need early enough. This lack of early identification increases their chances of academic failure, school alienation, and social behaviors that place them at further risk. A study conducted by the National Council on Disability (2000a) on federal monitoring and enforcement of IDEA found that every state was out of compliance to some degree with IDEA requirements and that these conditions can lead to systematic underidentification of students and lack of access to needed services. Furthermore, many students with emotional and behavioral disorders are particularly at risk of school failure and fall into diagnostic categories (e.g., conduct disorder, substance abuse, or social maladjustment) that make them ineligible for special education under IDEA. This group, which represents a growing number of youth in alternative education programs, will be discussed in greater detail later in this section.

Defining "At-Risk."   There is no standard definition for the student at risk of needing alternative education (White & Kochhar-Bryant, 2007). Although the term **at risk** has been defined in a variety of ways, it typically refers to students who are in school but at risk of school failure, those who have dropped out of high school and are seeking a General Education Diploma (GED), and those who have experienced an unstable family life, family poverty, single-parent homes, divorce, physical abuse, and substance abuse (Hallahan & Kauffman, 2003; Jerald, 2006; Kidscount, 2003; Riccomini et al., 2005; Smith et al., 2001; Sum et al., 2003; Vaughn, Bos, & Schumm, 2003).

Although transition through adolescence and into adult roles is difficult for all youth, it is especially challenging for youth with either visible or hidden disabilities such as learning, emotional and behavioral, ADD/ADHD, and language and sensory integration dysfunction. These groups represent 95% of all students with disabilities. These students are among those most at risk of poor school attendance, dropout, delinquency, unemployment, and failure to transition to adult independence. About one quarter of all students drop out of the K–12 educational system before receiving their high school diploma and 41.1% of students aged 14 and older with disabilities drop out. In some states, these figures reach 56%, 57%, or 60% (25th annual report to Congress).

States report that anywhere from 19% to 60% of alternative education students have disabilities (whether they are or are not identified before placement), and a majority have learning and emotional or behavioral disabilities, most often co-occurring (Lehr, Moreau, Lange, & Lanners, 2004). On the basis of a study of 49 state directors of special education, approximately 12% of all students in alternative education were special education students with IEPs and many more students are unidentified (Lehr, 2004). The number of students with mental health problems, conduct disorders, and traumatic brain injuries attending alternative schools is increasing.

Students considered at risk fall behind academically and generally exhibit antisocial behaviors toward adults and their peers. They come from every ethnic, religious, and socioeconomic group. They may or may not be eligible for special education services, yet they are in need of special learning strategies, interventions, or supports to be successful in school (Smith et al., 2001). These risk factors and their influence on learning demand nontraditional learning environments and close collaboration among professionals providing supportive services (Kochhar-Bryant & White, 2007).

Multiple studies have identified additional risk factors that can be attributed to school failure as early as the third grade. These factors include (a) reading below grade level, (b) math ability that is two years below grade level, (c) limited English proficiency, (d) at least one year grade retention, and (e) having a parent who has not completed high school (Abrams, 2002; Blechman, Fishman, & Fishman, 2004; Brendtro & Shahbazian, 2003; Huffman & Speer, 2000; Patrikakou, 2004). Because these students have a long history of academic difficulty, they often experience a negative academic climate with teachers who have low expectations of them, may not be aware of how their disabilities impact their learning, and lack the skills to provide appropriate instruction.

School Dropout and Alternative Education. Although schools in many states are making great gains in achieving their education goals, many state leaders are concerned with rising dropout rates. Six states graduate fewer than 25% of students with special needs (Orfield, 2004; U.S. Department of Education, Office of Special Education, 2003). Furthermore, in the 2000–2001 school year, more than 91,000 special education students were removed from their educational settings for disciplinary reasons (U.S. Government Accountability Office, 2003a). In three of the six states studied by GAO, special education students who were removed for longer than 10 days for disciplinary reasons were primarily placed in alternative schools or homebound placements.

Researchers examining school dropout over the past decade are also concerned that high-stakes testing and the resulting retention will cause the dropout problem to increase by 50% over the next five years (Beatty, Neisser, Trent, & Heubert, 2001; Schargel, 2003). High dropout rates reflect a breakdown of collaboration and coordination systems among professionals and agencies within a school or district and failure to provide adequate transition supports for students in middle and high school.

Dropout rates for students with disabilities vary by type of disability; however, the rate is 33.6% for all disabilities and 55.9% for students with emotional and behavioural disabilities (U.S. Office of Special Education, 2007). As high school graduation rates have declined over the past 10 years, the rate at which American children have been turning to alternative education has more than doubled. Many observers contend that traditional schools are failing to engage a significant number of such students and meet their complex and multiple needs (Olson, 2007). States report that they are now more likely to rely on alternative placements for students with learning and behavioral problems, particularly in response to the pressure of new student achievement accountability requirements.

Benefits of Alternative Education.   The primary goal of most alternative programs is to meet the needs of students who would benefit from nontraditional approaches to learning. Although Raywid (1994) describes three types of alternative programs, the majority of alternative placements have been created to address the chronically disaffected group of students at risk. Many programs are therapeutic, working to change or modify behaviors in order to assist students with successful assimilation into a mainstream environment (Raywid, 1998). The majority of these placements, however, are temporary:

> Students who succeed or shape up in such alternative schools are permitted to return to the mainstream. Not all do, and some of these schools are understood to be permanent placements. Nevertheless, the idea is to "beef 'em up and send 'em back." (Raywid, 1998, p. 12)

Regardless of the reasons for alternative placement, these students require special supports to meet their unique needs. Because of their disassociation from the mainstream, students are usually reluctant to participate in any decisions that impact their lives.

Research has shown that quality long-term alternative education programs can have positive effects on school performance, attitudes toward school, and self-esteem (Leone & Drakeford, 1999; White & Kochhar-Bryant, 2007). "Alternative" school or programs are often part of the continuum of middle or high school offerings, and students typically are underachieving and deficient in credits to graduate or to be with their same-age peers. In some cases they are placed in the school by the court system, but most desire to stay in school and earn their diplomas. A review of legislation on alternative schools in 48 states indicated they were most frequently defined as nontraditional settings that serve students at risk of school failure (Lehr, 2004). Long-term alternative schools and programs (more than five days) have also emerged as one educational option for students with and without disabilities who have a history of failure and are at risk of dropout from traditional public schools (Aron, 2003; National Governors Association, 2001).

Youth in the Correctional System

Another population participating in alternative education programs is youth who are involved in the juvenile justice system. A number of these individuals may have received educational services through correctional settings or may be reintegrating back to their communities after a period of detention. Educational programs in juvenile detention centers or less secure detention facilities provide a spectrum of services including basic academic skill instruction, remedial and tutorial services, high school courses with Carnegie credits, General Education Diploma (GED) preparation, special education, preemployment training, and programs focused on cognitive, social, and life skills development (Meisel, Henderson, Cohen, & Leone, 2000; Miller, Ross, & Sturgis, 2005).

Youth with disabilities are substantially overrepresented in the juvenile justice system (Miller et al., 2005; Rutherford & Quinn, 1999). Youth with specific learning, emotional, or behavioral disabilities are more vulnerable to alternative placement outside their base school or in juvenile or adult corrections than are youth who are not identified as having a disability. Rutherford and Quinn found that 46% of youth with a disability in the juvenile justice system had a primary diagnosis of specific learning disability and 45% were identified with an emotional disability.

Although it is not well understood why individuals with disabilities are so highly represented in the juvenile justice system, some evidence suggests that police officers, attorneys, judges, corrections staff, and probation officers are typically unaware of characteristics associated with youths with disabilities (Leone & Meisel, 1997). Adolescents may be more vulnerable to involvement in the juvenile or criminal justice system when poorly developed reasoning ability, inappropriate affect, and inattention are misinterpreted by professionals as hostility, lack of cooperation, and other inappropriate responses. This phenomenon has several implications. Youth placed at risk for involvement in the juvenile justice system, including students with disabilities, must receive support and preventative services to minimize their vulnerability. Early identification and intervention can reduce chances of incarceration and long-term dependence.

Ethnic minorities are dramatically overrepresented in the population of young offenders. A study conducted from 1988 to 1997 of youth held in public and private juvenile detention, correctional, and shelter facilities revealed that more than three quarters (86.5%) of the 105,000 juveniles studied were young men from ethnic minority backgrounds (40% African American, 18.5% Hispanic, 28% other ethnicity), ranging in age from 13 to 17 years old (Gallagher, 1999). Although young women make up a smaller number of incarcerated youths, they tend to be younger in age than their male counterparts. About 21.4% of incarcerated females are 13 years of age.

NCLB and Youth Placed at Risk.   NCLB addresses the needs of at-risk youth in a variety of institutional settings. The Prevention and Intervention Programs for Children and Youth Who Are Neglected, Delinquent, or At Risk provides financial assistance to educational programs for youths in state-operated institutions and correctional or community day programs. The program makes this population of students a priority for local educational agencies, requiring them to focus on the transition and academic needs of students returning to their base schools from correctional facilities. Often, there is disconnect between the programs of local schools and correctional facilities, which affects transfer of information, continuity of support services, and ultimately student achievement (Miller et al., 2005). As students transition from correctional facilities back to their local schools, follow-up services can ensure that their education and support services continue so that they can meet the same challenging state standards required of all students. The NCLB program for at-risk youth responds to research affirming widespread neglect of students who are failing in public schools.

→ **WHAT OTHER RISK FACTORS AFFECT SUCCESSFUL TRANSITION TO ADULT LIFE?**

Students Who Do Not Qualify for Special Education

Typically, students who are at risk of failure in their base schools, or for placement into an alternative education program may have poor grades, chronic truancy, disruptive behavior, be pregnant, suspended from school, or any factors that are associated with an exit from school before completion of a high school degree. Often, these students do not qualify for special education services although their behaviors and school performance may seriously impede their ability to learn and succeed in a traditional school environment (Smith, Polloway, Patton, & Dowdy, 2003). Although these students attend class in the mainstream, they often become alienated from their peers as a result of negative behaviors and social relationships. The students often have difficulty learning basic skills and keeping up with their peers. As mentioned earlier, these students may be referred to an alternative school program often located in a separate facility from the traditional school.

Educators and other service providers have expressed concerns about placing at-risk students into more restricted alternative settings because they may have unidentified disabilities and will lack the protection and benefits provided under IDEA 2004. Many of these students are labeled as socially maladjusted and exhibit behaviors associated with oppositional defiant disorder and conduct disorder and may also have the co-occurring diagnosis of substance abuse. These disorders *are not included in the definition of* disability *under IDEA and therefore students are ineligible for services* (American Psychiatric Association, 2000; Bazelon Center for Mental Health Law, 2003). Students, however, may qualify for accommodations under §504 of the Vocational Rehabilitation Act of 1973 (Pub. L. No. 93-112) (see chapter 4).

Divorce and Risk of Failure in Transition

Research estimates that about half of new marriages will end in divorce. As a result, divorce forces children to live in single-parent homes or between two homes. The research supports that a female heads the vast majority of these households in which divorced children live. Further, the Decennial Census (U.S. Census, 2000) showed that about 40% of children in female-headed families were poor in 2000, compared to only 8% of children in households of married couples. Divorce often creates problems for many children as they struggle to reorganize their lives. Children respond in different ways to divorce—from guilt to anger, grief, anxiety, hopelessness, and antisocial behaviors. Although divorce has different effects on different children, the separation destroys continuity in the family unit.

When divorce occurs during the adolescent years, youth experience greater difficulties adjusting to the transition to postsecondary settings, including employment. There is research evidence that children who grow up in an intact, two-parent family with both biological parents present do better on a wide range of outcomes than children who grow up in a single-parent family (McLanahan, Garfinkel, & Mincy, 2001;

McLanahan & Sandefur, 1994). Although single parenthood is not the only, nor even the most important cause of the higher rates of school dropout, teenage pregnancy, and juvenile delinquency, it does contribute independently to these problems. Furthermore, marital hostility associated with divorce is associated with increased aggression and disruptive behaviors on the part of children which, in turn, lead to peer rejection, academic failure, and other antisocial behaviors (Webster-Stratton, 2003).

Abuse and Risk of Failure to Make a Successful Transition

Child abuse occurs at every socioeconomic level, ethnic background, and religion. The literature describes two major types of abuse—emotional and physical. Thompson and Kaplan (1999) suggest that emotional abuse can be defined as excessive demands placed on children by parents, peers, and siblings and the failure of parents to provide an emotional support system. Students who have experienced emotional abuse may exhibit a low self-esteem, thoughts of suicide, depression, antisocial behaviors, and have difficulty initiating and maintaining relationships with adults and peers. These are the characteristics of many students who attend alternative education programs.

Children who are physically abused are more likely to be disciplined in the school setting than those children who do not experience abuse. These students have difficulty forming relationships with their peers, exhibit physically aggressive behaviors, and are deficit in social skills (U.S. Department of Heath and Human Services, 2003). Research suggests that deficits in cognitive functioning are more likely in students who are physically abused (National Center for Education Statistics, 2001). The effects of abuse on social skills, behavior, relationships, and cognitive functioning impede the process of transition and adjustment to adult roles. Therefore, students who have experienced past abuse need additional support and mentorship during this period and may need mental health services and vocational rehabilitation supports.

Substance Abuse and Risk of Failure to Make Successful Transition

The illegal use of drugs and alcohol and abuse of prescription drugs is on the rise nationwide (Jerald, 2006; Volkow, 2005). Even after aggressive substance abuse education, the use of drugs and alcohol has not decreased. The National Center on Education Statistics (2001) reports that students who abuse substances have a difficult time keeping up academically with their peers. Substance abuse not only affects students' academic achievement but also may be characterized by poor attendance, difficulty concentrating, apathy, impulsivity and disordered behavior, and sleeping in class, which greatly impact cognition and thinking patterns. The effects of substance abuse also greatly impede or can greatly delay the process of transition and adjustment to adult roles. Therefore, students who are recovering from addictions typically need intensive support and mentorship during this period. They may also need mental health services and close coordination is needed between school and community service agencies.

WHO ARE CULTURALLY AND LINGUISTICALLY DIVERSE STUDENTS?

Humans differ greatly in the language they speak and in their cultural heritage. For example, even among those who speak English, regional accents and lexicon in states across the United States often create barriers to communication and relationships. Accents and vocabulary can disclose levels of education, social status, personal biases, and a range of other personal characteristics. These differences, however, also add richness to our experience if we are willing to step outside our own cultural confines and examine how our own ethnic identities influence our interactions with people who are different from us.

For immigrants struggling to learn the English language, the challenge of learning in American schools is enormous. The phrase **culturally and linguistically diverse** (CLD) is descriptive of students whose culture and language are different from that of the dominant culture and language in American society. Because diversity implies a multidimensional learning environment, CLD is also descriptive of students who will need *accommodative programming and instruction* to facilitate their cultural and linguistic development within the general education curriculum (American Association of Colleges for Teacher Education [AACTE], 2002). CLD students now constitute the fastest growing group in the U.S. educational system. This population demonstrates low levels of achievement, coupled with the highest dropout rates, in comparison with their non-CLD peers. Policy makers and educators have identified several challenges associated with the transition needs of the rapidly growing number of English language learners (ELL), or limited English proficient (LEP) students in schools across the United States, both with and without disabilities.

If culturally and linguistically diverse students and parents were one homogeneous group, then discussing effective educational strategies with this population would be easier. However, it is important to consider the spectrum of linguistic possibilities that this population represents, examine the concept of culture, and recognize the importance of acknowledging and respecting native cultures. This understanding is essential to the successful application of the principles presented later in this chapter.

Linguistic diversity is generally defined as students who speak, or whose families speak, a language other than English (English language learners, ELL). Approximately 15% to 20% (one in five) of students in schools speak a foreign language at home and this percentage is growing rapidly (Avoke & Wood-Garnett, 2001; Capps et al., 2005; National Clearinghouse for English Language Acquisition, 2005). According to the U.S. Department of Education, the percentage of 5- to 24-year-olds who spoke a language other than English in their homes more than doubled between 1979 and 1999 (Wirt et al., 2003). Some are in families that are in or near poverty status, but many are in technical or professional families who earn high incomes. The term *non-English speakers* represents a great range in English language skills. For example, some students and their parents may not speak English at all. Some parents may not speak English, but their children have acquired conversational English, though they may not be fully proficient (limited English proficient, or LEP). Many parents and students are bilingual. The possible combinations of language proficiency among students and families from the same linguistic background are numerous and, therefore, educators should be cautious not to generalize their experiences with non-English speakers to all students and families.

Changing Demographics in the United States

As the demographics of the U.S. population changes, so do the demographics of student populations. Here are some important facts to consider:

1. One in five Americans speaks languages other than English in the home. Students speak 400 languages across the nation, although students whose native language is Spanish represent 76.9% of students learning English in America (Zehler, Fleischman, Hopstock, Pendzick, & Stephenson, 2003).

2. By the year 2010, one in five children will be Hispanic (Wiley, 2005), and by 2030 it is estimated that more that 40% of all students in the K–12 population will have culturally and linguistically diverse backgrounds, not of European–American heritage (U.S. Department of Education, 2004b).

3. More immigrants have come to the United States in the last decade than compared to any other decade (Fix & Passel, 2001)

4. California has the highest ELL population in the United States with 33% and Texas is second with 12% (California Department of Education, 2004).

5. There is a severe shortage of CLD teachers in the workforce; 45% of U.S. teachers have at least one student with limited English proficiency (LEP) in their classrooms (National Clearinghouse for English Language Acquisition, 2005).

6. It is estimated that 9% of all ELL students in U.S. public schools have disabilities (U.S. Department of Education, 2004b).

In the face of NCLB accountability requirements for state testing of students, many school districts are struggling to address the needs of this population to achieve annual yearly progress (AYP) (McLeod, 2005; Northwest Evaluation Association, 2005; Ruiz-de-Velasco, Fix, & Clewell, 2000). States must now provide data on how English language learners (ELL) are performing on state assessments and ELL students must participate in these assessments (Albus, Lieu, & Thurlow, 2002; Albus & Thurlow, 2005; Education Policy Reform Research Institute, 2004; U.S. Department of Education, 2005a). The research and education policy community is divided on whether bilingual education or English immersion is best for non-English speakers, and more research is needed.

The needs of CLD students are currently largely unmet in today's schools, as reflected by two important statistics. First, a disproportionate percentage of Hispanic, black, and Native American students drop out or do not obtain a high school diploma (Garcia, 2005; Ingels et al., 2007; National Center for Education Statistics, 2002). Second, and equally important, is the disproportionate percentage of Hispanic, black, and Native American students who are placed in special education classes (Artiles, 2003; Cummins, 2001; Northwest Evaluation Association, 2005; Obiakor & Wilder, 2003; Salend, Garrick-Duhaney, & Montgomery, 2002). Although special education may meet the needs of students with disabilities, it can be inappropriate for students *without* disabilities. Recent research has demonstrated that improperly placing CLD students in special education can negatively impact their educational outcomes and potential career possibilities (Greene & Kochhar, 2003; Nieto, 2000). School personnel have difficulty distinguishing between language acquisition-based learning difficulties and actual LD (Zehler et al., 2003). Students therefore, have difficulty obtaining services from both special education and ESL (English as a second language) departments when they have both challenges.

Special Education and Transition Issues

Persons with disabilities usually must overcome a variety of challenges not faced by their peers without disabilities to successfully transition to postsecondary education settings. These challenges are especially difficult for persons with disabilities who are also culturally and linguistically diverse. Compared to non-CLD students with disabilities, CLD students with disabilities are more likely to face language and social barriers, the negative effects of having grown up in poverty, and difficulty processing "standard English" oral and written information, all of which may contribute to their risk of academic difficulty (Greene & Nefsky, 1999). It has also been argued that persons with disabilities comprise a minority group whose members, like members of other minorities, are often stereotyped and subjected to negative perceptions and low expectations (Leake & Cholymay, 2004). CLD students with disabilities should be supported to gain self-advocacy skills during high school.

Cultural and linguistic experiences greatly affect the ease with which CLD students can adapt and progress within the mainstream American society. Second language acquisition takes about 5 to 7 years (to reach content proficiency), but students can reach conversational language proficiency well before that (Winzer & Mazurek, 1998; Zehler et al., 2003). Although parents may appear to fully understand conversations and discussions, it is important that professionals are sensitive to language capabilities.

Unfortunately, language differences often appear to be communication disorders, such as language delays or deficiencies (Obiakor & Wilder, 2003). In many instances, these perceived delays or deficiencies trigger referrals to special education. Once a CLD student is referred to special education, it is likely that he or she will be found eligible (Ysseldyke, Olsen, & Thurlow, 1997; Zehler, 2003). To ensure that students are being fairly assessed, collaboration among speech and language therapists, bilingual specialists, and general and special education teachers is essential in the early intervening services stage to determine whether the student is exhibiting a communication disorder or expected language differences.

Many schools are creating school-based community resource centers to expand participation of CLD families. Resources fall into two main categories: (a) family oriented resources such as support groups that provide opportunities for families to discuss issues such as daily demands, triumphs, and obstacles they encounter (Perez & Pinzon, 1997) and (b) service-oriented resources that identify service-based resources for culturally and linguistically diverse students and families. The resource center becomes a logical hub for facilitating frequent and regular participation and linking with school-based and community services (Riehl, 2000). Service-oriented resources include health care options, child care options, coordination of services through mental health facilities, housing, language instruction, economic resources, and other social resources available through public agencies.

Self-advocacy skills can be challenging for CLD students because of cultural values against disclosing disabilities or requesting help from persons perceived to be of higher status. One strategy that has demonstrated promise is that of *cultural brokering,* in which an individual familiar with both cultures negotiates on behalf of the student to achieve a compromise. Furthermore, technical assistance and training should be available to students, staff, and faculty to enhance cultural competence for serving students in postsecondary education (Leake & Cholymay, 2004).

In summary, CLD students with disabilities face multiple barriers to obtaining post-secondary degrees. Postsecondary faculty and staff can have a significant influence in the success of these students by gaining awareness of the supports they need.

 ## WHO ARE MIDDLE SCHOOL STUDENTS AND WHAT ARE THEIR TRANSITION NEEDS?

There is a growing attention to the unique needs and experiences of middle school students. Who are middle school students? They are part children, carefree and ebullient, and part adolescents, restless and intense. They are in transition from the protection and support of the smaller elementary environment to a larger school with greater demands. Although most families celebrate this passage to a new stage in the child's development, some students and parents harbor great apprehension about the move, uncertain about how prepared they are for the new expectations. Some children adjust well but others, with and without disabilities, need extra support. Students' success in transition into and from middle school can predict their long-term transition to adult life (Repetto, Webb, Neubert, & Curran, 2006; Weidenthal & Kochhar-Bryant, 2007).

Transition to Middle School: A Sudden Event

The middle years represent major transformations in the student and in the educational environment, and expectations and needs of students at this stage are complex. Researchers and educators have come to view early adolescence as a unique period of development in all domains—cognitive, social, emotional, and physical (Ames & Miller, 1994; Billig, 2001; Doyle & Moretti, 2000; Steinburg & Baier, 2003; Stoffner & Williamson, 2000). Two of the nation's leading educational organizations—National Association of Elementary School Principals (2004) and the National Middle School Association (2006), as well as a variety of disability associations, have called for a collaborative partnership among parents, teachers, principals, counselors, and students to support them as they change from childhood to adolescence and move from elementary to middle school.

With the exception of infancy, early adolescence is the time when a child's body and brain grows and changes faster than in any other phase of life. The student is in a process of change from child to adolescent, yet the change in environment from elementary to middle school is a sudden event. There are new social demands, demands for time management skills, new expectations for independence and personal responsibility, multiple classrooms, more homework and a cadre of teachers. They leave their self-contained elementary classrooms, their relationship with a single teacher and a small group of peers, and shift to a large, often impersonal middle school. Here they attend up to six or seven different classes with seven sets of students, taught by a variety of teachers with different personalities and standards. They have important choices to make about courses and curriculum and extracurricular activities. Students are assigned lockers that may be located in a far corner of the building, out from under adult watch, and locker combinations must be memorized. They must organize their books and materials and transport them from class to class. Daily class schedules may vary throughout the week, and students must record and track their homework assignments daily or over a period of weeks.

The combination of changes in the student and the environment naturally creates stress, which for some students proves too great and they may "call out" for help. They may react to the stress by exhibiting behaviors or changes in personality that are quite different from their behavior in the elementary years. For example, they may for the first time exhibit fearfulness about school, disengagement from learning and general apathy toward schooling, loss of interest in home activities, resistance to completing or turning in homework, uncooperative or aggressive behavior, and even depression.

Students with disabilities are more likely than their nondisabled peers to experience these problems and are twice as likely to drop out of school in middle and high school (Blackorby & Wagner, 1996; Christenson & Thurlow, 2004). Because most children are developing at different rates, some come into middle school ready for changes, others struggle to keep up, and still others fall behind. In contrast, the transition to middle school occurs as a one-size-fits-all event to which all children are expected to adapt.

Recent brain research also reveals that during the teen years up to age 15, the areas in the middle and back of the brain associated with associative thinking and language reach their peak growth rates (Wilson & Horch, 2004). The growth spurt is most predominant just before puberty in the prefrontal cortex, the part of the brain crucial to information synthesis. The prefrontal cortex is the area of the brain that also controls planning, working memory, organization, and mood modulation. This area of the brain is not mature until about 18 years of age (Spinks, 2002). The prefrontal cortex appears to be the last region of the brain to mature (Casey, Giedd, & Thomas, 2000; Dahl, 2004), undergoing major changes throughout puberty. These findings about adolescent brain development have major implications for classroom practices and student supports. Only recently have educational researchers and practitioners begun to relate new brain research to learning. The challenge for middle school teachers and administrators, however, is to integrate this research in classroom practice and organization of middle schools for all students, including special needs learners (Hough 2003; Niogi & McCandliss, 2006; Sylwester, 2006).

During the middle school years, relationships with parents, peers, and other adults become very challenging for adolescents. There are conflicting influences—pushes and pulls from the family, school, and peers. These pushes and pulls often send mixed messages about what is expected of them. Young people are caught in a vortex of physical, psychological, and social growth. They constantly feel competing demands for how and with whom they should invest their time; how to improve their status with peers and adults, how to relate to authority figures, and how to define themselves. Yet, in the midst of all this change, young people, particularly those who are special learners, need stability and people on whom they can rely. The adults in their families and schools, acting in partnership, must fill these critical needs (Billig, 2001; Mizelle & Mullins, 1997; Roeser, Eccles, & Sameroff, 2000; Stoffner & Williamson, 2000).

For these reasons, the transition from elementary to middle school for special needs students—indeed for all students—should be made as smooth and seamless as possible, and parents, teachers, and support personnel must remain vigilant in their watch for the signs of stress. Open and continuous communication among professionals and with families is particularly important during these years because of the complexity of the changes the child and the family face. Attention to the process of transition into middle from elementary and from middle to high school is essential to sustaining children's progress through the latter years of schooling and preventing dropout.

Middle School Students at Risk

The transformations of adolescence, compounded by the change that the move to middle school brings, leave many students particularly vulnerable. They are at greater risk for alienation and dropout. The dropout rate for students with disabilities is approximately twice that of general education students and peaks at the late middle and early secondary levels (Christenson & Thurlow, 2004). Students with emotional disabilities are particularly vulnerable during the transition to middle school. A 2001 report from the U.S. Surgeon General estimates that 21% of young people in the United States between ages 9 and 17—about 15 million children—have diagnosable emotional or behavioral health disorders but less than a third get the help they need for these problems (Olbrich, 2002; U.S. Department of Health and Human Services, 2001). These young Americans—fully one quarter of adolescents 9 to 17 years old—may be at risk of failing to achieve productive adult lives.

Results of a large Youth Risk Behavior Survey (Simeonsson, McMillen, McMillen, & Lollar, 2002) indicated that students with disabilities were more likely to report (a) engaging in risky behaviors that result in injuries (not wearing seatbelts or bicycle helmets, riding with a drinking driver, carrying weapons, fighting); (b) feeling depressed or considering suicide; (c) using alcohol, tobacco, marijuana, and other drugs; and (d) engaging in unhealthy weight loss behaviors. Students with disabilities were also more likely to report having had property stolen or damaged at school, a low quality of life, and poor health status (Frank Porter Graham Child Development Institute, 2002). In 2000–2001, 12% of all students in alternative schools and programs for at-risk students were special education students with an IEP (Baer, Quinn, & Burkholder, 2001). This number excludes those who fail to qualify for special education services and are failing in the school setting (Bazelon Center for Mental Health Law, 2003).

Increased concerns about the dropout problem are also emerging because of state and local education agency experiences with high-stakes accountability and standardized testing. A growing number of students are having difficulty with these assessments (Thurlow, Sinclair, & Johnson, 2002). The use of high-stakes tests have been associated with higher dropout rates—6 to 8 percentage points higher just between 8th and 10th grades (Heubert & Hauser, 1999; Warren & Edwards, 2001). A variety of dropout prevention strategies, therefore, are now targeted at middle school students, when the pressures of schooling related to a more complex curriculum, a less personal environment, and the growing need for peer acceptance pose a danger to students who are already disadvantaged (Anderman, Maehr, & Midgley, 1999; Butler & Hodge, 2004; Elias, 2001; Gil-Kashiwabara, Hogansen, Geenen, Powers, and Powers, 2007).

Many middle school students have "hidden disabilities" such as learning, emotional and behavioral, ADD/ADHD, or language and sensory integration dysfunctions. These groups represent 95% of all students with disabilities. Many go undiagnosed, particularly those with learning and emotional disabilities and ADHD, and do not receive services until school age, many not until the middle school years (U.S. Department of Education, 2005b).

Estimates of students with ADD/ADHD range from 3% to 7.5% of all school-age children (National Institute of Mental Health, 2003). It is not unusual for ADD/ADHD students with high intellectual abilities to go undiagnosed until middle school because they can learn how to compensate enough to "get by" in elementary grades (Wagner, Marder, & Cardoso, 2002). Often, disabilities are not manifested until the demands of middle school become too great. At this stage, students may be labeled as inattentive, lazy, bored, alienated, oppositional, or behaviorally or conduct disordered. Furthermore, fewer students with disabilities receive accommodations at the middle and secondary levels than in elementary grades, which undermine learning and test taking (Blackorby & Wagner, 2002; U.S. Department of Education, 2005b).

Middle schools are undergoing reforms to become more developmentally appropriate for young adolescents, building in greater collaboration and coordination among educators, parents, students, and outside agencies. Promptness in identifying possible disabilities is essential for preventing more serious and perhaps lifelong problems.

Career Education and Transition Issues.   Career education is an important element in the curriculum for both middle and high school, particularly for students with special needs who have employment as their postsecondary goal. In the middle school, adolescents are beginning to learn about careers and some participate in service learning (unpaid work experiences) in their communities. Involving students in real-life apprenticeships allows them to shadow workers in various jobs or learn skills in a short internship that either connects to an area of study or helps them understand one of the problems they have posed themselves and are interested in finding answers. Career education provides the opportunity for youth to learn, in the least restrictive environment possible, the academic, daily living, personal–social and occupational knowledge, and specific career-related skills necessary for attaining their highest levels of economic, personal, and social fulfillment (Bailey, 2001; Brown, 2000; Eisenman, 2001; Sarkees-Wircenski & Scott, 2003).

LET'S SEE IT IN ACTION! CASE EXAMPLE

Saving Eric

The following example is based on a true story.

ERIC: When I started at Waymans Middle School, I was afraid, but I did not want anyone to know. There was so much pressure. Things were easy at my other school because I only had one teacher and one classroom and I always kept my books and papers in one desk. Now I have a locker, a combination to remember, and a bunch of classes to get to with so little time. I have to keep all my subjects organized, my papers and stuff organized, get different homework in to different teachers, prepare for lots of different tests on different days, and there's so many big projects that take weeks. I have trouble with remembering things and keeping all my papers together and no one gave me help with this. I started falling behind everyday and feeling bad about myself. Then I just gave up.

ERIC'S MOTHER: Since he was a toddler, Eric was always a very active child and had trouble with attention. Conversations were difficult with him because his mind was always flitting away like a butterfly. During his elementary school years, this high activity level and lack of attention began to create some difficulty, but he was very bright and could always compensate. We didn't have him diagnosed because he seemed to find a way to keep up. He was never identified as needing special education because he was getting average or better grades. Each year, though, his teachers reported problems with minor disruption in class, disorganized behavior, and trouble paying attention. Because I had continuous communication with his elementary teachers, I could stay on top of the problems and provide support at home. When Eric was 10, he was diagnosed with attention deficit and hyperactivity disorder (ADHD).

Once Eric hit 7th grade, though, everything changed. He had to develop organizational skills for homework assignments, subjects, and schedule of classes, teachers, long-term projects, and papers. Organization was his Achilles heel. He began to change, became distant, hung out with friends whom I was very concerned about. I thought at first this was Eric just being a preteen but by the end of the year his grades had plummeted and by the end of 8th grade he was nearly failing in every subject. More frequently, he was refusing to go to school and we had to start using structured behavioral strategies. During the 7th grade, no teachers had attempted to communicate with me about his situation and no one provided any extra help to Eric to organize himself. When I went to back-to-school night I expressed my concerns and one teacher said, "In middle school we expect them to manage independently. This isn't elementary school and they have to take more responsibility for themselves." I asked—"What if they have difficulty with this and need extra help? What if they fall too far behind?" The teacher responded, "Well, if they're in the general education class, we treat everyone alike. No special treatment." Eric did pass 8th grade by a small margin and I feared for the following year when he shifted to 9th grade.

HIGH SCHOOL COUNSELOR: Eric's mother made an appointment to talk to me just before the end of his 8th grade year. She was very concerned about her son's experience in 7th and 8th grades and worried about his near failure and what that meant for the coming year. Unfortunately, I have a caseload of 300 students, so it's hard for me to spend much time with each child. But, I was interested in this case and appreciated the mother's genuine concern and involvement. I pulled his file and found that, yes indeed, Eric had nearly failed all of his classes. Yet, what was amazing was that he had taken the state assessment tests in 8th grade and had scored "advanced proficient" on all of them. Moreover, he had early psychological

(Continued)

tests that showed that he was indeed a very bright student. How could he be failing his grades yet scoring "advanced proficient"? Something was terribly wrong.

I spoke with some of his teachers in middle school and they reported that Eric was known to sleep in class, routinely failed to turn in homework, and often showed disruptive and attention-seeking behavior in class. I asked if any of the teachers had let his parents know about this behavior or had provided any extra support for Eric, and they all said no. They believed Eric could do the work, could pass the tests, but was just unmotivated. They did not believe he needed special education. They were reluctant to report on his behavior because they wanted to "give him every chance to make the changes on his own." Furthermore, the special education screening team refused to evaluate Eric for services because of his high SOL scores and teacher reports. And so, in my opinion—and his mother's—we had failed him in the middle school. This student clearly needed help and was at particular risk of academic failure or dropout once he entered 9th grade. His marginal adjustment in middle school and growing sense of isolation had left him even more vulnerable to the pressures and demands of high school.

I met Eric and talked with him about his feeling of being overwhelmed with the work and promised to get him some help with organization

and time management during the year. We set up a time to visit the high school and meet with a few of the teachers and classrooms. I discussed what he could expect in terms of schedule and workload and other expectations. I also stayed in close touch with his mother for the balance of the year to give suggestions about how she might provide extra support at home and prepare him for the transition at the end of summer. During 9th grade, we held a teacher's roundtable with Eric and his mother and the high school counselor to discuss progress at midyear and share what supports were being used in his classes. By the middle of the year, Eric's grades had improved from failing to B's and C's and his attitude toward school was improving. The frequency of disruptive and attention-seeking behavior began to decline (Kochhar-Bryant, in press, by permission).

Questions for Discussion

1. How did middle school teachers characterize middle school expectations for Eric? How were these expectations different from those in elementary school?
2. How does Eric characterize the new demands placed on him?
3. Why was Eric not screened for special education services in the elementary years even though he was diagnosed with ADHD?
4. How did the school counselor intervene and provide support to Eric and his mother?

What can we learn about this case? First, Eric's experience of change in his educational environment placed great stress on his coping skills. He was predisposed to being at risk of poor adjustment to the new demands of middle school. He had not received professional help during his elementary years because he was bright and able to compensate for his learning challenges. Eric also had no one with whom to share his feelings and fears. Second, Eric's parents had little communication from the middle school teachers about Eric's behavior so they missed many opportunities to intervene at home. Although the teachers may have been well meaning in "hoping" and giving Eric a chance to "change on his own," they inadvertently contributed to his deterioration. Opportunities were lost to intervene early, to provide supports in school, and to help Eric turn around his sense of failure and defeat.

A serious situation was diffused, however, because of the persistence of Eric's mother, the support of an astute and caring school counselor, and the willingness of 9th grade teachers to coordinate and provide support. Close collaboration around Eric's needs was achieved. Without such a response on the part of the school, Eric may well have deteriorated further in 9th grade and may have become a dropout statistic. Eric's case mirrors that of a growing number of middle school students who may or may not be diagnosed as having disabilities and yet are at significant risk for alienation, academic failure, and dropout.

➡ HOW DO FAMILIES' NEEDS CHANGE ALONG THE DEVELOPMENTAL PATH TO TRANSITION?

Together, the IDEA 2004 and NCLB set expectations for parent-professional partnerships that are unprecedented for the public school system. Parents were given important roles in identifying and evaluating their children with disabilities and in the development, implementation, and revision of their educational programs. IDEA 2004 encouraged parents to become more involved in their children's education and, additionally, to work in other ways as partners with educators and policymakers (Abrams & Gibbs, 2002; Christie, 2005; Henderson et. al., 2003).

In summary, IDEA and NCLB convey three messages to parents, teachers, and service providers: (a) the importance of the parent-professional partnership in service delivery and improving educational outcomes for children and youth, (b) the inclusion of the family unit (system) as the target for intervention and support by the schools and community agencies, and (c) the importance of strengthening the family's role in decision making and educational improvement.

Consider the case example in Box 2-1 as you discuss the following:

1. What biases or fears can you identify in the parents about the school and teachers?
2. What factors threatened Andrew's high school completion?
3. How did teachers engage the parents in helping Andrew prepare for the exit examination?
4. What is Andrew's postsecondary goal and how supportive are his parents of the goal?

In this example, Andrew's parents negotiated carefully and persistently for accommodations in testing for their son. It is a story of competing needs between parents and professionals as well as parents' sometimes unhelpful misperceptions about teachers and schools that can impede constructive communication and collaboration.

There are many ways that parents participate in the coordination of services, particularly when they have children with disabilities who need extra support services in the classroom. Because most schools do not provide direct help to parents to coordinate services needed outside the school, parents are frequently their own children's

BOX 2–1

LET'S SEE IT IN ACTION! CASE EXAMPLE

The Importance of Family Engagement

Andrew's mother and father, Michelle and Richard, have felt that because Andrew started at the high school (a small rural school) in a general education class, they have not had the same level of connection with his school program as they had in middle school. The last few IEP meetings have included discussions around transition but they get the sense that the special education teachers really do not think Andrew will be able to achieve a regular diploma. Although Andrew is maintaining C's and D's, he has great difficulty with the standardized tests. At the last meeting, Andrew's father felt that he had to "get in a few faces" in order to get the accommodations they thought Andrew needed. His mother, of course, tried to smooth things over. She did not want the school perceiving them as hostile or overly demanding parents. She has been warned by her friend from the autism support group, who also had a son at the high school a few years ago, that if they asked for too much, then they would be labeled with a "reputation for trouble." Everyone seems to be anxious about improving the school's test scores and more families are becoming concerned.

Attending transition meetings at school is difficult for Andrew's father, Richard. He dropped out of school when his mother died in order to help his father with the family plumbing business. He was not upset about that because he did not like school. He always believed that the teachers were only interested in students who were going to college—the ones from the "good side of town." So school left him with bad memories. He prefers to let his wife go alone, and only when she is really worried about a specific meeting will he attend with her. He does not want his children to have the same experiences, and so he is pushing for them to continue their education beyond high school. According to Michelle and Richard, the only person at the school who seems to understand is the young man, Mr. Harris, the transition coordinator, whose job is to make sure that "this thing called transition" happens for Andrew. He dropped by their house last summer before the school year began to talk with them about Andrew's plans and goals for the future. According to Richard, that is where "this crazy idea about going to the Community College came from." But as long as Mr. Harris thought Andrew could do college-level work, and if Andrew wanted to try it, then he would support Andrew. The personal home visit by Mr. Harris really convinced him that this could be a possibility for his son.

Andrew and his mother met with Mr. Harris and his resource room teacher. The teachers had recently attended a workshop and learned new strategies to help students with special needs take the high school exit examination. They offered to meet with Andrew and Michelle to work through some of their concerns and help them better understand the testing process. The teachers explained to them about the different types of testing accommodations such as having Andrew take the test in a quiet place to reduce distraction. They also shared information about other types of accommodations. They discovered that some of the possible accommodations had not been made available to Andrew when he took and failed the practice I-STEP+ (high school exit examination).

This process really helped Andrew and his family relieve some of the pressure they were feeling. The family could focus on the next phase of Andrew's life—a job for the summer and a search for the right college with services to accommodate Andrew.

"case managers" or "service coordinators" during the school years, and particularly at transition points. They participate in their child's IEP meeting, learn about the in-school services needed, and take recommendations for external or community-based services.

For example, in the case example of Eric, presented earlier in this chapter, the parents were working among four agencies—county mental health services, private psychological services, substance abuse services, and juvenile services and the courts—as well as the school system—to provide multiple services to their son. Their weeks and months that turned into years involved numerous hours doing a variety of coordination activities. These included communicating by e-mail and telephone with teachers, contacting and coordinating appointments with agencies, visiting representatives of the agencies involved, tracking and maintaining files related to each agency so as not to duplicate services or evaluations, completing applications and evaluations, participating in team meetings and family counseling sessions, remaining close to home for probation officer visits, and providing documentation to insurance companies to obtain needed specialized services not provided by the school. Although this is a complex case, parents are often overwhelmed with the complexity of their lives when the needs of a special child must come first in the family's life.

Educators and policy makers have recognized the need to strengthen parent participation in schools as well as increase schools' support of families (Kreider, Caspe, Kennedy, & Weiss, 2007; Morningstar & Wehmeyer, in press). It is important that schools be explicit in their communication with parents about the role they are expected to have at all levels. In addition to having strong collaborative relationships in schools, and being a full partner in their child's IEP, parents should be partners in the policies, program decisions, and reforms. To achieve such participation, however, parents need help with their complex lives. In a recent study by Chambers, Hughes, and Carter (2004) of parent and sibling perspectives on transition, parents and siblings believe that they lacked knowledge with respect to postschool options, and parents report assuming more active roles in the transition process than siblings did.

Research on Family Engagement in Transition

National Longitudinal Transition Study of Parents. The National Longitudinal Transition Study-2 (2005), sponsored by the U.S. Office of Special Education, surveyed 9,230 parents and guardians of students with disabilities to examine the involvement of families in their children's (ages 13 to 16) education. This study provides the first national picture of family involvement and its impact on student achievement. The study supports the findings of others that parents' activities in support of their children's education is associated with consistent differences in several achievement domains, independent of disability, functioning, or other differences among youth. Youth whose families are more involved in their schools are less far behind grade level in reading, tend to receive better grades, and have higher rates of involvement in organized groups and with individual friendships than youth with less family involvement in school. In the domain of independence, youth whose families are more involved in their schooling are more likely than youth from less involved families to have had regular paid jobs in the preceding year. Family expectations for the future also help shape the achievements of youth with disabilities, particularly with regard to academic engagement and achievement (Newman, 2004). These findings support decades of research that have recognized parent and family participation as the most crucial factor in the development and educational success of a child with disability.

Parent and family resource centers provide training and information to parents and connect children with disabilities to community resources. Each state has at least one parent center, and states with large populations may have more. There are about 100 parent centers in the United States (Technical Assistance Alliance for Parent Centers, 2001; U.S. Government Accountability Office, 2003a). At the local level, these centers provide an inviting place where parents can chat with other parents and teachers, watch informational videos, and learn about school activities. In addition, they often provide resources and information about health and social service agencies, adult educational opportunities, child development, school policies and procedures, and how to support their child's education. Most important, family resource centers are a highly effective way to communicate to parents that they are welcome at school.

The Harvard Study: Family Involvement in Middle and High School Students' Education. Family involvement in academics and learning remains important in the adolescent years, yet such involvement in education tends to decrease across middle and secondary school, due in part to adolescents' increasing desire for autonomy and in part to changes in school structure and organization (Kreider et al., 2007). Yet, family involvement in education remains a powerful predictor of various adolescent outcomes. It has been related to higher rates of college enrolment as well as successful transition directly from high school to employment (Kreider et al., 2007; Zarrett & Eccles, 2006).

Last, unique to the middle and high school years, parents' participation in school or community-sponsored college-outreach programs also supports adolescent learning and development by influencing students' postgraduation plans. This is particularly true for low-income, minority, and immigrant youth, for example, when parents attend meetings at the school that provide basic information about college-entrance processes, SAT preparation, financial aid, and course placements. Parents begin to imagine their children as college students, feel more comfortable in the school setting, build support groups with other parents, and are more likely to assist their children in navigating the school and college application system (Jacobs & Bleeker, 2004). Youth whose parents possess these qualities are more likely to graduate high school and attend college (Dearing, McCartney, Weiss, Kreider, & Simpkins, 2004; Kreider et al., 2007).

SUMMARY

This chapter examined various populations of special learners and their transition needs, explored the transition choices and challenges that they face, and examined the needs of families in the dynamic interaction with their children along the developmental path of transition to adulthood. For many diverse groups of individuals in

U.S. history—women, people with disabilities, and cultural and language minorities—have initiated social movements to fight for civil rights for social recognition and access to the benefits of society. Today schools share the responsibility with community agencies for creating a transition service system for all students with disabilities. CLD students now constitute the fastest-growing segment of the educational systems in the nation. The challenge of making a successful transition through school and into postschool roles is particularly difficult for those with disabilities involving CLD.

Many schools are creating school-based community resource centers to expand participation of families in the education of their children. Together, the IDEA 2004 and NCLB set expectations for parent–professional partnership that is unprecedented for the public school system. IDEA and NCLB emphasize the importance of the parent–professional partnership in educational services and improving educational outcomes for children and youth and the importance of strengthening the families' role in decision making and educational improvement.

KEY TERMS AND PHRASES

alternative education program

at risk

autism

correctional system

culturally and linguistically diverse

disability

dropout

economically disadvantaged

emotional and behavioral disabilities

human variation

intellectual disability

learning disability

other health impairment

parent and family resource centers

sensory impairments

special population

traumatic brain injury (TBI)

QUESTIONS FOR REFLECTION, THINKING, AND SKILL BUILDING

1. Identify 3 to 5 factors that affect successful transition to adult life.

2. Why are educators and policy makers concerned about student performance in the middle school years?

3. What is an alternative education program? Describe the characteristics of students who attend them.

4. Why is there increasing concern about the number of students placed into alternative education settings?

5. Describe some of the benefits of alternative education.

6. How does NCLB address the needs of youth in institutional settings?

7. Why are transition services and supports important for youth in the correctional system, juvenile justice system, or other institutional settings?

8. Why do some students who are at risk of educational failure not qualify for special education services?

9. Who are culturally and linguistically diverse students, and what unique transition needs do they have?

10. How have IDEA and NCLB enhanced the role of parents and families in their children's education and transition planning?

Chapter 3

History and Philosophy of Transition

Carol A. Kochhar-Bryant

Chapter Questions

- What are the historical roots of career education and transition?
- What philosophies form the foundation for transition practices?
- What theories form the foundation for transition practices?
- How are philosophies and theories applied to the developmental pathways to transition?

INTRODUCTION

Since the turn of the 20th century, expectations for the schooling of adolescents in the United States have changed markedly. The very notion of adolescence as a phase of life distinct from both childhood and adulthood came into common vocabulary only in the first decades of the 20th century, at about the same time that educators began to develop increasingly ambitious goals for the schooling of students beyond the eighth grade (Beatty, Neisser, Trent, & Heubert, 2001; Furstenberg, Rumbaut, & Settersten, 2005). At the turn of the century, very few teenagers attended high school and fewer completed it. Today, people living in the United States generally attend school by age 6, enter their first jobs in their early 20s, and retire from full-time work at age 70 or 75. These experiences create, and in turn reflect, the expectations about the timing and progression of human experiences, and people who fail to meet these expectations or norms often meet with unwanted advice or outright hostility (Dorn, 1993). More youth today are extending their education, living at home longer, and moving more gradually along the pathway to adulthood. A new period of life is emerging in which young people are no longer adolescents, but not yet adults (Settersten, Furstenberg, & Rumbaut, 2004).

Professionals who implement transition services require a shared understanding of the values and philosophical principles that undergird the practices and policies they choose. As Skrtic (1991) advised almost two decades ago, each profession must have an operating paradigm or accepted way of interpreting the world that will guide their practices and standards. Philosophy is much broader than law and has had a greater effect on public attitudes toward individuals with disabilities and on the response of our social institutions in providing education and human services. This chapter traces the history, philosophies, and theories that have shaped the evolution of transition as a field and applies them to the recent development of transition practices for youth with disabilities.

WHAT ARE THE HISTORICAL ROOTS OF CAREER EDUCATION AND TRANSITION?

Over the past 20 years, major transformations have occurred in educational, social, political, and economic arenas that continue to impact the education and development of youth with disabilities and the institutions that support them. Youth with disabilities are now typically educated with their nondisabled peers. Antidiscrimination laws have improved access to postsecondary education and employment for youth and young adults with disabilities in a variety of occupations. A greater national investment is being made to assist all individuals to access education and employment preparation programs and to increase social and economic independence. Furthermore, interest in youth development and transition is greater than it has been in the past, both in the United States and in other nations (Gordon, 1999; Kochhar-Bryant, 2008; National Center on Secondary Education and Transition, 2000; U.S. Department of Education, 2007).

Although career development for children, youth, and adults of all exceptionalities has been evolving since the turn of the century, the concept of high school *transition* and preparation for careers has only emerged since the 1950s. More recently, educators and policy makers are recognizing how important it is to understand the role of career development and high school diploma options within the overall framework of adolescent development.

Youth development, transition, and adjustment to adult roles have emerged as a new subfield within education. Preparation for transition from school to adult life involves changes in the self-concept, motivation, and development of the individual and is a fragile passage for the adolescent seeking to make difficult life choices (Blum, 2005; Burgstahler, Crawford, & Acosta, 2001; German, Martin, Marshall, & Sale, 2000; Judd, 2006; Kochhar-Bryant, 2008; Michaels, 1994). This passage is even more delicate for youth with disabilities who need additional support and preparation to make the journey. For professionals seeking to help students on this journey, the process involves forming linkages with education and other human service agencies, including employment and training, adult services, and rehabilitation.

History of the Debate over Academic and Occupational Education

Historical context is important for understanding the continuing tensions between academic and career–vocational curriculum in today's standards-based educational environment. In the following historical overview, the terms manual arts, vocational education, career, and technical education are used. Over the past few decades, however, the use of the terms career and technical education has become preferred over manual arts and vocational education.

Philosophers from the Aristotelian era to the modern day have disputed the role of career and vocational preparation in the educational development of children and youth. Aristotle, like Plato, distinguished between liberal education and technical training, viewing the liberal arts as enlarging a person's horizons, consciousness, and choices and viewing vocational training as an interference with intellectual development (Ornstein & Levine, 1997). The philosophical debate about the concept of career development and vocational choice and their role in the social and educational development of children and youth continues today.

Educational historians have observed that as the public schools emerged in the United States over the past two hundred years, they mirrored this schism in philosophy, breaking the curriculum into *academic* subjects and separating it from *career-oriented* learning. Different pathways to graduation and diploma options emerged as students made forced choices between college and employment. Furthermore, concerns about the image of *vocational* education and conflicting opinions about what students belong in the programs have plagued policy makers and educational practitioners since the emergence of the first vocational education programs. In other words, should students with disabilities be tracked into vocational education, or should vocational education be de-stigmatized by renaming it career-technical education and by offering more technical courses? By separating the concept of *academic education* from that of *career development,* educators perpetuated the dichotomy between life and work, intellectual pursuit and manual activity, and individual success and social responsibility. Since before the beginning of this century, statesmen and educators such as Ben Franklin, Horace Mann, and John Dewey have spoken against this artificial dichotomy (Cremin, 1957; Dewey, 1916; Spring, 1988).

Early Emergence of Career–Vocational Education.   Career, vocational, technological, or practical arts education has a long history that spans centuries. In Europe, at the beginning of the industrial revolution, Denis Diderot (1713–1784) and Jean-Jacques Rousseau (1712–1778) began to stimulate a wider interest in the mechanical arts in France. In his *Discourse on the Sciences and Arts of 1750,* Rousseau criticized the arts and sciences (especially the arts in the luxury trades) for what he believed to be their undesirable effects on social values. His essay described the detrimental effects of the arts and sciences on civilization, criticizing urban high society of its self-serving promotion of the arts and sciences. Diderot, however, wanted to elevate the status of the mechanical arts and promote among the literate a better understanding and appreciation for craftsmen, their work, and their contribution to technological progress (Pannabecker, 1996). He called for craftsmen to think more critically about their craft through more systematic and analytical reflection and to systematize their practice in a manner similar to arts and sciences. These two philosophers contributed greatly to the development of technological education. Elements of the differences between Diderot and Rousseau are still part of the mix in contemporary technological education and will continue to be a part of future patterns in curriculum and instruction (p. 21).

Manual Arts Enters the Public School Curriculum.   The shop system, based on the early theories of Rousseau, Diderot, and others, remains a central part of career-technical education today. In the United States, career and vocational education is rooted in the old apprenticeship system in which adolescents lived with their masters who taught them a craft and also how to be responsible members of society. In that system, career and life were intimately connected. The manual arts movement emerged in the late 1800s, when several vocal educators advocated an increase in the availability of manual training to all students as part of the public schools (Walter, 1993). Manual arts training signaled a shift away from the belief that college preparatory curriculum should be the sole purpose of high school to a belief that it should be broadened to prepare students for a variety of career options (Gordon, 1999).

Many social and economic forces influenced the rise of vocational and technical education in the 1800s and 1900s. The mass production, automation, and technological explosion that occurred in this period accelerated the expansion of vocational and technical educational opportunities for youth. Addressing the massive social, cultural, and demographic changes brought about by the industrial revolution, **John Dewey** reasoned that the new transformations demanded that schools be capable of educating pupils in a manner that reflects the larger society, not just the privileged society:

> The obvious fact is that our social life has undergone a thorough and radical change. If our education is to have any meaning for life, it must pass through an equally complete transformation . . . To do this means to make each one of our schools an embryonic community life, active with types of occupations that reflect the life of the larger society and permeated throughout with the spirit of art, history, and science. When the school introduces and trains each child into membership within such a little community, saturating him [*sic*] with the spirit of service, and providing him with the best instruments of self-direction, we shall have the deepest and best guaranty of a larger society which is worthy, lovely, and harmonious. (Dewey, 1916, pp. 28–29)

Dewey challenged educational arrangements that isolated learning from life and found the model for his experimental school at the University of Chicago in the interactions and experiences of the home, neighborhood, and community. Dewey believed that as students joined the daily exchanges and participated in occupational experiences of these communal settings, they would acquire valuable knowledge, develop habits of industry and order, develop regard for the needs of others, and learn how to temper individual desire with a sense of cooperative service. Dewey was aided and inspired in these efforts by his friendship and collaboration with Jane Addams, who, in her work with the emerging immigrant community in Chicago, also demonstrated in the concrete what many others merely preached—a vital, inclusive concept of American democracy grounded in community learning, cooperative education, and cultural inclusion (Addams, 1916).

Career Education Becomes a National Priority and Includes Disadvantaged Populations.
The federal government has had an important role in the expansion of vocational and technical education, with the creation of the Commission on National Aid to Vocational Education (Wilms, 1979) and passage of the National Vocational Education (Smith-Hughes) Act (1917, Pub. L. No. 64-347) that provided the basis for the vocational education movement. Vocational rehabilitation programs for individuals with disabilities were also built into this act (Meers, 1980, p. 9). The career education movement in the United States gained additional momentum in the 1960s, when it became a high priority of the then U.S. Office of Education's Bureau of Adult, Vocational and Technical Education (Halpern, 1985, 1999). In 1963, the Vocational Education Act (Pub. L. No. 88-210) was passed to maintain, extend, and improve upon existing programs of vocational education, as well as to use funds for persons who have academic, socioeconomic, or other disadvantages that prevent them from succeeding in regular vocational education (Gordon, 1999). In 1971, the U.S. Commissioner of Education, Sidney Marland, Jr, proclaimed career education as a major educational reform. Marland believed that the high dropout rate in the United States was partly because of the failure of the educational system to provide students with a relevant education that was aligned with their future goals and potentials (Brolin & Kokaska, 1995; Kokaska & Brolin, 1985).

Students with disabilities were not included in the initiative originally, but in 1977, the Career Education Implementation Incentive Act (Pub. L. No. 95-207) was passed to help states infuse career education into school curricula. Students with disabilities were included as a target population (Michaels, 1994). In 1984, the Vocational Education Act (Pub. L. No. 98-524) was passed and named for House Representative **Carl D. Perkins**, a civil rights supporter who introduced the bill that still bears his name.

Career Education Expanded to Include Youth with Disabilities. During this period, federal involvement in youth development was primarily characterized by an ad hoc approach to policy making in which special population groups that had previously been left out were added into existing programs. For example, many employment training policies were aimed at easing the transition for all youth and included the 1965 Manpower Development and Training Act (MDTA) in the 1960s, the 1973 Comprehensive Employment and Training Act (CETA), the 1977 Youth Employment Demonstration Act, and the Job Training Partnership Act in the 1980s. Many youth advocates view this era of policy making as aimed at leveling the playing field and providing leverage to state and local educational and human service agencies to build their own foundations for equity and productivity (Horne & Morris, 1998).

During the 1970s and 1980s, federal policies increased education and training resources that provided extra help to all youth, particularly those special populations who faced severe disadvantages in schools and the workplace. These special populations included those with disabilities, limited English proficiency, the economically disadvantaged, teen parents, and those in correctional settings. Educators cautioned policy makers that students with disabilities continued to experience limited access to educational and employment programs. The work of Gary Clark through the 1980s and 1990s greatly influenced practice and policy related to the career development of children and youth with disabilities. His life span approach to career development represents a major contribution that builds upon the early development of the concept of career development (Clark, Carlson, Fisher, Cook, & D'Alonzo, 1991). This theory will be discussed in greater detail later in this chapter.

Defining Transition: An Evolving Idea

Educators and policy makers recognized that career-vocational preparation was not enough to assist youth with disabilities to make the difficult passage from high school to the adult world. Specialized transition services were needed as an important adjunct to career-vocational legislation. The 1983 Amendments to the Education of the Handicapped Act (Pub. L. No. 98-199) encouraged states and local school districts to develop systems of transition supports and services. By the end of the 1980s, all 50 states and territories and local school districts had voluntarily developed transition supports and services for youth with disabilities (Halloran & Simon, 1995; Johnson & Rusch, 1993; Ward & Halloran, 1993).

Over the past 50 years, many definitions of transition have emerged, but what they have in common is that they refer to a continuing process of movement toward independent adulthood. One of the earliest discussions of transition was presented by Hill in 1969, who reported on the changing perceptions of work in children aged 7 through 18. Hill found that older youths placed more emphasis on the social values of work, that the transition stage produced anxiety in the individuals, and that youths found it difficult to connect the world of school with the world of work. In 1976, Scharff and Hill described the transition process as a critical stage in life in which an individual brings together his or her internal resources and those gained from adults at school and home to make the first major independent choice that has lasting implications for the future. Young people are required to cope with the personal turbulence inseparable from adolescence while experiencing an abrupt change in their institutional environment (p. 68). This collision between the *personal turbulence* of adolescence and the institutional demands on youth presents many barriers to successful transition for all youth, but particularly for those with disabilities.

1977: Transition Defined as a Responsibility of the Schools.   In 1977, a federal report on education and work examined barriers to the transition of youth to employment and postsecondary education. Successful transition activities were determined to be the responsibility of the schools and included

1. providing students with information about the nature and requirements of different occupations, employment prospects, and educational and experience requirements for career entry and progression;
2. providing students with information about their own abilities and aptitudes;
3. providing early socialization of young people into occupational roles;
4. ensuring that occupational competencies learned in school qualify them for continued education or for entry and progression into various occupations;
5. providing job seeking skills and assistance in finding work; and
6. strengthening students' work habits and basic skills required for entry level employment and preparation for advancement in careers (Berman, McLaughlin, Bass-Golod, Pauley, & Zellman, 1977; U.S. Department of Health, Education and Welfare, 1977).

That same year, the Youth Employment and Demonstration Projects Act of 1977 (Pub. L. No. 95-93) established a youth employment training program that included, among other activities, promoting education-to-work transition, literacy training and bilingual training, and attainment of certificates of high school equivalency. In 1975, Public Law 94-142, the Education for All Handicapped Children Act (Pub. L. No. 94-142, 20 U.S. C. §1401 *et seq.*) established and reaffirmed the responsibility of the schools to provide appropriate programs of education and employment preparation for students with disabilities.

1983: Transition Services Are Authorized Under Special Education Law.   The introduction of transition services represented a major policy initiative for special education during the 1970s and 1980s. The continuing difficulties that youth were having as they exited from high schools were brought to the attention of lawmakers by parents, educators, and the research community. Follow-up studies conducted in the early 1980s (Edgar, 1991; Edgar, Levine, & Maddox, 1986; Hasazi, Gordon, & Roe, 1985; Mithaug & Horiuchi, 1983) revealed that despite this emphasis on equality, integration, and independence (seen in Pub. L. No. 94-142 and other legislation), large numbers of special education students leaving public education were entering segregated, dependent, nonproductive lives (Halloran, 1993). Two thirds of adults with disabilities were not employed, and others were served in segregated programs or no program at all.

Transition services were first introduced in federal legislation in the 1984 Amendments to the Education of the Handicapped Act (Pub. L. No. 98-199), and the components of transition included the following:

1. Effective high school programs that prepare students to work and live in the community
2. A broad range of adult service programs that can meet the various support needs of individuals with disabilities in employment and community settings
3. Comprehensive and cooperative transition planning between education and community service agencies for the purpose of developing needed services for completers, leavers, and graduates

The interest in transition and the success of early initiatives led to the expansion of federal funding to states through the Education of the Handicapped Amendments of 1986, (Pub. L. No. 99-475). These amendments included more specific language to shape transition policy and state interagency agreements for the provision of transition services and to require states to report on the status of students with disabilities exiting secondary education (Halloran, 1993).

In the 1990s, Madeleine Will, then director of the Office of Special Education and Rehabilitative Services of the U.S. Department of Education, defined transition as an *outcome-oriented process* encompassing a broad array of services and experiences that lead to employment and which are designed to be a bridge from secondary school to employment. Services to assist youth to make a successful transition into employment were divided into three categories: no special services, time-limited services, and ongoing services (Will, 1984) (Figure 3–1).

Will's model focused attention on the *shared responsibility* of school and community service agencies (e.g., vocational rehabilitation, mental health services, public health, & independent living centers) for improving outcomes for youth as they exit

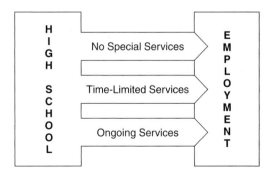

Figure 3–1 OSERS 1984 Transition Model
Source: From "Transition: A Look at the Foundations," by A. S. Halpern, 1985, *Exceptional Children, 51,* pp. 479–486. Copyright 1985 by the Council for Exceptional Children. Reprinted with permission.

secondary education for employment and adult life. Will realized that school-based career education and similar services for youth with disabilities were ineffective without the connection to adult service programming (Busby & Danek, 1998). This definition has been modified and expanded since 1983, adding new services and expected outcomes for youth.

Transition Definition and Goal Expands Beyond Employment.   During the 1980s, transition experts argued that the definition of transition should not be confined solely to an employment outcome or goal for students but should be expanded to include other life domains. For example, Halpern (1985) expanded upon Will's definition to include *community living* and *social and interpersonal* domains (Halpern, 1985). Halpern's definition was further extended by Wehman, Kregel, Barcus, and Schalock (1986) and redefined as an extended process of planning for the adult life of persons with disabilities and included the domains of employment, *independent living,* and *recreation*. Wehman et al. (1986) viewed transition as beginning in the early secondary school years and involving students, families, school-linked agencies, employers, and other organizations. Wehman et al. recognized the importance of a student's informal networks and home environment for the success of transition services.

Similarly, Bates, Suter, and Poelvoorde (1986) defined transition as a dynamic process involving a partnership of consumers, school age services, postschool services, and local communities that results in maximum levels of employment, independent living, integration, and *community participation*. Halpern (1987) augmented his earlier definition, adding four pillars for secondary education and transition curriculum: academic skills, vocational skills, social skills, and independent living skills (Figure 3–2).

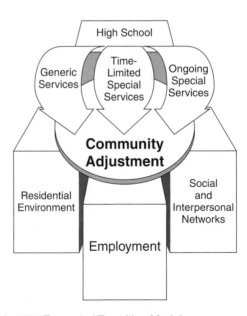

Figure 3–2   Halpern's 1985 Expanded Transition Model
Source: From "Transition: A Look at the Foundations," by A. S. Halpern, 1985, *Exceptional Children, 51,* pp. 479–486. Copyright 1985 by the Council for Exceptional Children. Reprinted with permission.

Figure 3–3 illustrates the development of transition definitions through the 1980s.

Polloway, Patton, Smith, and Rodrique (1991) added another dimension, referring to transitions as both vertical and horizontal. *Vertical transitions* are life span developmental transitions associated with major life events such as beginning school, leaving school, and growing older (p. 3). *Horizontal transitions* refer to movement from one situation or setting to another, such as the movement from a separate setting to a less restrictive, more inclusive setting (Figure 3–4).

These broader conceptions of the transition outcomes helped shape transition policy in the United States and have been reflected in the 1997 and 2004 amendments to the Individuals with Disabilities Education Act (IDEA) and the Rehabilitation Act Amendments of 1998 and 2006 (Greene & Kochhar, 2003).

In 1994, the Council for Exceptional Children's Division on Career Development and Transition (DCDT) developed a definition of transition that reflected recent advances in transition practices. The DCDT definition *combined the concepts of continuous career development from early schooling through high school, recognized the multiple life domains encompassed by the term, and emphasized the central role of the individual in the planning process.* The DCDT definition is as follows:

Transition refers to a change in status from behaving primarily as a student to assuming emergent adult roles in the community. These roles include employment, participating in postsecondary education, maintaining a home, becoming appropriately involved in the community and experiencing satisfactory personal and social relationships. The process of enhancing transition involves the participation and coordination of school programs, adult agency services, and natural supports within the community. The foundations for transition should be laid during the elementary and middle school years, guided by the broad concept

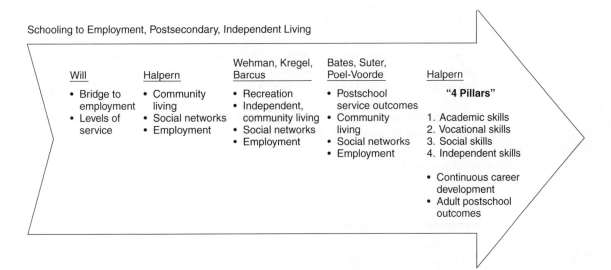

Figure 3–3 Definition of Transition Evolving Through the 1980s

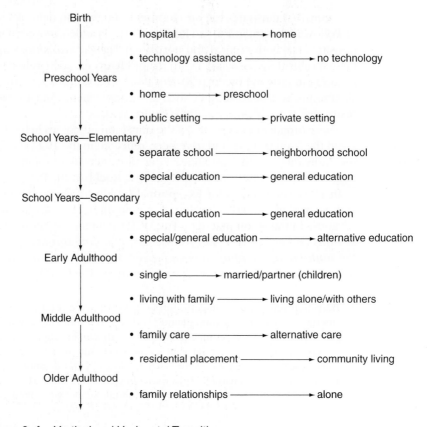

Figure 3–4   Vertical and Horizontal Transitions
Source: From *Transition from School to Adult Life for Students with Special Needs: Basic Concepts and Recommended Practices,* by J. R. Patton, 1995, Austin, TX: PRO-ED. Copyright 1995 by PRO-ED. Reprinted with permission.

of career development. Transition planning should begin no later than age 14, and students should be encouraged to the full extent of their capabilities, to assume a maximum amount of responsibility for such planning. (Halpern, 1994, p. 117)

In 1996, Patton and Blalock advanced the notion that transition involves many interrelated domains, including the following:

- advocacy and legal
- career–vocational training
- communication
- community participation
- daily living
- employment
- financial, income, or money management
- health

- independent living
- leisure or recreation
- lifelong learning
- personal management
- postsecondary education
- relationships or social skills
- self-determination or self-advocacy
- transportation or mobility
- vocational evaluation

During the 1990s, transition research indicated that effective transition programs could not rely on the efforts of the school system alone but required partnerships with school-linked agencies and postsecondary institutions (Johnson & Sharpe, 2000; Kochhar-Bryant, 2008; National Council on Disability, 2000b; Storms, O'Leary, & Williams, 2000). In recognition of the persistent need to improve transition outcomes for youth, the 1997 and 2004 Amendments to IDEA modified the definition of transition to emphasize a shared role between school and community agencies.

Recent Efforts to Expand Transition

The 1990s and 2000s have been marked by intense education policy development and efforts to build the capacity of state and local educational agencies to improve education, provide employment preparation, and transition to postsecondary education for the nation's youth. Special attention has been given to the most disadvantaged populations who continue to experience poor postsecondary outcomes (Thompson & Wehmeyer, in press).

Educational Reforms and Transition. In the 1990s, partly in reaction to public concerns about the eroding quality of education in the United States and weakening economic competitiveness, policy makers turned their attention to improving student academic achievement. Policy initiatives reflected the belief that improving education depends upon the creation of national standards that define what every student should know and be able to do (Jennings, 1995, 2000). The *standards-based reform movement* has led to a shift in the attention of educators from work and career-preparation to academic performance outcomes (Halloran, 1993; Kochhar-Bryant, 2006; Kochhar-Bryant & Vreeburg-Izzo, 2006a, 2006b; Vreeburg-Izzo, Hertzfeld, Simmons-Reed, & Aaron, 2001).

In the 1990s, six additional events contributed to the expansion of transition services: (a) the passage of the Americans With Disabilities Act (ADA) (Pub. L. No. 101-336) that prohibited workplace discrimination against individuals with disabilities; (b) the shortage of prepared adults in the workforce; (c) research findings that demonstrated the relationship between transition services and postsecondary success for youth; (d) federal initiatives to promote state development of transition services; (e) amendments to the Rehabilitation Act that promote coordination with secondary schools to improve transition services; and (f) the School to Work Opportunities Act (STWOA) of 1994 (Pub. L. No. 103-239). The STWOA was passed to assist all students to make a smooth transition from high school to the workplace or postsecondary education. Although the ad hoc nature of policy making across many government agencies has contributed to an uncoordinated patchwork of youth programs and initiatives, efforts to develop and expand transition practices have increased.

Leaders in education and job training are demanding a systematic redesign of secondary education and transition service delivery for all youth, particularly those with disabilities (Education Policy Reform Research Institute, 2004; Jorgensen, 1998; Patton & Trainor, 2002). Reformers are promoting comprehensive and flexible youth development programs that integrate academic development, social–psychological development, career development, and preparation for work and broader life roles. For students with the postsecondary goal of employment, educators recommend a curriculum that blends both school-based and community-based learning opportunities, particularly during the transition grades 9–12 and if needed, through age 21.

On August 11, 2006, Assistant Secretary of Education, John H. Hager, announced new priorities for the Office of Special Education and Rehabilitative Services (OSERS). These priorities include (a) creating a culture of student achievement, (b) achieving self-sufficiency through postsecondary education and/or employment, (c) expanding access to and use of assistive technology, (d) advancing the use of evidence-based practices, (e) improving accountability for OSERS programs, and (f) strengthening management excellence. These priorities signal a dual challenge to educators to focus both on student achievement and on helping prepare youth for postsecondary and employment settings. Figure 3–5 depicts the evolution of transition services from its earlier roots in career development.

WHAT PHILOSOPHIES FORM THE FOUNDATION FOR TRANSITION PRACTICES?

Why Are Philosophy and Theory Important?

Transition practices are rooted in philosophies and theories that have emerged within a variety of fields, including education, organizational development, sociology, psychology, and the health professions. The process of transition to adulthood and the experience of the adolescent in the process have fascinated researchers and philosophers for decades. Both emerging *theories* about the process of transition and *philosophies* about how adults and society ought to help youth through such transitions are helpful in understanding sound practice.

The English word *theory* comes from the Greek root word *theorós,* meaning spectator. This derives from the same root as the word theater. A theory is a logical explanation, general group of principles, or model that is based on extensive observation, analysis of facts, testing of hypotheses, and reasoning that attempts to explain a phenomenon (Montiel-Overall, 2005). Theories help explain complex natural phenomena such as transition to adulthood. Christman (2001) referred to theories of action as a key element for change. She observed that people's understanding of how their beliefs, values, and intention result in action ultimately produces positive results.

In science, a theory states a relationship between two or more things (scientists call them *variables*) that can be tested by factual observations. A theory emerges from and

```
┌──────────────────────────────────────────────────────────────────┐
│ 1900–1960: The concept of career development evolves, " centering on │
│ preparation for work.                                              │
└──────────────────────────────────────────────────────────────────┘
                                  ↓
┌──────────────────────────────────────────────────────────────────┐
│ 1960–1970: The concept of career development broadens beyond the work │
│ role, to include the full range of life roles.                     │
└──────────────────────────────────────────────────────────────────┘
                                  ↓
┌──────────────────────────────────────────────────────────────────┐
│ Early 1970s: The term transition is introduced and refers to both transition │
│ from school to employment and transition of society to a world of  │
│ advancing technology.                                              │
└──────────────────────────────────────────────────────────────────┘
                                  ↓
┌──────────────────────────────────────────────────────────────────┐
│ 1970s: Employment and training legislation emerges to facilitate transition of │
│ youth and young adults from school or unemployment into jobs.      │
└──────────────────────────────────────────────────────────────────┘
                                  ↓
┌──────────────────────────────────────────────────────────────────┐
│ Early 1980s: Transition services for youth with disabilities are promoted in the │
│ States and a decade of experimentation begins.                     │
└──────────────────────────────────────────────────────────────────┘
                                  ↓
┌──────────────────────────────────────────────────────────────────┐
│ 1983: P.L. 98-199 established services to facilitate school-to-work transition │
│ through research and demonstration projects. The 1980s is marked by │
│ dialog and debate about the definition of transition.              │
└──────────────────────────────────────────────────────────────────┘
                                  ↓
┌──────────────────────────────────────────────────────────────────┐
│ 1990: IDEA incorporates transition into the definition of special education and │
│ mandates statewide transition services under Part B.               │
└──────────────────────────────────────────────────────────────────┘
                                  ↓
┌──────────────────────────────────────────────────────────────────┐
│ 1990s: Statewide systems develop focus on measuring transition impacts and │
│ outcomes.                                                          │
└──────────────────────────────────────────────────────────────────┘
                                  ↓
┌──────────────────────────────────────────────────────────────────┐
│ 2000s: Focus on aligning education, rehabilitation, employment preparation │
│ systems, and postsecondary institutions to prepare all youth and adults for │
│ the high-technology work environments of the new century (Kochhar, West, & │
│ Taymans, 2000).                                                    │
└──────────────────────────────────────────────────────────────────┘
```

Figure 3–5   Transition: An Evolving Idea

is supported by experimental evidence or data. A theory is an organized system of knowledge that is generally accepted and applies in a variety of circumstances to explain a phenomenon. A theory can be a well-substantiated explanation of some aspect of the natural world. For example, the theory of gravity addresses the phenomenon of objects that fall to the ground from a height and predicts the speed at which two objects will fall toward one another. Theories also apply to the social world and human behavior. For example, the theory of aggression, based on social learning theory (Bandura, 1977, 1986) is the most well-supported and documented theory of aggression that is widely applicable to males and females of all age levels. It has been developed and modified over the past 40 years so as to incorporate new findings. In the field of transition, through numerous research studies and data collection, a theory has been developed about how self-determination training for youth with disabilities increases their ability to advocate for their own services while in college. A scientific hypothesis that survives repeated experimental testing becomes a scientific theory.

Philosophy differs from theory because it is concerned with broader questions of how one should live (ethics), the nature of human existence and the essential nature of things (metaphysics), the meaning of genuine knowledge and how humans inquire into it (epistemology), and the principles of reasoning (Rutherford, 2006). Philosophers differ from scientists who are concerned with validating theories based on the collection of experimental evidence or data. Applied philosophies include political and economic philosophies that shape and justify government actions. In the field of education, for example, progressive philosophy championed by John Dewey in 1916 continues to have a profound impact on educational practices in the United States today. Philosophies in which transition services are rooted include the human potential movement, youth development movement, and the philosophies of normalization, community integration, inclusion, self-determination, and individual liberty.

The Human Potential Movement

The past century has witnessed the emergence of a **human potential movement**, referred to by many philosophers in the field of psychology. This movement represents an emerging philosophy founded on the belief that all individuals have a basic desire to grow and to develop in positive ways (metaphysics). Programs that embrace the human potential ideology subscribe to the following principles and beliefs:

1. Our social policies should reflect the imperative that society has a responsibility to provide supports and opportunities to disadvantaged citizens.
2. Society must defend the basic right of all citizens to "life, liberty, and the pursuit of happiness," which includes equal educational and social service opportunities for all.
3. All children can learn and have a right to education and support services appropriate to their developmental level.
4. All citizens have an inalienable right to resources and environments that support positive growth and development in children, youth, and adults whether they are disabled, ill, or disadvantaged.

This movement has been called a philosophical revolution in psychology and human services for persons with disabilities and disadvantages. The movement is actually a mix of several emerging new philosophies or ideologies that are driving many practical reforms in education and human services.

What Does This Mean for Career Development and Transition?   The human potential movement advanced the philosophy that all individuals have a basic desire to grow and to develop in positive ways, and therefore, it is the right thing for schools and communities to collaborate to provide the appropriate resources and environments that support positive growth and development in youth with disabilities as they prepare for transition to the adult world. Philosophies or ideologies are broader and much more comprehensive than laws and can be far more effective in influencing traditional practice. The philosophy of positive youth development has also helped shape a recent movement that advocates an optimistic view of youth as having great potential if they are given appropriate structure and support.

Positive Youth Development Movement

Positive youth development is a *philosophy* about youth, concerned with the broader ethical question of how adults should view adolescents and their relationship to them (ethics), as well as the nature of adolescence and how we can come to understand their view of the world (metaphysics and epistemology). Positive youth development addresses the broader developmental needs of youth and departs from the deficit-based models that focus solely on youth problems (Hall, Yohalem, Tolman, & Wilson, 2002).

   Much recent attention has been given to the task of distinguishing a "set of personal and social assets that increase the healthy development and well-being of adolescents and facilitate a successful transition from childhood, through adolescence, and into adulthood" (National Research Council and Institute of Medicine, 2002, p. 6). Individuals have various combinations and ranges of assets or strengths, and continued exposure to positive experiences, people, and settings increases the growth and acquisition of these strengths. Strengths-based principles involve a deliberate focus on strengths, assets, existing capacities and competencies; exploration of existing natural supports; development of plans that build on the full range of people's assets and strengths; and a matching of strengths to workplace or role functions (Cooperider & Whitney, 1998). Rather than seeing young people as problems, this positive and optimistic development approach views them instead as capable of building on their strengths and talents and contributing to their communities.

   For example, parents and teachers of adolescents often focus on the problems and needs and fail to ask—What is right with this teen? What is working in their lives? What are their special talents and interests? The answers to these questions—which also involve asking the youth—can often serve as essential levers for motivating adolescents during the delicate passage through adolescence. The National Youth Development Information Center (2001) defines youth development as a process that prepares young people to meet the challenges of adolescence and adulthood through a coordinated, progressive series of activities and experiences that help them to become socially, morally, emotionally, physically, and cognitively competent. Positive youth development addresses the broader developmental needs of youth, in contrast to deficit-based models that focus solely on remediating youth problems.

The positive youth development movement has emerged as a reaction to the problematic assumptions around deficit models of development. Approaching development as a healing of maladaptions has proven to be ineffective in addition to being an uninspirational approach to a young person or to building human potential. Positive youth development views youth with the glass half full—seeing what can go right with youth, rather than what can go wrong. It is more productive to understand what kinds of attitudes and behaviors might promote thriving and optimal development, rather than focus on deterring antisocial development (Damon, 2004; Jelicic, Bobek, Phelps, Lerner, & Lerner, 2007).

What Does This Mean for Career Development and Transition?   The youth development approach calls for a national dialogue about youth that is centered on their strengths, capabilities, and developmental needs rather than on their problems, risks, and vulnerabilities. It is an appreciative, health-based approach that assumes that as young people prepare to transition to adulthood, they can overcome life challenges and can gain lifelong resilience if they have appropriate and positive supports from adults and peers and are engaged in planning for their futures.

Transition is not a linear process, for it must take into account the wide variation in the development of adolescents and their particular needs for long-range planning and services. Successful transition services require an understanding of the activities and program elements that have shown evidence of effectiveness: a coordinated program of study and challenging and interesting activities, a sense of belonging, supportive relationships with adults, opportunities for leadership, and involvement in community and decision making (Bremer, Kachgal, & Schoeller, 2003; Gambone & Arbreton, 1997; Skinner, 2004).

Programming for youth becomes part of a larger developmental space and should be intentionally linked to other settings in which young people grow and develop, particularly postsecondary settings. Effective youth development programs are characterized by several qualities: (a) promote comprehensive and flexible youth development; (b) engage youth in planning for the future; (c) integrate multiple developmental domains: academic, social–psychological, and career; (d) include a curriculum that blends school-based and community-based approaches; (e) design programming as part of a larger developmental space linked to other settings; (f) design programs to be intensive during middle to high school transition years, in grades 9–12 and through age 21 if needed; (g) account for variation in the development of adolescents and their needs for long-range planning and services before age 16; and (h) focus the IEP postsecondary goals to help students move away from home, establish a social life, become lifelong learners, and work a part- or full-time job (Roth & Brooks-Gunn, 2003; Sagawa, 2003).

Normalization Philosophy and Community Integration

The concept and principles of *normalization* have resulted in a major shift in what we believe about the potential abilities and rights of individuals with disabilities. The principle of normalization originated in Scandinavia and gained popularity in North America through the 1970s (Bank-Mikkelson, 1980; Nirje, 1976; Wolfensberger, 1972,

1983). The principle formed the early foundations of a civil rights movement for persons with disabilities and is closely related to the principle of individual rights and freedoms in a democracy.

Bank-Mikkelson (1980) defined normalization as letting the individual with a disability obtain an existence as close to the normal as possible. Later, Wolfensberger (1972) brought the concept of normalization to the United States and defined it as "the use of culturally normative means to offer persons life conditions at least as good as those of average citizens, and as much as possible, to enhance or support their behavior, appearances, experiences, status, and reputation" (p. 8). This concept reflects a shift in society's response to persons who have been viewed as different, or deviant, from one of banishment and segregation to an effort to reverse deviancy by restoration, rehabilitation, and reintegration. The normalization principle can be applied to any type of profession, agency, individual student consumer, or client. The principle of normalization is the only developed and articulated value system that is

1. consistent with the ideals on which western democracies and their legal structures are based;
2. readily disseminated and applied through established training and evaluation methods;
3. well known in the field and routinely included in the curricula of manpower development programs across North America (Wolfensberger & Thomas, 1983); and
4. relevant to human services in general, rather than to a narrow specialty (Wolfensberger & Thomas, 1983).

Community integration practices have resulted directly from the influence of the principle of normalization. The **community integration philosophy** incorporates such concepts as civil liberty, least restrictive environment, right to treatment and to refuse treatment, care versus cure, quality of life, engaging natural helpers, and coordination of a *system* of services.

What Does This Mean for Career Development and Transition?   Transition services and interagency services coordination models that support transition are rooted in the normalization principle. Normalization of service environments, social integration, and advocacy for the individual have become hallmarks of transition and the *social enabling* (self-determination) philosophy. Specialized services for youth with disabilities, who need extra support as they transition from high school, help approximate life conditions experienced by their peers.

Philosophy of Inclusion

Recent demands to increase educational *quality (excellence) and equity* for all children are now being systematically addressed in education and human service policies throughout the states. Quality improvement refers to the general effort to define and improve standards in the services provided. Equity refers to efforts to decrease social inequality by providing equal access and equal opportunity for all to benefit from programs and services available to all (National Center for Education Statistics, 2000b; Nieto, 2000; Shapiro, 1980). Social equality refers to protecting the rights of the individual and a commitment to making cultural experiences and development of human potential (through education) generally available to all (Harvard Civil Rights Project, 2004; Shapiro, 1980). The way schools are organized, the way teachers collaborate to teach, the way curriculum is structured, and the manner in which children with particular disadvantages are supported and included in basic education can either decrease or perpetuate social inequality.

Education serves both an ideological and an economic role in improving equity in all societies (Hart, Zafft, & Zimbrich, 2001; Shapiro, 1980). The principle of inclusion and belief that children with disabilities should be served in educational settings to the extent possible with nondisabled peers is closely related to earlier philosophy of normalization and community integration. General and special education laws have civil rights provisions that protect access, participation, and progress in the general education curriculum. These laws are also grounded in principles of equal protection under law, based on civil liberty and social integration.

Although the term *inclusion* was not written into special education law, the concept of social inclusiveness was expressed in several principles. Inclusion generally refers to social and legal mandates designed to ensure that children have access to educational programs and services without regard to race, gender, ethnic origin, age, level of education, or disability. Full participation is a broader term more recently used in the United States that refers to educational policies that also emphasize social integration and student progress in a program in addition to access. Full participation also refers to the provision of the range of necessary support services and guidance needed by a student to make necessary progress and to complete an educational program. The term *full participation* has emerged because of the concerns of educators, policy makers, and families who have access to educational programs, and support services alone have not resulted in improved educational, economic, or social outcomes for children and youth. *Once children gain access to educational programs and services, professionals within the system* are also accountable for their progress and successful completion. Public Law 94-142 (1975) guaranteed that children with disabilities would have a right to an appropriate education in the *least restrictive environment.* The term generally refers to the philosophy that students should, to the extent possible, be educated with their nondisabled peers. Special classes, separate schooling, or other removal of children with disabilities from the general education environment occurs only when the severity of the disabilities is such that education in regular classes with the use of supplementary aids and service cannot be achieved satisfactorily.

The law reflects a public recognition of the historical struggle of children and adults against segregation and exclusion from mainstream society. Special education due process provisions, such as protection of their rights to social integration, have shaped educational practices for children with disabilities. These significant historical events include

1. broad philosophical influences in the 20th century on educational practices that promoted an acceptance of exceptionality within the human experience that does not diminish the right of individuals to participate in or to contribute to society;

2. in the mid-20th century the movement of adults with exceptionalities out of institutions and community residential opportunities to assist adults' integration into the mainstream;

3. the expanding roles of federal and state governments and advocacy organizations to protect civil rights of children to education and support services in their schools and communities;

4. the expansion of laws and regulations that protect the rights of children and adults to be included in all aspects of education and community life;

5. interpretation of laws and regulations by the courts that has further defined fair and effective practices for children with exceptional needs (e.g., the *Brown* decision, *Pennsylvania Association of Retarded Citizens* decision, *Mills v. Board of Education*);

6. the expansion of teacher preparation to educate children with exceptional needs in community schools and in the general education classroom; and

7. the support and broadening of research efforts that have led to effective practices in special education and teaching.

These philosophical and legal processes have contributed to new assumptions about educating students with special learning needs and have advanced society's shared belief that all children have the right to be educated in settings with their peers, to receive an education appropriate for their educational and developmental needs, and to maximize their potential for growth into productive adulthood.

What Does This Mean for Career Development and Transition?   An equitable and inclusive education system offers programs and services for all children and youth for whom continuing education, productive employment, and community participation are long-term goals. Recognizing the connections among the social goals of equity (social equality), personal decision making (liberty), and educational preparation for adult life, educational policy makers support shifting resources from supporting young people in states of dependency to the arena of independence and self-sufficiency (Lynch, 1994; National Collaborative on Workforce and Disability, 2005). The philosophy and practice of ensuring full participation and social inclusion also means that no one lives in isolation, but rather, each student is interconnected or interdependent with other people and with their communities. Furthermore, there is a close interrelationship between the economic participation (employment) and independence of individuals and the economic development of the community (Kochhar & Gopal, 1997; Lynch, 1994; Zuckerman, 2005).

The Philosophy of Self-Determination and Individual Liberty

The concept of self-determination is closely related to the youth development framework and the principles of normalization, social inclusion, and individual rights. It is based on the philosophical belief that the student is viewed as a central participant in educational planning and postschool goal setting. Many youth and young adults with disabilities have difficulty assuming control over their lives or in participating in decisions that professionals make about the youth's education and long-range transition goals. Self-determination philosophy is embraced by many human rights groups and is based on core social values of personal freedom, choice, responsibility, equal access, and support.

In 1993, the following working definition of *self-determination* was developed and adopted by the U.S. Office of Special Education: "Choosing and enacting choices to control one's own life to the maximum extent possible, based on knowing oneself, and in pursuit of one's own needs, interests, and values" (Campeau & Wolman, 1993, p. 2). Definitions of self-determination have been modified and expanded in the past decade to include some common themes. These themes are reflected in a summary of definitions offered by Field, Martin, Miller, Ward, and Wehmeyer (1998b) as part of a position statement for the Division on Career Development and Transition, Council for Exceptional Children:

> Self-determination is a combination of skills, knowledge, and beliefs that enable a person to engage in goal-directed, self-regulated, autonomous behavior. An understanding of one's strengths and limitations together with a belief in oneself as capable and effective are essential to self-determination. When acting on the basis of these skills and attitudes, individuals have greater ability to take control of their lives and assume the role of successful adults. (p. 2)

During the past 50 years, our philosophical views about freedom, autonomy, learning, and the potential to improve the mental, physical, and emotional capacities of individuals with disabilities have changed dramatically. These changes have affected the integration of persons with disabilities into community schools and settings (Benitez, Lattimore, & Wehmeyer, 2005; Shogren, Wehmeyer, Reese & O'Hara, 2006; Trainor, 2005; Wehmeyer, 2005, 2006; Wehmeyer, Agran, Hughes, Martin, Mithaug, & Palmer, 2007). For education and human service agencies, the following questions become important: How much accommodation and support should be given to assist the individual to achieve educational goals? How much should professionals intervene in the life of the individual? How does opportunity for individual decision making improve the motivation of youth and their ultimate educational and postsecondary outcomes?

Through this century, the progressive tradition in education and human services reflected a strong belief in *individuality and individual freedoms* and the belief that social support systems should facilitate the educational and human development of the individual, including development of productive skills and personal decision making. As an extension of the progressive philosophy, many communities are making efforts to transfer decision-making authority for educational and human services from large organizational units and professionals to students and their families. Table 3–1 summarizes steps in the philosophical shift toward individual liberty and **self-determination** and the individualization of services that have occurred during the past century.

Most individuals with disabilities in the United States remain in stage 2, characterized by limited access to education and the community in general. There is, however, an intensive national effort to lead education and human service agencies into stages 3 and 4. For example, IDEA 2004 mandates that students participate in their IEP meetings and their transition planning process to the extent possible. By doing so, it is expected that they will learn how to make decisions about their own futures, be more

Table 3–1 Philosophical Steps toward Individual Liberty, Self-Determination, and Full Participation for Persons with Disabilities

Stage 1: Dependence (1900–1950)	**Devalued status or neglect** Social concern or benevolence Physical intervention or medical treatment Segregated educational and psychological intervention
Stage 2: Partial integration (1950–1990)	**Access to special education** Limited access to general education classes Limited access to career-technical education and vocational rehabilitation services Limited access to employment preparation Limited access to transportation and communication Limited access to public facilities for persons with physical disabilities
Stage 3: Individual liberty and full participation (1990–2020)	**Self-determination and personal decision making is expected and actively facilitated** Access to general education with appropriate supports Full access to paid community-based work Full access to medical and life insurance Full access to career-technical education and employment training
Stage 4: Social Leadership (2020 and beyond)	**Full access to postsecondary and higher education** Access to political power (voting, access to congressional, judicial, and administrative roles) Access to private business enterprise and control General access to public facilities, transportation, and communication Access to media and entertainment roles

knowledgeable and realistic in their appraisal of their own abilities and goals, and advocate for themselves in the postsecondary world.

Self-Determination, Self-Advocacy, and Transition.   Two terms that are now in wide use in relation to transition planning are *self-determination* and *self-advocacy.* Many youth and young adults with disabilities have difficulty assuming control of their lives and participating in the educational decisions that are made each year about their educational programs. In 1974, a consumer-directed movement called self-advocacy was begun in Oregon by a group of individuals with disabilities. Now, most states have self-advocacy groups and organizations, such as People First, self-advocacy associations, or disability coalition groups, who are active in establishing peer support groups.

Self-advocacy is defined as a social and political movement started by and for people with disabilities to speak for themselves on important issues such as housing, employment, legal rights, and personal relationships (Smith, 1992). It is related to self-determination because the individual with a disability is directly involved in informed decision making about his or her education, support services, and short- and long-term transition goals. The term has emerged from the earlier concept of normalization, which meant enabling people with disabilities to live, work, and play in environments most close to those of "normal" or nondisabled persons in the mainstream of their community (Nirje, 1976). The concept of self-advocacy extends the idea of normalization to include the active participation of the individual in decision making for their own future, particularly as they prepare for the transition to adult roles.

The process of promoting self-determination and self-advocacy skills depends on the greater shared decision making among the individual, the family, and professionals in decisions that affect the future of the student (Thoma & Wehmeyer, 2005). With building individual capacity to make informed choices and decisions also comes a greater responsibility and accountability for the outcomes of those decisions. Individuals and parents, therefore, become equal partners and share the responsibility for developing individualized transition service plans as part of the IEP and for the results of those plans. Self-determination is also discussed as a theory in the next section.

⇨ WHAT THEORIES FORM THE FOUNDATION OF TRANSITION PRACTICES?

As mentioned earlier, a *theory* is an organized system of knowledge that is generally accepted and applied in a variety of circumstances to explain a phenomenon. Theories help explain why particular practices, such as transition practices, work or are effective for youth. Theories related to transition services are not fixed or static, but are constantly being tested, modified, and refuted as new ideas and evidence about human and organizational behavior emerge. Transition practices that are applied widely in society and aimed at improving outcomes for youth and young adults are based on theoretical principles and assumptions. Theories upon which transition services are grounded include general systems theory, adolescent development theories, social and cognitive development theory, career development theories, and self-determination theory.

General Systems Theory

General systems theory offers a framework for understanding complex relationships among organizations or social systems. The general systems theorist identifies ideas that have application across many disciplines and that are successful in solving problems that practitioners recognize as shared. Derived from the work of Von Bertalanffy (1969) and Sutherland (1973), an integrated set of general systems principles that can be broadly applied in many disciplines include the following: (a) individuals and social systems are viewed as whole systems; (b) individuals, families, and groups are viewed as open systems; and (c) interdisciplinary communication is essential. Applied to education, general systems theory *promotes interdisciplinary interchange and increased communication among specialists from widely diverse fields, creating a shared responsibility for the individual.*

What Does This Mean for Career Development and Transition? General systems principles are helpful in analyzing relationships within complex service systems. Three general systems principles are applied to transition and interagency service coordinators:

   1. *Individuals are viewed as wholes (holistically):* In general systems theory, individuals are viewed as wholes that are greater than the sum of their parts. This means that understanding human growth, development, or behavior cannot be accomplished by reducing behavior into parts and analyzing these parts in isolation of each other. The individual's behaviors and experiences must be viewed as a dynamic, whole system that interacts within a unique environment. When a student has multiple education and support needs, those needs must be considered in relation to one another, and not in isolation. For example, a guidance counselor should be concerned not only with academic performance of the student in his final year of high school, but also with the student's motivation, family circumstances, health and physical status, and other factors. Similarly, if a student preparing for transition to postsecondary education has a chronic health problem, requires special accommodations, and requires mental health counseling, intervention in one of these areas is likely to interact with the other two. It is therefore much more effective to unify these interventions and engage a team of professionals to address the needs.

   2. *Individuals, families, and groups are open systems:*   People are complex and *open systems* who are in continuous interchange with the environment in which they live—the individuals with whom they interact, the physical surroundings, and culture. The needs of the individual student preparing for transition to adulthood must be understood in the context of their family and community environment and the context of her postsecondary goals.

   3. *Interdisciplinary communication is essential:*   General systems principles suggest that specialists from diverse fields can better communicate if they develop a common vocabulary, a common set of guiding principles for action, and common practices for responding to individuals with disabilities. Within education and human services, general systems theory can help professionals recognize shared problems and solutions among disciplines or fields and agencies (Kochhar-Bryant, 2008). For example, to solve problems of youth transition and interagency collaboration between schools and social service agencies, we can explore and learn from the models for collaboration within the mental health and public health fields. Such models will be explored in depth in Chapter 5.

Transition professionals address the needs of the individual as a whole person and strive to develop service system responses that are unified and integrated. They make connections among professionals and agencies that can lead to collaborative relationships. In summary, transition professionals address the holistic needs of the student and help the service system develop responses that are integrated rather than fragmented.

Adolescent Development Theories

All adolescents vary in their rate of development, maturation, and ability to negotiate various tasks of childhood. Numerous theories have been developed over the past decades to explain the phenomenon of adolescent development. The physical and social effects of disabilities, however, can provide special challenges and can interfere with the successful passage through each of the transition domains. The following sections provide brief summaries of major theories and conceptual frameworks related to adolescent development and suggest implications for transition services. These are synthesized from the work of several theorists.

The Adolescent Brain.   With the exception of infancy, early adolescence is the period in which a child's body and brain grow and change faster than in any other phase of life. The student is in a process of change from child to adolescent, yet the change in environment from middle school to high school is a sudden *event*. Because most children are developing at different rates, some come into high school ready for the changes, others struggle to keep up, and still others fall behind. As with all school transitions, the transition to high school occurs as a one-size-fits-all event to which all youth are expected to adapt.

Recent brain research reveals that during the teen years up to age 15, the areas in the middle and back of the brain associated with associative thinking and language reach their peak growth rates (Wilson & Horch, 2004). The growth spurt is most predominant just before puberty in the prefrontal cortex, the part of the brain crucial to information synthesis. The prefrontal cortex is the area of the brain that controls planning, working memory, organization, insight, judgment, mood modulation, and inhibition of inappropriate behaviors (Arnsten & Shansky, 2004). This area of the brain is not mature until about 18 years of age (Spinks, 2002). The prefrontal cortex appears to be the last region of the brain to mature (Casey, Giedd, & Thomas, 2000), undergoing major changes throughout puberty and continuing until age 25. These recent findings about adolescent brain development have major implications for classroom practices, student supports, and transition. Only recently have educational researchers and practitioners begun to relate new brain research to learning.

Recent research also addresses new evidence that the nature of early adulthood is changing. The period before adulthood is lengthening, often spanning the 20s and even extending into the 30s. Pathways into and through adulthood have become less linear and predictable (Furstenber, Rumbat, & Settersten, 2005). These changes have significance for postsecondary institutions, employers, and policies that are aimed at supporting adolescents and young adults as they make the transition to adulthood.

Life Span Theory of Development Theorists.   Age or stage models form one school of thought in developmental theory in which life is described as a series of stages linked to specific ages and occurring in sequence. Major life span theorists include Adams, Gullotta, and Montemayor (1992); Blos (1962, 1979); Bosma, Graafsma, Grotevant, and De Levita (1994); Clark and Kolstoe (1995); Erickson (1968); and Kroger (1992). The life span approach to career development has been an important concept since the early development of the concept of career development (Clark et al., 1991). Life span theory of development involves the following propositions:

1. Over the life span, each individual passes through a series of distinct developmental periods with a developmental task at each stage.
2. The developmental periods are partially defined by the society in which the individual lives.
3. Any developmental task that is not successfully completed impedes or interferes with the accomplishment of later tasks.

Identity formation occurs between ages 13 and 18. Identity formation means the development of an internalized system for self-regulation that requires the individual to distinguish between the inner self and outer social world. The adolescent develops either a passive identify formation process, in which he or she either accepts the roles and self-images of others or experiences role confusion (the youth experiences self-doubt and uncertainty), or an active identity formation process based on a searching and self-selection process and commitment to the choices made. In the second, the youth experiences self-assurance and a sense of mastery (Adams et al., 1992). One's family and social context greatly influence this process.

Erikson's (1968) theory of psychosocial development included eight stages of development: trust versus mistrust (age 0–1); autonomy versus shame and doubt (2–3 years); initiative versus guilt (4–5 years); industry versus inferiority (6–12 years); identity versus role confusion (13–18 years); intimacy versus isolation (19–25 years); generativity versus stagnation (26–40 years); ego integrity versus despair (41 years and above). Each stage is characterized by a different conflict that must be resolved by the individual. When the environment makes new demands on the individual, conflicts arise. The person is faced with a choice between two ways of coping with each crisis—adaptive or maladaptive.

Rapp (1998) proposed three developmental stages that include the following: (a) early adolescence (12–14 years; characterized by strong influence of peer groups, emotional distance from parents, rapid growth, and interest in sex); (b) middle adolescence (14–17 years; self-discovery, performance orientation, and vital relationships); and (c) late adolescence (17–19 years; career focus, physical distance from parents, and self-sustaining living). Havinghurst (1972) proposed eight developmental tasks:

1. Achieving new and more mature relations with age-mates of both sexes
2. Achieving a masculine or feminine social role
3. Accepting one's physique and using the body effectively
4. Achieving emotional independence from parents and other adults
5. Preparing for marriage and family life
6. Preparing for an economic career
7. Acquiring a set of values and an ethical system as a guide for behavior
8. Desiring and achieving socially responsible behavior

Researchers are now questioning the validity of age-linked phases (Leonard, Mathews, & Bowes, 1987). A more eclectic approach is advocated by Schlossberg (1985) who describes four ways of viewing adult experience: (a) the cultural context or social environment, (b) the psychological developmental stages of the individual, (c) life events or transitions, and (d) continuity and change throughout the life span.

What Does This Mean for Career Development and Transition?　In considering appropriate transition education activities and needs, educators and transition specialists informally assess a student's developmental level and support needs to participate in career decision making. They provide supports and accommodations for self-directed IEP planning that are appropriate to the student's level. They provide maximum opportunity for students to develop self-determination skills to participate in their own education and career planning. The more we learn about adolescent development, brain development, and identity formation, the better we will be able to prepare students for the transition planning and decision making. Figure 3–6 depicts developmental tasks for adolescents and factors that can interact to create barriers to their successful transition to adulthood.

Cognitive Development Theory.   Cognitive development theorists (e.g., Piaget, 1929, 1970) emphasize the development and influence of thinking and mental growth rather than personality. The process of discovery and growth occurs primarily through a process of the child's involvement with and action on his or her environment. Piaget (1929) was interested in how infants and young children come to understand their world and proposed four developmental stages: (a) sensorimotor (ages 0–2); (b) preoperational (ages 2–7); concrete operational (ages 7–11); and formal operational (age 11 to adulthood). Piaget's theory is primarily domain general, meaning that it assumes that cognitive maturation (maturing of the mind) occurs concurrently across different domains (e.g., language and numeracy). More recent cognitive developmentalists, however, have been influenced by trends in cognitive science, away from such domain generality and toward the proposition that the mind is made up of different cognitive faculties that are independent of one another and develop at very different rates.

What Does This Mean for Career Development and Transition?   Effective educational and career-vocational programs are designed to (a) accommodate different

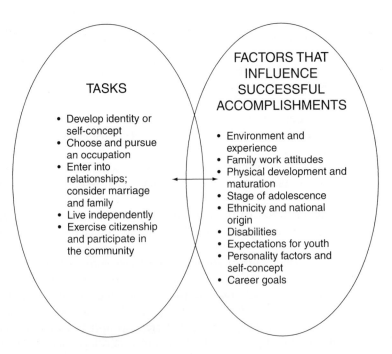

Figure 3–6   Developmental Tasks for Adolescents and Factors That Affect Successful Accomplishment

cognitive learning styles and (b) incorporate instructional approaches that include a variety of classroom and community-based learning experiences. Transition service planning is designed to respond to a wide range of developmental levels within different domains in the individual student. For example, a high school student may be developmentally advanced beyond his or her peers in mathematics, but may be delayed in social development. Disabilities may impact domains of development differently, which are also impacted by family and environmental circumstances.

Transition Adaptation Patterns. According to developmental theorists Phelan, Davidson, and Yu (1998), there are six transition and adaptation patterns identified among high school youths as they negotiate among their multiple worlds of family, school, peers, and self. Several types of *boundaries* or borders exist between each of these worlds that can create obstacles to successful transition among them. These borders include *sociocultural* (e.g., cultural differences between family and school), *socioeconomic* (e.g., economic differences between family and peers), *psychosocial* (e.g., anxiety, depression, or fear that disrupts ability to focus in the classroom), *linguistic* (e.g., communication differences between family and peers), *gender* (e.g., differential expectations of girls and boys), *heterosexist* (e.g., conflicts that arise when the individual assumes the world is heterosexual but comes in contact with homosexuality), and *structural* (features in the school environment that impede student learning, social or academic, including school rules, curriculum, etc.) (Phelan et al., 1998).

Phelan et al. (1998) eloquently describe adolescence as a "critical period fraught with promise and peril—a time of passage in which biological, emotional, and social factors converge to forecast the future of youth adults" (p. 2). The processes of crossing borders and adjusting and adapting to the various "worlds" of adolescents—home, family, teachers, and peer groups—requires competencies and skills for transitions to be successful, particularly for students with disabilities.

What Does This Mean for Career Development and Transition? Phelan, Davidson, and Yu point out that students' ability to move between these worlds of adolescents or settings and adapt to different settings has great implications for the quality of their lives and their chances of using the educational system as a stepping stone to further education, productive work experiences, and a meaningful adult life. Effective transition planning addresses these multiple borders and the complexity of youths' efforts to negotiate them.

Educators and transition specialists address borders between students' home, school, community, and postsecondary institutions in transition planning. They promote sensitivity toward cultural and family attitudes about work and the students' career aspirations and address language barriers in transition planning. They assess the need for student or family counseling or career counseling and ensure communication with family members who speak other languages. Furthermore, they consider supports and accommodations needed to enable the student to be included in the general secondary education classroom and work to increase acceptance among students of different backgrounds and between students and adults.

Social Competency Theory.   Several developmental tasks are associated with the development of social competency in adolescents (Adams et al., 1992; Bloom, 1990; Kirchler, Palmonari, & Pombeni, 1993). These include both psychosocial constructs and social–biological constructs. Psychosocial constructs include personal factors such as developing cognitive or intellectual structures, expanding affective structures (feelings), expanding behavioral repertoire, and changing relationships with others in educational and employment arenas. Social–biological constructs include the process of change in puberty and their effects on personal and interpersonal social competency (self-image, maturity, independence, concern over competence, physical self-satisfaction, and relationships with peers and parents) and physical appearance (height, weight, body image, and attractiveness).

What Does This Mean for Career Development and Transition?   Educators and transition specialists include activities in the student's IEP that support development of physical and social competence such as sports, music, and extracurricular activities. They provide students direct instruction about their own development, its impact on learning, and the tasks they must accomplish as they progress toward adulthood.

Social Learning Theory.   Social learning theory relies on an operant conditioning model that is based on the assumption that behavior of children is under the control of external environmental reinforcements (Bandura, 1977; Bee & Mitchell, 1980; Bijou & Baer, 1961; Patterson, 1975; Sears, 1972). Children and youth learn new behaviors largely through modeling. Behavior is strengthened by reinforcement, and this applies to aggression, dependency, sharing, competitiveness, or any other behavior. When behavior is reinforced on a "partial schedule," it is more resistant to extinction than behavior that is consistently reinforced.

Educators and transition specialists recognize that the individual's potential to change patterns of behavior, depending on the support of the environment, is considerable but is not necessarily consistent from childhood to adulthood. Transition planning reflects social learning theory when it incorporates skill development (self-determination, self-advocacy, career and employment, and social and behavioral) that is consistent and occurs over the long term.

Temperament Theories.   Temperament theories express several propositions that emphasize the biological basis of social interaction. First, each individual is born with characteristic patterns of responding to the environment and to other people. These temperamental qualities are genetically programmed, persist throughout the life span, and affect the way an individual responds to things around him or her or in relationships with others. Conversely, the individual's temperament affects the way others respond to him or her, so that temperament interacts with his or her environment. The child "shapes" others' behavior toward him or her (Buss, 1991; Buss & Plomin, 1984; Chess & Thomas, 1991; Diamond, 1957).

What Does This Mean for Career Development and Transition?   Educators and transition specialists recognize that, whereas behavior is malleable and patterns can change over time based on influences of the environment, some patterns related to temperament and personality are genetically determined and are therefore stable and predictable. Reflecting this understanding, educators avoid stereotyping individuals' career potential or goals based on individual personality characteristics.

Psychoanalytic Theories.   Psychoanalytic theory is based on the proposition that the child is focused throughout life on gratification of the basic instincts (Freud, 1960; Horney, 1945, 1950; Rank, 1927, 1958; Sullivan, 1953). The child passes through a series of distinct psychosexual stages from birth through adolescence. At each stage, the specific experiences a child encounters will affect his or her overall psychological "health" or "illness." In the course of development, children discover that instant gratification is not always possible, so they are forced to develop cognitive skills (language and intellectual strategies) that allow them to plan and manipulate the environment more effectively. The ego, once developed, will defend itself against any perceived threat, and the child develops defense mechanisms to handle them.

What Does This Mean for Career Development and Transition?   On the basis of this theory, educators and transition specialists help teachers and parents to understand and view adolescents' attempts to manipulate and engage with their environment and to seek gratification as a natural part of development. They harness this natural tendency by coaching students to direct their own individualized education and transition planning. They help adolescents understand their own developmental stages and develop self-controls.

Self-Determination Theory

Self-determination philosophy, discussed earlier as a philosophy, can also be viewed as a theory. The theory is based on the assumption that people have inborn tendencies to grow and develop psychologically, to strive to master challenges in their environment, and to integrate new experience into their self-concepts (Deci & Ryan, 1985, 2000, 2006; National Research and Training Center, 2002; Ryan & Deci, 2000). Self-determination is a broad theory of human motivation and personality concerned with the development and functioning of personality within social contexts. The theory focuses on the degree to which human behaviors are based on reflection and personal choice.

   Self-determination theory is comprised of four mini-theories: (a) *cognitive evaluation theory* that addresses the effects of social contexts on individual motivation; (b) *organismic integration theory* that addresses the concept of how experiences are "internalized" and contribute to the development of motivation; (c) *causality orientation theory* that describes individual differences in people's tendencies toward self-determined behavior; and (d) *basic needs theory* that addresses the concept of basic needs and its relationship to psychological heath and well-being. Self-determination theory begins with the assumption that young people have a natural tendency toward psychological growth and development and they have a desire to master ongoing challenges and develop a strong sense of self. This natural tendency toward growth, however, does not operate automatically, but requires a supportive social context to function effectively (Deci & Ryan, 1985, 2000, 2006).

What Does This Mean for Career Development and Transition?   Educators and transition specialists informally assess the student's motivation in participation and decision making, along with their ability to participate. They recognize that students of the same age may vary widely in their motivation to participate, but that all youth do prefer to become self-determined. Transition education programs incorporate self-determination skill training as an essential element and help students understand how these skills apply in postsecondary environments.

Career Development Theory

Although **career development theory** has its origins in ancient Greek culture, contemporary theory has been shaped by the work of organizational and adolescent development theorists in the 1940s and 1950s. Several theories of career development have emerged and are in application today, but there remains little consensus on the definition of *career development* and **career education**. The career development movement in the United States was launched without a commonly accepted definition (Kokaska & Brolin, 1985). *Furthermore, there is little agreement on the appropriate role of career development in the K–12 curriculum; in adolescent cognitive, social, and emotional development; or in the preparation of youth for transition from school to employment and postsecondary education.* There has, however, been a great deal of searching to define the concept. Ever since former U.S. Commissioner of Education, Sidney P. Marland, made a plea for "career education now" in 1971, educators and policy makers have been asking the question—what is career education? A few recent definitions of career education include the following:

1. Educational programs and curriculums at many different developmental levels, provided by several types of delivery systems, that provide experiences designed to help individuals become oriented to, select, prepare for, enter, become established, and advance in an individually satisfying and productive career (Bailey & Stadt, 1973, pp. 346–347).
2. A process of systematically coordinating all school, family, and community components to facilitate each individual's potential for economic, social, and personal fulfillment (Brolin, 1973, p. 1).
3. An effort aimed at refocusing American education and acting for the broader community in ways that will help individuals acquire and utilize the knowledge, skills, and attitudes necessary for each to make work a meaningful, productive, and satisfying part of his or her way of living (Hoyt, 1975, p. 5).
4. The totality of experiences through which one learns to live a meaningful, satisfying work life (Halpern, 1994).
5. Career education is believed to produce several outcomes for students: knowledge about careers; orientation and attitudes about careers; and specific skills required to enter a specific occupation, including self-identity, educational identity, economic understanding, career decisions, employment skills, career placement, and social fulfillment. Basic to the concept of career education is the recognition that *preparation for a career role must begin in early childhood if*

*the individual is to develop the concepts, attitudes, and skills that insure free-
dom of choice and expand career options* (Clark & Kolstoe, 1995).

6. The totality of experiences through which one learns about, and is prepared to
   engage in, work as part of his or her way of living, and through which he or she
   relates work values to other life roles and choices (such as family life) (Pub. L. No.
   95-207).

Although there may not be clear consensus among career development theorists, the
definitions described here have several important features in common: emphasis on
individual needs, developmental processes, preparation for work, community involvement, expansion of options, and preparation for adult life. Transition services, defined
in Chapter 1, are viewed as a component of the broader career development process
that begins in early childhood and continues throughout the life span. There are five
distinct frameworks for career development theory that have emerged within the past
century:

1. *Trait-factor theories:*　　**Trait-factor theories** are based on the assumption that
career–vocational choice is stable, patterned, and predictable and that individual abilities and interests can be matched with career opportunities to facilitate vocational
choice (Crites, 1981; Hull, 1928; Kitson, 1925; Parsons, 1909). Such theories place less
emphasis on career choice factors outside the individual such as cultural and sociological influences. An expected outcome of "successful" matching would be an individual occupational choice that is appropriate and enduring for the individual. A
range of interest inventories and aptitude tests have emerged from this framework,
which remains a major focus in vocational education and rehabilitation.

2. *Sociological (ecological) model of career choice:*　　A sociological model of
career development (also called the reality theory or accident theory) is based on the
assumption that societal circumstances beyond the control of the individual contribute significantly to **career choice** (Caplow, 1954; Harmony, 1964; Hollingshead,
1949; Szymanski & Hanley-Maxwell, 1996; Szymanski & Hershenson, 1998; Szymanski,
Hershenson, Enright, & Ettinger, 1997; Wehman, 1992, 2006). The principle task for the
individual is to learn techniques for coping with those pushes and pulls of his or her
particular environment or *ecology*. Factors that influence an individual's expectations
and aspirations in careers, as well as the expectations of others, become important in
this framework. The new ecological paradigm for services to persons with disabilities
is strengthening, but there has not yet been a systematic examination of these principles for current career development and counseling practices.

3. *Developmental or self-concept theory:*　　This theory combines the psychological theory of self-actualization and self-image with a developmental model of career
development. Propositions include the following: (a) the individual's self-concept
becomes more clarified as he or she grows older and matures; (b) people develop
images of the occupational world that they compare with their self-image in trying to
make career decisions; and (c) the adequacy of the career decision ultimately made is
based on the congruence or match between the individual's self-concept and his or her
concept of the chosen career (Dudley & Tiedeman, 1977; Ginzberg, Ginsburg, Axelrod, &
Herman, 1951; Osipow, 1983; Osipow & Fitzgerald, 1996; Rogers, 1951; Super, 1957).

What Does This Mean for Career Development and Transition?   The self-concept framework has led to current practice in which early career development is not emphasized in schools, because it is assumed that career interventions are "premature" unless the individual is old enough to have "crystallized" career interests and preferences. Such assumptions of pre-maturity appear to be more pronounced for persons with disabilities, who are often perceived by educators as younger than their chronological age, "childlike" and in need of care, and not ready for career development activities until later in adolescence or early adulthood. The result is that career development and supports are often provided much later for individuals with disabilities than they are for nondisabled individuals. When this occurs, it creates an added disadvantage for these individuals who would benefit from early career planning.

The concept of transition was introduced as part of Ginzberg, Ginsburg, Axelrod, and Herman's (1951) developmental or self-concept theory. Ginzberg et al.'s (1951) vocational choice theory described three stages—the fantasy period, the tentative period, and the realistic period. The fantasy period reflects the young child's arbitrary and unrealistic preferences about occupations and choices (Osipow, 1983; Osipow & Fitzgerald, 1996). In the tentative period, children consider what they are interested in and like to do, their abilities, and the value of different vocations. Ginzberg et al. define the transition stage as the closing of the tentative period, which occurs at about age 17 or 18. In this stage, individuals begin to make immediate, concrete, and realistic decisions about their career future. The realistic period involves the actual entry into work or college and the development of a career pattern and ultimately a career focus or specialization. As Ginzberg's theory demonstrates, the logic of transition planning is rooted in several assumptions about the tasks of adolescent development, one of which is career decision making and vocational awareness.

Understanding the characteristics of the stages of adolescence helps educators design the types of education and transition services most appropriate for middle and high school age youth. Adolescence is recognized as a stage, or passage, in which the adolescent undergoes substantial transformations, physically, psychologically, emotionally, and socially (Adams et al., 1992; Blos, 1962, 1979; Erikson, 1968). Krup (1987) synthesized literature to yield the following definitions of *transition:* A transition is a natural process of disorientation and reorientation, caused by an event or nonevent, that alters the individual's perception of self and the world, demands a change in assumptions or behavior, and may lead either to growth or deterioration; the choice rests with the individual (p. 4).

4. *Vocational choice and personality theories:*   Personality theories are based on the assumption that there are personality types associated with career areas and that personality factors are involved in career choice and career satisfaction (Holland, 1959; Roe, 1957; Schaffer, 1953; Small, 1953). The propositions include the following: (a) workers choose their jobs because they see potential for the satisfaction of their individual needs, (b) certain personality characteristics are common among people who choose certain occupations, (c) certain common lifestyles are associated with certain occupations, (d) certain psychopathologies are associated with professional activities, and (e) people become more like each other the longer they remain in a certain occupation together.

When personality theories are applied to the career development of individuals with disabilities, they may be distorted by myths or generalizations that are detrimental to persons with disabilities and can negatively affect career development services. For example, such generalizations may lead to inaccurate assumptions that persons with disabilities only prefer certain types of jobs, such as manual labor, because they "suffer from personality deficits." They either generally prefer construction or "hands-on" trades rather than white-collar office work, or they accept low-paid, dead-end jobs because of certain personality factors or because they prefer not to enter jobs with challenges or high demands. Such assumptions are not only false but lead to continuing societal discrimination against individuals with disabilities.

5. *Behavioral approaches:*   This theoretical framework borrows from behavioral theory and is concerned with the effect of the environment on behavior. The more recent social learning approaches assert that individuals are "socialized" into careers by external factors such as family and culture, and individual personality factors or traits have less to do with career choices than environmental factors (De Leon, 1996; Herring, 1998; Osipow & Fitzgerald, 1996). The career choice of an individual is thought to be shaped primarily by such environmental factors.

Gottfredson's Theory of Career Development

Gottfredson's (1996) theory offers a developmental, sociological perspective on career development that is focused on the types of compromises people make in formulating their occupational aspirations. This process of compromise, termed *circumscription,* involves the process of eliminating unacceptable occupations based primarily on gender and social class. *Compromise* involves the process of modifying career choices because of limiting factors. Gottfredson proposes four stages of cognitive development:

Stage 1:   *Orientation to size and power* (ages 3–5). Children orient themselves to differences in size and power between themselves and adults.

Stage 2:   *Orientation to sex roles* (ages 6–8). Children develop their "tolerable sex-type boundary." That is, they believe that certain jobs are only for boys, and others are only for girls.

Stage 3:   *Orientation to social valuation* (ages 9–13). Children and early adolescents develop a zone of occupations as acceptable based on social class and ability level. In other words, they rule out careers they consider "beneath" them and those that are above the upper limit of effort and risk that they are willing to take.

Stage 4:   *Orientation to internal, unique self* (age 14 and above). Adolescents, and adults, become more introspective and self-aware, establishing a self-identity or self-concept and related personal goals. Compromise occurs as preferred careers are eliminated by external realities such as job opportunities in the community.

Gottfredson (1996) highlights the importance of career education programs to promote systematic exploration of career choices. Although research on the theory has not been extensive, her concepts describing boundaries and motivation related to choice and aspiration are noteworthy.

Levinson's Stages of Career Development

Figure 3–7 depicts Levinson's (2002) stages of career development. Levinson defined growth stages and sub-stages that children progress through during the career development process.

Figure 3–7   Levinson's Development Tasks by State of Career Development and Age

Growth Stage	Exploration Stage
Fantasy Substage (0–10 years) 1. Imagination and play themes revolve around work	**Tentative (15–17 years)** 1. Adolescents become aware of their own aspirations 2. Adolescents identify career options and set tentative goals 3. Adolescents explore their tentative career options and goals
Interest Substage (11–12 years) 1. Children form a healthy self-concept and become aware of their personal qualities 2. Children become aware of and consider a variety of careers and learn about what workers do and about the value of work 3. Children identify with a gender role and think of jobs in terms of gender 4. Children develop positive attitudes that lead to competence, cooperation, and achievement	**Transition (18–21 years)** 1. Young adults make a career choice 2. Young adults learn skills needed for entry-level employment in their career of choice
Capacity Substage (13–14 years) 1. Adolescents become aware of their own values and abilities 2. Adolescents develop planning, decision-making, and problem-solving skills 3. Adolescents recognize that not all jobs are the same, that there are differences in requirements, duties, pay, and rewards among careers 4. Adolescents realize that academic choices may affect their post–high school life 5. Adolescents take on increased responsibility for making their own career-related decisions	**Trial (22–24 years)** 1. Young adults follow through with obtaining a job in their career of choice

Source: From "Best Practices in School-Based Vocational Assessment," by E. M. Levinson in *Best Practices in School Psychology IV* (pp. 1569–1584), by A. Thomas and J. Grimes (Eds.), 2002, Bethesda, MD: National Association of School Psychologists. Copyright 2002 by the National Association of School Psychologists, Bethesda, MD. Reprinted with permission of the publisher.

What Does This Mean for Career Development and Transition?   The transition process, defined in Chapter 1, is viewed as a broad framework for preparing youth to successfully move through the passages through schooling and into the adult life roles—academic, vocational, social–psychological, and civic. Transition incorporates the career development process that begins in early childhood and continues throughout the life span. Educational programs that incorporate career development help students become oriented to, select, prepare for, and enter individually satisfying and productive careers. It is a process of systematically coordinating all school, family, and community components to facilitate each individual's potential for economic, social, and personal fulfillment (Brolin, 1973, p. 1).

Comprehensive career transition assessment is also an underpinning for effective career development programs and is designed to identify the extent to which individual students are meeting career development objectives in a manner consistent with career development theory (Leconte, 1994; Smith & Leconte, 2005). Students identified as not meeting objectives can then be provided with interventions to assist them in career development. Activities designed to facilitate acquisition of career-related objectives should occur both as part of (for all students) and outside of (for students needing additional assistance) regular education. Student populations who are at high risk for career-related difficulties (women, minorities, and individuals with disabilities) will require targeted career development services and transition supports from high school to postschool life as part of a comprehensive K–12 career education program.

→ HOW ARE PHILOSOPHIES AND THEORIES APPLIED TO THE DEVELOPMENTAL PATHWAYS TO TRANSITION?

How does the discussion of philosophy and theory apply to transition planning and the developmental pathways introduced in Chapter 1? Transition planning involves a variety of decisions that can be quite confusing for students and families. Students and families must choose among postsecondary goals, course choices in high school that support the goals, assessments to inform the decisions, support services and accommodations that will be needed during high school and beyond, planning and services required at the point of transition, and agency services that might be needed. Although some students need time-limited transition supports and others need ongoing services, the transition planning process for students with disabilities should begin early in the middle school years and as they enter secondary education. For students without disabilities, such long-range vision and secondary planning to achieve postsecondary goals is the typical model that begins as the student prepares to exit middle school and makes choices for a high school course of study.

A pathways approach—individualized for each student—provides a framework for matching planning strategies with students' postsecondary goals early enough to provide adequate time to define and implement the plan. Inadequate time for this process places students at risk of incomplete or unsuccessful transition. As introduced in Chapter 1, the four pathways include (a) academic or postsecondary education, (b) career-technical training, (c) employment, and (d) supported setting.

Effective transition services are structured to facilitate each student's potential for personal, social, and economic fulfillment and participation in family, society, and community. Such a structure can only be possible when people put into action a coordinated system of transition services that addresses the goals and needs of the whole student and is both flexible and rational. Rational refers to the degree to which the transition services match and are appropriate to the unique needs and goals of the individual student preparing to enter the adult world in a variety of domains: academic, career and social, vocational, and social and independent living.

A rational system aligned with individual needs and goals reflects a history rooted in the philosophies and theories reviewed in this chapter (Figure 3–8). A transition service system, therefore, is individualized and flexible to provide a spectrum of

Figure 3–8   Summary of Philosophy, Theory, and Transition Practices

Transition Assumptions and Practices

Philosophy

Human potential movement	All students have an inalienable right to resources and environments that support positive growth and development.
Positive youth development	Career development and transition services are based on a positive and optimistic developmental approach that views youth as capable of building on their strengths and talents and contributing to their community. They promote thriving and optimal development.
Normalization and community integration	Normalization of service environments, social integration, and advocacy for the individual have become hallmarks of transition and the "social enabling" (self-determination) philosophy. Specialized services for youth with disabilities, who need extra support as they transition from high school, help approximate life conditions experienced by their peers.
Inclusion and full participation	The principle of inclusion and belief that children with disabilities should be served in educational settings, to the extent possible, with nondisabled peers is closely related to earlier philosophy of normalization and community integration. Full participation is a broader term more recently used in the United States that refers to educational policies which also emphasize social integration and student progress in a program in addition to access. The term least restrictive environment generally refers to the philosophy that students should, to the extent possible, be educated with their nondisabled peers and that special classes, separate schooling, or other removal of children with disabilities from the general education environment occurs only when the severity of the disabilities is such that education in regular classes with the use of supplementary aids and service cannot be achieved satisfactorily.
Self-determination and individual liberty	Self-determination is based on the philosophical belief that the student is viewed as a central participant in educational planning and postschool goal setting. Self-determination philosophy is based on core social values of personal freedom, choice, responsibility, equal access, and support. With building individual capacity to make informed choices and decisions also comes a greater responsibility and accountability for the outcomes of those decisions.

Theory

General system theory	In general systems theory, individuals are viewed as wholes that are greater than the sum of their parts. This means that understanding human growth, development, or behavior cannot be accomplished by reducing behavior into parts and analyzing these parts in isolation from each other. The individual's behaviors and experiences must be viewed as a dynamic, whole system that interacts within a unique environment. The needs of the individual student preparing for transition to adulthood must be understood in the context of their family and community environment and the context of their postsecondary goals. Transition professionals address the needs of the individual as a whole person and strive to develop service system responses that are unified and integrated. Transition professionals address the holistic needs of the student and help the service system develop responses that are integrated rather than fragmented.
Adolescent development theory	The period before adulthood is lengthening, often spanning the 20s and even extending into the 30s. Pathways into and through adulthood have become less linear and predictable (Settersten, Furstenberg, & Rumbaut, 2005). These changes have significance for postsecondary institutions, employers, and policies that are aimed at supporting adolescents and young adults as they make the transition to adulthood. The more we learn about adolescent development, brain development, and identity formation, the better we will be able to prepare students for the transition planning and decision making.
Cognitive development theory	Effective educational and career–vocational programs are designed to (a) accommodate different cognitive learning styles, and (b) incorporate instructional approaches that include a variety of classroom and community-based learning experiences. Transition service planning is designed to respond to a wide range of developmental levels within different domains in the individual students.
Self-determination theory	Self-determination theory begins with the assumption that young people have a natural tendency toward psychological growth and development and they have a desire to master ongoing challenges and develop a strong sense of self. This natural tendency toward growth, however, does not operate automatically, but requires a supportive social context to function effectively (Deci & Ryan, 1985, 2000, 2006).
Career development theories	Understanding the characteristics of the stages of adolescence helps educators design the types of education and transition services most appropriate for middle and high school age youth. Adolescence is recognized as a stage or passage in which the adolescent undergoes substantial transformations physically, psychologically, emotionally, and socially (Adams et al., 1992; Blos, 1962, 1979; Erikson, 1968). Educational programs that incorporate career development help students become oriented to, select, prepare for, and enter individually satisfying and productive careers. It is a process of systematically coordinating all school, family, and community components to facilitate each individual's potential for economic, social, and personal fulfillment. Preparation for a career role must begin in early childhood if the individual is to develop the concepts, attitudes, and skills that insure freedom of choice and expand career options (Clark & Kolstoe, 1995).

service options or pathways for students with a variety of disabilities to select and plan for individual postsecondary goals. The pathway is determined by the postsecondary goal established jointly among the student, the parents, and the IEP team. Transition planning is the coordination of the postsecondary goal with the curriculum, assessment, and related services that the student needs to achieve that goal. It is a process of backward design or backward planning that begins with the postsecondary goals. Transition becomes the unifying concept for the process of decision making throughout the secondary years.

SUMMARY

Although career education and transition has a long history, the debate about their role in the social and educational development of children and youth continues today. During the last 50 years, career development and transition systems have remained enduring concepts and instruments in federal policy for improving secondary and postsecondary outcomes for youth with disabilities. The emergence of the human potential movement—a philosophical revolution in psychology and human services for persons with disabilities—has had a broad effect on society's beliefs about the career potential of individuals with disabilities.

Transition service models are grounded in the broad theoretical frameworks of adolescent development and career development. There remains a lively dialogue on the definition of career development and career education. The theory of development, however, has provided a foundation for building a social responsibility to (a) provide supports and opportunities to disadvantaged citizens, (b) defend the basic right of all citizens to equal educational and social service opportunities, (c) establish a right to education and support services appropriate to the developmental level, and (d) define the right to resources and environments that support positive growth and development.

KEY TERMS AND PHRASES

adolescent development theory

career development theory

career–vocational education

Carl D. Perkins Act

community integration philosophy

general systems theory

human potential movement

John Dewey

normalization philosophy

philosophy of inclusion

self-determination theory

vocational choice and personality theories

QUESTIONS FOR REFLECTION, THINKING, AND SKILL BUILDING

1. Is career-vocational education new? Explain your answer.
2. What forces have influenced the emergence of career-vocational education in the United States?
3. Do you believe the human potential, normalization, and community integration philosophies reflect core principles of democracy in the United States? Explain why or why not.
4. What is the historical "tension" between academic and career education?
5. How do career development and transition fit together?
6. Identify three theories of adolescent development. What are their distinguishing assumptions?
7. Identify three theories of career development. What are their distinguishing assumptions?
8. How have fundamental beliefs and assumptions about people with disabilities changed over the past few decades? How have these beliefs and assumptions affected career development and transition practices?
9. Which of the career development theories makes most sense to you? Which best reflects your own career pathway? Discuss this in a group.
10. Develop your own career development profile. To do this, trace your own career development path in terms of (a) the information you received as a child or youth about careers, (b) your early career awareness or exposure to careers or jobs, (c) your early career experiences or jobs, (d) career skills and training that you have gained, (e) contacts with career role models (those in occupations), and (f) help you received with career decision making.

Federal Legislation, Research, and State Initiatives Advance Transition Services

Carol A. Kochhar-Bryant

You can't mandate what matters but . . . mandates are important. They put needed pressure on local reform, and they provide opportunities for legitimizing the efforts of local change agents working against the grain. Top-down mandates and bottom-up energies need each other.

—Change Forces, Michael Fullan, 1993

Chapter Questions

- How has transition policy evolved? Four generations
- How have broad education reforms affected the development of transition services?
- How has case law shaped transition practices?
- How does the Individuals with Disabilities Education Act of 2004 strengthen transition services?
- How does the No Child Left Behind Act of 2001 promote transition services?
- How do NCLB and IDEA differ in principles and policies?
- What related laws promote transition services?
  a. Americans with Disabilities Act
  b. Carl D. Perkins Career and Technical Education Improvement Act of 2006
  c. Workforce Investment Act Amendments of 2005
  d. Rehabilitation Act Amendments
  e. Higher Education Act Amendments
  f. Social Security administration initiatives to promote employment for individuals with significant disabilities
  g. Fair Labor Standards Act
  h. Assistive Technology Act of 2004
  i. Developmental Disabilities Assistance and Bill of Rights Act of 2000

INTRODUCTION

The development of current transition policy can be traced in federal legislation over the past 25 years—a period of intense focus on education and employment preparation for youth in the United States. Waves of legislation and experimental policy initiatives at national, state, and local levels have emerged to help high school youth prepare for changing work environments and make a successful transition to adult life. A primary goal of the United States is to preserve democracy and build the national economy by promoting full participation of all citizens in the work of the nation. To achieve these aims, educators and policy makers have concluded that educational institutions must make commitments to directly assist young people to make successful transitions from school to adult life and productive citizenship.

New educational reform laws have also been shaped by and grounded in research that provides scientific evidence of the benefits of career development and transition planning and processes. *Research* means the systematic investigation (i.e., the gathering and analysis of information) on a subject to contribute to our general knowledge (U.S. Department of Health and Human Services, Office for Human Research Protection, 2001). Today, the definition of transition is rooted both in federal legislation and in the broad efforts by researchers, practitioners, and professional organizations to develop and test effective field-based practices. Interpretation of laws in our federal system differs widely among the states, producing substantial variations in "transition" services within communities. The sharing of research-based practices at the state and national levels, however, is reducing these differences.

Comprehensive systems for transition from school to postsecondary life require partnerships dedicated to linking the worlds of school, home, community, and family. Programs authorized by the Individuals with Disabilities Education Act of 2004 (IDEA 2004) are now expected to be coordinated with programs under a variety of education, employment, and related disability laws. The cumulative result of these interrelated policies has been the permanent embedding of transition services into special education and general education, rehabilitation, and other human service systems (Abrahams, Boyd, & Ginsburg, 2001; Bates, Bronkema, Ames, & Hess, 1992; Kochhar-Bryant, 2008). In other words, taken together, these laws establish and reaffirm the responsibility of the broader education and human services system to provide appropriate programs of education and training for youth. Federal and state policies, however, emerge out of a complex interplay of social and political forces, resources, and available research evidence on what works. Research can be instrumental in understanding whether particular policy choices, programs, and collaborative partnerships are actually helping to solve or eliminate problems while meeting their intended goals for students and families.

This chapter reviews federal laws and national policy initiatives that give states and local educational agencies the mandate and authority to implement and improve transition service systems. Recent case law that has established new precedents for transition services is also presented.

➡ HOW HAS TRANSITION POLICY EVOLVED? FOUR GENERATIONS

Transition policies can be viewed as developing in a series of stages or generations.

First Generation

The *first generation* of transition services (1960s–1980s) was characterized by early definition of transition services, establishment of services and supports, and emerging evidence of the relationships between transition planning and successful student transition to postsecondary education and employment. Beginning in 1986, transition service initiatives struggled to take root during the Reagan administration, when federal involvement in educational policy was minimal and states had maximum discretion in how they defined and delivered transition services (Repetto, Webb, Garvan, & Washington, 2002; Repetto, White, & Snauwaert, 1990).

Second Generation

The *second generation* of transition services that began in the 1990s was characterized by federal policy initiatives aimed at further defining transition services and providing resources to build capacity in the states and local communities. In 1990, the amendments to IDEA (Pub. L. No. 101-476) defined transition services and activities and the relationship between the individualized education program (IEP) and needed transition services. IDEA 1990 mandated formal agreements with school-linked agencies to share the responsibility for long-range transition planning and described the responsibility of state and local educational agencies to monitor and sustain the provision of services. These initiatives were based on early research evidence of the relationship between transition planning and student postsecondary outcomes and evidence of underdeveloped implementation of the legal requirements for transition services in the states. Educators and advocates worked with legislators to promote more specific guidance for IDEA implementation that would help expand transition services.

Example.   In several studies of transition implementation, State Department of Education leaders reported that although there are many promising initiatives at the state level, at the LEA level, challenges to implementing transition services include the following:

1. State and local leadership capacity for the development of transition services has been slow to develop.
2. Formalized interagency linkages and agreements between local education agencies, community-based agencies, and state workforce or employment development initiatives remain underdeveloped.
3. Transition components of IEPs required by IDEA remain partially implemented throughout the states.
4. Students and families need greater encouragement to become engaged in the process.
5. Career-technical education and assessments have diminished in local education agencies during the past decade, in response to increased attention to academic performance in basic subjects.
6. General education secondary programs lack the flexibility to incorporate transition-related activities.
7. General education teachers have less knowledge of students' transition needs and available school and community resources.

Transition outcomes (postsecondary enrollment, employment, access to adult services, etc.) are not systematically tracked across states and data collection remains a challenge for states (Academy for Educational Development, 1999; Kochhar, 1999; Kohler & Hood, 2000; National Alliance for Secondary Education and Transition, 2005; National Council on Disability, 2004).

Third Generation

The *third generation* of transition services (2000s) has been characterized by more explicit definition and guidance in IDEA 2004 for developing a comprehensive and systematic transition planning process that is individualized for each student. In secondary education, for students with disabilities to have meaningful access to the general curriculum, transition planning and services must be tailored to individual needs and preferences, relevant to postsecondary goals, and use flexible curricula and environments. Such a transition program (a) recognizes different pathways to graduation for students, (b) incorporates the concept of integrated transition planning and participation in a general education course of study, and (c) employs flexible combinations of academic, career-technical education classes and community-based work experiences to achieve different pathways to graduation.

Research Advances Transition Practices.   The third generation is also characterized by efforts to validate effective transition practices—that is, what works? For example, research related to transition has demonstrated that effective high schools are characterized by strong *professional collaboration* for postsecondary planning (Deshler, Schumaker, & Bui, 2005; McLaughlin & Talbert, 2001). Relationships between students' involvement in their own individualized educational planning and transition goal-setting (*self-determination*) have been associated with an improved postsecondary outcome (Bremer, Kachgal, & Schoeller, 2003; Martin, 2002; Repetto, Webb, Neubert, & Curran, 2006). Written agreements among agencies are essential for *interagency coordination* and are a defining characteristic of model transition programs (Harley, Donnell, & Rainey, 2003; Hasazi, Furney, & DeStefano, 1999; Kohler, 2003; Research and Training Center on Service Coordination, 2001). Results from case studies showed that in *model sites* (those that demonstrated the best results for youth), one or more persons known as *transition facilitators* or coordinators were designated to implement transition services. Participation in *work-based learning* is also associated with successful outcomes for youth with disabilities.

Transition coordination can increase the likelihood that *incarcerated youth* will be reenrolled in their home school, complete high school, and become gainfully employed in their communities (Stephens & Arnette, 2000). Studies of service-coordination strategies for young offenders have shown that these services can improve *positive adjustment,* decrease negative behaviors, and reduce the likelihood of reincarceration (Bullis & Cheney, 1999; Stephens & Arnette, 2000).

Research has demonstrated that with the change in their status as they leave secondary education, students show a greater ability to advocate for themselves if they have gained an understanding of their strengths and disability in high school. When they are better prepared to make decisions and choices about their future, then they are more likely to *enroll in and complete* advanced education and to enter and sustain employment (Benz, Lindstrom, & Yovanoff, 2000; National Center on Secondary Education and Transition, 2004; U.S. Government Accountability Office, 2003; Wehmeyer, 2003). Several professional and research organizations and federal agencies have contributed to strengthening transition services through research.

Federal and Professional Organization Initiatives.   Several federal and professional organization initiatives have been instrumental in advancing transition services in the third generation:

1. National Council on Disability (NCD) report on disability policy (2004) called for clearer policy guidance on regulations affecting youth with disabilities.

2. U.S. Government Accountability Office (GAO) report (2003a, 2003b, 2004, 2005) addressed the challenges of increasing high school completion rates, transition-implementation problems, and strategies to improve postsecondary outcomes for youth.

3. In 2000, the U.S. Office of Special Education's Expert Strategy Panel on Secondary Education, Transition and Employment identified five primary issues as critical to the improvement of secondary education and transition services for students with disabilities: (a) self-determination and self-advocacy, (b) participation in a rigorous and relevant education curriculum, (c) enhancement of service coordination and collaboration, (d) improved accountability for results and postsecondary outcomes, and (e) engagement of practitioners in rigorous professional development programs.

4. In 2001, Congress approved an Office of Disability Employment Policy (ODEP) within the U.S. Department of Labor to improve access for adults with disabilities to employment services through the One-Stop system and to dramatically increase the employment rate of people with disabilities.

5. President's Commission on Excellence in Special Education (2002) recommended federal interagency collaboration to focus on improving coordination of services to reach students with disabilities early, an increase in federal enforcement of interagency agreements now required between state educational agencies (SEAs) and state vocational rehabilitation (VR) agencies, and greater attention to collaboration between schools and families.

Fourth Generation

The nation is now on the frontier of a *fourth generation* of transition-service development. This phase is characterized by redefining national priorities for youth development and transition services based on accumulating transition research, defining transition outcome performance indicators for states, developing program guidelines and standards, and sharing knowledge about what is working in the states. Fourth-generation transition leaders will advance the mandate for a shared responsibility for transition outcomes by raising expectations for institutions of higher education, employers, and community service agencies to assist in transition of youth.

HOW HAVE BROAD EDUCATION REFORMS AFFECTED THE DEVELOPMENT OF TRANSITION SERVICES?

In the 1980s and 1990s, Congress and the federal government recognized the urgent need to respond to persistent poor outcomes for youth with disabilities as they transition from schooling to employment, postsecondary education, and adult independence. Federal efforts were expanded to identify promising practices and increase states' capacity to develop transition service systems. Although these federal initiatives have stimulated significant efforts in the states, they have produced modest improvements in secondary and postsecondary outcomes for youth with disabilities (Benz, Lindstrom, & Yovanoff, 2000; National Council on Disability, 2004; National Longitudinal Transition Study-2, 2005; Wagner, Newman, Cameto, & Levine, 2006). Adding to the challenge to expand transition services is the call to align transition services systems with general education reforms. The emerging standards-based policy framework with standardized testing is significantly altering secondary education and transition services for youth with disabilities.

States Implement High-Stakes Exit Examinations

By the 2003–2004 academic year, 26 states had implemented—or have plans to implement by 2008—mandatory high-stakes exit examinations that assess competency in mathematics and language arts. In addition, 5 of the 24 states that do not have state-mandated exit examinations give school districts the option of requiring that a student pass a test to graduate from high school (Center on Education Policy, 2005; Clark, 2002; Milou & Bohlin, 2003). Tests are considered *high-stakes* when results of the testing have important consequences for students, personnel, or schools (Manzo, 1997; Walker, 2000). For example, student graduation and promotion, staff incentives, and allocation of school resources are often based on testing results.

Many states use tests to make other types of high-stakes decisions, such as whether a student is eligible for scholarships, advanced placement, and honors classes. By 2012, three quarters of all American public school students (72%) will be required to take the examinations, including English language learners (87%) (Center on Education Policy, 2005). Despite state efforts to boost pass rates, they have not changed much in the past few years. Achievement gaps between white, black, and Latino students and students with disabilities remain very large, averaging 20–30 percentage points in most states. In two states, less that 60% of students with disabilities passed after multiple attempts (Center on Education Policy, 2005). The recent emphasis on standards-based education (SBE) and uniform testing as a federal policy is rooted in widespread concern about the effectiveness of public education today and the belief that all students can master more rigorous curriculum content.

SBE has introduced a set of policies and practices that are based on uniform state learning standards within a curriculum that is focused on those standards (standards-based curriculum). The students' mastery of the curriculum content is measured by standardized tests or assessments. The implications of uniform learning standards and more rigorous accountability requirements for the achievement of students with disabilities are being carefully examined in the states. The 2004 Amendments to the IDEA emphasized the importance of an equitable accountability system and required states to include students with disabilities in general state- and district-wide assessments. States are now required to revise their state improvement plans to establish goals for the performance of children with disabilities. They must assess their progress toward achieving those goals by establishing indicators and measurements such as assessments, dropout rates, and graduation records. States must also develop guidelines for alternate assessment of children with disabilities.

Standards-based reforms have introduced a set of policies that are based on uniform student learning standards rather than individual learning needs, outcomes rather than process (McDonneld, McLaughlin, & Morison, 1997). The challenge for educators are the inherent tensions created as they attempt to align SBE policies with those under IDEA, which are based on individual rights and an individualized educational process. Policies based on individual rights and procedural requirements have been the primary tools for effecting sweeping changes in secondary education, transition, and postsecondary outcomes for students with disabilities.

Implementation of transition programs within an SBE framework also presents a conceptual and practical challenge for educators, many of whom see the principles and goals as mutually exclusive. Yet, IDEA 1997 and 2004 *emphasized both transition services and*

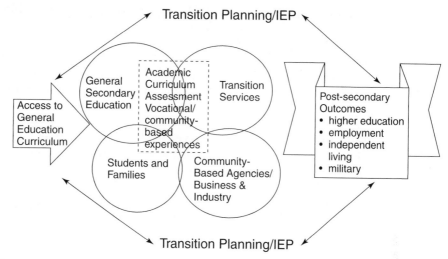

Figure 4–1   Transition Planning and Access to General Education

access to the general education curriculum and therefore placed expectations on state and local educational agencies to seek practical solutions for aligning the systems (Kochhar-Bryant, 2007; Kochhar-Bryant & Bassett, 2002). Many experts agree that it is possible to design education based on both common standards and the right of students with disabilities to an individualized and appropriate education. Indeed, it is imperative. IDEA 1997 and 2004 have given shape to that practical bridge between special education and general education with provisions that strengthen academic expectations and accountability for the nation's 5.8 million children with disabilities (U.S. Department of Education, Office of Special Education, 2002). Figure 4–1 depicts the transition planning process as it supports access to the general education curriculum.

Emerging Emphasis on Results, Standards, and Outcomes in Education and Transition

The effects of standards-based reforms and high-stakes testing on students with disabilities are only beginning to be examined systematically for youth with disabilities. This is particularly important because although federal and state educational reforms and a stronger economy have led to increasing employment rates and postsecondary enrollments of youth in general, only modest outcomes have been achieved by young adults with disabilities as they make the transition to postsecondary settings and adult life (Center on Education Policy, 2005; Gladieux & Swail, 2002; Wagner, Newman, Cameto, & Levine, 2006; Ward & Berry, 2005).

Educational reforms in the 1990s and 2000s to improve educational outcomes for all children and youth were leveraged chiefly through enhanced accountability for student outcomes, school improvement, and personnel performance (McDonnel, McLaughlin, & Morison, 1997). Two fundamental changes have taken place as a result of this demand for educational reform: (a) attention has *shifted to educational outcomes rather than inputs* and (b) political systems have become far *more active in evaluating the performance of students and schools*. These changes have influenced schools to focus more heavily on student outcomes such as attendance, dropout rates, and successful instructional programs measured against specific standards and accountability requirements.

Educators, policy makers, and the public have been concerned about the effectiveness of public education programs and, consequently, 50 states have implemented accountability measures (National High School Center, 2007a). A similar public emphasis on results, standards, and outcomes in the provision of transition services offers some interesting parallels.

Federal Education Performance Goals and Transition Indicators. Concerned over waste and inefficiency in federal programs and insufficient attention to program performance and results, Congress passed the Government Performance and Results Act (GPRA) in 1993. The purpose of the act was to improve program performance by setting program goals and measuring program performance against them, reporting publicly on their progress, and holding federal agencies accountable for achieving program results. Federal managers are required to submit strategic plans that include general goals and objectives, including outcome-related goals and objectives, for the major functions and operations of the agency (Bassett & Kochhar-Bryant, 2006).

In the U.S. Department of Education's strategic plan for 2002–2007 (2002), Goal 1 was aimed at helping all students reach challenging academic standards so that they are prepared for responsible citizenship, further learning, and productive employment. In conjunction with the 2004 reauthorization of IDEA in December 2005, the U.S. Office of Special Education Programs, which administers special education funds, required states to develop 6-year State Performance Plans around *20 indicators*. States were required to submit data in Annual Performance Reports, beginning February 2007. The *13th Indicator* relates to transition services for students: "The percentage of youth aged 16 and above with an IEP that includes coordinated, measurable, annual IEP goals and transition services that will reasonably enable the student to meet the postsecondary goals" [20 U.S.C. 1416(a)(3)(B)].

Indicator 14 refers to the percentage of youth who had IEPs, are no longer in secondary school, and who have been competitively employed, enrolled in some type of postsecondary school, or both within 1 year of leaving high school. Once the state has finalized the methods for collecting performance data on these two indicators, improvement plans can be developed, if needed, to improve outcomes for all students with disabilities. Indicator 13 results will need to show 100% compliance by 2010. IEP teams must, therefore, be trained in the necessary components of an effective transition IEP. In addition, Indicator 14 will provide information about the effectiveness of postschool planning for students that will serve as a basis for training and improvement strategies to be implemented over the same time period. The process of transition to adulthood is a shared responsibility among students, parents, educators, and others that does not end until an initial postsecondary placement goal has been achieved.

➡ HOW HAS CASE LAW SHAPED TRANSITION PRACTICES?

The federal, state, and district courts interpret our laws and issue administrative judgments when disputes (lawsuits) arise over the application of laws written in Congress and in State Legislatures. Transition services have become a significant area of litigation (lawsuits) by parents who have been dissatisfied with services provided to their children. To examine the nature of this litigation, in 2006, Etcheidt reviewed 36 state level administrative and district court rulings related to school-to-postsecondary transition plans published between 1997 and 2004. The types of disabilities involved varied and included male and female students, those with learning disabilities, emotional disabilities, autism or Asperger's syndrome, and multiple disabilities. She identified five transition themes most salient in the decisions reviewed: agency contact, student involvement, individualization of the transition plan, district obligations, and the appropriateness of the transition plan. A part of all the decisions reviewed, however, addressed the importance of *individualizing transition planning* on the basis of student strengths, needs, preferences, and interests. This author also reviewed additional recent cases.

Theme 1: Agency Contacts

The IDEA 1997 and 2004 and the Vocational Rehabilitation Act required formal agreements for sharing the responsibility between schools and community agencies for providing and paying for transition services to students with disabilities. Failure to involve these agencies creates a barrier to successful postsecondary outcomes for special education students. Districts prevailed (i.e., won their cases) when they could demonstrate that they made good-faith efforts to obtain information about agency services, to include those agencies in transition planning, and to develop action steps to link parents and students with agency resources.

Theme 2: Student Involvement

The 1997 IDEA required that all students 14 and older must be invited to attend IEP meetings to participate in planning their transition services. Even when a student does not attend, their preferences, interests, and concerns must be considered by the IEP team. Districts are not required to address each student's preferences; the team may determine a course of study that is aligned with interests and a set of services that are designed to assist the student to achieve transition goals. The requirement to include the students is essential for districts.

Theme 3: Individualization of the Transition Plan

Of central importance for districts is the individualization of transition plans on the basis of assessed student strengths, preferences, and interests. Districts cannot substitute sound, coherent programs of study with activities that do not adequately individualize services (e.g., providing generic information, brochures, or catalogs to students and families). When districts demonstrate that they have provided appropriate course work, work-related activities, and have helped students develop realistic postsecondary goals, then errors that are procedural have been excused. In two cases, the IEPs that were being disputed did not contain a formal statement of transition service needs, but because students and parents were involved in developing the IEP and the program of study, activities, and IEP goals were individualized, the districts prevailed (case was ruled in their favor). When transition services have not been provided, courts can require districts to create a variety of solutions that include community-based programming in "real world" settings and functional skill development that can take place after a student has participated in graduation ceremonies with his peers.

Theme 4: District Obligations

Interpreting earlier precedents set in relation to a "free, appropriate public education," districts are not required to guarantee or ensure that the student actually achieves his or her employment or independent living goal, but they must do more than simply provide information, opportunity, and the skills to apply to postsecondary programs. They must provide a *coherent program of study and services* that are calculated to *provide benefit* to the student. Districts have prevailed in hearings when they have demonstrated that they have provided opportunities to participate in a variety of school and community experiences and that the individual programs are designed to meet students' social and career goals and graduation requirements. In one important case, the fact that the student met graduation requirements *did not mean that the district was relieved of its obligation to provide transition services* that the student needs to complete their IEP goals (Etcheidt, 2006).

Theme 5: Appropriateness of the Transition Plan

Many of the cases pertained to the issue of how the transition plan appropriately addressed the needs of the student. In several cases, the districts failed to provide adequately designed communication aids, reading instruction, or proper evaluations while students were in secondary school. As a result, the districts were mandated to provide and fund additional or compensatory services to students who had graduated or were in the process of enrolling in a postsecondary program. When districts demonstrated that they offered a free, appropriate public education and ensured the successful participation in and completion of IEP goals, then parents' requests for compensatory or additional services were not granted.

Recent Case Law on Transition Signals a Shift in Interpretation of IDEA

In summary, Etcheidt's research as well as more recent case laws related to transition since 2004 have important lessons for the development of transition services. Most importantly, IDEA requires public schools to provide a free, appropriate public education (FAPE) to students with disabilities. The interpretation and application of FAPE remains a challenge for schools and the courts. Box 4-1 presents the complex case of a secondary level student who did not receive adequate educational, transition, or support services to benefit from her IEP. The case reinterprets the historic **Rowley case** of 1982 (*Hendrick Hudson Central School District Board of Education v. Rowley,* 458 U.S. 176, 200, 1982), which required that educational services provide students with some educational benefit. The following summary is based on an analysis by Wright & Wright (2007).

In the Mercer case, the court determined that the administrative law judge (ALJ) misapplied the IDEA statute and failed to uphold its requirements (***J.L. v. Mercer Island School District***, No. C06-494P, 2006). IDEA requires that the IEP confer a

Box 4–1

J.L., M.L., and Daughter K.L. v. Mercer Island School District, 2006

J.L., M.L., and Daughter K.L. v. Mercer Island School District, 2006, involves the case of K.L., a 17 year old of average intelligence with severe learning disabilities that affect her ability to read and write. Before the commencement of 10th grade, the parents unilaterally removed her from public school and enrolled her in a private residential educational facility in Massachusetts where she remains at present. At issue in this action are the Individualized Education Plans (IEPs) developed for K.L.'s 8th-, 9th-, and 10th-grade education, in which the parents claim they were denied adequate participation. The parents further claim that the IEPs failed to meet the requirements of the IDEA, resulting in a failure to provide K.L. with a free appropriate public education (FAPE).

K.L.'s eighth-grade IEP called for special instruction in reading, writing, and math, and accommodations included a peer note-taker, peer or adult reader, oral examinations, extended time for testing and assignments, reduced assignments, and the use of a calculator. At the end of her eighth-grade year, K.L. scored in the second percentile on the Iowa Test of Basic Skills and failed the Washington Assessment of Student Learning (WASL); her Wechsler Individual Achievement Test (WIAT) results showed her to have fallen further behind her classmates than when she was tested 3 years earlier. The reevaluation report was prepared to reflect these findings but was not shared with the parents. The school district's report on K.L.'s progress in eighth grade reflected that she had met zero of three IEP objectives in writing and two of four in reading.

By ninth grade (2003–2004), K.L.'s IEP was essentially unchanged from her eighth-grade plan, with the same specialized instruction and accommodations (plus an additional hour of "reading assistance" per day). Standardized reading tests (Gates-MacGinitie) administered in January and June of 2004 resulted in scores in the first percentile for her age, results which were not shared with her parents. K.L. met zero of three of her IEP writing objectives for this grade and one of three reading objectives. The parents reported a steep decline in their daughter's self-esteem and confidence with a corresponding reluctance to participate in her education during this time.

K.L.'s 10th-grade IEP called for specialized instruction in reading, writing, math, and study skills (but did not specify the methodologies to be used or time to be devoted to each). At the IEP meeting, the school failed to staff the meeting with the general education teacher called for by the regulations. In relation to transition goals, the IEP contemplated that K.L. would attend "community college or college" and engage in "competitive employment" and noted that the school district's program "is aimed at [K.L.] attending a community or technical college," while parents were investigating colleges for her.

In June 2004, the school district paid for an independent educational evaluation by a neuropsychologist who concluded that K.L. had a language-based learning disorder that required intensive reading intervention and had a mood disorder and, therefore, could benefit from placement at a private residential facility. She was placed into the facility. In September 2004, the school district produced an IEP for 2004–2005 and adopted some of the neuropsychologist's recommendations about reading instruction. They did not accept the recommendation related to residential placement. In November 2004, K.L. returned home on a break from Landmark and was evaluated by two school district experts who concluded that K.L. did not have a language-based learning disorder and did not require the type of reading program offered by the residential school. Furthermore, the evaluation

(continued)

by a psychiatrist, Dr. Golden, resulted in a finding of no mood disorder. In March 2005, the parents provided a statement of what they believed should be in the IEP. The IEP reflected some of the neuropsychologist's recommendations as well as all of the recommendations of the school district's experts. The IEP included an increased list of accommodations that conformed with the assessment of the districts' experts that K.L. did not have a phonologic disorder that required the special attention; it did not allocate time for specific activities nor did it indicate which specific methodologies would be used to accomplish its goals.

During the due process or administrative hearing, the parents sought compensation from the district for the out-of-state placement on the grounds that the previous educational programs were inadequate. The district refused and the parents sought an administrative review of that determination. After 12 days, the administrative law judge (ALJ) ruled in favor of the district, finding that (a) the June 2003 and 2005 evaluations were appropriate, (b) the special education programs provided were appropriate and provided K.L. with FAPE, and (c) the parents were not entitled to reimbursement for the residential placement or for compensation for K.L.'s earlier education. The parents, however, appealed the ruling of the ALJ and requested a judicial review on the basis that the district provided inadequate and inappropriate special education programs for eighth and ninth grade and proposed an inadequate program for 10th grade that caused K.L. to lose educational opportunities. They argued that they were entitled to reimbursement for all costs associated with the residential placement and legal fees. As a result of the appeal, the parents were awarded attorneys fees and costs, and the ALJ was required to review the case again and reconsider the previous findings and conclusions. The court determined that the findings of the ALJ were thorough but represented a misunderstanding of the intent of IDEA.

From Harbor House Law Press, Inc., Hartfield, VA, by permission.

---

meaningful educational benefit toward the goals of self-sufficiency (*Deal v. Hamilton County Board of Education.,* 392 F.3d 840, 862, 864 [6th Cir. 2004]). This means that the benefits or results must be significant and measurable. In other words, when a child is in a mainstream class, the attainment of passing grades and regular advancement from grade to grade are generally accepted indicators of satisfactory progress (Capistrano, 59 F.3d at 896.[5] [CL 49, AR 365]). A school district is not required by IDEA to maximize a student's potential, but the standard is whether the program provided by the District is *reasonably calculated to provide educational benefit*. In the Mercer case, the ALJ did not apply the correct standard for determining whether K.L. received a meaningful educational benefit. The parents were correct that the failure of the IEPs to focus on progressing K.L. toward *self-sufficiency* (i.e., independent living) and her desired goal of postsecondary education represented a failure to confer the benefit embodied in IDEA (Wright & Wright, 2007).

Laws related to the education of individuals with disabilities underwent a major change about a decade ago. Before 1997, the framework for fundamental provisions under IDEA was based on the Education for Handicapped Children Act of 1975 (EHA). The sole purpose of EHA was to provide *access* to education for students with disabilities who had been marginalized in the public school system. Satisfied that the goal of "access" had been reached, in 1997, Congress enacted the IDEA with the express purpose of addressing implementation problems resulting from "low expectations, and an insufficient focus on applying replicable research on proven methods of teaching and learning for children with disabilities" [20 U.S.C. §1400(c)(4)]. The statute clearly stated its commitment to "our national policy of ensuring equality of opportunity, full participation, independent living, and economic self-sufficiency for individuals with disabilities" [20 U.S.C. §1400(c)(1)].

This represented a significant shift in focus from the disability education system in place prior to 1997 (Wright & Wright, 2007). In defining the applicable standard, the District and the ALJ place much reliance on the Supreme Court case of *Hendrick Hudson District Board of Education v. Rowley,* 458 U.S. 176 (1982), a case which interprets the 1975 EHA. To the extent that the Supreme Court at that time was interpreting a statute which had no requirement (a) that programming for disabled students be designed to transition them to postsecondary education, independent living, or economic self-sufficiency or (b) that schools review IEPs to determine whether annual goals were being attained, the Court had to consider that opinion, superseded by later legislation, and the District's and ALJ's reliance on it, to be misplaced.

The IDEA is not simply about "access," but rather it is focused on "transition services, . . . an *outcome-oriented* process, which promotes movement from school to postschool activities . . . taking into account the student's preferences and interests" (20 U.S.C. §1401(30); 34 CFR §300.29). This is such a significant departure from the previous legislative scheme that any citation to pre-1997 case law on special education is suspect. The federal regulations interpreting IDEA speak to an increased focus on self-sufficiency. One of the key purposes of the IDEA Amendments of 1997 was to promote improved education results for children through educational experiences that prepare them for postsecondary challenges and employment(H.Rep. No. 105–195, p. 82, 1997; S.Rep. No. 105–117, p. 4, 1997). Therefore, throughout preschool, elementary, and secondary education, IEPs for children with disabilities must focus on providing instruction and experiences that *enable the child to prepare himself or herself for later educational experiences and for postschool activities, including formal education—if appropriate—employment, and independent living.* IDEA 2004 reinforces this expectation, as does the No Child Left Behind Act (Wright & Wright, 2007).

The ALJ and the District in the Mercer case set the bar too low. The District relied heavily on "accommodations" for K.L. which allowed her to progress through material, but it is at odds with the IDEA goals of self-sufficiency and independent living. Using accommodation and other compensatory strategies without increasing a student's skill level does not represent compliance with IDEA.

The IDEA calls for disability education programs that guide the student toward posteducation independence and self-sufficiency. In pursuit of that goal, students such as K.L. must receive educational opportunities that significantly advance them toward that end. The IEPs developed in accordance with this statutory scheme must specifically define the methodologies to be used to achieve these goals and the time to be allotted to each of the services employed to that end and furthermore must be geared toward the achievement of these goals. The IEPs for K.L.'s 8th, 9th, and 10th grade years were deficient in their failure to adhere to the IDEA requirement for specialized education aimed at achieving independence and self-sufficiency for the student and to provide *meaningful (i.e., significant) educational benefits.*

Lessons Learned for The Development of Transition. These cases have important lessons for the development of transition services. First, adult service agencies must be involved if their services are needed to support students' transition goals and plans, and such agency services must be written into the IEP. Second, IDEA modified the definition of transition from an "outcome-oriented process" (1997)—which promotes movement from school to postschool activities to a "results-oriented process" (2004)—that is focused on improving the academic and functional achievement of the child to facilitate the child's movement from school to postschool activities. Therefore, transition planning means more than helping a student earn the required academic credits for graduation—both academic and functional skills goals and supports must be addressed. It is a blueprint for direction setting and for constructing a plan that is aimed at high school exit goals most appropriate for the individual.

Third, school districts are not expected to ensure that students achieve specific outcomes, but they are responsible for developing individualized comprehensive, coordinated transition programs that are aligned with the student's strengths, preferences, and interests. Transition planning is expected to be a thoughtful, unified set of goals and plans that will lead to an individualized course of action for each student. The transition plan, as part of the IEP is a document intended to reflect the IEP team's post-secondary plan and vision for the student (Cameto, Marder, Wagner, & Cardoso, 2003). Box 4–2 provides an example of a state guidance framework for standards-driven IEPs (Virginia Department of Education, 2005).

Box 4–2

VA Individualized Education Program: Standards-Driven IEPs

Standards-driven IEPs are related to the general curriculum and should be based upon the long-range educational outcomes of the student.

All IEPs in Virginia must contain a present level of performance, goal statements, list of accommodations and/or modifications, and service statements. Short-term objectives or benchmarks are required for goals of students working toward alternate achievement standards (i.e., VAAP). It is permissible to include objectives or benchmarks for other students' IEP goals.

In addition, standards-driven IEPs contain

- Curriculum-based assessment information;
- Statements of educational performance related to classroom instruction and state and district assessments;
- Goal statements linked to content standards, their key components, or a skill required to access the content;
- Measurements of progress that include descriptions of classroom performance and classroom/district assessments;
- Accommodations and modifications that allow meaningful participation in content instruction; and
- Progress measures that are assessed and measured in relation to the general education curriculum.

Academic Achievement

In Virginia the local academic curriculum is based on the state's Standards of Learning (SOL) in

- English (Reading, Writing);
- Mathematics;
- Science; and
- History/Social Sciences.

These have state assessments. Other curriculum areas include physical education/health, fine arts, foreign languages, career-technical education, and elective courses.

Functional Performance

Any deficiencies in age-appropriate functional skills should be addressed in the student's IEP. Functional skills and behaviors across different environments include

- Social interaction, including communication;
- Self-care skills, including safety;
- Self-determination; and
- Mobility, etc.

Annual Goals

The academic and functional goals are based on the information in the Present Level of Performance. Goal statements should be linked to content standards, their key components, or a skill required to access the content (for example literacy, numeracy, learning strategies, social skills, and other functional skills). Goals should be stated so student progress is measurable.

Annual goals are prioritized based on individualized needs and identified outcomes. IEP teams may discuss

- Where is the student functioning now?
- Where is the student headed?
- What is needed this year for the student to progress to where he/she is headed?

Refer to *IDEA 2004 Guidance Document Section VI,* May 2005.

Finally, if school districts fail to provide individualized and comprehensive transition planning, then plaintiffs (individuals filing the lawsuit) could be awarded extended or compensatory services and supports may be awarded as a result of substantive failure to provide transition programs. Districts, however, are more likely to be upheld if they can demonstrate that they have made good faith efforts to develop goals and supports that benefit students and put them on an appropriate pathway to successful transition.

The systematic, cumulative, and long-range nature of the transition planning and decision-making process is not made explicit in IDEA statutory language, and consequently state implementation is hampered. The continuing high dropout rates, low graduation rates, and continuing poor postsecondary outcomes for youth with disabilities, however, point to the crucial importance of initiating transition planning within the IEP process as early as possible in the student's secondary years. The change in IDEA 2004 from age 14 to 16 for initiating transition planning may be challenged in the future on the basis of equity and intent of the IDEA statute. IDEA requires that beginning no later than the first IEP in effect, when the student is 16 and updated annually, must include a statement of "appropriate measurable postsecondary goals based on age appropriate transition assessments related to training, education, employment, and independent living skills" (IDEA, 2004, §614). Furthermore, the coordinated set of activities must be (a) based on the individual student's strengths, preferences, and interests and (b) include needed activities in the areas of instruction, community experiences, the development of employment and other postschool adult living objectives, and if appropriate, daily living skills and functional vocational evaluation. These requirements suggest a systematic, long-range process.

Although some students need time limited transition supports, some need ongoing services, the transition planning process for students with disabilities should begin early as they enter secondary education. For students *without disabilities,* such long-range vision and secondary planning to achieve postsecondary goals is the typical model that begins as the student exits from middle school and makes choices for a high school course of study. Because planning for transition assessments and a comprehensive, coordinated postsecondary transition plan and course of study is at least a 4-year process that should begin as the student moves from middle to high school.

In a final note, it is important to understand that in all areas of the law, given the same facts and the same statutes such as IDEA, judges may offer different decisions (Wright & Wright, 2007). One decision might apply to one geographical area but not another, and state regulations may differ greatly in procedures for applying federal statutes.

➡️ HOW DOES THE INDIVIDUALS WITH DISABILITIES EDUCATION ACT OF 2004 STRENGTHEN TRANSITION SERVICES?

The following sections summarize the laws that provide the authority for transition services in the states and promote cooperation among schools, community agencies, and postsecondary institutions. Appendix 4-1 contains a comparison of IDEA 1997 and 2004 provisions related to transition.

Transition Provisions in IDEA 2004

Definition of Transition Services.   On December 3, 2004, IDEA 2004 (Pub. L. No. 108-446) was signed into law and made several important changes in transition related provisions. It was effective on July 1, 2005. The term *transition services* means a "coordinated set of activities" for students that

1. is designed within a results-oriented process, which promotes movement from school to postschool activities, including postsecondary education, career-technical training, integrated employment (including supported employment), continuing and adult education, adult services, independent living, or community participation;

2. is based upon the individual student's strengths, taking into account the student's preferences and interests; and

3. includes instruction, related services, community experiences, the development of employment and other postschool adult living objectives, and when appropriate, acquisition of daily living skills and functional-vocational evaluation (IDEA, 2004, §602).

The IEP, beginning no later than the first IEP in effect when the student is 16 and updated annually, must include a statement of "appropriate measurable postsecondary goals based on age appropriate transition assessments related to training, education, employment and independent living skills" (IDEA, 2004, §614). Students' success will depend on their active participation in setting postsecondary goals and planning a coordinated set of services to achieve those goals.

Understanding a "Coordinated Set of Activities" Under IDEA.   Since the IDEA leaves the phrase "coordinated set of activities" open to interpretation, the states are challenged in their efforts to implement a "systematic, cumulative, and long-range transition planing and decision-making process."

> coordinated set of activities aimed at a specific student outcome (e.g., employment, referral to rehabilitation services, enrollment in college); activities which promote the movement of a student from school to postschool activities which may include postsecondary education, vocational training, integrated employment (including supported employment), continuing and adult education, adult services, independent living, or community participation. [§602 (34) (A)]

The coordinated set of activities (above) must be (a) based on the individual student's strengths, preferences, and interests and (b) include needed activities in the areas of instruction, community experiences, the development of employment and other postschool adult living objectives, and, if appropriate, daily living skills and functional vocational evaluation.

The word *coordinated* is the only reference—and an oblique one—to a systematic approach to transition. The term was first defined in the 1990 IDEA (Pub. L. No. 101-476) regulations to mean both "(1) the linkage between each of the component activities that comprise transition services, and (2) the interrelationship between the various agencies that are involved in the provision of transition services to a student" (U.S. Department of Education, 1992, p. 48694) (see Figure 4-2). Thus, the various transition activities must complement and be coordinated with each other. The agencies responsible for providing the services must do the same, making sure that the services they provide to the student meet, in a coordinated, nonduplicating fashion, his or her transition needs. Because the transition process relies on the involvement of many professionals and many service providers, this coordination of effort is essential. Transition—viewed as a systematic, individualized process that incorporates a coordinated set of activities—

1. is a long-range planning and decision-making framework for students and families that addresses a variety of domains of education and life preparation;

2. is a continuous process through transition from middle school and through high school;

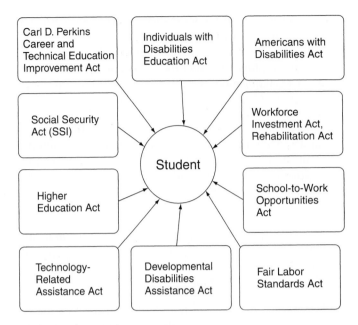

Figure 4–2   Major Laws Promoting Transition

3. incorporates a coordination strategy that provides continuity of planning and links each student with a transition coordinator, counselor, or mentor;
4. considers students' anticipated postsecondary goal;
5. addresses curriculum options, including participation in the general education curriculum, career–technical, **community-based learning**, nonacademic learning activities, and standardized assessments;
6. incorporates related and supportive services (opportunities for learning) identified by students, parents, and professionals; and
7. incorporates the coordination of appropriate community-based and adult service agencies, vocational rehabilitation, health and mental health agencies, postsecondary institutions, and employment development services.

Transition planning is foundational for the IEP planning process. Long-term transition planning provides an over-arching framework that guides the development of the IEP and provides continuity in the process about the immediate and long-term future of the student (Kochhar-Bryant & Bassett, 2002). It is a blueprint for direction setting and for constructing a plan that is aimed at high school exit goals most appropriate for the individual. The transition plan is vital to accessing and progressing in the secondary education curriculum because it defines specific needs and services in regard to the secondary curriculum and associated assessments, related services, and supports. Although IDEA 2004 initiates transition once again at age 16, many states are choosing to continue their practices (begun under IDEA 1997) to initiate planning when the student turns 14 (Grack, 2005).

Shift in Emphasis to "Results" in IDEA 2004.   IDEA 2004 placed greater emphasis on accountability of the educational system for improving transition outcomes for youth. The statute modified the definition of transition from an "*outcome-oriented* process, which promotes movement from school to post-school activities" to a "*results-oriented* process, that is focused on improving the academic and functional achievement of the child to facilitate the child's movement from school to post-school activities . . ." *This subtle shift from "outcomes" to "results" signaled to educational institutions that they were to be held accountable, not just for defining outcomes and measuring them but also for producing results for students.* IDEA 2004 requires that the student's IEP include "appropriate measurable postsecondary goals based upon age-appropriate transition assessments related to training, education, employment, and, where appropriate, independent living skills . . . and the transition services (including courses of study) needed to assist the child in reaching these goals" (IDEA, 2004, §614).

Initiation of Transition Services Is Moved from Age 14 to 16.   Public Law 94-142, **Education for All Handicapped Children Act** of 1975 provided free appropriate public education to all children with disabilities and in the 1980s, established and expanded transition programming to help youths prepare to move from school to postsecondary education, employment, and independent living. Under the 1990 amendments to IDEA, transition services were required to be provided to youth no later than age 16 or earlier where appropriate. It is important to note the statements in the Report of the House Committee on Education and Labor with respect to the provision of transition services to students younger than 16:

> Although this language leaves the final determination of when to initiate transition services for students under age 16 to the IEP process, it nevertheless makes it clear that *Congress expects much consideration to be given to the need for transition services*—for students by age 14 or younger. The Committee encourages that approach because of their *concern that age 16 may be too late for many students, particularly those at risk of dropping out of school and those with the most severe disabilities.* Even for those students who stay in school until age 18, many will need more than two years of transitional services. Students with disabilities are now dropping out of school before age 16, feeling that the education system has little to offer them. Initiating services at a younger age will be critical. (House Report No. 101-544, 10, 1990)

IDEA 1997 moved the date of initiation of transition services to age 14 (or younger, if determined appropriate by the IEP team), to be updated annually. Congressional records justified the reasons for the decision by Congress in 1997: waiting until age 16 was simply too late for many students to plan an academic or career-technical course of study and to provide the needed transition services consistent with the student's postsecondary goals.

> The purpose of this requirement is to focus attention on how the child's educational program can be planned to help the child make a successful transition to his or her goals for life after secondary school. This provision is designed to augment, and not replace, the separate transition services requirement, under which children with disabilities beginning no later than age sixteen receive transition services, including instruction, community experiences, the development of employment and other post-school objectives, and, when appropriate, independent living skills and functional vocational evaluation. (H.R. 105-195, 1997, p. 102)

The IDEA 2004, however, again shifts the age at which transition services are initiated *from 14 back to age 16*. The federal regulations, however, leave the door open for flexibility:

> Beginning not later than the first IEP to be in effect when the child turns 16, *or younger if determined appropriate by the IEP team,* and updated annually thereafter, the IEP must include
>
> 1. appropriate measurable postsecondary goals based upon age-appropriate transition assessments related to training, education, employment and, where appropriate, independent living skills and
> 2. the transition services (including courses of study) needed to assist the child in reaching those goals [34 CFR 300.320(b)] [20 U.S.C. 1414(d)(1)(B)].

Whether the student chooses employment or postsecondary education, they will have to direct their own lives and navigate among a spectrum of community-based service providers and federal, state, and local programs. For many youth this is an overwhelming challenge for which they must be prepared for long in advance. The process, therefore, must begin earlier than the final year of high school (before 16) to provide enough time to

1. prepare the student to be actively engaged in decision making and the IEP process during high school;
2. develop a course of study and related transition services that are aligned with the postsecondary goal;
3. conduct assessments needed to determine appropriate postsecondary goals, transition services, and supports;
4. prepare the student for self-determination and self-advocacy in the postsecondary setting; and
5. prepare the youth for adult life in a variety of domains including academic, social, career-vocational, and independent living.

Recognizing the central importance of advanced planning for successful transition, many local educational agencies are continuing the practice of beginning comprehensive transition planning at age 14, as was promoted under IDEA 1997 (Grack, 2005). Many are also integrating transition planning into the standards-based framework for students who are in general education classes.

Research had shown that when the student is actively involved in the IEP team and in planning his or her educational program, then he or she is more likely to view school as relevant and remain invested in staying in school (Bremer, Kachgal, & Schoeller, 2003; O'Leary & Collision, 2002; O'Leary, Lehman, & Doty, 2001). The age 14 provision was also designed to assist youth in their transition from middle to high school, a crucial year of development and adjustment for all youth. As a result, postsecondary outcomes began to improve for some students in school districts that provided early planning (New York State Department of Education, 2005; Pennsylvania State Department of Education; Repetto et al., 2006; Weidenthal & Kochhar-Bryant, 2007).

Recognizing the central importance of advanced planning for successful transition, many local educational agencies are continuing the practice of beginning comprehensive transition planning at age 14, as was promoted under IDEA 1997. Many are also integrating transition planning into the standards-based framework for students who are in general education classes. Box 4–3 reflects a school administrator's perspective on early transition planning.

BOX 4–3

An Administrator Comments on the Value of Early Transition Planning

Special Education Directors serve as change agents directly responsible for generating the bottom-up energies that foster the creative thinking and committed action necessary to effect positive change in the area of transition services for youth with disabilities. We rely on top-down mandates to complement these energies. Therefore, we must carefully consider the potential impact that the elimination of the age 14 requirements may have on the transition services we provide for our youth with disabilities, their families, and our communities.

Students usually turn age 16 sometime within their sophomore year of high school. In most school systems eighth grade students choose either an academic or a vocational course of study that begins in ninth grade. Regardless of the age 16 requirement, schools should continue to use the existing time frame for selecting a course of study. Given this time frame it is "best practice" to conduct a functional-vocational assessment during the eighth grade so students, their families, and teachers can use the assessment results to discuss the student's interests, aptitudes, and abilities when choosing a course of study and planning for the student's future. It is also best practice to begin offering direct instruction in self-determination and self-advocacy at this time as well. Research consistently reflects the benefits of such assessment and instruction and reinforces that the earlier it starts the better.

Typically, states, school districts, local school boards, and communities allocate their respective resources *for mandated services first.* . . . when budgets are being formed and presented to superintendents and school boards, they ask—Is this program really necessary? Is it mandated by state or federal guidelines? Do we have to do this? . . . Despite the demonstrated benefits to our youth with disabilities, their families, and our communities, these programs fall victim to red ink. Two recent transition training efforts conducted for secondary special education teachers on how to design, develop, and implement effective IEPs for secondary youth with disabilities were affected. . . . One of our school districts was not sending middle school teachers, claiming that it was no longer mandated and, therefore, they decided not to allocate their resources for this effort. In the second example, we are working closely with five of our member school districts to conduct functional vocational assessments of every eighth-grade student with a disability in an effort to plan a "high school experience with a purpose." Once again, the same district chose not to participate even though all costs associated with the training and subsequent assessments were covered by the regional service agency. Thankfully, some proactive states have already demonstrated exemplary leadership by providing direction to their respective school districts maintaining the age 14 requirement for beginning transition services.

Source: Hal Bloss, a long-time CASE member, is the Assistant Executive Director of Luzerne Intermediate Unit 18 in Kingston, PA, with permission.

An Exception to the Requirement to Evaluate the Student Before a Change in Status.
The 1997 IDEA required a local educational agency to evaluate a student with a disability before there was a change in his or her eligibility status for special education (i.e., determined to no longer be a child with a disability). IDEA 2004 includes an exception to the 1997 requirement. For students who are (a) ending their eligibility due to graduation from secondary school with a regular diploma or (b) exceeding the age of eligibility for special education under State law, the school need not conduct such an evaluation. Instead, the LEA or district must provide the students with a "summary of academic achievement and functional performance, which shall include recommendations on how to assist the youth to meet their postsecondary goals" [§300.305 (e)(3)].

New Requirements for Interagency Responsibilities in the IEP.   The 1997 IDEA required that the IEP contain a "statement of needed transition services for the child, including, when appropriate, a statement of the interagency responsibilities or any needed linkages." IDEA 2004 deleted this language in relation to transition services. The law preserved language under the definition of the IEP, however, requires that the IEP include

> [the] projected date for the beginning of services and modifications, the anticipated frequency, location and duration of those services [(D)(1)(A)(VII)]. . . . If a participating agency, fails to provide the transition services described in the IEP, the local educational agency shall reconvene the IEP team to identify strategies to meet the transition objectives for the child set out in the IEP[(D)(6)].

Interagency responsibility to provide needed services to support students' programs of study and postsecondary goals continues to be an expectation.

Self-Determination and the "Age of Majority."   The 1997 IDEA included a requirement that relates to the **age of majority** or the age at which the student is considered an adult rather than a minor under state law. IDEA 1997 outlined, and IDEA 2004 maintained, a procedure for the transfer of parental rights to the student when he or she reaches that age. Public agencies must notify both the parents and students about their rights upon reaching the age of majority. Under this provision, 1 year before the student reaches the age of majority under state law, the IEP must include a statement that the student has been informed of the rights, if any, that transfer to him or her upon reaching the age of majority. This provision is important because the postsecondary, adult service, and rehabilitation systems deal directly with individuals and not their parents (Cashman, 1998; National Center on Secondary Education and Transition, 2002). Like the rehabilitation and adult service systems, educational policy makers are becoming more alert and cautious about policies designed to intervene in the decision of the individual. This "transfer of rights" was an enormous step toward empowering students as adults and encouraging them to become much more involved in their education and future planning (Kupper, 1997; Siegel, 2007). This shift was also important in shaping the public's view of the competence of persons with disabilities to engage in their own self-determination.

➡️ HOW DOES THE NO CHILD LEFT BEHIND ACT OF 2001 PROMOTE TRANSITION SERVICES?

The No Child Left Behind Act of 2001 (Appendix 4-2) (NCLB) is the most sweeping reform of the Elementary and Secondary education Act (ESEA) since it was enacted in 1965. It redefines the federal role in K–12 education and aims to help close the achievement gap between disadvantaged and minority students and their peers. The ESEA is the principal federal law that affects education from kindergarten through high school. The four "pillars" of the Act are (a) accountability for results, (b) emphasis on doing what works based on scientific research, (c) expanded parental options, and (d) expanded local control and flexibility. The new law requires states to test children annually in reading and math from third to eighth grades and to analyze and report the results publicly by race, English proficiency, income, and disability. The year 2014 marks the final year that schools have to ensure that all students reach the levels of proficiency on standardized tests that are established by the states.

The goals are ambitious, but there is broad recognition that schools cannot work alone to achieve the results expected. NCLB incorporates service coordination and school-community collaboration as a primary policy instrument for creating change. There are many provisions within the act that support transition services and require new levels of formal coordination between schools and community agencies in order to share responsibility for improving education to help students achieve new academic standards.

Transition Services That Target Special Populations

There are several funding streams in NCLB that can be used to support transition services and used as supports for youth with disabilities, including (a) 21st Century Community Learning Centers Program, (b) Title I School Improvement and Supplemental Educational Services, (c) Title I, Part D, Prevention and Intervention Programs for Children and Youth Who Are Neglected, Delinquent, or At-Risk; (d) Safe and Drug-Free Schools and Communities; and (e) Comprehensive School Reform. These programs can use funds to coordinate federal, state, and local services and programs; violence prevention; adult education; counseling; career–technical education; and job training. For example, under Title 1, Part D, transition services can be provided for students who are moving out of state-operated facilities. In the case of a student who is not more than 20 years old and already has earned a high school diploma, the transition services may help the youth transition into postsecondary education or career–technical training.

Transition Support for At-Risk Populations.   At-risk youth are more likely than their peers to drop out of school, experience educational failure, or be involved in activities that are detrimental to their health and safety. Available research shows that children raised in economically disadvantaged families are at greater risk of low academic achievement, behavioral problems, poor health, and have difficulties with adjustments to adulthood (Hale, 1998; Land & Legters, 2002). NCLB devotes Title I, Part D to prevention and intervention programs for children and youth who are neglected, delinquent, or placed at risk of high school noncompletion.

NCLB provides support for youth who are in transition out of institutions into home schools. Nearly one third of the U.S. adult population does not advance beyond high school and this proportion has remained relatively constant for nearly 30 years (Friedman, 2000). It is estimated that approximately 1 million youth per year leave school without completing their basic educational requirements (Barr & Parrett, 2001). Adolescents with emotional and behavioral disabilities (EBD) have only a 41.9% graduation rate and the highest dropout rate of any disability category (U.S. Department of Education, Office of Special Education, 2001). Box 4–4 describes Alaska Department of Education's (2007) invitation for school districts to apply for Title I, Part D, funds with a focus on transition services.

Youth in Transition from Correctional Facilities.   NCLB also strengthens transition services and supports for youth transferring into the community from correctional facilities such as adult jails, juvenile detention, less secure detention facilities, or protective shelters. The law strengthens the ability of youth exiting correctional facilities to enter postsecondary education or employment. Under NCLB, the school district program is required to focus on the transition and academic needs of students returning from correctional facilities. Often, there is a disconnect between the programs of local schools and correctional facilities, which results in low student achievement. As students transition from correctional facilities back to their local schools, follow-up services can ensure that their education continues and they can meet the same challenging state standards required of all students.

Youth with disabilities are substantially overrepresented in the juvenile justice system (National Center on Education, Disability and Juvenile Justice, 2004; Rutherford & Quinn, 1999). Youth with specific learning, emotional, or behavioral disabilities are more vulnerable to alternative placement outside their base school or in juvenile or adult corrections than youth not identified as disabled. Ethnic minorities are also dramatically

---

Box 4–4

Alaska Application for Title I Funds for Neglected and Delinquent Youth

A Focus on Transition Supports

The purpose of this program is

1. to improve educational services for children and youth in state institutions for neglected or delinquent children and youth so that such children and youth have the opportunity to meet the same challenging state academic content standards and challenging state student academic achievement standards that all children in the state are expected to meet;

2. to provide such children and youth with the services needed to make a successful transition from institutionalization to further schooling or employment; and

3. to prevent at-risk youth from dropping out of school and to provide dropouts and children and youth returning from correctional facilities or institutions for neglected or delinquent children and youth with a support system to ensure their continued education.

From Alaska Department of Education, §1401(a), 2007.

overrepresented in the population of young offenders. A study conducted from 1988 to 1997 of youth held in public and private juvenile detention, correctional, and shelter facilities revealed that more than three quarters (86.5%) of the 105,000 juveniles studied were young men from ethnic minority backgrounds (40% Black and 18.5% Hispanic) ranging in age from 13 to 17 years old. NCLB includes specific provisions for assisting minority youth who are offenders returning from correctional facilities into their communities. NCLB mandates that states provide supportive and preventative services to youth placed at risk for involvement in the juvenile justice system, including students with disabilities, to minimize their vulnerability.

Women and Children in Poverty. Women and children account for more than three quarters of households with incomes below the poverty level. Children from racial minority groups are much more likely to live in poverty than are white children. Unmarried teen mothers need access to day care, transportation, and other supports that will enable them to complete high school, enter employment, and pursue advanced education (National Council for Research on Women, 1998, 2001). NCLB focuses attention on the needs of women in poverty to assist them in completing high school and entering employment.

Transition Support for Native Americans. Native American students with disabilities face unique challenges to successful transition. Lack of familial support, lack of support networks for students with disabilities who enter higher education institutions, chemical dependency, all play a role in the high dropout rates and in the level of difficulty in transitioning into adulthood successfully. These issues coupled with other factors, e.g., lack of employment opportunities, limited resources, and high poverty levels, impede the ability of Native Americans to succeed in higher education and independent living. Employment rates run as high as 70% in some reservations, placing Native American youth, as a whole, at a heightened risk for failure to assume adult responsibilities after leaving high school (Blasi, 2001; Leake, Kim-Rupnow, & Leung, 2003; Shafer & Rangasamy, 1995). NCLB devotes Title VII to Indian, Native Hawaiian, and Alaska Native education and support for career preparation and postsecondary education.

How Do NCLB Requirements for Adequate Yearly Progress Impact Transition?

Like IDEA, the NCLB promotes school-wide reforms to improve results for all children in the school and particularly the needs of low-achieving children and those at risk of not meeting the state academic achievement standards.

Adequate Yearly Progress and Transition. Under NCLB, schools are expected to make **adequate yearly progress** (AYP) toward meeting state academic achievement goals. In passing NCLB, Congress recognized that some schools experience chronic underachievement and the performance of students on standardized tests in those schools was unacceptable. The AYP status of a school is determined using student assessment data, but the data must be broken out by subgroups of students (general education, students in special education, English language learners, low-income students, and specific ethnic groups). One hundred percent of students in general education (with a 2% AYP exception for students with disabilities) and in each subgroup must reach the state-defined *proficient* levels in reading and math assessments by 2013–2014 (U.S. Department of Education, 2004). States may develop modified academic achievement standards with alternative assessments for students served under IDEA, but in making AYP, they may only include the proficient scores from such assessments up to a cap of 2% of the total tested population (U.S. Department of Education, 2006a). A lack of progress (10% improvement is required each year) by any of these sub-groups could cause an entire school to be designated as *needing improvement*.

Districts and schools that fail to make AYP toward that goal face a series of escalating consequences. If a school fails to achieve AYP, then a system of corrective actions come into play to help the school improve. These include the following:

Level 1—School Improvement Status (Missed AYP for 2 Years): Revise the school improvement plan for a 2-year period, seek technical assistance, and provide students with an option to transfer to another school.

Level 2—School Improvement Status (Missed AYP for 3 Years): Make supplemental educational services (e.g., tutoring) available to students through approved providers and continue to make transfer options available.

Level 3—Corrective Action Status (Missed AYP for 4 Years): Implement a corrective plan identified by the District and continue requirements in Level 2.

Levels 4 and 5—Restructuring Status (Missed AYP for 5 or 6 Years): Prepare a plan for major restructuring of the school and its governance (NCLB, 2002).

NCLB requires that each school have a plan for implementing the law, including processes for coordination and integration of services for all children. For example, in many schools seeking to improve the performance of all students, especially those with disabilities, specialists are being trained as in-school service coordinators with caseloads of students for whom they are responsible. These coordinators become the main contacts for the students, help arrange support services when needed, obtain assessments, and maintain records of service needs and progress of each student. Examples of service coordination activities, which support broad change efforts or restructuring, include those that (a) restructure preschool programs to incorporate health and social services to improve general readiness for elementary school; (b) restructure schools, classrooms, teaching, and curriculum to improve basic academic and career-related outcomes for students in K–12, and incorporate social service and family supports; and (c) restructure secondary schools to better link with 2- and 4-year colleges and provide outreach to adults in need of retraining and continuing education (Volpe, Batra, Bomio, & Costin, 1999). Administrators report that coordinating with other organizations to meet the needs of special learners improves student outcomes, expands schools' access to resources, increases efficiency and effectiveness by engaging students and families, and builds stronger schools and communities (American Association of School Administrators, 2003).

State standards assume that all students can achieve high levels of learning if they are in environments with high expectations, clearly defined standards, and effective teaching. Although some states develop specific standards for students with disabilities, most states simply created standards that are the same for all students (McDonnell,

McLaughlin, & Morison, 1997). These high expectations in state education standards are at odds with the core rulings in *Rowley* that school districts only need to provide access to education and to minimally meet the "some educational benefit" standard (*Rowley,* 458 U.S. at 189, 200–201). The NCLB focus addresses the substance of quality of services once students have access, including postschool outcomes, independent living, and self-sufficiency. Box 4–5 provides an example of coordination of transition goals and the student's educational program.

How Do NCLB and IDEA Differ in Principles and Policies?

In considering the twin educational goals of *equity* (access for all) and *excellence* (high standards) in education, it is important to understand the differences between the principles that underlie NCLB and IDEA. For more than two decades, the primary policy tool for improving outcomes for students with disabilities has been the IDEA and its provisions for free and appropriate education and protection of individual rights. SBE under NCLB has introduced a fundamentally different set of policies and practices that are based on uniform learning standards within a *standards-based curriculum*. The students' mastery of the curriculum content is measured by standardized tests or assessments. SBE is based on the assumption that *common standards for all students* are a catalyst for improved educational results and serve as a basis for what should be taught and for measuring what students should be expected to know (McDonnel, McLaughlin, & Morison, 1997). SBE is also based on the assumptions that content and performance standards can be clearly and precisely defined, student performance can

---

Box 4–5

Linking the Transition Goals and Objectives to the Educational Program (Course of Study)

Once transition goals and objectives have been developed for a student, transition activities and the course of study are then designed to help the student achieve those goals. Courses should relate directly to the student's postsecondary goals, increasing the chances the student will be invested in their program of study. Courses of study for many students with disabilities match those of the general population. For students with moderate or severe disabilities, courses of study are likely to be different. Instead of the listing specific course titles, for students with moderate to severe disabilities one should list general content areas (e.g., mobility, self-determination, independent living, money management, personal relationships) (O'Leary & Collision, 2002; O'Leary, Lehman, & Doty, 2001). For example, the student may need to strengthen basic mathematics skills and learn to apply them in a work setting. This can be accomplished by blending academic course work with vocational education. Investigating supervised community living opportunities to address the student's independent living domain, however, is an activity that falls outside the typical curriculum. The community is necessarily the site of many transition activities.

From Alaska Application for Title I Funds, §1401(a), 2007.

be measured validly and reliably, and accountability can be strengthened through public reporting of aggregate data on student performance (Kochhar & Bassett, 2003).

In contrast to the assumption of common performance standards, special education services are guided by the special education framework which defines the rights of students with disabilities to a free and appropriate education and specifies the responsibilities of school systems to accommodate their individual needs (McDonnel, McLaughlin, & Morison, 1997). Individualized education relies on a *private process*— the IEP and transition plans are centered on the *needs of the individual student,* and *students' individual rights* are enforced through a set of procedural safeguards. Also, in contrast to the focus on academic outcomes that are the hallmark of SBE, the special education framework for students with disabilities encompasses a broader range of educational outcomes for students with disabilities.

Also in contrast to the focus on academic outcomes that are the hallmark of SBE, the transition service framework for students with disabilities includes a broad range of educational outcomes for students with disabilities. For example, Ysseldyke (1997) and Ysseldyke, Thurlow, Kozleski, & Reschly (1998) clustered outcomes into eight domains: presence and participation, accommodation and adaptation, physical health, responsibility and independence, contribution and citizenship, academic and functional literacy, personal and social adjustment, and satisfaction. Critics of SBE for all students claim that states have crafted standards that are too narrow and do not allow educators to include nonacademic learning objectives such as those that are focused on social and behavioral skills, career development, physical and health development, and functional skills (Izzo, Hertzfeld, Simmons-Reed, & Aaron, 2001; Kochhar & Bassett, 2003). To address the broader life domains of the student, the foundation for transition must be laid during the elementary and middle school years, guided by the broad concept of career development and preparation of the whole person for postsecondary life (Clark et al., 1991; Clark & Kolstoe, 1990, 1995). Table 4–1 compares the assumptions of individualized (IDEA) and standards-based (NCLB) education.

Table 4–1   Comparing the Assumptions of Individualized Education and Standards-Based Education

Transition under IDEA	Standards-Based Education
Emphasizes a range of educational outcomes	Focuses on academic and basic literacy outcomes
Is an individualized process	Emphasizes common rigorous learning standards for all students
Aligns the curriculum with the student's post-school goals	Assumes that performance can be measured validly and reliably through testing
Emphasizes a career-oriented curriculum for student not bound for postsecondary education	Decreases "low-track" English, mathematics, science classes
Involves interagency coordination and support	Increases enrollment in college preparatory courses
Improves transition outcomes	Assumes that greater inclusion in general education improves transition outcomes

Source: From *Aligning Transition and Standards-Based Education* (pp. 15–16), by C. Kochhar-Bryant and D. Bassett, 2003, Arlington, VA: Council for Exceptional Children.

The challenge for educators is to align SBE policies with those under IDEA that are based on individual rights and individualized educational processes. Transition, therefore, must be viewed as a comprehensive framework (a) to ensure effective alignment between secondary education and transition services and (b) to guide planning and decision making among students, families, and professionals.

➡️ WHAT RELATED LAWS PROMOTE TRANSITION SERVICES?

Americans with Disabilities Act (Pub. L. No. 101-336)

The **Americans with Disabilities Act** (ADA) guarantees equal access for all individuals with disabilities in employment, public accommodations, state and local government services, transportation, and telecommunications. As a civil rights act, the act requires employers (as well as other entities) to make reasonable accommodations for qualified individuals with disabilities to perform essential job functions (Horne & Morris, 1998). Under the ADA, **reasonable accommodations** in the workplace include making facilities physically accessible and usable by individuals with disabilities. Other examples of reasonable accommodations, however, include job restructuring, modified schedules, the acquisition of equipment and devices, modifications to examinations or training materials, and the provision of qualified readers or interpreters.

The disabilities act promotes nondiscrimination in any private entity (including colleges and universities, postsecondary career–technical schools, employer-based training programs, and other private training programs) on the basis of disability. The law promotes collaboration among general, special, career–technical, and postsecondary personnel to assist young adults to exercise their rights to access postsecondary programs.

Americans with Disabilities Act and Transition to PostSecondary Institutions. The ADA promotes collaboration to provide accommodations in both public and private organizations, including public and private schools, colleges and universities, postsecondary career–technical schools, employer-based training programs, and other private training programs. Under ADA, transition activities can include preparation for college interviews, knowledge about reasonable accommodations provided in the programs, assistance with applications and supporting documentation. ADA prohibits discrimination against individuals with disabilities in postsecondary applications, postsecondary education, job training, job application procedures, hiring, advancement, and employee compensation.

According to ADA regulations, reasonable accommodations at the postsecondary level include modifications to a postsecondary education, admission procedures to enable individuals to be considered for admission, modifications in classrooms, test taking, and instructional modifications that would help the student participate and learn in the college setting. Through antidiscrimination provisions, the ADA encourages postsecondary institutions to consider applicants with disabilities in their recruitment of teachers, professors, and support personnel.

What Does This Means for the Student? In most colleges and universities, students can expect to apply for and receive services from an office with a title such as "student support services" or "office of disability services." Although a student may not have an

IEP or 504 plan in college, postsecondary institutions are required under ADA and the Higher Education Act of 1998 to provide reasonable accommodations (Brinckerhoff, McGuire & Shaw, 2002; Ekpone & Bogucki, 2003; HEATH, 2003). Often, students have support service plans that are similar to 504 plans because they specify the kinds of accommodations that the student is to receive in classrooms and in nonacademic activities. Accommodations that can be requested in postsecondary education include testing accommodations, physical accommodations, adaptations of technology, special software for large print, note takers, supplemental online tutorials, extensions of time for papers and homework, tutors, and group support sessions. If students plan to use telecommunications equipment as part of the educational program or in their work on campus, then accommodations for sensory deficits must be made.

Americans with Disabilities Act and Transition to Employment.   The ADA prohibits discrimination by employers against "qualified individuals with disabilities (visible or hidden)"—those who possess the skills, experience, education, and other job-related requirements of a position and who, with or without reasonable accommodations, can perform the essential functions of the job. This antidiscrimination provision covers all aspects of employment, including application, testing and medical examinations, promotion, hiring and layoffs, assignments and termination, evaluation and compensation, disciplinary actions and leave, and training and benefit. Examples of reasonable accommodations include job restructuring, modified work schedules, reassignments of position, modifications to equipment, modifications of examinations, training materials or policies, and provision of readers or interpreters (Dixon, Kruse, & Van Horn, 2003). Employers are not required to lower their standards to make such accommodations, nor are they required to provide accommodations if they impose "undue hardships" on the business through actions that are very costly or disruptive of the work environment (National Information Center for Handicapped Children and Youth, 1999). Most accommodations, however, cost less than $500.

Carl D. Perkins Career and Technical Education Improvement Act of 2006 (Pub. L. No. 109-270)

The 1998 Perkins Act Amendments were signed into law in August 2006 as the Carl D. Perkins Career and Technical Education Improvement Act of 2006 (§20 U.S.C. §2301 *et seq.,* Pub. L. No. 109-270). The Act authorizes funding for career–technical education and envisions that all students will achieve challenging academic and technical standards and be prepared for high-skill, high-wage, or high-demand occupations in current or emerging professions. The act provides an increased focus on the academic achievement of career and technical education students, improves state and local accountability, and strengthens the connections between secondary and postsecondary education.

The federal legislation that authorizes funding for career–technical education, the Perkins Act, requires a national study of career–technical education before each reauthorization (renewal) of funds. The most recent evaluation, *National Assessment of Vocational Education: A Final Report to Congress* showed that the progress toward these goals has been uneven and that the system as a whole has been plagued by a lack of clarity about purpose and goals (Silverberg, Warner, Fong, & Goodwin,

2004). As a result, the reauthorization plan linked the Career Technical Education system to the principles of the No Child Left Behind Act. The plan also called for higher academic achievement rates and *more pathways and smoother transitions* into technical education programs in community college and workforce investment systems, and allowed states more freedom in how they spend their Perkins dollars (Association for Career and Technical Education [ACTE], 2005).

Changes in the Perkins Act.   The most notable provisions of the 2006 statute is the use of the term *career and technical education* instead of *vocational education* throughout and the continuation of the Tech Prep program as a separate federal funding stream within the legislation. Perkins 2006 authorizes the legislation through FY 2012, for a total of 6 years instead of the current 5 years. Other major changes include a section on local accountability that did not exist in the 1998 law, the separation of performance indicators for secondary and postsecondary programs, and requirements for "Career and Technical Programs of Study" (ACTE, 2005).

The Perkins Act builds on the efforts of states and localities to develop challenging academic and technical standards and to assist students in meeting such standards, including preparation for high-skill, high-wage, or high-demand occupations in current or emerging professions. The act calls for significantly higher levels of academic achievement, including 4 years of English, 3 years of mathematics and science, and 3 years of social studies. It promotes the development of services and activities that integrate rigorous and challenging academic and career and technical instruction and that link secondary education and postsecondary education for participating career and technical education students.

The act supports partnerships among secondary schools, postsecondary institutions, baccalaureate degree granting institutions, area career and technical education schools, local workforce investment boards, and business and industry. It provides individuals with opportunities throughout their lifetimes to develop, in conjunction with other education and training programs, the knowledge and skills needed to participate in today's workforce.

What Does This Mean for Students Who Are Special Populations?   A student is eligible for the Perkins Special Populations Program if he or she is enrolled in a career and technical program, has the intent of entering the workplace immediately following the completion of a degree of certificate in a career and technical education program, and meets one or more of the following criteria (Carl D. Perkins Act of 2006, §3, Definitions):

1. *Economically disadvantaged:* The term *economically disadvantaged family* or *individual* refers to such families of individuals who are determined to be low income according to the latest available data from the Department of Commerce.
2. *Academically disadvantaged:* An individual is considered academically disadvantaged if his or her disadvantaged condition is a contributing factor to a lack of success and/or he or she is not succeeding or cannot be expected to succeed in career–technical education without special assistance.
3. *Individual with a disability:* A student with a disability is one with any disability as defined in the ADA of 1990, including one who is physically, mentally, emotionally,

learning, and/or developmentally disabled or impaired. Students with IEPs and §504 plans are eligible (U.S. Department of Education, 2006b).

4. *Nontraditional:* The term *nontraditional* refers to individuals from one gender who comprise less than 25% of the individuals employed in each such occupation or field of work.

5. *Limited English proficiency:* A student with limited English proficiency (LEP) is an individual who has limited ability in speaking, reading, writing, or understanding the English language and whose native language is other than English.

6. *Single parent:* The term *single parent* means an individual who is unmarried or legally separated from a spouse and has full or partial custody of a minor child or children or is pregnant.

7. *Displaced homemaker:* A student who has worked primarily without pay in caring for a home and family and for that reason has a lack of marketable skills. This person has been dependent on the income of another family member but is no longer supported by that income. This person also is unemployed or underemployed and is experiencing difficulty in obtaining or upgrading employment.

What Does This Mean for Students with Disabilities?   Perkins 2006 requires the development and implementation of a program of study for each student or participant. Each program of study must (a) incorporate secondary education and postsecondary education elements; (b) include academic and career and technical content in a coordinated, nonduplicative progression of courses; and (c) the program must lead to an industry-recognized credential or certificate at the postsecondary level, or an associate or bachelor's degree. States are required to develop the programs of study in consultation with local programs and each local program receiving funds under the bill must implement at least one of the programs of study.

The 2005 amendments reflect a recognition by lawmakers that career–technical education offers unique benefits for many youth with disabilities and, therefore, the act requires states to ensure equal access to career–technical education, including access to recruitment, enrollment, and placement activities in the full range of career-related education programs in the public schools, including tech-prep programs. Youth with disabilities must be provided the same opportunity as all other youth to enter career–technical education. Local school districts, area career–technical schools, and other agencies that receive funding under this law must provide information to special populations, including youth with disabilities, about career–technical education opportunities at least 1 year before they are eligible for such opportunities, or as indicated by their IEP. Student service offices in 2-year colleges receive funds under the Perkins Act to provide special services for students with disabilities who are enrolled in certificate or associate degree programs and career–technical programs. Services may include tutoring, psychoeducational assessments, classroom modifications, and instructional aids and devices. Box 4–6 illustrates the benefits for a student with disabilities.

Tech-Prep Program.   Tech-Prep programs funded under the Perkins Act must lead to technical skill proficiency, an industry-recognized credential, a certificate or a degree in a specific career field, must utilize CTE programs of study to the extent practical, and must coordinate with activities conducted with Basic State Grant funds. Additional

Box 4–6

Colin Prepares for a Career

Colin, a student with emotional and severe learning disabilities, participated in career exploration classes during the middle school years to help assist him in making career decisions. During seventh and eighth grade, he had an opportunity to rotate through several exploratory classes. In high school, Colin was told that he could elect to take classes in one of seven major occupational areas defined by the Association of Career and Technical Education (ACTE), a professional organization of teachers in career and technical programs.

1. Agriculture (careers related to food and fiber production and agribusiness)
2. Business (accounting, business administration, management, information technology, and entrepreneurship)
3. Family and consumer sciences (culinary arts, fashion design, interior design, home maintenance, employment and career development, child care, and other life skills)
4. Health occupations (nursing, dental, and medical technicians)
5. Marketing (management, entrepreneurship, and merchandising and retail)
6. Technology (production of consumer electronic goods, communication systems, and transportation systems)
7. Trade and industrial (skilled trades such as automotive technician, carpenter, and computer technician)

Colin was interested in becoming a computer technician like his father. In addition to the classroom experience, Colin participated in both in-school and on-the-job learning and training experiences in business settings through a cooperative education or work experience program. This program was made possible through Carl D. Perkins funds. A high school teacher trained to work in the program selected and developed job sites in the community. Local businesses were committed to providing on-the-job training for a student who is ready to go to work in the community although still in high school. This teacher coordinated services between the school and the community, providing site supervision and, when required, job coaching for Colin. When Colin was ready to transition from high school, he chose to enter a community college and major in computer technical services. He also worked part time in a computer support services firm, to gain experience in the field.

activities that are authorized are designed to strengthen career guidance and counseling provisions and encourage transition between secondary and postsecondary education.

Workforce Investment Act Amendments of 2005 (Pub. L. No. 105-220), currently under consideration in Congress, will revise and reauthorize appropriations through FY 2011 for (a) workforce investment systems for job training and employment services under title I of the Workforce Investment Act (WIA) of 1998; (b) adult basic skills education, including adult education and family literacy programs, under WIA Title II (WIA-II); and (c) vocational rehabilitation services under the Rehabilitation Act of 1973 (Title IV). Authorization for WIA is operating under an extension, awaiting action in the 109th Congress.

WIA is a large public sector job training and employment system that gives authority to local regions and the private sector to guide public sector education and training programs. Its goal is to improve the quality of the workforce, reduce welfare dependency, and enhance the productivity and competitiveness of the nation's economy by providing a wide variety of career development services for individuals, including services for adults, youth, and for individuals employed, underemployed, and unemployed. WIA provides the framework for the publicly funded workforce development system. Title I of the legislation authorizes the Workforce Investment System, Title II reauthorizes adult education and family literacy programs, Title III amends the Wagner–Peyser and related acts, Title IV reauthorizes Rehabilitation Act programs, and Title V contains general provisions.

WIA replaced the Job Training Partnership Act (JTPA) that had been in place from 1982 to 2000. The legislation placed new emphasis on universal access to services, sequenced service delivery, interagency coordination, consumer choice, service provider accountability, and local planning. The JTPA was preceded by the Comprehensive Employment and Training Act of 1973 (CETA, Pub. L. No. 93-203) and the amendments of 1978 (Pub. L. No. 95-524) that launched federal involvement in job training to target economically disadvantaged youth and adults and required that persons with disabilities be addressed in planning and application for funds. This law improved the efficiency and performance of the program. It also established procedures to involve private business and industry in partnerships with the public sector to provide programs and services to assist young people to prepare for and enter employment. The act targeted disadvantaged youth and adults, which included individuals with disabilities. The partnership act also established Job Corps centers for disadvantaged youths who needed additional education, career and job skills training, and other support services to make a successful transition into employment. The partnership act was consolidated under the WIA of 1998.

WIA Programs and Services.   Universal access is one of the underlying principles of WIA. A young adult who needs employment assistance can access services at a One-Stop Career Center that provides information and services from the various federal agencies that help people get jobs and advance in the labor market. WIA legislation requires agencies to partner through the One-Stop system, including the Department of Labor, the Department of Education, the Department of Health and Human Services, and the Department of Housing and Urban Development.

WIA services fall into three categories of service: *core, intensive,* and *training.* Core services are available to all job seekers, including access to job listings, information about careers and the local labor market, and assistance with job search activities. Intensive services are only available after core service efforts are exhausted and include life-skills workshops, case management, and comprehensive assessments leading to the development of an individual employment plan. Training services, such as employer-linked programs and classroom-based skills training leading to a specific occupation, can only be accessed by individuals who have failed to obtain or maintain employment through core and intensive services. Title II of WIA is the Adult Education and Family Literacy Act replacing the Adult Education Act and the National Literacy Act of 1991. The goals of Title II are to assist adults to become literate, gain knowledge and skills needed for employment, complete secondary education, and to help young parents become engaged in their children's educational development.

One-Stop System.   Title III amends the Wagner–Peyser Act that was authorized in 1933 to establish a nationwide system of public employment offices (the Employment Service). WIA required the Employment Service activities to become unified as a *One-Stop system* that integrates a once fragmented service-delivery system into a convenient, comprehensive process that addresses local labor market needs. Because older youth (ages 18–21) are eligible for core, intensive, and training services, they have increased access to comprehensive career counseling, job search assistance, and skill building opportunities. WIA programs create lifelong access to career development assistance in that these services are not only available at the time of transition but eligible individuals may tap into these services throughout their adult lives.

Box 4-7 provides the case of Mariana, who finds a way to employment through the One-Stop system in her community.

WIA, through the One-Stop system and youth services, considerably expands the resources available to youth with disabilities. It also offers the promise of a more

Box 4–7

Mariana Finds a Way

Mariana is an 18-year-old school dropout and a single parent living with her mother and grandmother, who was battling bone cancer. When she was young, her family had moved around the country, and so Mariana was never in one school for very long. It was not until the sixth grade that Mariana was diagnosed with severe learning disabilities, and she was far behind grade level in reading and writing. She enjoyed mathematics and science, but her reading skill deficiencies were a barrier in all her subjects. In the ninth grade, Mariana walked out during a standardized test that she could not complete and never returned to school. For 3 years she worked in a variety of minimum-wage jobs to contribute to the family finances and had two incidents in which she was charged with theft and possession of marijuana and received probation for a year.

While waiting for a bus one day Mariana discovered a brochure with information about a One-Stop Career Center in the community (a Workforce Investment Act program). The program offered educational options for persons aged 14–21 who were no longer in a school setting. The program offered employment services, unemployment insurance, vocational rehabilitation, adult education, welfare-to-work, and postsecondary vocational education. All these services were coordinated under a one-stop system at one physical site. What really caught her attention was the passage that—students with learning disabilities qualify for this program because all youth between the ages of 14 and 21 who are experiencing one or more of the following six barriers to successful workforce entry qualify: pregnant or a parent; school dropout; juvenile or adult offender (aged 14–21); in need of help to complete an educational program or to secure and hold a job; has a basic literacy skills deficiency; is homeless, runaway, or a foster child.

Mariana visited the career center, was introduced to the services by a counselor, and discussed her strong interest in getting her GED and trying to find work in the health care field. She learned that she could get job search assistance to find entry level employment in the health field, while attending GED classes in the evening. The career center would also provide tutoring to improve her reading and writing skills. After receiving her GED, she planned to apply for a scholarship and enroll in a career-technical school to study to become a radiology technician.

inclusive system that builds determination of accommodation needs into mainstream workforce investment services, thus reducing the stigma people with disabilities often feel when they are singled out by receiving services in a separate location. WIA also extends the reach of employment and training programs that are designed to address the specific needs of individuals with disabilities (National Center on Secondary Education and Transition, 2002b).

WIA, Youth Programs, and High School/High Tech.   The WIA youth-focused programs and activities hold tremendous potential to support career development activities for young people with disabilities. WIA can play an important role in addressing the dropout crisis among youth with disabilities and connect with other systems to create a comprehensive approach for challenged youth (e.g., those with disabilities, homeless, out of school, or transitioning from foster care of the justice system). One way of accomplishing this is to increase the participation of youth with disabilities in transition programs like the WIA youth programs and High School/High Tech (HS/HT).

In 2002, the U.S. Department of Labor launched a grant program to assist states in developing statewide HS/HT programs that would be integrated into youth services provided through the One-Stop Center System. HS/HT is a series of nationally established programs designed to provide young people with disabilities with an opportunity to explore careers or further education leading to technology-related careers. These programs, which have generally been locally directed and supported, serve both in-school or out-of-school youth with all disabilities in a year-round program of corporate site visits, mentoring, job shadowing, guest speakers, after school activities, and summer internships. HS/HT graduates demonstrate at least a doubling of postsecondary education achievements. At some HS/HT sites, as many as 70% of HS/HT graduates move on to postsecondary education (U.S. Department of Labor, 2002).

Recommendations related to youth development include allowing more flexibility in use of funds so programs can prioritize services to youth in high-risk situations, targeting communities with the highest level of youth distress and promoting a community collaboration process that establishes partnerships among education, justice, and child welfare systems (Center for Law and Social Policy, 2007; Strawn & Duke, 2007).

Rehabilitation Act Amendments of 2003

The Rehabilitation Act prohibits discrimination against individuals with disabilities in federally funded programs and activities. The *Rehabilitation Act programs* are now embedded in the WIA, which links them to state and local workforce systems. The Rehabilitation Act Amendments of 2003, also under consideration in Congress, makes up the major portion of the WIA of 2005. The Rehabilitation Amendments extend the state/federal vocational rehabilitation program for 5 years. Several provisions apply to *secondary and postsecondary schools*. Section 504 of the Rehabilitation Act of 1973 requires that

> No otherwise qualified individual with a disability in the United States . . . shall, solely by reason of her or his disability, be excluded from the participation in, be denied the benefits of, or be subjected to discrimination under any program or activity receiving Federal financial assistance.

Section 504 prohibits the arbitrary and discriminatory assignment of students who are disabled to segregated classes or facilities. In elementary and secondary schools, students who are disabled may be assigned to separate facilities or courses of special education only when this placement is necessary to provide equal educational opportunity to them. Any separate facilities and the services provided in separate facilities must be comparable to facilities and services for individuals without disabilities. To determine what the educational needs of a student with disabilities may be, schools must carry out preliminary evaluation and placement procedures. Specific elements that must be considered include the following:

1. *Evaluation and placement procedures:* Before placing students with disabilities in any educational program, schools must evaluate each student using tests and evaluation materials that are chosen to assess specific areas of the student's needs. For example, a student may not be assigned to special education classes only on the basis of intelligence tests. When a student with impaired sensory, manual, or speaking skills is evaluated, the test results must accurately reflect what the test is supposed to measure and not the student's impaired skills, except where those skills are what is being measured. Only trained people may administer the tests or evaluation materials, and placement decisions must be made by a team that includes people who know about the student and understand the meaning of the evaluation information. The placement team must consider a variety of documented information for each student from several sources, including the results of aptitude and achievement tests, teacher recommendations, and reports on the student's physical condition, social or cultural background, and adaptive behavior.

2. *Educational setting:* The law requires that students with disabilities be educated along with nondisabled students to the maximum extent appropriate. This means that disabled students must be assigned to regular courses or classes if the students' needs can be met there. Also, decisions on academic placement must be based on an individual student's needs. Students with disabilities may be placed in a separate class or facility only if they cannot be educated satisfactorily in the regular educational setting with the use of supplementary aids and services. For example, students who are blind may be assisted by readers or may use Braille equipment or specially equipped computer equipment and remain in the regular classrooms. Students with severe learning disabilities, however, may be assigned to special education classes for part of the day. Schools that do not offer the special educational programs or facilities that may be required by a student with disabilities may refer that student to another school or educational institution. The student's home district, however, remains responsible for providing the student a free and appropriate education. Transportation must be provided at no greater cost than would be incurred if the student were placed in the home district.

3. *Reevaluations:* The performance and skill levels of students with disabilities frequently vary, and students, accordingly, must be allowed to change from assigned classes and programs. A school, however, may not make a significant change in a student's placement without a reevaluation. Schools must conduct periodic reevaluations of all students with disabilities.

4. *IEP:* The IDEA requires schools to develop, according to specific standards, an IEP for each eligible student with disabilities. An individualized program that meets

the requirements of the IDEA also fulfills the requirements of §504 and Title II of the ADA for an appropriate education for a student with disabilities.

5. *Procedural safeguards:* Schools must establish procedures that allow the parents or guardians of students in elementary and secondary schools to challenge evaluations, placement procedures, and decisions. The law requires that parents or guardians be notified of any evaluation or placement action and that they be allowed to examine their child's records. If they disagree with the school's decisions, parents or guardians must be allowed to have an impartial hearing with the opportunity to participate in the discussions. A review procedure must be made available to parents or guardians who disagree with the hearing decision.

6. *Transition services:* Several provisions of the Rehabilitation Act affect schools and the delivery of transition services. Recognizing that some youth with disabilities leaving school will require assistance, the Rehabilitation Act includes many provisions related to transition using essentially the same definition of transition services as used by the IDEA. State vocational rehabilitation (VR) agencies are encouraged to assist schools to identify transition services and to participate in the cost of transition services for any student with a disability who is determined to be eligible for VR services. Transition services that promote or facilitate the accomplishment of long-term rehabilitation goals and intermediate objectives were added to the scope of rehabilitation services under the act (Grossi, 2000; Horne & Morris, 1998).

Recommendations for Reauthorization Related to Transition.   Every year increasing numbers of students with disabilities are leaving schools and seeking adult services, including VR services. Youth with disabilities represent the single largest category of children and youth who do not complete school. Four out of every 10 high school dropouts are youth with disabilities (Prokop, 2006). Many of these youth seek assistance from VR and greater emphasis is being placed on the provision of transition services before students with disabilities leave the school system. VR administrators and advocates indicate that VR's ability to address the need of transition age students is severely limited by inadequate VR resources. National studies of transition services show that access to VR assistance for students with disabilities significantly increases the likelihood that these students will complete school and continue on to postsecondary education and training or enter competitive employment (Council of State Administrators of Vocational Rehabilitation, 2006).

Higher Education Act Amendments of 1965 (Pub. L. No. 107-139)

The Higher Education Act, administered by the U.S. Department of Education, is designed to strengthen the educational resources of the nation's colleges and universities and to provide financial assistance to students in postsecondary and higher education. This law was first enacted as Pub. L. No. 89-329 in 1965 and most recently on February 8, 2002, Amendments to the Higher Education Act (HEA, §1762) were signed into law as Pub. L. No. 107-139. The HEA is currently up for reauthorization by Congress. The HEA authorizes programs and activities most of which fall into four main categories: (a) student financial aid, (b) support services to help students complete high school and enter and succeed in postsecondary education, (c) aid to strengthen institutions, and (d) aid to improve K–12 teacher training at postsecondary institutions (Congressional Research Service, 2004b; Stedman, 2003).

HEA authorizes the federal government's major student aid programs, as well as other significant programs such as those providing aid to special groups of higher education institutions and support services to enable disadvantaged students to complete secondary school and enter and complete college. It allows for early counseling of youth about postsecondary opportunities available to them and what they need to do to prepare for these opportunities. The law provides institutions of higher education with grant funds to develop and implement support services for disadvantaged youth, including those with disabilities. The 2002 amendments extended the authorization of programs under the 1965 act.

Title I of the Higher Education Act encourages partnerships between institutions of higher education and secondary schools serving low income and disadvantaged students, including students with disabilities. Such partnerships may include collaboration among businesses, labor organizations, community-based organizations, and other public or private organizations. Title IV is aimed at increasing college retention and graduation rates for low-income students and first-generation students with disabilities. A high priority is placed on serving students with disabilities and low income. This priority challenges colleges and universities to collaborate with schools and other community agencies for outreach and support of students.

Title II, Improving Teaching Quality, is designed to improve the quality of the current and future teaching force by improving the preparation of prospective teachers and enhancing professional development activities (Higher Education Act amendments of 2002). Title II also holds institutions of higher education accountable for preparing teachers who have the necessary teaching skills and are highly competent in the academic content areas in which the teachers plan to teach, such as mathematics, science, English, foreign languages, history, economics, art, civics, government, and geography, including skills in the effective uses of technology in the classroom. The act calls for the recruitment of highly qualified individuals, including individuals from other occupations, into the teaching force.

Chapter 4 of Title IV, Student Aid Programs, allows for grants for experimentation and development of model programs that provide counseling for students about college opportunities, financial aid, and student support services. It also encourages creative collaboration among colleges, universities, financial aid organizations, and support service agencies.

Part D of Title VII, Graduate and Postsecondary Improvement Project, authorizes national graduate fellowship programs to attract students of superior ability and achievement, exceptional promise, and demonstrated financial need, into high-quality graduate programs and provide the students with the financial support to complete advanced degrees. A second purpose is to support model demonstration projects, to provide technical assistance or professional development for faculty and administrators in institutions of higher education, and to provide students with disabilities a quality postsecondary education.

Title XI provides incentives to career-technical schools, colleges, and universities to encourage them to work with private and civic organizations to address problems of accessibility of students with disabilities to institutions of higher education. Title XI is also aimed at reducing attitudinal barriers that prevent full inclusion of individuals with disabilities within their academic communities, including the social and cultural community of the campus. Such activities can include visits by students to postsecondary settings, provision of information about student support services on campus, special seminars for college teachers and administrators about student accommodation needs, and accommodations in the classrooms and on campus.

Social Security Administration Initiatives to Promote Employment for Individuals with Significant Disabilities

Plans to Achieve Self-Support.   The Social Security Administration (SSA) operates the federally funded program that provides benefits for people of any age who are unable to do substantial work and have a severe mental or physical disability. Several programs are offered for people with disabilities, including Social Security Disability Insurance (SSDI), Supplemental Security Income (SSI), Plan to Achieve Self-Support (PASS), Medicaid, and Medicare. Examples of employment services include cash benefits while working (e.g., student-earned income), Medicare or Medicaid while working, help with extra work expenses the individual has as a result of the disability, and assistance to start a new line of work. Postsecondary services generally include financial incentives for further education and training (see chapter 12 for more discussion).

An increasing number of youth apply for SSI or SSDI each year, despite significant federal, state, and local investments in special education; about 60,000 between ages 18 and 24 come onto the rolls annually (Berry & Jones, 2000; Social Security Administration, 2001) and less than 1% ever leave. An increasing number of young people with disabilities apply for SSI or SSDI each year.

To provide incentives for young people to enter the workforce, the SSA developed the Plan for Achieving Self-Support (PASS) to help individuals make the transition without losing disability benefits (U.S. Department of Labor, Office of Disability Employment Policy, 2004). A PASS lets the young worker use his or her income or other assets to achieve employment goals. For example, a young high school graduate could set aside money to go to school to get specialized training for a job or to start a business. The job that the individual wants should allow him or her to earn enough to reduce or eliminate the need for benefits provided under both the Social Security and SSI programs. A plan is designed to help the individual to obtain services, items, or skills that are needed to reach employment goals.

Three requirements are needed to qualify for a PASS plan: (a) desire to work, (b) currently receiving SSI (or can qualify for SSI by having this plan) because the person is disabled or blind, and (c) have other income or resources to get a job or start a business (U.S. Department of Labor, 2004). Under SSI rules, any income that the individual has reduces the SSI payment for disability. But, with an approved PASS plan, the individual can use that income to pay for the items needed to reach their employment goal. Money that is set aside toward work-related goals is not counted under this plan when the SSI payment amount is determined. Money set aside can be used for transportation to and from work; tuition, books, fees, and supplies needed for school or training; child care; attendant care; employment services, such as job coaching and resume writing; supplies to start a business; equipment and tools to do the job; or uniforms, special clothing, and safety equipment. If the plan is approved, the coordinator or specialist will stay in contact to make sure that the plan is followed and the goals are being met.

Setting up a PASS Plan.   First, the young person decides on a work goal and determines the items and services he or she needs to achieve it. The individual can get help in setting up the plan from a VR counselor, an organization that helps people with disabilities, a benefits specialist or protection and advocacy organizations who have contracts with SSA, an employment network involved in the Ticket to Work program, or the local Social Security office. Next, the individual contacts the local SSA office to obtain a PASS form, completes it, and mails it to the Social Security office. If the goal is self-employment, there must also be a business plan.

Ticket to Work and Work Incentives Improvement Act of 1999.   In late 1999, the Congress enacted the Ticket to Work and Work Incentive Improvement Act (TWWIIA, Pub. L. No. 106-170). The law takes significant steps toward removing some of the most serious barriers to work faced by people with disabilities by providing quality, affordable health insurance for people with SSI and SSDI who work and by making it easier for people to choose their own provider of employment services in the private or public sector.

The SSA administers the act and the Department of Health and Human Services administers the health care component. The TWWIA was developed through a coordinated effort between the Federal Administration, Congress, and the disability community. TWWIILA was designed to provide better health care options for people with disabilities who work, extend Medicare coverage for people on disability insurance who return to work, and enhance employment-related services.

Under the voluntary Ticket to Work Program, individuals with disabilities can obtain job-related training and placement assistance from an approved provider of their choice. For example, youth in transition to work can receive employment services, career-related services, or other services to help them enter employment. Under the program, individuals with disabilities receiving SSI or Title II (SSDI) benefits may receive a "ticket" or voucher to obtain employment services of their choice from within employment networks. Employment networks may include both state VR agencies and private and other public providers. Examples of employment services include VR counseling, assistive technology, or job coaching. Employment networks are private organizations or government agencies that have agreed to work with SSA to provide employment services to persons with disabilities at no cost.

The second measure expands health care coverage so that individuals with disabilities will be able to become employed without fear of losing their health insurance (U.S. Department of Labor, Office of Disability Employment Policy, 2001a). The Ticket to Work Program has helped many young people make the transition into employment. Two federally funded studies published in 2000 (Bruyere, 2001; Loprest & Maag, 2001) show that much remains to be done to improve access to employment for persons with disabilities. Key national and local initiatives are needed in the areas of preparation, education, and training of persons with disabilities; outreach by the employment community to recruit persons with disabilities; a better understanding of reasonable accommodation in the workplace; and a concerted effort to break through attitudinal barriers that are detrimental to full integration of people with disabilities into the employment arena (Justesen & Justesen, 2000).

Fair Labor Standards Act

The Fair Labor Standards Act (FLSA) protects workers from unfair employment practices. The law was passed in 1938 after the Depression, when many employers took advantage of the tight labor market and subjected workers to dismal conditions and impossible hours. In 1985, however, Congress mandated that the act apply to all state and local government employees. It is one of the most complex laws of the workplace and has been amended many times.

The U.S. Department of Labor is responsible for monitoring child-labor laws, minimum wages, overtime pay, and subminimum wage certification. The law states that if an employer–employee relationship exists, then the youth (or adult) must be paid the prevailing or minimum wage as well as overtime pay. The law includes specific criteria that define an employer–employee relationship and it applies to all youth, including youth with disabilities, whether they participate in transition programs as trainees or as employees (Fair Minimum Wage Act of 2007). The act also addresses work-related issues such as minimum wage, labor standards protection for prison inmates, strengthening of child-labor law, status of "model garment" workers and industrial home workers. The act also addresses labor standards for workers who are blind and disabled, overtime pay revisions to allow flexibility, and a provision to allow employers to benefit from services of a volunteer for a 6-month period without wages.

FLSA Supports Employment of Youths with Disabilities.   The FLSA has many provisions that allow for training and work internships at modified wage structures. Many youths with disabilities participate in work-based training using special wage arrangements with businesses in coordination with career-technical education programs in secondary schools (Abrahams et al., 2001). Pertinent provisions of the act that support youth in employment while they are in high school include the following:

1. *Subminimum wage provisions:* The act provides for the employment of certain individuals at wage rates below the statutory minimum. Such individuals include student learners (career-technical education students), as well as full-time students in retail or service establishments, agriculture, or institutions of higher education. Also included are individuals whose earning or productive capacity is impaired by a physical or mental disability, including those related to age or injury, for the work to be performed. Employment at less than the minimum wage is authorized to prevent curtailment of opportunities for employment. Such employment is permitted only under certificates issued by the U.S. Department of Labor, Wage and Hour Division (Fair Minimum Wage Act of 2007).

2. *Youth minimum wage:* A minimum wage of not less than $4.25 an hour is permitted for employees younger than 20 during their first 90 consecutive calendar days with an employer. Employers are prohibited from taking any action to displace employees in order to hire employees at the youth minimum wage. Also prohibited are partial displacements such as reducing employees' hours, wages, or employment benefits.

3. *Nonagricultural jobs (child labor):* Regulations governing youth employment in nonfarm jobs differ somewhat from those pertaining to agricultural employment. In nonfarm work, the permissible jobs and hours of work, by age, are as follows:

a. Youths 18 years or older may perform any job, whether hazardous or not, for unlimited hours.

b. Youths 16 and 17 years old may perform any nonhazardous job, for unlimited hours.

c. Youths 14 and 15 years old may work outside school hours in various nonmanufacturing, nonmining, nonhazardous jobs under the following conditions: no more than 3 hours on a school day, 18 hours in a school week, 8 hours on a nonschool day, or 40 hours in a nonschool week. Also, work may not begin before 7 a.m., nor end after 7 p.m., except from June 1 through Labor Day, when evening hours are extended to 9 p.m. Under a special provision, youths 14 and 15 years old enrolled in an approved work experience and career exploration program (WECEP) may be employed for up to 23 hours in school weeks and 3 hours on school days (including during school hours). The minimum age for most nonfarm work is 14. At any age, youths, however, may deliver newspapers; perform in radio, television, movie, or theatrical productions; work for parents in their solely owned nonfarm business (except in manufacturing or on hazardous jobs); or gather evergreens and make evergreen wreaths (Abrahams et al., 2001).

Recent Amendments.   On May 25, 2007, a supplemental appropriations bill (H.R. 2206) was signed into law which contains the Fair Minimum Wage Act of 2007. This provision amends FLSA to provide for the increase of the federal minimum wage to $7.25 an hour by the summer of 2009.

The Assistive Technology Act of 2004

The **Assistive Technology Act** of 2004 (Tech Act, Pub. L. No. 108-364) assists states to develop comprehensive, consumer-responsive programs of technology-related assistance and to extend the availability of technology to individuals with disabilities and their families (Congressional Research Service, 2004a). The AT act extends through FY 2010 funds for (a) State grants for AT and for national activities and (b) State grants for AT related protection and advocacy services.

For some individuals with disabilities, assistive technology devices and assistive technology services are necessary to enable the individuals to (a) have greater control over their lives; (b) participate in, and contribute more fully to, activities in their home, school, and work environments, and in their communities; (c) interact to a greater extent with individuals who do not have disabilities; and (d) benefit from opportunities that are taken for granted by individuals who do not have disabilities. Progress has been made in the development of assistive technology devices, including adaptations to existing equipment, which significantly benefit individuals with disabilities of all ages. Such devices can be used to increase the involvement of such individuals in, and reduce expenditures associated with, programs and activities such as early intervention, education, rehabilitation and training, employment, residential living, independent living, recreation, and other aspects of daily living (Tech Act of 2004).

AT and Transition.   There are many reasons for the increase in demand for assistive technology. First, students in special education often rely on assistive technology to participate in educational programming. As these youth transition to adult services, they will need similar technology to assist them in their pursuit of higher education and employment (CSAVR, 2005; 2006). Second, America's reliance on an information-based economy has made the use of computers ubiquitous in the workplace. Individuals with disabilities often require additional software or customized assistive technology that enables them to make use of the computer systems that are widely needed to perform in the workplace.

New Provisions.   The 2004 Amendments added several new provisions: (a) a national public awareness toolkit to inform individuals and organizations about the availability of AT devices and services, (b) research and development grants and contracts, (c) a training and technical assistance program to disseminate information and provide training and technical assistance to states, and (d) data collection and reporting assistance.

Developmental Disabilities Assistance and Bill of Rights Act of 2000 (Pub. L. No. 106-402)

The Developmental Disabilities Assistance and Bill of Rights Act was authorized in 2000 as Pub. L. No. 106-402. The purpose of the act is to provide federal financial assistance to states and public and nonprofit agencies in order to assure that individuals with developmental disabilities and their families participate in the design of and have access to needed community services, individualized supports, and other forms of assistance. Such assistance is designed to promote independence, productivity, and self-determination in the lives of these individuals and create opportunities for them to participate fully in community life through programs authorized under the act (Association of University Centers on Disability, 2007). The Developmental Disabilities Act is currently under consideration in Congress. The Administration on Developmental Disabilities, Administration for Children and Families, in the U.S. Department of Health and Human Service administers DD Act programs.

Federal funds support the development and operation of state councils, protection and advocacy systems, and university centers (formerly known as university-affiliated programs), and projects of national significance. Projects of National Significance focus on emerging areas of concern and support local implementation of innovative programs that offer practical solutions and provide results and information for possible national replication.

The 2000 reauthorization added a new authority to provide services and activities for families of individuals with developmental disabilities and workers who assist them. These programs have made community living possible for individuals across our nation with significant disabilities. Currently, four programs are funded under the act: (a) State Councils on Developmental Disabilities (DD Councils) that seek to improve services and supports, design or deliver services that promote positive and meaningful outcomes for individuals with developmental disabilities and their families; (b) Protection and Advocacy Systems that protect and advocate for the rights of individuals with developmental disabilities and their families and to assure that they have access to needed community services, individualized supports, and other forms of assistance that promote self-determination; and (c) University Centers for Excellence in Developmental Disabilities (UCEDD) that conduct interdisciplinary research and training, develop best practices, and provide technical assistance to local and state agencies serving individuals with developmental disabilities and their families (Association of University Centers on Disability, 2007; SABE USA, 2000).

SUMMARY

During the past few decades, several laws have emphasized the need to improve transition services nationally. The federal government has assumed a major role in stimulating state and local effort through a variety of policy, interagency, systems change, model demonstration, and research initiatives. The federal government has initiated these programs to shape systemic reform, service improvement, and capacity building in the states by involving a broad spectrum of stakeholders in the change process, including parents and individuals with disabilities. The major goals of these initiatives were to (a) increase availability and quality of transition assistance; (b) improve the ability of professionals, parents, and advocates to work with youths to promote successful transition; (c) improve working relationships among those involved in delivery of transition services; and (d) create an incentive for collaboration among agencies concerned with transition, including postsecondary agencies.

This chapter reviewed many education and related laws and recent case laws that give states and local educational agencies the mandate, authority, and guidance to implement transition service systems. The chapter examined the new provisions for transition services in the reauthorization of the Individuals with Disabilities Act of 2004, the No Child Left Behind Act, and the responsibility of nonschool agencies as partners in the provision of transition services. Laws that provide the authority and funding for programs and services for youth and adults with disabilities frequently change as Congress seeks to improve, align, and consolidate established programs and services. It is important that youth, families, transition service providers, educators, employers, and others become familiar with these laws and their impact on transition services for youth with disabilities.

Two central goals in the United States are to preserve democracy and build our national economy by promoting full participation of all citizens in the work of the nation. To increase the likelihood that all youths can and will prepare for participation in their communities, educational institutions are seeking to provide direct assistance in transition from school to adult life and constructive citizenship. Although implementation remains incomplete in most states, in local communities where the commitment and leadership are strong and research-based practices are implemented, youth outcomes show significant improvement. Although still in early stages of development, transition practices are advancing at a promising pace.

KEY TERMS AND PHRASES

adequate yearly progress
age of majority
Americans with Disabilities Act
Assistive Technology Act
Carl D. Perkins Career and Technical
    Education Improvement Act
community-based learning
Developmental Disabilities Assistance
    and Bill of Rights Act
Education for All Handicapped Child-
    ren Act

four generations of transition
Higher Education Act Amendments
Individuals with Disabilities Education
    Act of 2004
J.L. v. Mercer Island School District
No Child Left Behind Act of 2001
reasonable accommodations
Rehabilitation Act Amendments
Rowley case
standards-based education (SBE)
Workforce Investment Act Amendments

QUESTIONS FOR REFLECTION, THINKING, AND SKILL BUILDING

1. Identify several broad educational reforms that have impacted transition services. How have they impacted transition services?

2. Why did Congress revise IDEA in 1997 to include 14- to 16-year-old youth in the requirements for transition services? Discuss how the IDEA 2004 shift to age 16 impacts transition planning for youth.

3. What recommendations would you make to policy makers for revising transition requirements in the next reauthorization of IDEA?

4. Provide a rationale for why nonschool agencies should share responsibility with schools for transition services. Identify some of the nonschool agencies that IDEA 2004 refers to. What do IDEA regulations require of nonschool agencies?

5. After two decades of implementation of transition services, outcomes for youth with disabilities are very slowly improving. What do you believe to be the greatest barriers the states face in implementing transition services?

6. Discuss in a group the implications of the *J.L. v. Mercer Island School District* case for transition services. What does it mean for you?

7. In a small team, develop an outline for an inservice training curriculum for teachers that addresses important things to know about transition services and the laws that authorize and promote it. Present that outline to the class.

8. Conduct a mock hearing before "Congress" in which members of the class divide into two groups: (a) a group of members of Congress inquiring about the status of transition services in the states and (b) a group of administrators, teachers, parents, students, and others who will provide testimony on the status of transition services from the state and local perspective. Construct the questions from members of Congress and the responses from those testifying.

Comparison of IDEA 1997 And 2004 Provisions Related to Transition Services

IDEA 1997	IDEA 2004 (changes in boldface)
PART A: GENERAL PROVISIONS	
Section 601: Short Title; Table of Contents; Findings; Purposes	**Section 601: Short Title; Table of Contents; Findings; Purposes**
(d) PURPOSES: The purposes of this title are—	(d) PURPOSES: The purposes of this title are—
(1)(A) to ensure that all children with disabilities have available to them a free appropriate public education that emphasizes special education and related services designed to meet their unique needs and prepare them for employment and independent living	(1)(A) to ensure that all children with disabilities have available to them a free appropriate public education that emphasizes special education and related services designed to meet their unique needs and prepare them **for further education,** employment, and independent living
Section 602: Definitions	**Section 602: Definitions**
(30) TRANSITION SERVICES: The term "transition services" means a coordinated set of activities for a student with disability that—	(34) TRANSITION SERVICES: The term "transition services" means a coordinated set of activities for a **child** with a disability that—
(A) is designed within an outcome-oriented process, which promotes movement from school to postschool activities, including postsecondary education, vocational training, integrated employment (including supported employment), continuing and adult education, adult services, independent living, or community participation;	(A) is designed to be **within a results**-oriented process, **that is focused on improving the academic and functional achievement of the child with a disability to facilitate the child's** movement from school to postschool activities, including postsecondary education, vocational **education,** integrated employment (including supported employment), continuing and adult education, adult services, independent living, or community participation;
(B) is based upon the individual student's needs, taking into account the student's preferences and interests; and	(B) is based on the individual child's needs, taking into account the **child's strengths,** preferences, and interests; and
(C) includes instruction, related services, community experiences, the development of employment and other postschool adult living objectives, and when appropriate, acquisition of daily living skills and functional vocational evaluation.	(C) includes instruction, related services, community experiences, the development of employment and other postschool adult living objectives, and when appropriate, acquisition of daily living skills and functional vocational evaluation.

(Continued)

PART B: ASSISTANCE FOR EDUCATION OF ALL CHILDREN WITH DISABILITIES

IDEA 1997	IDEA 2004 (Changes in bold)
Section 614: Individualized Education Programs	**Section 614: Individualized Education Programs**
(c) Additional Requirements for Evaluation and Reevaluations	(c) Additional Requirements for Evaluation and Reevaluations
(5) Evaluations Before Change in Eligibility—A local educational agency shall evaluate a child with a disability in accordance with this section before determining that the child is no longer a child with a disability.	(5) Evaluations Before Change in Eligibility—
	(A) In General—**Except as provided in subparagraph (B)**, a local educational agency shall evaluate a child with a disability in accordance with this section before determining that the child is no longer a child with a disability.
	(B) Exception—
	(i) In General—The evaluation described in subparagraph (A) shall not be required before the termination of a child's eligibility under this part due to graduation from secondary school with a regular diploma, or due to exceeding the age eligibility for a free appropriate public education under State law.
	(ii) Summary of Performance—For a child whose eligibility under this part terminates under circumstances described in clause (i), a local education agency shall provide the child with a summary of the child's academic achievement and functional performance, which shall include recommendations on how to assist the child in meeting the child's postsecondary goals.
Section 614: Individualized Education Programs	**Section 614: Individualized Education Programs**
(d) Individualized Education Programs	(d) Individualized Education Programs
(1) Definitions	(1) Definitions
(A) Individualized Education Program	(A) Individualized Education Program

(VII) the projected date for the beginning of services and modifications, the anticipated frequency, location and duration of those services . . .

(VIII) beginning not later than the first IEP to be in effect when the child is 16, and updated annually thereafter—

(aa) appropriate measurable postsecondary goals based upon age appropriate transition assessments related to training, education, employment, and, where appropriate, independent living skills;

(bb) the transition services (including courses of study) needed to assist the child in reaching those goals; and

(cc) beginning not later than 1 year before the child reaches the age of majority under State law, a statement that the child has been informed of the child's rights under this title, if any, that will transfer to the child on reaching the age of majority under section 615(m).

(ii) Rule of Construction—Nothing in this section shall be construed to require—

(I) that additional information be included in a child's IEP beyond what is explicitly required in this section; and

(II) the IEP Team to include information under 1 component of a child's IEP that is already contained under another component of such IEP. [Note: The following text appears in Part B, Section 614 (d)(1)(A)(i), as part of the definition of what an IEP includes.]

(II) a statement of measurable annual goals, including academic and functional goals, designed to—

(aa) meet the child's needs that result from the child's disability to enable the child to be involved in and make progress in the general education curriculum; and

(bb) meet each of the child's other educational needs that result from the child's disability;

(Continued)

(vii)(I) beginning at age 14, and updated annually, a statement of the transition service needs of the child under the applicable components of the child's IEP that focuses on the child's courses of study (such as participation in advanced-placement courses or a vocational education program);

(II) beginning at age 16 (or younger, if determined appropriate by the IEP Team), a statement of needed transition services for the child, including, when appropriate, a statement of the interagency responsibilities or any needed linkages; and

(III) beginning at least one year before the child reaches the age of majority under State law, a statement that the child has been informed of his or her rights under this title, if any, that will transfer to the child on reaching the age of majority under section 615(m); and

(viii) a statement of—

(I) how the child's progress toward the annual goals described in clause (ii) will be measured; and

(II) how the child's parents will be regularly informed (by such means as periodic report cards), at least as often as parents are informed of their nondisabled children's progress of—

(aa) their child's progress toward the annual goals described in clause (ii); and

(bb) the extent to which that progress is sufficient to enable the child to achieve the goals by the end of the year.

(III) a description of how the child's progress toward meeting the annual goals described in subclause (II) will be measured and when periodic reports on the progress the child is making toward meeting the annual goals (such as through the use of quarterly or other periodic reports, concurrent with the issuance of report card) will be provided.

(D)(6). If a participating agency, fails to provide the transition services described in the IEP, the local educational agency shall reconvene the IEP team to identify strategies to meet the transition objectives for the child set out in the IEP.

(3) Development of IEP—
(A) In General—In developing each child's IEP, the IEP Team, subject to subparagraph (C), shall consider—

(i) the strengths of the child;
(ii) the concerns of the parents for enhancing the education of their child;
(iii) the results of the initial evaluation or most recent evaluation of the child; and
(iv) **the academic, developmental, and functional needs of the child.**

The IEP team **shall consider special factors** for children:

- whose **behavior** impedes learning
- who have **limited English proficiency**
- who are **blind or visually impaired**
- who are **deaf or hard of hearing** (Section 1414(d)(3)(B))

Multiyear IEPs:
Fifteen states may request approval to implement optional "comprehensive, multiyear IEPs" for periods of no longer than three years. IEP review dates must be based on "natural transition points."

---

(3) Development of IEP—

(A) In General—In developing each child's IEP, the IEP Team, subject to subparagraph (C), shall consider—

(i) the strengths of the child and the concerns of the parents for enhancing the education of their child; and
(ii) the results of the initial evaluation or most recent evaluation of the child.

Multiyear IEPs (no comparative language)

Parents have the right to opt-out of this program. The parent of a child served under a multiyear IEP can request a review of the IEP without waiting for the "natural transition point." (Section 1414(d)(5))

(6) Children with Disabilities in Adult Prisons—

(A) In General—The following requirements do not apply to children with disabilities who are convicted as adults under State law and incarcerated in adult prisons:

(i) The requirements contained in section 612(a)(17) and paragraph (1)(A)(v) of this subsection (relating to participation of children with disabilities in general assessments.)

(ii) The requirements of subclauses (I) and (II) of paragraph (1)(A)(vii) of this subsection (relating to transition planning and transition services), do not apply with respect to such children whose eligibility under this part will end, because of their age, before they will be released from prison.

(7) Children with Disabilities in Adult Prisons—

(A) In General—The following requirements **shall** not apply to children with disabilities who are convicted as adults under State law and incarcerated in adult prisons:

(i) The requirements contained in section 612(a)(16) and paragraph(1)(A)(i)(VI) (relating to participation of children with disabilities in general assessments).

(ii) The requirements of items (aa) and (bb) of paragraph (1)(A)(i)(VIII) (relating to transition planning and transition services), do not apply with respect to such children whose eligibility under this part will end, because of **such children's age, before such children** will be released from prison.

Appendix 4-2

The No Child Left Behind Act of 2001
Provisions Related to Transition

Provisions	Comment
Title I: Improving the Academic Achievement of the Disadvantaged	At-risk youth are more likely than their peers to drop out of school, experience educational failure, or be involved in activities that are detrimental to their health and safety. Available research shows that children raised in economically disadvantaged families are at greater risk of low academic achievement, behavioral problems, and poor health and have difficulties with adjustments to adulthood (Hale, 1998; Land & Legters, 2002).
Part C. Education of Migratory Children	
Section 1301 Program Purpose	
(5) design programs to help migratory children overcome educational disruption, cultural and language barriers, social isolation, health-related problems, and other factors that inhibit the ability of such children to do well in school, and to prepare such children to make a successful transition to postsecondary education or employment.	
Part D. Prevention and Intervention Programs for Children and Youth Who Are Neglected, Delinquent, or At-Risk	Provides transitions out of institutions into home schools. Nearly one third of the U.S. adult population does not advance beyond high school, and this proportion has remained relatively constant for nearly 30 years, according to Friedman (2000). It is estimated that approximately 1 million youth every year leave school without completing their basic educational requirements (Barr & Parrett, 2001). Adolescents with emotional and behavioral disabilities (EBD) have only a 41.9% graduation rate and the highest dropout rate of any disability category (U.S. Department of Education, Office of special Education, 2001).
Section 1402 Purpose and Program Authorization	
(2) to provide such children and youth with the services needed to make a successful transition from institutionalization to further schooling or employment;	
(3) to prevent at-risk youth from dropping out of school and to provide dropouts, and children and youth returning from correctional facilities or institutions for neglected or delinquent children and youth, with a support system to ensure their continued education	
Section 1414 State Plan and State Agency Applications	Strengthens transition services and supports for youth transferring into the community from correctional facilities such as adult jails, juvenile detention, less secure detention facilities, or protective shelters.
(B) for assisting in the transition of children and youth from correctional facilities to locally operated programs;	

Section 1415 Use of Funds

(B) concentrate on providing participants with the knowledge and skills needed to make a successful transition to secondary school completion, vocational or technical training, further education, or employment.

Section 1416 Institution-Wide Projects

(3) describes the steps the State agency has taken, or will take, to provide all children and youth under age 21 with the opportunity to meet challenging State academic content standards and student academic achievement standards in order to improve the likelihood that the children and youth will complete secondary school, attain a secondary diploma or its recognized equivalent, or find employment after leaving the institution.

Section 1418 Transition Services

Transition services—Each State agency shall reserve not less than 15% and not more than 30% of the amount the agency receives for any fiscal year to support

(1) projects that facilitate the transition of children and youth from State-operated institutions to schools served by local educational agencies; or

(2) the successful reentry of youth offenders, who are age 20 or younger and have received a secondary school diploma or its recognized equivalent, into postsecondary education, or vocational and technical training program, through strategies designed to expose the youth to, and prepare the youth for postsecondary education, or vocational and technical training programs, such as

(A) preplacement programs that allow adjudicated or incarcerated youth to audit or attend courses on college, university, or community college campuses, or through programs provided in the institution;

Strengthens the ability of youth exiting correctional facilities to enter postsecondary education or employment.

The school district program is required to attend to the transition and academic needs of students returning from correctional facilities. Often, there is a disconnect between the local schools and correctional facilities, which results in low student achievement or dropout. As students transition back to their local schools, follow-up services can ensure that their education continues and that they can meet the same challenging state standards required of all students.

Youth with disabilities are substantially overrepresented in the juvenile justice system (Rutherford et al., 1999). Youth with specific learning, emotional, or behavioral disabilities are more vulnerable to alternative placement outside their base school or in juvenile or adult corrections than youth not identified as disabled. Youth placed at risk for involvement in the juvenile justice system, including students with disabilities, must receive support and preventative services to minimize their vulnerability.

Ethnic minorities are dramatically overrepresented in the population of young offenders. A study conducted from 1988 to 1997 of youth held in public and private juvenile detention, correctional, and shelter facilities revealed that more than three quarters (86.5%) of the 105,000 juveniles studied were young men from ethnic minority backgrounds (40% Black and 18.5% Hispanic), ranging in age from 13 to 17 years.

(Continued)

Provisions	Comment

Provisions

(B) worksite schools, in which institutions of higher education and private or public employers partner to created programs to help students make a successful transition to postsecondary education and employment;

(C) essential support services to ensure the success of youth, such as— personal, vocational, technical and academic counseling; placement services designed to place the youth in a university, collage or junior college program; counseling services, and job placement services.

Title V: Promoting Informed Parental Choice and Innovative Programs

Subpart 21 Women's Educational Equity Act

Section 5611(2) Support and Technical Assistance

(A) (iv) school-to-work transition programs, guidance and counseling activities, and other programs to increase opportunities for women and girls to enter a technologically demanding workplace and in particular to enter highly skills, high-paying careers in which women and girls have been underrepresented;

Title VII: Indian, Native Hawaiian, and Alaska Native Education

Subpart 2 Special Programs and Project to Improve Educational Opportunities for Indian Children

Section 7121 Improvement of Educational Opportunities for Indian Children

(C) Grants authorized;

(E) special compensatory and other programs and projects designed to assist and encourage Indian children to enter, remain in, or reenter school, and to increase the rate of high school graduation;

Comment

Women and children account for more than three quarters of households with incomes below the poverty level. Children from racial minority groups are much more likely to live in poverty than are white children. Unmarried teen mothers need access to day care, transportation, and other supports that will enable them to work and pursue their education (National Council for Research on Women, 1998, 2001).

Native American students with disabilities face unique challenges to successful transition. Lack of familial support, lack of support networks for students with disabilities who enter higher education institutions, and chemical dependency play a role in the high dropout rates and the challenges in transitioning into adulthood successfully. In addition, other factors such as lack of employment opportunities, limited resources, and high poverty levels impede the ability of Native Americans to succeed in higher education and independent living. Unemployment rates run as high as 70% in some reservations, putting Native American youth, as a whole, at a heightened risk for failure to assume adult roles and responsibilities after leaving high school (Biasi, 2001; Leake, Kim-Rupnow, & Leung, 2003; Shafer & Rangasamy, 1995).

(F) comprehensive guidance, counseling and testing services;

(H) partnership programs between local educational agencies and institutions of higher education that allow secondary school students to enroll in courses at the postsecondary level to aid such students in the transition from secondary to postsecondary education;

(I) partnership projects between schools and local businesses for career-preparation programs designed to provide Indian youth with the knowledge and skills they need to make an effective transition from school to a high-skill wage career.

Chapter 5

Coordinating Systems and Agencies for Successful Transition

Carol A. Kochhar-Bryant

Collaboration is like dancing with an octopus. The work of building and sustaining school/community collaborations is a dance with multifaceted partners.

—Levine, 1998

Chapter Questions

- Why is service coordination important for transition services?
- What is service coordination?
- How has service coordination evolved as a practice?
- What philosophies have shaped the development of service coordination?
- What national and state policies promote service coordination?
- What is the role of the family in system coordination for transition?

INTRODUCTION

Efforts to coordinate services for children and youth with special learning needs have been a central focus of federal, state, and local governments and the schools for several decades. Over the past few decades, the benefits of case management and interagency coordination in systems such as health care, mental health, rehabilitation, and adult disability services have caught the attention of educators and policy makers.

This chapter defines *interagency* **service coordination (system coordination)** and its relationship to transition services. It also provides an overview of the ideas, philosophies, and public policies that have guided interagency coordination for transition services for youth with special learning needs and examines the role of the family.

➡ WHY IS SERVICE COORDINATION IMPORTANT FOR TRANSITION SERVICES?

Introduction to Service Coordination

In education and human services, a systematic approach to transition service delivery means developing goals, activities, and approaches to address the holistic needs of children and youth with disabilities in a coordinated manner. The individual is viewed as having interconnected needs that often require coordinated responses from services within the school and between school and community agencies (e.g., vocational rehabilitation, mental health, adult services, public health, social services, juvenile services, and family services). Coordination is about connecting people within systems and the extraordinary commitment that is required to accomplish it.

The Individuals with Disabilities Education Act (IDEA) 2004 holds schools responsible for ensuring that students with disabilities receive appropriate transition services and planning. Reflecting the understanding that schools cannot do it alone, however, *IDEA and No Child Left Behind (NCLB) also require that schools establish linkages with community and postsecondary agencies and share the responsibility for transition services.* Furthermore, IDEA requires states to have interagency agreements among state and local education agencies and public agencies. After several decades of mandates for "interagency collaboration," research shows that the concept of collaboration for transition services is not well understood at state and local levels, nor has it been widely tested and adopted (Research and Training Center on Service Coordination, 2001). There is a need for further development of models and best practices for school–community coordination for transition services.

Because approximately half of all students with disabilities (2003–2004) spend 80% or more of their day in a regular classroom (National Center on Education Statistics, 2005), there is a growing interest in linking the educational and community-based human service systems to provide comprehensive supports for children in general education (Dunst & Bruder, 2002; Hart, Zimbrich, & Whelley, 2002; Kendziora, Bruns, Osher, Pacchiona, & Mejia, 2001; National Center on Outcomes Research, 2001; Research and Training Center on Service Coordination, 2001; U.S. Department of Education, 2003; U.S. Government Accountability Office, 2004; Whelley, Hart, & Zafft, 2002). Such an approach requires that schools reach out beyond their boundaries and seek a shared responsibility from the many agencies that provide services for students.

The following example is based on an actual case and highlights the complexity of working across systems and services when students have complex and layered educational needs.

LET'S SEE IT IN ACTION! CASE EXAMPLE

A Family's Desperate Struggle

The worried family of Eric, a very bright 16-year-old, recently attended an interagency team meeting that included representatives from the County Public Schools, Mental Health Services, Alcohol and Drug Services, and Juvenile Services/Probation. Eric was failing ninth grade a second time, was on a CHINS petition (Child in Need of Supervision) through Juvenile Services, was participating in Alcohol and Drug Services by court order, and had been in weekly private mental health therapy. He was participating in outpatient alcohol and drug treatment services but was failing urine tests regularly. His behavior was deteriorating at home and he was becoming a danger to his family. His parents and former therapists all believed he needed intensive behavioral therapy in a residential treatment program. The school special education evaluation team would not refer him for special education because they believed his primary problems were conduct disorder and substance abuse, and IDEA did not provide services for students with these problems. The private mental health counselor said he could not continue to work with Eric because he needed to "get clean first," otherwise the family was wasting its money. He recommended residential treatment. The Alcohol and Drug Services Counselor said they could not refer Eric for residential treatment as long as he was willing to participate in outpatient treatment, and the parents would need to make a formal charge against him before he could be court ordered into residential treatment.

An interdisciplinary team (IDT) meeting was arranged that gathered representatives of all participating agencies. After all of the reports were reviewed, the IDT team leader explained that because Eric was over age 14, under state law this team could not forcibly place Eric into residential treatment unless he had a charge filed against him; the team could only recommend a "level of service." They recommended a dual diagnosis program and specifically referred him to an intensive Adolescent Day Treatment program in the local community. Eric's mother asked for copies of all reports from the agencies being represented at the IDT. They said they could not release them to her, because Eric was aged 16 and permission was needed.

Eric's mother, a monolith of patience and a master of record-keeping after years of being Eric's "case manager," proceeded to contact each of the agencies separately to obtain the reports.

She immediately made an appointment to visit the Day Treatment program. She learned that the program was a "dual diagnosis" program for youth with mental health and substance abuse problems and seemed to be what Eric needed. The program accepted 22 students each year and had a classroom ratio of 1:5. It was combined with an alternative school that was part of the public education system and aligned with the state curriculum. It had a structured behavioral component, a mental health counseling component, and family counseling services. Eric and the family would have a case manager and would also continue to receive outreach services by his probation officer during the evening and weekends. After the completion of the one-year program, program staff and the case manager would provide transition support for Eric's reentry into his home school. The family believed that this program represented hope for Eric's future.

From *Collaboration and System Coordination for Students With Special Needs: From Early Childhood to Post-secondary* (p. 69), by C. A. Kochhar-Bryant, 2008, Upper Saddle River, NJ: Pearson/Merril.

Service Coordination Is Central to Transition Service Delivery

Over the past few decades, the successes and benefits of interagency coordination in systems such as health care, mental health, rehabilitation, and adult disability services have caught the attention of educators and policy makers. Service coordination and multiagency collaboration continue to be primary factors in the transition success or failure for individuals with disabilities and their families. Among the purposes of a systematic approach to transition are (a) to facilitate interagency linkages, (b) to improve the ability of systems to respond to changing population needs, and (c) to reduce fragmentation of local services.

The term *service coordination* builds upon earlier terms that emerged in the fields of health, mental health, mental retardation, and rehabilitation in the 1960s—case management and interagency coordination. More than two decades ago, Bachrach (1986) defined case management within the mental health discipline as

> The integration of services on the patient level . . . someone in the system is taking charge and seeing to it that all the little bits and pieces of the fragmented service system begin to come together in some coherent way for the chronically mentally ill individual. It embodies the concepts of continuity and comprehensiveness in a personalized manner. (p. 174)

Figure 5–1 depicts the complexity of this shared system today.

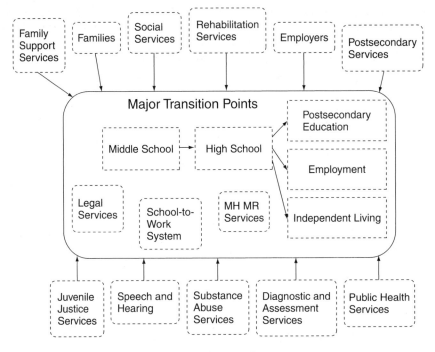

Figure 5–1   Shared Responsibility for the Service System
Source: Adapted from *Successful Inclusion: Practical Strategies for a Shared Responsibility* (p. 20), by C. A. Kochhar, L. L. West, & J. M. Taymans, 2000, Upper Saddle River, NJ: Merrill/Prentice Hall. Reprinted with permission.

A **systematic approach to transition services** means developing strategies to address the complex needs of youth with disabilities in an organized and coordinated manner that supports multiple pathways to successful transition. Research on system coordination reveals that effective interagency collaboration requires a comprehensive restructuring of our educational and employment preparation systems to better support youth with disabilities in the critical transition stages (Dunst & Bruder, 2002; Hasazi, Furney, & DeStefano, 1999; Johnson, Sharpe, & Stodden, 2000; Minnesota System of Interagency Coordination Communication Project, 2003; National Center on Secondary Education and Transition, 2002c; Research and Training Center on Service Coordination; 2001; Stodden, Jones, & Chang, 2002; Whelley et al., 2002).

Almost two decades ago, DeStefano and Wermuth (1992) explained that transition has shaped secondary school reform in at least three areas: (a) the development of linkages between school and postschool environments and a cadre of coordinators inside and outside the traditional secondary school setting; (b) a broadening of the secondary curriculum and programs and the provision of instructional and educational experiences and related services beyond those generally associated with academic outcomes; and (c) a change in the roles and skill requirements of secondary teachers and transition personnel to reflect expanded relationships outside the school and broadening of school programs and curricula. This emphasis on linkages between schools and communities challenges educational personnel to develop a systematic approach to transition service delivery based on bold reforms in the way education, employment, rehabilitation, and community service agencies work together to assist youth to make successful transitions to adulthood. Figure 5–1 depicts the complexity of the service system that shares the responsibility for youth transition.

The Value and Role of Service Coordination

Communities across the nation have been working to develop a systematic approach to transition service through interagency service coordination for a variety of reasons:

1. *Complexity of the service system:* The increasing complexity of the service system can be especially burdensome for students and families with complex needs who require a variety of support services to prepare for successful transition from school to postsecondary life. Families of youth with disabilities often need many support services to help the family cope as a family unit and, ultimately, the individual to participate and progress in education and work settings and function as independently as possible.

2. *Service disconnects:* Gaps or disconnects in the service system refers to several perplexing challenges for education and human service personnel:

a. The frustrations and anxieties that arise when a single individual in need must acquire transition services and supports from several separate and uncoordinated sources

b. The risk that the youth or family will be unable to find help because of the gap in services (e.g., absence of speech and hearing services in the school, or career assessments, when they are needed)

c. The variations among families in their capacity to access and effectively use services within the system (Kochhar-Bryant, 2008)

As a result of these gaps, families must retell their stories and provide background to each of the separate services agencies or professionals involved. When a system gap exists, there are typically incomplete, weak, or broken links between schools and community service agencies. There may be no formalized agreement between school and agency or among agencies, and there is often no single access or entry point to help the individual and family select and access the services they need.

3. *Interest in interdisciplinary linking:* Interest has surged for integrating educational and support services across disciplines. For example, in high schools, teachers and administrators are collaborating across curriculum areas. In middle schools, the needs of students and families with multiple challenges are being addressed by coordinating the expertise and resources of professionals in public health, social services, mental health and psychological services, counseling, and many others.

4. *The expanding role of early intervening services for students in transition from middle school to secondary school:* Recent research and practice have confirmed the value of early intervening services and systematic planning in preparing preadolescents to make the often-precarious transition from smaller middle school environments to large high school settings (Akos & Galassi, 2004a; Mizelle & Irvin, 2000; Morgan & Hertzog, 2001; National Middle School Association, September 2006; Smith,

2006; Zeedyk et al., 2003). In response to this new knowledge, IDEA 2004 legislation has mandated an expanded role for educators and related services personnel in preparing students for such transitions.

5. *The expanding role of business partnerships:* Business and industry have also become important partners in youth development and transition initiatives. Through active commitment and involvement, the private sector is linking with educational and community-based agencies to address the health, academic, career-vocational, and independent living needs of all youths, particularly those with disabilities (Hubbard, Bell, & Charner, 1998; Luecking, Fabian, & Tilson, 2004). Expanded private sector involvement is based on the assumption that effective school and community programs produce a better work force and citizenry and improve the quality of life for the individual and the community.

6. *Educating the whole person:* Schools and school-linked agencies are finding that as they improve their work together, outcomes for students improve as well. Shared approaches to and a shared responsibility for addressing student educational and developmental needs of the "whole child" bring to bear the combined thinking, planning, and resources of many professionals within the schools and in a variety of agencies (Conzemius & O'Neill, 2001). There is a growing recognition of the economic value of sharing resources across agencies to close persistent gaps in services for children and families who need them.

Service Coordination Is Essential to Larger System Change Initiatives

Interagency service coordination can be instrumental in supporting other broad school change efforts. For example, in many school systems, coordination of services between schools and community agencies have provided the necessary supports to help youth participate in community-based training in local businesses and to prepare for transition to postsecondary training and employment. Resources for systematic service delivery systems are typically shared among agencies such as the local educational agency, rehabilitation agencies, the workforce system, community mental health, and private nonprofit funds and may be supplemented by state and federal funds. In some states, interagency agreements are being used to coordinate large system change initiatives aimed at expanding and improving transition services.

Many states are forming partnerships among workforce development and rehabilitation agencies (authorized by the Workforce Investment Act [WIA]) and school-based transition services (authorized under IDEA). Most funding for state and local transition programs that serve youth with disabilities depends on the authority of three federal laws—the Individuals with Disabilities Education Act, Title I of the Workforce Investment Act, and the Vocational Rehabilitation Act found under Title IV of WIA (Crane, Gramlich, & Peterson, 2004; Timmons, 2007). Agencies are experimenting with blended funding, formal interagency agreements or memoranda of understanding (MOU), and single points of entry for services. Many states have existing interagency transition teams—for example, in Minnesota, the state legislature has put in place the Minnesota System of Interagency Coordination that is designed to encourage partnerships among groups serving youth with disabilities from birth to young adulthood (Timmons, Podmostko, Bremer, Lavin, & Wills, 2004).

Service coordination processes can facilitate school restructuring efforts. In the following examples, service coordination activities support broad change efforts designed to:

1. create connections among community services agencies (e.g., health and mental health services, social services, and family services) to improve secondary education and transition services;
2. create linkages between residential programs or state facilities for adolescents with disabilities to improve reentry into base schools; and
3. create pathways from high school to community college programs and provide outreach to adults in need of retraining and continuing education.

Processes of change and restructuring in schools represent new demands on professionals to change the way they function in their roles and the way they communicate and coordinate with each other—working outside their "scripts" (Smylie & Crowson, 1996). For example, in schools seeking to improve the performance of all students, especially those with disabilities, guidance counselors or specialists are being trained as in-school service coordinators with "caseloads" of students for whom they are responsible. These coordinators become the main contacts for the students, help arrange support services when needed, obtain assessments, and maintain records of service needs and the progress for each student.

State and Local Communities Recognize the Value of School-Linked Services

Recent arguments for implementing coordinated school-linked services rest on six basic premises. First, educators and policy makers have come to recognize that all facets of a child's well-being impact his or her potential for academic success and successful transition. Second, demographic trends indicate that an increasing number of American school-age children can be considered placed at risk for school failure and social problems such as substance abuse and delinquency (Center for Educational Research and Innovation, 1998; Cuban & Usdan, 2002; Hodgkinson, 2003). Third, prevention is more cost-effective for society than correction or remediation. Hodgkinson (2002) reports, for example, that there is an established relationship between dropping out of school and the probability of committing a crime and that dropout prevention is cheaper in the long run than the cost of incarceration.

Fourth, children who are at risk in the educational setting come to school with multiple problems that cut across conventional health, social, and education systems boundaries, problems that schools are often ill-equipped to handle alone (Cuban & Usdan, 2002; Kirst & Jehl, 1995; Rubin, 1992). Fifth, the current system of child-related service delivery is fragmented, often characterized by duplication, waste, and lack of coordination (Abrams & Gibbs, 2002; Kirst & Jehl, 1995; Timmons, 2007). Finally, because schools maintain long-term contact with children, they are the logical gateway for providing multiple services to children (Adelman & Taylor, 1997).

➡ WHAT IS SERVICE COORDINATION?

A Framework for Defining Service Coordination

Coordinated services refer to the delivery of services across systems to address the *holistic (whole person)* needs of students. When families seek services from two or more agencies with different rules for eligibility, a mechanism for connecting them with the agencies is extremely helpful. School–community partnerships can facilitate coordinated services by providing liaisons between families and service providing agencies (Bonner-Thompkins, 2000). System coordination should be viewed as a process that occurs on many levels, including (a) the individual and family, (b) the school, (c) the local educational agency and collaborating community agencies, and (d) the state educational agencies and collaborating state agencies (Figure 5-2).

Two Levels of Service Coordination.   Service coordination is essential for delivery of transition services at two levels: the transition service system or program level, and the *individual/family level.* At the individual/family level, a *transition program* refers to a coordinated local program of services designed to address the individual needs and postsecondary goals of a student. The expected outcome is individual achievement of transition goals.

The *transition service system* involves all of the school and community agencies, at the local and state levels, that collaborate to assist youth with transition from school to postsecondary education, employment, and independent living. The expected outcome at the local and state system level is to expand or make more responsive and flexible the entire service network that affects all students and all schools. The goal of larger system coordination at the local and state levels becomes one of broader system change and improvement, rather than one of change in the individual. At the system level, schools and community agencies work to (a) make services more available to students and families; (b) make services easier to coordinate among schools

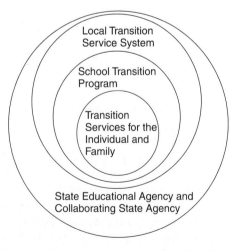

Figure 5–2   Service Coordination and Levels of the Transition System

and agencies; (c) improve linkages among services at key transition points for students; (d) improve projections of services and close gaps in services; (e) improve interagency training of professionals; and (f) evaluate service outcomes. **Service coordination functions** are focused on expanding or sustaining the availability of school-linked services to a whole population of students within a state, a local school district, or school cluster.

Several functions or tasks also make up the process of system coordination at state, local, and school levels. These can be categorized into eight sets of activities, as follows: information and referral, identification and preparation, assessment and evaluation, transition program planning and development, service coordination/linking, service monitoring and follow-along, individual and interagency advocacy, and service evaluation and follow-up (Kochhar-Bryant, 2008). These functions will be discussed in greater detail later in this chapter.

Dimensions of Service Coordination. Service coordination also involves several dimensions that, when aligned with one another, contribute to the effectiveness of service coordination. The dimensions include service philosophy and principles, policies and legal requirements, procedures for interagency agreements, and service coordination outcomes. If these dimensions are not in agreement, then the effectiveness of service coordination will be diminished. In other words, if a local system's interagency agreement is not consistent with its service philosophy (e.g., student self-determination), then the service coordination will be less effective than it could be. Similarly, if the local level system is seeking to develop interagency coordination but state interagency requirements or guidelines are weak, then the strength of the local coordination may be reduced. Furthermore, if a local system is not addressing the legal requirements for interagency coordination under IDEA, then it is unlikely that the basic functions of service coordination will be implemented. Figure 5–3 depicts these dimensions, levels, and functions of system coordination.

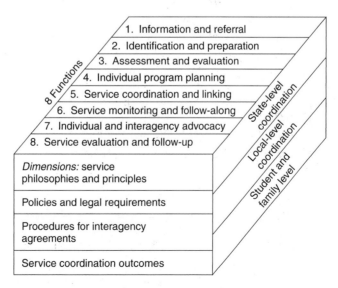

Figure 5–3 Dimensions of System Coordination

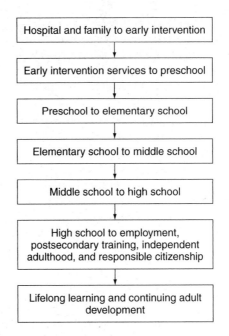

Figure 5–4   The Continuum of Transition Passages

System-level service coordination represents a range of relationships among disciplines and service agencies *because no single solution for improving coordination can be applied to all individuals or all communities.* Educational needs are thought to be best addressed, not from the perspective of a single institution such as the school but from multiple perspectives and a broadly shared understanding. Many community sectors must bring their collective knowledge and skills together to address the complex developmental and educational needs of individuals with disabilities as they make difficult transitions throughout their lives. These transitions, or *passages,* are depicted in Figure 5-4.

Many educators and human services personnel remain focused on the "here and now" for the student or are concerned with the current developmental stage. For example, just as it is typically difficult for a ninth-grade teacher to look back along the continuum or consider what has occurred in earlier years in the family of a student she now teaches, similarly, she may not look ahead along the continuum to get to know the postschool options and appreciate the complex choices that students face upon leaving school. Professionals who collaborate to provide transition services are more effective when they understand the full continuum of passages in a young person's life.

Defining Interagency Service Coordination for Transition

Interagency partnerships have typically been viewed as relationships that involve at least two key disciplines or agencies collaborating for a common purpose. To meet the complex education and transition needs of individuals today, schools must collaborate with a broad range of service agencies, parents, consumers, and the private sector to create *connected and supportive systems in the community*. This means that each component part of the system is connected and is working together for a common goal. Each part of the system is dedicated to ensuring that each youth preparing for transition from the school system is connected with the services he or she needs before leaving, at the time of exit, and in the postsecondary environment. Yet, these complex connections or relationships are much more than collections of agencies with a common purpose. *Each agency in a system is dedicated to contributing to the well-being and development of individuals with disabilities and to appraising and responding to the changing needs of the service population and the service environment.* Because of the changing environment of service organizations, the relationships among them must be *dynamic and continually evolving*.

Systematic Strategy.   In a *system*, elements are assembled to form a coordinated and unitary whole. In education and human services, a *systematic strategy* for transition means developing goals, activities, and approaches to addressing the complex needs of youth in an organized, connected, and coordinated manner. The individual is viewed as having complex and interconnected needs that require coordinated responses from service agencies. Such responses involve several service organizations that coordinate their goals, efforts, and resources to address problems and create solutions that will improve the service system as a whole for all individuals served. The definition of *service coordination*, therefore, should reflect three assumptions:

1. Interagency and interdisciplinary relationships are *formalized* and the respective roles of agencies and personnel are *clarified*.
2. Interagency and interdisciplinary relationships are *dynamic and responsive* to change in the service environment.
3. The system relationships should result in goals, strategies, and outcomes that systematically address the priority needs of persons being served by the system (Kochhar-Bryant, 2008).

A coordinated interagency service system is a systematic, comprehensive, and coordinated system of secondary education and transition for individuals with disabilities, which is provided in their communities in the most integrated settings possible and in a manner that promotes individual choice and decision making. Interagency service coordination may also be defined as a strategy for mobilizing and organizing all of the appropriate resources to link the individual with needed services to achieve individualized education program (IEP) goals and successful transition outcomes. Transition, therefore, is not a single passage or bridge between school and adult life for students with disabilities. It is a comprehensive and coordinated planning process that provides ample time and support to prepare the youth to successfully complete a secondary program of study and to achieve post-school goals.

In applying this definition, a coordinated interagency service system for transition

1. includes activities, goals, and strategies to improve the availability of and access to needed services by individuals and groups;

2. includes systematic strategies explicitly designed to restructure and improve education or community services;
3. uses both local and statewide system change strategies to assist local education and community service organizations to develop interagency collaboration;
4. values student- or consumer-centered goal-setting that focuses the coordination efforts on (a) end results expected for the individual and (b) maximizing the individual's level of potential and capacity for personal decision making (self-determination).

The general goal of service coordination is to ensure that students who may need services from both school and community agencies receive the services they need in a timely manner—to do whatever it takes (Friesen & Poertner, 1997; National Center on Outcomes Research, 2001; National Center on Secondary Education and Transition, 2002).

Introduction to Eight Basic Functions of Service Coordination

This section defines the essential elements or functions of service coordination that have been applied to assist youth in transition. In 1979, the Joint Commission on Accreditation of Healthcare Organizations published a set of functions that became widely accepted: assessment, planning, linking, monitoring, and advocacy. On the basis of a broad study of service coordination in several service sectors, Kochhar-Bryant (2008) identified additional discrete functions or clusters of activities that represent the mechanisms that agencies create to meet the common needs of their consumers in collaborative and systematic ways:

1. Information and referral
2. Identification and preparation
3. Assessment and evaluation
4. Individual program planning and development
5. Service coordination and linking
6. Service monitoring and follow-along
7. Individual and interagency advocacy
8. Service evaluation and follow-up

These eight functions can be applied at the *individual, program, and system (interagency) levels* and each will be discussed separately in the following sections (see Figure 5–5).

Function 1: Information and Referral. Information and referral activities vary widely among interagency systems which define the function in one of two ways:

1. *Very narrowly,* as information-giving to the public and the referral of youth and families to agency services for which they are eligible, or

8 SERVICE COORDINATION FUNCTIONS	SELF-DETERMINATION OPPORTUNITIES FOR STUDENTS
Information and referral	• Proactively request information about available transition services and supports (both in-school and out-of-school youth). • Talk to other students receiving transition services.
Identification and preparation	• Ask peers about transition service supports and opportunities. • Talk with the family about goals and interests. • Get involved in early planning.
Assessment and evaluation	• Understand one's own learning needs, interests, and goals. • Understand one's own career–vocational interests and levels of functioning. • Seek to understand the assessments and evaluation information.
IEP/transition planning and development	• Learn self-determination skills. • Learn how to choose short-term and long-range goals and understand what the time lines mean. • Learn how to direct an IEP meeting.
Service coordination and linking	• Learn about community agencies and the services they provide. • Keep in regular contact with the coordinator or case manager. • Help the case manager stay in touch with the family.
Service monitoring and follow-along	• Help teachers and service coordinators know what has been accomplished at school and at home (they may miss things). • Have regular meetings.
Individual and interagency advocacy	• Joint support groups and self-advocacy groups in the high school or postsecondary institution. • Join youth advisory groups and disability-rights groups. • Join youth policy advisory groups.
Service evaluation and follow-up	• Let service coordinators know what services and supports were most helpful through high school. • Let service coordinators know what happens after high school. • Let them know what adult or community services you enroll in, and which benefit you the most. • Return to high school as a guest to help others plan for transition. • Get back in touch if you do not complete high school.

Figure 5–5 Aligning Self-Determination and Service Coordination

2. *Broadly,* with extensive outreach activities, aggressive parent and community education, and interagency case-finding activities to identify different groups of individuals needing transition services. (IDEA now requires that schools reach out to youth who have dropped out or who wish to reenter and complete high school.)

For some students and families with complex needs, creative attempts at outreach are needed. Often, outreach and referral activities must be conducted in places that are closest to the student and family. For example, special education students who need rehabilitative services can often be encouraged to accept such assistance if services are offered at the local school. *Individual* information and referral includes activities such as the following:

1. Identifying and conducting outreach to eligible in-school students who are not currently benefiting from transition services
2. Identifying and conducting outreach to eligible students who are out of school or in alternative placements and who could benefit from transition services
3. Disseminating information to students and families about community resources and how to access them
4. Developing a single point of entry or *first contact* for transition services
5. Managing referrals and follow-up for transition services
6. Decreasing the amount of time between the individual's initial contact and entry into services or programs
7. Managing expanding caseloads

Many cooperating agencies are working toward improved outreach and identification of eligible target groups to ensure that transition services reach the populations in the greatest need. When the public learns about transition services and supports through an organized and coordinated public information and referral strategy, the service system is more likely to be perceived as accessible, responsive, and supportive.

Function 2: Identification and Preparation.   At the individual level, identification and preparation involve procedures for determining individual readiness for transition planning and services and matching individual service needs with appropriate supportive agencies. Identification and preparation activities may include the following:

1. Developing criteria for early transition assessment and planning at age 14 (as IDEA 2004 permits) or at the time of transition from middle or junior high to high school
2. Making services accessible for the student and family (i.e., physical access, hours of operation, transportation, and costs)
3. Obtaining and documenting informed consent
4. Developing and maintaining student records on early planning and assessment
5. Involving families in early planning processes

At the *interagency or system level,* identification and preparation mean developing an interagency database on student support needs. Through joint data collection, agencies can compare information about different groups of students and can help each other anticipate future service needs. Function 2 also involves developing policies and procedures for identifying students who need early transition support before age 16 and for implementing such supports.

Function 3: Assessment and Evaluation.   Needs assessment is the process of gathering and interpreting information about the education, health, or human service needs of individuals in the service system and using this information to establish service priorities and individual goals and objectives (as documented in their IEPs and transition plans). Needs assessments are used for decision making in a collaborative way among the service coordinator, student, family, teachers, and other relevant personnel to address the following key questions:

1. What is the current functioning of the student (social, intellectual, physical, career-vocational, etc.), and what are his or her strengths and needs in relation to post-secondary goals?
2. What features of the individual's environment or milieu support or inhibit improved functioning?
3. What are the career-vocational preferences, interests, and current level of functioning of the individual?
4. What goals and objectives for improved functioning should be identified and included in the IEP and transition plan, and what are the priorities?
5. What resources and services are necessary to accomplish these goals and objectives?
6. What procedures and schedule will be used for monitoring progress toward these goals and objectives?
7. What outcome criteria will be used to evaluate results? (Clark, 1996; Epstein, Rudolph, & Epstein, 2000; Kortering, Sitlington, & Braziel, 2004; Miller, Lombard, & Corbey, 2006; Neubert, 2003; Sitlington, Neubert, Begun, Lombard, & Leconte, 2007).

Evaluation refers to the interpretation of assessment information for the development of educational and transition goals and plans.

A needs assessment should focus on both the individual's current level of functioning and his or her highest level of functioning before seeking services. A needs assessment should also address the whole person, including academic, social, career-vocational, and independent living domains (Epstein et al., 2000; Leconte, 1994; Leconte & Newbert, 1997; Sax & Thoma, 2002; Sitlington et al., 2007; Timmons et al., 2004). On the basis of a thorough assessment of individual needs, the service coordinator can establish priorities for services to the student. Assessment activities at the *individual level* include the following:

1. Conducting comprehensive assessments of strengths and developmental needs in relevant functional domains (physical development, independent functioning, social, family or natural support, behavioral, academic and career-vocational, employment, legal, transportation, recreation or leisure, health, physical, psychological, and psychiatric status)
2. Reviewing assessments and renewing them periodically
3. Communicating and interpreting assessment information
4. Adapting assessment tools for individuals with disabilities and eliminating cultural bias
5. Documenting assessment and diagnostic information
6. Making specific recommendations for interventions on individual transition plans on the basis of assessment information in all relevant functional domains

An important step for teachers and service coordinators is to gather and share all available assessment information, including with families, to define new goals or expectations that should be established for students in the transition plan. Table 5–1 lists the elements of a comprehensive individual functional needs assessment for youth

Table 5–1 Elements of a Comprehensive Individual Functional Needs Assessment
for Youth Preparing for Transition

Educational placement and academic skills
Current school placement and grade level
Nature of disability
School attendance patterns and record
Extracurricular school activities
School performance and grades
Diplomas or certificates

Career–vocational and technical skills
Employment history and patterns of performance
Career preferences and interests
Employment and training program participation
Career–vocational/technical skills gained
Career–technical certificates or licenses
Work behaviors and readiness assessments
Work ethic and beliefs

Independent living and self-determination skills
Self-determination skills
Meal preparation
Self-help skills (dressing, bathing, cleaning, etc.)
Maintenance of home or personal space
Basic safety and self-protective skills (locking doors, turning off stove, knowledge of Emergency numbers, etc.)
Community participation history
Mobility

Management of personal health
Personal hygiene
Nutrition and eating habits
Using medications appropriately
Routine health visits, vision, and dental care
Cooperation with ongoing medical treatment
Contacting physician in an emergency

Social supports and social functioning
Relationships with family, sibling(s), and others
Presence of other adults who are cared for in the home
Social skills and peer relationships
Sexual behavior and functioning
Record of antisocial activities or problems, criminal record
Leisure and recreational activities
Marital status and number of children
Presence of children with difficulties who are also in, or in need of, services

Financial resources and management
Personal income and additional sources
Eligibility for public support (e.g., SSI/SSDI, food stamps, subsidized housing, Medicaid, etc.)
Personal financial management skills
Financial health

History of previous services (or the exit summary of functional performance)
History of previous services, IEP goals, and transition plans
Outcomes of previous services
Current services in use

preparing for transition (Alper, Ryndak, & Schloss, 2001; IDEA, 2004; Sitlington et al., 2007). It is important to remember that needs assessment is not a one-time event but an ongoing process that extends throughout the student's school program and beyond. Furthermore, the needs of students change over time (Miller et al., 2006). For this reason, assessments must be conducted at least every three years.

Assessment activities performed at the transition system level (the school) or interagency level, which typically occurs at a district level, involve the following:

1. Defining the range of local services available in the existing system to identify an existing foundation for an interagency agreement
2. Identifying service gaps and service needs that are currently not being met within the system
3. Determining the level of "readiness" of cooperating agencies to establish formal interagency agreements
4. Determining the expertise and resources that each organization brings to the partnership
5. Assessing the needs of the cooperating partners to address transition as a common goal

An interagency needs assessment can provide important information for determining how prepared each agency is to perform the eight core service coordination functions. Ongoing needs assessment is as important at the interagency level as it is at the individual level. Also, as individual needs change over time so do the needs of cooperating agencies, and ongoing needs assessments can help the system remain sensitive to future change.

Function 4: Transition Planning and Development. The development of a comprehensive transition plan as part of the IEP is an essential function of service coordination. At the individual level, individual transition plans represent the service "agreement" or contract among the student, parents, the school, and providers of needed services. The transition component of the IEP should include long-range postsecondary goals, a plan of study, career-vocational and community-based learning needs, and related service and technology needs. It documents the responsibilities and commitments of the students, teachers, family members, and other agency service providers. The plan is based on information obtained from the individual assessments described in Function 3. At the individual level, program-planning activities may include the following:

1. Engaging the interdisciplinary team and families in transition planning
2. Developing IEP transition plans that address all the functional domains, including family supports in some instances
3. Including plans for continuity of needed services as the student moves from middle or junior high to high school and from high school to postsecondary settings
4. Including regular review of IEP transition service plans
5. Ensuring active participation and decision making of students and their families.

Program planning also occurs at the *system level* and typically results in the development of an *interagency cooperative agreement at the state or local level.* The cooperative agreement includes the mission statement, interagency goals and objectives, and a timetable for activities. The mission statement describes the broad parameters for the cooperative partnership, the purpose of the agreement, and broad areas of joint responsibility for service delivery (see *Chapter 10* for a detailed discussion of developing interagency agreements for transition).

Function 5: Service Coordination or Linking.   At the individual level, service linking means identifying appropriate service agencies and/or individual professionals to deliver the services represented in an IEP. For example, for families of youth with disabilities, it may mean providing a central point of contact to link the student and family with a variety of in-school services such as academic supports, speech and hearing, school counseling, and assistive devices or equipment. For individuals with chronic health or behavioral health needs, it might mean providing information and linking with community-based services such as health and mental health clinics, physician services, and providers of in-home health-related and adaptive equipment. For youth preparing for postsecondary placement, it may mean providing additional linking services in the event that the first postsecondary linkages or planned placement is not achieved.

At the *individual level,* linking activities may include the following:

1. Establishing a service coordinator or point of contact for each individual or family
2. Identifying and contacting needed services within the agency's catchment area (service boundary) or outside, if appropriate
3. Arranging contacts between the individual or family and the service agency involved
4. Linking students and families with needed services during transition from middle or junior high to high school or from high school to postsecondary education (e.g., providing extra counseling or guidance during the transfer or transition, providing information to families about new services and how to access them, and arranging meetings with service agencies)

At the *interagency or system level,* linking means coordinating and sharing resources among agencies on behalf of youth preparing for transition. Shared resources include financial, human and intellectual, and material resources that belong to cooperating agencies, which could be allocated for transition-service coordination activities defined by a cooperative agreement. Interagency linking activities can help prevent duplication of services among many agencies and can make the service system more efficient.

Function 6: Service Monitoring and Follow-Along.   Service monitoring and follow-along are essential functions of service coordination. At the individual level, the purpose of monitoring is to (a) ensure that the student receives services that are described in the IEP or transition service plan and that they are appropriate and (b) evaluate the student's progress in achieving the goals and objectives included in the plan. Monitoring requires that the service coordinator and IEP or transition planning team maintain ongoing contact with the student receiving services and the agencies providing them. Monitoring of the student's IEP or transition plan also permits the service coordinator to observe and gain direct knowledge of the nature and quality of the services received.

Another important aspect of monitoring is that it allows the student and family to evaluate the services received and allows the service coordinator to understand the appropriateness of services from the consumer's perspective. Service monitoring activities at the individual level include the following:

1. Documenting and maintaining a chronological record of services received by each student
2. Measuring and documenting progress made by students in their daily functioning, academic, and career-vocational skills; family relationships; social relationships; and/or independent living skills
3. Documenting student achievement of goals included in the service plan and modifying the plan
4. Documenting services actually received, services requested but not received, and reasons why services were not received
5. Documenting gaps in services for the student and efforts to locate services within and outside the community or catchment area
6. Documenting barriers in services for the student
7. Maintaining continuity in service coordination from middle or junior high school, through secondary education, and during transition to postsecondary settings (college or employment)

Service monitoring at the *interagency or system level* means ensuring that the services of cooperating agencies and contract service providers

1. are delivered according to the intended schedule;
2. reach the students they were intended to serve;
3. are delivered in a manner that complies with established local, state, and national laws; regulations; guidelines; standards; and ethics;
4. are delivered with an acceptable level of quality.

Monitoring activities at the interagency or system level include the following:

1. Documenting performance of cooperating agencies and contract service providers and the achievement of interagency goals, objectives, and timetables
2. Collecting data on support services used by individuals or families
3. Collecting data on referrals to agencies for services
4. Collecting information from students and families about how they perceive the quality, appropriateness, and accessibility of services
5. Examining and improving interagency policies related to eligibility criteria, admission criteria, termination criteria, and policies governing supports for participation in the program of service
6. Conducting projections of student needs for services from cooperating agencies

The monitoring function can offer valuable information about the quality and effectiveness of service coordination in the service-delivery system.

The follow-along function is an important part of the monitoring function. The **follow-along** function includes those activities by the service coordinator that provide emotional support, foster relationships of trust with the student, and maintain close contact and communication with the family. In some schools and community agencies where caseloads are high, the monitoring function is often a "paper-tracking" activity (Kochhar, 1995, 2008). In others, monitoring includes ongoing and close contacts with the student and family to provide direct support. Follow-along activities may include the following:

1. Home visits to families
2. Visits to youth in their school- or work-based programs
3. Informal and supportive counseling with students or families
4. Providing for regular face-to-face contact with a service coordinator
5. Addressing family support needs
6. Providing behavioral (or other) crisis intervention

The follow-along function includes the personal support component of service coordination assistance. It can be instrumental in retaining students in needed services or programs and preventing service dropout or school dropout.

Function 7: Individual and Interagency Advocacy.   Advocacy is a broad term that means different things to different groups of people, but it is a particularly important function of service coordination. At the individual level, advocacy means advocating on behalf of a student for services he or she needs, or it can mean assisting the student to advocate on his or her own behalf for services (self-advocacy). More recently, individual advocacy has come to mean ensuring that schools and service agencies promote student self-determination, participation in educational planning, and informed decision making by individuals and their families.

Self-determination is the act of making independent choices about personal goals and directions, based on accurate information about one's own strengths and needs and the available service or program options (Field, Hoffman, & Spezia, 1998; Field, Martin, Miller, Ward, & Wehmeyer, 1998a; Racino, 1992). Self-determination is most effective and rewarding within an environment that promotes and facilitates independent decision making (Algozzine, Browder, Karvonen, Test, & Wood, 2001; Bremer, Kachgal, & Schoeller, 2003). Self-determination does not mean "going it alone" or relying only on oneself. Rather, the idea should be placed within the context of shared decision making, interdependence, and mutual support. **Self-advocacy** is an important part of self-determination. Table 5-2 provides examples of individual advocacy activities that service coordinators can perform on behalf of students or to assist them to *advocate on their own behalf in pursuing transition goals.* These two sets of activities can be viewed as two poles of a *continuum* rather than as separate from one another. Service coordinators continually strive to empower students and families to make decisions about short-term and long-range transition goals in as independent and self-sufficient a manner as possible.

Interagency or system advocacy means advocating in similar ways to those described above but doing so on behalf of a whole system or group of individuals. Examples of interagency advocacy activities include the following:

1. Developing a shared interagency understanding of the needs of students with disabilities

Table 5.2 Individual Advocacy Activities (Two Poles of a Continuum)

Advocacy on Behalf of the Individual	Assisting Individuals to Advocate on Their Own Behalf (Self-Advocacy and Self-Determination)
Intervening to ensure that student human rights and due process procedures are protected	Providing information about human rights and due process procedures to the student or family for their own self-advocacy
Helping the student gain access to a service from which he or she has traditionally been excluded	Offering strategies to the student to help him or her independently gain access to a service or program from which he or she has been excluded
Directly intervening on behalf of the student to negotiate enrollment in a service or program	Offering strategies, information, or coaching that will help the student negotiate his or her own admission to a program and supports services or accommodation that will make it possible to participate in a service
Negotiating with a service agency to provide special supports services or accommodations that will enable a student to participate in a service	Helping students negotiate with their family to support participation in a needed service or program, or to agree to enroll as a family in a needed service
In instances in which the family is fearful of having their son or daughter participate in a needed service, the service coordinator helps educate the family, allay fears, and encourage cooperation and participation	Offering strategies, information, or coaching to help the student explain the special language or cultural conditions and barriers that prevent enrollment or make it difficult to participate in a service or program
Helping an agency understand the special language or cultural conditions and barriers that prevent enrollment and participation in a service and negotiating special supports for such a student	Providing coaching to help the student as a potential employee to describe his or her own strengths and weaknesses, relevant job skills, and training needs
Collaborating with potential employers to provide information about students tr aining and supervision needs	

Source: From *Successful Inclusion: Practical Strategies for a Shared Responsibility* (p. 116), by C. A. Kochhar-Bryant, L. L. West, & J. M. Taymans, 2000, Upper Saddle River, NJ: Merrill/Prentice Hall. Reprinted with permission.

2. Addressing issues of cultural and linguistic diversity with service agencies to negotiate the development of special supports or accommodations
3. Communicating service barriers and service gaps to decision makers
4. Communicating and protecting human rights and due process procedures for groups of students
5. Promoting an emphasis on self-determination and informed decision making for students and their families
6. Linking students with legal advocacy services, or working with local agencies to help them meet new legal requirements
7. Providing attitudinal leadership to improve internal agency, interagency, or community attitudes toward students served or their families
8. Working to increase supports during the movements or transitions between services or to more integrated settings

As local agencies respond to new requirements for interagency coordination, advocacy can help build a shared capacity to meet the multiple needs of students and their families. Advocacy activities can help stimulate creativity in reducing resistance and barriers to interagency coordination. When service-system coordinators set specific goals related to the advocacy function, transition services are more likely to promote empowerment of the student and to be more closely connected to individual goals and needs.

Function 8: Service Evaluation and Follow-Up.   Service evaluation and follow-up are essential to effective service coordination. Although evaluation may be a final step in assessing the value and quality of services to consumers, it is the first step in their improvement. Evaluation is a process by which we collect information about the services or the service partnership to

1. find out how powerful the effects of the services and programs are on students, families, and the educational environment;
2. determine whether the interagency partnership is achieving the goals that it set for itself;
3. help in making decisions about the future of the interagency partnership.

Evaluation activities, according to Rossi, Lipsey, and Freeman (2003), help improve social conditions and community life for humankind. Because evaluation is closely linked to the decision making process for cooperating agencies, it is considered successful *if the information it generates becomes part of the decision-making process.* Evaluation seeks answers to questions such as the following:

1. How do we know the services are helping students and families to achieve individual transition goals?
2. What can we do to improve the interagency partnership to increase the effects or benefits of the services included in students' IEP/transition plans?
3. How do students and families judge the quality, accessibility, and appropriateness of the services?
4. How well are the interagency partners accomplishing the goals in their cooperative agreements?
5. To what extent are students and families benefiting from the services provided?

Evaluation, therefore, provides us information about whether services and programs are actually helping students and families achieve their transition goals. Such information supports management because it assists in decision making. A coordinated interagency system should combine individual and interagency service evaluation activities to measure its effectiveness and contribute to decision making. Furthermore, interagency evaluation is most useful and effective when it takes into consideration the perspectives and judgments of consumers, families, and the cooperating agencies.

Follow-Up.   Follow-up activities are used to track the path or disposition of students once they have exited the program or service agency. Follow-up activities are designed to answer questions such as the following:

1. What happens to students once they have left the school and the services in which they have been participating?
2. Do the students return to community agencies for additional services, and are they more likely to access services again in the future?

3. Do students experience long-term benefits or effects as a result of receiving services (e.g., improved independent living, physical health, mobility, continuing education, social skills, financial aptitude, family relations, employment, and general functioning)?
4. Is there a change in the way students perceive the quality and appropriateness of services after a period of time away from them?
5. Can we predict the effect of services by examining what happens to students when they leave?

Follow-up information informs us about whether the benefits or progress made by students while they are participating in services endures over time. Activities related to evaluation of interagency coordination and follow-up at the *individual level* include the following:

1. Student or family surveys of perceptions about quality, accessibility, appropriateness of services
2. Surveying or interviewing individuals who have discontinued participation in services or programs to determine whether the benefits have endured over time for the individual
3. Providing outreach to students who did not complete high school to determine what additional services are needed
4. Evaluating individualized transition planning for students and their families

Activities related to service evaluation and follow-up at the *interagency/system level* include the following:

1. Evaluating interagency agreements and policies at the state or local levels
2. Evaluating the effectiveness of interagency service coordination functions and agreements
3. Evaluating individualized transition planning procedures and outcomes across the state or local district
4. Evaluating communication barriers among agencies
5. Evaluating systematic use of evaluation information for service improvement at state and local levels

Follow-up activities are an important part of interagency evaluation, because they *help determine the long-term effects of agency services in helping students achieve their transition goals.* Chapter 11 will explore follow-up processes in greater detail.

→ HOW HAS SYSTEM COORDINATION EVOLVED AS A PRACTICE?

In the United States, there is a long history of providing noneducational services to children within a school setting—a shared responsibility between schools and communities. Initially, as part of social reform efforts early in the 1900s, health services were provided primarily by public health doctors and dentists who volunteered their services. As health and social services became embedded in the schools, the services became more school-centered and less family-oriented, focusing on improving school attendance and academic performance. Over the past 50 years, the number of non-educational staff and the ratio of these staff to students have increased dramatically. The goals for providing school-linked health and social services was to (a) improve academic performance, (b) improve international competitiveness, or (c) meet the health and social needs of underserved children (children at risk) (Tyack, 1992).

From the 1950s through early 1980s, schools and community agencies reported little formal interagency collaboration and minimal use of formal interagency agreements, even though there was a strong consensus on the need to develop such agreements (Neubert, 2000; Storms, O'Leary, & Williams, 2000). During the 1990s, however, several factors stimulated the development of interagency coordination to advance the development of children and youth in the schools. These included (a) better definitions of interagency coordination goals and functions; (b) laws that encouraged interagency coordination in order to carry out transition planning requirements for students with disabilities; (c) greater willingness of agencies to reduce barriers that have hindered collaboration; (d) development of state and local resources to develop interagency cooperative activities; and (e) lessons learned about the effectiveness of interagency coordination in other disciplines (e.g., social work, mental health, public health, and rehabilitation). Recent outcome data now confirms the effectiveness of interagency services coordination activities in improving access, quality of services, and outcomes for students and families (Dunst & Bruder, 2002; Kohler & Hood, 2000; National Center on Outcomes Research, 2001).

National Policies Promote Coordination

Over the past two decades, the cornerstone of the Regular Education (Inclusion) Initiative has been collaboration among teachers, specialists, and parents (Villa, Thousand, Stainback & Stainback, 1992; Welch & Brownell, 2002). More recently, collaboration and system coordination strategies together have become central policy tools or instruments embedded in major education and disability related laws. The IDEA of 1997, IDEA Amendments of 2004, No Child Left Behind Act of 2001, and Rehabilitation Act Amendments expanded cooperative arrangements at the federal, state, and local levels. Service coordination has been central for implementing free and appropriate public education for students with disabilities and for improving educational outcomes.

➡ ## WHAT PHILOSOPHIES HAVE SHAPED THE DEVELOPMENT OF INTERAGENCY SERVICE COORDINATION?

Over the past few decades, service models have focused less on "fixing problems" or ameliorating "deficits" within the individual and more on seeking ways to change or improve the individual's environment to improve the secondary education and transition process for youth with disabilities. The following sections provide a brief review of philosophical ideas and principles that have had a major effect on the way we view individuals with disabilities in the human-service system during the past 50 years.

Principles for System Coordination: Protecting Access to Transition Opportunities

Researchers concur that service system coordination through shared responsibility is vital for sustaining the hard-earned gains made in the past two decades to integrate individuals with disabilities into general education, postsecondary programs, the workforce, and the community (Baer et al., 2003; National Center on Secondary Education and Transition, 2002a; Timmons, 2007). Interagency coordination experts believe there are several principles that facilitate effective coordination and guide model development. Interagency coordinators agree on the importance and relevance of these philosophical principles in assisting persons with disabilities to maximize their potential. *Consumer-centered goal-setting focuses attention upon the end result expected for the individual or family.* As mentioned earlier, it incorporates the principle of self-determination—the student must learn to exercise as much personal decision making in life planning as is possible. Table 5–3 presents a synthesis of eight consumer-centered principles that can help to focus goals for service coordination activities.

Table 5–3   Consumer-Centered Principles for Interagency Service Coordination

Principle 1 Service coordination assists the individual to achieve the maximum level of potential and promotes self-determination	Some students with disabilities require short-term support in education and community settings and during periods of transition from one setting to another. Others require extended support services or intermittent intensive support services. Service coordination activities are flexible and responsive to student needs. They assist him or her to achieve as much independence as possible in as many areas of functioning as he or she is assessed to have needs. Finally, they promote self-determination in planning for support services and future linkages with community agencies.
Principle 2 Service coordination activities result in improvements in the quality of life and learning environment of the individual	Interagency personnel work together to seek opportunities to strengthen the service system and the linkages among service organizations and advocate for improvements in services on behalf of the individual. For example, the linking of a student and family to counseling services prevented a student from dropping out of school and enabled him to participate successfully in a career-technical program operated by the high school and community college.
Principle 3 Service coordination promotes community integration	Service coordination helps individuals obtain services in the most integrated environments. Assistance to the individual is provided only at the level actually needed to promote independence and self-reliance.
Principle 4 Service coordination assists the individual to improve health, mental health, and physical well-being	A coordinated system of services addresses the physical development and the improvement of overall health and mental health. Access to education or support service does not simply mean enrollment in it but also the ability to remain in and

(Continued)

Table 5–3   *Continued*

	benefit from the service. An individual does not really have educational access if he or she is in ill health and unable to fully participate in the service or program. Developmental, educational, and support services cannot be effective unless the health, mental health, and physical well-being of the participant are attended to.
Principle 5 Service coordination assures equitable access to a range of needed services	An important goal of service coordination is the development of a range of developmental and educational settings that meet the different developmental needs of the student. Service coordination activities also give priority to individuals who are at risk of failing to progress in integrated settings.
Principle 6 Service coordination reinforces the informal support network	Service coordination activities strengthen or reinforce self-help and informal support networks, which include the individual's parents, siblings, and extended family. Cooperating agencies recognize that the informal support network for the individual is an important factor in his or her ability to be successful through high school and during the period of transition. Therefore, service coordination activities also address the support needs of the family as part of service provision to the individual.
Principle 7 Service coordination promotes access to community services	Service coordination activities link individuals with the range of services in the community and create a bridge between the individual and the agencies.
Principle 8 Service coordination evaluation methods focus on individual outcomes and service improvements	Measures of the performance of service coordination activities are centered on the quality of the process as well as on individual outcomes in the domains for which services are provided (e.g., health, education, employment training, and family involvement).

The **consumer-centered principles** described in Table 5–3 represent recurring themes and guiding principles that have helped shape existing models for interagency service coordination.

⇒ WHAT NATIONAL AND STATE LAWS PROMOTE SERVICE COORDINATION?

The philosophical principles described above are reflected in many of the laws and policies that govern education and human services at the national, state, and local levels. Congress has recognized that education, health and mental health, and employment outcomes for children and youth with disabilities remain a great concern throughout the United States. As a result, several recent laws have extended state and local efforts to create coordinated systems of services through interagency cooperation and linkage. New provisions in these laws were designed to improve working relationships among those involved in delivery of transition services and to create incentives for collaboration between schools and community agencies, including postsecondary agencies. Furthermore, these laws have been crafted and interconnected in such a way to create a durable framework for a broader system of shared responsibility that promotes successful transitions to postsecondary life.

IDEA 2004 holds the schools responsible for ensuring that students with disabilities receive appropriate transition services and planning. Besides encouraging a shared responsibility for youth in transition, *IDEA also requires that schools establish linkages with community and postsecondary agencies and share the responsibility for transition services.* Furthermore, IDEA requires states to have interagency agreements among state and local education agencies, as well as public agencies. States and local districts are expected to create interagency or multiagency agreements to provide the kinds of transition services incorporated in students' IEP. The *IEP must include a statement of each participating agency's responsibilities or linkages before the student leaves the school setting.* This includes a commitment to meet the financial responsibility it may have in the provision of transition services (IDEA, 2004).

Recent transition experts have found that transition services are most effective when there is (a) involvement of all stakeholder systems and (b) coordination among transition initiatives such as those under IDEA, NCLB, Carl D. Perkins Career and Technical Education Act, Workforce Investment Act, and Rehabilitation Act (Dunst & Bruder, 2002; Knight & Boudah, 2003; National Center on Outcomes Research, 2001; Wagner & Gomby, 2000). National and state legislation includes two important elements that guide the delivery of services at the state and local levels:

1. Guidelines on how services are to be implemented, structured, and funded
2. Statements about the principles and values that are expected to be reflected in program implementation and use of funds.

The state and local regulations that are written to interpret the laws and guide implementation at the program level are often ambiguous. Recent education, employment training, and disability-rights laws and regulations, however, have clearly been aimed at (a) improving the quality of services, (b) increasing the participation of special populations in the full range of programs and services available, and (c) ensuring coordination and collaboration among service sectors to improve access to and efficient delivery of services.

Role of the State Education Agency for Coordination

The transition of youth with disabilities is a shared responsibility under the Individuals with Disabilities Education Act (IDEA) and the Rehabilitation Act of 1973, as amended in 1998. Primary responsibility for the transition of children with disabilities under IDEA rests with state educational agencies (SEAs). The State Vocational Rehabilitation (VR) Services Program, however, authorized under the Rehabilitation Act also has a key role facilitating the transition of youth with disabilities, including providing consultation and technical assistance to SEAs, participating in transition planning, identifying youth who are in need of VR services, and providing transition services to eligible individuals. Federal and state efforts to improve the postschool outcomes of youth with disabilities have resulted in some important gains over the past decade, including increases in graduation rates, enrollment in postsecondary education, and the number of youth entering the workforce (Cameto & Levine, 2005; Newman, 2005; Office of Special Education Programs, 2006). Despite these gains, far too many youth with disabilities continue to experience difficulties in achieving successful postschool outcomes (National Longitudinal Transition Study 2, 2005).

LET'S SEE IT IN ACTION! CASE EXAMPLE

Successful Interagency Coordination for Transition

While he was in high school, Bill participated in community-based nonpaid work experience at a local hospital and at a hotel through his high school's Occupational Work Experience program. Upon completion of these experiences, Bill, his parent, and the work-study coordinator agreed that he needed a job in the community. He was referred to the Rehabilitative Services Commission's Pathways program for VR support services in a community-based work experience. In discussing Bill's employment options with his Pathways VR counselor and his parent, a referral was made to the Ladders to Success employment program for job development in Bill's senior year.

With the Ladders' help, Bill secured a job as a houseman at a hotel. Rehabilitative services purchased job coaching services. Just before graduation, Bill was determined to be eligible for County Board of Mental Health Services. Rehabilitative services made Bill's mental-health case manager aware of his need for supported employment services. One month after graduation, a meeting was held with Bill, his father, the job coach, the Ladders job developer, the mental-health case manager, and the employer to assure there were no unaddressed issues. Two months later, the Pathways VR counselor closed Bill's case, confident that support services were in place.

What agencies are coordinating services for Bill? What laws can you identify that underpin these linkages and the services that Bill is receiving?

A synthesis of the literature on state planning for transition services for students with disabilities yields the following essential components for a coordinated system of appropriate educational and transition services and supports for individuals with disabilities:

1. A *long-range, coordinated interagency plan for a system of education and support services* for students in integrated settings, from early intervention through postsecondary transition, and special supports for the critical "passages" or transitions between educational settings
2. A *statewide system of personnel development* dedicated to the long-range coordinated interagency plan for the system of services that includes preservice and in-service personnel preparation and the training of parents
3. *Innovative cooperative partnerships* among public schools, area colleges and universities, private providers, related service agencies, parents, and the private sector to achieve common goals for the inclusion of students with disabilities into the mainstream of education and in all aspects of educational reform
4. Ongoing evaluation of systematic service delivery efforts and transition outcomes (Aspel, Bettis, Test, & Wood, 1998; Benz, Lindstrom, & Yovanoff, 2000; Johnson &

Halloran, 1997; Kim-Rupnow, Dowrick, & Burke, 2001; Luecking & Certo, 2002; Neubert, 2000; Stodden, 2001; U.S. Office of Special Education, 2006).

Implementing transition services is complicated by several factors. First, many different parties developing and implementing effective programs can be difficult. Interagency partnerships at the state and local level are needed to ensure effective agency collaboration, including coordination of policies and practices, sharing of knowledge, information, and other resources, and providing technical assistance and training. A state level interagency transition team can promote effective collaborative models, provide training and technical assistance across the state, and maintain communication and support for the transition community. *Local community transition teams* identify common goals and action plans, problem-solve through interagency collaboration, create community-based options for students, seek funding, and implement action plans (Miller, 2002, Twenty-Eighth Institute on Rehabilitation Issues, 2002).

WHAT IS THE ROLE OF THE FAMILY IN SYSTEM COORDINATION FOR TRANSITION?

Parents as Partners: The Role of Families in Interagency Service Coordination

Parents have been very powerful advocates in initiating services for children and adults with special needs during the past century. Parents have also stimulated major change in education and human service systems nationally and locally. The participation of parents and families is among the most crucial factors in the success of the individual in education and human services.

Reaffirming the role of parents in education, recent legislation has expanded family-centered service coordination to an extent that is unique in law and in practice. The IDEA of 1997 and 2004, NCLB 2001, and the Higher Education Act Amendments of 1998 all strengthened the role of parents in their children's IEPs and transition plans in school decision making and in teacher preparation.

Together, the IDEA 2004 and NCLB set expectations for parent–professional partnerships that are unprecedented for the public school system. Parents have been given important roles in identifying and evaluating their children with disabilities and in the development, implementation, and revision of their educational programs. IDEA 2004 encouraged parents to become more involved in their children's education, and additionally, to work in other ways as partners with educators and policymakers (Abrams & Gibbs, 2002; Christie, 2005; Henderson, et al., 2003). Parents are encouraged to be involved in policymaking at the state and local levels as members of the advisory panels and in developing school improvement plans.

In summary, IDEA and NCLB convey three messages to parents, teachers, and service providers: (a) the importance of the parent–professional partnership in service delivery and improving educational outcomes for children and youth; (b) the inclusion of the family unit (system) as the target for intervention and support by the schools and community agencies; and (c) the importance of strengthening the families' role in decision making and educational improvement. IDEA 2004 and NCLB require schools to transform the traditional notions of parent involvement from signing report cards, reading newsletters, and chaperoning holiday parties to include activities such as participating in school decision-making processes, providing input to teachers about how to assist their child, and forming genuine partnerships with the school community.

Barriers to Family Participation in Transition

Surveys of parent centers across the country indicate there is a critical need for additional staff to be able to assist families transitioning from high school into the world of work, higher education, and adult service systems (Henderson et al., 2003). Once a student leaves the special education system, however, families are often unsure how to help their young adults find and receive the support they need to continue their education, develop career and independent living skills, or find employment (Briar-Lawson & Lawson, 2001; Dounay, 2006; Epstein, 2001; Ferguson, 2005; Lee, Palmer, Turnbull, & Wehmeyer, 2006; Morningstar & Wehmeyer, in press). When families do identify postsecondary, vocational rehabilitation, or employment programs, they may find it difficult to have input into decisions about the services their family member receives (Technical Assistance on Transition and the Rehabilitation Act, 2007).

Principles for Family-Centered Service Coordination

Research has demonstrated that effective parent involvement programs are built on several assumptions: (a) the primary educational environment is the family; (b) parent involvement in a child's education is a major factor in improving school effectiveness, the quality of education, and a child's academic success; (c) the benefits of parent involvement extend from preschool and elementary school through high school; and (d) low-income and minority children have the most to gain when schools involve parents (Ames & Dickerson, 2004; Lightfoot, 2001; National Center for Family Literacy, 2004; Newman, 2004; Perna & Titus, 2005; Raimondo & Henderson, 2001; Zhang, Wehmeyer, & Chen, 2005).

It is important to understand the difference between strategies that call for more *parent involvement* and strategies that are *family-centered* or aimed at promoting family empowerment and decision making. Current models of interagency coordination are taking a family-centered approach in which the service coordinator incorporates assessments of family needs into the IEP for students through to the age of majority. A family-centered perspective and increased coordination between schools and human service agencies are crucial in the move toward service integration (Gonzalez-DeHass, Willems, & Holbein, 2005; Novick, 2001; Turnbull, Turnbull, & Wehmeyer, 2007; Zhang et al., 2005).

The coordination functions are guided by **family support principles**, which emphasize family strengths, and principles of family empowerment, including parents as lead decision makers with their sons or daughters in planning for their educational progress and later for postsecondary life. Family-centered strategies are based on the following principles:

1. Informed choice among service options is ensured for the individual and his or her family.

2. Services are coordinated around the life of the individual and family, not around the needs of the school or program.

3. The ability of ordinary citizens to help people to participate in community life is recognized.

4. Parents are children's first teachers and have a lifelong influence on their values, attitudes, and aspirations.

5. Most parents, regardless of economic status, educational level, and/or cultural background care deeply about their children's education and can provide substantial support if given specific opportunities and knowledge.

6. Schools must take the lead in eliminating, or at least reducing, traditional barriers to parent involvement (Ames & Dickerson, 2004; Christie, 2005; Education Commission of the States, 2004a; Field et al., 1998; Novick, 2001; Turnbull et al., 2007).

As mentioned earlier, a family-support philosophy emphasizes an empowerment model that builds on family strengths and develops home–school relationships that are based on mutual respect and responsibility. The important themes for the participation of parents and family members in the service coordination process are summarized in Table 5–4.

Table 5–4   Themes for Participation of Families in Service Coordination and Transition

Theme	Description of Positive Practices
1. Parents/families as active partners	Parents and families are partners with professionals in the service-delivery process and must be viewed as collaborators, not *service recipients*. The collaborative view fosters a perception that parents and families are active and not passive in the service-delivery process and should enjoy equal status with professionals in the team decision-making process.
2. Parents/families as team members	Parents and families are involved in the assessment of their child's transition needs and participate with members of the interdisciplinary team in developing individualized service plans and transition plans. Parents are invited and participate in each annual IEP meeting for their children who need special services; they participate in any change of placement decision or change in level of services. Parents should be invited into the service planning, policy development, and service evaluation processes and in the planning for training of service coordinators (adapted from Hausslein, Kaufmann, & Hurth, 1992).
3. Parents as transition coordinators	Parents are encouraged to be closely involved and supportive of their adolescent children in the process of preparing for and making the transition between services, such as between secondary school to postsecondary settings and employment. They partner with transition coordinators to provide parent-training seminars or to speak in classes about transition and preparation for employment and self-advocacy.
4. Parents as decision makers	Parents/families are lead decision makers regarding the assessments and the services to be provided, in cooperation and consultation with professionals.
5. Parent/family training for advocacy	Parent training and resources are provided to help family members and guardians better advocate and coordinate services for their children or wards. Families are educated and empowered to acquire and to assist in the creation of transition services and supports and are informed about available community and outreach services. Parents or guardians

(Continued)

Table 5–4   (Continued)

Theme	Description of Positive Practices
	are provided training to understand concepts such as self-determination, self-advocacy, services coordination, transition, IEP, least restrictive environment, and other concepts. Parents are informed about the legal and human rights of their children to educational services and supports.
6. Families as peer supports	Parents and families are encouraged to provide basic support to one another to achieve satisfactory outcomes for their children. Parents collaborate to organize parent support groups, in which experienced parents of children with disabilities help less-experienced parents.
7. Parent supports	Funding for parent resource centers are provided from local, state, or national sources.

The principles of family-centered approaches are receiving some attention in public schools as well as in community-based agencies. Educational leaders recognize that their efforts to improve students' learning and performance are integrally related to family circumstances and home life (Gutman, 2005; Hong & Ho, 2005; Jeynes, 2005; Spera, 2006). For example, research has demonstrated that one reason for the continuing poor outcomes of school-to-work transition programs is the absence of family-focused approaches that promote the students' and families' determination of transition goals and services (Ames & Dickerson, 2004; Education Commission of the States; 2004a; Gerry & McWhorter, 1990; Morningstar, 2002; Turnbull et al., 2007). Some schools are beginning to have an impact on family circumstances and needs by offering parents special supports. Examples of such supports include basic academic skills classes, language classes, career-vocational skills training, or employment counseling to parents in the schools in the evening.

SUMMARY

Educators and policy makers concerned with transition outcomes of youth are emphasizing the importance of interagency coordination for children and youth with special learning needs. This chapter defined *interagency or system coordination* and its relationship to transition services. It also reviewed ideas, philosophies, and strategies that have shaped the development of interagency coordination for transition services for youth with disabilities. National and state laws that promote service coordination and the barriers to their implementation were also discussed. Finally, the role of the family in service coordination for transition was introduced.

Service coordination processes are an important tool in the overall improvement in transition and support services. Effective service coordination relies upon the presence of a constructive process for (a) analyzing and communicating interagency information in a manner that is understandable and usable by students, families, and partner agencies and (b) applying the information for service system change and improvement. The new legal requirements for transition services demand a new kind of system collaboration among disciplines and service sectors if transition and employment outcomes are to be improved for the nation's youth with disabilities. Under current laws, agencies are *required* to coordinate their services (a) at the state level to ensure coordination between major service sectors such as education and rehabilitation, (b) at the local level to ensure that schools are linked with community agencies and that there is a shared responsibility for transition services, and (c) at the individual level to ensure that needed agency services are received and documented in the students' individualized education and transition programs. These new requirements for coordination are transforming the transition service system. They mandate formal linkages between schools and community agencies to affect outcomes for students with disabilities and promote self-determination and greater independence.

KEY TERMS AND PHRASES

consumer-centered principles
family support principles
family-centered service coordination
follow-along
follow-up
self-advocacy

self-determination
service coordination
service coordination functions
systematic approach to transition
   services
system-level service coordination

QUESTIONS FOR THINKING, REFLECTION, AND SKILL BUILDING

1. Why is service coordination central to transition service delivery? In what ways can service coordination activities lead to improvement in overall transition services?

2. What is meant by "family-centered approaches" to service coordination?

3. Why are self-determination and self-advocacy important concepts for students and families?

4. How is increased parent and student involvement in transition planning likely to improve postsecondary outcomes? What examples of this have you observed?

5. Find out in your school or local school district whether there is a student transition team and an interagency agreement (or memorandum of understanding) for transition coordination. Do you see evidence of (a) consumer-centered planning and student involvement, (b) use of interagency teams to ensure coordination and quality of services, and (c) a lead transition services coordinator?

6. Find out in your school or district who is responsible for interagency coordination for transition. What roles are involved—teacher, guidance counselor, administrator, transition coordinator, or others?

7. If there is no interagency agreement or memorandum of understanding, what steps are being taken to develop one? What steps are being taken to form a local interagency coordination transition team?

8. Contact the parent training and information center or parent advocacy center in your area for information about services and transition. What services are provided, and what information related to transition can you find?

9. Examine a local college or university curriculum for the preparation of special education teachers. Does it include interagency service coordination or system coordination content? In your judgment, how adequate is the teacher preparation content related to interagency service coordination?

Chapter 6

Best Practices in Transition

Gary Greene

Chapter Questions

- What does the term *best practices* in transition mean?
- What are best practices for transition collaboration?
- What are best practices for transition education programming?
- What are best practices for transition planning?

INTRODUCTION

Much has been written on the subject of transition since the mid-1980s, when transition became a high priority in the fields of special education, vocational education, and vocational rehabilitation. The term ***best practices in transition*** frequently appeared throughout the literature in these fields of study. In the early 1990s, it was important to exercise caution when discussing the term best practices in transition because the majority of the literature on the subject was nonempirically based (Greene & Albright, 1995; Johnson & Rusch, 1993). This lack of empirical evidence prompted Greene and Albright (1995) and many others to view the field of transition services as a very *soft* science, similar to the field of special education in its early years. More recently, however, attempts have been made to identify promising, evidence-based transition practices and programs that result in improved outcomes for youth with disabilities (Kohler & Hood, 2000; Phelps & Hanley-Maxwell, 1997).

The purpose of this chapter is to review both historical and recent literature on best practices in transition to identify a set of recommendations for personnel working in agencies and schools that provide transition services to youth with disabilities. This material should allow transition personnel to evaluate the quality of services they are providing and identify potential areas for program improvement.

WHAT DOES THE TERM *BEST PRACTICES IN TRANSITION* MEAN?

Best practices in transition refers to a number of specific recommendations for facilitating successful movement from school to adult life for youth with disabilities. These recommendations have been derived from both empirical (e.g., scientific, experimental investigations) and nonempirical sources (e.g., field studies and clinical practice). Examples of these sources include (a) follow-up and follow-along studies of youth and adults with disabilities, (b) surveys of transition specialists and transition program administrators, (c) field observations and summaries of model transition programs, such as state policy and systems-change efforts in transition, and (d) consensus of opinion from scholars in the field of transition services.

Kohler (1993) noted in a review of literature on best practices in transition that most published research on the subject consisted of follow-up studies. Moreover, she found that only 4 of 11 key components of transition considered to be *best practices* were supported by empirical data. These were (a) vocational training, (b) parent involvement,

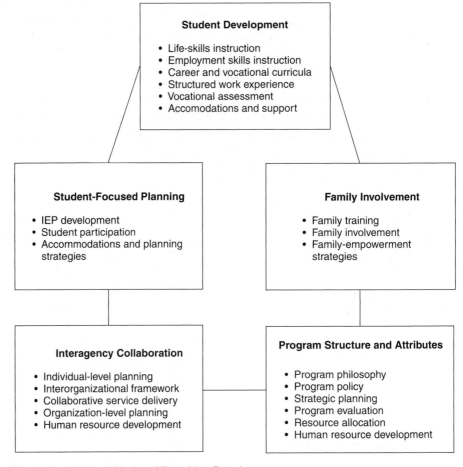

Figure 6–1   Emerging Model of Transition Practices
Source: From "Implementing a transition perspective," by P. D. Kohler in *Beyond High School: Transition from School to Work,* (p. 208), by F. R. Rusch and J. G. Chadsey (Eds.). Copyright 1998. Reprinted with permission from Wadsworth Publishing, a division of Thomson Learning.

(c) paid work, and (d) social-skills training. Kohler and her colleagues suggested a need for more evidence to determine the relationship between what is accepted as best practice in transition and postschool outcomes. This is essential, because without such evidence it is difficult to know which transition practices truly facilitate positive postschool outcomes for youth with disabilities.

Kohler (1996) subsequently published a model entitled *Taxonomy for Transition Programming* based both on empirical and validation studies, as well as model demonstration projects funded by the Office of Special Education and Rehabilitation Services (OSERS) in Washington D.C. (see Figure 6–1). Best practices emphasized in the model include (a) student-focused planning, (b) student development, (c) family involvement, (d) interagency collaboration, and (e) program structure. Phelps and Hanley-Maxwell (1997, p. 197) in a review of the literature noted that "two educational practices appear to consistently align with higher quality outcomes for youth with disabilities." These include (a) school supervised work experiences and (b) functionally oriented curricula in which occupationally specific skills, employability skills, and academic skills are systematically connected for students.

With these thoughts in mind, we used a cautious and systematic approach to defining best practices in transition by reviewing multiple sources of information on the subject. These included empirical and nonempirical publications such as journal articles, monographs and papers, and major transition textbooks, as well as state transition policy, practice, and educational materials. From these combined sources, a comprehensive list of 12 best practices was created. This list is shown in Table 6–1, along with the sources from which they were derived. The most frequently cited transition best practices included

1. person-centered or student-focused planning;
2. parent or family involvement in transition planning;
3. student self-determination and advocacy;

Table 6–1 Literature-Derived Best Practices in Transition

Best Practices in Transition	Deshler and Shumaker (2006)	Flexer et al. (2005)	Kohler and Hood (2000)	Phelps and Hanley-Maxwell (1997)	Powers et al. (2005)	Test, Aspel, and Everson (2006)	Wehman (2001)
1. Person-centered/ student-focused planning	✓	✓	✓	✓	✓	✓	X
2. Parent/family involvement in transition planning	✓	✓	✓	✓	✓	✓	X
3. Student self-determination and advocacy	✓	✓	✓		✓	✓	X
4. Interagency/ interdisciplinary collaboration and service coordination	✓	✓		✓	✓	✓	X
5. Integrated schools, classrooms (i.e., general education participation and inclusion), and employment	✓		✓	✓	✓		X
6. Career and vocational assessment/ education			✓	✓	✓	✓	X
7. Business and industry linkages with schools	✓		✓	✓			X
8. Community-based educational experiences		✓		✓	✓		X
9. Postsecondary education participation and supports	✓	✓			✓		X
10. Competitive paid work experience in high school and beyond	✓			✓	✓	✓	
11. Functional life-skills education	✓			✓	✓		
12. Social-skills training and competency	✓	✓					X

4. interagency–interdisciplinary collaboration and service coordination;
5. integrated schools, classrooms (i.e., general education participation and inclusion), and employment;
6. career and vocational assessment and education;
7. business and industry linkages with schools;
8. community-based educational experiences;
9. postsecondary education participation and supports;
10. competitive paid-work experience in high school and beyond;
11. functional life-skills education; and
12. social-skills training and competency.

We organized these 12 items under three common categories of best practices in transition. These are shown in Figure 6–2, and include (a) **transition services agency** best practices, (b) transition education programming best practices, and (c) transition planning best practices. A discussion of these three major categories and related 12 best practices in transition will subsequently be presented. A case study is presented after each category illustrating the respective transition best practices reviewed.

 ## WHAT ARE BEST PRACTICES FOR TRANSITION COLLABORATION?

Interagency Collaboration

Helping youth with disabilities transition from school to a quality adult life is a complex task involving the coordination of multiple personnel, agencies, programs, and services. The Individuals with Disabilities Education Act (IDEA) 2004 stated that transition services must be a "coordinated set of activities for a child with a disability that is designed to be within a results-oriented process, that is focused on improving the academic and functional achievement of the child with a disability to facilitate the child's movement from

---

Transition Services Agency Best Practices

  1. Interagency collaboration
  2. Interdisciplinary collaboration

Transition Education Programming Best Practices

  3. Integrated schools, classrooms, and employment
  4. Functional, life-skills curriculum, and community-based instruction
  5. Social and personal skills development and training
  6. Career and vocational assessment and education
  7. Competitive paid work experience
  8. Business and industry linkages with schools

Transition Planning Best Practices

  9. Post secondary education participation and support
 10. Person-centered/student-focused planning
 11. Student self-determination, and advocacy
 12. Family/parent involvement

Figure 6–2   Best Practices in Transition

school to postschool activities including postsecondary education, vocational education, integrated employment (including supported living), continuing and adult education, adult services, independent living, or community participation" [§ 602(34)(A)].

It is difficult, if not impossible, for any single agency to comprehensively address all of IDEA 2004 mandated transition activities for youth with disabilities. IDEA 2004 removed the previous requirement for schools to include in the Individualized Education Program (IEP), when appropriate, a statement of interagency responsibilities and linkages. It did, however, retain language stating that schools shall reconvene the IEP team to identify alternative strategies to meet transition objectives for the child if a participating agency other than the local school fails to provide the agreed-upon transition services. Historically, IDEA has strongly encouraged collaboration among schools and community agencies in the design and delivery of transition services for youth with disabilities. The importance of this best practice in transition is underscored by the widely documented history of problems related to interagency collaboration. These problems include (a) lack of collaboration among vocational, special education, and vocational rehabilitation personnel; (b) isolation, fragmentation, and duplication of services among various transition services agencies; and (c) competition for external funding for services among agencies within the same community (Asselin, Hanley-Maxwell, & Szymanski, 1992; Baer & Kochhar-Bryant, 2008; Bates, Bronkema, Ames, & Hess, 1992; Harley, Donnell, & Rainey, 2003).

How should community-based adult service agencies collaborate in ways that will facilitate the successful transition of a youth with a disability? The formation of state and local interagency transition committees or core teams made up of multiple transition service agencies has been frequently suggested in the literature as an effective means for accomplishing this objective. The ultimate goal of an interagency team is to form agreements that promote communication and transfer of information among transition services agency personnel, as well as sharing of resources and services for individuals with disabilities and their families (see chapters 5 and 10 for more information on creating interagency transition teams and agreements).

Despite widespread support in transition literature for the formation of interagency teams and agreements, local practitioners may not be able to wait for formal agreements to be put in place. Most high school special education teachers do not have time in their daily schedules to participate or expedite the development of local interagency transition teams. Hence, an interim and responsive interagency activity for these personnel would be to identify local transition services agencies and programs, followed by the establishment of positive collaborative relationships with transition personnel working for these agencies and programs. Figure 6–3 contains a list of potential federal, state, local, private, and school transition services agencies and organizations to consider contacting. Visitations, if possible, to these transition programs and agencies by school special education personnel are highly recommended.

In summary, transition personnel from multiple disciplines and agencies must learn about each other's programs and services and collaborate when planning and implementing transition services for youth with disabilities. No single agency is capable of offering the vast array of transition services and programs needed by the full range of youth with disabilities (e.g., mild, moderate, and severe). Interagency collaboration, in ideal circumstances, involves the formation of **interagency transition**

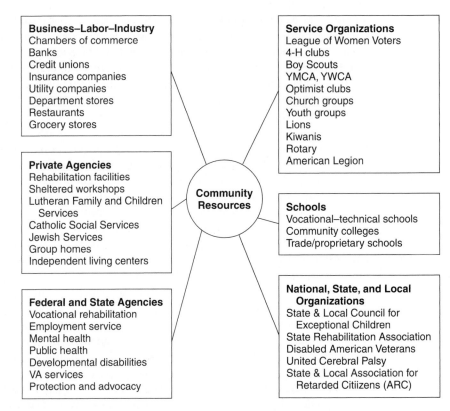

Figure 6–3   Some Community Resources Important to Career Development of Individuals with Disabilities and Who Are Disadvantaged

teams and the writing of interagency agreements. Although formalization of these teams is emerging, transition personnel from multiple agencies should at least discuss and share the programs and services available in their local region.

Interdisciplinary Collaboration

This best practice is covered extensively in chapter 5 and, hence, will not be repeated here.

Summary of Interagency Collaboration for Transition Best Practices

Interagency and interdisciplinary collaboration are frequently cited best practices in transition literature. Promoting positive outcomes for youth with disabilities in multiple domains such as education, employment, community independence, and recreation and leisure takes a team of transition professionals working together. Sharing knowledge, time, and resources between and within agencies is the key to interagency and **interdisciplinary collaboration.** Formation of interagency and interdisciplinary core teams is a highly recommended strategy for accomplishing this objective. If teams are not yet formed, school personnel can begin by making concerted efforts to learn the roles and responsibilities of colleagues in their own agency, as well as available transition services and programs in their local community and region.

A case study illustrating transition services agency best practices is presented next. We then review and discuss the second major category of best practices in transition, **transition education programming.**

LET'S SEE IT IN ACTION! CASE EXAMPLE

Transition Services Agency Best Practices

The special education program at Willard High School recently participated in a program quality review from the state. The state found that the transition services offered at the school were limited to on-campus and district programs, with little collaboration with other community-based transition service agencies. The special education staff subsequently attempted to identify transition service agencies in their local area that provided postsecondary education, employment, independent living, transportation and mobility services, and recreation and leisure activities for persons with disabilities. The county and state departments of education and special education services division were contacted to provide local transition services agency names and telephone numbers. Each member of the Willard High School special education and related services staff were subsequently assigned the task of contacting and meeting with transition personnel at these various agencies to determine the services they provide and program eligibility requirements. This information was then shared at a later special education department meeting that resulted in the creation of a transition services agency resource guide. The guide was distributed to all special education department and related services staff and used in the **transition planning** process, as well as to invite transition services agency representatives to attend future IEP meetings or provide parents with agency information where appropriate.

WHAT ARE BEST PRACTICES FOR TRANSITION EDUCATION PROGRAMMING?

Integrated Schools, Classrooms, and Employment

Numerous pieces of legislation reviewed in chapter 4 support the rights of individuals with disabilities to participate in integrated settings within society. IDEA 2004 and the No Child Left Behind Act (NCLB) in 2001 are perhaps the most prominent pieces of legislation supporting access to and inclusion in general education classrooms for youth with disabilities. The field of special education has a long and well-documented history of seeking ways to better integrate this population into mainstream environments. Examples include the following:

1. Lloyd Dunn's (1968) seminal article criticizing the justification of special education placement for children with disabilities

2. The concept of mainstreaming and least restrictive environment brought forth in the Education of the Handicapped Act of 1975 (Pub. L. No. 94-142)
3. The Regular Education Initiative, which called for the reform of separate systems, resources, and educational services for youth with disabilities, along with a merger of general and special education into one unified system (Reynolds, Wang, & Walberg, 1987)
4. The full inclusion or inclusive education movement advocating education for youth with disabilities at their neighborhood school, along with full integration in general education classrooms in order to be educated with their nondisabled peers (Stainback, Stainback, & Ayers, 1996)

In the past, some professional groups within the ranks of special education, such as the Council for Learning Disabilities (CLD), did not endorse fully **inclusive education** for all youth with disabilities and urged the field not to abandon the continuum of service options outlined in IDEA (Andregg & Vergason, 1996; Council for Exceptional Children [CEC], 1993). Professionals and consumers on both sides of the debate, however, have agreed that it is unreasonable to expect persons with disabilities to successfully transition into an integrated society as adults if they are not provided with integrated learning experiences during their childhood and adolescent years.

With these thoughts in mind, we concur that the path to successful transition for youth with disabilities begins with their participation in integrated schools and programs, preferably at their neighborhood school. Fortunately, segregated school sites for youth with disabilities are far less common today than in the past. At one time, segregated schools were considered the least restrictive environment for many youth with disabilities, primarily those with moderate and severe disabilities. Segregated schools were created in response to the lack of public school service options that existed for these individuals prior to the passage of the Education for All Handicapped Children Act in 1975. This is no longer the case, as evidenced by recent data from the U.S. Department of Education (2002) which indicated that 96% of all students with disabilities received their education at neighborhood schools. Most special education professionals agree that a major shortcoming of a segregated education for youth with disabilities is a lack of "normal" role models, resulting in limited opportunities for the development of adequate and appropriate social skills and friendships with nondisabled peers.

Integrated classrooms and programs, in addition to integrated school sites, are equally important transition education programming best practices that contribute to successful transition of youth with disabilities. The vast majority of youth with disabilities (e.g., 97% of those in middle school and 95% of those in high school) receive their education during at least 40% of the school day in general education classrooms (Smith, 2007), with well over half of them participating in general education classes more than 80% of their school day. Resource specialist programs afford opportunities for youth with mild disabilities to interact both socially and academically with their nondisabled peers and with general education teachers. Research has demonstrated a relationship between participation in integrated classrooms and improved transition outcomes (Blackorby & Wagner, 1996; Wagner, Newman, Cameto, Levine, & Garza, 2006).

Despite these encouraging statistics, some individuals with more severe learning disabilities and those with moderate to severe disabilities continue to be educated in segregated special day classrooms or community-based programs around the country. Although most of these classrooms exist on integrated school campuses, the factor of colocation alone cannot overcome the negative effects of a segregated education. Typically, students with more moderate to severe disabilities educated in self-contained special day classes only experience integration with their nondisabled peers during recess, lunch, and/or limited academic activities such as art, music, and physical education. Furthermore, it is not uncommon to find segregated special education classes located in isolated places on the school grounds such as detached trailers or bungalows placed far away from the general education population and in less than desirable classroom spaces. Likewise, segregated community experiences for persons with disabilities still exist, such as supported employment in sheltered workshops or recreation activities for persons with disabilities without participation of their nondisabled peers (e.g., art therapy and bowling).

In summary, successful transition to a quality adult life in an integrated world is less likely to occur for youth with disabilities if they spend the majority of their school years segregated from their nondisabled peers. We must provide youth with disabilities not only the opportunity to attend their neighborhood school on an integrated campus, but also provide access to and education in general education classrooms and community programs. It is in these settings that they can best learn appropriate social interaction skills and develop friendships.

A second transition education programming best practice frequently cited in the literature is the use of a functional life-skills curriculum, along with community-based instruction. This best practice in transition is covered next.

Functional Life-Skills Education

Providing youth with disabilities a **functional life-skills education** is frequently cited in transition best practices literature. Traditional models of secondary education emphasizing academic skills alone have been shown to be inadequate for preparing most youth with disabilities for the demands of postschool life (Brolin & Loyd, 2004; Zigmond & Miller, 1992). Evidence supporting this statement can be seen in the findings that youth with disabilities, compared with their nondisabled peers, experience higher dropout rates, lower academic achievement or performance levels, significantly poorer employment rates and wages, limited postsecondary school enrollment, and poorer residential independence after high school (Wagner, Cameto, & Newman, 2003). In response to similar statistics, over a decade ago several researchers called for fundamental changes in public school educational programming practices and curriculum for all students, particularly those with disabilities (Clark, Field, Patton, Brolin, & Sitlington, 1994; Kohler, 1996; West, Taymans, & Gopal, 1997). Kohler, for example, argued that educational programming for youth with disabilities must be based on postschool goals in a variety of transition areas, with curricular options offered in school that are related to these goals.

Functional life skills are those that are both academic and critical for successful functioning in the community and in adult life (Brolin & Loyd, 2004; Cronin, 1996). A functional life-skills curriculum emphasizes learning in areas such as personal–social skills, independent living, occupational skills, recreation and leisure, health and grooming, communication skills, and other skills and abilities that generalize to the community (Clark, 1991, 1994). All of these skill areas have appeared in transition literature historically under various terms such as *functional competency, literacy, functional literacy, functional academics,* and *daily living skills.*

A number of life-skills curriculum models and materials are available for special educators interested in this educational approach for youth with disabilities (see Brolin & Loyd, 2004, for a review of these models and materials, and see Appendix 6-1 for a list of published transition curricula). Perhaps the most widely known and used is the *Life Centered Career Education (LCCE) Curriculum,* developed and written by Donn Brolin and published by the CEC (1997). This curriculum, shown in Table 6-2, contains 22 major life-skill competencies and 97 subcompetencies, organized into three major domains (daily living skills, personal–social skills, and occupational guidance and preparation). Two versions of the LCCE curriculum are available, one for youth with mild disabilities and a second, modified version designed for youth with more moderate disabilities. The curriculum is based on the concept of career development that emphasizes the infusion of career education and work (paid or unpaid) in all school subjects, beginning in kindergarten and continuing throughout the K–12 system, as shown in Figure 6-4 (see the Career and Vocational Assessment and Education section in this chapter for a more complete review of this topic).

Community-Based Educational Experiences

A key component to the successful implementation of the LCCE or any functional life-skills curriculum is the provision of *community-based educational experiences* for youth with disabilities. A common characteristic of this population of learners, particularly those with moderate to severe disabilities, is their inability to generalize classroom-based learning to real-life situations. To address this problem, special education teachers have frequently used classroom simulations of various life skills such as filling out job applications, conducting mock interviews, role-playing social interactions, newspaper searches for rental property, and planning and preparing a snack or meal. Although these activities may appear to be useful in preparing youth with disabilities for postschool life demands, they neither fully address the problem of generalization of learning nor offer participants the breadth and depth of experience needed to function fully independently as adults. Hence, it is important to take youth with disabilities out into the community to practice life skills and explore various community businesses, agencies, and resources in which they are likely to interact as adults. Trips to banks, grocery stores, restaurants, malls, department stores, and other businesses are recommended places where youth with disabilities can practice daily living and personal–social skills.

In summary, an important and frequently recommended transition education programming best practice is to teach youth with disabilities in community-based settings, paired with specific life skills (e.g., social skills) that they will need to function independently in the adult world. What are effective ways to promote the development of social and personal skills in youth with disabilities? This transition education programming best practice is covered next.

Social-Skills Training and Competency

Lack of adequate social skills is a frequently cited problem affecting the successful transition of persons with disabilities, particularly in employment settings. Social development and training programs have subsequently become highly recommended transition education programming best practices (Brolin & Loyd, 2004; Deshler & Schumaker, 2006; Gajar, Goodman, & McAfee, 1993; Halpern, 1994; Kohler et al., 1994). Unfortunately, valid and functional changes in social integration of individuals with disabilities in the workplace and other settings have failed to be clearly demonstrated in transition research literature (Chadsey & Sheldon, 1998; Chadsey-Rusch & O'Reilly, 1992; Crites & Dunn, 2004; Rutherford, 1997). As a result, the value of social-skills training for this population is an important emerging area of research. What types of social skills are critical for youth with disabilities to demonstrate?

Deshler and Schumaker (2006) and others (Elksnin & Elksnin, 2001) affirm the importance of social behaviors that facilitate the ability of youth with disabilities to communicate with, relate to, and work with peers, teachers, employers, and other adults. A survey by Williams, Walker, Todis, and Fabre (1989, as reviewed in Chadsey-Rusch & O'Reilly, 1992) attempted to validate social skills that were most highly valued by secondary teachers and students. Student behaviors that teachers rated most highly were (a) behavioral compliance, (b) task engagement and completion, (c) responsiveness to the teacher, and (d) socially mature behavior. They rated behavior related to peer relationships very low. In contrast, students rated peer relationship behaviors much higher, thereby demonstrating their concern with effectively coping with the demands and pressures of social relationships and the quality of their friendships in school. Chadsey-Rusch and O'Reilly identified particular conditions in postsecondary educational and employment settings that promote the successful social integration of individuals with disabilities. These conditions included having (a) equal access and participation in a variety of social activities, (b) equal treatment and acceptance by others, and (c) personal satisfaction with the level of interactions and relationships one achieves.

Chadsey-Rusch and O'Reilly (1992) reviewed literature on the type of social skills valued by college and community college professors and vocational instructors in postsecondary school settings. The authors indicated that very little valid information on this topic exists. Aune (1991), however, discussed the importance for postsecondary-bound youth with learning disabilities to develop self-advocacy skills, study habits, and the ability to ask for and use classroom accommodations. Youth with learning disabilities in Aune's study were taught their rights and responsibilities under § 504 and trained to use self-advocacy skills needed in postsecondary settings. Examples of these skills included asking for help, accepting criticism, and discussing a grade with a teacher. Gajar, Goodman, and McAfee (1993) mentioned the following specific workplace-related social skills to be taught to persons with disabilities: (a) complying with instructions, (b) asking a supervisor for assistance, (c) responding to criticism and suggestions, (d) getting information about a task, (e) communicating feelings to a supervisor, and (f) conversing with a supervisor. A second set of social skills mentioned by the authors related to interpersonal communication with coworkers are (a) offering to help coworkers, (b) conversing, (c) expressing feelings, (d) developing close relationships,

Table 6–2   Life-Centered Career Education Competencies

Curriculum Area	Competency	Subcompetency: The student will be able to:	
Daily living skills	1. Managing Personal Finances	1. Count money & make correct change	2. Make responsible expenditures
	2. Selecting & Managing a Household	7. Maintain home exterior/interior	8. Use basic appliances & tools
	3. Caring for Personal Needs	12. Demonstrate knowledge of physical fitness, nutrition, & weight	13. Exhibit proper grooming & hygiene
	4. Raising Children & Meeting Marriage Responsibilities	17. Demonstrate physical care for raising children	18. Know psychological aspects of raising children
	5. Buying, Preparing & Consuming Food	20. Purchase food	21. Clean food preparation areas
	6. Buying & Caring for Clothing	26. Wash/clean clothing	27. Purchase clothing
	7. Exhibiting Responsible Citizenship	29. Demonstrate knowledge of civil rights & responsibilities	30. Know nature of local, state, & federal governments
	8. Using Recreational Facilities & Engaging in Leisure	33. Demonstrate knowledge of available community resources	34. Choose & plan activities
	9. Getting Around the Community	38. Demonstrate knowledge of traffic rules and safety	39. Demonstrate knowledge & use of various means of transportation
Personal-social skills	10. Achieving Self-Awareness	42. Identify physical & psychological needs	43. Identify interests & abilities
	11. Acquiring Self-Confidence	46. Express feelings of self-worth	47. Describe others' perception of self
	12. Achieving Socially Responsible Behavior—Community	51. Develop respect for the rights & properties of others	52. Recognize authority & follow instructions
	13. Maintaining Good Interpersonal Skills	56. Demonstrate listening & responding skills	57. Establish & maintain close relationships
	14. Achieving Independence	59. Strive toward self-actualization	60. Demonstrate self-organization
	15. Making Adequate Decisions	62. Locate & Use sources of assistance	60. Anticipate consequences
	16. Communicating with Others	67. Recognize & respond to emergency situations	68. Communicate with understanding
Occupational guidance and preparation	17. Knowing & Exploring Occupational Possibilities	70. Identify remunerative aspects of work	71. Locate sources of occupational & training information
	18. Selecting & Planning Occupational Choices	78. Make realistic occupational choices	77. Identify requirements of appropriate & available jobs
	19. Exhibiting Appropriate Work Habits & Behaviors	81. Follow directions & observe regulations	82. Recognize importance of attendance & punctuality
	20. Seeking, Securing & Maintaining Employment	83. Search for a job	88. Apply for a job
	21. Exhibiting Sufficient Physical-Manual Skills	94. Demonstrate stamina & endurance	95. Demonstrate satisfactory balance & coordination
	22. Obtaining Specific Occupational Skills		

Source: From *Life Centered Career Education: A Competency-Based Approach* (4th ed., pp. 12–13), by D. E. Brolin, 1993. Reston, VA: Council for Exceptional Children. Copyright 1993 by Council for Exceptional Children. Reprinted with permission.

3. Keep basic financial records
4. Calculate & pay taxes
5. Use credit responsibly
6. Use banking services

9. Select adequate housing
10. Set up household
11. Maintain home grounds

14. Dress appropriately
15. Demonstrate knowledge of common illnesses, prevention & treatment
16. Practice personal safety

19. Demonstrate marriage responsibilities

22. Store food
23. Prepare meals
24. Demonstrate appropriate eating habits
25. Plan/eat balanced meals

28. Iron, mend, & store clothing
31. Demonstrate knowledge of the law & ability to follow the law
32. Demonstrate knowledge of citizen rights & responsibilities

35. Demonstrate knowledge of the value of recreation
36. Engage in group & individual activities
37. Plan vacation time

40. Find way around the community
41. Drive a car

44. Identify emotions
45. Demonstrate knowledge of physical self

48. Accept & give praise
49. Accept & give criticism
50. Develop confidence in oneself

53. Demonstrate appropriate behavior in public places
54. Know important character traits
55. Recognize personal roles

56. Make & Maintain friendships

61. Demonstrate awareness of how one's behavior affects others

64. Develop & evaluate alternatives
65. Recognize nature of a problem
66. Develop goal-seeking behavior

69. Know subtleties of communication

72. Identify personal values met through work
73. Identify societal values met through work
74. Classify jobs into occupational categories
75. Investigate local occupational & training opportunities

78. Identify occupational aptitudes
79. Identify major occupational interests
80. Identify major occupational needs

83. Recognize importance of supervision
84. Demonstrate knowledge of occupational safety
85. Work with others
86. Meet demands for quality work
87. Work at a satisfactory rate

90. Interview for a job
91. Know how to maintain post-school occupational adjustment
92. Demonstrate knowledge of competitive standards
93. Know how to adjust to changes in employment

96. Demonstrate manual dexterity
97. Demonstrate sensory discrimination

There are no specific subcompetencies, as they depend on skill being taught

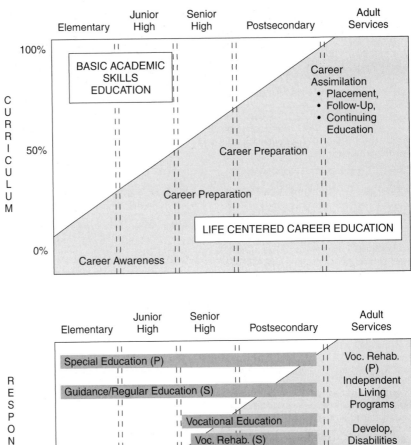

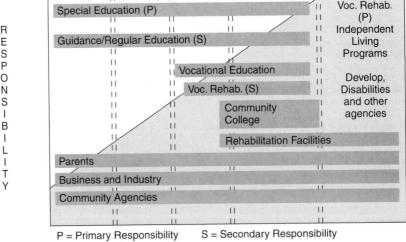

P = Primary Responsibility   S = Secondary Responsibility

Figure 6–4   Curriculum/LCCE Transition Model
Source: From *Life Centered Career Education: Professional Development Activity Book* (p. 43), by
Council for Exceptional Children, 1993, Reston, VA: Council for Exceptional Children. Copyright 1993
by Council for Exceptional Children. Reprinted with permission.

(e) contributing to the group, (g) respecting the rights of others, (h) showing honesty
and fairness, (i) negotiating conflict, (j) giving and receiving positive and negative feedback, (k) resisting peer pressure, (l) accepting assistance, and (m) handling teasing and
provocations.

Special educators interested in social-skills training curricula should consider the LCCE curriculum. Brolin (1997) emphasized the following social-skill development objectives in the LCCE curriculum: (a) develop respect for the rights and property of others, (b) recognize authority and follow instructions, (c) demonstrate appropriate behavior in public places, (d) know important character traits, and (e) recognize personal roles. In addition, the LCCE curriculum contains several social–interpersonal skill objectives: (a) demonstrate listening and responding skills, (b) establish and maintain close personal relationships, and (c) make and maintain friendships. Activities in the classroom and community for helping students with disabilities master these various social skills are included in the LCCE curriculum guide. The Council for Exceptional Children (CEC) offers many publications related to teaching social skills to youth with disabilities (see books by Crites & Dunn, 2004; Elksnin & Elksnin, 2001; Mannix, 1998; Sargent, 1998; Simpson, Myles, Sasso, & Kamps, 1997). An overview of these books, along with ordering information, can be found at the CEC Web site www. cec.sped.org/bk/catalog2/social.html

Deshler and Schumaker (2006) describe three types of social skills programming to consider when teaching adolescents with disabilities: (a) positive behavioral supports, (b) instruction in specific social skills, and (c) self-advocacy and problem-solving training. With respect to the first of these three programs, Deshler and Schumaker describe positive behavioral support programs to be a *school-wide system* designed to establish rules and expectations for social behavior for all students (e.g., show respect for others), including those with disabilities. These involve establishing norms for behavior throughout the school setting where all students spend their time, such as hallways, the cafeteria, or the auditorium. Simultaneously, *setting specific policies and rules* that are more rigid for the classroom are developed by teachers to facilitate learning and classroom productivity (e.g., maintain eye contact when the teacher is talking). Finally, *individual student systems* focus on specific behaviors for students whose needs are not met within the broader school context and program (e.g., cognitive behavior modification techniques). Prevention of social problems and interventions vary in the system, depending on the context in which the problems occur. For example, universal or school-wide interventions used for typical students would apply to those with disabilities as well, such as conflict resolution training or strategies. For students at risk for serious social and behavioural difficulties, more individualized interventions should be used, such as positive behavioral interventions, counseling and anger management. Finally, for students with chronic or severe social problems, more comprehensive interventions are required, such as connection to community social service agencies, law enforcement personnel, or drug and alcohol treatment programs.

Instruction in specific social skills is the second program mentioned by Deshler and Schumaker and involves social skills packages that focus on teaching both verbal and nonverbal behaviors that individuals can apply to particular categories of social tasks (e.g., giving positive feedback, dealing with peer pressure, and handling negative situations). Strategies are taught to students, along with a corresponding set of behaviors to use in a specific situation. Students are taught to know and understand the reasons why each step in a social strategy is important, the benefits of using each step, and the social rules associated with using the steps.

Finally, Deshler and Schumaker propose self-advocacy and problem-solving train-ing as a means to help adolescents with disabilities become independent and empow-ered to meet their social needs. Programs of this nature typically teach adolescents with disabilities how to identify and prioritize their needs, set and monitor learning and developmental goals for themselves, and work toward the attainment of their goals. The authors describe a social strategy called SHARE that can be applied in self-advocacy situations (*S*it up straight, *H*ave a pleasant tone of voice, *A*ctivate your think-ing, *R*elax, *E*ngage in eye communication).

In summary, social-skills training and competency in youth with disabilities is important to consider when designing quality transition education programs and services (Elksnin & Elksnin, 2001). Which specific social skills are to be taught depends on the context in which the skills must be applied. Employers, teachers, and youth with disabilities may value different social skills (Chadsey-Rusch & O'Reilly, 1992). Moreover, it is unclear whether teaching particular social skills results in desired social integration outcomes, but recent research is demonstrating more posi-tive results in this regard, particularly for youth with learning disabilities (Deshler & Schumaker, 2006). Continued research is needed in this area. The LCCE curriculum, along with others published by the CEC offer specific social-skills training activities to special educators interested in this type of material.

Career and Vocational Assessment and Education

A consistent finding in vocational special-needs literature is that career and vocational assessment, career and vocational education programs, and paid work experience in high school leads to positive postschool employment outcomes for youth with disabili-ties (Schwarz & Taymans, 1991; Sitlington & Clark, 2006; Sitlington, Frank, & Carson, 1993; Sitlington, Neubert, Begun, Lombard, & Leconte, 2007). The purpose of career and vocational assessment is to introduce youth with disabilities to a wide variety of career and vocational opportunities. Traditional assessment involves determining a person's career and vocational interests, aptitudes, achievement, and likely future suc-cess or failure in particular work situations. Assessment can be conducted in clinical settings, using formal and standardized testing instruments and procedures, or in simu-lated and real-work settings (authentic assessment), where the actual work adjustment and job performance capabilities of an individual are evaluated (see Chapter 7 for a more complete review of vocational assessment models, instruments, and procedures).

Curriculum-based vocational assessment (CBVA) has been offered as an alternative to traditional vocational assessment. CBVA is a process for determining career develop-ment and vocational needs, based on a student's ongoing performance within existing vocational and academic courses (Albright & Cobb, 1988; Ianacone & Leconte, 1986; Schloss, Schloss, & Schloss, 2006). The advantage of this approach over traditional vocational assessment is that it (a) allows for data collection on the student over multiple points in time within social and employment contexts, (b) addresses student needs and evaluation through the identification of key personnel and resources, (c) promotes the development of an operational plan for implementation and evaluation, and (d) increases the accuracy of predicting the student's future performance in social and employment contexts (Gajar et al., 1993; Schloss et al., 2006).

An overview of career education and vocational education will be presented next.

Career Education

The term **career education** was first introduced in 1971 by Sidney Marland, Jr., former U.S. Commissioner of Education. Marland called for major education reform in response to the high dropout rate in schools and sought an educational system that was more capable of providing students with knowledge and skills relevant to adult functioning. In 1985, Kokaska and Brolin defined career education as the "process of systematically coordinating all school, family, and community components together to facilitate each individual's potential for economic, social, and personal fulfillment and participation in productive work activities that benefit the individual or others" (p. 43). Gajar et al. (1995) reviewed a host of definitions of career education and indicated that the term *career education* has encompassed both a narrow and broad perspective during the past 25 years. A common theme in all definitions, however, is a focus on lifelong learning, beginning in early childhood and extending throughout adulthood, and emphasis on the preparation of an individual for the various demands of adult life, including daily living, social and interpersonal relationships, and occupational guidance and preparation. A major feature of career education is an emphasis on the classroom as a workplace for both teachers and students (Hoyt, 1993).

The possession of a disability can potentially have a substantial negative effect on the career development of such an individual (Miller, Lombard, & Corbey, 2007). Examples of this for youth with disabilities include (a) limitations in career exploration and experiences, (b) limited opportunities to develop decision-making skills, and (c) lower self-concept. Youth with disabilities are often less career-mature compared to their nondisabled peers and thereby less ready to make career decisions that will help them prepare for the responsibilities of adult life (Field et al., 1998a; Sitlington et al., 1996). This, in turn, can contribute to their having greater difficulty obtaining employment. For these reasons, it is imperative that career education be addressed in the adult life preparation of youth with disabilities.

A number of authors have conceptualized various models of career education (see Sitlington, 1996, pp. 52–53, for a review of these models). A common theme in all of these models is the view of career education as a progression through various stages involving several interrelated activities. Brolin and Loyd (2004) identified the following stages and activities of career education:

1. *Career awareness* begins during the elementary school years and is focused on helping students develop awareness of the world of work, both paid and unpaid. Students gain an understanding during this stage of career education of how they will fit into the work-oriented society in the future.

2. *Career exploration* occurs during the middle and high school years and is focused on helping students explore their interests and abilities in relation to desired lifestyle and potential occupations.

3. *Career preparation* is emphasized during the high school years and involves career decision-making and acquisition of the necessary skills for achieving a desired lifestyle. Students identify their interests and aptitudes at this stage of career education.

4. *Career placement, assimilation, follow-up,* or *continuing education* occurs during the postsecondary years and is focused on postsecondary training and community adjustment. Students successfully engage in quality adult life activities such as vocational, family, and civic or volunteer work, as well as obtain paid employment. Continuing education and follow-up support services is provided, as needed, to students at this stage of career education.

A second model of career education is Clark's *School-Based Career Development and Transition Education Model for Adolescents with Handicaps* (Clark & Kolstoe, 1990; Sitlington & Clark, 2001). This model, shown in Figure 6–5, advocated a school-based curriculum on life-career development that spans preschool through adulthood. In the early school grades, the model emphasized the teaching of values such as courage, honesty, cooperation, courtesy, and respect, as well as a host of other values associated with individual and group success in life. Human relationship instruction is also emphasized in the early grades, with a focus on personal–social skills needed for creating and maintaining positive relationships with others. The third and fourth components addressed in the first phase of the model are occupational information (e.g., prevocational skills and preparation) and job and daily living skills. The remaining two phases of the model emphasized postsecondary career and vocational preparation and continuing education and adult independence.

In summary, career education is a core best practice in transition education programming. A number of career education models have been proposed over the years, containing common elements of career awareness, exploration, preparation, and maintenance for youth with disabilities. School-based activities throughout elementary, middle, and high school should focus on helping youth with disabilities become aware of their career interests, aptitudes, and capabilities, as well as the world of work. The ultimate goal of career education is to provide youth with disabilities the necessary skills and education to function independently in all aspects of their adult life.

Vocational Education (Career and Technical Education)

The field of vocational education has gradually undergone a shift in the past decade in an attempt to find its role and place in the standards-based reform movement and other systems-change efforts in the public schools (Sitlington & Clark, 2006). For example, these authors point out that the term *vocational education* evolved to the term *vocational and technical education* and now is referred to the current title of *career and technical education* (CTE). No matter the terminology used, the focus of programs of this nature is to prepare individuals for gainful employment as semiskilled or skilled workers, technicians, or subprofessionals in recognized occupations and in new and emerging occupations or for enrollment in advanced technical education, excluding occupations that generally require a professional or advanced degree (American Vocational Association, 1998). The National Assessment of Vocational Education (NAVE) (U.S. Department of Education, 2004) identified 10 broad occupational areas that are typically the focus of CTE programs. These include

1. Agriculture (and renewable resources)
2. Business, including business services and business management

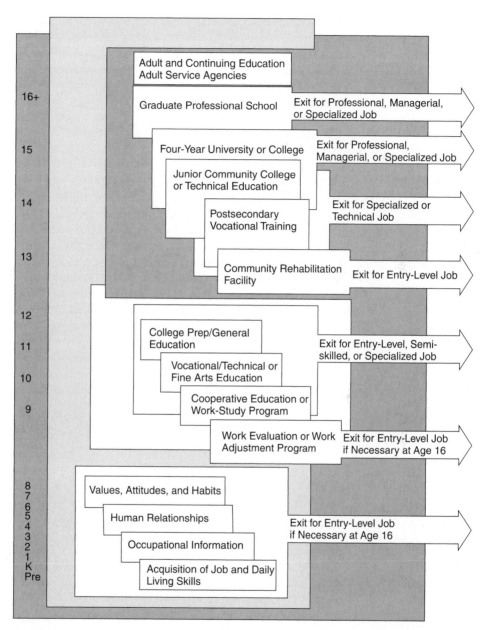

Figure 6–5 A School-Based Career Development and Transition Education Model for Adolescents with Handicaps

Source: From *Career Development and Transition Education for Adolescents with Disabilities,* by G. M. Clark and O. P. Kolstoe, 1990, Boston: Allyn & Bacon. Copyright 1990 by Allyn & Bacon. Reprinted with permission.

3. Marketing
4. Health care
5. Protective services (and public service)
6. Technology, including computer technology, communication technology, and other technology
7. Trade and industry, including construction, mechanics and repair, precision production, and transportation
8. Food service and hospitality
9. Child care and education
10. Personal and other services.

CTE should begin after the completion of career and vocational assessment and prevocational education activities. The purpose of these assessments and activities are to identify and match the interests, aptitudes, and capabilities of the individual with a disability with appropriate CTE (see Chapter 7 for more information). Cobb and Neubert (1992, 1998) described a vocational education planning model for youth with disabilities that begins in the middle school years and lasts well into postsecondary and adult life (Figure 6–6). The model includes prevocational education, vocational education, work experience, postsecondary options, and change and advancement activities.

According to Sitlington and Clark (2006), the three basic administrative arrangements for delivering CTE are (a) general high schools, (b) comprehensive high schools, and (c) vocational technical centers and career academies. A successfully greater number of vocational training areas are available across these three settings, with as few as two or three in general high schools and as many occupations as are reflected by local

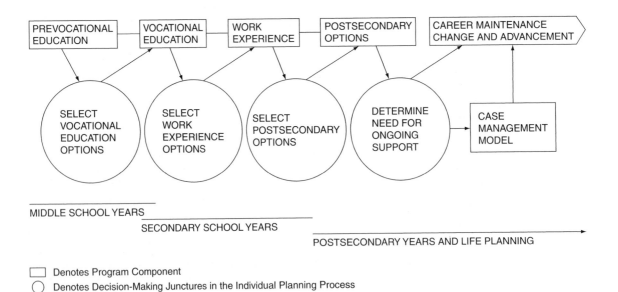

Figure 6–6   Vocational Education Planning Model

labor market needs in vocational technical centers. Vocational classes in any or all of these settings utilize traditional lectures, reading assignments, homework, and tests, as well as actual hands-on training, supervised skill development, and possible on-the-job work in the community. Important factors to consider when choosing a vocational education program for a youth with a disability include the program's required prerequisite knowledge and skills, opportunities for entry-level employment, and availability of support services. Once a youth with a disability has been placed in a vocational education program, vocational resource personnel should provide instructional support, curriculum modification, monitor progress, linkages between the school and community, and assistance in writing the employment component of the individualized education plan (Sarkees & West, 1990).

In summary, the importance of career and vocational assessment and education for youth with disabilities consistently appears in transition best practices literature. Prevocational education should be provided to youth with disabilities during the middle school years, leading to paid work experience during high school. Youth with disabilities may require time-limited or ongoing support from job developers and job coaches to successfully participate in competitive employment. This transition education programming best practice is reviewed next.

Competitive Paid Work Experience in High School and Beyond

Work experience, preferably paid, is an additional component of a quality transition education program for youth with disabilities. The School-to-Work Opportunities Act of 1994 (which sunset in 2002) helped promote school-to-work transition programs for all students, including those with disabilities, by emphasizing school-based learning activities, along with work-based learning components and connecting activities. Many states still have programs of this nature that provide paid work experience for students with disabilities while in high school (e.g., California's Work Ability Program, "What Makes Workability Work?" 2004). Work experience promotes enhancement and application of acquired career and vocational education knowledge and skill. Special assistance in the form of job development, job placement, and job coaching may be necessary to facilitate work experience in the community for youth with disabilities (see Griffin & Targett, 2001 and, Steere, Rose, & Cavaiuoo, 2007, for recommendations on how to find, develop, and provide job support for youth with disabilities). Career counseling should also be offered, with an emphasis on exploration of future community-based employment and postsecondary education and training options. Finally, observations and visitations to prospective career/vocational training programs, employment sites, and community colleges and universities are recommended to allow youth with disabilities to investigate actual job and training requirements, talk with prospective employers, and develop realistic postsecondary educational goals.

Employment of youth with disabilities is significantly facilitated when businesses and industries are linked with local schools. This transition education programming best practice is discussed next.

Business and Industry Linkages with Schools

The 1990s were dominated by calls for school reform and restructuring in response to the discrepancy between high school graduates' skills and the demands of available jobs in business and industry. Major federal legislation was passed, such as Goals 2000 and the School-to-Work Opportunities Act, that encouraged the establishment of partnerships between business and industry and local schools to promote improved occupational skills training and career education for youth with disabilities. Brolin and Loyd (2004) offered the following suggestions for building collaborative relationships between schools and businesses in career development:

1. Identify trends in the economy
2. Further contacts with business and industry
3. Become advocates
4. Serve as a classroom resource
5. Provide program consultation
6. Provide work experience
7. Participate in conferences and workshops
8. Provide instructional and resource materials.

Additional thoughts on building connections between schools and employers are provided by Wehman (1996). This author suggested (a) including employers on advisory committees, (b) developing an employer speakers' bureau, (c) having local businesses review school curricula and teaching strategies, (d) providing job shadowing, mentoring, and internship experiences for students, and (e) promoting awareness of students with disabilities in local businesses. More recently, Wehman (2001) reviewed opportunities that employers can offer to help students understand what business and industry can do to help connect school-based learning with what is needed in the workforce. The Employer Participation Model, published by the National Employer Leadership Council (1996) presented the following examples, ranging from minimal to intense:

1. Career talks (i.e., visits to the classroom)
2. Career fairs
3. Workplace and industry tours
4. Job shadowing
5. Job rotations
6. Internships
7. Cooperative education
8. Youth apprenticeships
9. Mentoring

Initially, establishing contacts with business and industry representatives can be a potentially challenging task for educators. Brolin and Loyd (2004) suggested using the resources of vocational rehabilitation; state, regional, and local employment services departments; and other organizations that have contacts with business and industry. The use of newspaper advertisements, yellow pages, private employment agencies, civil service bulletins, business pages of newspapers, union or trade publications, and the Internet are other possible resources. In response to the mandates of the Americans with Disabilities Act, many large corporations have become actively engaged in advocacy activities for people with disabilities. Numerous corporations and companies in the United States have special employment outreach programs for persons with disabilities (see Brolin & Loyd, 2004, pp. 150–151, for a complete listing).

In summary, finding employment for youth with disabilities can be facilitated greatly by linking local schools with business and industry. Many companies today are interested in hiring youth with disabilities and welcome connections with special education, vocational special needs, and vocational rehabilitation personnel. Positive relationships between business and industry and transition personnel can subsequently produce a win-win situation for all parties involved. This is particularly true for persons with disabilities, who become the recipients of valuable employment opportunities.

The final best practice for transition education programming, postsecondary education participation and support, is reviewed next.

Postsecondary Education Participation and Support

Compared with their nondisabled peers, youth with disabilities have had historically lower participation and completion rates in postsecondary education, and these trends have continued over the past 15 years (Wagner, D'Amico, Marder, Newman, & Blackorby, 1992; Wagner et al., 2006). Recommendations have appeared in the literature on how to best support individuals with disabilities, particularly those with learning disabilities, who choose to participate in postsecondary education. Hitchings et al. (2001) interviewed college students with learning disabilities and asked them to discuss their career development needs. The study found that the majority of these students had difficulty describing their disability and its impact on their college career exploration and planning. They would have benefited from career development services, training in self-advocacy and career exploration in their first two years of college, and ongoing instruction in career self-management skills.

Lehman, Davies, and Laurin (2000) interviewed 35 college students with a variety of disabilities to explain their experiences in college. Four themes emerged: (a) lack of understanding and acceptance concerning disabilities on the part of people in general, fellow students, staff, and faculty; (b) lack of adequate services for helping them with academic and nonacademic responsibilities; (c) lack of sufficient financial resources and knowledge of how to acquire them; and (d) lack of self-advocacy skills and training. Recommendations for eliminating barriers and providing support for postsecondary education students with disabilities included (a) conducting faculty and staff development workshops on the nature of various disabilities, as well as adaptations, and accommodations to meet the learning needs of these students, (b) providing summer classes to teach entering students compensatory strategies for use in college classes, (c) role-playing how to effectively communicate their disability and learning needs to faculty, and (d) encouraging networking among college students with disabilities. Finally, a publication by CLD (2001) offered guidance on how to select effective postsecondary support services and outlined specific professional and program standards for institutions of higher education that could be considered state of the art.

"Of particular importance to students with LD are standards related to fostering self-advocacy, providing instruction in learning strategies, specifying policies and procedures for students with disabilities, and doing program evaluation" (p. 6). In addition, CLD notes that postsecondary education support programs for students with disabilities should be able to satisfactorily answer all of the questions of their consumers and provide written information and evaluation data to support their claims.

In summary, students with disabilities choosing to attend postsecondary education are at a distinct disadvantage compared to their nondisabled peers. Although federal law supports the need to provide access and accommodations to individuals with disabilities on college campuses, the onus of responsibility for accessing these services on the students themselves and the quality of the services offered may vary from campus to campus. Academic, career, and self-advocacy skills appear to be the major supports identified in existing literature on the subject of postsecondary education support for individuals with disabilities.

Our review of best practices for transition educational programming ends with the presentation of a case study. This is followed by a discussion of the third and final category of transition best practices, specifically, transition planning.

LET'S SEE IT IN ACTION! CASE EXAMPLE

Best Practices in Transition Education Programming

Jaime Martinez is a 17-year-old youth with multiple disabilities, including low cognitive functioning and visual impairments. He recently received the outstanding special education student award from the local county office of education, special education division. His parents and Jaime credited the special education staff and program at Madison High School for helping Jaime achieve this award.

Jaime participated in an inclusive education at his neighborhood school beginning in the ninth grade. He was assigned a full-time paraprofessional to attend all of his classes. The paraprofessional was bilingual and spoke Spanish. The special education staff collaborated weekly with Jaime's teachers and developed modified and adapted assignments, when appropriate. They also consulted with his teachers regarding partial participation for Jaime and the importance of his developing good social and communication skills, as well as peer interaction. Jaime also received

mobility training from the special education staff at Monroe High School.

A functional vocational evaluation was completed for Jaime in 10th grade and it was determined that he enjoyed physical work involving use of his hands and preferred to be outdoors. The special education staff contacted the local office of the Department of Rehabilitation when Jaime was in 11th grade and they agreed to help explore supported employment options for Jaime. He was eventually trained to be a member of a mobile work crew that washed cars for auto dealers in the local community. Jaime enjoyed the work very much. He was hired full time at a local auto dealership and they offered to train him in other jobs that he was capable of doing. The Department of Rehabilitation agreed to pay Jaime's wages during training, as well as cover the costs for any specialized or modified equipment needed for Jaime to perform the essential functions or jobs for which he could be trained.

WHAT ARE BEST PRACTICES FOR TRANSITION PLANNING?

Person-Centered or Student-Focused Planning and Student Self-Determination and Advocacy

Student input in transition planning "remains the missing link in most transition programs in the United States. . . . In far too many instances, professionals determine what they 'think' students need or want rather than seek student input and representation" (Wehman, 1996, p. 35). Powers et al. (2005) reviewed research studies examining the status and quality of transition planning documents and procedures and concluded that "additional quality transition practices, such as student-led IEPs, student-centered planning, and mentorship, do not yet appear to be commonplace" (p. 48). Unfortunately, it appears that schools often force youth with disabilities to accept available curricula and service delivery models without considering their individual needs, preferences, and interests (see Eisenman & Chamberlin, 2001). These practices are in direct conflict with the mandates of IDEA 2004, which require students' preferences and interests to be taken into account when planning transition services. Moreover, the law requires districts to include students as participants in their transition planning meetings.

Despite these disappointing findings, terms such as *person-centered* or *student-focused planning, self-determination,* and *self-advocacy* have been common best practice recommendations in transition literature in the past decade (for a review of self-determination literature, see Deci & Ryan, 2006; Field, 1996a; Wehmeyer, Agran, & Hughes, 2000; Wehmeyer & Schwartz, 1998). Self-advocacy and self-determination are related terms that are often used interchangeably in the literature (Patton & Blalock, 1996). *Self-determination* is defined by Wehmeyer et al. (2000) as "acting as the primary causal agent in one's life and making choices and decisions regarding one's quality of life free from undue external influences or interferences" (p. 58). "Self-advocacy refers to taking action on one's own behalf; acts of self-advocacy lead to greater self-determination" (Patton & Blalock, 1996, p. 65).

Wehman, Everson, and Reid (2001) emphasized the importance of using person-centered practices (a.k.a. student-focused planning) to individualize the transition planning process and outcomes. Person-centered planning is based on the philosophy of self-determination and focuses on the wants and needs of individual youth with disabilities and their families as opposed to simply placing youth with disabilities into available transition services and programs in the community (e.g., one-size-fits-all approach). Key aspects of person-centered planning models reviewed by Wehman et al. and derived from Everson and Reid (1999) include the following:

1. Driven by the individual and family
2. Focuses on an individual's gifts and capacities
3. Visionary and future-oriented
4. Dependent on community membership and commitment
5. Emphasizes supports and connections over services
6. Enables individualized plans to be developed
7. Changes services to be more responsive to consumers

1. Convene IEP teams to do the following:
   • Identify all transition-age students.
   • Identify appropriate school and adult service personnel.
   • Identify appropriate members of the student s support network.
2. Review transition assessment data and conduct additional assessment activities, if necessary.
   • Use nonstandardized assessment instruments and procedures, such as learning styles inventories, observation, situational assessment, mapping procedures, interviews, rating scales, and self-determination checklists.
3. Develop transition portion of IEP and related academic portion of IEP by doing the following:
   • Schedule the IEP meeting.
   • Conduct the IEP meeting.
4. Implement the transition portion of the IEP and all other IEP portions as well.
5. Update the IEP annually and implement follow-up procedures.
6. Hold an exit meeting.

Figure 6–7   Person-Centered Transition Planning Steps
Source: Adapted from "Beyond Programs and Placements: Using Person-Centered Practices to Individualize the Transition Process and Outcomes, by P. Wehman, J. M. Everson, and D. H. Reid in *Life Beyond the Classroom: Transition Strategies for Young People with Disabilities,* 3rd ed., by P. Wehman (Ed.), 2001, Baltimore: Paul H. Brookes.

Wehman et al. (2001) have outlined the basic steps to follow when using a person-centered IEP transition planning process. These are shown in Figure 6–7. Step 1 involves convening the IEP team, whose job it is to identify for a transition-age youth with a disability appropriate school and adult service personnel and members of the individual's support network (e.g., people who know the youth best and whom the youth trusts for advice and support). Review of transition assessment data occurs in Step 2, and additional assessment activities take place if needed. Wehman et al. recommended mapping procedures, a group process that includes the youth with a disability, families, and support personnel and employs the use of colors, symbols, words, and pictures to record information about the youth with a disability. Maps developed should focus on the goals, wants, and needs of the individual. This information can then be used for writing the transition portion of the IEP, which is Step 3 in the process. Step 4 is to implement the IEP, including the transition goals and objectives. Step 5 involves close monitoring of the IEP, with annual reviews and accompanying follow-up procedures implemented as needed. Finally, Step 6 is implemented toward the end of the last year in school for the youth with a disability. An exit meeting is held in which transition culmination takes place (see chapter 8, for a more complete review of this step).

The importance of empowering youth with disabilities to develop and demonstrate self-determination skills to facilitate their transition to adult life has been strongly advocated by transition leaders during the past several years. The Division on Career Development and Transition (DCDT) from the CEC issued a position statement strongly endorsing the need to promote self-determination skills in youth with disabilities (Field et al., 1998b). Moreover, several model demonstration projects to promote self-determination were funded in the early 1990s by the U.S. Department of Education Office of Special Education Programs (OSEP). Self-determination models, methods, and materials for educators working with transition-aged youth with disabilities emerged from these OSEP funded projects (see Field, 1996, for a review of several models).

SELF-DETERMINATION

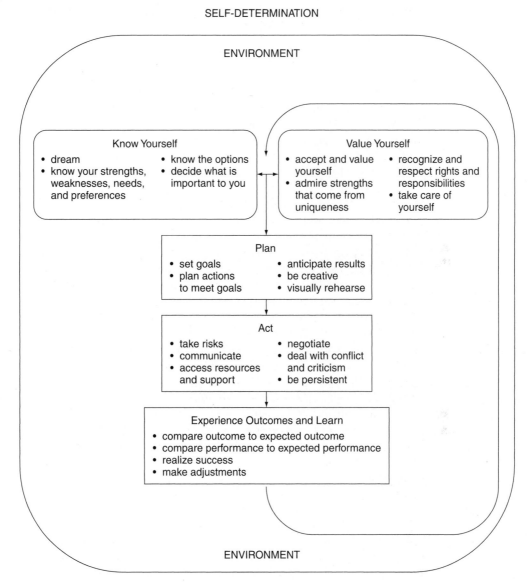

Figure 6–8   Model for Self-Determination

A model of self-determination proposed by Field and Hoffman (1994) is shown in Figure 6–8. This model posits that self-determination is affected both by factors within the individual's control, such as values, knowledge, and skills, as well as by environmental variables (e.g., opportunities for choice making and attitudes of others). Five major components were included in the model: Know Yourself, Value Yourself, Plan, Act, and Experience Outcomes and Learn. One must have self-awareness, self-esteem, and the skills to plan and act to fully experience being self-determined. To have either the foundation of self-awareness and self-esteem but not the skills, or the skills but not the inner knowledge and belief in the self is insufficient to achieve self-determination. The model presumed that behaviors generating self-determination are also expressions of self-determination.

Martin et al. (2006) reviewed literature that demonstrates that students can be effectively involved in their IEP meetings when they are taught effective leadership skills, are provided the opportunity to participate, and adult IEP team members expect them to participate. The self directed IEP, developed by Martin, Marshall, Maxson, and Jerman (1997), has been shown to substantially increase student IEP participation behaviors (see Martin et al., 2006, for a review of studies related to the self directed IEP). The program uses video modeling, student assignments, role-playing, and the teaching of leadership skills to get students to demonstrate goal setting, planning, self-evaluation, mediation, public speaking, and self-advocacy skills.

Another promising curriculum, *Steps to Self-Determination,* developed and filed-tested by Field and Hoffman (1996b), contains strategies and materials that promote knowledge, skills, and values that lead to self-determination (see also Deci & Ryan, 2006; Field, Hoffman, & Spezia, 1998; Field, Martin, Miller, Ward, & Wehmeyer, 1998a). Significant positive gains in pre- and postcognitive knowledge and observed behavior associated with self-determination were achieved in experimental subjects compared to control group subjects. Other self-determination curricula recommended for potential adoption and reviewed by Field (1996), as well as by Test, Karvonen, Wood, Browder, and Algozzine (2000) include (a) *The Choicemaker Self-Determination Transition Curriculum* (Martin & Marshall, 1994), targeted to help students acquire knowledge and skills that will give them a stronger voice in the IEP planning process, (b) the *IPLAN* (VanReusen & Bos, 1990), designed to promote increased student involvement in educational planning, and in some cases, student directed IEPs, and (c) the *Life-Centered Career Education Curriculum* (Brolin, 1995), which was previously reviewed. Wehman (2001) comprehensively reviewed a number of programs designed to teach self-determination skills. A common element of these self-determination curricula, along with other transition curricula briefly described in the appendix to this chapter, is that they offer teachers ways to develop in youth with disabilities the skills needed to take a leadership role in their IEP transition planning meeting.

Teachers can also play an important role in helping prepare youth with disabilities to voice their transition needs and direct their own planning process. Adoption of any of the self-determination or student-directed IEP curriculum and materials reviewed in this chapter is a good place to begin. Youth with disabilities should be educated about their rights and responsibilities. Objectives on the IEP should include and reflect self-determination training and planning for the future. Finally, it is recommended that teachers, with the help of counselors, develop peer support groups as a means for promoting and teaching assertiveness, discussing transition goals, and increasing involvement of youth with disabilities in decisions related to their future lives.

In summary, a key transition planning best practice recommendation is to actively engage youth with disabilities in planning their future and to focus the planning around their personal interests and strengths. Numerous self-advocacy and self-determination programs, models, and curricula exist for youth with disabilities. The skills they can potentially gain through self-advocacy training can lead them to taking a more active role in their IEP meeting, resulting in greater expression of their future hopes and desires in a variety of transition outcomes.

TAKE CHARGE for the Future (Powers, Ellison, Matuszewski, Wilson, & Turner, 1997) contains four major components or strategies designed to develop self-determination skills in both youth with and without disabilities: (a) skill facilitation, (b) mentoring, (c) peer support, and (d) parent support. The program provides youth with self-help materials, coaching, and a process for being matched with successful adults of the same gender who have experienced similar challenges and share common interests with them. Parents are provided with information and support to help promote their child's active involvement in transition planning.

Whose Future Is It Anyway? A Student-Directed Transition Planning Program (Wehmeyer & Kelchner, 1995) consists of 36 sessions that introduce the concept of transition and transition planning, using student-directed materials and instruction. The sessions focus on (a) self- and disability awareness, (b) making decisions about transition-related outcomes, (c) identifying and securing community resources to support transition services, (d) writing and evaluating transition goals and objectives, (e) communicating in small groups, and (f) developing skills to become an effective team member, leader, or self-advocate.

Next S.T.E.P.: Student Transition and Educational Planning (Halpern et al., 1997) is designed to teach students transition planning skills and the skills they need to successfully engage in the process. The curriculum contains 16 lessons, with four units titled (a) Getting Started: introduces transition planning and motivates student involvement; (b) Self-Exploration and Self-Evaluation: activities that help students identify their interests, strengths, and weaknesses in adult-oriented outcome areas; (c) Developing Goals and Activities: helps students identify their hopes and dreams and identify related goals; and (d) Putting a Plan into Place: teaches students skills to help them prepare for their transition planning meeting.

The next transition planning best practice to be reviewed is family or parent involvement.

Parent or Family Involvement in Transition Planning

Family or parent involvement in transition planning is considered an important best practice in transition for several reasons. IDEA 2004 requires parent notification when transition planning is scheduled as part of an IEP, and parents must be invited to attend the meeting. Parent–professional collaboration is important because it promotes (a) real change in children, (b) child development and learning across multiple environments, and (c) coordination and linkages between home and school (Anderson, Christenson, & Lehr, 2004; Christie, 2005; Sinclair & Christenson, 1992). Brolin (1995) pointed out that the youth with a disability and his or her family are the only participants who will be potential members of every IEP meeting; "teachers, administrators, related service personnel, and adult service providers will all change from year to year and school to school" (p. 97). Moreover, families often represent the hopes and dreams of a youth with a disability and possess a wealth of information about the youth's strengths, abilities, likes, dislikes, limitations, and idiosyncrasies.

Despite this rationale favoring parent or family involvement in the IEP planning process, the literature shows a historically low participation rate of these individuals in such meetings (Salembier & Furney, 1997). Parent involvement in IEP meetings has been characterized as passive in nature and focused primarily on attendance, as opposed to genuine participation. Several barriers to more active parent participation were identified by Salembier and Furney in their review of the literature on the subject. These barriers included (a) parent lack of information and skills, (b) negative teacher perceptions of parent participation in the IEP planning process, (c) use of educational jargon in the reporting of test results, (d) insufficient amount of time for meetings, (e) incomplete development of documents prior to the planning process, and (f) conferences focused on compliance with legal procedures rather than on collaborative development of individualized plans for students. Additional studies of transition planning practices indicated that (a) parents may not have received all of the support and services they needed to deal with the stressful challenges of transitioning their son or daughter with disabilities from school to adult life (Gallivan-Fenlon, 1994), (b) strategies were not being employed to promote active parent roles in developing and implementing transition plans (Boone, 1992; McNair & Rusch, 1991), and (c) transition plans were not being developed based on students' individual interests, needs, and preferences (Kohler, 1996; Lichtenstein, 1993; Lichtenstein & Michaelides, 1993).

More recently, a number of authors have written on the subject of families of individuals with disabilities. Steere et al. (2007) review Turnbull, Turnbull, Erwin, and Soodak's (2006) family system model, which conceptualizes a family as consisting of a system and several component subsystems (e.g., the *interaction subsystem, functions subsystem, and life cycle transitions subsystem*). Each of these subsystems interacts over the course of the family's lifetime to affect the dynamics of the family. For example, the birth of a child with a disability dramatically affects the relationship and interactions of mother-to-father behaviors with other children in the family, as well as the relationship of husband and wife. Turnbull et al. emphasize the importance of ensuring that school personnel know the family system model in order to effectively collaborate with and support families of children with disabilities. Likewise, Steere, Rose, and Cavaiulo reviewed literature suggesting that the transition years for families of children with disabilities are a particularly difficult time, resulting in greater intensity of stress experienced as compared to families of students without disabilities (see Challenges Faced by Families in Transition, p. 63 in Steere et al., 2007). Finally, a wealth of literature has been written on the unique challenges faced by culturally and linguistically diverse families of children with disabilities, including the transition years (see Chapter 2).

How can school personnel effectively empower families in the transition planning process? Singer and Powers (1993) and Brolin and Loyd (2004) have identified several basic principles of family support, which facilitate empowerment of family involvement in educational planning and decision making.

1. Emphasize the common needs of all families (e.g., both those of children with and without disabilities) when interacting with families of children with disabilities in order to enhance a sense of community and to improve linkages with the broader community.
2. Focus more broadly on the family's needs versus just the child's individual needs.
3. Encourage shared responsibility and collaboration by viewing parents as equal partners and professionals who are capable of solving their own problems and empower them by providing opportunities and resources to accomplish their goals.
4. Reexamine and change educators' perceptions and expectations of people with disabilities. This includes (a) replacing negative, outdated stereotypes; (b) eliminating

the use of medical model explanations and perceptions of disability as an aberrant, outside the norm, pathological condition; and (c) using *people first* language to describe individuals with disabilities.

Brolin and Loyd (2004) added that educators should view students and families as *consumers,* a term that connotes a collaborative relationship allowing families greater control over desired actions and services needed.

Several activities or conditions present during the IEP meetings were identified by parents in Salembier and Furney's (1997) study as factors that made it easier for parents to participate. These included the following:

1. The meeting was held in a comfortable place.
2. People listened to me.
3. The purpose of the meeting was explained to me.
4. The time of day of the meeting was good.
5. There was enough time to meet.
6. The meeting was well organized.

The study also identified ways to enhance parent-professional relationships and increase communication among parents, school, and agency personnel. Factors enhancing parent-professional relationships included the following:

1. Parents having an established and ongoing relationship with teachers and/or agency representatives both during and outside formal meeting times
2. Having ongoing opportunities to meet and interact
3. Teachers knowing the interests and needs of parents' sons or daughters
4. Teachers using specific strategies to encourage active parent and student participation

Factors identified as enhancing communication among parents, school, and agency personnel were the following:

1. Communication that is constant and open
2. Communication that centers on shared goals for the student
3. Parents being knowledgeable regarding the IEP planning process
4. Parents being informed of their legal rights and responsibilities
5. Parents being informed of community resources

Finally, Kohler (1996) offered the following four recommendations for increasing family involvement in transition planning meetings: (1) provide pre-individual education program planning activities for parents, (2) identify and provide information about transition services and program and/or curriculum options, (3) facilitate parent attendance at individual education planning meetings, and (4) actively include parents and family members in planning and decision making.

In summary, despite the intent and mandates of IDEA 2004, many parents and families of youth with disabilities do not play an active role in the IEP planning process. This situation has been a historical problem in special education and continues to be a cause for concern with transition planning. Special education personnel often lack adequate time in meetings to form effective partnerships with parents of youth with disabilities. Nevertheless, research clearly shows that parents desire a more active role in the IEP planning process. The recommendations of many of the authors reviewed here, if effectively implemented by special education personnel, will greatly enhance opportunities for parents and families to participate more fully in planning the future for their son or daughter with a disability.

Summary of Best Practices for Transition Planning

Several transition planning best practices consistently appear in the literature: (a) person-centered/student-focused planning, (b) promoting student self-determination and self-advocacy, and (c) parent/family involvement in transition planning. With regard to the first recommended best practice, IDEA 2004 requires transition planning to take into consideration the student's interests, preferences, and needs. A wealth of literature exists on how to effectively involve youth with disabilities in the decision-making process regarding their future and several excellent self-directed IEP curricula were reviewed that can promote a more active role of youth with disabilities in transition planning during IEP meetings. Likewise, training them in self-advocacy and self-determination skills helps accomplish this objective. Finally, research shows that parents and families have historically low participation rates in IEP meetings, not because they lack desire or interest but rather because of multiple barriers. Parents and families need to play a more active role in the IEP process. A number of strategies were presented that can be used by transition personnel to increase active involvement of parents and families during the IEP meeting.

A case study illustrating transition planning best practices is presented next.

Case Study: Transition Planning Best Practices

Representatives from middle and high school special education departments in the Golden Unified School District were paid summer stipends to help create a new IEP form that could be used for transition services language requirements and to identify ways to increase parent and student participation in IEP meetings involving transition planning. They contacted the state department of education, special education services division, and were able to obtain sample copies from other school districts of IEP forms used for writing transition goals. The state department of education also loaned the team copies of various published self-determination curriculum materials.

The team reviewed many IEP forms, but the one they most preferred was a two-page document, with the first page containing spaces for writing the student's vision for the future, career interests, perceived strengths, and current level of performance data in all required transition outcome areas. The second page contained spaces for writing in the student's transition services needs in each outcome area, along with transition goals and related IEP annual goals and benchmarks. The team agreed to adopt this form and have new IEP documents printed by the school district office and readily available by the start of the next school year. In addition, the team discussed ways to train teachers, parents, and students in the use of this IEP form and in the IPLAN self-determination training program, which they liked best.

New IEP forms were printed and the IPLAN was purchased for all middle and high school special-education programs in the district. Training was provided at the district-required staff development day the week before school started on how to use the new IEP documents and the IPLAN program.

SUMMARY

Effective and quality transition for youth with disabilities is promoted by a number of best practices. Although not all of those reviewed in this chapter are supported by empirical evidence, clearly there is consensus among professionals across multiple transition-related fields regarding what are considered best practices in transition. We reviewed empirical and nonempirical literature and sources on the subject and compiled a list of the 12 most frequently cited transition best practices (see Table 6-1). These were subsequently grouped into three major categories: (a) transition services agency best practices, (b) transition education programming best practices, and (c) transition planning best practices.

With respect to transition services agency best practices, collaboration both between and within agencies promotes efficient use of people and resources for meeting the postschool needs of youth with disabilities. The formation of interagency transition teams and agreements greatly facilitates a more user-friendly system for consumers. Equally important is collaboration between professionals within the same agency. Colleagues should be well-versed in each other's roles and responsibilities and be able to work together effectively when assisting families and youth with disabilities involved in transition.

A second major category of best practices is transition education programming. This begins with school foundation experiences that prepare youth with disabilities for quality adult life, such as (a) providing integrated classrooms, programs, and community experiences; (b) providing a functional life-skills curriculum; (c) offering vocational assessment, career and vocational education, paid work experience, and community-based educational experiences in high school; and (d) providing competitive paid work experience in high school and beyond. In addition, we highlighted the importance of helping youth with disabilities develop appropriate social skills and friendships with nondisabled peers. A final recommendation was forming business and industry linkages with local schools. Partnerships of this nature offer career awareness, exploration, mentoring, job try-outs, job shadowing, and paid work experience opportunities for youth with disabilities during their high school years.

The final category of best practices in transition discussed was transition planning. The IEP process should involve multidisciplinary personnel from schools and community agencies when transition planning is being discussed. Moreover, youth with disabilities should engage in self-determination and person-centered planning during this process. Published curricula exist to train youth with disabilities in these skills. Finally, we discussed the historical problem of the lack of active participation of parents and families in the IEP planning process. Important literature was reviewed containing recommendations for how to increase parent and family involvement. Active involvement of youth with disabilities is not only encouraged by IDEA 2004 but is one of the most frequently cited transition planning best practices found in the literature.

In closing, we offer a transition best practices evaluation instrument for adoption consideration by school and transition agency personnel (see Table 6–3). This instrument

Table 6–3 Transition Best Practices Evaluation Instrument

Transition Services Agency Best Practice Indicators					
1. Degree of interagency collaboration	0	1	2	3	4
2. Degree of interdisciplinary collaboration	0	1	2	3	4
Transition Education Programming Best Practices					
3. Degree to which students with disabilities participate in integrated schools, classrooms, and employment	0	1	2	3	4
4. Provision of functional, life-skills curriculum and community-based educational experiences to students with disabilities	0	1	2	3	4
5. Provision of social-skills training and competency for students with disabilities	0	1	2	3	4
6. Provision of career and vocational assessment and education for students with disabilities	0	1	2	3	4
7. Provision of competitive paid work experience in high school and beyond	0	1	2	3	4
8. Degree of business and industry linkages with schools	0	1	2	3	4
9. Degree of postsecondary participation and support	0	1	2	3	4
Transition Planning Best Practices					
10. Degree of person-centered or student-focused transition planning	0	1	2	3	4
11. Degree of student self-determination and advocacy	0	1	2	3	4
12. Degree of parent or family involvement in transition planning	0	1	2	3	4

Rate the quality of transition services in the categories below provided by your school or agency based on the following scale: 4 = outstanding, 3 = very good, 2 = adequate, 1 = inadequate or needs improvement, 0 = not applicable.

incorporates all of the recommendations contained in this chapter and can be used by professionals to evaluate the degree to which the transition services and programs they provide for youth with disabilities are of high quality. It is hoped that this instrument will be useful in promoting the best practices in transition recommended in this chapter.

CASE STUDY 6–1

Transition Best Practices

Use the transition best practices evaluation instrument to analyze the strengths and weaknesses of transition practices in the following case studies.

Case Study #1

Sean Blackwell is a 14-year-old youth with severe disabilities. His overall IQ is 55. He has poor oral communication skills and experiences difficulty with social relationships. He is very good with his hands and follows directions well. Sean has been enrolled in segregated special education classes on integrated school campuses throughout his school years. A functional life-skills curriculum has been taught to him, delivered entirely in a special

education classroom. He has had some preemployment experience, working in nonpaid jobs in the school cafeteria and around campus with the school janitor. He seems to enjoy these activities. The special education staff has identified appropriate transition goals and objectives for Sean's IEP and is planning on presenting these to Sean and his parents for their approval at an upcoming IEP meeting.

Case Study #2

Becky Evans is a 16-year-old student with a learning disability. She would like to attend a community college or 4-year university. She is currently enrolled in a departmentalized special education program at her high school and receives all of her core academic subjects in self-contained classes taught by special education teachers to small groups of students with identified learning disabilities. The curriculum is modified significantly for these classes and Becky receives tutoring and support one period a day in the resource room. She has a good group of friends in school and participates in several extracurricular activities, such as school plays and chorus. Becky would like to take a career-technical education class in health occupations, but there is no time in her current schedule and her parents are hesitant to enroll her in a community-based program because the center is located in a dangerous part of town. Becky is hoping to be able to graduate from high school and enroll in health occupations courses when she enters community college. Her special education teachers believe this is unrealistic because Becky currently lacks the necessary study skills to succeed in college classes. They are trying to encourage Becky to get a job at the McDonalds in her neighborhood and hope she will get married someday and raise a family.

Case Study #3

John Benoit is an 8-year-old student with physical disabilities and uses a wheelchair. Intellectually, he is bright, gets along well with others, and has many friends in the school and community. John is fully included in a third-grade class in his neighborhood school and, other than adaptive physical education, participates in all classroom and school activities with his nondisabled peers. He is doing well in school, both academically and socially. His parents, however, wonder what the future holds for him and are unsure how to determine in what direction his education should move. John wonders this as well. Because he participates in the mainstream curriculum, he is not receiving some of the educational experiences he needs to function independently at home or in the community. His parents, however, have not complained about this because they are so happy he is being fully included in general education classrooms.

Case Study #4

Sara Winfield is an 11-year-old child with autism. She lacks verbal communication skills and is socially withdrawn, rarely interacting with others. She is enrolled in a full-day special education class at a segregated school for children with autism. Her behavior is quite manageable and she rarely disturbs others. Her parents are pleased with the school and plan to have Sara complete her education there. Unfortunately, the school is not well connected with other agencies in the community, and the students tend to continue to live at home and receive full-time care from their families after graduating. The students are taught a functional curriculum but are not taken out into the community because of liability concerns on the part of the school administration and owners. Few of the students learn career skills. Nevertheless, the parents are very pleased with the program and think it meets the majority of their children's needs.

KEY TERMS AND PHRASES

best practices
business and industry linkages with schools
career education
community-based instruction
functional life skills and other transition curricula
inclusion
inclusive education

interagency agreements
interagency transition teams
interdisciplinary collaboration
self-determination, self-advocacy, and person-centered planning
transition education programming
transition planning
transition services agency

QUESTIONS FOR REFLECTION, THINKING, AND SKILL BUILDING

Transition Services Agency Reflection and Thinking Activities

1. What does the term *best practices in transition* mean, and how was the term derived?
2. What are the key transition services agencies in your region that provide transition services to youth with disabilities?
3. Complete an agency report on a transition services agency in your region. Prepare a written summary on the following aspects of this agency:
   a. Name of agency and contact information
   b. Legislative mandates governing transition services the agency provides
   c. Consumers served by the agency
   d. Transition services provided by the agency
   e. Degree of collaboration and cooperation with other agencies in the region
   f. Degree of linkages with business, industry, and schools
4. Create a transition services agency resource guide for your region. Include information outlined above on each agency.
5. Write a hypothetical interagency agreement between two or more transition services agencies. Describe the reason why an agreement is needed and address key aspects of interagency agreements presented in this chapter.

Transition Education Programming Reflection and Thinking Activities

6. Analyze the quality of transition education programming that currently exists in a middle or high school in your local area. What best practices in transition education programming exist, and what could be improved?

7. Create the ideal transition education program for youth with disabilities during the school years. Specify the ages of your students and the transition education personnel, services, and supports your ideal program would offer.
8. What transition curricula would you recommend be used with transition-age youth with disabilities at middle and high schools in your local area?

Transition Planning Reflection and Thinking Activities

9. Compare current transition planning documents and process in a school or agency with which you are familiar to those recommended in this chapter. What is reflective of best practices, and what can be improved?
10. Create an IEP transition planning document and process that reflect best practices recommended in this chapter.
11. Use the transition best practices evaluation instrument and analyze the transition practices in a school or agency. Develop an action plan for any needed improvements, and discuss the plan with supervisory or administrative personnel.
12. Organize an interagency transition team in your region and develop an interagency agreement specifying transition services and collaboration between transition personnel. Use the steps for creating interagency transition teams and agreements outlined in this chapter.
13. Review various transition curricula, and select one that is most appropriate for your target population of transition-age youth with disabilities.

Transition Curricula

1. *Career Choices.* A curriculum that teaches self-awareness, decision making, and career exploration. Academic Innovations, 1386 Rio Virgin Drive, Washington, UT 84780, (800) 967-8016. www.academicinnovations.com

2. *Career Ideas for Kids Roadmap CD-ROM.* (2002). Provides children with a personalized roadmap to take them from daydream to dream job. Meridian Education Corporation, P.O. Box 2053, Princeton, NJ 0543-2053, (800) 257-5126. www.meridianeducation.com

3. *Career Exploration Inventory* (CEI). JIST Publishing, 8902 Otis Avenue, Indianapolis, IN 4621, (800) 648-JIST. www.jist.com

4. *Career Occupational Preference Survey* (COPS). EDITS, P.O. Box 7234, San Diego, CA 92167, (800) 416-1666. www.edits.net

5. *Windmills: Hiring and Working with People with Disabilities,* Richard Pimantele. This program is designed for human resource managers and trainers to successfully include persons with disabilities as an excellent labor source. Milt Wright & Associates, Inc., 17939 Chatsworth Street, Suite #530, Granada Hills, CA 91344, (800) 626-3939. www.miltwright.com

6. *Helping Students Develop Their IEP: A Student's Guide to the IEP.* Teacher and student guides and audiotape/CD overview. A free publication of NICHCY—the National Information Center for Children and Youth with Disabilities. P.O. Box 1492, Washington, DC 20013, (800) 695-0285. www.nichcy.org

7. *How to . . . Career Development Activities for Every Classroom* (2nd ed.) (1999). Classroom activities to develop: self-knowledge, educational and occupational exploration, and career planning. Separate books for K–3, 4–6, 7–9, and 10–12. Center on Education and Work, University of Wisconsin—Madison, School of Education, 964 Educational Science Building, 1025 W. Johnson Street, Madison, WI 53706-1796, (800) 446-0399, (608) 262-9197. http://www.cew.wisc.edu.

8. *Individual Program Plan Resource Manual: A Person-Centered Approach* (1995). Available free from California Department of Developmental Services, 1600 9th Street, Sacramento, CA 95814, (916) 654-2198.

9. *Individual Transition Plans,* (2nd ed.), (2002), Paul Wehman. Manual for writing transition goals. Includes samples for students with a variety of cognitive, learning, physical, and behavioral disorders. Pro-Ed, 8700 Shoal Creek Blvd., Austin, TX 78757-6897, (512) 451-8542. www.proedinc.com (product number 9336)

10. *It's Your Future* (2001). A 23-minute video, produced by the California Department of Education, Special Education Division, for students on the importance of making a transition plan. CalSTAT/CIHS, 1801 E. Cotati Avenue, Rohnert Park, CA 94928, (707) 849-2275. www.calstat.org

11. *Next S.T.E.P.* (2000). A comprehensive curriculum for transition and education planning. Pro-Ed, 8700 Shoal Creek Blvd., Austin, TX 78757-6897, (512) 451-3246. www.proedinc.com (product number 9265)

12. *One-a-Day Language Lessons* (2007). Each lesson focuses on a single job and includes writing, thinking or speaking questions, and vocabulary. Pearson AGS Globe, 5910 Rice Creek Parkway, Shoreview, MN 55126, (800) 328-2560. www.agsglobe.com

13. *Pathfinder—Exploring Career & Educational Path,* (3rd ed.), (2007). Lindsay, Norene. Allows young people to explore their interests and skills at a junior and senior high level so they can make informed education and career choices. JIST Publishing, 8902 Otis Avenue, IN 46216-1003, (800) 648-5478. www.jist.com

14. *Promoting Successful Outcomes for Students with Emotional Disorders* (1994). Manual with techniques for supported employment, program evaluation, and case studies. Center for Community Participation, 303 Occupational Therapy Bldg., Colorado State University, Fort Collins, CO 80523, (907) 491-5930. www. ccp.colostate.edu

15. *Self-Directed IEP,* Martin, J. E. et al. (2005). Self-directed IEP kit with closed caption videos. Sopris West Educational Services, 4093 Specialty Place, Longmont, CO 80504, (800) 547-6747. www.sopriswest.com

16. *Self-Advocacy Strategy for Education and Transition Planning,* Van Ruesen et al. (1994). Lawrence, KS: Edge Enterprises.

17. *A Student's Guide to the IEP,* McGahee-Kovac, M. (1995). Washington, DC, National Information Center for Children and Youth with Disabilities.

18. *The Career Game.* Career-interest inventory with color graphic format for beginning sessions on self-awareness and career investigation. Includes a software program that generates a report. Rick Trow Productions, P.O. Box 29, New Hope, PA 18938, (800) 247-9404. www.careergame.com

19. *Tools for Transition—Preparing Students with Learning Disabilities for Postsecondary Education* (2007). Video, teacher's manual, and student materials. Pearson AGS Globe, 5910 Rice Creek Parkway, Shoreview, MN 55126, (800) 328-2580. www.agsglobe.com

20. *Transitions Curriculum* (1998). Three-part curriculum: Personal Management, Career Management, and Life Management. Teacher-developed lessons and student worksheets. James Stanfield Co., Inc., P. O. Box 41058, Santa Barbara, CA 93140, (800) 421-6534. www.stanfield.com

21. *Tuning in to My Future* (1997). A middle school career guidance program in three units: student workbook, teacher guide, and parent guide. PrepWorks Publishing, P.O. Box 292239, Kettering, OH 45429, (937) 294-5057. www.prepworks.com

➡ TRANSITION-RELATED WEB SITES

1. California Department of Education—Special Education Division—Resources http://www.cde.ca.gov/sp/se/sr
2. Center for Innovation in Transition and Employment http://www.meridianfilm.com
3. Council for Exceptional Children http://www.cec.sped.org
4. Council for Exceptional Children, Division on Career Development and Transition http://www.dcdt.org
5. Disability Resources, Inc. http://www.disabilityresources.org

6. Employment Support for People with Disabilities http://www.ssa.gov/work/
7. Health Resource Center—The National Clearinghouse on Postsecondary Education for Individuals with Disabilities http://www.health.gwu.com
8. Institute on Community Integration http://www.ici.umn.edu
9. Job Accommodation Network (JAN) http://www.jan.wvu.edu/
10. National Center on Educational Outcomes http://www.education.umn.edu./nceo/
11. National Center for Research in Vocational Education http://vocserve.berkeley.edu/
12. National Center on Secondary Education and Transition http://www.ncset.org
13. National Center on Research in Career and Technical Education (HEATH Resource Center) http://www.heath.gwu.edu/
14. National Clearinghouse on Postsecondary Education for Individuals with Disabilities http://www.heath.gwu.edu
15. National Coalition on Self-Determination http://www.nconsd.org/
16. National Information Center for Children and Youth with Disabilities (NICHCY) http://www.nichcy.org
17. National Institute on Disability and Rehabilitation Research http://www.ncddr.org
18. National Longitudinal Transition Study-2 http://www.nlts2.org/
19. National Transition Network http://ici2.umn.edu/ntn/
20. National Transition Research Institute at Illinois http://www.ed.uiuc.edu/sped/tri/institute.html
21. National Youth Employment Coalition http://www.nyec.org/
22. Office of Special Education and Rehabilitative Services http://www.ed.gov/about/offices/list/osers/
23. Parent Advocacy Coalition for Educational Rights (PACER) http://www.taalliance.org
24. Research and Training Center on Independent Living http://www.rtcil.org
25. The ARC http://www.thearc.org
26. The Association for Persons in Supported Employment (APSE) http://apse.org
27. The IDEA and transition http://www.ldonline.org/ld_indepth/transition/law_of_transition.html
28. The U.S. Department of Labor, Office of Disability Employment Policy http://www.dol.gov/odep/welcome.html
29. Transition Research Institute http://www.ed.uiuc.edu/sped/tri/institute.html

Chapter 7

Transition Assessment

Gary Greene

Chapter Questions

- What is transition assessment and how does it differ from traditional assessment in special education?
- Who are the people involved in the transition assessment process and what skills do they need?
- What is involved in the development of a transition assessment plan?
- What transition assessment models and methods are recommended?
- How can transition assessment data be used to help select and evaluate an appropriate high school course of study and transition pathway for youth with disabilities?

INTRODUCTION

One of the most challenging and important tasks for transition personnel, parents, and youth with disabilities is to make decisions about the future. It is an awesome responsibility to discuss and identify career and occupational goals, postsecondary education plans, and adult living options while a youth with a disability is still in school. And yet, IDEA 2004 requires (a) this planning process to begin no later than the first individual education program (IEP) to be in effect when the child is 16, and updated annually thereafter [§614(d)(1)(A)(i)(VIII)], and (b) appropriate measurable postsecondary goals based upon age appropriate *transition assessments* related to training, education, employment, and where appropriate, independent living skills must be developed [§614(d)(1)(A)(i)(VIII)(aa)].

This chapter reviews the subject of transition assessment of youth with disabilities and its central role in transition planning. The chapter will present case studies illustrating various aspects of transition assessment. The discussion begins with an overview of transition assessment.

WHAT IS TRANSITION ASSESSMENT AND HOW DOES IT DIFFER FROM TRADITIONAL ASSESSMENT?

Miller, Lombard, and Corbey (2007) define transition assessment as

1. the process of determining a student's abilities, attitudes, and interests;
2. work behaviors, levels of self-determination and self-advocacy;
3. skills, interpersonal skills, academic skill level, and independent living;
4. skills over an extended period of time for the purpose of planning; and
5. an appropriate individual education program (IEP) (p. 5).

Transition assessment, in this way, is the first step in helping youth with disabilities plan for their future. These individuals and their families are faced with a number of important questions, concerns, and decisions in the transition planning process. For example, youth with disabilities may ask the following questions:

1. What are my interests, aptitudes, and capabilities in school, work, and community living?
2. Where do I want to live, work, or go to school after completing high school?
3. What courses do I need to take in high school to graduate and prepare for my future?
4. What are my strengths and areas where I need to improve my transition skills?
5. What do I need to learn to be a fully functional, independent member of my community?
6. What supports and resources do I need in high school and beyond to achieve my hopes and dreams?

Transition assessment plays a critical role in answering these and many other key questions. Despite its importance, transition assessment has frequently been overlooked, ignored, or misunderstood by professionals working with youth enrolled in special education in high school. This prompted the Division of Career Development and Transition (DCDT) of the Council for Exceptional Children to publish a position paper on the subject (Sitlington, Neubert, & Leconte, 1997). The division views *transition assessment* "as an umbrella term that includes career assessment, vocational assessment, and ecological or functional assessment practices" (p. 70).

Transition assessment, when properly implemented, helps individuals with disabilities make informed choices and determine their individual strengths, needs, preferences, and interests in the areas of career development, vocational training, postsecondary education, community functioning, and personal and social skills. Ideally, transition assessment should occur in a variety of environments that are natural to the person's life and involve the individual with disabilities, his or her family, related school personnel, and community service providers. Collaboration among these individuals should take place during the initial phases of transition assessment to determine what types of data are needed and the methods to be used to obtain such information. Other important characteristics of transition assessment discussed by Test, Aspel, and Everson (2006) are that transition assessment should be (a) student-centered, (b) useful and understandable to all people involved, and (c) sensitive to cultural and ethnic diversity (e.g., awareness of the student's and family's cultural values and desires). Flexer, Simmons, Luft, and Baer (2005) add that transition assessment should have a clearly specified purpose. Such purposes include (a) determining current levels of ability, interest, and preferences; (b) predicting and prescribing potential programs and strategies to promote achievement of adult outcomes; (c) identifying tasks or activities that facilitate exploration and skill development in specific adult outcome areas; and (d) developing profiles to help students and their families advocate for themselves in high school and beyond. In addition, Flexer et al. state that "many assessments were not normed on persons with disabilities, resulting in problems in administering them or analyzing them" (p. 112). For this reason, transition assessment should be individualized, relevant, and appropriate to the unique characteristics and disability of the student.

In contrast to **traditional assessment** in special education, which is an annual process, transition assessment is a broader, ongoing process that focuses not only on current capabilities but also on an individual's "future role as worker, lifelong learner, family member, community citizen, and participant in social and interpersonal networks" (Sitlington et al., 1997, p. 72). A second key difference between transition and traditional assessment in special education is that the former assessment process is a person-centered one that emphasizes individual capabilities rather than disabilities. Traditional assessment in special education has been criticized for focusing too heavily upon student weaknesses rather than strengths. A final difference between transition and traditional assessment relates to the degree of involvement and self-determination of the youth with a disability in the assessment process. Person-centered transition assessment models and activities, discussed in detail in this chapter, are predicated by the unique needs and expressed desires of the individual youth with a disability and his or her family. Traditional assessment does not typically promote or facilitate this same level of self-determination.

WHO ARE THE PEOPLE INVOLVED IN THE TRANSITION ASSESSMENT PROCESS AND WHAT SKILLS DO THEY NEED?

Any or all of the following individuals can participate and contribute important information in the transition assessment process: (a) student, (b) parent(s), (c) general education personnel, (d) special education personnel, (e) both general and vocational special-needs educators, (f) supplementary and related service providers (e.g., school psychologists, speech therapists, occupational therapists, physical therapists), and (g) community transition service agency personnel, such as college and university disabled-student services personnel, assistive technology specialists, rehabilitation counselors, employers and employee coworkers, financial-aid personnel, Social Security counselors, residential counselors, and housemates. It is very important for all of these individuals to maintain a person-centered focus when gathering transition assessment information to accurately *make a match* among the strengths, needs, preferences, and interests of the youth with a disability and the demands and culture of current and future environments (Sitlington & Neubert, 2004; Sitlington, Neubert, Begun, Lombard, & Leconte, 1996).

A list of skills or competencies for personnel conducting transition assessments has been developed by the Division of Career Development and Transition and appears in Sitlington et al. (1997, p. 78). These include being able to

1. function as a member of an interdisciplinary team, which may include identifying assessment needs, collecting assessment data in a variety of settings through various methods and using data to plan;
2. select, adapt, or develop methods to determine students' strengths, needs, preferences, and interests related to their current and future role as a worker, lifelong learner, family member, community citizen, and participant in personal and social networks;
3. select, adapt, or develop valid assessment activities in authentic contexts;
4. develop assessment sites and conduct behavioral observations in work, vocational training, educational, community, and social settings;

5. conduct ecological analyses, such as job and task analyses, vocational training analyses, postsecondary education surveys, community living surveys, and community resources surveys;

6. recommend accommodations, assistive technology devices and services, and related services for students who require support to participate in inclusive worksites, vocational training programs, postsecondary educational program, community settings, and social programs;

7. interpret, communicate, and use assessment data to develop transition goals and activities in individualized education programs, individualized written rehabilitation plans, and individualized habilitation plans;

8. work in concert with students and parents throughout all phases of the assessment process to ensure understanding of assessment options and outcomes;

9. train students and families to assume responsibility for ongoing assessment and transition planning;

10. follow up with students who have been assessed to validate the processes used; and

11. research, understand, and interpret new policies that support the transition assessment process.

Personnel working with youth with disabilities should be mindful of these competencies and obtain the training needed to properly conduct transition assessments. DCDT recommends that personnel serving as vocational assessment specialists or vocational evaluators be certified and meet the knowledge and performance areas required by the Commission on Certification of Work Adjustment and Vocational Evaluation Specialists (1996). The commission is the national accrediting body for personnel from all disciplines who are involved in vocational evaluation and assessment activities.

➡ WHAT IS INVOLVED IN THE DEVELOPMENT OF A TRANSITION ASSESSMENT PLAN?

The development of a **transition assessment plan** prior to engaging in the assessment process is highly recommended, given the limitations of time and available personnel for conducting transition assessments. The relationship of transition assessment to the transition planning portion of the IEP is an important one. The type of information gathered from transition assessment should feed directly into the areas of the IEP that focus on transition of a youth with a disability from school to postschool environments. Figure 7–1 presented by Sitlington and Clark (2006) provides examples of various knowledge and skill domains to consider for transition assessment. These domains are the major outcomes associated with a quality adult life for a youth with a disability and should be addressed when developing the transition portion of an IEP. Miller et al. (2007) created a transition assessment model (see Figure 7–2) containing a different but similar set of components to consider when developing a transition plan for a youth with a disability. Regardless of which domains or components one chooses to consider when developing a transition assessment plan and related IEP, Sitlington et al. (1997) mention several key questions to help guide the process:

1. What do I already know about this student that would be helpful in developing postsecondary outcomes?

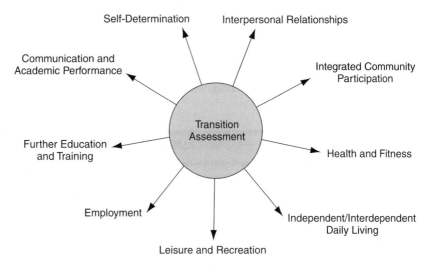

Figure 7–1   Knowledge and Skill Domains for Transition Assessment
Source: Reprinted from *Transition Education and Services for Students with Disabilities* (4th ed.),
by P. L. Sitlington and G. M. Clark, 2006, Boston: Pearson/Allyn and Bacon.

2. What information do I need to know about this individual to determine postsecondary goals?
3. What methods will provide this information?
4. How will the assessment data be collected and used in the IEP process?

Figure 7–3 contains a blank transition assessment planning form that can be used by transition personnel involved in the transition assessment process. Figure 7–4 shows an example of a completed form on a case study of Marcos, a 17-year-old Hispanic youth with a disability (see the case study presented later in this chapter). Transition assessment personnel are encouraged to use this form in planning the transition assessment process for youth with disabilities. This will increase the probability of selecting transition assessment instruments and procedures that are varied and based on the characteristics and stage of career development and transition for the person being assessed.

A review of recommended transition assessment models and practices, along with specific transition assessment procedures, occurs next. Case studies illustrating these models and practices are presented as well.

WHAT TRANSITION ASSESSMENT MODELS AND METHODS ARE RECOMMENDED?

Two transition assessment models were presented in the previous section, one developed by Sitlington and Clark (2006) and the other by Miller et al. (2007). Each of these models offers domains or components for determining the future desires, needs, and preferences of youth with disabilities. Additional models of transition assessment are

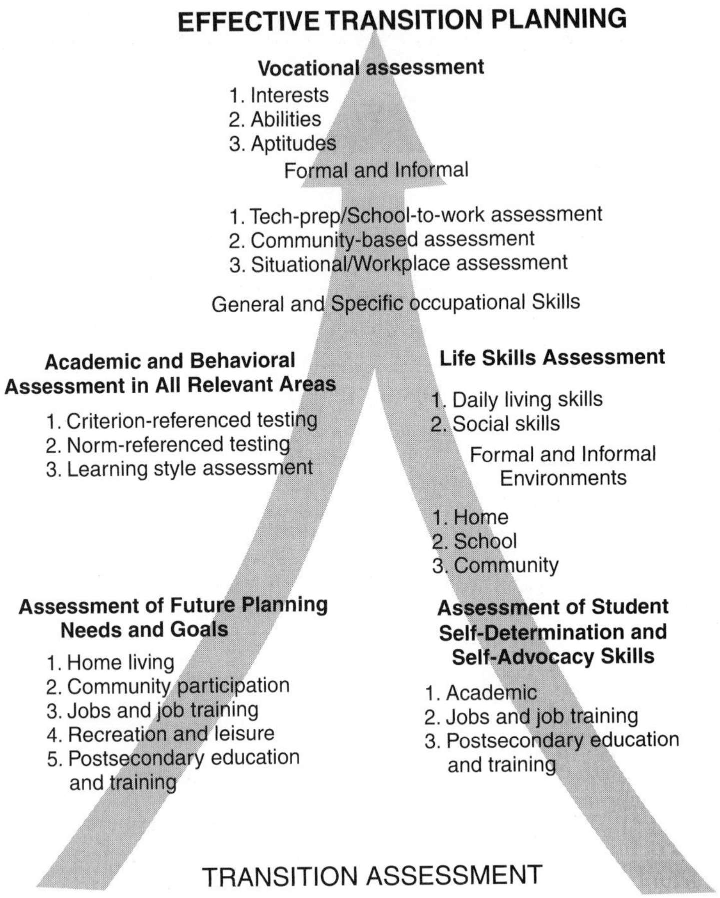

EFFECTIVE TRANSITION PLANNING

Vocational assessment

1. Interests
2. Abilities
3. Aptitudes

Formal and Informal

1. Tech-prep/School-to-work assessment
2. Community-based assessment
3. Situational/Workplace assessment

General and Specific occupational Skills

Academic and Behavioral Assessment in All Relevant Areas

1. Criterion-referenced testing
2. Norm-referenced testing
3. Learning style assessment

Life Skills Assessment

1. Daily living skills
2. Social skills

Formal and Informal Environments

1. Home
2. School
3. Community

Assessment of Future Planning Needs and Goals

1. Home living
2. Community participation
3. Jobs and job training
4. Recreation and leisure
5. Postsecondary education and training

Assessment of Student Self-Determination and Self-Advocacy Skills

1. Academic
2. Jobs and job training
3. Postsecondary education and training

TRANSITION ASSESSMENT

Figure 7–2   Transition Assessment Model
Source: Reprinted from *Transition Assessment: Planning Transition and IEP Development for Youth with Disabilities,* by R. J. Miller, R. C. Lombard, and S. A. Corby, 2007, Boston: Pearson/Allyn and Bacon.

reviewed in this section, which can be used by personnel involved in the transition planning process. Each of these models offers a unique perspective or method for transition assessment that deserve consideration.

Person-Centered Transition Assessment and Planning

Wehman, Everson, and Reid (2001) and Story, Bates, and Hunter (2002) offer comprehensive reviews of person-centered transition assessment and planning practices. According to Story et al., *person-centered* is a general term describing a variety of approaches to transition that empower self-determination in youth with disabilities and their families, thereby enabling them to assume more active involvement in the transition assessment and planning process. A variety of person-centered approaches have appeared in transition literature in the past 15 years, including (a) personal

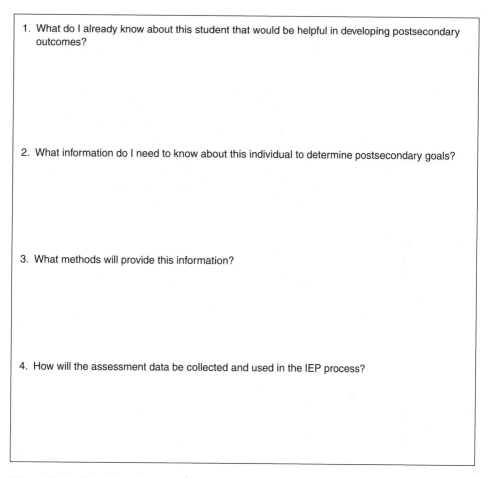

1. What do I already know about this student that would be helpful in developing postsecondary outcomes?

2. What information do I need to know about this individual to determine postsecondary goals?

3. What methods will provide this information?

4. How will the assessment data be collected and used in the IEP process?

Figure 7–3 Transition Assessment Planning Form

futures planning (Mount & Zwernik, 1988), (b) the McGill action planning system (Vandercook & York, 1989), (c) outcome-based planning (Steere, Wood, Pancsofar, & Butterworth, 1990), (d) Essential Lifestyle Planning (Smull & Harrison, 1992), (e) Group Action Planning (Turnbull & Turnbull, 1997), and (f) Transition Planning Inventory (TPI) (Clark & Patton, 1997). A common goal of these approaches is that they encourage youth with disabilities to express their vision for the future and develop needed supports to achieve this vision.

Person-centered transition assessment focuses on assisting youth with disabilities to discover their unique preferences, experiences, skills, and support needs. Specific assessment tools and strategies uncover the individual's gifts and abilities, wants, needs, and dreams for the future. Capacity building occurs in person-centered transition assessment by identifying community connections and natural supports that can help the youth with a disability gain membership in the community, a greater sense of independence, and ultimately the realization of his or her future hopes and dreams.

Answer the following questions in narrative form to obtain critical information related to transition planning. Include potential transition assessment data sources (i.e., formal, informal, standardized, and criterion-referenced instruments related to academics, employment, independent living, and social and interpersonal skills of the individual being assessed).

1. **What do I already know about this student that would be helpful in developing postsecondary outcomes?**
   - Marcos speaks Spanish and English.
   - Cognitive functioning is significantly below average.
   - Marcos gets along well with his peers and adults.
   - Current academic functioning is around first-grade level; can read functional words, write his name, address, and phone number.
   - Possesses good grooming, hygiene, dressing, and feeding skills.
   - Marcos is good at following directions and staying on task; completes most tasks with limited assistance provided.
   - Requires assistance with independent living skills.
   - Likes to listen to music and watch television in free time.
   - Likes animals.
   - Marcos is mobility trained and can use public transportation independently.

2. **What information do I need about this individual to determine postsecondary goals?**
   - A functional vocational evaluation is needed to determine his occupational interests, needs, preferences, and abilities.
   - Where do Marcos and his family want him to live after completing school?
   - Does Marcos want to work in the community after completing school and what type of employment would best match his skills?
   - Is Marcos qualified to be a consumer of the Department of Rehabilitation?

3. **What methods will provide this information?**
   - Have Marcos and his family complete the *Life Planning Inventory.*
   - Referral to and screening by Department of Rehabilitation.
   - Obtain a functional evaluation of Marcos's career and occupational interests and skills.
   - Explore supported employment and living options in the community for Marcos if desired by him and his family.

4. **How will the assessment data be collected and used in the IEP process?**
   - Marcos and his parents will complete the *Life Planning Inventory* at least one month prior to the IEP meetings and the results will be discussed at the meeting.
   - A representative from the Department of Rehabilitation will be contacted and invited to attend the IEP meeting and asked to assess Marcos for eligibility and to perform a functional vocational evaluation.

Figure 7–4   Completed Transition Assessment Planning Form

The most important individuals involved in person-centered transition assessment are the youth with a disability and their family members. Additional team members may include extended family members, family friends or neighbors, school and transition services agency personnel who know the family well, or anyone else in the family's close circle of support.

Group graphics, mapping, and *mapping a circle of support* are all terms to describe assessment procedures used in person-centered transition approaches. A number of different types of maps or graphic organizers can be created containing important information about the youth with a disability. Story et al. (2002) reviewed and presented several examples of personal profile maps and lists, such as the interpersonal relationships in an individual's life (circle of support map), places within the community the person uses (community presence map), a preference list, and gifts and capacities list. These transition assessment procedures are completed in a group meeting with the assistance of a facilitator, who can be anyone committed to the process (e.g., school personnel, social worker, family member, and youth with a disability). The purpose of the meeting is to assist all the individuals involved to construct a personal profile of the youth with a disability, describing his or her unique capabilities and capacities. Additional information can include the individual's "background, preferences, connections to people and places, communication style, medical health behaviors, hopes, goals, and fears" (Wehman et al., 2001, p. 97). Transition assessment maps typically take 15–30 minutes to create and are not meant to take the place of traditional transition assessment tools. The following case study illustrates the use of mapping.

LET'S SEE IT IN ACTION! CASE EXAMPLE

Mapping

Dora is a 16-year-old girl with Down syndrome. Her cognitive functioning is below average, and according to the AAMR (2002) definition of mental retardation, she requires limited intensity of supports in order to function successfully in school and in other transition environments (e.g., home, community, and employment). She has relatively good oral communication skills and is capable of engaging in self-determination activities.

The IEP team is in the process of completing various transition assessment procedures with Dora and will be meeting in the near future to discuss transition planning with Dora and her family. The team has chosen to use a mapping procedure to facilitate discovery of Dora's unique gifts, capacities, and support needs. They offer to complete this transition assessment in Dora's home, with the help of Dora, her family, Dora's best friend from school, and a few members from the family next door, who know Dora very well.

Five pieces of butcher paper are taped to the wall, containing the following labels: (a) relationships, (b) places, (c) background, (d) personal preferences, and (e) dreams, hopes, and fears. Colored marking pens are used to complete each map. The meeting begins with introductions and a statement of purpose. Dora's special education teacher acts as the facilitator of the group, and her older brother volunteers to write information on the maps with the colored markers. The special education teacher asks the following questions, which are directed to Dora but can be answered by anyone in the circle:

1. Who are the people in your life that interact with you on a regular basis?
2. Where do you typically spend your time?
3. What are things about you that people see as positive and make you likeable?
4. What are things about you that people see as negative and make you dislikeable?
5. What types of choices do you make?
6. What things do you prefer, motivate you, and make you happy?
7. What are things that you do not prefer, frustrate you, and make you unhappy?
8. What are your personal goals and dreams?

(Continued)

9. What are your most important priorities in the next several months to a year and in the next 1 to 5 years?
10. What people or agencies can help you achieve these personal goals and dreams?
11. What, if any, are potential barriers that can interfere with you achieving your personal goals and dreams?
12. What strategies can be used to help you overcome these obstacles or barriers?

After all the maps are completed, the special education teacher asks Dora to summarize them by discussing what she has learned about herself. Her family is then asked to do the same. The special education teacher tells Dora and her family that at their upcoming IEP meeting, transition planning will take place and the maps that were created here will be very helpful in the planning process. The remaining time is spent socializing and talking about the value of what took place.

According to Wehman et al. (2001), a number of commercially available self-determination curricula, such as *Next Step, Steps to Self-Determination, TAKE CHARGE for the Future,* and *Whose Future Is It Anyway?,* contain mapping procedures and other self-discovery activities to promote more active involvement of youth with disabilities in their own transition planning (see Chapter 6 for a review of several of these curricula).

Comprehensive Transition Assessment Model

A second model to be presented comes from a Sitlington (1996) publication entitled "Transition Assessment—Where Have We Been and Where Should We Be Going." This model is shown in Figure 7–5 and combines three historical assessment approaches that contribute to the development of the transition portion of the IEP: (a) vocational evaluation and assessment, (b) career assessment, and (c) transition assessment. The first of these, vocational evaluation and assessment, emerged from the field of vocational rehabilitation and focuses on determining the type of skills and abilities required by a person with a disability to allow him or her to work. This type of assessment, as shown in the model, typically begins around junior high school age and continues through senior high school and beyond and helps determine potential jobs that the individual can perform in the world of paid employment. Vocational assessment, however, falls under the larger category of career assessment in the model. Career assessment is a lifelong assessment process that begins at birth and continues throughout school and life. It involves becoming aware of various careers at a young age, exploring career possibilities through the school years, preparing for a career in high school, and eventually entering a career of interest or choice after completing high school. The model shows, however, that career assessment, vocational assessment, and education and training may continue in the postsecondary years as the individual with a disability matures. This takes into account the possibility of one's career interests and vocational abilities changing over the course of one's life. Likewise, the model shows that as one enters adult life, the concept of a career expands beyond

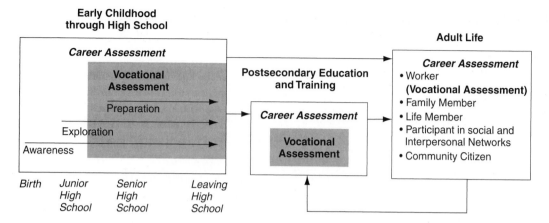

Figure 7–5 Transition Assessment
Source: Reprinted from "Transition Assessment: Where Have We Been and Where Should We Be Going?"
by P. L. Sitlington, 1996, *Career Development for Exceptional Individuals, 19,* p. 163. Copyright 1996 by
Council for Exceptional Children.

simply the role of worker to include family member, lifelong learner, participant in
social and interpersonal networks, and community citizen. These roles feed back to
inform the career and vocational assessment process, thereby helping the individual
understand better their capabilities, interests, and preferences throughout the course
of their adult life.

Making the Match Transition Assessment Model

The final model to be presented was published by Sitlington et al. (1996). It emphasizes the importance of making the match between an individual's strengths, needs,
preferences, and interests and the demands and culture of current and future environments. This model is shown in Figure 7-6. The upper left box contains various transition assessment methods. Information on the youth with a disability obtained from
these data sources must be compared with an analysis of the various environments in
which this individual will possibly participate after completing high school. **Methods
for analyzing the environment**s are presented in the upper right box in Figure 7-6.
These include analysis of the living environment, job, program, and resources available
to the student in the target environment. Last, the lower box in the model asks the
question "Is there a match?" An answer to this question is obtained by comparing individual transition assessment data results with the demands of the transition environment. If a match exists (*Yes*), the youth with a disability should be placed in the
transition environment and periodically monitored for progress toward achievement
of specified transition outcomes on the IEP. If possibly a match exists (*Possibly*), the
transition team should attempt to *identify needed supports, accommodations,* and
instruction to better facilitate a match. Finally, if a match does not exist (*No*), the transition team should *continue to collect data on other environments and on the individual and initiate the matching process again.*

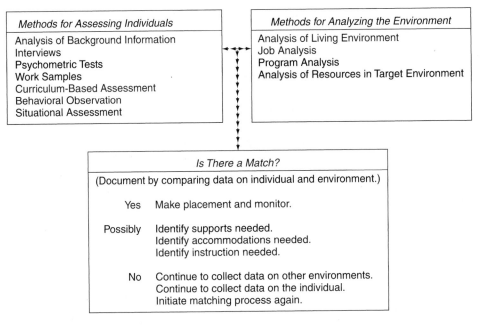

Figure 7–6   Making the Match
Source: Reprinted from *Assess for Success Handbook on Transition Assessment* (p. 99), by
P. Sitlington, D. A. Neubert, W. Begun, R. C. Lombard, and P. J. Leconte, 1996, Reston, VA: Council
for Exceptional Children. Copyright 1996.

What transition assessment methods exist for determining the individual character-istics of a youth with disabilities (upper left box in the model, Figure 7–6)? What tran-sition assessment methods exist for analyzing transition environment characteristics (upper right box in the model, Figure 7–6)? How can these combined assessment results be used effectively in the selection and evaluation of an appropriate high school course of study and transition pathway for a youth with a disability? These aspects of transition assessment are discussed next.

Methods for Assessing Individuals

A variety of methods exist in special education, rehabilitation, and vocational educa-tion that can be used for transition assessment of individuals with disabilities. These methods can generally be grouped into one of two categories: standardized assess-ments or informal assessments. A review of each type of transition assessment follows.

Standardized Assessments

Clark (1996) reported "the following types of standardized assessment procedures or instruments are available commercially or through professional services" (p. 81):

1. Learning style inventories
2. Academic achievement tests

3. Intellectual functional assessment
4. Adaptive behavior scales
5. Aptitude tests
6. Interest inventories
7. Personality scales
8. Quality of life scales
9. Social skills inventories
10. Prevocational or employability scales
11. Vocational skills assessments
12. Transition knowledge and skills inventories
13. Medical laboratory procedures

Owing to space limitations, it is not possible to present a comprehensive review of all the published standardized assessment instruments mentioned here. Instead, we offer a summary of recommended transition-related assessment instruments in Figure 7–7. These instruments are the ones that are most frequently cited in transition assessment literature.

It is important to emphasize avoiding selection and adoption of transition-related standardized assessment instruments that are isolated from actual life contexts, such as paper-and-pencil tests. Transition assessment instruments and procedures should be conducted within natural or actual employment, postsecondary, or community settings. Equally important is the adoption of transition assessment instruments and procedures that promote individual choice and self-determination. A transition questionnaire to be completed by a youth with a disability and his or her family is an excellent example of this. A sample transition questionnaire (Life Planning Inventory) can be found in Appendix 7–1. Samples of published transition questionnaires are presented in Figure 7–7.

Informal Assessments

Clark (1996) noted that "in addition to selected standardized assessment instruments, nonstandardized assessments can be used as designed or with appropriate adaptations" (p. 83) for most youth with disabilities. Types of nonstandardized transition assessment instruments and procedures mentioned include the following:

1. Situational or observational learning styles assessments
2. Curriculum-based assessment from courses taken in school
3. Observational reports from teachers, employers, and parents or guardians
4. Situational assessments in home, community, and work settings
5. Environmental assessments (specific to the individual's placement options)
6. Personal-future planning activities or procedures
7. Structured interviews with parents, guardians, advocates, or peers
8. Adaptive, behavioral, or functional skill inventories and checklists
9. Social histories
10. Rating scales of employability, independent living, and personal–social skills
11. Applied technology or vocational education prerequisite skills assessments
12. General physical examinations

Student Self-Report Measures

Quality of Life Questionnaire (QOL.Q) (Schalock & Keith, 1993)

This instrument can be used to assess quality of life for persons with developmental disabilities or any other population, according to the authors. The subscale contains 40 items focusing on Satisfaction, Competence/Productivity, Empowerment/Independence, and Social Belonging/Community Integration. The scale is administered in an interview format, requires forced-choice answers using a 3-point scale, and takes about 20 minutes to administer. Total scores and percentile scores are provided for each subscale.

Quality of School Life Questionnaire (QSL.Q) (Keith & Schalock, 1995)

This scale focuses on psychological and social indicators of secondary and postsecondary student's subjective reactions to and perceptions of life experiences while in school. The scale contains 40 items measuring Satisfaction, Well Being, Social Belonging, and Empowerment/Control and may be administered through an interview or written questionnaire format in approximately 15 minutes. It requires students who have sufficient receptive and expressive language (natural or augmented) to understand and respond to the questions. Percentile ranks can be estimated manually or through software scoring programs. Norms are based on secondary and postsecondary student populations.

Arc's Self-Determination Scale (Weymeyer, 1995)

This scale is a student self-report instrument designed for use with adolescents with cognitive, developmental, and learning disabilities. Students can evaluate their own beliefs individually or work with others to identify areas of strength, limitations, self-determination goals and objectives, and progress in self-determination over time.

Transition Skills Inventory (Halpern, 1996)

This is a curriculum-based inventory consisting of six lessons that deal with student self-exploration and self-evaluation. The student, parent, and teacher complete the inventory. Students learn about their interests, strengths, and weaknesses in different areas related to adult life roles they will assume following high school completion (e.g., personal life, jobs, education and training, independent living). Students are responsible for conducting and interpreting the assessment and for selecting specific transition goals to include in their transition plans.

Transition Scale Measures

Transition Behavior Scale (McCarney, 1989)

This scale contains 62 items to be completed by at least three persons (preferably employers and teachers) with primary observational opportunities who measure the interpersonal skills and behaviors related to employment and independent living readiness of the individual being observed. The scale takes about 15 minutes to complete and can be used to identify desirable employee and social transition behavior, compare student behavior with nationwide standards, and identify areas of concern for transition readiness. An accompanying intervention manual is available for identifying possible goals, objectives, and interventions for each of the 62 scale items.

Enderle-Severson Transition Rating Scale (Enderle & Severson, 2005)

The criterion-referenced assessment device can be used with individuals age 14–21 with any type of disability to develop statements for needed transition services. The classroom teacher, parent, and primary caregiver can complete it. The scale contains 136 items divided into 5 subscales: (a) job and job training, (b) recreation and leisure, (c) home living, (d) community participation, and (e) postsecondary training and learning opportunities. Percentages are obtained for subscales and total performance.

Transition Planning Measures

McGill Action Planning System (MAPS) (Vandercook & York, 1989)

This is a published structured interview containing systematically posed questions across a variety of life situations and environments designed to elicit individual answers related to planning for the future. It is used primarily with students with severe or multiple disabilities but can also be used for students with learning disabilities. In addition to student input, it allows parents or guardians, friends, and interested others to express their hopes, dreams, and fears about the future for the individual with disabilities.

Figure 7–7 Tools for Transition Assessment

Transition Planning Inventory (Clark & Patton, in press)

This inventory allows for comprehensive transition planning for students and can be used by student, parent, teacher, and local education agency personnel in identifying and meeting the student's needs, preferences, and interests. Three forms are to be completed (school, home, and student form) to provide information related to transition planning and goals. A manual is included that provides an overview of the instrument, administration procedures, technical information, a comprehensive resource list, and more than 600 transition goals correlated to each planning statement.

Transition Knowledge-Based Measures

Social and Prevocational Information Battery (SPIB) (Halpern, Irvin, & Munkres, 1986)

This test measures knowledge of vocational and community adjustment skills and competencies for adolescents and adults with mental retardation. Nine subtests assess knowledge of (a) job-search skills, (b) job-related behavior, (c) banking, (d) budgeting, (e) purchasing, (f) home management, (g) health care, (h) hygiene and grooming, and (i) functional signs. The nine subtests consist mostly of true/false, orally administered items and are intended for middle- and high-school level students.

Test for Everyday Living (Halpern, Irvin, & Landman, 1979)

This test can be used to assess knowledge of daily living and community adjustment skills in mildly low-achieving adolescents and young adults. Seven subtests are included in the battery and reflect on the same long-range educational goals as those in the SPIB.

Life-Centered Measures

Life-Centered Career Education (LCCE) Curriculum (Brolin, 1995)

This comprehensive curriculum is designed to prepare students with disabilities with critical skills needed to successfully function as productive workers, in the home, and in the community. Curriculum-based measures that accompany the curriculum are the LCCE Knowledge Battery, Performance Battery, and Competency Rating Scale. These allow for a determination of student knowledge and skill in 22 competency areas and 97 subcompetencies related to the areas of Daily Living Skills, Personal-Social Skills, and Occupational and Preparation Skills. Individually appropriate instructional goals can subsequently be written using this information.

Career Interest and Aptitude Surveys

Career Orientation and Placement Survey (COPS Interest Inventory, 1995), EdITS, San Diego, California

This inventory helps individuals define the kinds of work they are interested in doing. The test booklet lists activities in many kinds of occupations and asks respondents to decide, using a 4-point scale, whether they would like to perform the activity listed.

Career Ability Placement Survey (CAPS, 1976),EdITS, San Diego, California

This survey determines a variety of career placement abilities of the respondent. Career abilities surveyed include (a) mechanical reasoning, (b) spatial relations, (c) verbal reasoning, (d) numerical ability, (e) language usage, (f) word knowledge, (g) perceptual speed and accuracy, and (h) manual speed and dexterity.

Career Orientation Placement and Evaluation Survey (COPES,1995), EdITS, San Diego,California

This survey contains statements that represent values that people consider important in their work and activities. Each value statement is paired with a contrasting statement. Respondents are to decide which of the two statements best describes their values.

Support for these types of informal assessment instruments and procedures can be found in IDEA 2004, which placed a greater emphasis on informal assessment data. This represented a significant shift in assessment process recommendations of prior years in IDEA legislation. Hence, data from informal transition-related assessment instruments and procedures are valid and important to consider for youth with disabilities.

Additional Transition-Related Assessment Recommendations

In addition to the use of standardized and informal transition-related assessment instruments and procedures, Sitlington et al. (1997) suggest the following guidelines for selecting methods used in the transition assessment process for individuals with disabilities:

1. Assessment methods must be tailored to the types of information needed and the decisions to be made regarding transition planning and various postsecondary outcomes.
2. Specific methods selected must be appropriate for the learning characteristics of the individual, including cultural and linguistic differences.
3. Assessment methods selected must incorporate assistive technology or accommodations that will allow an individual to demonstrate his or her abilities and potential.
4. Assessment methods must occur in environments that resemble actual vocational training, employment, independent living, or community environments.
5. Assessment methods must produce outcomes that contribute to ongoing development, planning, and implementation of next steps in the individual's transition process.
6. Assessment methods must be varied and include a sequence of activities that sample an individual's behavior and skills over time.
7. Assessment data must be verified by more than one method and by more than one person.
8. Assessment data must be synthesized and interpreted to individuals with disabilities, their families, and transition team members.
9. Assessment data and the results of the assessment process must be documented in a format that can be used to facilitate transition planning. (p. 75)

Analyzing the Transition Environment

The upper right box in Figure 7-6 lists methods for gathering information on the demands of future working, educational, and community environments for youth with disabilities. These include analysis of the living and job environment of the individual with a disability, as well as analyzing the programs and resources available in these environments. An effective means for analyzing living and job environments is through the use of an ecological inventory. A sample ecological inventory can be found in Table 7-1. Ecological inventories help identify the specific tasks to be performed in various environments, such as home, school, work, and community. Ecological inventories often use a rating scale or other recording system for quantifying the degree of competency on a specific task performed by the individual with a disability in the observed environment. For example, daily living skills such as dressing, hygiene, or preparing a simple meal can be observed and rated for a person with a severe disability. Ecological inventories often use ratings such as + or − to indicate if the individual performed the task successfully or unsuccessfully. Examples of tasks to be rated in a job or school setting include

Table 7–1   Ecological Inventory

Student Name:
Curriculum Domain: Personal Hygiene
Setting: Bathroom
Activity: Washing and drying hands

Skills	Date									
Turn on hot and cold water										
Place hands under water										
Lather wet hands with soap										
Place soapy hands under water										
Rub soapy hands together										
Remove clean hands from water										
Turn off hot and cold water										
Wipe hands dry with towel										

Assessment Code
  + = skill performed fully
  ✓ = skill performed partially
  − = skill not performed

(a) following directions, (b) working independently, (c) completing assigned tasks, and (d) interacting in a socially appropriate manner with peers, coworkers, or supervisors.

Analysis of the program and resources in the target transition environment focuses on (a) the degree of correspondence between the specific transition goals on the IEP for a youth with a disability and the environment, (b) the personnel available to assist and support the individual with a disability in the environment, and (c) funds available to support the transition program, personnel, needed equipment, and supplies in the environment. People with disabilities frequently require job development and job coaching, for example, to gain work experience and obtain successful competitive, integrated employment. An analysis of the work environment would assess the degree to which these resources and personnel are available prior to placing an individual with a disability in a specific work setting.

In addition to these methods for analyzing the environment, Sitlington et al. (1997) caution that an effective environmental transition assessment also requires analysis of the culture within the environment. For example, what is the culture of the workplace, school, or community, and what effect does this culture have on an individual with a disability interacting within this environment? Observations and interviews with coworkers, supervisory personnel, classmates, or others in the community should be conducted to gather necessary information regarding the cultural demands and expectations placed on the individual with a disability in a given setting. Relevant questions to ask are

1. What are the formal and informal rules, expectations, and standards for behavior in the workplace, school, or community?
2. How are these cultural expectations communicated and enforced?
3. How does the person with a disability respond to the cultural expectations and demands in the environment?

4. What strategies or methods can potentially be employed to improve the ability of the person with a disability to better meet the cultural expectations and demands of the environment?

Sitlington et al. also recommend the use of available resources such as assistive technology for enhancing the capabilities of persons with disabilities to adapt to both cultural and general characteristics of the environment before, during, and following transition assessment.

A case study illustrating the making the match transition assessment model is presented next, followed by a summary of transition assessment models and methods.

LET'S SEE IT IN ACTION! CASE EXAMPLE

Making the Match Transition Assessment Model

Marcos is a 17-year-old Hispanic youth with a developmental disability. Marcos and his parents completed the Transition Planning Inventory before the annual IEP meeting at which transition planning was to be discussed. Marcos and his parents indicated that their primary transition goal was for Marcos to get a paying job in the community after completing school, although they were unsure of how to help Marcos achieve this goal. Marcos would continue to live at home with his family after completing school and use public transportation to get around in the community. A representative from the Department of Rehabilitation was invited and attended the IEP meeting. The counselor agreed to complete the department's eligibility process for Marcos and to conduct a full transition assessment using standardized and informal assessment instruments and procedures. This included completing a functional vocational evaluation using the following assessment instruments and procedures: (a) Enderle–Severson transition rating scale, (b) social and prevocational information battery, and (c) McGill action planning inventory. A summary of the transition assessment findings and results for Marcos appears below:

1. Cognitive functioning significantly below average
2. Limited but understandable speech

3. Bilingual in oral communication skills in English and Spanish
4. Limited written-language skills in both languages
5. Good social and behavioral skills; well-liked by peers and adults
6. Performs well at following directions, initiating and staying on task, and task completion
7. Is interested in jobs working with people, prefers to be indoors, and performs best in jobs that do not require long periods of sitting and concentration
8. Capable of successfully performing the following daily living skills independently: dressing, preparing simple meals, feeding himself, and personal hygiene and grooming
9. Capable of successfully completing the following daily living skills with support: laundry, grocery shopping, clothes shopping
10. Requires supported living and desires to continue to live at home with parents and family after completing school
11. Capable of using public transportation fully independently to complete trips in the community within 5 miles of home

Next to be discussed in this case study is the assessment results of the transition environment for Marcos.

As previously stated, the Department of Rehabilitation counselor was told at the IEP meeting that the main transition environment desired by Marcos and his family was competitive employment, because plans were for him to continue to live at home with his family after school completion. Because Marcos was interested in jobs indoors and working with people, the counselor arranged for several job tryouts in a local luxury hotel close to Marcos's home (e.g., within a 5-mile radius). Marcos was observed working in food services, housekeeping, and at the bell station. He appeared to be most interested and capable of working successfully as a bell person. This job environment was a good match with his social skills, ability to follow directions, and the opportunity to experience frequent movement at work.

The counselor arranged for a job coach to assist Marcos for the first 30 days at the position at the hotel. The coach assisted the bell station staff in providing natural supports to Marcos in the workplace, such as occasional reminders of whom to serve first, how to be courteous to hotel guests, where to store luggage, and how to perform other appropriate tasks. Marcos performed the job to the satisfaction of his supervisor and coworkers and was subsequently hired for a full-time paid position as a bell person for 30–40 hours a week.

Summary of Transition Assessment Models and Methods

A number of transition assessment models have been proposed over the years. The person-centered approach to transition assessment emphasizes the active involvement of the youth with a disability and their family and focuses on gathering information that promotes self-determination with respect to future living arrangements and other dreams and hopes for the future (e.g., employment, social networks, community access, recreation and leisure activities, family life). The comprehensive transition assessment model combines historical approaches to assessment of individuals with disabilities that include vocational assessment and evaluation, career assessment, and adult life focused assessment (i.e., family roles, social and interpersonal networks, community citizen). This particular assessment model covers the entire lifespan (birth to death) of the individual with a disability, as opposed to other models that focus on the transition years and beyond. Finally, the making the match model of transition assessment was presented. This model is both logical and practical to implement. It focuses on gathering data on the transition characteristics of the individual with a disability, the potential environments to which this person will transition to upon completion of school, and determining if a proper match exists between the two.

Methods reviewed for assessing individuals with disabilities for transition include both standardized and informal assessment instruments and procedures. Clark (1996) offers a comprehensive list of both types of assessments. In addition, we have outlined in Figure 7-7 a number of transition assessment instruments and procedures that are commonly cited in transition assessment literature. These include (a) student self-report measures, (b) transition scale measures, (c) transition planning measures, and (d) transition knowledge-based measures. Methods for analyzing transition environments and the cultural expectations and demands of these environments, emphasized in the making the match model, were reviewed and include (a) ecological inventories, (b) observations, (c) personal interviews, and (d) reviewing resources and supports available to the person with a disability.

How Can Assessment Data Be Used to Select and Evaluate a Course of Study and Transition Pathway?

The relationship between transition assessment and transition pathways (presented and discussed in greater depth in the next chapter) is an important one. Numerous transition programming options and choices are faced by transition-age youth with disabilities as they move through middle school, high school, and beyond to postschool life. Middle school youth with disabilities have an important decision to make in selecting a high school course of study and transition pathway that will best prepare them for life after completing school. Most 14-year-old individuals, however, let alone those with disabilities, typically do not have a clear picture of their career interest, aptitude, or capabilities. Transition assessment can help them determine these things, along with the course of study and transition pathway to pursue in high school.

Several of the transition assessment instruments described in Figure 7–7 can be offered as examples. The McGill action planning system (Vandercook & York, 1989) and the Transition Planning Inventory (Clark & Patton, 1998) are excellent for assisting middle school youth with disabilities self-determine an appropriate high school course of study and transition pathway. Both instruments assess an individual's future interests, needs, and preferences across a variety of transition situations and environments, including school (see sample case study following this section for an illustration).

For high-school-age youth with disabilities, transition assessment is even more critical because transition goals on their IEP require greater specification and detail than that necessary for their middle school counterparts. Transition goals for high-school-age youth with disabilities must address the areas of instruction, community, employment, and other postsecondary education needs, as well as a functional-vocational evaluation and daily living skills, if appropriate.

Several of the transition assessment instruments described in Figure 7–7 provide data and information useful in constructing present level of performance statements and transition goals and objectives on an IEP. The Transition Behavior Scale-2 (McCarney & Anderson, 2000), for example, estimates the current level of social behavior of an individual with a disability in an employment setting compared with a standardized sample and identifies areas where social growth is needed on the job (e.g., the individual will develop appropriate social interactions with coworkers and supervisors in the workplace). The Enderle–Severson transition rating scale (Enderle & Severson, 2005) estimates the degree to which a youth with a disability possesses the competencies for success in recreation and leisure activities, independent living, community participation, and postsecondary learning environments. This data can be used for writing all IDEA 1997 required transition services language on an IEP for high-school-age youth with disabilities (see sample case studies at the end of this section for examples).

The transition-related assessment instruments in Figure 7–7 can also help transition personnel evaluate the appropriateness of the course of study requirements and transition pathway selected by high-school-age youth with disabilities and their families. For example, several of the student self-report measures, such as the Quality of Life and Quality of School Life Questionnaires (Schalock & Keith, 1993, 1995) assess the current satisfaction of a youth with disability in regard to social well-being, empowerment, and a sense of belonging in school and life in the community. This type of data can be reviewed and discussed at an annual IEP meeting to determine the satisfaction of a youth with a disability with his or her chosen transition pathway and high school course of study. Adjustments can subsequently be made when indicated.

Case studies illustrating the relationship between transition assessment, high school course of study, and transition pathways are presented next.

LET'S SEE IT IN ACTION! CASE EXAMPLE

Casey (Transition Pathway 1)

Casey is a 16-year-old ninth-grade student who is deaf and functions cognitively in the above-average range. He attended a special school for the deaf during most of his elementary school years and began receiving an inclusive education in sixth grade at his request and that of his parents. This program continued through middle school and into high school. Prior to the IEP meeting when Casey turned 14, he and his parents completed the life skills inventory. Results of this informal transition assessment instrument indicated that he would like to go to college, engage in full-time career-oriented employment, live on his own in an apartment, and participate in recreation and leisure activities in his community. His middle school IEP team agreed that a college preparatory course of study in high school was appropriate for Casey and that with related services and supports, he would likely be successful in Transition Pathway 1.

An IEP meeting was scheduled for Casey midway through his ninth-grade year in high school to evaluate the degree to which he was achieving success in Transition Pathway 1. Transition assessment data gathered during middle school and in Casey's ninth-grade year were shared at the meeting. The high school resource specialist had administered the McGill Action Planning System to Casey, along with the Transition Skills Inventory. In addition, the specialist had gathered informal

transition assessment data such as curriculum-based measures, obtained grades, and had interviews with several of Casey's teachers.

Transition assessment results showed that Casey was performing above average in most academic subjects, particularly in science and math. Casey had the most difficulty in high school subjects involving written language, an area in which his achievement throughout school had been consistently about a year and a half below grade level due to his hearing impairment. He, however, was earning "B" or better grades on most written assignments with resource specialist study skills support and curriculum modifications. Collectively, transition assessment data showed that Pathway 1 was an appropriate course of study for Casey and that his transition goal to participate in a college preparatory program, leading to obtainment of a high school diploma, was being achieved. In addition, results from the McGill Action Planning System led the IEP team to suggest the following transition goals be added to Casey's IEP: (a) complete career and occupational assessment in the high school career center, (b) explore careers in math and science, (c) participate in driver's education and training, (d) participate in integrated high school or community recreation and leisure activities. Casey and his parents agreed to add these transition goals to his IEP.

LET'S SEE IT IN ACTION! CASE EXAMPLE

Marion (Transition Pathway 4)

Marion is a 14-year-old eighth-grade student with multiple disabilities. Her cognitive functioning is significantly below average and she has limited oral communication skills. She functions academically around the mid-first-grade level and requires extensive supports in school. She is well-mannered, somewhat shy, and a bit of a loner in school, at home, and in the community. Marion has been in special day classes since she started school.

A person-centered transition assessment session was recently completed with Marion and her family at their home. Also in attendance were a few members of her extended family, a case worker from the regional center who had worked with the family since Marion's birth, and Marion's special education teacher from school, who acted as the facilitator of the meeting. After introductions of all in attendance, the special education teacher explained person-centered transition assessment and planning to the group and proceeded to develop a personal profile of Marion, using a number of different maps. A *Circle of Support Map* revealed that outside her immediate family, teachers, and classmates, Marion had a limited number of important relationships in her life. A *Community Presence Map* showed that the primary places Marion spent time in her community were home, school, occasional visits to the local mall or grocery store with her mother, and attending her older brother's recreational sporting events (e.g., soccer and baseball). Lists of her preferences, gifts, and capacities were completed and showed that she loves animals, is very good caring for her pets, enjoys music, and likes to sing.

Traditional transition assessment had been previously completed with Marion and her family, using the Quality of School Life Questionnaire and the Transition Skills Inventory. In addition to these instruments, school-based transition assessment results from ecological inventories and curriculum-based measures were shared at the meeting. The

results of all of these assessment instruments and procedures revealed the following:

1. Marion has a limited social network and desires more friendships, particularly with nondisabled peers.
2. Marion thinks that most of her teachers in the past have liked her, especially her current special day-class teacher.
3. She would like to participate more in some general-education classrooms in high school and in extracurricular activities such as chorus or drama.
4. Marion would like to live on her own after graduating from high school.
5. Marion's academic skills are relatively low, and she would benefit from more of a functional life-skills education emphasizing daily living skills, community integration, and career exploration and preparation leading to supported employment.

A summary of all the transition assessments completed showed that Marion's hopes and dreams for the future revolved around a desire for greater integration in school and in the community, greater contact with nondisabled peers, and the opportunity to live and work semi-independently in the future. Marion's family thought that Pathway 3 or 4 would be the best option for her in high school. Her current special education teacher agreed to invite the high school special day-class teacher to Marion's upcoming IEP meeting. At this meeting, discussions would focus on promoting greater integration of Marion into some general education classes next year. The special education teacher would recommend collaboration or consultation to modify the general education curriculum in a way that would promote Marion's achievement of functional daily living skills in several general education classes (e.g., math, social science, health, and science).

In addition, enrollment in elective classes, such as chorus and drama, would offer Marion an opportunity to have greater social contact and develop possible friendships with nondisabled peers. Marion's time in special day class in high school would focus on reinforcing acquisition of social and daily living skills, community-based skills, and career exploration and preparation in the field of animal care.

SUMMARY

Transition assessment is an essential part of transition planning and evaluation for youth with disabilities. Transition assessment data are needed to help youth with disabilities and their families decide an appropriate future high school course of study, the transition pathway to pursue beyond high school, and the degree to which the individual is achieving success in their chosen course of study and transition pathway. Transition assessment, in contrast to traditional annual-based assessment in special education, is an ongoing process of collecting data on the needs, preferences, and interests of a youth with a disability in the areas of work, education, independent living, and personal and social skills.

Three major approaches to transition assessment were presented in this chapter. Person-centered approaches are designed to promote active involvement of youth with disabilities and their families in transition assessment, empowering them through various self-determination activities to discuss and express their hopes and dreams for the future. The use of mapping procedures and other personal-future planning activities is effective for accomplishing these objectives. A second approach to futures planning for youth with disabilities is the comprehensive transition assessment method. This focuses on gathering transition-related information on the youth with a disability across their lifespan, including career awareness, exploration, preparation, and vocational assessment data during their school years, followed by adult life role information after completing school. The final model presented and discussed was the making the match model. This model conceptualizes the steps of transition assessment to include the following:

1. A determination of the transition characteristics of an individual with a disability
2. The demands and culture of potential transition environments
3. Judging the degree of match that exists between the two

A number of standardized and informal transition assessment methods were presented to help transition personnel obtain relevant data to help develop the transition portion of the IEP for a youth with a disability. Regardless which of these transition-related assessment instruments or procedures is used (e.g., standardized, informal, or a combination of the two), transition assessment should take place in real life versus simulated contexts and allow for self-choice and determination by youth with disabilities. In addition, we have suggested a wide variety of individuals be involved in administering various transition assessment instruments and procedures. These personnel include general and special educators, general and vocational special needs personnel, parents, youth with disabilities, and transition service agency support representatives. Transition assessment competencies to be possessed by these individuals have been suggested by the Division of Career Development and Transition. Perhaps the most important of these competencies are (a) the ability to select, adapt, develop, administer, and interpret valid transition assessment instruments and procedures and (b) serving and contributing as a member of an interdisciplinary team in the ongoing transition assessment process.

What process should individualized educational program teams use to write required transition services language and related annual IEP goals and objectives for various transition pathways? This important transition planning skill is the topic of the next chapter.

KEY TERMS AND PHRASES

making the match	transition assessment
methods for analyzing the environment	transition assessment personnel
methods for assessing the individual	competencies
traditional assessment	transition assessment plan

QUESTIONS FOR REFLECTION, THINKING, AND SKILL BUILDING

1. What is involved in the development of a transition assessment plan for a youth with a disability?

2. What methods and procedures are recommended for performing a transition assessment?

3. Which personnel in your school or agency are most qualified to conduct transition assessment of youth with disabilities? Describe their qualifications and roles.

4. What transition assessment tools are available in your school or agency?

5. How can transition assessment be improved in your school or agency?

6. Conduct an evaluation of transition assessment personnel, instruments, and procedures in a local school or district and write commendations and recommendations based on your findings.

7. Investigate and review one of the transition assessment instruments listed in Figure 7-7 and write a report on your findings.

8. Conduct a transition assessment of an individual with disabilities, the environments to which the individual will potentially transition, and the degree of match that exists. Make recommendations based on your findings.

9. Create a staff development program to train transition personnel in effective ways to conduct transition assessment of youth with disabilities.

Life Planning Inventory

Student Name: _____   Date: _____

Directions: Circle all appropriate answers.

WORK OPTIONS

What type of work do you plan to do upon leaving school?
1. Volunteer work
2. Part-time work
3. Full-time work
4. Other _____

SUPPORT AGENCIES

Which of the following agencies would you like information about?
1. Department of Rehabilitation
2. Irvine Youth Employment
3. Employment Development Department
4. Other _____

EDUCATIONAL OPTIONS

Please indicate the possible educational choice upon leaving high school.
1. Adult school
2. Community college
3. State university
4. University of California
5. Private college
6. Other _____

VOCATIONAL TRAINING OPTIONS

Please indicate possible vocational program choice upon leaving high school.
1. Coastline Regional Occupational Program
2. California State Work Ability Program
3. Job Corps

(Continued)

(Continued)

4. California Conservation Corps
5. Private trade or technical school
6. Other _____

INCOME-RELATED SERVICES

Which of the following issues need to be resolved?
1. Medical insurance
2. Dental insurance
3. Income
4. Medical issues
5. Taxes
6. Tuition
7. Other _____

RESIDENTIAL OPTIONS

Where do you plan to live upon leaving school and 2 years from now?
1. Apartment
2. Dormitory
3. Family home
4. Other _____

TRANSPORTATION OPTIONS

What type(s) of transportation will you be using upon leaving high school?
1. Bicycle
2. Public transportation (bus)
3. Car

Which issues need to be resolved?
1. Driver's license
2. Car insurance
3. Public transportation route information

INDEPENDENT LIVING SKILLS

Which of the following skills needs to be addressed before leaving school?
1. Money management
2. Advocacy

RECREATION AND SOCIAL OPTIONS

Which recreational activities do you want to participate in?
1. City- or community-sponsored activities
2. Church-sponsored activities
3. College activities
4. Workplace activities
5. Other _____

Chapter 8

Transition Pathways

Gary Greene

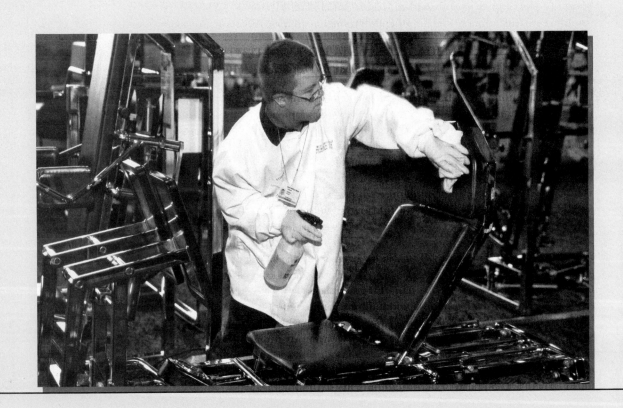

Chapter Questions

- What is the model and philosophy of transition pathways for youth with disabilities?
- What are the various pathways to transition that youth with disabilities can choose as they move into, through, and beyond high school to a quality adult life?
- How are these pathways similar and different from one another with respect to transition planning and programming considerations?

Children and their families experience numerous transitions as the child grows and develops from infancy to adulthood. Some of the more significant ones include entrance *into* school, movement between or *through* schools, and transition *beyond* school. This final phase, *transition beyond school,* is critical for youth with disabilities because they achieve less positive postschool outcomes in comparison with youth without disabilities (Wagner, Newman, Cameto, Levine, & Garza, 2006). This chapter focuses on potential pathways to achieving a quality adult life *beyond* school for youth with disabilities.

The model illustrating the **transition pathways** concept, presented in Chapter 1, is discussed in greater detail in this chapter. The model reflects the transition services requirements of IDEA 2004 and is applicable to all youth with disabilities who are eligible under federal definitions. Moreover, the model is responsive to special transition considerations such as inclusive education, access to the general education curriculum, participation in standardized tests required for graduation, self-determination, and cultural and linguistic diversity. A review of this model and the philosophy upon which the model is based are discussed in this chapter.

⇒ WHAT IS THE MODEL AND PHILOSOPHY OF TRANSITION PATHWAYS FOR YOUTH WITH DISABILITIES?

A Pathways Model to Successful Transition for All Youth with Disabilities

Table 8-1 shows a model of four distinct pathways to successful transition beyond school for youth with disabilities. The unique characteristics of the model are that it (a) is applicable to individuals with a broad range of disabilities, (b) offers course of study specifications for youth with disabilities, (c) contains IDEA 2004 IEP transition services requirements for youth with disabilities age 16, and (d) outlines transition programming components for each pathway.

The first column of the model contains IDEA 2004 transition services language requirements for the individualized educational program. Columns for Pathways 1 through 4 are shown across the top horizontal axis of the model, with corresponding

Table 8–1 Pathways to Successful Transition Model

IDEA 2004 Transition Services Language Requirements	Pathway 1	Pathway 2	Pathway 3	Pathway 4	Transition Programming Components
Instruction	Fully integrated high school college preparatory curriculum leading to passage of high school exit examination, obtainment of standard high school diploma, and entrance into a 2- or 4-year college or university	Fully integrated high school curriculum of blended academic and career–vocational courses leading to passage of high school exit examination with necessary accommodations, obtainment of a standard high school diploma, and entrance into a career–technical school or career apprenticeship	Semi-integrated high school curriculum of blended academic and career–vocational courses leading to obtainment of high school certificate of completion and entrance into community-based paid competitive employment with time-limited supports	Semi-integrated high school curriculum emphasizing functional academics, social skills, and life skills leading to obtainment of a high school certificate of completion and entrance into community-based competitive or supported employment	Assessments General education curriculum access and school foundation Instructional setting Related services and supports
Community experiences	Function fully independently in the community	Function fully independently in the community	Function semi-independently in the community with time-limited supports	Function semi-independently in the community or with ongoing supports	
Employment and other postsecondary adult living objectives	Career exploration and paid-work experience in high school, college degree-based full-time competitive career employment with salary and benefits, and independent living as an adult	Career exploration and paid-work experience in high school, vocational–technical school or career apprenticeship-based full-time competitive employment with salary and possible benefits, and independent living as an adult	Career exploration and paid-work experience in high school, community-based paid competitive employment with time-limited supports, and full or semi-independent living as an adult	Career exploration and paid-work experience in high school, community-based paid competitive or supported employment, and semi- or supported living as an adult	Transition planning considerations
Functional vocational evaluation and daily living skills	Not needed	Career–vocational and community-based authentic assessments	Functional career and life skills assessment in authentic or simulated settings	Social, adaptive behavior, and independent living skills assessments in authentic or simulated settings	Transition culmination considerations

IEP sample transition services language to be written in the IEP for a youth with disability in each respective pathway. Finally, transition programming components to consider during high school for youth with disabilities in all pathways is presented in the far right column of the model. Figure 8–1 contains a summary of the complete IDEA language for transition services for each pathway shown in the model.

Transition Pathways Model Philosophy: Keeping Options Open for Youth

In the past decade, the educational program options available to youth with disabilities have been dramatically reduced and restricted as a result of the standards-based reform movement, No Child Left Behind (NCLB) Act of 2001, and related high-stakes testing (i.e., passage of high school exit examination as a graduation requirement).

Pathway 1

The youth with disabilities will (a) participate in a fully integrated high school college preparatory curriculum leading to passage of high school exit examination, obtainment of a standard high school diploma, and entrance into a 2- or 4-year college or university; (b) function fully independently in the community; (c) complete career exploration activities and paid work experiences in high school; (d) obtain a college degree that leads to full-time competitive employment with salary and benefits; and (e) live fully independently as an adult.

Pathway 2

The youth with disabilities will (a) participate in a semi-integrated high school curriculum of blended academic and career–vocational courses leading to passage of high school exit examination with necessary accommodations, obtainment of a standard high school diploma, and entrance into a career–technical school or career apprenticeship; (b) function fully independently in the community, including independent living; (d) complete career exploration and paid-work experience in high school; and (e) obtain full-time competitive employment with salary and possible benefits in their career interest.

Pathway 3

The youth with disabilities will (a) participate in a semi-integrated high school curriculum of blended academic and career–vocational courses leading to obtainment of a high school certificate of completion and entrance into community-based paid competitive employment with time-limited supports, (b) function semi-independently in the community with necessary supports, (d) obtain functional daily living skills needed for full or semi-independent living, (e) participate in a functional vocational evaluation that identifies competitive employment skills, and (f) participate in integrated paid competitive employment with necessary supports.

Pathway 4

The youth with disabilities will (a) participate in a semi-integrated high school curriculum emphasizing functional academics, social skills, life skills, and self-determination and self-advocacy skills leading to obtainment of a high school certificate of completion and entrance into community-based competitive or supported employment; (b) function semi-independently in the community with necessary supports; (c) obtain daily living skills needed for independent or supported living; (d) participate in a functional vocational evaluation that identifies competitive employment skills; and (e) participate in community-based competitive or supported employment.

Figure 8–1   Transition Pathways Model Language

Although alternative options for graduation of students with disabilities are currently being discussed at the U.S. Department of Education, these alternatives have not yet been fully realized. Hence, today's public schools are operating perhaps more than ever before in a *one size fits all* atmosphere. This is problematic for youth with disabilities and their families when it comes to choosing educational program options during one's high school years and beyond. Although IDEA 2004 requires access to the general education curriculum, the law still emphasizes the importance of providing an individualized educational program for a youth with a disability based on his or her unique needs. With respect to transition, this educational program must take into account the individual's interests and preferences. In short, we suggest that a potential conflict exists between the standards-based reform movement, NCLB 2001, and IDEA 2004 with respect to the transition educational program options available to youth with disabilities in today's public schools.

The intent of our transition pathways model is to provide youth with disabilities and their families a variety of educational program options during high school, regardless of the current atmosphere of the public schools, categorical label of a youth with a disability, or the school district in which they reside. We fully support a noncategorical, individualized approach to transition for all youth with disabilities, inclusive of educational practices, self-determination, and access to the general education curriculum, as required by IDEA 2004. The pathways model presented in this book is meant to reflect this philosophy and set of educational practices. Although different pathways may reflect educational program practices that have historically been associated with certain types of students with disabilities, the pathways themselves should not be interpreted as representing educational tracks for mild, moderate, or severe disabilities. Each pathway is meant to be an option available to any youth with a disability and his or her family to consider, regardless of categorical label or severity of disability. The pathway selected depends greatly on the hopes and dreams of these individuals, their cultural values and beliefs, and desires for the future. We present four distinct pathways which we believe represent the best range of options for youth with disabilities and are those that have been historically and, in many instances, still available to youth with disabilities in many school districts today.

Each pathway in the model is available to any youth with a disability, regardless of the severity of his or her disability. The degree of intensity of support needed to do this, however, may vary, depending on the severity of the individual youth's disability. It is our recommendation, therefore, that as early as possible *the youth and his or her family engage in self-determination activities, such as person-centered planning,* with the guidance of the IEP team and decide the most appropriate pathway, as well as the necessary supports for success to occur in the pathway of their choice. Although youth with disabilities and their families have the option at any time to change pathways as the youth matures and matriculates through his or her middle school and high school years, it is important for everyone to understand the school program and community implications of making such a change. In other words, transition pathways should be selected carefully and changes approached cautiously, with full collaboration from the IEP team.

It should also be pointed out that the pathways model should be viewed as flexible or fluid. By this, we mean that components from different pathways in the model can be combined to form unique, new pathways not shown in the model. For example, a youth with a physical disability with average to above average cognitive ability and academic skills may decide that he or she is college-bound and would like to pursue Pathway 1. Given their physical disabilities, however, this individual may benefit from a functional-vocational evaluation and supported employment to gain competitive, paid work experience before entering college (Pathway 3 components). Thus, in this example, a combination of components from Pathways 1 and 3 would be appropriate to select during person-centered planning for transition.

A narrative description of the four pathways will subsequently be presented containing the following information: (a) recommended assessments; (b) general education curriculum access or effective school foundation, including self-determination and self-advocacy skills; (c) instructional setting; (d) related services and support; (e) transition planning recommendations; and (f) transition culmination considerations, including recommended transition services agencies. Note with regard to transition planning recommendations that adoption of person-centered planning practices applies to all pathways in the model. Review of person-centered planning occurred in chapters 6 and 7 and therefore will not be discussed in this chapter. Sample case studies of transition-age youth with disabilities for each pathway will be presented following the review of key information for each pathway.

⇒ PATHWAY 1

The youth with disabilities will (a) participate in a fully integrated high school college preparatory curriculum leading to passage of high school exit examination, obtainment of a standard high school diploma, and entrance into a 2- or 4-year college or university; (b) function fully independently in the community; (c) complete career exploration activities and paid work experiences in high school; (d) obtain a college degree that leads to full-time competitive employment with salary and benefits; and (e) live fully independently as an adult.

Recommended Assessments

Assessment for youth with disabilities who plan to attend a 2- or 4-year university may include any or all of the following tests:

1. Preliminary Scholastic Aptitude Test (PSAT): An examination similar to the SAT and taken early in the high school years to measure verbal and mathematics aptitude for college entrance.
2. Scholastic Aptitude Test (SAT): An examination measuring verbal and mathematics aptitude for college and taken during the 11th-grade year. Submission of scores on this examination is required on most 4-year college and university applications.
3. American College Test (ACT): An examination measuring verbal and mathematics aptitude for college and taken during the 10th-grade year. It is an alternative examination to the SAT. Scores on the ACT can be submitted in place of SAT scores on many 4-year college and university applications.

4. Advanced Placement (AP) Examinations: Examinations measuring aptitude in specific advanced placement courses completed in high school (e.g., science, social science, mathematics, English, foreign language).

These tests are typically administered at the end of the youth's sophomore year through the junior year of high school. High school youth may consider taking preparatory classes or working independently with published SAT, ACT, and AP manuals or computer programs to prepare for these tests. In addition to these assessments, regular admission requirements for 4-year colleges and universities include the possession of a high school diploma or general education diploma (GED), submission of high school transcripts showing courses completed, grade point average and/or class rank, and in some instances a personal interview with an admissions officer.

Career and vocational interests, aptitudes, values, and strengths are equally important to assess in college-bound youth. Tests of this type are typically available and administered in most high school career centers. Youth with disabilities are highly encouraged to meet with high school career counselors as early as their ninth-grade year to begin exploring career interests and later, in their 11th-grade year, to begin the college search and application process. For a more complete review of career and vocational assessment instruments, readers are encouraged to see Chapter 7.

General Education Curriculum Access and Effective School Foundation

Youth with disabilities pursuing Pathway 1 have full access to and participate in a college preparatory general education curriculum in high school if planning to attend a 4-year college or university. For this reason, youth with disabilities choosing Pathway 1 are encouraged to visit their high school career center to determine the actual requirements for the colleges or universities of interest. In California, for example, the following requirements apply for admission into the University of California system (www.universityofcalifornia/edu/admissions/undergrad_adm/):

1. Two years history and social science
2. Four years English 9th–12th grade (honors, AP, challenge recommended)
3. Three years math (Algebra I, Geometry, Algebra II, 4 years recommended)
4. Two years laboratory science (3 years recommended)
5. Two years foreign language (3 years recommended)
6. One year visual and performing arts
7. One year (two semesters) college-preparatory electives

In addition to fully participating in these general-education courses in high school, maintaining a minimum grade point average of 3.0 and ability to pass the high school exit examination is important for college-bound youth with disabilities in California and elsewhere. High-stakes testing and its effect on graduation from high school for youth with disabilities has become a subject of great concern in recent years to professionals in the field of special education. Figure 8–2 presents information from

Thurlow (2002), in an issue brief published by the National Center on Secondary Education and Transition, discussed assessment (e.g., high school exit exam) accommodations for students with disabilities in high school. According to Thurlow, "Accommodation is just one of many terms that have been used to indicate a change in instructional or assessment materials or procedures" (p. 5). The author further states that the term *modification* "is generally (but not always) used to refer to a change in which scores produced are invalid or otherwise not comparable with other scores." IDEA 1997 uses both of these terms but intends for them to be considered synonymous with one another. Data presented and reviewed by Thurlow showed that, in most states, accommodations are used by greater percentages of students at the elementary school level compared with middle and high school levels. Furthermore, we do not know what is happening in the majority of situations in which accommodations are being used and whether these accommodations promote better performance on state-level assessments for students with disabilities. A list of examples of instructional and assessment accommodations for students with disabilities can be found in the appendix to Chapter 6.

Figure 8–2   Assessment Accommodations for Students with Disabilities

Thurlow (2002) and the National Center on Secondary Education and Transition regarding state assessment accommodations for youth with disabilities in high school. A list of accommodations reviewed by Thurlow can be found in Appendix 8–1.

Pathway 1 youth with disabilities receive the majority of their instruction in general education classrooms. King-Sears (2001) has outlined three steps for gaining access to the general education curriculum for learners with disabilities:

Step 1. Analyze the general education curriculum for learners with disabilities.
Step 2. Enhance the general education curriculum parts that need strengthening.
Step 3. Accessibility through minor and major changes.

Key components of each step are presented in Figure 8-3. In addition, King-Sears provided an excellent curriculum evaluation guide for teachers in deciding the ease in which the general education curriculum can be used to instruct students with a range of disabilities (see Figure 8-4).

Instructional Setting

Youth with disabilities in Pathway 1 are fully included in general education classrooms to the maximum extent possible, with minimum, if any, enrollment in departmentalized special education college preparatory classes; note that since the implementation of NCLB 2001, departmentalized special education academic courses have been drastically reduced, if not fully eliminated in many high schools. Resource specialist (RSP) enrollment for a period a day as an elective is an optional instructional setting for youth with disabilities who can potentially benefit from academic support and specific skills training, such as the type provided in the strategies intervention model (see next section). Full community participation, as well as integrated community-based career and vocational training are additional instructional settings for Pathway 1 youth with disabilities.

King-Sears (2001) presented a three-step process for helping teachers determine how accessible their general education curriculum is for students with disabilities. These steps are outlined below.

Step 1. Analyze the General Education Curriculum

1. How well does the curriculum describe what learners should be able to know and do by the end of the course?
2. What resources are included in the curriculum that provide teachers with materials and research-based methods for diversifying instruction?
3. How many universal design elements are included in the curriculum?

Step 2. Enhance the General Education Curriculum Parts That Need Strengthening

Determine poorly designed curriculum features for learners with disabilities and build them in (e.g., describe more explicit standards, schedule judicious review, prime student background knowledge).

Step 3. Accessibility Through Minor and Major Changes

1. Minor curriculum changes include providing students with disabilities:
   a. *Accommodations:* Change the input and/or output method used by the teacher or student related to the intended instructional outcome (e.g., books on tape, graphic organizers).
   b. *Adaptations:* Hold the curriculum content the same as it is for other students (e.g., science) but change slightly the conceptual level for the standards (e.g., match 20 science terms versus recall them from memory).
2. Major curriculum changes include providing students with disabilities:
   a. *Parallel Curriculum Outcome:* Hold the curriculum content the same as it is for most students (e.g., English) but make major changes in the outcome within the content (e.g., most students are writing lengthy book reports on a novel they have read, whereas a student with mental retardation is writing a brief report describing one of the characters in the same or different novel).
   b. *Overlapping Curricula:* Allows a student with a disability to work on his or her IEP goals in a general education setting while accomplishing very different content or curriculum (e.g., a student with moderate mental retardation participates in general education curriculum science activities, but the targeted curriculum area for the youngster is to follow directions during science experiments).

Figure 8–3   Steps for Gaining Access to the General Education Curriculum for Learners with Disabilities
Source: From "Three Steps for Gaining Access to the General Education Curriculum for Learners with Disabilities," by M. E. King-Sears, 2001, *Intervention in School and Clinic, 37,* pp. 67–76. Austin, TX: PRO-ED. Reprinted with permission.

Related Services and Support

Youth with disabilities in Pathway 1 can benefit from the following related services and support in preparation for college and a career:

1. Study skills and strategies intervention model (SIM) instruction beginning in the seventh-grade year or no later than the ninth-grade year (see Figure 8–5 for an overview of SIM).
2. Exploration of career options, on the basis of interests, aptitudes, values, and career area strengths.

Directions: Carefully read through all curriculum materials. Decide how easily the curriculum can be readily used by teachers to effectively instruct students with a range of learning strengths and needs. Then rate the curriculum on each of the 22 items using the following scale:

3 Curriculum is well designed as is
2 Curriculum needs minor modifications and enhancements
1 Curriculum needs substantial revisions and resources

General Adequacy	1	2	3
1. Substantive rationale and purpose, including research that supports curriculum content			
2. Clearly defined goals and objectives (used synonymously with standards, outcomes, competency-based criteria)			
3. Curriculum content appropriate to objectives			
4. Significant content appropriate to the discipline/subject-matter area			
5. Emphasis on critical thinking and problem solving			
6. Coherent structure and order to content			
7. Global, multicultural perspective			
8. Instructional strategies appropriate to objectives			
9. Appropriateness for developmental levels and styles of intended learners			
10. Responsiveness to affective and social needs of intended learners			
11. Varied strategies for both individuals and groups			
12. Authentic, curriculum-based evaluation procedures			
13. Technical adequacy of media and technology			
14. Additional supportive resources for teachers and learners			
Considerations for Students with Disabilities	1	2	3
15. Relevance of the curriculum to present and future environments			
16. Emphasis on data-based instructional decision making			
17. Attention to development of independence and social competence			
18. Structured lessons geared to stages of learning			
19. Appropriate teacher modeling, cueing, and reinforcement			
20. Varied formats and pacing for guided and independent practice			
21. Provision for appropriate assistive technology			
22. Attention to maintenance and generalization			
TOTAL # of items with each score			

Figure 8–4 Curriculum Evaluation Guide

Source: From "Three Steps for Gaining Access to the General Education Curriculum for Learners with Disabilities," by M. E. King-Sears, 2001, *Intervention in School and Clinic, 37,* pp. 67–76. Austin, TX: PRO-ED. Reprinted with permission.

SIM training for adolescents with learning disabilities is one of the most highly research-validated models of instruction for this population of learners. SIM focuses on teaching learning strategies as a means to more effective learning and performance. Task-specific learning strategies available to be taught in this model include the following:

1. reading strategy instruction
2. writing strategy instruction
3. memory and test-taking strategies
4. note-taking strategy instruction
5. social skills strategy instruction
6. strategic instruction in the content areas
7. strategies for transition to postsecondary education settings
8. strategies for transition to employment settings

Figure 8–5   Strategies Intervention Model
For a comprehensive review of these strategies and the SIM model, see *Teaching Adolescents with Learning Disabilities: Strategies and Methods,* 2nd ed., by D. D. Deshler, E. S. Lewis, and B. K. Lenz, 1979, Denver: Love. Also see *Teaching Adolescents with Disabilities: Accessing the General Education Curriculum,* by D. D. Deshler and J. B. Schumaker, 2006. Thousand Oaks, CA: Corwin Press.

3. Exploration of postsecondary career preparation options, such as career-technical schools, community college career training, and 4-year university degree programs.
4. Self-determination and self-advocacy skills training in the ninth-grade year for use in general education classrooms. Self-determination skills training should focus on exploring hopes and dreams for the future, education planning, decision making, and self-selection of IEP goals and objectives. Self-advocacy skills training should teach youth with disabilities acceptance of their disability, how to explain their disability to others, and how to ask for reasonable accommodations in general education classrooms, in the workplace, and in the community.
5. Continuation of self-determination and self-advocacy skills training during the 11th-grade year to prepare for successful postsecondary participation in college and community, with a focus on locating available resources, such as disabled student services or Department of Vocational Rehabilitation services.
6. Development of a personal youth profile and portfolio for use in the college application process and/or job search.

With respect to related supports, the resource specialist and other special education personnel provide collaborative consultation in general education classrooms for Pathway 1 youth with disabilities. This collaboration includes (a) planning the design and delivery of core academic instruction; (b) curriculum modification, adaptations, and accommodations; and (c) coteaching, when possible. A list of accommodations for students with learning disability (LD) published by the National Center Learning Disabilities (2006) can be obtained from LD online and is found in Appendix 8–2.

Youth with more severe disabilities who possess the cognitive and academic capabilities to pursue Pathway 1 may need the support of an inclusion facilitator in areas such as written and oral communication, curriculum modification, and alternative ways to demonstrate course competency. The inclusion facilitator will need to possess considerable collaborative consultation skill and ability. A review of CLASP, an acronym for a collaborative problem-solving approach, is presented in Figure 8–6. Use of CLASP may prove to be highly beneficial for this purpose.

Voltz, Brazil, and Ford (2001) presented a relatively simple five-step model of collaborative problem solving that is an adaptation of the collaborative consultation process developed by West and Idol (1990). The essential steps in collaborative problem solving, represented by the acronym CLASP, are as follows:

1. *Clarify the Problem:* General and special education teachers developing a problem statement that is specific enough to enable both parties to have a common understanding of the central issues.
2. *Look at Influencing Factors:* Analyze the context in which the problem occurs. What tends to precipitate the problem? What seems to reinforce it? The purpose of this step is to identify possible underlying causes and aspects of the context that may affect the problem.
3. *Actively Explore Intervention Options:* The special and general education teachers brainstorm to develop strategies that may positively affect the problem. At this point, to increase the quantity and diversity of ideas being generated, evaluating intervention options is discouraged.
4. *Select the Option:* During this step, the general and special educators evaluate interventions generated during the brainstorming state and attempt to reach a consensus regarding which of the interventions is most feasible and has the highest probability of success.
5. *Plan to Implement the Selected Strategy:* Here, teachers outline responsibilities regarding who will do what when, as well as how and when the effectiveness of the selected strategy will be assessed.

Figure 8–6   CLASP: Collaborative Problem Solving

Transition Planning

College preparatory and high school graduation requirements are the primary topics of discussion during a person-centered IEP transition planning meeting for youth with disabilities aged 16 and older. Annual reviews of academic performance occur to determine whether adequate progress is being made toward meeting college admissions requirements and if Pathway 1 remains an appropriate option. A review of necessary supports (e.g., resource specialist, inclusion facilitator) and the outcomes of supports provided should also be discussed at annual IEP meetings.

Additional transition planning topics to be discussed for Pathway 1 youth with disabilities involve community participation and employment. Driver's education or training, obtainment of a driving license, or community mobility training are the most likely options for transition goals in the area of community access. Participation in school and community youth group activities, sports leagues, and other areas of interest are likely transition goals in the area of recreation. With respect to employment, transition planning and goals should focus on career and vocational assessment that leads to paid work experience in high school for Pathway 1 youth with disabilities.

Transition Culmination

As the Pathway 1 youth with a disability reaches the 11th- or 12th-grade year in high school, a culminating IEP check should take place in the fall semester to determine whether

1. all of the necessary high school completion requirements appear on the youth's transcript and a summary of performance document has been prepared by the IEP team;

2. the youth has taken the necessary college, university entrance, and/or community college placement tests;

3. the youth has had paid-work experience in high school and demonstrated appropriate knowledge and skills in the workplace;

4. the youth has explored, visited, and/or applied to desired community colleges or 4-year universities;

5. the youth demonstrates awareness of his or her disability;

6. the youth is aware of and capable of obtaining assistance from disabled-student services at desired community colleges and universities, as well as other necessary community services, to support transition in postsecondary education;

7. the youth knows how to seek reasonable accommodations in education and employment settings and uses appropriate self-advocacy skills; and

8. the youth possesses the recreation and leisure skills needed for community participation.

In addition to the above, it is important to determine whether the youth or family has the financial ability to pay for all college expenses and has completed the necessary financial aid forms, such as scholarships and grants. Employment training and opportunities during college to support financial needs should also be discussed with Pathway 1 youth with disabilities and their families. Determining the living arrangements for the youth while attending college must be addressed as well. Finally, Pathway 1 youth with disabilities should know how to connect with postschool transition services agencies such as disabled-student services at the college or university they plan on attending, regional occupational training program for additional employment training, and the Department of Vocational Rehabilitation.

LET'S SEE IT IN ACTION! CASE EXAMPLE

Pathway 1

Angela is a 15-year-old student with a learning disability participating in a college preparatory program in high school. Her primary academic problems are reading comprehension and written language. She received pull-out resource specialist services for up to 50% of her day through middle school. Angela and her parents decided in her eighth-grade year that this would be reduced to one period a day in high school so that she could participate in a more inclusive college preparatory educational program. The resource specialist sees Angela for one period a day and provides her direct instruction in strategies intervention model training, advanced organizers, paraphrasing, and

text look-backs to better comprehend what she reads. Angela is also receiving direct instruction in how to construct paragraphs and essays and use editing strategies to correct her work. The resource specialist regularly collaborates with Angela's classroom teachers to check assignments, examinations, and obtained grades and to offer curriculum and assignment modifications. At this point in her sophomore year, Angela is maintaining a 3.2 grade-point average. She has visited the career center in her high school and has taken career-interest surveys and vocational assessments that show she is interested and capable of working in the fashion industry. Angela will enroll in a regional occupational program fashion design course in her junior year and eventually be placed in a paid position in a department store at her local mall. The transition portion of her IEP also states that she will enroll in driver's education in the second semester of her sophomore year and obtain her learner's permit, followed by her driver's license when she turns 16. Her community participation transition goal is to be capable of independently transporting herself by car to school, employment, shopping, and recreation and leisure activities.

 # PATHWAY 2

The youth with disabilities will (a) participate in a fully integrated high school curriculum of blended academic and career-vocational courses leading to passage of high school exit examination with necessary accommodations, obtainment of a standard high school diploma, and entrance into a career-vocational school or career apprenticeship; (b) function fully independently in the community, including independent living; (c) complete career exploration and paid work experience in high school; and (d) obtain full-time competitive employment with salary and possible benefits in their career interest.

Recommended Assessments

Assessment for youth with disabilities in Pathway 2 focuses heavily on career and vocational interests, aptitudes, and strengths. The primary goal of this pathway is transition from high school to a vocational-technical school or career apprenticeship, leading to full-time competitive employment with salary and benefits. Career and vocational assessment can take place in the classroom, a high school career center, or regional occupational training program, using standardized tests, career interest surveys, informal measurements, work samples and simulations, or online career and occupational tests (see Chapter 7 for a complete review of this material). The high school exit examination is the other important test that must be successfully completed by the Pathway 2 youth with a disability. Although passage of this test may not be required for entrance into career-technical school or career apprenticeship, it is wise for Pathway 2 youth with disabilities pass this examination in order to maximize their postsecondary career options.

General Education Curriculum Access and Effective School Foundation

Youth with disabilities pursuing Pathway 2 participate in the general education curriculum to the maximum degree possible and complete all high school graduation requirements leading to a diploma. Many of the Pathway 1 suggestions for successful participation in the general education curriculum are applicable to Pathway 2 (see Figures 8-2, 8-3, 8-5, and 8-6 for specific information). Pathway 2 youth with disabilities, however, may require a greater degree of special education support (e.g., one period a day of resource room placement and possible special educator coteaching in more challenging academic classes). In addition to obtainment of a high school diploma, an effective Pathway 2 curriculum should produce an academic and career-occupational portfolio containing samples of a Pathway 2 student's best work in school subjects, career, and vocational skills. Successful completion of prevocational training and a career-vocational course along with high school paid-work experience in the student's career interest are also components of an effective school foundation for Pathway 2. Finally, it is important for youth with disabilities in Pathway 2 to develop computer literacy skills.

All the training and skills reviewed in Pathway 1 apply to Pathway 2 youth with disabilities. The postsecondary education outcome for Pathway 2, however, is entrance into a career-technical school or career apprenticeship as opposed to entrance into a 2- or 4-year college or university. Training and skills for Pathway 2 can include any or all of the following:

1. Study skills and strategies intervention model instruction beginning in the ninth-grade year.
2. Exploration of career-technical school or career apprenticeship options based on the youth's interests, aptitudes, values, and career area strengths.
3. Exploration of postsecondary training options, such as career-technical schools or career apprenticeship programs.
4. Self-determination and self-advocacy skills training in the ninth-grade year for use in general education classrooms. Self-determination skills training should focus on exploring hopes and dreams for the future, education planning, decision making, and self-selection of IEP goals and objectives. Self-advocacy skills training should teach youth with disabilities acceptance of their disability, how to explain their disability to others, and how to ask for reasonable accommodations in general education classrooms, in the workplace, and in the community.
5. Continuation of self-determination and self-advocacy skills training during the 11th-grade year to prepare for successful postsecondary participation in career-technical school or apprenticeships and the community, with a focus on locating available resources, such as the Department of Vocational Rehabilitation.
6. Development of a personal youth profile and portfolio to share with career-technical schools, career apprenticeship programs, and potential employers (note that this meets the Summary of Performance requirement under IDEA 2004; see Chapter 4).

Instructional Setting

The primary instructional setting for Pathway 2 youth with disabilities is the general education classroom, along with resource specialist support for up to one period a day and coteaching in more challenging general education classrooms. In rare instances where school districts still permit departmentalized special education instruction in core academic subjects, this represents a less restrictive instructional setting for Pathway 2 students; however, NCLB 2001 requirements for highly qualified teachers has drastically restricted this option and many school districts are no longer offering this type of instructional setting. The instructional setting for Pathway 2, in addition to emphasizing the core academic subject, should focus on teaching related study skills, self-determination, self-advocacy, career awareness and exploration, occupational training, and social-interpersonal skills (note that many of these skills are the primary responsibility of related service personnel, particularly special education teachers). Community businesses and employment sites are other important instructional settings for Pathway 2 youth with disabilities, particularly for obtaining paid-work experience in high school.

Related Services and Support

Pathway 2 youth with disabilities receiving an inclusive education in high school require the support of a resource specialist or an inclusion facilitator to be successful in general education classrooms (see recommendations in Pathway 1). Time-limited supports, such as job development and job coaching, may be needed for youth with disabilities pursuing Pathway 2 to obtain successful paid work experience in high school.

Transition Planning

A person-centered IEP **transition planning** meeting held in the ninth-grade year focuses on determining the desired postsecondary education plans of the youth with a disability and whether this includes vocational–technical school, career apprenticeship, or full-time competitive employment. If the individual desires to obtain a 2- or 4-year college degree, it is recommended that he or she pursue Pathway 1. If his or her primary interest and that of the family, however, is obtainment of training and skills leading to a future career in their area of interest, then transition goals in instruction should include (a) successful completion of high school graduation requirements, exit examination, obtainment of a diploma, and admission to a career–technical school or apprenticeship program and (b) enrollment in one or more career-related courses and paid work experience in their career interest area during high school. Transition goals in the area of community participation focus on successful independent living and community access, as well as social and interpersonal skills, if needed. Finally, employment and other postsecondary transition goals for a Pathway 2 youth with a disability include (a) developing career awareness and decision-making skills, (b) developing job seeking and maintenance skills, and (c) obtaining paid work experience in high school.

Transition Culmination

As the Pathway 2 youth with a disability reaches the 11th- or 12th-grade year in high school, a culminating meeting is scheduled in the fall semester to determine whether

1. all the necessary high school completion requirements appear on the youth's transcripts and a summary of performance document has been prepared by the IEP team;
2. the youth has visited and/or applied to desired career–technical schools or apprenticeship programs;

3. the youth has had paid-work experience in high school in his or her career interest area and has developed job-seeking and maintenance skills;
4. the youth has developed career decision-making skills and has explored career and occupational options;
5. the youth demonstrates awareness of his or her disability;
6. the youth is aware of and capable of obtaining assistance from the Department of Vocational Rehabilitation and community-based support services to promote community participation;
7. the youth knows how to seek reasonable accommodations in postsecondary education and employment settings and can apply appropriate self-advocacy skills; and
8. the youth possesses the recreation and leisure skills needed for community participation.

In addition, it is important to determine whether the youth and family have the financial ability to pay for all postsecondary expenses, such as career–technical school or career apprenticeship program fees, books, materials, and transportation costs. The youth may wish to apply for Supplemental Security Income (SSI) benefits and acceptance into the Department of Vocational Rehabilitation to help with these expenses. Living arrangements for the youth with disabilities should also be addressed in the culminating meeting (e.g., will the youth continue to live at home or in an apartment during his or her initial postsecondary school years?).

LET'S SEE IT IN ACTION! CASE EXAMPLE

Pathway 2

Alejandro is a 17-year-old student with a severe learning disability. He has been in special education since second grade and is currently functioning at about a fourth-grade level in reading, spelling, and writing skills. His strength is in mathematics, with current functioning around a seventh-grade level. Alejandro and his parents want him to graduate high school with a diploma but do not see college as a priority; rather, they desire participation in a vocational–technical career in which he can obtain full time competitive paid employment with possible salary and benefits as an adult. The special education staff designed a high school program for him that blends his interest in pursuing a career and academic requirements by utilizing coteaching, resource specialist pull-out services for one period a day, and enrollment in vocational training courses throughout high school. He is passing all his courses and is on target to graduate from high school with a diploma next year.

Alejandro has a strong interest in automotive repair and wants to work in his father's auto shop business upon graduation from high school and attend vocational–technical school for advanced training in automotive repair. He is currently enrolled in a high school automotive repair class and works part time in the parts department at his father's shop. His special education teachers have taught him about the nature of his learning disability and how to ask his high school teachers for (a) reasonable accommodations (b) peer assistance in note taking, and (c) extended time and a reader for tests. A representative from the Department of Vocational Rehabilitation attended Alejandro's recent IEP meeting and explained how Alejandro could obtain support for his postsecondary education, such as books on tape, financial assistance with school costs, and purchase of automotive repair tools. Alejandro has a driver's license and will be able to transport himself by car to school and work. He and his parents mutually decided that he would live at home while he attends school. Eventually, he would like to get an apartment and live independently in the community.

⇒ PATHWAY 3

The youth with disabilities will (a) participate in a semi-integrated high school curriculum of blended academic and career–vocational courses leading to obtainment of a high school certificate of completion and entrance into community-based paid competitive employment with time-limited supports, (b) function semi-independently in the community with necessary supports, (d) obtain functional daily living skills needed for full or semi-independent living, (e) participate in a functional vocational evaluation that identifies competitive employment skills, and (f) participate in integrated paid competitive employment with necessary supports.

Recommended Assessments

Assessments for Pathway 3 youth with disabilities are completed in the areas listed below (see chapter 7 for a review of many of these assessments):

1. Student self-report measures
2. Social-interpersonal skills and adaptive behavior
3. Independent living skills and life-centered measures
4. Transition scale measures
5. Career and occupational interest and skills tests
6. Achievement tests

Curriculum-based assessments are also recommended for providing valuable transition related information on Pathway 3 youth with disabilities.

General Education Curriculum Access and Effective School Foundation

Pathway 3 is most appropriate for youth with disabilities who may require any or all of the following:

1. Extensive modifications in the general education curriculum, partial participation in academic classes, or social integration into high school elective classes.
2. Obtainment of a certificate of attendance instead of a diploma upon completion of high school.
3. Special accommodations and modifications on high school proficiency tests required for graduation and other state standardized tests.

4. Choice to remain in school beyond age 18 with participation in a community-based transition class, if offered by the school district.

The most appropriate curriculum for a Pathway 3 youth with a disability is one that emphasizes blended academic and career–vocational courses, community-based employment experiences, and self-determination and self-advocacy development. The primary goal of this pathway is for the individual to be able to function as independently as possible upon graduation from high school, with community access and mobility, semi-independent living, and participation in paid competitive employment. This type of curriculum may be difficult to offer in a typical high school college preparatory program emphasizing core academic subjects. Access to the general education curriculum, in this instance, will require significant modifications and accommodations to be made by special education personnel and/or coteaching (see recommendations in the section on Related Services and Supports).

The Pathway 3 curriculum includes opportunities for development in any or all of the following areas:

1. Social and interpersonal
2. Self-awareness and advocacy
3. Prevocational
4. Independent living
5. Career and occupational
6. Mobility and community access
7. Family life or health education

The Life-Centered Career Education Curriculum (Council for Exceptional Children, 1997), as well as other transition curricula listed in the chapter 6 appendix are excellent resources for providing an effective school foundation for Pathway 3 youth with disabilities.

Instructional Setting

Youth with disabilities in Pathway 3 participate in integrated settings to the maximum extent possible to properly prepare them for transition to a quality adult life. They attend school on an integrated campus and participate in any or all education and recreation activities with their nondisabled peers. Many advocate for an inclusive education for Pathway 3 youth with disabilities (e.g., The Association for the Severely Handicapped). IDEA 2004, however, preserved the continuum of services options for youth with disabilities. With this in mind, we believe that a special day-class setting emphasizing functional, life, and career and occupational skills, along with community-based instruction, is the best instructional setting for a Pathway 3 youth with disabilities. Ultimately, the decision regarding an inclusive education and the degree of integration into general education classes for a Pathway 3 youth with disabilities rests with the individual and his or her family. For this reason, providing self-determination training throughout the school years is very important (see Chapter 6).

The decision about an inclusive education should be made in collaboration with the IEP team, and the desires of the family and youth with a disability should be fully honored and supported.

Related Services and Support

School personnel must promote self-determination and in so doing, be sensitive to the wishes and desires of the family and youth with a disability. This includes making a concerted effort to meet their needs, rather than attempting to get them to accept only the available transition program options in the school district or surrounding community. Families desiring an inclusive education for a Pathway 3 youth with disabilities are provided the necessary supports, regardless of the level of intensity, for their child to have access to general education classrooms. This may involve providing an inclusion facilitator throughout the day for the youth with a disability. In addition, the primary goals for the youth with a disability receiving an inclusive education need to be clearly articulated (e.g., social, academic, and/or functional) for general-education teachers who will be including this individual. Ongoing collaborative consultation occurs between general and special education personnel, with consistent support provided to the general education teacher who is instructing a Pathway 3 youth with a disability (see CLASP model in Figure 8–6).

Additional possible supports for Pathway 3 youth with disabilities in general education or special day-class settings include (a) job development and job coaching, (b) mobility specialist training, (c) supported-living specialist training, and (d) adapted Physical Education (PE) specialists. Parents of Pathway 3 youth with disabilities may need to speak with other families whose youth have successfully achieved full or semi-independent living and employment in the community. Meetings of this nature can help reduce parent fear and anxiety.

Transition Planning

Perhaps the most important transition planning consideration for a Pathway 3 youth with a disability and family involves their vision for the future and desired degree of inclusion in the general education program. Use of person-centered IEP transition planning is critical for this reason. It is challenging, though not impossible, to provide a blended academic and career–vocational academic program, along with community-based employment to a youth with a disability. Discussions of this nature need to take place as early as possible, preferably in the middle school years, among the family, youth with a disability, and members of the IEP team. If the youth and family opt for an inclusive education, then transition planning focuses on identifying the necessary supports and services for general education teachers so they can emphasize these aspects of the curriculum in the classroom. Together, parents and youth will specify how much time per day should be dedicated to teaching transition-related skills (i.e., career–vocational, self-determination, self-advocacy) with the assistance of an inclusion facilitator in the general education classroom. The amount of time per day or week for participation in community-based employment participation is specified as well.

Modification of the general education curriculum is discussed with families and youth with disabilities who desire a less inclusive educational placement, such as a special day class or transition class. Because these instructional settings allow for greater flexibility in terms of access to the community and for teaching transition-related skills, transition planning can focus on alternatives in the general education classroom. Nevertheless, IDEA 2004 requires all youth with disabilities in special education to be provided access to this curriculum and so it is still important to connect Pathway 3 instructional goals with those of the general education curriculum.

Transition Culmination

A culminating meeting should take place for a Pathway 3 youth with a disability in the fall semester of the 11th- or 12th-grade year to determine whether

1. the youth has adequately mastered the skills needed to function in the community in employment and independent living;
2. career and vocational training and paid work experience in high school has been completed and paid competitive employment and supports are available in the community upon high school completion;
3. the youth wishes to obtain certificate of attendance and exit school or remain in school till age 22 and participate in a community-based transition classroom; or
4. linkages have been made with the appropriate transition service agencies in the community, such as the Department of Vocational Rehabilitation, independent living agencies, department of recreation, and public transit district and a summary of performance document has been prepared by the IEP team.

LET'S SEE IT IN ACTION! CASE EXAMPLE

Pathway 3

Ahmed is a 14-year-old individual with Down syndrome and has been in special education since preschool, primarily educated in a special day classroom. His cognitive abilities are somewhat limited: he possesses understandable speech, listens and understands verbal directions, and has good social skills. He is functioning academically at about a second-grade level in most subjects. He needs further training in daily living skills, community and mobility training, and employment skills. At his eighth-grade annual IEP meeting, Ahmed and his parents were asked what type of academic program (e.g., course of study) they desired for high school. After weighing all the options, the family decided to continue Ahmed's placement in a special day class and for him to receive community-based instruction, daily living skills, and employment training. Ahmed would be included in several elective courses in high school that offered reinforcement and training in life skills, such as home economics, health, and a career exploratory class. Ahmed's special education teacher would offer collaborative consultation, coteaching, and a paraprofessional to these general education teachers when needed. Transition goals for Ahmed were for him to graduate with a certificate of attendance, develop semi-independent daily living skills, obtain paid competitive employment in a career interest area of his choice, and learn to use public transportation for access to employment and the community.

 # PATHWAY 4

The youth with disabilities will (a) participate in a semi-integrated high school curriculum emphasizing functional academics, social skills, life skills, self-determination and self-advocacy skills leading to obtainment of a high school certificate of completion and entrance into community-based competitive or supported employment; (b) function semi-independently in the community with necessary supports; (c) obtain daily living skills needed for independent or supported living; (d) participate in a functional vocational evaluation that identifies competitive employment skills; and (e) participate in community-based competitive or supported employment.

Recommended Assessments

Youth with disabilities in Pathway 4, compared with those in Pathways 1–3, typically require more intensive levels of support to function semi-independently in society. Hence, assessments should be completed in the areas of daily living skills, social skills, adaptive behavior, and academic ability. In addition, a functional vocational evaluation is recommended to identify work-related interests, preferences, and abilities. Suggested assessments reviewed in Pathway 3 are appropriate for individuals in Pathway 4 as well (see recommended assessments in Pathway 3). A functional vocational evaluation is also needed for youth with disabilities in Pathway 4. A review of these types of assessments is presented in Chapter 7.

General Education Curriculum Access and Effective School Foundation

Pathway 4 is designed for individuals who would benefit primarily from a functional life-skills curriculum with community-based instruction, preparation for supported employment and supported living, and the obtainment of a certificate of completion from high school. The school program for Pathway 4 is focused on life-skills and community-based experiences and, therefore, will not likely result in attainment of a standard diploma. Access to the general education curriculum occurs primarily through partial participation in school academics through major curriculum modifications, and in many instances, occurs in elective versus core academic subjects and extra curricular activities. The Pathway 4 learning foundation is community-based and emphasizes daily living skills, orientation and mobility, personal-social skills, family life or health education, personal safety and sexuality, and occupational guidance and preparation. The Life-Centered Career Education Curriculum (Council for Exceptional Children, 1997) is highly recommended for Pathway 4 youth with disabilities.

An effective school foundation for Pathway 4 youth with disabilities also promotes productivity, independence, socialization, the development of friendships, and participation to the maximum extent possible in integrated settings, such as school, community, and employment. Pathway 4 should be offered in the neighborhood school of the youth with a disability, with access to and participation in general education classrooms and integrated settings occurring whenever possible.

Instructional Setting

Any of the following instructional settings can potentially be selected by Pathway 4 youth with disabilities and their families: (a) inclusion in a general education classroom; (b) partial integration in a general education classroom, along with a resource specialist or special day-class placement; or (c) full-time special day-class placement. The most appropriate instructional setting depends on the individual's unique needs, individualized educational program goals and objectives, and the transition priorities expressed by the youth with a disability and his or her family in collaboration with the IEP team, such as academic, social-emotional, daily living, and career–occupational. The choice of an inclusive education instructional setting may result in less time available for teaching daily living skills, functional vocational skills, and for community-based instruction; most general education teachers do not offer community-based instruction or functional skills as part of their daily instructional program. Therefore, the responsibility of modifying the general education curriculum to include these components will rest mainly with an inclusion facilitator, special education teacher, or other transition personnel (see the section on Related Services and Support). In contrast, greater amounts of time and flexibility are available to teach daily living, functional vocational skills, and community-based instruction in a special day class. For this reason, a more restrictive instructional setting may be preferred by Pathway 4 youth with disabilities and their families. If such is the case, more frequent opportunities will be needed for social interaction and friendship development between Pathway 4 youth with disabilities and their chronological-age peers. Suggested means for accomplishing this include (a) participation in general education elective classes; (b) participation in integrated community youth group activities such as sports leagues, recreation classes, clubs, or scouting groups; and (c) integrated employment opportunities. Activities of this type are essential to ensure that Pathway 4 youth with disabilities educated in more restrictive instructional settings can successfully transition into the community in the future. Parents and youth with disabilities must carefully weigh all of these factors when choosing instructional settings in Pathway 4.

A community-based transition classroom for 18- to 22-year-old youth with disabilities is another instructional setting option to consider for Pathway 4. Many school districts today offer this transition program to youth with disabilities who decide to remain in school past their 18th birthday. In some instances, these classrooms are offered on integrated college or community college campuses or out in the community. Parents may wish to consider an inclusive education for their Pathway 4 youth with disabilities during the middle and high school years and subsequently enroll them in a transition class at age 18 to focus on functional daily-living skills, community-based instruction, and integrated employment skills training. This option is currently the preferred choice of the Association for the Severely Handicapped.

Related Services and Support

It is possible for Pathway 4 youth with disabilities to learn functional, social, prevocational, and occupational skills in general education settings. This, however, typically requires (a) extensive support and assistance from an inclusion facilitator, (b) collaborative instruction and general education curriculum modification by special education personnel, and (c) allowances for partial participation of the individual in the more academically demanding portions of the general education curriculum and classroom. Other nonacademic supports needed by Pathway 4 youth with disabilities include community and mobility training, adaptive PE, supported employment, and supported living training. Specialists in these areas are employed by some school districts and/or adult transition service agencies. These types of specialists will be needed to deliver training and instruction to Pathway 4 youth with disabilities.

Transition Planning

Person-centered IEP transition planning for a Pathway 4 youth with a disability frequently focuses on the degree of independence desired both by the individual and his or her family. The primary instructional goals for a Pathway 4 youth with a disability range from an inclusive education to partial participation in the general education classroom curriculum, along with acquisition of skills in daily living, orientation and mobility, personal-social, family life or health education, personal safety, and sexuality. Transition goals in employment and other postsecondary needs include following directions, completing tasks, working inside and outside the classroom, and obtaining integrated paid work experience in high school. Transition goals in community participation should emphasize (a) activities of daily living, such as grocery shopping, meal preparation, and housekeeping; (b) safety skills; (c) participation in integrated community recreation activities and programs; and (d) exploration of potential living options, such as continuing to live at home with family, living in a group home, or other supported-living options within the community such as a staffed apartment.

Establishing linkages with adult transition service agencies is a particularly important transition planning objective for Pathway 4 youth with disabilities. These individuals typically require greater intensity of support than that needed by youth with disabilities in Pathways 1 through 3. For a list of adult transition service agencies that provide extensive supports to persons with disabilities, see Chapters 5 and 6. Collaboration between Pathway 4 families and representatives from these transition service agencies occurs early in the transition planning process to form lasting and productive linkages and to obtain the necessary supports needed during and after school completion. This is best accomplished by having adult transition service agency representatives in attendance at the transition planning meeting to discuss the support services they have to offer to the Pathway 4 individual and his or her family.

Transition Culmination

A culminating meeting should be held early in the 12th-grade year of a Pathway 4 youth with a disability to decide (a) whether the individual wishes to remain in school and receive special education services past age 18, as well as enroll in a transition class; (b) complete high school and exit special education, in which case a summary of performance document should be prepared by the IEP team; and (c) whether the youth with a disability wishes to exercise his or her age of majority rights. Transition culmination also focuses on the future living arrangements, financial and medical services and supports, and supported work or special vocational training programs desired by the youth with a disability. Equally important is to make sure that the transition service agencies that have agreed to provide services and supports have made the proper connections with the individual and his or her family and are ready to begin providing these services after school completion takes place (see Chapter 5 for a list of transition services agencies to consider).

LET'S SEE IT IN ACTION! CASE EXAMPLE

Pathway 4

Ya-Ling is a 14-year-old girl with multiple disabilities, including blindness, limited speech, and very low cognitive functioning. She is about to enter high school and her parents have been requested at the annual IEP meeting to discuss the information they completed on a transition planning inventory provided by the high school special education department. Ya-Ling's parents would like her to be included in general education classrooms for a portion of the day in academic subjects that promote student interaction and oral communication, such as drama, science, and health. They are making this request because Ya-Ling loves social interaction with her chronological age peers. In addition, her parents have requested assistance from (a) a speech and language therapist for augmentative and facilitated communication for Ya-Ling in general education classrooms,

(b) a vision specialist to help modify the general education curriculum in a way that will allow Ya-Ling to participate to the maximum extent possible, and (c) collaborative consultation services of the high school special day-class teacher for assistance with curriculum modification. Ya-Ling's parents also want her to participate in community-based instruction and receive a functional vocational evaluation to determine her employability skills. They believe, based on Ya-Ling's enthusiastic behavior when out in the community, that she would like to develop semi-independent living skills and work in the community with ongoing support. She will live at home after completing high school while developing semi-independent living skills and eventually move into a supported living situation in the local community.

SUMMARY

IDEA 2004 guarantees the rights of youth with disabilities to a free and appropriate public education designed to meet their individual needs. No two individuals with disabilities should be treated exactly alike when it comes to the educational programs and services they receive in school. This is equally true with respect to transition services and programs. With these thoughts in mind, we have attempted in this chapter to identify four potential pathways to transition that fit the needs of most youth with disabilities, ranging from mild-moderate to moderate-severe. Each transition pathway specifies postschool outcomes in IDEA 2004 transition services requirements for instruction, community experiences, employment, and other postsecondary adult living objectives, and when appropriate, functional vocational evaluation and daily living skills. Also specified in each pathway are the transition assessments, **school curriculum and foundation** experiences, instructional settings, supports, transition planning, and transition culmination considerations for youth with disabilities and their families. We have placed all this information in a transition pathways model (see Table 8-1) to illustrate the multiple options available to youth with disabilities and their families during the transition years (i.e., starting at age 16 and possibly lasting until age 22). It is vitally important to reiterate that our pathways to transition model does not represent disability categorical group tracking but, rather, is a fluid and dynamic model that allows for all youth with disabilities to be treated individually and provided access to any and all pathways to transition or combinations thereof. Self-determination training and person-centered transition planning practices are critically important for this reason. One must remember, however, that youth with disabilities have a limited time in school during their transition years and must take full advantage of the opportunity to prepare themselves for their adult lives. Hence, it is important for these individuals and their families to carefully consider the options available in the various pathways shown in our model and, when engaged in self-determination and person-centered transition planning, decide the most appropriate pathway (or combination of pathways) to pursue. This, is turn, will determine the types of supports, transition services, and programs to be provided. It subsequently becomes the responsibility and legal obligation of transition personnel in schools and transition service agencies in the community to provide these components to youth with disabilities as they pursue their path to the future.

KEY TERMS AND PHRASES

instructional setting	transition pathways
school curriculum and foundation	transition planning
transition culmination	transition supports

QUESTIONS FOR REFLECTION, THINKING, AND SKILL BUILDING

1. What is the conceptual model and framework for transition pathways for various youth with disabilities?

2. What process is recommended for youth with disabilities and their families to use when considering a potential transition pathway?

3. What transition pathways for youth with disabilities exist in your local school, region, or state?

4. How can the transition pathways for youth with disabilities be improved in your local school, region, or state?

5. Form a committee of interagency or intra-agency transition personnel to discuss ways to implement the transition pathways model in your local school district.

6. Evaluate the current transition pathways options for youth with disabilities in your local schools, write a report, and present recommendations to special education administrative personnel and teachers.

7. Create a staff development program to train transition personnel in the transition pathways model and concept. Include sample transition plans and case studies in the training package.

Examples of Instructional and Assessment Accommodations

INSTRUCTIONAL ACCOMODATIONS

Materials and Curriculum

- Alternative assignments
- Substitute materials with lower reading levels
- Fewer assignments
- Decrease length of assignments
- Copy pages so students can mark on them
- Provide examples of correctly completed work
- Early syllabus
- Advance notice of assignments
- Tape-recorded versions of printed materials

Methods and Strategies

- Highlight key points to remember
- Eliminate distractions by using a template to block out other items
- Have student use a self-monitoring sheet
- Break task into smaller parts to do at different times
- Use study partners whenever reading or writing is required
- Secure papers to work areas with tape or magnets
- Present information in multiple formats
- Use listening devices

ASSESSMENT ACCOMMODATIONS

Setting

- Study carrel
- Special lighting
- Separate room
- Individualized or small group

Timing

- Extended time
- Frequent breaks
- Unlimited time

(Continued)

(*Continued*)

Scheduling

- Specific time of day
- Subtests in different order

Presentation

- Repeat directions
- Larger bubbles on multiple-choice questions
- Sign-language presentation
- Magnification device

Response

- Mark answers in test booklet
- Use reference materials (e.g., dictionary)
- Word process writing sample

Other

- Special test preparation techniques
- Out-of-level test

Source: From *Testing Students with Disabilities: Practical Strategies for Complying with District and State Requirements* (Boxes 3.2 and 3.3), by M. L. Thurlow, J. L. Elliott, and J. E. Ysseldyke, 1998, Thousand Oaks, CA: Corwin Press. Reprinted with permission.

Appendix 8–2

Accommodations for Students with LD

PRESENTATION

- Provide on audio tape
- Provide in large print
- Reduce number of items per page or line
- Provide a designated reader

RESPONSE

- Allow for verbal responses
- Allow for answers to be dictated to a scribe
- Allow the use of a tape recorder to capture responses
- Permit responses to be given via computer
- Permit answers to be recorded directly into test booklet

TIMING

- Allow frequent breaks
- Extend allotted time for a test

SETTING

- Provide preferential seating
- Provide special lighting or acoustics
- Provide a space with minimal distractions
- Administer a test in small group setting
- Administer a test in private room or alternative test site

TESTING SCHEDULING

- Administer a test in several timed sessions or over several days
- Allow subtests to be taken in a different order
- Administer a test at a specific time of day

OTHER

- Provide special test preparation
- Provide on-task or focusing prompts
- Provide any reasonable accommodations that a student needs that does not fit under the existing categories

Source: Accommodations for Students with LD, National Center for Learning Disabilities (2006), LD Online (http://www.ldonline.org/indepth/accommodations or http://www.ldonline.org/article/8022).

Chapter 9

Transition Planning

Gary Greene

Chapter Questions

- What are IEP transition services requirements and how are they written into the IEP?
- What should be written first on an IEP: academic or transition goals and objectives?
- What do transition goals look like in middle and high school?
- What steps are involved in planning and conducting a professionally driven IEP transition planning meeting?
- How can youth with disabilities be prepared to conduct student-directed IEP transition planning meetings?

Most special education teachers are well trained and skilled in writing annual individualized education plan (IEP) goals and objectives to meet their students' academic, behavioral, and social–emotional needs. Many special educators, however, report feeling ill-equipped and ill-prepared for writing transition goals for youth with disabilities. The purpose of this chapter is to present information that will help special education and transition personnel effectively complete the transition planning process and write the transition portion of an IEP for high-school-age youth with disabilities. Information on transition planning for middle-school-age youth with disabilities is also discussed, although this is no longer required according to the Individuals with Disabilities Education Act (IDEA) 2004.

We begin with a review of IEP transition services requirements of IDEA 2004 and explore IEP format differences for writing transition goals versus annual goals and objectives.

WHAT ARE IEP TRANSITION SERVICES REQUIREMENTS AND HOW ARE THEY WRITTEN IN THE IEP?

IDEA 2004 requires that beginning at age 16, and younger if appropriate, a statement by the IEP of transition services needs to be included under the applicable components of the IEP for each youth with a disability in special education. The transition services portion of the IEP must address (a) instruction, (b) related services, (c) community experiences, (d) development of employment and other postschool objectives, and, when appropriate, (e) daily living skills, and (f) functional vocational evaluation. Transition goals and objectives in these areas are to be part of the IEP as opposed to being written on a separate document (i.e., individual transition plan [ITP]). Technically, the acronym ITP is inappropriate, because IDEA 1997 discouraged school districts from using a separate document for drafting transition services. Therefore, we refer to the transition portion of the IEP when discussing transition goals and objectives.

Complaints about excessive paperwork demands by special educators have been common in the past and have led to IDEA 2004 no longer requiring benchmarks in IEPs. In addition, many school districts today utilize computerized banks of prewritten

IEP goals, including those for transition. The Life-Centered Career Education (LCCE) curriculum can be used for this purpose (see LCCE curriculum shown in Table 6–2). Caution must be exercised, however, when using the LCCE bank of transition goals or ones similar to it, so as to guarantee that the transition services portion of an IEP (a) is *individualized* and based on current level of performance data, student interest, and choice; (b) *does not* contain a preprogrammed set of transition goals selected by special education personnel without input from the individual youth with a disability and the youth's family; and (c) is unique for each student, rather than containing the same transition goals for large numbers of youth with disabilities enrolled in special education. Failure to adhere to any of these cautions may result in the transition services portion of an IEP being out of compliance with IDEA 2004 and could trigger a legal challenge (see chapter 4).

In addition to these recommendations, the transition services portion of an IEP should contain spaces for the following information: (a) current level of performance data in needed transition services (see Chapter 7), (b) a summary of the future dreams and visions or long-range goals of the youth with a disability, (c) instruction, community experiences, related services, employment and other postsecondary objectives, daily living skills, and functional vocational evaluation, if appropriate, (d) persons or agencies responsible, and (d) timeline. A sample transition portion of an IEP with this format is shown in Figure 9–1.

Our discussion now turns to which portion of the IEP to write first, annual goals and objectives or required transition services.

➡ WHAT SHOULD BE WRITTEN FIRST ON AN IEP: ACADEMIC OR TRANSITION GOALS AND OBJECTIVES?

Beginning with the end in mind, transition goals should drive the annual goals and objectives on an IEP for transition-age youth with disabilities. Therefore, the transition services portion of the IEP should be written first, followed by the academic annual goals and objectives. This implies a shift in focus for special educators from short-term, annual academic goals to those that are more long-term in nature, and extend from transition into, through, and beyond high school. This relationship is illustrated in Figure 9–2. Note that IEP goals and objectives are written for a youth with a disability every year throughout high school, whereas transition goals apply for multiple years, including up to 2 years beyond high school. Adopting this approach to transition planning results in (a) annual IEP goals and objectives that have a close relationship to transition and postsecondary goals and (b) provision of a solid foundation for helping youth with disabilities in special education make yearly progress toward their long-term transition goals. Although this approach to writing IEPs may seem foreign and uncomfortable initially to special education personnel, it is highly recommended. *In short, the transition services portion of the IEP should function as the roadmap for identifying future life plans, activities, and directions for transition-age youth with disabilities.*

Although IDEA no longer requires transition goals for all middle school students, doing so is still considered a best practice. *IDEA regulations, however, do preserve flexibility in the process,* stating that "Beginning no later than the first IEP to be in

Student Name _____ _____ IEP Date _____ / _____ / _____

Last   First   Page _____ of _____

LONG BEACH UNIFIED SCHOOL DISTRICT
INDIVIDUALIZED EDUCATION PROGRAM

XXI. (D) INDIVIDUAL TRANSITION PLAN

Transition Services (For students 14 and older)

Instruction	ACTIVITIES FOR THE NEXT YEAR	AGENCY/PERSON RESPONSIBLE	TIMELINE
• Present Level of Performance: • Long-Range Goal:			

Community Experiences			
• Present Level of Performance: • Long-Range Goal:			

Employment			
• Present Level of Performance: • Long-Range Goal:			

Services not needed because _____

See pages _____ for designated instructional services as they relate to my school-to-work transition needs.

Figure 9–1 Blank Section IEP Transition Plan Format

297

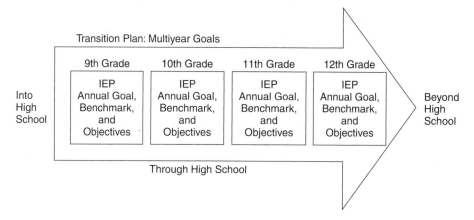

Figure 9–2 Relationship among Transition Plan and Annual Goals, Objectives, and Benchmarks Sections of an IEP

effect when a child turns 16, or younger if determined appropriate by the IEP team, and updated annually thereafter" [34 CFR 300.320 (b) and (c); 20 U.S.C. 1414]. For this reason, we present information in this regard next, along with transition goals for high-school-age youth with disabilities.

WHAT DO SAMPLE TRANSITION GOALS LOOK LIKE IN MIDDLE SCHOOL AND HIGH SCHOOL?

Figure 9–3 presents transition services requirements for 16-year-old youth with disabilities, as well as for 14-year-olds. Because flexibility by the IEP team to initiate services before age 16 is permitted under the IDEA regulations, this information is presented in Figure 9–3, because it represents best practice and encourages families of youth with disabilities and schools to continue to address the transition needs of this age group. Four areas must be addressed on the transition portion of the IEP for 16-year-olds and should be based on the individual's needs, preferences, and interests. *This requirement implies that special education personnel complete various transition assessments with youth with disabilities before scheduling and conducting an IEP meeting to discuss transition* (see Chapter 7 for recommendations on transition assessment). For 14-year-olds, it is recommended that the family and IEP team explore the course of study to pursue in high school and the related transition pathway for the individual (see Chapter 8).

Is it necessary to write transition services in all required areas on the IEP? This question is frequently asked by members of IEP teams, particularly when a youth with a disability in special education is functioning appropriately in a given transition domain, such as community participation. IDEA 1997, in attempts to reduce the paperwork requirements for special educators, eliminated the requirement to write transition services in all domains on the IEP. In addition, the final regulations deleted the requirement that the IEP must contain a justification for not providing a particular

- **Beginning at age 14, a statement of** *transition service needs* **(course of study) is required.** The focus is planning the student's educational program to help achieve a successful transition by including advanced placement courses or vocational education programs.

- **At age 16, a statement of** *needed transition services* must include each of these areas:
  1. **Instruction**—typically provided in schools (e.g., general education classes, academic instruction, tutoring arrangements). There may be other ways to deliver skill development using other agencies, adult education, and postsecondary schools.
  2. **Related services**—include any designated instructional service as it relates to the student's school-to-work transition needs. This area may also address assistive or augmentative devices. Related services may be provided by the public school or other public agencies. These services are provided by qualified personnel and focus on career development, employment preparation, achieving independence and integration in the workplace and community of the student with a disability.
  3. **Community experiences**—provided outside the school building, in community settings, by schools or other agencies. Experiences may be activities such as banking, shopping, transportation, community counseling, recreational services, independent living centers, and adult service providers.
  4. **Development of employment and other postschool adult living objectives**—services that lead to a job or career, such as work experience and job site training, and important adult activities that are done occasionally, such as registering to vote, filing taxes, obtaining medical services, and applying for Supplemental Security Income (SSI). This type of training could be provided by schools or other agencies.

If appropriate:
  5. **Daily-living skills**—training in tasks or activities adults do every day, such as preparing meals and paying bills. This training could be provided by schools or other agencies.
  6. **A functional vocational evaluation**—provides information about job or career interests, aptitudes, and skills. Information may be gathered through observation or formal measures. It should be practical. The evaluation may be conducted by the school or other agencies.

Figure 9–3   Required Transition Service Language for the IEP
Source: Adapted from *Individuals with Disabilities Education Act (IDEA), Amendments of 1997 P. L. 105-17, Revised Transition Services Language Survival Guide for California,* by M. Kent and R. Stodden, 1998. California Department of Education, Special Education.

transition service. Therefore, transition services need only be written for appropriate areas of need for a youth with a disability in special education.

One additional and important transition requirement that was added in IDEA 1997 and continued in IDEA 2004 is the *age of majority* requirement. If a youth with a disability in special education is at least one year from reaching the age of majority, considered 18 years of age, the IEP must include a statement that the individual has been informed of his or her rights under Part B of the IDEA 1997. Part B specifies that the responsibility for approval of the IEP document will transfer from the parent to the youth with a disability upon reaching the age of majority. Language reflecting age of majority notification must be included on all IEP documents for youth with disabilities who will reach age 18 within one year of their current IEP.

IDEA 2004 added the *summary of academic and functional performance* (SOP) requirement. It is a relatively new requirement for school districts and is in an early stage of exploration, development, and implementation. A model SOP template in

Appendix 9-1, developed by the National Transition Documentation Summit, reflects the contributions and suggestions of numerous stakeholders in professional organizations, school districts, universities, and state departments of education. A specific form has not been mandated by IDEA or the Department of Education, so the template is intended to be shared, adapted, and modified to fit the unique needs of state and local educational systems. It is available to be freely copied or adapted for educational purposes (Shaw, Kochhar-Bryant, Izzo, Benedict, & Parker, 2005). One of the primary purposes of the SOP document is to reduce delay time in determining eligibility for postsecondary transition services for the youth with a disability and his or her family, thereby facilitating a smoother hand-off process between school and adult transition service agencies. For more information on the hand off process, see Chapter 11.

Sample IEP Transition Services Goals for Middle School Youth with Disabilities

Transition services for middle school youth remain at the discretion of the IEP team and represent best practice. The transition goals and services should focus on the student's desired course of study in high school. High school course of study descriptions presented in Chapter 8 can be appropriately used for this purpose. Course of study descriptions for each of the four transition pathways follow.

Pathway 1

The youth with disabilities will (a) participate in a fully integrated high school college preparatory curriculum leading to passage of high school exit examination, obtainment of a standard high school diploma, and entrance into a 2- or 4-year college or university; (b) function fully independently in the community; (c) complete career exploration activities and paid work experiences in high school; (d) obtain a college degree that leads to full-time competitive employment with salary and benefits; and (e) live fully independently as an adult.

Pathway 2

The youth with disabilities will (a) participate in a fully integrated high school curriculum of blended academic and career–vocational courses leading to passage of high school exit examination with necessary accommodations, obtainment of a standard high school diploma, and entrance into a career–technical school or career apprenticeship; (b) function fully independently in the community, including independent living; (c) complete career exploration and paid work experience in high school; and (d) obtain full-time competitive employment with salary and possible benefits in their career interest.

Pathway 3

The youth with disabilities will (a) participate in a semi-integrated high school curriculum of blended academic and career–vocational courses leading to obtainment of a high school certificate of completion and entrance into community-based paid competitive employment with time-limited supports, (b) function semi-independently in the community with necessary supports, (c) obtain functional daily living skills needed for full or semi-independent living, (d) participate in a functional vocational evaluation that identifies competitive employment skills, and (e) participate in integrated paid competitive employment with necessary supports.

Pathway 4

The youth with disabilities will (a) participate in a semi-integrated high school curriculum emphasizing functional academics, social skills, life skills, and self-determination and self-advocacy skills leading to obtainment of a high school certificate of completion and entrance into community-based competitive or supported employment, (b) function semi-independently in the community with necessary supports, (c) obtain daily living skills needed for independent or supported living, (d) participate in a functional vocational evaluation that identifies competitive employment skills, and (e) participate in community-based competitive or supported employment.

It is extremely important for school special education personnel to honor the high school course of study or transition pathway selected by a middle school or high school youth with a disability and his or her family, even if it seems unrealistic. There are several reasons for this. First, IDEA 2004 requires that IEP transition goals be based on the interests and preferences of a youth with a disability. Second, the intent of the law is to promote individual and family self-determination. Person-centered transition assessment and planning, discussed in previous chapters, are highly recommended for this purpose (also see discussion of student-directed IEP transition planning meeting in this chapter). It would be inappropriate for IEP team members to discourage a youth with a disability from pursuing his or her hopes and dreams for the future or desired transition pathway in high school. IEP team members can express their opinions on these matters but, nevertheless, must promote and facilitate self-determination.

The responsibility of school special education personnel is to provide the maximum possible resources and supports to help the youth with a disability achieve successful outcomes in his or her designated high school course of study and transition pathway, documenting along the way the services provided and results. This information should subsequently be shared at annual IEP meetings with the family and youth with a disability. If at any time the desired results within the selected course of study and transition pathway are not being achieved, despite the best efforts of all concerned, it is then appropriate to discuss alteration of the course of study and transition pathway. Any attempt to do so on the part of special education personnel prior to this set of circumstances is premature and does not reflect best practices in transition.

Sample transition activities and objectives for middle school students in the areas of education, community skills, career–vocational skills, daily-living skills, and functional vocational assessment can be found in Appendix 9–1.

Sample Transition Goals and Objectives for High School Students

The transition services requirements for high school youth with disabilities are much more extensive compared with those for middle school youth with disabilities. As shown in Figure 9–3, required transition services for a 16-year-old youth with a disability include instruction, related services, community experiences, development of employment and other postschool adult living objectives, and, if appropriate, daily-living skills and a functional vocational evaluation.

Case studies with accompanying IEPs containing transition services requirements for four 16-year-old youth with disabilities are presented next. Each individual case study corresponds to one of the four transition pathways we have outlined in this text. One should assume that person-centered transition planning practices have been implemented and that the designated transition pathway and course of study presented are based on self-determination by the youth with a disability and his or her family during the middle school or high school years. The transition services in each IEP span the high school years and up to 2 years beyond completion of school. Annual IEP goals, benchmarks, and state standards that support the transition goals on the IEP are presented and illustrated in the accompanying figures. State standards should be included on all IEPs, when appropriate, because they demonstrate compliance with IDEA 2004 requirements of access to the core general education curriculum for youth with disabilities. For this reason, we have included them on the sample IEPs.

LET'S SEE IT IN ACTION! CASE EXAMPLE

Lawrence (Transition Pathway 1)

Lawrence is an athletic, 10th-grade boy who is very popular in school, as evidenced by his having lots of friends and strong social and interpersonal skills. He is a star player on the high school football, basketball, and baseball teams. He has a learning disability and has been in special education since third grade. His major difficulties are in reading comprehension, written language, and study skills.

Lawrence received resource specialist pullout services in elementary through middle school for academics. He and his family requested at his eighth-grade annual IEP meeting that he be fully included in a core curriculum, college-preparatory academic program in high school, with collaborative consultation resource specialist services provided in regular classrooms. Transition assessment data supported this desired high school course of study and transition pathway, as evidenced by the fact that Lawrence was found to be generally happy with the quality of his school and social life and deemed academically capable of participating in a college-preparatory program with inclusive education supports. Career interest survey results indicated that Lawrence was interested in careers in sports, business, and law. Lawrence and his parents want him to go to a 4-year university, perhaps earning an athletic scholarship, and perhaps pursue a career in professional sports and/or sports-related business and law.

Lawrence is well adjusted in the community and is considered a model citizen by many. His family is active in the church and in community service. His father owns and operates a local sporting goods store and Lawrence has worked for his father part time during the summer months. Lawrence has completed driver's education and training and intends to get his driver's license later this year.

Transition Portion of Lawrence's IEP. A copy of the transition services portion of Lawrence's IEP is shown in Figure 9-4. Figure 9-5 shows the portion of his IEP containing annual goals and objectives and state standards in reading comprehension and study skills (to be reviewed in the next section). Owing to space limitations, it is not possible to show and review all of Lawrence's IEP annual goals and objectives or the Persons and Agencies Responsible section of the document.

As can be seen in Figure 9-4, Lawrence's vision, career interests, and strengths are summarized in the top portion of his IEP. Lawrence's dreams for the future are to earn a high school diploma, attend a 4-year university, and play professional sports or work in a business, law, or sports-related career. The Current Level of Performance section shows his academic achievement scores and information in a number of required transition services areas. This data demonstrates that Transition Pathway 1 appears to be appropriate for Lawrence. Note that the current levels of performance data from a functional vocational evaluation are not shown because this is not needed for Lawrence.

Below the Current Level of Performance section of the IEP are the Transition Service Needs and Needed Transition Services for Lawrence. The transition service needs for Lawrence focus on facilitating successful academic achievement in general education classes in high school and in college after graduation. Needed transition services include collaborative consultation from a resource specialist in general education high school classrooms, driver's education and training, and prevocational and occupational special needs services in high school. Assistance and academic support from disabled-student services personnel are needed in college.

Finally, transition goals for Lawrence have been written in the areas of instruction, community, employment, and supplementary and related services, as required by law. All the transition goals appropriately reflect Lawrence's vision, career interests, strengths, desired course of study in high school, and transition pathway.

Lawrence's IEP: Annual Goals, Benchmarks, and State Standards. Shown in Figure 9-5 are IEP annual goals, objectives, and corresponding state standards for Lawrence in the areas of instruction and employment. (Note that although IDEA 2004 eliminated the requirement to include objectives in the IEP, we have chosen to include them in all case studies in this chapter, because they represent best practice in special education.) The instructional annual goal and benchmarks for Lawrence focus on study skills and examination preparation, corresponding to the Transition Service Needs and Needed Transition Services sections of the transition portion of Lawrence's IEP (see Figure 9-5). Likewise, the annual goal and objectives for employment focus on Lawrence's successful participation and completion of a business occupations class. Related transition services of this nature are present in the Needed Transition Services section of the transition portion of Lawrence's IEP. Hence, the IEP annual goals and objectives are driven by the goals on the transition portion of his IEP, thereby demonstrating a strong and direct relationship between these two portions of the IEP.

A case study for Transition Pathway 2 is presented next.

Vision
* High school diploma
* Attend 4-year university and obtain law or business degree
* Play professional sports
* Live independently and own a home

Career Interests
* Business
* Sports careers
* Law

Strengths
* Good social skills and citizenship
* Well-liked by others, has many friends
* Good athlete
* Works hard in school

Current Level of Performance:

Academics: Woodcock-Johnson: Broad Reading 7.2; Comprehension 5.2; Word Attack 6.9; Written Language 6.2; Mathematics 11.3. Lawrence requires resource specialist support to be successful in general education classes in college-preparatory high school course of study.

Community: Functions fully independently in community; capable of obtaining driver's license and driving own car for travel within local community.

Employment: Capable of working fully independently in paid competitive employment.

Postsecondary Training and Learning: Capable of participating in postsecondary education at 4-year university or community college.

Recreation and Leisure: Enjoys football, soccer, and basketball and plays on school and community club teams. Goes to movies and mall with friends.

Daily-Living Skills: Capable of full independent living; performing necessary daily-living skills.

Transition Service Needs:
* Lawrence requires academic support from an inclusion facilitator or resource specialist to be successful in mainstream academic classes.
* Lawrence needs academic support in reading comprehension, written language, study skills, self-advocacy, and how to ask teachers for reasonable accommodations in mainstream academic classes.
* Lawrence will need assistance from disabled-student services to be successful in academic classes in college.

Needed Transition Services:
* *Instruction:* Lawrence will receive instruction in reading comprehension, written language, study skills, and exam preparation.
* *Community:* Lawrence will enroll in driver's education/training course leading to obtainment of driver's license.
* *Employment:* Lawrence will participate in prevocational training class and business occupations and computer applications course, with special assistance.

Transition Goals:

Instruction: Lawrence will (a) participate in a fully integrated high school course of study emphasizing college preparatory instruction, (b) maintain a minimum GPA of 3.00, (c) complete all graduation requirements necessary for obtainment of a diploma and all application requirements for acceptance into a 4-year university, and (d) complete a career occupational training course in business occupations and computer applications.

Community: Lawrence will obtain a driver's license and maintain a safe driving record through graduation from high school.

Employment: Lawrence will (a) complete career awareness activities in high school and select a career occupation of interest, (b) participate in paid competitive part-time employment in his career interest during high school, and (c) pursue postsecondary education and training in his career interest at a 4-year university.

Supplementary and Related Services: Lawrence will maintain a minimum GPA of 3.00 with the help of an inclusion facilitator or resource specialist in all college-preparatory classes in high school and will obtain academic support and assistance from disabled student services at a 4-year university upon graduation.

Figure 9–4 Lawrence's IEP: Transition Plan

Annual Goal No.1—Instruction: By the end of the year, Lawrence will improve his study skills as evidenced by his maintaining a B average in all core academic classes.

Or

By the end of the year, given direct instruction on how to prepare and study for written examinations, Lawrence will be able to use effective study skills leading to scores that average 80% or higher on all multiple-choice, true-false, matching, and short-answer examinations in core academic subjects.

State Standard(s): No California State Standards exist for study skills.

Benchmarks: By November, given direct instruction in study skills, Lawrence will create accurate written summaries or outlines of information presented from text and lectures in his core academic subjects four out of five successive times, based on teacher observation and judgment.

By March, given direct instruction in study skills, Lawrence will independently create accurate reconstructive elaborations (e.g., graphic organizers, pictures, and illustrations) that use keyword visual mnemonics to facilitate recall of fact-based information four out of five successive times, based on teacher observation and judgment.

By May, given direct instruction in study skills and practice examinations, Lawrence will correctly use item-elimination strategies for multiple-choice, true-false, and matching examinations four out of five successive times, based on teacher observation and judgment.

Annual Goal No.2—Employment: By the end of the year, Lawrence will enroll in and successfully complete a course in business occupations, earning a passing grade in the course.

Or

By the end of the year, given direct instruction in reading comprehension, Lawrence will achieve at least an 80% average on all reading comprehension tests on material from a business occupations textbook.

State Standard(s)—Comprehension and Analysis of Grade-Level-Appropriate Text: 2.3 Generate relevant questions about readings on issues that can be researched. 2.4 Synthesize the content from several sources or works by a single author dealing with a single issue; paraphrase the ideas and connect them to other sources and related topics to demonstrate comprehension. 2.5 Extend ideas presented in primary or secondary sources through original analysis, evaluation, and elaboration.

Benchmarks: By November, given direct instruction in reading comprehension strategies, Lawrence will correctly use Survey, Question, Read, Recite, Review (SQ3R) when reading textbook chapters four out of five successive times, as determined by teacher observation and judgment.

By March, given direct instruction in reading comprehension strategies, Lawrence will create graphic organizers of main ideas from business occupations textbook chapters four out of five successive times, based on works samples and teacher observation and judgment.

By May, given direct instruction in reading comprehension strategies, Lawrence will write an outline of a business occupations textbook chapter that summarizes key points four out of five successive times, based on teacher judgment.

Figure 9–5   Lawrence's Annual Goals, Benchmarks, and State Standards

LET'S SEE IT IN ACTION! CASE EXAMPLE

Maria (Transition Pathway 2)

Maria is a bilingual 10th-grade Hispanic youth with a learning disability. She comes from a large family and is the oldest of five children. Her parents are immigrants from Mexico and do not speak English. Maria was classified as English as a Second Language (ESL) student through second grade but has been fully proficient in English since third grade. She has a receptive language processing disorder that interferes with her ability to comprehend spoken language, either Spanish or English. This affects her ability to listen and follow directions in class, engage in sustained conversations with others, and take lecture notes efficiently. Her primary academic difficulties are in word attack skills in reading and in written language, as evidenced by achievement scores significantly below grade level in each of these subjects on standardized tests.

Maria was in a special day-class in third and fourth grade and then transitioned to a resource specialist program, receiving pullout services for reading and written language from fifth grade through middle school. She loves working with children and is a very popular babysitter in the community. She would like to go to community college and pursue training and employment in child care, as a school instructional aide, or as a preschool or elementary school teacher. Her parents are very supportive of this plan.

Transition Portion of Maria's IEP.   The transition portion of Maria's IEP is shown in Figure 9-6. The top portion of the IEP indicates that Maria desires to obtain a high school diploma, attend community college, pursue a career in child care, and work and live independently in her community. The Current Level of Performance section displays achievement test scores in reading and written language that justify Maria's placement in special education, her high school course of study, and Transition Pathway 2. All other data demonstrate that Maria has the capability to achieve successful postschool outcomes in the community, employment, and postsecondary training.

The Transition Service Needs portion of Maria's IEP indicates she needs special education assistance in reading and written language to be successful in academic subjects in high school and community college. She also requires career–vocational special needs support to help her obtain occupational training and paid competitive employment in child care. Needed transition services will be provided to Maria in instruction for reading and written language, driver's education and training, and pre-vocational and occupational education.

Maria's transition goals specify (a) participation in a semi-integrated instructional program in high school, leading to obtainment of a diploma, (b) obtainment of a driver's license, (c) prevocational occupational training and paid competitive employment in child care, followed by advanced occupational training in her career interest after high school graduation, and (d) provision of assistance and academic support from special education personnel in high school, community college, and vocational technical school.

Maria's IEP: Annual Goals, Benchmarks, and State Standards.   Owing to space limitations, we have included only two of Maria's IEP annual goals and objectives for review. These are shown in Figure 9-7. Maria's annual goal for instruction is to improve in

Vision
* High school diploma
* Attend community college with possible transfer to a 4-year university
* Work with children and live independently in the community

Career Interests
* Careers in child care
* Preschool teacher
* School instructional aide
* Elementary school teacher

Strengths
* Excellent relationships with children
* Bilingual in English and Spanish
* Very polite, pleasant personality

Current Level of Performance:

Academics: Woodcock-Johnson: Broad Reading 5.0; Word Attack 4.9; Reading Comprehension 4.0; Written Language 5.2. Maria requires resource specialist pullout services for reading and written language.

Community: Functions semi-independently in community; capable of obtaining driver's license and driving own car for travel within local community.

Employment: Capable of working fully independently in paid competitive employment.

Postsecondary Training and Learning: Capable of participating in postsecondary education at community college or occupational training program.

Recreation and Leisure: Enjoys helping in home with domestic chores and child care; likes listening to music and watching television and going to mall with friends.

Transition Service Needs:
* Maria requires academic support from an inclusion facilitator, resource specialist, or special day-class instructor to obtain diploma, with differential standards applied, in academic classes involving reading and written language.
* Maria needs support from vocational special needs personnel to obtain paid competitive employment in child care while in high school and after graduation.
* Maria will need assistance from disabled student services to be successful in academic classes in community college.

Needed Transition Services:
* **Instruction:** Maria will receive special education instruction for reading and written language.
* **Community:** Maria will enroll in driver's education/training course leading to obtainment of driver's license.
* **Employment:** Maria will participate in prevocational training class and in childcare occupations courses in high school and community college.

Transition Goals:

Instruction: Maria will (a) participate in a semi-integrated high school course of study that leads to passage, of district proficiency exams, graduation requirements, and community college entrance requirements, and (b) complete a child care occupations course.

Community: Maria will obtain a driver's license and maintain a safe driving record through graduation from high school.

Employment: Maria will (a) complete career awareness activities in high school and select a career or occupation of interest, (b) participate in paid competitive part-time employment in her desired career during high school, and (c) pursue postsecondary education and training in her career interest at a community college or vocational technical school.

Supplementary and Related Services: Maria will receive assistance and academic support from an inclusion facilitator, resource specialist, or special day-class instructor to maintain passing grades in all high school courses required for graduation with a diploma. She will obtain academic support and assistance from disabled student services at a community college or career–technical school after graduation from high school.

Figure 9–6   Maria's IEP: Transition Plan

Annual Goal No.1—Instruction: By the end of the year, Maria will improve in written language skills.

Or

By the end of the year, given direct instruction on the five-step writing process for reports, short essays, and short stories, Maria will produce at least three writing samples containing at least five paragraphs with proper capitalization, organization, punctuation, and spelling and score at least four out of five on a teacher-made writing rubric.

State Standard(s): Organization and Focus 1.1 Establish a controlling impression or coherent thesis that conveys a clear and distinctive perspective on the subject, and maintain a consistent tone and focus throughout the piece of writing.

1.2 Use precise language, action verbs, sensory details, appropriate modifiers, and the active rather than the passive voice.

Grammar and Mechanics of Writing: 1.1 Identify and correctly use clauses (e.g., main and subordinate), phrases (e.g., gerund, infinitive, and participial), and mechanics of punctuation (e.g., semicolons, colons, ellipses, and hyphens). 1.2 Understand sentence construction (e.g., parallel structure, subordination, and proper placement of modifiers) and proper English usage (e.g., consistency of verb tenses).1.3 Demonstrate an understanding of proper English usage and control of grammar, paragraph, and sentence structure, diction, and syntax.

Manuscript Form 1.4 Produce legible work that shows accurate spelling and correct use of the conventions of punctuation and capitalization.

Benchmarks: By November, given direct instruction on paragraph writing, Maria will be able to write a complete paragraph containing a topic sentence, at least three supporting details, and a concluding sentence with proper capitalization, organization, punctuation, and spelling, and score at least four out of five on a teacher-made writing rubric on three successive occasions.

By March, given direct instruction on the five-step writing process, Maria will be able to plan, draft, edit, revise, and write a final draft of a report, short essay, or short story of at least three paragraphs in length with proper capitalization, organization, punctuation, and spelling, and score at least four out of five on a teacher-made writing rubric on three successive occasions.

Figure 9–7   Maria s Annual Goals, Benchmarks, and State Standards

written language skills. Resource-specialist instruction will focus on the five-step writing process and promotion of writing proficiency in the creation of written reports, short essays, and short stories. A second annual goal in Maria's IEP is in the area of employment. Maria will successfully participate in and complete a prevocational training class emphasizing career exploration. Activities will involve her finding several reference materials on careers in child care, visiting local child-care facilities in her area, and writing a career exploration report on child care.

Note that both of these annual goals and benchmarks are directly related to the transition portion of Maria's IEP and reflect her vision for the future. In addition, they appropriately reflect her transition service needs, needed transition services, and transition goals. Finally, the annual goals and objectives are aligned with her high school course of study and chosen transition pathway.

Next we present a case study for Transition Pathway 3.

Transition Portion of Jamie's IEP.   The transition portion of Jamie's IEP is shown in Figure 9–8. The top portion of the IEP indicates that Jamie and her family desire a certificate of attendance and for her to work and live semi-independently in the community. She has strong career interests in animal care and graphic arts. The Current Level of Performance section of her IEP transition plan shows her academic

By May, given direct instruction on informative and creative writing, Maria will be able to plan, draft, edit, revise, and write a final draft of a report, short essay, or short story of at least five paragraphs with proper capitalization, organization, punctuation, and spelling, and score at least four out of five on a teacher-made writing rubric on three successive occasions.

Annual Goal No.2—Employment: By the end of the year, Maria will participate in a prevocational training program and successfully complete career exploration activities.

Or

By the end of the year, given direct instruction and guidance by vocational special needs personnel in the career center, Maria will conduct a career exploration of child care and produce a written report of at least five paragraphs, with proper capitalization, organization, punctuation, and spelling, which specifies the educational requirements, necessary workplace skills, and salary and benefits in at least one child care job of her choice, and score at least four out of five on a teacher-made writing rubric.

State Standard(s)—Education, Child Development, and Family Services Sector 1.0 Academics: Students understand the academic requirements for entry into postsecondary education and employment in the education, child development, and family services sector.

Benchmarks: By November, given direct instruction and guidance by vocational special needs personnel in the career center, Maria will select three reference materials that she can use to complete a career exploration written report on child care, based on teacher observation.

By March, given assistance by vocational special needs personnel, Maria will visit at least three child care sites in her local region and gather relevant information to include in her written career exploration report, as measured by visitation logs maintained by vocational special needs personnel.

By May, given direct instruction on how to write a career exploration report, Maria will complete a rough draft of a report on child care and receive editorial feedback by vocational special needs personnel, based on teacher records.

LET'S SEE IT IN ACTION! CASE EXAMPLE

Jamie (Transition Pathway 3)

Jamie is a 10th-grade girl with mild Down syndrome. Her cognitive functioning is in the below-average range and her current grade level achievement in most academic skills is around mid-fourth-grade level. She is well-mannered, works hard in school, and always tries to please her teachers and parents. She has difficulty with auditory processing and memory and has received speech and language services from elementary through middle school. Her parents were given the choice in elementary school to have Jamie receive an inclusive education, but they thought she would progress better academically and be able to receive a more functional, community-based program in a special day class. She was subsequently placed in a special day class in first grade for all academic subjects and mainstreamed for music, art, and physical education.

Jamie is liked by others, has a few friends in school and in her neighborhood, but does not possess a wide social and interpersonal network. She participates in some after-school, integrated activities, such as soccer and Girl Scouts. She rarely goes into the community on her own because her parents are somewhat worried about her safety. She loves animals and has several pets at home, providing them with excellent care. She also loves to draw and is a very fine artist. In her free time, she likes to play with her pets, draw, and listen to music.

Vision
* High school diploma or certificate of attendance
* Work and live semi-independently in the community

Career Interests
* Animal care
* Graphic arts

Strengths
* Works hard in school
* Artistic
* Good with animals and pets

Current Level of Performance:

Academics: Woodcock-Johnson: Broad Reading 4.5; Comprehension 4.2; Word Attack 4.7; Written Language 4.4; Mathematics 4.5. Current oral and receptive language skills are around fourth-grade level. Jamie requires major modifications in curriculum and support of inclusion facilitator or special day-class teacher to be successful in academic classes.

Community: Currently not able to function independently in community.

Employment: Capable of working independently with time-limited support in paid competitive employment.

Postsecondary Training and Learning: Capable of participating in postsecondary occupational training with support.

Daily-Living Skills: Currently unable to prepare simple meals, grocery shop, maintain a bank account and budget.

Recreation and Leisure: Enjoys caring for animals, drawing, and listening to music.

Transition Service Needs:
* Jamie requires major curriculum modifications and academic support from an inclusion facilitator or special day-class teacher to be successful in general education classes.
* Jamie needs continued speech and language services to promote improved oral and receptive language development.
* Jamie needs instruction in daily-living skills and community-based instruction to be able to function semi-independently at home and in the community.
* Jamie needs time-limited supports to obtain paid competitive employment.

Needed Transition Services:
* **Instruction:** Jamie will receive instruction in (a) academic subjects required for graduation and (b) daily living skills and community-based instruction.
* **Community:** Jamie will participate in a community-based instructional program.
* **Employment:** Jamie will participate in prevocational training class and occupational training classes in animal care, as well as graphic arts.
* **Related Services:** Jamie will continue to receive speech and language therapy throughout high school.
* **Daily Living:** Jamie will participate in a daily-living skills training program in high school.

Transition Goals:

Instruction: Jamie will (a) participate in a semi-integrated high school course of study that leads either to passage of district proficiency exams and graduation requirements or obtainment of a certificate of attendance, (b) successfully complete a daily-living skills and community-based instructional program that promotes semi-independent functioning in the home and community, and (c) complete occupational training courses in animal care or graphic arts.

Community: Jamie will be able to function semi-independently in the community after completing school.

Employment: Jamie will (a) complete career awareness activities in high school and select a career occupation of interest, (b) participate in paid competitive part-time employment in her career interest during high school, and (c) obtain postsecondary occupational training or paid competitive employment in her career interest after completing school.

Supplementary and Related Services: Jamie will receive (a) speech and language services in high school, (b) academic support from an inclusion facilitator or special day-class teacher, (c) community-based instructional support, and (d) time-limited supported employment services.

Figure 9–8 Jamie's IEP: Transition Plan

achievement level around mid-fourth-grade in most subjects. Her oral and receptive language skills are at the fourth-grade level. She is not currently able to function independently in the community, needs supports for employment, and lacks daily-living skills needed to live independently. She is capable of participating in postsecondary training if provided supports.

The Transition Service Needs portion of Jamie's IEP indicates that she needs major curriculum modifications and academic support from an inclusion facilitator or special day-class teacher to participate in high school academic classes. She also needs continued speech and language services, instruction in daily-living skills, community-based instruction (CBI), and supportive employment training. Needed transition services for Jamie will focus on all of these areas.

Jamie's transition goals specify (a) participation in a semi-integrated high school course of study leading to obtainment of a certificate of attendance, (b) daily living skills and community-based instruction, (c) career and occupational exploration, (d) occupational training in animal care or graphic arts, as well as paid competitive employment, and (e) supports from a variety of related services personnel.

Jamie's IEP: Annual Goals, Benchmarks, and State Standards. Again, owing to space limitations, we have selected two of Jamie's annual goals and objectives to highlight, specifically employment and community. These are shown in Figure 9–9. With respect to employment, Jamie's annual IEP goal and benchmarks specify that she will successfully complete a prevocational training class that results in her gaining the necessary skills to apply for, interview, and obtain a part-time competitive employment position in animal care in a business in her local community. The second annual goal and benchmarks shown on Jamie's IEP focus on CBI skills and, specifically, the ability to successfully use public transportation to travel between home and employment. Jamie will receive time-limited supports for both employment and community-based training.

Finally, we present a case study for Transition Pathway 4.

LET'S SEE IT IN ACTION! CASE EXAMPLE

Phong (Transition Pathway 4)

Phong is a 15-year-old Vietnamese boy with multiple disabilities. He has very limited cognitive functioning and oral language ability. His parents emigrated from Vietnam 20 years ago. His father is a dentist in the local community and his mother is a homemaker, caring for Phong and his three younger siblings. Phong has been in special education since starting school and is very low functioning academically. He is usually cooperative and compliant with his teachers and family but, when frustrated, can be defiant because of his inability to communicate his desires and needs in language. Positive behavioral support plans have been implemented over the years with Phong and have produced generally favorable results, such as reduction in tantrums, increased instances of cooperative behavior, and ability to communicate his needs through augmentative communication. Phong has a good sense of humor and when interested in a task, will work diligently to complete it.

Phong and his parents would like him to live at home after graduation from high school, because they are concerned that his presence in the community would reflect poorly on them as a family

(Continued)

LET'S SEE IT IN ACTION! CASE EXAMPLE   *(Continued)*

(e.g., a culturally related concern). They have expressed a desire for him to work on a limited basis in the nearby community in a job of his interest but are unsure of what he is capable of doing vocationally. Phong has a limited social network, mostly consisting of friends at school and relatives. He likes sports and often watches televised sporting events in football, basketball, and baseball. He has never played on a local recreational sports team.

Annual Goal No.1—Employment: By the end of the year, Jamie will be successfully competitively employed in a paid, part-time job in animal care in the community.

Or

By the end of the year, given direct instruction by vocational special needs personnel in prevocational training, Jamie will apply for and obtain a part-time, paid competitive job in animal care in the community.

State Standard(s)—Animal Science: D1.0 Students understand the necessary elements for proper animal housing and animal handling equipment.

D2.0 Students understand key principles of animal nutrition.

Benchmarks: By November, given counseling and guidance from vocational special needs personnel, Jamie will enroll in and maintain at least a B average in a prevocational training class on or off campus, based on teacher records.

By March, given assistance from vocational special needs personnel, Jamie will visit at least three animal care businesses in her local community and discuss with potential employers her interest and the job requirements for employment, based on teacher records.

By May, given assistance from vocational special needs personnel, Jamie will complete job applications and interviews from at least three animal care businesses in her local community and obtain a part-time, paid job in animal care, based on teacher records.

Annual Goal No.2—Community: By the end of the year, Jamie will use public transportation to access employment, local businesses, recreation, and leisure activities in her community.

Or

By the end of the year, given time-limited support and direct instruction from CBI personnel, Jamie will independently use public transportation to travel between home and community destinations (at least three) of her choice, based on teacher observation, judgment, and records.

State Standard(s): No California Standards exist for mobility training.

Benchmarks: By November, given time-limited support and direct instruction from CBI personnel, Jamie will correctly read a bus schedule and walk from her home to the bus stop at a designated time and wait for the arrival of the bus, based on teacher observation, judgment, and records.

By March, given time-limited support and direct instruction from CBI personnel, Jamie will successfully use public transportation to travel from her home to at least one destination in the community, based on teacher observation, judgment, and records.

By May, given time-limited support and direct instruction from CBI personnel, Jamie will use public transportation to travel from her home to at least one destination in the community and her place of employment, based on teacher observation, judgment, and records.

Figure 9–9   Jamie's Annual Goals, Benchmarks, and State Standards

Transition Portion of Phong's IEP. The transition services portion of Phong's IEP is shown in Figure 9–10. Phong's parents' vision for him is to participate in a semi-integrated program in high school, leading to a certificate of attendance, development of daily living and semi-independent living skills for the home, and semi-independent work in the community. Current Level of Performance data for Phong indicate that his levels of functioning in academics, community, employment, and daily-living skills are commensurate with the vision his parents hold for him.

The Transition Services Needs portion of Phong's IEP indicates that he needs major curriculum modifications and support from an inclusion facilitator or special day-class teacher to be successful in general education classes. In addition, Phong will require continued speech and language services, daily living skills instruction, positive behavioral supports, CBI, and supported employment assistance. Needed Transition Services on his IEP are written in all of these areas. In addition, a functional vocational evaluation is on Phong's IEP to determine his occupational abilities and aptitudes.

Phong's transition goals specify (a) participation in a semi-integrated high school course of study emphasizing functional daily living skills, community-based instruction, and obtainment of a certificate of attendance; (b) completion of a functional vocational evaluation, career awareness activities, and participation in paid, competitive supported employment in high school and beyond; and (c) supports from a variety of related services personnel.

Phong's IEP: Annual Goals, Benchmarks, and State Standards. As in previous case studies, we have chosen to focus on only two sample IEP annual goals and objectives for Phong, owing to space limitations. The areas highlighted in Phong's IEP, shown in Figure 9–11, include instruction or daily living skills and employment or functional vocational evaluation. With respect to the first of these two areas, Phong's IEP contains an annual goal and objectives designed to teach him to prepare a simple, nutritionally balanced breakfast, lunch, and dinner. Phong's employment or functional vocational evaluation IEP annual goal and objectives are aimed at using augmentative communication and maintained concentration to determine his career interests, aptitudes, and abilities.

Summary of Case Studies for Transition Pathways

We have attempted to illustrate in the four case studies the various components and sections of an IEP and the relationship among required transition services, annual goals, benchmarks, and state standards. As stated previously, it is our recommendation that the transition services portion of an IEP drive the annual goals and objectives section of the document. Though IDEA 2004 no longer requires IEP objectives, we have included them in all four case studies and recommend them because they represent best practice in special education. This is also true of state standards on IEPs. The four case studies and supporting IEP documents reflect this approach to transition planning. The case studies and IEP documents illustrate the various high school courses of

Vision

* High school certificate of attendance
* Live semi-independently at home
* Work semi-independently in the community

Career Interests

* Athletics and sports careers

Strengths

* Good sense of humor
* High task completion rate
* Enjoys watching sports

Current Level of Performance:

Academics: Developmental scales, cognitive, and academic tests show functioning in significantly below average range, with academics at the kindergarten to first-grade level. Very limited oral language skills; requires augmentative communication devices.

Community: Currently not able to function independently in the community.

Employment: Capable of working independently with ongoing support, possibly in paid competitive employment.

Postsecondary Training and Learning: May potentially benefit from ongoing supported training and employment after completing school.

Recreation and Leisure: Enjoys attending and viewing sports and athletic events.

Daily-Living Skills: Currently unable to prepare simple meals, grocery shop, or do laundry.

Transition Service Needs:

* Phong requires major curriculum modifications and academic support from an inclusion facilitator or special day-class teacher to be successful in general education classes.
* Phong needs continued speech and language services to promote ability to communicate with augmentative communication devices.
* Phong needs instruction in daily-living skills, positive behavioral support, and community-based instruction to be able to function semi-independently at home and in the community.
* Phong needs time-limited or ongoing support to obtain paid competitive employment.

Needed Transition Services:

* **Instruction:** Phong will receive instruction in functional skills, social and behavioral skills, and community-based instruction.
* **Community:** Phong will participate in a community-based instructional program.
* **Employment:** Phong will participate in a prevocational training class and occupational training classes in sports and athletics careers.
* **Related Services:** Phong will continue to receive speech and language therapy throughout high school, community-based instructional services, positive behavioral support services, and supported employment services.
* **Daily Living:** Phong will participate in a daily-living skills training program in high school.
* **Functional Vocational Evaluation:** Phong will receive a functional vocational evaluation to determine his occupational aptitudes and abilities.

Transition Goals:

Instruction: Phong will participate in a semi-integrated high school course of study emphasizing (a) functional, daily-living skills, community-based instruction, and obtainment of a certificate of attendance, (b) semi-independent functioning in the home and community, (c) completion of occupational training in sports and athletics careers, and (d) obtainment of paid competitive employment.

Community: Phong will be able to function semi-independently in the home and community after completing school.

Employment: Phong will (a) receive a functional-vocational evaluation and career-awareness activities in high school and select a career-occupation of interest; (b) participate in paid, competitive, part-time supported employment in his career interest during high school; and (c) obtain paid, competitive supported employment in his career interest after completing school.

Supplementary and Related Services: Phong will receive (a) speech and language services in high school, (b) academic support from an inclusion facilitator or special day-class teacher, (c) community-based instructional support, (d) positive behavioral support services, and (e) time-limited or ongoing supported employment services.

Figure 9–10 Phong's IEP: Transition Plan

Annual Goal No.1—Instruction and Daily Living Skills: By the end of the year, Phong will prepare a simple, nutritionally balanced meal for himself in his home.

Or

By the end of the year, given direct instruction in daily living skills, Phong will prepare a nutritionally balanced breakfast, lunch, and dinner, based on teacher observation, judgment, and records.

State Standard(s)—California Alternative Performance Assessment (CAPA) Standards, Moderate–Severe Health and Knowledge, Positive Health Behaviors: Develop basic food preparation skills.

Benchmarks: By November, given direct instruction in daily living skills, Phong will prepare a nutritionally balanced breakfast on three successive occasions, based on teacher observation, judgment, and records.

By March, given direct instruction in daily living skills, Phong will prepare a nutritionally balanced lunch on three successive occasions, based on teacher observation, judgment, and records.

By May, given direct instruction in daily living skills, Phong will prepare a nutritionally balanced dinner on three successive occasions, based on teacher observation, judgment, and records.

Annual Goal No.2—Employment or Functional Vocational Evaluation: By the end of the year, Phong will identify through augmentative communication his vocational interests, aptitudes, and abilities.

Or

By the end of the year, when given a functional vocational evaluation by vocational special needs personnel, Phong will identify through augmentative communication his vocational interests, aptitudes, and abilities.

State Standard(s): No California State Standards exist in the area of functional vocational evaluation.

Benchmarks: By November, given direct instruction, Phong will maintain concentration and focus on a functional vocational evaluation task requiring his response through augmentative communication for up to 15 minutes on three successive occasions, based on teacher observation, judgment, and duration recording data.

By March, given direct instruction, Phong will maintain concentration and focus on a functional vocational evaluation task requiring his response through augmentative communication for up to 30 minutes on three successive occasions, based on teacher observation, judgment, and duration recording data.

By May, given direct instruction, Phong will respond with augmentative communication to a series of functional vocational evaluations, each lasting up to 30 minutes in length, and communicate his career interests, aptitude, and abilities.

Figure 9–11   Phong's Annual Goals, Benchmarks, and State Standards

study requirements and transition pathways advocated in this text. It is our hope that readers now have a clear picture of what an IEP document looks like for the transition pathways model and can begin to draft sample IEPs of this nature.

This chapter concludes with information on how to plan and conduct an IEP meeting in which transition planning is to take place.

➡ WHAT STEPS ARE INVOLVED IN PLANNING AND CONDUCTING A PROFESSIONALLY DRIVEN IEP TRANSITION PLANNING MEETING?

In a *professionally driven* IEP transition planning meeting, the primary persons responsible for planning and conducting the proceedings are school personnel—such as the school psychologist and special education teacher—and related services personnel. In the vast majority of school districts in this country, the IEP meeting is still a professionally driven process, although there has been much discussion and advocacy in special education literature to make the IEP a more student-directed process. We concur with this recommendation and will discuss how to do this more extensively in the next section. Nevertheless, we think it is important to present information and recommendations on how to best conduct professionally driven IEP transition planning meetings.

Transition planning meetings that are professionally driven should be conducted in conjunction with annual IEP meetings, beginning when youth with disabilities in special education reach age 16, and for best practices, as early as age 14. This often results in a longer-than-usual IEP meeting (one to two hours) because the transition planning process is considerably more complex and time consuming than what is required in a typical IEP meeting. In addition, more personnel are typically in attendance at an IEP meeting in which transition planning is being discussed. Persons in attendance can include the youth with a disability and his or her parents, high school special education personnel, adult transition service agency representatives from the departments of vocational rehabilitation or mental health, and community college or university disabled-student services.

Professionals responsible for planning and conducting an IEP transition planning meeting need to attend to a number of tasks associated with three phases of the meeting: (a) before the meeting, (b) during the meeting, and (c) following the completion of the meeting (see Figure 9–12). The most important task to attend to before holding an IEP transition planning meeting is to designate a *case coordinator*. This will usually be the special education teacher case carrier to whom the student is assigned. Some school districts, however, have a transition coordinator or program specialist serve as the case coordinator. These are often special education or vocational special needs personnel on special assignment. Regardless of the individual serving in this role, it is the case coordinator's responsibility to (a) determine the school and transition agency personnel to invite to attend the meeting (see Figure 9–13 for a list of potential participants in transition planning meetings); (b) schedule the meeting date and time that is most convenient for all team members; (c) send out written notices to all participants invited to attend the meeting; (d) send out a written transition planning worksheet or questionnaire to the youth with a disability and his or her family well in advance of the meeting; (e) make sure that all the necessary paperwork, test results, and other relevant information is available for the meeting; and (f) reschedule the meeting if necessary.

A transition planning worksheet or questionnaire is one of the most critical pieces of information to attend to for the case coordinator. A sample document of this type can be found in Appendix 7–1. Transition planning worksheets or questionnaires provide the IEP team with a wealth of information regarding the future vision across a variety of transition outcomes of the youth with a disability and his or her family. Examples of these outcomes include postsecondary education and training, employment, independent living, and community access for the youth with a disability.

Before the Meeting

Designate IEP case manager(s). This will usually be the special education teacher and/or administrator. The case manager

1. determines which individuals/agencies make up a comprehensive IEP team;
2. proposes a meeting date and time;
3. assures that written notices are sent to all appropriate participants in a timely manner;
4. encloses the written invitation to the IEP meeting, parent/student questionnaire, and transition planning worksheet with the notice to the student's family;
5. assures that required information is available at the meeting (e.g., IEP assessment data).
6. reschedules as necessary.

At the Meeting

Establish a chairperson to conduct the meeting according to the following agenda (the exact order of the following items is not important):

1. Introductions (who, position, reason for attendance). Make the parent feel welcome as an equal member of the team. The chairperson might want to state an approximate time frame for the meeting, if appropriate.
2. State purpose of meeting:
   a. Review parent/student questionnaire responses.
   b. Review assessment data.
   c. Determine student eligibility for special education.
   d. Review IEP forms.
   e. Develop IEP.

Conducting the Meeting

1. Explain *transition* and the purpose of the transition planning portion of the IEP, which is (a) to develop long-range goals for the student's movement into the adult world, and (b) to plan activities that need to be accomplished if the student is to achieve these goals. It should be emphasized to the student and family that this is their meeting, that their values and desires are the focus.
2. Review parent/student questionnaire and transition planning worksheet responses.
3. Review current level of performance data (Section IIA, page 2 of IEP packet).
4. Check ( ) transition goals for the student (Section I, page 2 of the IEP packet).
5. Review other transitional/support services goals, if applicable (Section II B, page 2 of IEP packet).
6. Review various columns of the education/transition planning record form (page 3 of the IEP packet).
7. Identify competencies and subcompetencies from LCCE curriculum (pages 4 and 5 of the IEP packet) to place on education/transition planning record (page 3).
8. Write transition goal competency and subcompetency numbers/letters in column 1 of education/transition planning record.
9. Fill in relevant information in columns 2–5 on education/transition planning record (e.g., special services needed, special media/materials and equipment, individual's or agencies' responsibilities, beginning date, evaluation).
10. Review and complete district IEP forms and procedures (refer to district guidelines and procedures).

After the Meeting

Case manager

1. reviews the transition planning portion of the IEP at appropriate intervals as indicated by the "timeline" and the "date to be evaluated";
2. in the case where a participating agency, other than the educational agency, fails to provide agreed-upon services, the educational agency shall reconvene the IEP team to identify alternative strategies to meet the transition objectives;
3. Makes sure that the IEP is properly filed.

Figure 9–12 Conducting an IEP Meeting

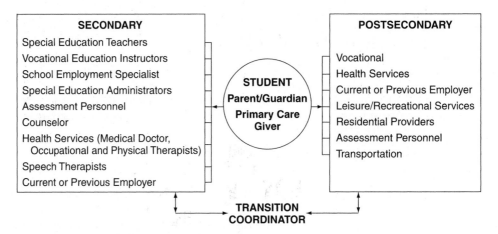

Figure 9–13 Participants in Transition Planning

Source: From *Transition Manual: TRIAD Telecommunications Project* (p. 76), by I. D. Cook and M. Thurman-Urbanic, 1990, Institute, West Virginia Graduate College. Copyright 1990 by West Virginia Graduate College. Reprinted with permission.

A chairperson should be designated to lead the proceedings once the IEP transition planning meeting begins. Best practice recommendations state that the youth with a disability, if capable, should chair his or her own IEP meeting to maximize the opportunity for self-determination and person-centered planning (see previous chapter and next section). The meeting should begin with introductions and a statement of purpose. A brief review of assessment data should occur, followed by an opportunity for the youth with a disability and parent(s) to share their responses to the transition planning worksheet or questionnaire. Available programs and services in both school and community should then be discussed, based on the transition interests and preferences of the youth with a disability and the family. It is appropriate to begin drafting required transition services on the IEP transition planning form (e.g., current level of performance, transition goals and activities, persons responsible, and timelines). Corresponding IEP annual goals and objectives can also be discussed and written. Any additional IEP goals and objectives unrelated to transition can be drafted as well. A final review and summary of all portions of the IEP document should take place, followed by obtainment of the necessary signatures. Copies should be provided to all participants at the conclusion of the meeting or mailed to them shortly thereafter.

Following the completion of the IEP meeting, it is critically important for the case coordinator to monitor and review the transition goals and IEP annual goals and benchmarks periodically to determine that specified services are being delivered and the progress to date on all goals and objectives are specified in the IEP. The case coordinator should document this in writing, preferably on the actual IEP forms, using one of the following terms: *met, continued, revised,* or *deleted.* Dates should be written next to these respective terms on the IEP document designating when the plan was last monitored and reviewed. Note that IEP goals and benchmarks cannot be revised or deleted without the written consent of the youth with a disability and his or her family. If necessary and as required by law, the case coordinator should reconvene the IEP team if agreed-upon transition services fail to be delivered. A revised IEP transition plan must subsequently be written in this instance.

➡ HOW CAN YOUTH WITH DISABILITIES BE PREPARED TO CONDUCT STUDENT-DIRECTED IEP TRANSITION PLANNING MEETINGS?

Halpern (1996) noted that the transition planning meeting is the culminating event in the process of developing a transition plan and should be student-directed. And yet, he cautioned, "The history of student involvement in the IEP process is not very encouraging" (p. 12). IEP meetings have typically been controlled by teachers, with parents or students having very little engagement or active involvement. IDEA 1997 and 2004 strengthened the involvement of youth with disabilities in the decision-making process about their own futures. Self-determination and person-centered transition planning, reviewed in previous chapters in this book, provide the foundation skills needed by youth with disabilities to direct their own IEP transition planning meeting. With sufficient preparation and support, students can successfully direct their own IEP meetings (ERIC/OSEP Special Project, 2000; Martin, Marshall, & DePry, 2002; Test, Mason, Hughes, Konrad, Neale, & Wood, 2004; Tindle, Leconte, Buchanan, & Taymans, 2005; Togerson, Miner, & Shen, 2004; VanDycke, Martin, & David, 2006).

A specific set of skills has been identified to teach to youth with disabilities throughout their school years to help them become more active participants in IEP transition planning meetings. These come from a variety of sources, and we have attempted to summarize what we believe are the most important ones in Figure 9–14.

In addition to those presented in Figure 9–14, there are several other student-directed IEP transition planning meeting skills and recommendations that bear mentioning. According to ERIC/OSEP Special Project (2000), teachers experienced in involving their students in the IEP process have suggested that self-determination instruction begin as early as possible, preferably in the elementary school years. Teachers may need to support students with more sensitive issues, because some youth with disabilities may never have seen their IEP, they may not know what it means, or they may find it uncomfortable to read about their disability. In addition, teachers need to realize that developing IEP participation skills takes time; therefore, they may wish to consider teaching these skills as a semester course. Halpern (1996) has suggested that courses of this nature use self-determination, transition curricula that contain six desirable components. The curricula must

1. address and enhance student motivation to participate;
2. build on a foundation of student self-exploration;
3. address the most important areas of student transition in a manner that is responsive to student interests and needs;
4. teach students how to set goals and develop a concrete transition plan;
5. provide students with an opportunity to direct their own transition planning meeting involving other significant people; and
6. teach students how to implement and monitor their own transition plans.

1. Learn about your disability:
   - Clarify the exact nature of your disability.
   - Learn about your strengths and weaknesses.
   - Understand how your disability affects your life.
   - Understand what you need and how to get help (e.g., self-advocacy and accommodations).

2. Learn about IEP laws:
   - Know and understand federal laws for students with disabilities.
   - Understand IDEA 2004 transition mandates.
   - Read and understand your current IEP.

3. Learn how to choose goals across transition areas:
   - Identify your interests.
   - Identify your strengths.
   - Identify your limitations.
   - Identify your hopes and dreams for the future.

4. Learn how to participate in and lead your IEP transition planning meeting:
   - Identify whom to invite to the meeting.
   - Schedule the meeting.
   - Prepare refreshments and name tags.
   - Wear appropriate clothes for the meeting.
   - Sit at the head of the table.
   - Lead the meeting, with support as needed by others.
   - Express concerns, show preferences, and give opinions based on personal experience during the meeting

Figure 9–14   Student-Directed IEP Transition Planning Meeting Skills

A publication by the Parent Advocacy Coalition for Educational Rights (PACER) Center (1999) contained specific grade-level recommendations related to student self-directed IEP skills. Elementary school students should "learn how you learn best; know your strengths and weaknesses" (p. 5). In intermediate school, they should learn what goes into an IEP. Finally, in high school, they should learn about laws that require IEPs, learn how to read their IEPs, learn about their strengths and weaknesses, and practice asking for reasonable accommodations.

For those interested in obtaining published materials specifically designed for teaching student-directed IEP skills, Russell (2001) recommended a valuable guide produced by The National Information Center for Children and Youth with Disabilities (NICHCY): *A Student's Guide to the IEP: Helping Students Develop Their IEPs* and an accompanying audiotape available from NICHCY, P.O. Box 1492, Washington, D.C. 20013, (800) 695-0285. These materials can be downloaded from the NICHCY Web site http://www.nichcy.org/stuguid.asp. Finally, specific suggestions have been made about what a youth with a disability can do before, during, and after the IEP meeting to prepare for a direct role in the process. A publication titled *Transition to Adult Living: An Information Resource Guide (2007)*, published by the California Department of Education, Special Education Division, offers an excellent list in this regard. Figure 9-15 contains this information. In addition to these excellent suggestions, Halpern (1996) mentioned that youth with disabilities who desire to participate

---

What Students Can Do Before the IEP Meeting

1. Understand what is supposed to happen during the IEP meeting and ask your teacher to explain the process if you are unsure.
2. Brainstorm with others about who you should invite to the meeting.
3. Invite people to the meeting who know, value, and support you.
4. Review your dreams and goals for the future.
5. Write out questions that you may want to ask during your meeting. Have someone help you write the questions if necessary.
6. Learn to lead the meeting.
7. Create a transition portfolio with
   • test or assessment results,
   • employment history,
   • letters of reference,
   • employer evaluations,
   • personal information.

What Students Can Do During the IEP Meeting

1. Use your transition portfolio and notes as a reference.
2. Speak clearly about your thoughts, feelings, and dreams for the future.
3. Be open to the suggestions and ideas of others, but make sure the transition activities help you reach your goals and dreams for the future.
4. Always ask questions about things you do not understand.

What Students Can Do After the IEP Meeting

1. Continue to talk with teachers, counselors, family, and community agencies about your transition plan.
2. Do what you agreed to do as best you can.
3. Check in regularly with the people who agreed to help you.
4. Ask your teacher for help if you have difficulty making contact with the people who agreed to help you.
5. Make sure that the activities of your IEP take place.
6. Modify your plan as you mature or if your career interests change.
7. Don't be afraid to take risks!

Figure 9–15   What Students Can Do Before, During, and After the IEP Meeting

actively in IEP meetings need to learn and practice a variety of skills, including the following:

1. Selecting and inviting the participants to the meeting
2. Introducing the participants
3. Presenting their plans
4. Encouraging and processing feedback from other participants
5. Responding positively to suggestions from others
6. Closing the meeting and arranging follow-up activities

In summary, a number of important skills need to be taught, practiced, and learned by youth with disabilities throughout their school years for them to become proficient in student-directed IEP meetings. Teachers need to be cognizant of the fact that youth with disabilities may demonstrate varying levels of ability, involvement, and assertiveness at differing points in time in their school careers. According to Halpern (1996), developing student-directed IEP skills in youth with disabilities is not an all-or-nothing proposition but rather one that may take years for students to reach their full potential.

A case study illustrating a student-directed IEP transition planning meeting for Transition Pathway 2 is presented next.

LET'S SEE IT IN ACTION! CASE EXAMPLE

Alex (Transition Pathway 2) Student-Directed
IEP Transition Planning Meeting

Alex is a 16-year-old, 11th-grade youth with a severe learning disability in reading and language arts. He currently reads around a fourth-grade level, has difficulty with reading comprehension, and struggles with language assignments that require him to write extensively, such as essays and topic reports. He is close to grade level in math, participates in school sports, and has a limited number of friends. Alex has been in special education since second grade and has received resource specialist support throughout his school years.

A major part of the special education curriculum throughout his education has focused on teaching him self-determination and self-advocacy skills. Alex learned in elementary school that he was good in math but struggles with reading and writing. The components of an IEP were taught to him in middle school and he learned how to read his own IEP at that time. In high school, he learned about what it means to have a learning disability from adult guest speakers with learning disabilities that were brought to class by his resource specialist to discuss their disabilities and long-term effects on their lives. Alex is now quite able and willing to discuss his learning disability with others, how it affects him in school and in life, and he is proficient in asking his general education teachers for accommodations when he experiences difficulty with class assignments. For example, he recently asked his biology teacher to allow him to write a shorter report on the topic of environmental biomes, agreeing to cover the

major points of the topic in less detail than his classmates.

Alex has taken on increasing responsibility over the years in directing his IEP meetings. He opted in eighth grade to pursue Transition Pathway 2 in high school, because he desired to continue to visit the resource room for at least one period a day to receive support in his general education classes that required a lot of reading and writing (e.g., English and social science). He has achieved passing grades in all general education classes in high school and is on track to graduate with a diploma. This year, he has decided he wants the full responsibility of conducting his IEP transition planning meeting. He has completed a number of formal and informal transition assessments in the past several months and reviewed the results with his teacher and parents. He clearly understands his disability, strengths, and weaknesses and has identified his hopes and dreams in a number of transition areas. He plans to graduate from high school with a diploma and enroll in the local community college to pursue an associate arts degree, specializing in fine arts. His career interest is in graphic arts or animation; he is an excellent illustrator, and he has a cartoon column in the school newspaper.

The IEP transition planning meeting for Alex was scheduled to take place three weeks ago. Alex sent an invitation letter to a representative from disabled-student services at the local community college, who confirmed that she would attend. He also invited and received confirmation from all special education and related services personnel at his school, as well as his parents. He checked with his resource specialist to be sure all of the necessary forms and documents were ready for the meeting and a room had been scheduled.

Alex chaired his IEP transition planning meeting. He had practiced what to say and do with his resource specialist for several months prior to the meeting. He began the meeting by having all participants introduce themselves. He then shared with everyone his hopes and dreams for the future, which were to earn his high school diploma, go to community college and learn graphic arts skills, and work in this career in the future. He said he would like to live at home initially after high school graduation, but eventually have his own apartment. He listened to the feedback and suggestions from others at the meeting. The disabled-student services representative from the community college suggested Alex meet with guidance counselors to determine the requirements for a bachelor of fine

arts degree, so he could see what courses he should be taking in community college if he decided to transfer to a 4-year university some day. It was also suggested that Alex schedule an appointment to meet with the learning assistance center for help in classes involving heavy reading and writing. His special education teacher suggested that he enroll in a graphic arts occupational studies course in his first semester of his senior year and look for potential part-time paid work as an apprentice in a local studio. Alex thought all of these were good suggestions.

The transition portion and academic portion of his IEP were subsequently finalized and written. Alex closed the meeting by thanking everyone for attending and agreed to keep track of his progress toward his transition goals and objectives. He would meet quarterly with his resource specialist and report the results to his parents regarding his progress toward achievement of his transition goals.

SUMMARY

Transition planning is the culminating process for a youth with a disability in special education. If properly implemented, transition planning provides a roadmap and bridge to the future for the youth with a disability and his or her family. In the instance of a middle school youth with a disability, minimally, the roadmap specifies the desired course of study in high school. Once a youth with a disability in special education reaches age 16, a transition plan must specify, if needed, transition services in the areas of instruction, related services, community, employment and other postsecondary adult living objectives, and functional vocational evaluation and daily living skills. Age-of-majority provisions must also be included on IEPs for youth with disabilities the year prior to age 18. A summary of performance document must be completed prior to the student's exit from school.

Case studies and sample IEP documents for youth with disabilities pursuing various courses of study and transition pathways in high school have been provided in this chapter. It is important to remember that the transition portion of the IEP should serve as the driving force for the annual goals and benchmarks portion of the document. Moreover, the IEP annual goals and benchmarks should have a direct relationship to the transition services requirements written in the IEP.

In this chapter, we outlined the tasks associated with an IEP meeting in which transition planning takes place. Professionally driven and student-directed IEP transition planning meetings were discussed. In professionally driven meetings, the role of the case coordinator is critical, because this individual is responsible for organizing and conducting all phases of the meeting. Student-directed IEP transition planning meetings, in contrast, place responsibility for many aspects of the meeting in the hands of a transition-age youth with a disability. Considerable knowledge, skill, and preparation learned throughout the school years must occur in youth with disabilities for them to successfully conduct a student-directed IEP transition planning meeting. Many of these skills were reviewed, including when and how they should be taught, as well as transition curricula recommendations.

Regardless of whether the IEP transition planning meeting is professionally driven or student-directed, IDEA 2004 requires that school personnel (a) monitor the implementation of all portions of the IEP, noting progress to date toward achievement of stated goals and benchmarks, (b) reconvene the IEP team if agreed-upon services should fail to be provided, and (c) draft a revised IEP should this circumstance occur. Recommendations for how to do many of these tasks will be covered in Chapter 11.

KEY TERMS AND PHRASES

steps for planning and conducting a person-centered IEP transition planning meeting

steps for planning and conducting a professionally driven and student-directed IEP transition planning meeting

transition goals for high school students

transition goals for middle school students

transition services requirements in the IEP

QUESTIONS FOR REFLECTION, THINKING, AND SKILL BUILDING

1. What is the transition planning portion of an IEP, and how does it differ from the annual goals and objectives portion of the document?

2. For a youth with disability, which should be written first and why—the transition planning portion of an IEP or annual goals and objectives?

3. What is the format of your IEP transition planning document, and how does it compare with the format recommended in this chapter?

4. What is the quality of required transition services on current IEP documents in your school or district, and how can it be improved?

5. How does the transition planning process and IEP meeting in your school or district compare with that recommended in the text?

6. Organize an interdisciplinary team to analyze current transition planning practices, procedures, and forms. Develop an action plan specifying needed improvements and share the plan with supervisory or administrative personnel.

Appendix 9-1

Summary of Functional Performance
Transition for Junior High School Students
Suggested Objectives and Activities
for 14- and 15-Year-Olds

1. Student will write down the required electives at school that correlate with his or her field of interest.
2. Student will investigate high school elective courses in [field of interest] and report to the teacher about requirements and course content.
3. Student will enroll in an elective course in [field of interest] and successfully complete the class.
4. Student will investigate Regional Occupational Program/Regional Occupational Center (ROP/ROC) course offerings in [field of interest] and report to the teacher about requirements and course content as measured by teacher observation and records.
5. Student will obtain information on registration and register for classes at high school as measured by teacher observation and records.
6. Student will enroll in high school as measured by teacher observation and records.
7. Student will investigate and obtain information regarding available support services and accommodations available at high school pertaining to his or her disability area as measured by teacher records.
8. Student will investigate extracurricular activities at a chosen high school measured by student report.
9. Student will participate in the school peer tutoring program, tutoring individual students _____ hours per week as measured by observation and record.
10. Student will participate in one or two situational assessments on campus.

Chapter 10

Implementing Interagency Agreements for Transition

Carol A. Kochhar-Bryant

Chapter Questions

- What are interagency agreements?
- Why are interagency agreements important for transition?
- What kinds of service coordination models exist?
- What is the service coordination role?
- How is an interagency agreement established? (10 steps in development)
- How can the success of interagency agreements be measured?

INTRODUCTION

Although schools have recognized the value of formal interagency agreements to implement transition services, they are complex to establish and to sustain. For youth with special needs preparing for transition, such agreements are an essential part of the solution for fragmented and hard to access services discussed in Chapter 5. Interagency service coordination is the organizational glue that cements together a coordinated transition and postsecondary plan and system of supports for youth. During the 1990s, several factors stimulated the development of interagency collaboration to strengthen transition services for youth: (a) better definitions of interagency coordination goals and functions; (b) systematic outcome data on the effectiveness of interagency coordination in other disciplines such as social work, mental health, public health, and rehabilitation; (c) greater willingness of agencies to reduce barriers that have hindered collaboration; (d) increased state and local resources to develop interagency cooperative activities; and (e) legislation that encouraged or required interagency coordination to carry out transition planning requirements for students with disabilities.

As mentioned in chapter 5, IDEA 2004, NCLB, and related legislation require local educational agencies to provide related and supportive services to all youth with disabilities in coordination with community-based agencies (see Chapter 5). More specifically, IDEA 2004 requires interagency service agreements between schools and community agencies, either through formal interagency agreements or memoranda of understanding (MOU), informal guidelines for coordinating with service providers, or assignment of service coordinators to work with participating agencies.

This chapter describes the steps for implementing interagency agreements for transition. It addresses practical aspects including development of the interagency agreement, management of transition service coordination, and lead agency considerations.

➡ WHAT ARE INTERAGENCY AGREEMENTS?

Interagency agreements are formed among schools and community agencies to provide transition services that are required by a student's individualized education program (IEP) in a coordinated manner. Such agreements define the activities, responsibilities, and resource contributions of each agency. The focus of the agreements is to (a) reduce the barriers that exist when a student and family must seek transition services and supports from several separate and uncoordinated sources and (b) achieve a successful transition to adult life. In planning the types of services students need to prepare for transition, the IEP team considers services that are provided by community agencies external to the school, including postsecondary education or vocational-technical training, adult services, job training and rehabilitation services, independent living services, and others. In this chapter the terms *interagency agreement* and *multiagency agreement* will be used interchangeably.

Interagency collaboration for transition is strongly encouraged under IDEA 2004, but specific relationships are not yet mandatory. The voluntary nature of these interagency linkages affects how they can and should be managed. As Hageback counseled in 1992 (still relevant today),

> Cooperation doesn't really work very well when it's mandated, because it depends so heavily on the attitudes of the people involved. You can't really buy a readymade cooperative human service system, although having some flexible funds to use in supporting the special mechanisms you develop can certainly help the process along. You've got to get close if cooperation is going to work. . . . [Y]ou have to work at it and keep it central to your purposes. . . . Cooperation is a contact sport and unless you build contact among administrators and managers, school and business staff and their boards, your effort will fail (pp. 73–74).

In voluntary or *discretionary* associations, relationships among people take on great importance and must be carefully nurtured if the interagency relationship is to endure.

➡ WHY ARE INTERAGENCY AGREEMENTS IMPORTANT FOR TRANSITION?

A shared responsibility and shared approaches to addressing student educational and developmental needs—helping the whole child—bring to bear the combined thinking, planning, and resources of many professionals in the schools and community agencies upon the needs and problems of a child and family (Conzemius & O'Neill, 2001). Educators, business leaders, and postsecondary personnel recognize the economic value of ensuring successful transitions for youth. They have come to appreciate how formalized agreements to coordinate support can improve outcomes and close gaps in services for students preparing for the postsecondary world.

Interagency agreements are instrumental in helping schools improve related and supportive services for students with special needs. Resources for systematic service delivery are shared among agencies such as rehabilitation, the workforce development system, community mental health, and other. In some states, interagency agreements are being used to coordinate large system change initiatives aimed at expanding and improving transition services. For example, many states are forming partnerships among workforce development and rehabilitation agencies (authorized by WIA) and school-based transition services (authorized under IDEA). Agencies are experimenting with blended funding, formal interagency agreements or memoranda of understanding (MOU), and single points of entry. Many states have existing interagency transition teams—for example, in Minnesota, the state legislature has put in place the Minnesota

System of Interagency Coordination that is designed to encourage partnerships among groups serving youth with disabilities from birth to young adulthood (Timmons, Podmostko, Bremer, Lavin, & Wills, 2004).

Interagency Agreements and the IEP

Each student's IEP should contain a statement of interagency responsibilities or linkages required to ensure that they have the transition services they need. The IEP coordinator must invite representatives from those agencies to attend the meetings. This new requirement for interagency collaboration and shared responsibility means that (a) schools must develop a seamless system of supports to help youth with disabilities make a successful transition to postsecondary life, (b) the youth and his or her family must be engaged in transition planning well before graduation, and (c) there must be formal interagency agreements between schools and cooperating agencies. The IEP team uses the following procedures that are aligned with IDEA 2004 requirements:

1. Before contacting any outside community agency, the school discusses the range of community services with the student and his or her family to reach agreement about which agencies are most appropriate to invite to the IEP meeting. This is accomplished well before the IEP meeting is scheduled.

2. The school then obtains a consent for release of information from the parent or student (if he or she has reached *age of majority* and is his or her own legal guardian) to contact the community agency and discuss their involvement in the student's IEP meeting. IDEA 2004 outlined procedures for the transfer of parental rights to the student when he or she reaches the age of majority under state law.

3. The IEP team is required to invite pertinent agencies to the IEP meeting and to obtain their participation. These agreements should be included in the IEP document, with a signature of the agency representative.

The school should not commit an outside agency to provide or pay for any transition service without the written consent and agreement of the agency. If the IEP team is unable to obtain the community agency's participation at the actual IEP meeting, then the school solicits their agreement to participate or provide linkages before or immediately after the IEP meeting. For example, if the IEP indicates that the student needs an assessment for vocational rehabilitation services by the VR agency but that agency cannot provide such an assessment, then the local educational agency is required to reconvene the IEP team to identify alternative ways to meet the transition objectives.

➡ WHAT KINDS OF SERVICE COORDINATION MODELS EXIST?

Several models for interagency coordination are in use across the nation today to facilitate transition services. These models of service coordination differ in the types of roles that interagency coordinators play, the functions that are performed, the scope of the authority for coordination (federal, state, or local level), and the kinds of interagency agreements developed. Some create *independent or dedicated* roles, meaning that service coordination is the only role of that agency, and others are *mixed or blended* roles, embedding the service coordination role in a team process (Hart, Zimbrich, & Whelley, 2002; Research and Training Center on Service Coordination, 2001). The following models have been defined and classified based on an examination of a variety of interagency coordination models in the United States (Kochhar-Bryant, 2007, 2008).

Generalist Model

A single school-based service coordinator or transition coordinator is responsible for all of the service coordination functions at the individual student level (information and referral, identification and preparation, assessment and evaluation, individual program planning and development, service coordination and linking, service monitoring and follow-along, individual and interagency advocacy, and service evaluation and follow-up) (see Chapter 5). This model most closely resembles the traditional social casework model but is applicable in a variety of disciplines. This type of model is particularly effective in long-term support systems for students with severe disabilities who need long-term assistance through the middle and high school years and into adult life. Under this model, each student is provided a single coordinator who is their primary point of contact and with whom they can communicate regularly (Woodside & McClam, 2002). Service coordinators use a variety of skills and perform the full range of functions. They have considerable autonomy in their daily activities, maintain complete records on a student, and maintain a high level of accountability.

Interdisciplinary Team and Specialist Models

The service coordination functions are distributed among professionals who work in a team to provide coordinated planning and a variety of services. The service coordination functions are divided into specialties in which one individual, for example, conducts individual planning, another conducts assessment and evaluation, and another conducts monitoring and follow-up. This model is most frequently used with individuals with severe and multiple disabilities and those who need comprehensive support services. Teaming among coordinators provides support and enhances shared problem-solving and creativity.

Embedded-Coordination Model

In the embedded model, the coordination function is attached to or embedded into the primary role of teacher, counselor, or therapist. Individuals who need ongoing support require a professional who knows them well and who can also help them link with other related support services in the community. This model is most effective when the professional is trained in coordination functions and carries a reasonable **caseload** (i.e., the numbers of students to whom they provide services does not exceed 80–100).

Family Model

The family model has traditionally meant that the service coordination rests with the individual's family. Parents or guardians act as primary coordinators for their child. This is common among families of young children with disabilities, children in school, youth entering employment, and in cases in which a family member becomes disabled or chronically ill. Some educational systems are recognizing the important role families play in negotiating services among agencies and are providing families with information, training, and supports to enable them to become more informed advocates. The family model is very much evolving.

Volunteer Natural-Support Model

Natural-support models are built around the natural-support structures in the community. Members of the community are selected as coordinators or ombudsmen who are matched with a single student. These coordinators may provide information to students, an ongoing mentor relationship, or supportive counseling; or they may conduct outreach and follow-up. They are provided regular training and supervision through the school system, often in cooperation with a local agency such as mental health. Volunteers can greatly extend the capacity of an agency or group of agencies to perform service coordination functions. This type of model has been particularly effective in rural and remote regions.

State Level Interagency Planning Model

State interdisciplinary and interagency initiatives typically result from federal initiatives or policies but sometimes emerge independently. They involve efforts to form partnerships among one or more state agencies for purposes of

1. conducting statewide assessment of transition needs;
2. identifying funds to support local interagency service coordination;
3. providing transition advocacy for target populations;
4. assuring continuity of transition services and access to the range of services;
5. developing professional development and training for transition and interagency coordination;
6. cooperative planning and policy development for transition; and
7. reducing duplication of services.

State governments and agencies play a pivotal role in stimulating and shaping local service coordination.

Local Systems Coordination Model

Interagency coordination can have the greatest effect on individual transition outcomes at the local level. Drawing from three decades of planning in the mental health and public health disciplines, many local service systems are adapting a core services model for linking the individual with transition services. Under the core services model, the cooperating agencies define the core service coordination functions that are considered absolutely essential for linking the student with needed services that support his or her individual transition plan (Kendziora, Bruns, Osher, Pacchiona, & Mejia, 2001; Lueking & Certo, 2002; New York State Office of Mental Health, 2001; Vinson, Brannan, Baughman, Wilce, & Gawron, 2001). The agencies that will provide these services are then identified and an interagency agreement is developed.

Federal-Level Systems Model

The federal-level model involves a variety of strategies designed to link the activities of several national health, education, and human service agencies. The purpose of federal-level interagency service cooperative initiative is to create interagency policies and to provide leadership to stimulate similar efforts at the state and local levels. Federal-level interagency cooperation establishes linkages when responsibility for a particular type of service or special population is distributed among several agencies. Such national-level coordination may include interagency planning, joint goal setting, priority setting, policy development, resource sharing, research and demonstration projects, joint training projects, or cooperatively funded programs and initiatives for state-level interagency coordination. Federal interagency activities can provide powerful leadership for encouraging state and local efforts (U.S. Department of Health and Human Services, 2003; U.S. General Accounting Office, 2000).

What Conditions Affect the Choice of Service Coordination Model?

Most local educational agencies developing transition services for students with disabilities apply combinations of the state interagency planning model, the local systems coordination model, and the generalist model (Timmons, 2007). A service system's decision about what type of model or approach to use must be based on the unique conditions of the system. In choosing a service coordination model, interagency teams must explore many factors, including the following: (a) complexity of the service needs of students in transition; (b) availability of a range of services in the community; (c) fiscal health of the system; (d) local or state leadership and politics; (e) demographics and cultural concerns of the student population and families; (f) geographic features of the area (e.g., rural versus urban setting); (g) policies and legal mandates that govern the service system; (h) degree of change occurring in the service system, requiring maximum flexibility in service coordination activities; and (i) service philosophies that are being applied.

➡ WHAT IS THE SERVICE COORDINATION ROLE?

The following sections describe several service coordination roles that assist youth to successfully navigate a transition from high school to postsecondary settings.

Role of the Service Coordinator and Transition Specialist

A taxonomy or set of categories for transition services was first developed by Kohler (1998) and has been expanded and revised through a CEC review process of the Council for Exceptional Children (CEC). The taxonomy included best practices recommended by transition experts and derived from the findings of empirical studies. These best practices were clustered and rated by another group of transition professionals as to their importance. From this work, Kohler (1995) developed a taxonomy of transition planning and services that included: (a) student development, (b) student-focused planning, (c) collaboration, (d) family involvement, and (e) program structure and attributes. The category of *student development* emphasized activities that include development of self-determination skills, learning strategies, accommodations, social skills, vocational skills, and career goals. The *student-focused planning category* emphasized the importance of developing measurable postschool transition goals, relevant educational activities, vocational objectives, student participation in IEP planning, and ongoing monitoring of services.

The third category, *collaboration,* included the development of system-level interagency teams, consultation with regular and vocational educators, and coordination of student assessment. The *family involvement* category addressed the importance of promoting family participation in IEP planning, family knowledge of school and postschool options, and individualized consideration of parent roles in the transition process. Lastly, the category of *program structure and attributes* stressed the importance of developing outcome-based programs, flexible curricula, integrated learning settings, identification of student outcomes and postschool needs, and development of transition resources.

Kohler's research established the foundation for defining the service coordination and collaboration competencies needed by secondary educators. This work led the CEC Subcommittee on Knowledge and Skills and the CEC Division on Career Development and Transition (DCDT) to identify the competencies needed by individuals preparing to be transition specialists. The transition specialist was defined as "an individual who plans, coordinates, delivers, and evaluates transition education and services at the school or system level, in conjunction with other educators, families, students, and representatives of community organizations" (Council for Exceptional Children, 2000a).

In many school districts, the transition specialist is a separate role, and in other districts (particularly rural regions), the transition specialist activities are embedded into existing teaching and consultation roles. The CEC DCDT specialist competencies were organized according to the competency areas for special educators as delineated in *What Every Special Educator Must Know: International Standards for the Preparation and Licensure of Special Educators* (Council for Exceptional Children, 2002).

Secondary Transition Coordinator: Bridge to the Postsecondary World

Secondary transition specialists typically begin work with students when they reach the age at which they are eligible for services and planning (16 under IDEA 2004, with an option to begin earlier if needed). The coordinator works with the student to identify preferences and goals. He or she collaborates with general educators to recommend a course of study through high school to prepare for careers and independent living in either college or employment settings. The coordinator arranges opportunities for the student (or a group of students) to learn about different careers through videos, job shadowing, visits to work environments, and hands-on work activities that allow the student(s) to try out a job. Finally, the coordinator makes connections with the adult service system, identifies the support services or accommodations the student may need in the postsecondary setting, assists students to assemble portfolios of academic records, job experiences, resumes, and postsecondary recommendations. Transition coordinators may follow-up with the student and continue their support services for a period of time after the student has graduated. Recent research on the role of transition coordinators shows that 94% of states employ one or more transition coordinators at the state level (Jackson, 2003; Schiller et al., 2003; U.S. Department of Education, Office of Special Education, 2003).

In many local communities there is a cadre of coordinators who function at individual and interagency levels and perform activities that affect students and the service system as a whole in broad ways, including the following:

1. Increasing transition service access to target groups: improving transition services for students who would not be able to participate without special accommodations and support
2. Affecting service priorities and service distribution: providing referral and assessment of students to ensure that they are given priority; they act as gatekeepers for access to services and as the *eyes and ears* of the system to communicate student needs to administrators and decision makers
3. Enhancing communication across agencies and disciplines: using a common language for sharing information about individuals in the service system, they assess transition service needs at the interagency level and assist with communication among service agencies
4. Providing quality assurance and monitoring: integrating local, state, and federal transition laws and guidelines and helping agencies adhere to guidelines related to service quality; they monitor the delivery of interagency transition services
5. Conducting interagency problem solving: intervening in interagency conflicts or disagreements, seeking alternative services as needed, intervening in human rights issues, troubleshooting interagency conflicts and procedural barriers
6. Monitoring service costs: procuring transition-related services for individual students and, in some systems, controlling a support budget for allocation to individuals

What Are Interagency Transition Teams?

Interagency transition services means a coordinated set of activities designed to achieve specific outcomes (National Center on Secondary Education and Transition, 2002). Such services are intended to prepare individuals with disabilities to live, learn, and earn in the community as adults. An interagency transition team brings together a variety of stakeholders who are supporting youth with disabilities so they can have the best chances for success as adults.

Interagency teams at both the local and state level are often comprised of representatives of all agencies involved in preparing, connecting, and receiving youth with disabilities as they transition from secondary school to postschool environments (Stodden, Brown, Galloway, Mrazek, & Noy, 2004). Interagency teams serve a variety of purposes. They identify local needs or discontinuity in policies, procedures, services, and programs that hinder youth with disabilities from achieving desired, valued outcomes. They increase the availability, access, and quality of interagency transition services through the development and improvement of policies, procedures, systems, funding, and other mechanisms for providing seamless transition services to youth with disabilities and their families. They help other service representatives understand the educational service system including: (a) laws, regulations, and policies related to transition services; (b) roles and responsibilities of families and district personnel; (c) roles of local or regional interagency planning teams; and (d) roles now expected of other service agencies involved in the transition process. Finally, they enable youth with disabilities to live, work, and continue to learn in the community, with supports if necessary, as adults (Stodden et al., 2004).

How Is an Interagency Agreement Established?

Planning for Interagency Agreements to Improve Transition Outcomes

Two terms that are important for understanding the development of **interagency cooperative agreements** are *strategic planning* and *planned change*. The first term relates to how a group of agencies and organizations makes decisions and acts in cooperation with one another (McClamroch, Byrd, & Sowell, 2001; Smith-Davis, 1991; Southeastern Louisiana University, 2000). The second term, *planned change,* relates to the implementation and management of interagency relationships or the implementation of agreed-upon actions through strategic planning. Both processes are essential to the development of new interagency relationships and agreements.

Strategic planning has been defined as a "disciplined effort to produce fundamental decisions and actions that shape and guide what an organization (or other entity) is, what it does, and why it does it" (Bryson, 1999). Strategic planning helps people identify ways in which schools and agencies can work together to improve quality and access to services for students to support secondary education and transition. Planning for interagency collaboration for transition must be viewed as a dynamic process. The planning process must support flexibility in the service system so that it can respond to changes in direction, environments, and system and student needs and outcomes (Birnbaum, 2003; Future Education Funding Council, 2002; Internet Nonprofit Center, 2000; Martinelli, 2002). The concepts of strategic planning provide a foundation for understanding, creating, and implementing interagency agreements that are responsive to the students and their families.

The Circle of Commitment

The circle of commitment concept is closely related to the idea of strategic planning. When applied to interagency coordination, the term ***circle of commitment*** helps to define the range of resources, both human and material, that must be invested in an interdisciplinary or interagency effort to improve transition services and outcomes for individuals and their families (Kochhar-Bryant, 2008). Key stakeholders responsible for transition, along with other material and financial resources, form the partnership's circle of commitment, which includes the following six elements (see Figure 10-1):

1. The human commitment: The key stakeholders, key staff, and advisors in the interagency partnership; students and families.

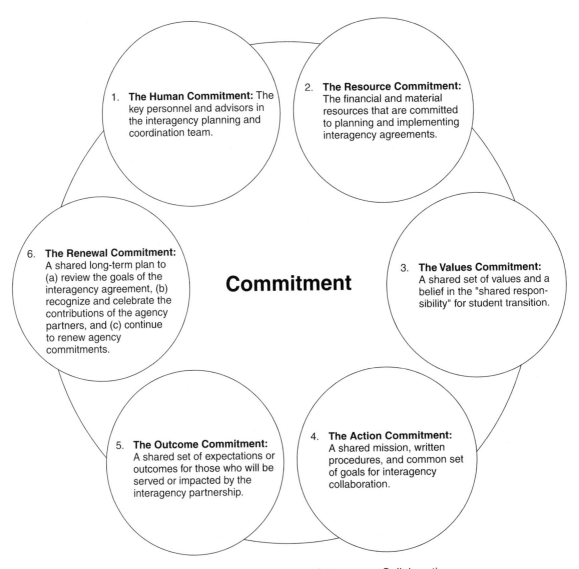

Figure 10–1   Six Elements in the Circle of Commitment to Interagency Collaboration
Source: From *Successful Inclusion: Strategies for a Shared Responsibility* (p. 174), by C. Kochhar, L. L. West, and J. Taymans, 2000, Upper Saddle River, NJ: Merrill/Prentice Hall. Reprinted with permission.

2. The resource commitment: The financial and material resources that cooperating agencies commit to the partnership for improving transition services and outcomes.

3. The values commitment: A shared set of values and a belief in the shared responsibility for the transition of youth with disabilities and their families.

4. The action commitment: A shared mission, written cooperative agreement for transition services, and a common set of goals for the interagency partnership.

5. The outcome commitment: A shared set of expectations for transition outcomes for those who will be served or affected by the interagency partnership (infants, toddlers, children, youth, and families).

6. The renewal commitment: A shared long-term plan to (a) continue to review the course of the interagency transition partnership, (b) recognize and celebrate the unique contributions that each agency and its staff make to the relationship, and (c) continue to renew those commitments.

This commitment represents the range of resources and tools that interagency coordinators need to improve transition services for students and their families. The following sections describe *10 strategic planning steps* for the development of interagency agreements to promote coordination of schools and community services for transition.

Ten Steps to Develop and Implement Interagency Agreements

The process of developing and implementing interagency agreements can be divided into the following 10 steps:

1. Engage the community
2. Conduct preplanning assessment
3. Assess interagency coordination needs
4. Identify opportunities for matched resources
5. Establish a shared mission for transition
6. Design cooperative agreements for transition
7. Define the management structure and the role of interagency transition planning teams (councils)
8. Develop an *adoption* plan: personnel development for transition
9. Develop problem-solving strategies
10. Evaluate for improvement

These steps are offered as a framework for developing local interagency agreements and action plans and are based on the practices of collaborating agencies around the nation. These steps provide a menu of options for the development of agreements and (a) can be initiated by a single school or agency, or jointly by several; (b) are relevant for service systems with very underdeveloped transition services and interagency relationships; (c) are useful for strengthening transition systems with more advanced interagency relationships; and (d) can form the basis for the design of evaluation of interagency partnerships. These steps are designed to provide a path of activities and strategies for those who are beginning the process of developing new interagency agreements and are suited to the local system and community. Each of these steps will be discussed separately.

Step 1: Engage the Community: The Spectrum of Key Stakeholders

The process of interagency collaboration begins by conducting activities that engage *key stakeholders,* or personnel within the cooperating agencies, in discussing transition services, legal requirements for cooperation, and intentions to improve the transition service delivery system. The quality and effectiveness of interagency agreements among service agencies relies on the commitment of a *spectrum of people* within those agencies to cooperate, including the following:

1. Parents and students
2. General and special educators and administrators
3. Career-vocational or technical educators
4. Related and support services personnel
5. Rehabilitation personnel
6. Adult and community-based services personnel
7. Public and private health services personnel
8. Postsecondary agency personnel
9. Employers, employment services, and private nonprofit agency personnel
10. Business-industry personnel and school-business liaisons
11. School-board members and key community decision makers
12. Probation and parole workers
13. Police
14. Advocacy agency workers and leaders
15. Recreation and leisure services providers
16. College and university personnel
17. Civic and religious group leaders
18. Local and state politicians concerned with the needs of children and youth
19. Job training program personnel
20. Social services personnel

There are several strategies for identifying stakeholders or interagency personnel who could be enlisted to initiate interagency collaboration.

Carefully Consider the Role of Students, Parents, and Parent Leaders and Enlist Them as Advisors and Planners.   Parent leaders are often the best champions for new initiatives— if they support the effort. Parent and student organizations can also serve as essential links between educational agencies and the community (Rosman, McCarthy, & Woolverton, 2001). Parent groups may include school alumni, parent association leaders, school board members who are parents of students with disabilities, PTA leaders, parents who are business leaders, parent volunteers, and advocates. The strongest champions for interagency collaboration can emerge from any sector of the community, once the value of the initiative is communicated.

Forge Partnerships with the Business Community.   In many communities, the business community is a key partner in developing transition initiatives for linking education and work environments. Table 10–1 provides examples of such business involvement.

Business leaders recognize that effective school-community programs help orient youth to work settings and expectations, and to the value of career planning.

Table 10–1 How Business Can Support Interagency Collaboration for Transition

Goals	Examples of Partnership Activities
1. Support schools' efforts to integrate academic, career-oriented, and community-based learning activities	Business employees can serve as tutors, mentors, career advisors; offer summer jobs, special courses, and after-school activities; create work-based programs for secondary youth to gain work experience; develop entrepreneurial clubs and sponsor activities in subject areas such as science fairs; help teachers and students link with community and social service agencies
2. Strengthen teachers' knowledge of industry environments.	Help teachers develop new instructional strategies to integrate academic and community-based learning, provide opportunities for teachers to learn more about the applications of a subject within an industry, provide teacher internships in business and industry, sponsor workshops, train volunteer teams, and help schools appeal for community support
3. Develop effective strategic planning models and tools.	Help schools generate, manage, and use needs assessment information for strategic planning; assist interagency teams to create effective organizations for coordination; institute an evaluation process

Planning for Interagency Collaboration for Transition.   Schools and districts use a variety of strategies for informing and engaging community agencies to provide needed services for students in transition. Effective interagency agreements, however, begin with community information activities that can help secure agency participation in the mission. Through the process of informing a wide spectrum of agencies about the interagency partnership, transition planners can begin to identify participants in the planning process. The first questions for an interagency transition team might be—Who among the stakeholders can best help define goals and make decisions? What combination of people could help address transition coordination needs? The strategic planning meeting brings people together in combinations that are likely to bring about new relationships and needed change. An interagency agreement depends on effective relationships among the representatives in the cooperating agencies who are most likely to be working together. Several questions may be helpful in deciding who to invite to strategic meetings:

1. Which agencies or service specialists are immediately needed to provide transition services for youth?
2. What agencies or individuals are the best champions for the cause to develop an interagency agreement for transition?
3. Who are the weakest links (need the most encouragement to get involved)?
4. Which agencies most need to understand each other's roles and begin working together first?
5. How can I get my state, regional, and local interagency personnel working together?

Meetings that are carefully crafted to strategically join people typically produce some very creative results and accelerate the development of interagency agreements.

Table 10-2 provides strategies for informing community agency personnel, parents, students, and community leaders about new transition initiatives for interagency services coordination.

Step 2: Conduct Preplanning Assessment: How Prepared Are Interagency Partners for Collaboration?

Assessment of the readiness or preparedness of community agencies for interagency coordination can benefit agencies developing new interagency partnerships as well as those seeking to improve existing relationships. Preplanning assessment at the interagency level helps you measure how ready the agencies are for entering into a partnership. It is important for interagency planners to know what each cooperating agency brings to the relationship in terms of resources, service missions, and service philosophies. It is also important to know something about the structure of the agencies that are collaborating, attitudes toward the interagency partnership, the extent of the knowledge of each agency about the population of individuals to be served, and the transition process.

Figure 10-2 provides a format for assessing the strengths and weaknesses of potential partner agencies in aspects of structure, attitudes, and knowledge about transition. Understanding what each agency can do to contribute in a collaborative relationship will help interagency transition planners understand how they can function together as an effective team.

Assessing Environmental Supports for Interagency Agreements for Transition. There are many aspects of the local environment that can support the development and effectiveness of interagency agreements for transition. The important questions related to the local environment are (a) are the key agencies in the community all represented in the development of the interagency coordination plan and (b) are the necessary resources available to implement the interagency plan? Figure 10-3 outlines environmental supports factors or conditions that are associated with effective interagency service coordination for transition.

If environmental supports are weak, then the system should focus its efforts on needs assessment and resource development.

Step 3: Assess Interagency Coordination Needs

The third step in the development of interagency agreements involves assessing the needs of each agency that will form the transition service network. Such needs may include resources and resource limitations, staffing, policy and procedural changes, and service delivery area considerations. The first set of goals and activities that are defined among coordinating agencies will provide only a blueprint or map for defining early relationships. As the agencies' activities expand or diminish, cooperative agreements must be revisited and modified. Ongoing needs assessments can help the system remain sensitive to changes in the needs of students and families. It is important that transition planners *show a clear relationship among the transition needs of students, the mission and goals of the interagency agreement, and the contributions of each cooperating agency.*

Table 10–2   Thirteen Strategies for Engaging the Community

1. Engage parents, student, and consumer organizations	Inform parents, student, consumer organizations such as the PTA, and parent advocacy groups about the plans for a transition interagency agreement. Distribute information and solicit input into the plans and roles of these groups in the development of the collaboration.
2. Engage educational leaders and school principals	Inform educational leaders and school principals who have primary responsibility for new transition initiatives that will affect instruction or student services. Principals and other administrators should be among the earliest to be informed of the effort and helped to see how the initiative will aid them in achieving their educational goals and objectives for students.
3. Engage personnel in community agencies	Inform staff and directors of relevant community and adult services agencies because their support is vital to a transition coordination initiative. Each cooperating (or potential) partner needs to know about an intent to collaborate and the process for forming or revising the interagency agreement.
4. Develop mission and goals statements	Develop mission and goals statements to help each potential cooperating agency understand the relationship between the transition initiative and their own individual agency mission, goals, and objectives. Each must understand how the new collaboration will help them to achieve their individual agency goals, improve outcomes for youth, improve their services and resources, or evaluate their efforts. The mutual benefits to all cooperating agencies must be defined early on.
5. Inform and engage relevant teacher unions and educational associations	Inform relevant teacher unions and educational associations about new transition initiatives that involve the teaching staff and help them understand the potential benefits of the collaboration for the students and professionals. It might also be helpful to have input from the county or district educational association.
6. Include the initiative in local education reform seminars	Include, in local education reform and accountability seminars, information about the transition initiative.
7. Conduct brainstorming meetings	Conduct special seminars or brainstorming meetings with heads of agency personnel to discuss the interagency agreement.
8. Develop informational brochures and materials	Develop informational brochures and materials that explain the mission and benefits of interagency collaboration for transition. Include information packets in the local budget documents that are distributed to educational and community agency planning boards. Develop interagency brochures to inform the community of the key partners in the initiative and to promote the interagency partnership as a distinct entity.
9. Conduct seminars with business	Include information about the initiative in local business-education seminars, or in Chamber of Commerce, Workforce Investment Council, or School-to-Work meetings.
10. Use local media newspapers	Feature articles about the transition initiative in local newsletters and newspapers.
11. Meet with community leaders	Conduct meetings with community leaders and solicit their assistance in championing the transition initiative.
12. Links with local universities	Link with local colleges or universities to develop meetings or seminars related to transition and interagency coordination.
13. Utilize annual reports	Include descriptions of interagency initiatives, accomplishments, and impacts in school improvement plans and report cards and in the annual reports of cooperating agencies.

Assessing the Organizational Structure of Cooperating Partners

1. *Understand the diversity of the agencies with which you will cooperate.* Diverse organizational structures make coordination a challenge. Each agency in the collaborative partnership (schools, businesses, community and social service agencies, postsecondary institutions, and others) has its own philosophy, service structure, procedures and regulations, service standards, and professional roles and responsibilities. This diversity enriches the process of setting shared transition goals and is also important in the evaluation of the service coordination effort.

2. *Determine what cooperative agreements and planning processes are already in place.* Many local districts have informal interagency relationships but lack formalized transition agreements to guide their activities. Formalized agreements are essential for the development of coordinated transition activities because they define the common goals and objectives and the local authority for action.

3. *Examine the policies and funding restrictions of the agencies forming the partnership.* Different agencies have evolved from separate funding streams and public laws and therefore have different eligibility requirements and different target groups or students. It is important to examine and understand these differences in developing transition agreements and cooperative activities and in defining outcomes. Also, recent changes in special education, general education, vocational–technical education, and related disability laws will affect organizational priorities and changes in the way programs are expected to operate.

4. *Examine geographic service boundaries of cooperating agencies.* Educational and human service agencies have different "service territories" or catchment areas, which may make defining a target population for a local interagency partnership difficult. These differences should be identified and discussed as partnership cooperative agreements are being crafted.

5. *Assess the existing transition data collection and reporting capability of cooperating partners.* Educational and community service agencies report their performance goals and outcomes differently from each other (e.g., referrals, services received, service goals achieved) and differently within different states and localities. Some have few reporting requirements. Each agency establishes its own reporting system, monitoring criteria, quality-assurance criteria, performance measurement criteria, and annual goals and plans for services. Agencies must examine their readiness to coordinate data collection and reporting systems for student services and transition outcomes if the partnership is to be a success.

6. *Consider the economic "health" of local educational and community service agencies because this could affect their ability to cooperate.* When funds for schools and community services are eroding, and local economies are unstable, there may be increased opportunity to advocate for the sharing of resources, which makes collaboration more attractive.

7. *Assess the level of parent involvement and family supports needed.* Because parent involvement considered one of the most important factors in the success of students transition, parent support services must be assessed. Parents can be essential players in the assessment of needs and in is the development of the partnership. Capacity for parent training, information dissemination, and opportunities for their direct involvement must be assessed early on.

Assessing Partnership Attitudes

8. *Be sensitive to political pressures and pressure groups.* In communities in which economic pressures are forcing agencies to economize, interagency planners must show how community linkages can contribute to more cost-effective services.

Figure 10–2   Assessing "Readiness" for Interagency Coordination

Source: Adapted from *Successful Inclusion: Strategies for Shared Responsibility* (pp. 204–205), by C. Kochhar, L. L. West, and J. Taymans, 2000, Upper Saddle River, NJ: Merrill/Prentice Hall. Reprinted with permission.

9. *Be sensitive to territorial attitudes.* Collaborative initiatives usually result in changes in the way everyone conducts business, and this should be made clear to all staff from the beginning of any partnership. Agency personnel, however, may think that a school system is encroaching on their "territory," and this can sometimes threaten people's comfort with traditional ways of operating and making decisions. *Attitudes and relationships are essential to the foundation of cooperative partnerships.*

10. *Consider issues in staff turnover and carefully select collaborators for continuity.* Many failures of interagency partnerships can be traced to high turnover rates among key personnel in the cooperating agencies. Established relationships, and the emergence of "champions" (energetic and enthusiastic leaders), contributes to confidence and trust among partners, and can accelerate collaborative efforts. As old links break apart through attrition, the initiative can weaken. For example, the loss of a respected champion for an interagency agreement who has fought to preserve the collaboration in a time of economic constraint can result in the loss of years of progress in interagency development.

Assessing Partnership Knowledge

11. *Work to build early understanding among agency personnel about their respective organizations and missions.* The education and community service sectors must understand each other's mission, and recognize each other's complementary strengths. This is essential to early crystallization of transition partnerships. Early seminars on interagency collaboration "readiness" are worth every hour of time, and continued interagency training can keep the momentum high.

12. *Explore and share existing models for interagency agreements.* There is a need to develop model practices for the development of interagency coordination to address the needs of individuals and families. Planning teams should explore a variety of organizational models and management practices, and discuss these ideas with cooperating agency leaders.

13. *Explore relationships with local universities to assist in the development process.* Many colleges and universities have entered relationships with local and state education agencies and community service organizations to provide resources and technical assistance for new initiatives. Universities can provide additional expertise and labor (students in training) to aid the effort. The university can offer the time and expertise of faculty and student and faculty expertise to design instructional materials, provide technical assistance, and develop funding proposals. Sometimes universities can help champion local and state partnerships in states with political or resource barriers. Frequently, the availability of grant funding for an interagency initiative can provide the stimulus for action.

What Should Be Assessed? Each agency that joins an interagency partnership for transition service coordination may have different reasons for cooperating and a different understanding of its role and responsibilities in providing transition services. How, then, can the transition planner help agencies determine a common mission to create a systematic and coordinated transition service program? What strategies are needed to form an effective working relationship that can achieve results? The first question has to do with what the collaborative relationship should focus on (principles, goals, and objectives) and the second with how (the processes). In thinking about what needs should be addressed by an interagency partnership, two propositions may be helpful:

Proposition No. 1: The primary focus for an interagency agreement for transition service coordination should be on helping agencies understand the nature of transition services and the legal authority for coordination across agencies, so that they build the necessary commitment to work together to help youth and families

1. Among cooperating agencies, there is a focus on *student or client outcomes and benefits* in the delivery and evaluation of interagency services.

2. Planning for *statewide interagency service coordination* has begun.

3. *State quality review and evaluation* of interagency agreements for transition has begun.

4. *Local quality review* of interagency agreements for transition has been planned for.

5. There already exists or there are plans to develop an information system for data collection on youth in transition from secondary education.

6. A *range of transition services* for youth with disabilities is being developed in the school system.

7. A *range of career/vocational–technical education programs* is being developed within the local education system and integrated with the academic curriculum.

8. A *range of postsecondary services and supports* are being developed in the community.

9. A *range of community living alternatives* are being developed in the community.

10. The cooperating agencies have acknowledged the *legal authority to establish interagency agreements* for transition.

11. The service system is exploring the development of a system for a *centralized interagency coordination and single point of referral* among all service sectors.

12. There is a student service coordination process with *established standards for maximum caseload* size.

13. State and local *technical assistance exists* for development of interagency agreements for transition.

Figure 10–3   Considering Environmental Support for Interagency Partnerships for Transition

prepare for and achieve a successful transition to postsecondary settings and adult living.

Proposition No. 2: The interagency partnership should focus on how it can better improve the coordination and linking of services to youth and families so they can achieve transition goals.

Assessment activities at the *transition system level* involve

1. defining the range of local services available to identify a foundation for a service coordination initiative;
2. identifying service gaps and service needs that are currently not being met within the system;
3. determining the level of readiness (structure, attitudes, and knowledge) of cooperating agencies to establish formal interagency agreements;
4. determining the expertise and resources that each organization brings to the partnership; and
5. assessing the needs of the cooperating partners to address a common goal.

A thorough needs assessment can help provide important information for determining how prepared each agency is to perform the eight core service coordination functions (see Chapter 5).

The criteria for interagency needs assessment are presented as a guide rather than as a prescription and should be adapted as the needs of educational and community agencies change over time. Cooperative agreements must be revisited and modified, and ongoing needs assessments can help the system remain sensitive to these needs for change.

Step 4: Identify Opportunities for Matched Resources

Once the interagency planning team has completed a needs assessment, the next logical questions are—How does the team find the resources to start the action? What should be asked from partner organizations? Should financial resources be requested, or should a different kind of investment be expected? IDEA 2004 permits the consolidation of a student's IEP with an individualized service plan under another federal program (Figure 10-4). Planning sessions among potential cooperating agencies and disciplines can also help stimulate creative thinking about resource sharing and matching. Table 10-3 reviews a variety of environmental resources or supports for interagency partnerships for transition.

It is rare that an interagency partnership begins with the sharing of resources in each of these areas. Often, new resources continue to be identified long after the cooperative relationship begins. Often, they emerge as a result of a needs assessment or evaluation of interagency activities.

Step 5: Establish a Joint Vision and Shared Mission for Transition

Once needs have been assessed and potential resources identified, the action phase of the collaboration process can begin—that of establishing the *shared mission.* This step involves discussing a joint vision for transition service improvement and hammering out broad goals and strategies for achieving that shared vision. The goal of this step is to develop a written *mission statement* for the cooperative relationship and a signed formal *interagency agreement* that embodies the principles of shared responsibility and community participation in transition development.

As the interagency planning team discusses the *common mission,* it is important to view the agreement as *much* more than a linkage, rather it is a *shared strategy for*

It is possible to develop a single consolidated individual service plan only if

1. it contains all of the information required in an IEP;
2. all of the necessary parties participate in its development.

Examples of individualized service plans that might be consolidated with the IEP include the following:

1. The individualized care plan under Title XI of the Social Security Act (Medicaid)
2. The Individualized Program Plan under title XX of the Social Security Act (Social Services)
3. The Individualized Service Plan under Title XVI of the Social Security Act (Supplemental Security Income)
4. The Individualized Employment Plan (former Individualized Written Rehabilitation Plan) under the Rehabilitation Act of 1973 (National Information Center for Children and Youth with Disabilities, 1997)

Figure 10–4 Coordinated Service Plans

Table 10–3   Potential Resources in the Service System

Educational agencies	Education budgets may provide seed funds for interagency planning activities.
	Educators, especially principals, special and general education teachers, guidance counselors, resource teachers, and others can aid in the planning and preparation for interagency services coordination.
	Education buildings and equipment may be used for special seminars and inservice training to inform community groups.
	Educational newsletters and brochures may include information about interagency service coordination initiatives.
Vocational rehabilitation agencies	Vocational rehabilitation (VR) agencies can establish in-school assessment, counseling, and information referral activities.
	VR can assist in planning for postschool VR services.
	VR can collaborate with education agencies to obtain local or state funds for special projects.
Postsecondary institutions	Vocational-technical institutions can collaborate in student vocational assessment.
	Community colleges can collaborate and pool funds for support services.
	Community colleges can work with local education agencies to provide summer skills academies to prepare students for transition to 2- and 4-year colleges.
Parent and advocacy organizations	PTAs may approve budget expenditures for local activities.
	Advocacy organizations can allocate grant funds to schools for interagency service coordination.
	Parent and advocacy organizations can provide assistance with community information campaigns.
	Parent volunteers can donate time to coordinate local seminars and community information exhibits.
State education agencies	Funds for statewide planning may be available to local districts to initiate interagency services coordination.
	State improvement funds or state personnel development funds can be used to support new inservice training.
	State funds may be used to initiate state-level interagency linkages.
Universities	University faculty and graduate students may provide expertise for technical assistance and inservice training.
	Faculty can develop planning resources and instructional materials.
	Faculty have expertise in planning, needs assessment, and evaluation.
Business and industry	Businesses or industries can contribute to the costs of printing community information materials.
	Businesses or industries can provide offices for meetings and seminars.
	Local media can help distribute information about interagency service coordination to the business and employer community.
	Business or industry leaders may donate their time to meet with educational leaders to discuss coordination.

effecting transition outcomes for youth in the community. The shared strategy can address both local and statewide transition implementation.

1. A *local change strategy* or intervention is designed to improve the availability of and access to transition services and to solve specific coordination problems among agencies that are identified in the local interagency needs assessment.

2. A *statewide systems change strategy* is designed to help all local education agencies build the capacity to develop transition services and agreements.

The mission statement should describe the transition issues or barriers that need to be addressed by the cooperating agencies and can be stated as opportunities for change. For example, interagency coordination activities aimed at improving transition outcomes for youth can help with some of the following challenges:

Local-Level Challenges

1. Problems with coordination between the school and vocational rehabilitation services in the final years before a student is due to graduate
2. Problems in transition adjustment from middle to high school programs and vocational-technical services
3. Problems with aligning transition activities with the general secondary education curriculum
4. Lack of career-vocational program options
5. Increased dropout rates and referrals to alternative educational programs

State-Level Challenges

1. Coordination of state special education, health and human services, vocational rehabilitation, adult services, and other relevant state agencies
2. Development of adequately trained personnel to implement and provide leadership for interagency coordination
3. Incorporation of transition outcomes into state improvement and accountability initiatives
4. Improving the coordination among educators, postsecondary personnel, private sector personnel, job-training personnel, parents, and advocates

Components of the Interagency Mission Statement.   Each community defines its interagency mission differently, so no two mission statements will look alike. A few fundamental elements, however, should be included in mission statements. The statement should describe the broad purpose of the transition interagency agreement and the areas of joint responsibility. The statement generally describes what each cooperating partner will contribute toward the goal of transition service delivery and improvement and may describe what the partnership is not designed to do. A mission statement generally includes several of the following four parts:

1. *A statement of context or history:* This is usually a brief introductory paragraph that broadly describes the interagency partnership; how it was initiated; how it addresses current transition needs; how it improves on current transition practices; and how the partnership may differ from, or expand, what has been in place before.
2. *A statement of the authority for the interagency agreement:* This is an introductory section in the mission statement that refers to the legal basis for the agreement and may list the local, state, and federal laws, statutes, regulations, or policies that give authority to this agreement.

3. General statement of purpose of the agreement and expected outcomes: This includes a broad statement of what the partnership expects to accomplish and what results it hopes to see for youth in transition.

4. The broad goal and outline of roles and responsibilities: Describes what the agreement provides and the roles and responsibilities of each cooperating partner.

Figure 10–5 provides an example of a local mission statement, a composite of many mission statements used in public schools (Kochhar & Erickson, 1993; Kochhar-Bryant, 2008).

A *mission statement* is a broad description of the vision of the interagency partnership and it is not a specific set of goals and objectives. Mission statements generally serve as a preamble to a **cooperative agreement** that defines specific goals, objectives, and actions for the partnership. The next step discusses how to develop the cooperative agreement and annual action plan.

Step 6: Design Cooperative Agreements for Transition

Once the mission statement is completed, the next step is to negotiate among collaborating agencies the *specific agreements for action* to achieve the mission. *The cooperative*

Context/history. Florence County Public Schools and the community it serves have recognized the need to expand upon and improve transition services for its youth. Therefore, in 1988, Florence County Public Schools established the transition Readiness Partnership, a countywide school-to-work skills development and employment training program with Pacific National Bank and Trust. This agreement establishes a partnership among the Florence County Public Schools, the Human Resource and Development Department of Pacific National Bank and Trust, and the Florence County Department of Social Services.

Purpose. The purpose of the partnership is to provide transition services and on-the-job skills development and employment experience at Pacific National Bank and Trust for Florence County high school juniors and seniors. Students will attend training sessions during the school day and receive school credit for course work and training. The purpose of this cooperative agreement is also to encourage and provide for the cooperation, collaboration, and integration of Florence County faculty and staff in the planning and implementation of Pacific National Bank and Trust's work training and transition program.

Authority. This agreement is in accordance with the School Board of Florence County's mandate to expand and improve upon existing vocational and career preparation programs and transition services for the youth of Florence County. The agreement is consistent with State Regulation 64-5678, which offers incentives to businesses to develop partnerships with educational and human service agencies, and with the Individuals with Disabilities Education Act of 1997.

Broad goal, roles, and responsibilities. To accomplish this mission each partner agrees to participate in the development of appropriate curriculum materials to assist in the needed career orientation and skills preparation for participating youth. While students are in training, Pacific National Bank and Trust will provide summer and part-time after-school employment. Upon completion of training and graduation from high school, Pacific National Bank and Trust will give priority hiring to Florence County High School graduates and will continue to coordinate with the Department of Social Services.

Figure 10–5   Partnership Mission Statement: Florence County Public Schools Partnership

agreement incorporates the mission statement and provides more detail about the commitments of the agencies involved. How does the team develop such a cooperative agreement to meet specific annual goals? How can goal statements be crafted in such a way that the team can measure the results of the interagency coordination activities? How does the team develop a timetable for action? This section discusses the development of a cooperative agreement and goals for coordinating and improving services.

Designing the Cooperative Agreement.   The *cooperative agreement* is essential to the development of effective interagency coordination. It defines the structure, processes, and local authority for action among the collaborating agencies. It also defines what can be expected from each agency—their activities, responsibilities, and contributions to the transition service delivery system. Cooperative agreements accomplish four things; they (a) identify resources to support the interagency relationship; (b) identify goals, objectives, and activities of cooperating agencies; (c) identify expected results of the interagency partnership; and (d) establish timetables for the activities.

1. *Resources:* Cooperative agreements outline the particular contribution from each cooperating agency and may include staff, funds, equipment, consultation time, vehicles, space, and other resources. Plans to transfer, redistribute, or match these resources are also defined.

2. *Goals, objectives, and actions:* Describes the goals, objectives, and actions to be performed by each of the cooperating agencies. The agreements should also describe the role and authority of the members of the interagency planning team.

3. *Expected results (outcomes):* Defines the expected results for students and families involved in transition services and for the cooperating agencies. Methods to evaluate results should be described along with the roles of cooperating agencies, students, and families in the evaluation process. The agreement should also clearly describe the interagency planning team's authority for evaluating and monitoring the coordination activities (more details on evaluation are provided in Step 10: Evaluating for Improvement).

4. *Timetable:* Includes the date the interagency relationship takes effect, the schedule for accomplishing objectives, and the dates for reviewing and modifying the agreement.

Though cooperative agreements look different in each service system, there is a basic blueprint for crafting an agreement to accomplish a set of goals within a specific time period.

Developing Goals and Objectives for the Agreement.   Two definitions are useful in developing goals and objectives for an interagency relationship.

1. An *interagency goal* is a broad statement about what two or more cooperating agencies intend to achieve.
2. An *interagency objective* is a specific statement of intent to carry out an activity to reach a goal and is stated in explicit, measurable, and time-limited terms. The objectives also form the basis for developing the intended outcomes of the interagency relationship (Fowler, Donegan, Lueke, Hadden, & Phillips, 2000; Mager, 1975; Milano & Ullius, 1998; Zemke, 1999).

The following compares objectives written in measurable and nonmeasurable terms.

1. Example objective written in *measurable* terms: By September 15, 2003, Vera County Public Schools will identify and enroll 20 high school juniors and 30 high school seniors in the Transition Work Readiness and Training Partnership at Pacific National Bank and Trust.

2. Example objective written in *measurable* terms: By January 30, 2004, Canyon Valley High School will identify all youths older than 14 who are in need of transition plans and will assign a transition coordinator to work with teachers to develop these plans for each student.

3. Example objective written in *nonmeasurable* terms: The Vera County Public Schools, in partnership with Pacific National Bank and Trust, will work to help Vera County High School graduates enter the field of banking and commerce.

4. Example objective written in *nonmeasurable* terms: Canyon Valley Health Department will seek to assess youth's transition needs using transition coordinators.

The first two objectives are preferable because they are specific and measurable. The first objective, for example, is time-limited (students will be enrolled by September 15), measurable, and quantifiable (20 juniors and 30 seniors), and the goal is clear (students will be enrolled in the Transition Work Readiness and Training Partnership at Pacific National Bank and Trust). The third and fourth statements (written in nonmeasurable terms) are written more as a broad goal that needs more specific, measurable objectives. The phrase *help graduates enter the field of banking* is vague and gives little information about the specific actions the partnership intends to take to accomplish this goal. Exactly how will it help graduates enter banking jobs? What does *enter the field of banking* mean? Does it mean taking nonskilled jobs as filing clerks with the banks? Or does it mean entering bank management training programs? How will the goal be measured?

If the interagency team defines its goals and objectives early in the development of the relationship, it is much easier to evaluate what is accomplished. It is also easier to determine whether students are benefiting from the coordinated transition services and if the quality of and access to services is being improved. Figure 10-6 provides an example blueprint for a cooperative agreement, which begins with or incorporates the framework of the mission statement. This blueprint reflects elements of many actual agreements used in the field today.

Comprehensive agreements are not token agreements but are "living," active, working documents that guide and direct a system of well-coordinated activities. Figure 10-7 provides a description of an urban school district in Ohio that faced its problems with coordination of services for transition.

Milestone Schedules for Comprehensive Interagency Agreements: An Example.

The cooperative agreement should include the following:

1. The dates the interagency relationship and the agreement take effect
2. The dates by which the collaborating agencies will accomplish annual objectives
3. The dates for review and modification of the agreement

Mission Statement

The mission statement describes the broad purpose of the interagency relationship and the areas of joint responsibility. The statement generally describes the transition service needs being addressed by the collaborating agencies and what each will do.

Parties

The cooperating partners are identified in full name (e.g., adult and community service organizations; state, local, or federal government agencies; businesses; educational agencies; health agencies; organized labor; employment services; and others).

Terms

The length of time the agreement will remain in effect before it is reviewed. Usually, agreements are reviewed annually by the cooperating agencies.

Purpose

This section describes the broad purpose of the agreements and broad areas of joint responsibility.

Commitments, Objectives, and Actions

Describes the specific commitments and actions to which the cooperating agencies agree. Examples include the following:

1. Resources which have been pledged for interagency service coordination by each cooperating agency
2. An annual calendar describing activities required by the agreement and schedule for annual review and modification
3. Ongoing interagency training and sharing of information, including interagency service coordinators, teachers, support personnel, counselors, administrators, instructors and supervisors, and others as appropriate
4. Annual goals and objectives for each cooperating agency
5. Joint review and evaluation (quarterly, biannually, or annually) of the service coordination efforts and goals
6. Data sharing among cooperating agencies, which might include resources shared among agencies, service assessments of student needs, service dropout rates, services provided to families, projections of individuals entering transition activities or programs, and other relevant information that helps cooperating agencies address the needs of joint clients
7. Meetings to determine which individuals or families are eligible for interagency services as appropriate
8. Interagency coordination evaluation meetings to determine how effective the partnership is for students and families and to solve problems related to collaboration

Partnership Evaluation

This section defines the criteria by which the interagency coordination activities will be evaluated, the expected benefits and outcomes for the students and the community.

Assurances for Participants

This section describes how collaborating agencies will comply with local, state, and federal laws to assure nondiscrimination in the provision of services on the basis of race, religion, national origin, sex, or disability.

(Continued)

Figure 10–6   Blueprint for a Cooperative Agreement for Service Coordination

---

Confidentiality

This section describes how collaborating agencies will assure confidentiality of individual records and information. It also describes procedures for getting written consents (if needed) from individuals served and parents/guardians, providing access to individual records, and sharing of information about individuals served. It may include mediation and procedures for settling conflicts over confidentiality or the services of the agencies.

Administrative Responsibility

This section identifies the interagency coordinator(s) and persons with responsibility and final authority within the collaborating agencies.

Terminating the Partnership

This section describes the procedures for ending the relationship among agencies and other related organizations. For example, an agency desiring to quit the partnership may have to give at least 60 days notice to other agencies of its intent to terminate.

Authorizing Signatures

Signatures of the responsible persons within each agency are entered with dates of signature.

Attachment to the Cooperative Agreement

Joint tools or forms may be attached to the agreement, such as referral forms, interagency coordination activities calendar, release and confidentiality forms, and evaluation forms.

Figure 10–6   (*Continued*)

A well-defined schedule of activities (Table 10–4) is important because it will help collaborating agencies ensure that milestones are met and that enough time is allowed for review of the agreement.

Step 7: Define the Management Structure and Role of Interagency Advisory Teams (Councils)

Often interagency collaboration begins with a few shared activities between agencies but as the relationship begins to grow, interagency coordinators may need to change the way they manage the coordination activities, communicate the mission of the interagency relationship, and measure the benefits or effects on students and families. This step offers case examples of how interagency relationships can be organized to manage the variety of service coordination activities.

Making Management Decisions.   In many communities throughout the United States, interagency linkages for transition service coordination are still largely informal and voluntary collaborations, and administrators are reluctant to impose federal regulations and procedures on these often fragile relationships. State annual reports indicate high needs for coordinated systems of services (Crane, Gramlich, & Peterson, 2004; Illinois State Board of Education, 2003; New Mexico Developmental Disabilities Planning Council, 2001). Instead, many choose approaches that encourage new collaboration

The Problem

In Hamilton County, Ohio, the transition of adolescents with special health care needs and/or disabilities to the adult world is not well coordinated. This is an urban county that contains the city of Cincinnati. Although many of the adolescents are involved in multiple public service systems, they do not have a comprehensive plan for transition that takes into consideration all their needs. The Cincinnati schools are facing typical urban problems of lack of funding and a high student dropout rate. They are attempting to comply with the requirements of IDEA, but need further guidance in planning and implementation. Many adolescents leave school prematurely, further cutting themselves off from supportive services. There is evidence that youth who lack a parental advocate for their transition have very limited success.

Project

Four strategies are used to develop transition services at the system level and at the level of individual students and their families: (a) development and presentation of a comprehensive life-skills curriculum for transition for professionals, families, and youth; (b) development of information and referral systems and products for transition resources; (c) transition coordination for youth with long-term conditions in Hamilton County and Cincinnati who are at high risk of dropout and unemployment; (d) support and facilitation of a transition network (roundtable) in Southwest Ohio of a wide range of stockholders; and (e) facilitation of interagency cooperation at the state level to improve the system of transition services.

Experience in FY 2000

Twenty-three training sessions were delivered to youth with special health needs in their school environment, with six sessions of a Teen Discussion group held at the program's offices. Seventy-seven parents participated in training activities. There were 14 training sessions for professionals working in the field, jointly produced by 10 agencies. New training segments were developed and already established segments refined on the basis of input from trainees. The information and referral services distributed 7,300 copies of six different transition information brochures. Transition coordination services were provided to 107 new students. Of these, 68 participated in a health care screening, 39 received transition services, and 26 received intensive transition coordination. Community planning and coordination services conducted by Career Connections included continued leadership of the Southwest Ohio Transition Roundtable, including participation with the County Board of Mental Retardation/Developmental Disabilities in developing a strategic plan. In collaboration with Cincinnati Public Schools, local rehabilitation agencies, the Bureau of Vocational Rehabilitation and County MR/DD Board a new program for orthopedically and multiply handicapped students was developed and delivered. The program participated with the Parent Information Center and the local Legal Aid Society in the redesign effort of Cincinnati public high schools to better retain special education students and accommodate their transition needs.

Figure 10–7   Hamilton County Transition-to-Work Project
Source: From *Healthy and Ready to Work; Career Connections for Students,* by Lighthouse Youth Services, Inc. 2001, Cincinnati, OH: Author Inc. Reprinted with permission.

through technical assistance, training, and sharing of models. How the interagency linkage is managed will depend on the number of agencies involved, which agency has the lead, and in which agency the center for coordination of the partnership is located.

There are often few rules governing interagency linkages, particularly in rural communities. Linkages tend to be loosely managed with a great deal of local flexibility and discretion over the types of relationships among service agencies. Local educational agencies have been the primary initiators for coordinating and managing activities of the interagency partnership. Large suburban and urban communities tend to have

Table 10–4   Example Timetable for Implementing a Cooperative Agreement

Time Period (flexible)	Activities
Six months to one year before developing the interagency agreement	Contact potential collaborating agencies and explore mutual needs, understanding, and capacity to participate in an interagency partnership for transition services. Conduct student and agency needs assessments.
One to three months before formal interagency commitment	Obtain informal agreements from committed agencies. On the basis of identified needs, determine human, financial, and material resources that each agency is willing to commit for transition coordination. Set a date to develop your cooperative agreement. Several weeks before the initiation of the formal interagency partnership, begin a media or public relations campaign to help initiate the interagency coordination initiative.
Immediate period after the agreement takes effect	Formalize the interagency partnership in a cooperative agreement document. The cooperative agreement should include all applicable components listed previously (goals, objectives, resources, activities, and expected results). Designate an interagency liaison or coordinator.
Summer or early fall of the current school year	Initiate the service coordination activities. Throughout fall, winter, and spring monitor the service coordination activities. Conduct periodic meetings with collaborating agencies. Through observations, and verbal and written communication, assess the ongoing effectiveness of the service coordination activities. Make adjustments in the activities as needed. Compile and share data collected from your informal monitoring. Set a date to initiate your evaluation process.
During the final month of the school year	During the last month of the school year, initiate formal measures to determine whether your interagency objectives have been met. Interview participants and disseminate surveys developed to assess the perceptions of effectiveness of coordination activities by students, families, and cooperating agencies.
At the close of the school year	At the close of the school year, analyze outcomes and determine whether objectives of the cooperative agreement have been met. Celebrate the success of the interagency partnership by conducting appreciation activities for cooperating agencies and personnel. Conduct a year-end meeting with the collaborating agencies to review and modify the agreement if needed.

central offices for coordinating interagency activities and are more likely to have extensive guidelines that agencies are encouraged to follow. In communities in which the service agencies are located close together, agencies are more likely to develop stronger linkages. They are more likely to focus greater resources on meeting priority transition service needs and often show the most significant positive effects on students in the system (Baer, Simmons, & Flexer, 1997; Crane, Gramlich, & Peterson, 2004; Johnson & Guy, 1997; Wagner & Gomby, 2000).

Because IDEA requires school systems to develop interagency partnerships for transition, the center for primary coordination of services typically lies with the school. The coordination, however, may be shared among agencies, through a transition council (discussed in the next section). There is no one way for managing or coordinating services among multiple agencies. There, however, are a few important considerations. Management models can be classified into three types, depicted in Figures 10-8, 10-9, and 10-10: (a) simple coordination, (b) joint coordination, and (c) centralized coordination.

Research on interagency coordination has found that coordination is more effective when the **lead agency,** typically the school, understands the different staffing constraints of the collaborating agencies and is sensitive to the individual economic circumstances that may be affecting each agency.

Lead Agency Considerations.   When Public Law 94-142 was passed in 1975, each child with a disability became entitled to a free and appropriate public education with services appropriate to his or her individual needs. Because special education is an entitlement program, special education units or departments in schools or at the district level have taken the lead to initiate interagency service coordination for youth and families in transition. IDEA 2004 requires schools to develop interagency partnerships to ensure that services that are required in students' IEPs are actually provided by nonschool agencies. Figure 10-11 provides a summary of issues the interagency planning team should consider when identifying the appropriate management structure and responsibilities of the lead agency.

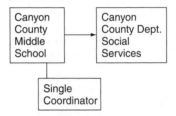

A lead coordinator from the middle school coordinates services with the social services department. A single agency agreement is in place.

Figure 10–8   Simple Coordination Model

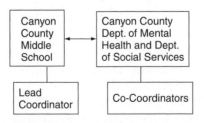

A coordination team includes a lead coordinator from the middle school and co-coordinators from mental health and social services who collaborate to identify service needs for students.

Figure 10–9   Joint Coordination Model

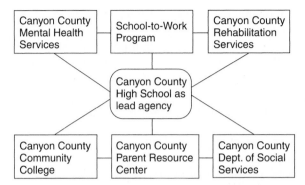

The school serves as the lead agency and center for administering multiagency coordination. A formal interagency agreement is established with roles defined for each of the agencies, and services specified. This model is common in urbanized communities with highly developed adult and community service agencies.

Figure 10–10   Centralized Coordination Model

1. Leadership for interagency coordination is best anchored within the educational agency, which has a clear state and federal mandate for transition service provision.

2. Interagency coordination is best led by the agency that administers a broad range of programs and services for a broad range of disabilities.

3. Interagency coordination is best led by the agency with highly developed local and state reporting mechanisms and data-based management capabilities.

4. Interagency coordination is best led by the agency with commitment to and strong evaluation capability for defining and measuring transition outcomes that are student-centered.

5. Interagency coordination functions should have high priority within the lead organization and allow transition coordinators proper authority to influence service provider agencies for system improvement.

6. Interagency coordination must be flexible and responsive to local school population needs and should develop and define transition outcomes that are locally relevant.

Figure 10–11   Rationale for Schools as Lead Agencies for Service Coordination

The lead agency role is crucial to the initiation, improvement, and renewal of interagency relationships. Strong state and local encouragement and support, through personnel training and technical assistance, can be quite powerful in assisting schools as lead agencies and in stimulating effective service coordination (Baer, Simmons, & Flexer, 1997; Guy & Schriner, 1997; Kochhar-Bryant, 2008).

What Is the Purpose and Role of an Interagency Transition Planning Team (Council)?   A central theme in this chapter is the importance of engaging the wider community in the interagency coordination process. There are many ways that interagency planners can organize to manage community representation in the partnership to improve transition. One strategy is to develop a **transition planning team or council** that implements the cooperative agreement and establishes a community transition advisory council representing the broader community. In each local service system, these teams have a different composition and serve different functions, depending on the type of linkages and agencies in the system.

An interagency transition planning team or council is one mechanism to increase the availability, access, and quality of transition services through the development and improvement of policies, procedures, systems, funding, and other mechanisms for providing services to youth with disabilities and their families. The community team or council may be purely advisory or have decision-making authority. As a decision-making body, the team or council may decide on the direction and operation of the interagency partnership, its goals and objectives, its management and staff, the use of resources, distribution of resources, and target populations (Washington Department of Education, 2000). The goals of the team or council typically include the following:

1. Coordinate services to ensure nonduplication and cost-effectiveness, including combining resources to maximize funding.
2. Share responsibility for helping students through the maze of services.
3. Provide a quality, local service delivery system that includes providing more effective transition services to students and families.
4. Review aggregate data to determine current and future needs for services and develop plans for providing services.
5. Increase positive student outcomes in adult living, learning, and working roles.
6. Develop a pool of adult services agency representatives who can attend IEP transition planning meetings and act as resources for the variety of service options available from different systems to aid in the transition process.
7. Identify local transition needs and develop local solutions, including identifying and addressing conflicts and gaps in services and service delivery patterns.
8. Share information about eligibility requirements for services and establish a local referral-eligibility process for students.
9. Provide information about, and advocate for, local options for living arrangements, transportation, employment, leisure activities, case management, and financial resources.
10. Become informed about the IEP and individualized written rehabilitation plan processes.
11. Develop service directories to clarify and describe organizational structures, including goals, objectives, and agency responsibilities; referral process; confidentiality process for exchanging individual student information; services and programs provided; due process and appeal; program evaluation; eligibility; methods of assessment; staff profile; experience, professional training, and functions; and community access (California Department of Education, 2004).

Organizing *community transition teams or councils* through a district, group of districts, or an educational service district is an effective way to share responsibilities, plan effectively for citizens leaving school, and promote awareness of transition issues, particularly for youth with disabilities.

Guidelines for Developing the Local Advisory Council Team.   The local advisory team or council should include a relatively small group of concerned, knowledgeable, and committed individuals. A small group is often more effective in directing interagency coordination than a large assembly. Members of the council can include representatives from special education, career-technical and regular education, community college, postsecondary education and career-technical training institutions, adults with disabilities (particularly those who have received transition services), parents of youth with disabilities, local businesses or industries, rehabilitation services, county human services, adult services providers, and additional public and private service providers as appropriate (Washington Department of Education, 2000). The following provides a few guidelines that may be useful in establishing a local transition advisory council. The team or council should

1. be balanced, including representatives from the cooperating agencies, individuals with disabilities, and parent representatives. The council should designate a chairperson who can also serve as the lead interagency coordinator or liaison;
2. formalize long-range plans (2- to 5-year) to ensure that the program is sustained;
3. participate in assessing the transition needs of students in the local system;
4. be responsive to local transition needs and define short-term and long-term transition goals and outcomes that are locally relevant;
5. be committed to evaluation of the interagency agreement to determine the benefits and effects on youth and families;
6. have the authority to shape the direction of the interagency partnership and its structure; they must be able to suggest program changes and review goals and objectives set by the partnership; and
7. establish a timetable for transition development activities.

To ensure the ongoing interest of members, it is helpful for the council to elect a chairperson, meet regularly, and develop goals and objectives that direct activities.

Step 8: Develop an Adoption Plan: Personnel Development for Transition

When people sense they are entering a new era of change and that old traditional ways of doing things are being abandoned, some may resist or become negative about the future of their roles. The interagency planner or leader needs special knowledge to help champion systemic change. How can interagency coordinators foster a sense of investment or ownership in an interagency partnership? How should agency personnel be oriented to the changes that the new collaboration may bring? What kinds of training will be needed? How can the agencies celebrate their successes and honor those who have made important contributions to the effort?

The Adoption Plan and Interagency Personnel.   Systemic change usually means that people will be traveling on new and unfamiliar paths in their work. These new paths will require different methods, relationships, procedures, norms, values, and attitudes from all who are involved in the process. No new transition initiative will be successfully adopted or fully accepted and implemented by agency personnel, unless the representatives are adequately trained in their field, understand the purposes of the collaboration initiative, and are prepared for systemic change. New training and development activities are needed to help key personnel adopt, sustain, and evaluate the effectiveness of new practices. Change cannot occur without the efforts of change agents who have new knowledge and can guide the needed changes. Chapter 14 includes a detailed plan for the preparation of interagency personnel working to improve transition.

Step 9: Develop Team Problem-Solving Strategies

Educators and human service professionals take pride in their professional status and independence. Such independence can sometimes create barriers to interagency cooperation. This section presents some of the common problems and barriers to building interagency relationships for transition and strategies to overcome them.

Common Barriers to Interagency Relationships.   Barriers to service coordination can be clustered into three categories: organizational, attitudinal, and knowledge.

1. Organizational barriers: Barriers related to the differences in the way interagency relationships are structured and managed, how they define their mission, how they operate and develop policies, and how they provide services. Personnel may fear that funds will not be available for the cooperative arrangement or that there will be competition for resources.
2. Attitudinal barriers: Barriers related to the beliefs, motivations, and attitudes that different agencies have about students and families, their roles in the transition service system, the role of families, and community participation. Personnel may fear control and scrutiny by other agencies that their jobs may be threatened or that quality of services might be compromised.
3. Knowledge barriers: Barriers related to the differences in the knowledge and skills of various agency personnel. Personnel may lack awareness and understanding of other organizations, be unable to imaging possibilities for cooperation, or may lack strategic planning skills.

The cornerstones of a cooperative interagency relationship are the personal relationships of the individuals involved. The most powerful of these relationships occurs among those closest to the students and families. Often, both the successes and difficulties with the cooperative process can be traced to problems in professional and personal relationships. Interagency coordination initiatives can be much more effective if agency personnel are alert to these barriers to cooperation. Diverse agency structures make transition coordination a challenge. Table 10–5 describes the many barriers (organizational, attitudinal, and knowledge) to interagency coordination and helpful strategies to overcome them. Most researchers studying interagency collaboration agree that *trust and active interpersonal relationships are the foundations for the success of cooperative efforts.*

Step 10: Evaluate for Transition Service Improvement

The final step in the development of an interagency agreement is evaluation—the measurement of effectiveness. The following section discusses factors that contribute

Table 10–5 System Level Barriers to Interagency Coordination

Organizational Barriers

Lack of transition cooperative agreements to empower interagency partnerships: Many interagency collaboration efforts lack formalized interagency agreements or have weak interagency agreements. These agreements are crucial to the development of interagency functions because they define the local authority for action and define common goals and objectives for the total program.

Problem-solving strategy: Carefully examine the cooperative agreement that exists in order to determine the interagency partners, the resources available, and the explicit goals of the transition initiative. Revise the cooperative agreement to make it more flexible and to allow for situational responsiveness. Model the cooperative agreement after those from experienced interagency programs.

Policy and categorical funding barriers: Different agencies have evolved from separate funding streams and public laws. Therefore, they have different eligibility requirements and different target groups. Coordinating funds among these agencies presents a challenge for transition program development and accountability for outcomes.

Problem-solving strategy: Incorporate interagency coordination activities into various aspects of coordination, including general education, career-vocational education, job training, and rehabilitation service plans. Discuss strategies for matching funds across agencies.

Legislative shifts and agency priorities: Changes in legislation and agency priorities mean changes in the way transition services are organized and delivered. Changes that affect a single agency's services within the interagency partnership will affect all cooperating partners.

Problem-solving strategy: Interagency coordinators should help personnel to be aware of public laws and local policies that affect the key agencies involved in the interagency transition partnership. Build this information into orientation and training of personnel.

Lack of incentives for coordination: Each cooperative agency may be evaluated according to different performance criteria. If coordination activities are not part of the evaluation reward system, then not much attention will be devoted to it by the individual partners and, over time, the collaboration might collapse.

Problem-solving strategy: Build interagency coordination efforts into the reward systems for each cooperating agency. Be cognizant of the kinds of incentives and disincentives that either encourage or discourage commitment to the interagency partnership. Design special recognition activities for staff of cooperating agencies to show appreciation for their contributions.

Data collection and reporting are inadequate: Cooperating agencies may each report their performance differently because their missions vary; however, some do not report at all. Therefore, each agency establishes its own reporting system, monitoring criteria, quality assurance criteria, performance measurement criteria, and annual goals and plans for services.

Problem-solving strategy: Coordinate agency efforts to collect and share data on the student in transition. Develop data collection procedures jointly with cooperating agencies and relate them directly to partnership goals and objectives. Collect a variety of data to get a comprehensive picture of transition activities and outcomes (school records, baseline data, interviews, observations, surveys of participants). Keep data collection methods ongoing throughout the development of the transition initiative.

Attitudinal Barriers

Political pressures and pressure groups: As the economic pressures force agencies to economize, interagency coordinators must show the community how interagency linkages can contribute to cost-effective services.

Problem-solving strategy: Involve stakeholder groups in the development of interagency initiatives and in the selection of outcome and performance measures. This involvement will assure that their interests will be acknowledged.

Territorialism: Encroachments of agencies on each other's service "territory" may threaten people and their comfort with traditional ways of operating. Interagency initiatives often result in changes in the way they conduct business.

Problem-solving strategy: Discuss with interagency personnel their perceptions of individual roles and responsibilities and staff satisfaction with their contributions or roles. Provide opportunities for staff to express feelings about changes in their roles and explain how change can contribute to student outcomes.

Staff turnover: Serious barriers to interagency relationships result from turnover rates among key personnel in cooperating agencies. Established relationships and the emergence of "champions" lead to leadership and trust and can accelerate interagency cooperative efforts. As old links break apart through attrition, the system can weaken. For example, the loss of a respected champion for the partnership, who has fought to preserve the program in a time of economic constraint, can result in the loss of years of progress.

Problem-solving strategy: Examine the staffing arrangement and loads. Examine orientation and training programs to determine how well training includes team-building strategies and helps foster cooperative attitudes and communications among agencies and their personnel. Decide if there are adequate materials for orientation and training of new and veteran staff.

Knowledge Barriers

Lack of understanding among interagency personnel about transition services and processes and their respective organizations and missions: Service providers need to understand each other, their distinctly different missions, and recognize each other's complementary strengths.

Problem-solving strategy: Develop interagency training sessions and share descriptions of agency missions, goals, and objectives. Build this information into orientation and training.

Lack of knowledge about interagency models for transition: There is a need to explore and design new models for interagency collaboration development and improvement of interagency relationships.

Problem-solving strategy: Develop common terminology for communication among cooperating agencies. Define common transition coordination activities and core activities, and define outcomes and target populations. Share information about interagency models in other local areas and states and discuss how they could be adapted to meet local needs.

to the success of an interagency cooperative agreement and strategies for designing and evaluation.

HOW CAN THE SUCCESS OF INTERAGENCY AGREEMENTS BE MEASURED?

Outcomes and Benefits: Evaluating Interagency Collaboration

Although IDEA 1997 and 2004 emphasized the need for a shared responsibility for transition between schools and community agencies, transition planning and service coordination continue to be a challenge for school systems. The assumption that underlies this emphasis is that system coordination has a positive effect on student outcomes and helps improve the system of transition services. Outcomes and benefits refer to that interagency which planners hope to see change as a result of the services or service coordination effort.

Effective interagency coordination must be viewed as an *intervention, or planned effort designed to produce intended changes or (outcomes), in a target population.* This "outcomes view" is consistent with IDEA 2004 transition requirements for agency involvement (see Chapter 4) and requires a change in the methods used to define the role and measure the effectiveness of the interagency coordinator. The intended student outcomes must be clearly specified and interagency resources focused to achieve those outcomes. As a result, orientation and vigorous focus on measuring student benefits and impacts becomes central to evaluating the performance of interagency collaboration and agreements. In a student-centered transition service system, individual benefits and impacts drive the development of interagency service coordination, from initial definition of the mission and goals to annual evaluation.

What Factors Contribute to Successful Collaboration?

Several factors contribute to the success of an interagency cooperative agreement:

1. Decisions are made jointly by consumers, families, and professionals who are involved with the student.
2. There is increased emphasis on innovativeness and flexibility.
3. A clear commitment for local cooperation comes from the top administrative levels of collaborating agencies.
4. Written policies describe ongoing roles and responsibilities to sustain organizational relationships even when personnel changes occur within one or more of the agencies.
5. Local agreements are kept current and there is a concerted effort to keep lines of communication open by maintaining active participation at regular meetings.
6. One agency serves as a team leader to facilitate local programming (typically the school system).
7. There is coordinated analysis of needs assessment data from each agency.
8. Sufficient time is allocated by agency administrators for staff to participate.
9. Agency representatives meeting with the group are empowered to recommend policy.
10. Participation is driven by interest in improving interagency linkages to enhance services.
11. Evaluation criteria are identified when planning activities are initiated (measurable short- and long-term goals).
12. There is ongoing follow-up of students who leave school to indicate program effectiveness (adapted from the California Department of Education, 2001).

Outcome evaluation of interagency coordination measures the extent to which interagency services cause desired change in the student or consumer population and in the collaborating agencies. Outcome evaluation addresses two questions: Are students really benefiting from the services in ways that can be measured? Are there improvements in service quality and accessibility? Additional questions related to improving transition outcomes for youth, questions that should be asked with respect to evaluation and accountability, include the following:

1. Do members of the interagency collaboration team define the goals for the collaboration in terms of specific transition outcomes for youth?
2. Do members share collective accountability for improving those outcomes?
3. Have a broad-based set of outcomes been identified, both short-term and long-range?
4. Are these outcomes being tracked regularly?
5. Is the information obtained from evaluation used to help improve the performance of the collaborative activity?
6. Are the successes achieved through collaboration well-publicized and used to sustain commitment to the effort?

Outcomes can be measured at the individual and interagency levels. *Individual level outcomes* include measures of achievement of transition goals by the students. *Interagency or system outcomes* include measures of improvements in the way agencies coordinate their services to serve students in transition, whether the processes and services match the interagency mission and objectives, and how well the system is assuring access to services for all students with transition plans.

Interagency activities positively affect students in indirect ways by improving the transition service system at the organizational level. These are referred to as *interagency-level outcomes* and are related to changes and improvements in the service system as a whole. Interagency-level outcomes are assumed to indirectly affect students and families served by collaborating agencies by improving linkages between students and services. Table 10–6 provides examples of indicators of positive interagency outcomes.

Action Steps for Evaluating Interagency Agreements

The following 10 action steps are useful for designing an evaluation of interagency agreements and collaboration.

Table 10–6   Interagency Level Outcomes

Category of Outcome	Example Outcome Indicators
Interagency planning	Cooperative agreements (formal and informal), agencies involved in cooperative planning and follow-up or follow-along, joint service assessments, joint projections of service needs and graduate placements (anticipated services)
Interagency training and staff development	Interagency training or cross-training activities for personnel of cooperating agencies
Parent and community outreach and dissemination	Parent and family training activities, linkages with parent training centers, and coordinated service information dissemination
Interagency management system	Coordinated database development to collect student data, coordinated information and referral services, interagency continuous improvement monitoring and quality assurance activities, coordinated follow-up and follow-along services, coordinated information-sharing among agencies, coordinated crisis management, or behavior management service
Interagency system advocacy	Individual and group advocacy to increase services and service responsiveness to student or family needs; human-rights protection and review activities; local, state, and national policy advocacy for improved services
Interagency evaluation	Interagency evaluation, which involves shared student data collection, joint design of service monitoring and quality assurance, and joint planning to use evaluation information to improve interagency coordination

Ten Action Steps for the Evaluation Process

1. Decide who will participate in developing the evaluation component. Engage a consultant if needed.
2. Select the components of the interagency agreement that you wish to evaluate (informing the community; assessing needs or developing shared resources, shared mission, cooperative agreement; or all of these).
3. Select the questions that you wish to ask for each of the components you are evaluating.
4. Select the evaluation methods.
5. Identify the documents that are sources of information needed to answer evaluation questions.
6. Decide on your data collection strategies (e.g., interviews, surveys, site visits and observations, and records reviews). Select your data analysis procedures (e.g., quantitative information on number of participants or measures of student progress or qualitative information such as analysis of interviews and surveys to determine students' judgments of the quality of the services).
7. Conduct your data collection activities.
8. Conduct your data analysis and develop your report of evaluation results.
9. Determine to whom you will distribute the evaluation report for review and input; develop your final report for distribution to stakeholders.
10. Ensure that your evaluation results are acted on and integrated into future interagency coordination planning, budgeting, and improvement. Have your evaluation design and methods evaluated by an external consultant.

Features of Effective Interagency Coordination Evaluation

Figure 10-12 provides a synthesis of suggestions and recommendations for designing evaluation of interagency agreements.

Sources of Evaluation Information. There is a great variety of sources of evaluation information and methods for data collection. Information can be obtained directly from students and families or indirectly through agency documents and staff. A comprehensive evaluation of interagency coordination agreements requires a broader review of many of these sources and would require some evaluation experience. The following presents a variety of information sources:

1. Review of individualized educational programs or transition plans
2. Student or participant survey or questionnaire
3. Staff and administrator
4. Parents or families survey or questionnaire
5. Interagency coordinator, liaison survey, or questionnaire
6. Interviews with students, families, staff, administrators, coordinators, and others
7. Observations in service delivery and agency site visits
8. Review of student records, assessment results, or test scores

9. Anecdotal records
10. Review of cooperative agreements and objectives accomplished
11. Review of agency budget documents and annual plans
12. Review of public relations materials
13. Review of previous evaluations and independent reports
14. Review of rehabilitation and career-technical education plans
15. Review of federal, state, and local policies and legislation affecting interagency coordination.

Asking the Right Questions. Surveys and questionnaires may ask several types of questions and they may include both quantitative and qualitative questions. The following examples may be helpful for developing survey questions.

Quantitative questions seek to answer questions of quantity, such as how many individuals or families were served by external agencies, what types of services were provided, how many transition goals were achieved with the support of agency services, or number of interagency training sessions that have been conducted. *Qualitative questions* seek to answer questions of quality, such as how satisfied are the families or

---

- Evaluation should assist the decision-making process throughout the life of the interagency partnership.

- Build evaluation into the transition cooperative agreement early in the planning stage and ensure that all cooperating agencies agree on the evaluation plan.

- Interagency coordinators should play central roles in the planning and implementing of evaluation.

- Interagency evaluation should be supported at the highest leadership level.

- Agency partners communicate about evaluation results and apply them in future planning.

- Preparation training for evaluation of service coordination should include all cooperating agencies.

- Interagency evaluation planning teams include representatives from all collaborating agencies, students, and families.

- Cooperative agreements permit modifications on the basis of a regular review process.

- Evaluation goals and measures are consistent with those addressed in the cooperative agreement and annual action plans.

- Evaluation should be designed to be supportive of effective coordination relationships.

- Evaluation should be flexible to allow for situational responsiveness as needs and service system environments change.

- Evaluations are based on shared goals and measurable objectives.

- Data collection should yield useful information about results and benefits for participants.

- Evaluation reinforces and supports program management, accountability, and continuous improvement.

Figure 10–12 Considerations in the Design of Effective Evaluations of Interagency Coordination

Table 10–7   Sample Quantitative and Qualitative Survey Questions

Examples of Quantitative Items in a Survey	Examples of Qualitative Items in a Survey
How many students or families are receiving transition services with service coordination support?	How satisfied are families with access to transition services and the quality of the services?
How many service coordination hours are provided to students?	What are the judgments of students or families about the benefits of service coordination support?
How many students are linked with needed agencies in accordance with their IEPs?	How satisfied are students with the amount of service coordinator contact?
How many transition IEP goals requiring agency services are accomplished?	What are the judgments of service coordinators about the quality of interagency training and preparation for their roles?
How many service agencies have joined the collaboration?	What are agency liaisons' perceptions of the effectiveness of service coordination efforts?
What are the total interagency training hours provided?	What are the judgments of local educational agency administrators about the effectiveness of coordination efforts?
What are the caseloads of service coordinators?	

students with services provided; are coordinators adequately trained; are cooperating agencies satisfied with the referrals of students and service planning activities in which they were involved? Qualitative questions involve judgments on the part of the evaluators and the service recipients (students and families) about the adequacy, appropriateness, or effectiveness of a service coordination activity. Table 10–7 provides examples of quantitative and qualitative survey questions.

Using Interagency Evaluation Information for Transition Systems Change.   This component involves the processes of acting on evaluation data collected from the multiple sources and agencies to improve the transition service system. Improvement requires a constructive process for

1. analyzing and communicating the information in a manner that is understandable and usable by different stakeholder groups (e.g., service coordinators, students or families, and administrators)
2. systematically applying the information for service system change and improvement

The system's change process involves identifying the weaknesses, barriers, and gaps in services and developing a plan of change to align the system with the actual assessed transition needs of students. Figure 10–13 depicts a series of steps for using evaluation information for transition system change.

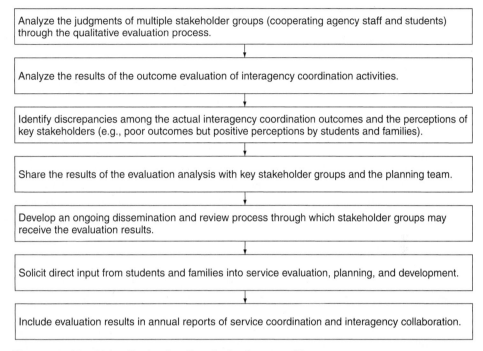

Analyze the judgments of multiple stakeholder groups (cooperating agency staff and students) through the qualitative evaluation process.

Analyze the results of the outcome evaluation of interagency coordination activities.

Identify discrepancies among the actual interagency coordination outcomes and the perceptions of key stakeholders (e.g., poor outcomes but positive perceptions by students and families).

Share the results of the evaluation analysis with key stakeholder groups and the planning team.

Develop an ongoing dissemination and review process through which stakeholder groups may receive the evaluation results.

Solicit direct input from students and families into service evaluation, planning, and development.

Include evaluation results in annual reports of service coordination and interagency collaboration.

Figure 10–13 Using Evaluation Results for Systems Change

Case Studies in Interagency Coordination for Transition

The following case examples from Virginia and Rhode Island illustrate how agencies work together to create a system of transition services.

LET'S SEE IT IN ACTION! CASE EXAMPLE

Interagency Coordination for Transition Case Example 1: Project FAST—Facilitating Successful Transition

Spotsylvania County Schools is implementing Facilitating Successful Transition (FAST). This is being achieved through an innovative curriculum approach to higher education transition based on the understanding that students with disabilities must be prepared with an array of skills to meet the demands of college. The traditional educational approach to prepare students with disabilities for transition after high school has only been successful for a small number of students. Project

FAST seeks to extend transition services to a greater number of students with disabilities entering college. Project FAST involves *interagency cooperation* among the Disability Resource Center, Department of Rehabilitative Services, Mary Washington College, Germanna Community College, Employment Resources Incorporated, and the school division's Parent Resource Center. The long-range goals of this project are to have 75% of participating students learn how to access support

(Continued)

services at the postsecondary level, to educate teachers and students about appropriate accommodations used at the postsecondary level, and to provide middle and high school teachers with the necessary resources to teach students the skills for transitioning successfully to postsecondary education.

Project FAST seeks to (a) increase the awareness and knowledge of school staff, students, and family members about postsecondary education opportunities and the resources and support services available; (b) provide opportunities for students with disabilities to engage in activities for career planning and preparation to determine their career goals and the postsecondary options that can help them reach their goals; and (c) assist students with disabilities in planning their course work to obtain the necessary academic requirements that students must fulfill to enter advanced degree programs (Spotsylvania County Schools, 2000).

LET'S SEE IT IN ACTION! CASE EXAMPLE

Interagency Coordination for Transition Case Example 2: Partnerships Promoting Employment for Graduates with Disabilities

Virginia's young adults with disabilities, particularly those with more significant disabilities, continue to face difficulties finding and retaining competitive employment upon graduation from high school. Although collaborative efforts between schools and adult services providers have improved in meeting transition needs, seamless transitions to long-term employment remain a challenge. Inexperience with job-keeping skills and living in communities with minimal follow-along services or supports contribute to the challenges facing these youths. Furthermore, education and adult service agencies continue to face barriers to seamless service provision such as policies and procedures that delay involvement with adult services or private providers. Resource limitations and coordination also contribute to the problem. The Virginia Department of Education (VADOE), in collaboration with the Virginia Department of Rehabilitative Services, the Virginia Department for the Visually Handicapped, and the Virginia Department of Mental Health, Mental Retardation and Substance Abuse services, seeks funds to promote community-based employment partnerships between local school districts and adult services, community organizations, and businesses.

The goal of this project is to strengthen the capacity of school divisions and local communities to improve employment outcomes for students with disabilities whose transition goals are immediate postschool employment. The project goal will be accomplished through the following objectives. The VADOE will

1. Implement a 3-year subgrant process that will enable up to 16 school divisions to receive competitive grant funding for 2 years to develop (in cooperation with the local Division of Rehabilitative Services and Community Services Board offices) community-based employment services that lead to stable postschool employment outcomes for a minimum 150 students with disabilities.

2. Strengthen transition service partnerships between education, human service agencies,

and the employment community at the state and local levels.

3. Evaluate, in cooperation with the Virginia Board for People with Disabilities, the effectiveness of this project and its effect on students with disabilities, their families, school division staff, employers, and community agencies.

4. Disseminate the outcomes of the local initiatives statewide and nationally through publications, presentations, and technical assistance.

The Virginia Department of Education is committed to improving postschool outcomes for youths with disabilities; this proposed project allows communities to develop local solutions to a problem faced by our state which, in turn, can be replicated in other communities (Virginia Department of Education, 2000).

LET'S SEE IT IN ACTION! CASE EXAMPLE

Interagency Coordination for Transition Case Example 2: Partnerships Promoting Employment for Graduates with Disabilities

On July 11, 1994, Governor Sundlun signed into law an act relating to disabled students that would establish a transition council. By definition, the transition process from school to self-sufficiency for all youngsters with disabilities must begin at 16 years of age or younger if appropriate. The transition process is an integral part of the student's IEP. The transition council is composed of administrators or their designees of the major state agencies and consumers and is managed by the Department of Elementary and Secondary Education. The goal of the council is to ensure preparedness of students with disabilities upon leaving school, to live and work in the community.

Before the transition council began, the Office of Special Needs of the Rhode Island Department of Education allocated a quarter of a million dollars to create transition centers in the four legislatively created collaboratives and the city of Providence. The major activities of these transition centers are the

1. creation and maintenance of an electronic data or information base for evaluating the effectiveness and outcomes of transition services;

2. coordination in the development and dissemination of information to parents, teachers, and administrators;

3. operation of a system of personnel development services on transition issues;

4. development of practices and procedures for establishing and accessing regional networks of state and local agency resources; and

5. program and curriculum development in the evaluation, skill development, and placement of students with disabilities based on the needs of business or industry.

Each transition center has a coordinator and a local transition advisory committee (TAC) that meets at least once a month. This committee is composed of special education teachers, Office of Rehabilitation Services (ORS) staff, and parents, who are involved in transition activities from within the region served by each collaborative. In addition, the transition coordinators have a close affiliation with the University Affiliated Program (U.A.P.) at Rhode Island College, the Rhode Island Technical Assistance Project (R.I.T.A.P.) at Providence College, the Rhode Island Parent

(Continued)

Information Network (RIPIN), and the Department of Education. One major activity that was accomplished by this consortium was the inservice training of approximately 400 individuals in IEP teams from local districts and agencies in designing and implementing effective IEPs for secondary students (Rhode Island Department of Education, 2002).

SUMMARY

Interagency coordination is most effective when it is viewed as an intervention or a planned effort designed to produce intended changes, or outcomes, in a target population. Where communities are implementing effective interagency agreements, they observe a positive effect on student transition outcomes. This chapter described the steps for implementing interagency agreements for transition. It addressed practical aspects including development of the interagency agreements, managing transition service coordination, models for service coordination, and considerations in choosing a lead agency. The chapter reviewed models for implementing interagency coordination and the components of interagency agreements. Ten steps in the implementation of interagency agreements were discussed. Strategies for evaluating interagency agreements were also provided.

A systematic approach to transition services, now required by IDEA, means developing strategies to address the complex needs of youth with disabilities in an organized and coordinated way. Provision of options for students, through multiple pathways to transition, requires that schools reach outside their boundaries and formalize the shared responsibility with community agencies through interagency agreements.

KEY TERMS AND PHRASES

adoption plan
caseload
circle of commitment
cooperative agreement
coordinated service plans
evaluating interagency collaboration

interagency cooperative agreement
interagency mission statement
lead agency
milestone schedule
strategic planning
transition planning team or council

QUESTIONS FOR THINKING, REFLECTION, AND SKILL-BUILDING

1. What would you look for if you were assessing agencies' readiness for entering into a cooperative partnership for transition?

2. What are the key components of a cooperative agreement? What are cooperative agreements designed to accomplish?

3. Identify five barriers to interagency relationships. Do you think interagency relationships are fragile? Why or why not?

4. Provide examples of local-level and state-level problems that interagency coordination activities can help ameliorate.

5. Examine your school's local interagency cooperative agreement or memorandum of understanding for transition services (find one in another locality if yours does not have one). Are the goals and objectives measurable? What would you recommend to improve them?

6. Discuss the elements of the circle of commitment. Which of these elements can you observe in action in your school or district in terms of implementation of transition services? Where are the strengths and weaknesses in terms of the six elements?

7. Interview one to three case managers or service coordinators who work with youth with disabilities in the transition phase and conduct a role analysis. What is their caseload size? What are their duties? Do they serve more than one role? How do they judge the effectiveness of their position? What barriers do they face? How do they overcome them? What training do they receive? What are their qualifications? How are they evaluated? What recommendations do *they* have for improving their services?

8. Find out what is being done in your school or district to promote collaboration and team-building among youth in transition, families, professionals, and agencies. Learn about what makes collaboration work. Examine what others are doing to work with people in the community to build partnerships around transition services for youth. How are they using community resources to help students achieve successful transitions?

Chapter 11

The Final Phases of Transition: Follow-Up and Evaluation

Gary Greene

Chapter Questions

- What is the *hand-off* process in the final phase of transition, and what models are available?
- What follow-up practices are recommended to monitor postschool transition services?
- How should transition services be evaluated after high school completion?

Most school districts today place a heavy emphasis on preparing students for transition to college as opposed to transition to a quality adult life. Data is gathered on average SAT scores of graduating seniors and percentages of graduates accepted into colleges and universities. This is unlikely to change in the future, given the emphasis on school accountability of No Child Left Behind (NCLB) and related standards-based reforms and high-stakes testing. Public schools must concentrate on raising standardized test scores as opposed to preparing well-rounded youth for independent living, careers, and other indicators of a quality adult life.

These statements hold true for students receiving special education services as well. Despite the intent of the Individuals with Disabilities Education Act (IDEA) 2004 and its predecessors to provide an individualized educational program (IEP) designed to meet the unique needs of a youth with a disability, the options for secondary students enrolled in special education have been markedly restricted in the past several years. Many school districts no longer offer a special education-based high school diploma, departmentalized special education classes in the core curriculum, or modified high school exit exam. Although collaboration and coteaching has been demonstrated as best practices for achieving greater access to the core secondary curriculum for youth with disabilities, many school districts lack the personnel, resources, and time necessary to implement this type of educational programming.

Despite these constraints, transition of youth with disabilities remains a high priority for special educators, particularly at the secondary level. Linking youth with disabilities to postschool agencies and support services during their transition years is a major intent of IDEA 2004. Furthermore, IDEA requires local education agencies to reconvene the IEP team if agreed-upon transition services fail to be provided by postschool transition services agencies after a youth with a disability completes or graduates from high school. Many special educators are unaware of this legal requirement. Hence, it is important for local education agencies to have in place methods and procedures that (a) promote a smooth transfer of youth with disabilities from school to postschool adult transition services agencies, (b) allow for monitoring the transition status of youth with disabilities after they complete or graduate high school, and (c) periodically evaluate the overall quality of the transition programs and services schools provide to youth with disabilities.

With these thoughts in mind, this chapter discusses the final phases of transition: the culmination and hand-off process, transition follow-up, and transition program evaluation. These important aspects of transition emphasize gathering accountability data on the overall quality of transition services and programs offered by school districts to youth with disabilities. Our discussion begins with a definition of the *hand-off process* and a review of models and case studies that illustrate this phase of transition. This is followed by a presentation of transition follow-up data gathering procedures. Finally, methods for evaluating the overall quality of transition programs and services in local school districts and adult services agencies are discussed.

> ## What Is the *Hand-Off Process* in the Final Phase of Transition and What Models Are Available?

The hand-off process occurs whenever a youth with a disability approaches the time to transfer from one educational setting or adult services agency to another, institution to school, school to school, school to adult services agency, or adult services agency to adult services agency. Critical tasks must be completed by personnel serving as the case carrier for a smooth transition to take place between these settings. A complete review of culmination steps for school-to-school transition was outlined in Chapter 8 (see *transition culmination* for each transition pathway). These steps alone, however, are inadequate for insuring a smooth hand-off process. Equally important is the degree of collaboration and cooperation that exists between school-based and agency-based transition personnel involved in the hand-off process. Several hand-off process models describing varying degrees of collaboration and cooperation between schools and transition services agencies will be reviewed next.

Models of the Hand-Off Process

Wehman, Moon, Everson, and Barcus (1988) presented three **models of interagency interaction** that illustrate varying degrees of collaboration and cooperation between transition services agencies and personnel. These three models, referred to as Models A, B, and C, are shown in Figure 11–1. This seminal work is still highly relevant today (see Chapters 5 and 10).

In Model A, little or no planned interaction exists between transition personnel and agencies; the hand-off process consists primarily of an exchange of paperwork and records on the youth with a disability, such as educational, psychological, vocational, social, and medical history. Hence, there is a high probability in this model that the informal, loosely established relationships between transition services agencies and personnel will result in a hand-off process that does not run smoothly. Records frequently get lost or are not sent in this model. In addition, sending agencies do not monitor the transition services provided by receiving agencies to youth with disabilities. Likewise, receiving agencies are unsure of what transition services were provided in the past to their new consumer or if transition planning occurred.

Model B represents a significantly better opportunity for a smooth hand-off process to occur because transition personnel from one or more agencies participate in the IEP meeting prior to the graduation or school completion of a youth with a disability. Close communication between schools and transition services agencies takes place during

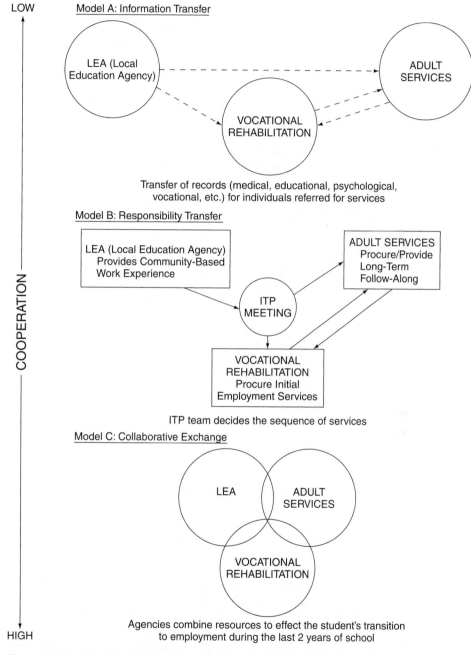

Figure 11–1 Models of Agency Interaction

Source: From *Transition from School to Work,* by P. Wehman, M. S. Moon, J. M. Everson, and J. M. Barcus, 1988, Baltimore: Paul H. Brookes. Adapted with permission.

the meeting, enabling transition personnel to gain an understanding of the services to be delivered by the sending agency and the future service commitments of the receiving agency. This increases the likelihood that the subsequent hand-off process will proceed smoothly. Other advantages of Model B over Model A are that (a) the sending agency can assist in preparing the necessary forms and paperwork before transferring the youth with a disability to the receiving agency, (b) the receiving agency obtains this information well in advance of the time transition services are scheduled to be provided, and (c) the receiving agency can attend to the necessary steps to provide agreed-upon transition services with little or no interruption following the transition of the youth with a disability. A further advantage of Model B is that it allows for relatively easy follow-up data gathering because of the preestablished relationships that exist between **sending and receiving agencies.** Note, however, that shared delivery of services to the youth with a disability does not occur in this model; each service agency has a distinct set of transition services it agrees to provide, and the receiving agency does not begin providing these services until scheduled to do so.

Model C represents the greatest degree of collaboration and cooperation between transition personnel and agencies. In this model, sending and receiving agency resources are combined for the youth with a disability during the last 2 years of participation at the sending agency (e.g., middle school or high school) and for up to 2 years after transition to the receiving agency occurs. All agencies are involved in the IEP meeting and mutual planning, and implementation of transition services takes place. Although there is no duplication of transition services between agencies, equitable cost-sharing arrangements are typically made and agreed upon at the IEP meeting. This model facilitates follow-up data gathering by the sending agency because there is continuous collaboration and cooperation with the receiving agency before, during, and after transition of the youth with a disability.

A short case study exemplifying Models B and C is presented next.

LET'S SEE IT IN ACTION! CASE EXAMPLE

Model B

Rico is an eighth grader with a learning disability and is fully included in general education classrooms, with resource specialist support and assistance. A transition plan is to be included with his annual IEP because he will be turning 14 years of age later this year. He will be attending his neighborhood high school next year. He has an older sibling at the high school and his parents are familiar with the school's academic program and many of the teachers. Rico and his family recently attended a high school orientation for entering freshmen and discussed the various academic and elective options, along with extrcurricular activities in which he was interested.

The resource specialist from the high school has been invited and is in attendance at Rico's IEP meeting. Rico's current level of performance data and academic goals and objectives are discussed, just as they have been in previous IEP meetings. At the meeting this year, however, the high school resource specialist asks Rico and his family to share Rico's interests and preferences in the areas of instruction, employment, and community participation. The specialist uses a survey developed by the high school special education department and administered by the middle school special education staff to all eighth-grade special education youth with disabilities.

Rico tells the high school resource specialist that in the area of instruction, he would like to pursue a college entrance course of study and thinks he will need assistance in language arts, social science, and science classes but not in other subjects. He is not sure what he would like to do for employment but may have a summer job this year helping with recreation camps at the local YMCA. He does not think he needs any assistance in the community, because he either uses his skateboard or gets a ride with his older brother or parents when going to the mall, movies, or a friend's house.

The high school resource specialist assists the middle school specialist in writing transition goals, annual goals, objectives, and benchmarks on Rico's IEP, in the areas of instruction and employment. The transition goals reflect Rico's desire to enroll in a high school course of study that will prepare him for college entrance. Transition goals in employment include his summer employment at the YMCA and the administration of vocational interest and aptitude tests during his ninth-grade year, along with a completion of a prevocational training class during his 10th-grade year. The high school resource specialist leaves the meeting with a copy of Rico's IEP after agreeing to provide all of the services contained in the plan and plans to meet with Rico at the high school next year during the first week of the fall semester.

Model C

Rosalina is an 11th-grade youth with a moderate-to-severe developmental disability. She attends her neighborhood high school and is fully included in academic classes most of the day, but spends the last two periods of school participating in community-based instruction with the special education staff.

Her transition goals in the area of instruction are to participate in mainstream classes for academics, life skills, and social skills with a modified curriculum and help from an inclusion facilitator. She plans to continue to live with her parents for a while after completing high school. Her community goals include mobility training and ability to access local businesses, recreation, and leisure facilities in her city. The high school special and vocational education staff has conducted functional vocational assessments and evaluations of Rosalina and has determined that she is interested and is able to work in retail sales.

An annual IEP meeting takes place, and in addition to the usual school personnel in attendance, a counselor from the local department of rehabilitation (DR) is present. The counselor tells Rosalina and her parents that a DR project exists at the high school that will provide Rosalina with job development, training, and support while she is in school. Furthermore, this program will help Rosalina obtain paid employment in retail sales at the local mall, along with ongoing job support and supervision from rehabilitation department personnel whenever she needs it. If Rosalina wishes to continue in the retail services industry after graduating from high school, the DR will pay for advanced training, including all expenses for tuition, fees, books, and supplies, enabling her to attend a vocational school or community college program specializing in retail services. Educational support is available for her at the vocational school or community college, if she chooses to attend.

Rosalina and her parents are very excited about this program and want her to start as soon as possible. She will begin the program next semester.

Summary of Culmination and Hand-Off Process

As has been illustrated in the case studies, important connections between high school special education personnel (sending agency) and adult transition services providers in the community (receiving agencies) must be established well in advance of school completion or graduation for a smooth transfer to occur for a youth with a disability from one transition services agency to another. Collaboration, cooperation, and participation of receiving agencies in all phases of the IEP process greatly facilitate the culmination and hand-off process. When this occurs, the transfer of responsibility from schools to postschool adult transition services providers happens smoothly, consumer records are handled efficiently and in a timely manner, and the startup of agreed-upon transition services occurs much more quickly.

⇒ WHAT FOLLOW-UP PRACTICES ARE RECOMMENDED TO MONITOR POSTSCHOOL TRANSITION SERVICES?

Follow-up and follow-along procedures are methods that allow sending agencies to track the outcomes and status of youth with disabilities transitioning between schools and from schools into the adult community and postsecondary education (Burgstahler, Crawford, & Acosta, 2001; Certo et al., 1997, 2003). Though not mandated by IDEA 2004, conducting a *follow-up* (i.e., assessing postschool status at a specific point in time) or *follow-along study* (i.e., assessing postschool status for a continuous period of time) enables transition services agencies and personnel to effectively and validly determine if the agreed-upon transition services specified in the IEP have been provided to youth with disabilities and the achieved outcomes of the transition services provided. In addition, follow-up and follow-along procedures allow for a determination of the success for youth with disabilities in general education courses during high school and enrollment and success in postsecondary education following high school completion.

Transition follow-up and follow-along procedures are not typically completed by special education teachers, because of their already busy schedules. It is our recommendation that school district special education administrative personnel, such as a program specialist, transition coordinator, or director of special education, be the individual(s) responsible for conducting follow-up or follow-along studies. Effective strategies for doing this are discussed next.

Guidelines for Conducting Follow-Up and Follow-Along Studies

Andrew Halpern (1990, 1996) has compiled perhaps the best set of guidelines and recommendations for conducting follow-up or follow-along studies of special education for youth with disabilities. Though this work is outdated, more recent literature on transition follow-up design does not exist. Halpern's work is therefore featured here. It is noteworthy in that it involved a thorough analysis of existing literature on the subject and produced a set of best practices that were research validated. Halpern subsequently presented a set of *desired features* that he believed should be incorporated into the design of follow-up or follow-along research studies:

1. Be longitudinal in nature.
2. Identify and use an appropriate subject-sampling strategy.

3. Use either personal or telephone interviews as the primary source of information.
4. Define variables in a clear and concise manner.
5. Include content that represents the important dimensions of transition.

Although these desired features are presented by Halpern in the context of conducting research, there is much that school personnel can learn from these recommendations with respect to tracking the between-school and postschool transition status of youth with disabilities. An overview and discussion of desired features recommended by Halpern that have implications and application for school special education personnel is presented next.

Adoption of a Follow-Along Versus Follow-Up Procedure.   A follow-along study periodically gathers tracking data on youth with disabilities over an extended period of time. In contrast, a follow-up study gathers tracking data on youth with disabilities on a single occasion after a predetermined period of time has elapsed. We highly recommend the adoption of a follow-along versus follow-up procedure for determining the effectiveness of transition programs and services. **Follow-up studies** are often ineffective because (a) school records of youth with disabilities who have changed, graduated, or left school(s) can be obtained only retrospectively and may be inadequate or lost, (b) there may be no baseline of information to determine the quality of between-school or postschool status of youth with disabilities, preventing one's ability to measure change (or lack of change) over time, and (c) the outcome of transition services can be only inferred when there is no baseline data available.

Obtain Sufficient or Representative Samples.   The number of youth with disabilities to be surveyed is an important consideration when tracking transition status. Sample sizes should be sufficiently large and representative of the population to which the findings are intended to be generalized. If, on the other hand, tracking the transition status of large numbers of youth with disabilities is not possible, school personnel should select and track a small, representative sample that will allow for generalization of the findings to the entire population. In this instance, sample subject variables to consider are gender, type of disability, socioeconomic status, cultural and linguistic diversity, special education setting in which the youth participated in school, and transition pathway during and after school completion or graduation.

Use an Effective Data Collection Method.   The most effective and recommended method for gathering between-school or postschool tracking data on youth with disabilities is face-to-face or telephone interviews. If this is not possible, owing to limited time and resources, mail surveys are an option. Mail surveys, however, are somewhat problematic and should be avoided because of inaccuracy or change of address of youth with disabilities who have completed school. Additional problems with mail surveys include the ability of a youth with a disability to (a) accurately read and comprehend the survey questions, (b) properly record appropriate and accurate answers, and (c) return the survey in a timely fashion. Another important consideration for school personnel who choose to use mail surveys is obtaining an adequate return rate. A return rate of somewhere between 60% and 80% is recommended if the results of a mail survey are to be considered valid and representative of the population measured. Second, and possibly even third, mailings may be necessary to obtain this rate of return, along with telephone reminders to those who fail to return the surveys.

Transition Outcomes Should Be Simply and Clearly Defined. A large number of transition outcomes can potentially be tracked for youth with disabilities, and it is important that these outcomes be defined in such a way that they are clearly understood and measured by all concerned. For example, an outcome such as success in school has vague meaning and is not written in observable and measurable terms. Such an outcome is more clearly defined for a youth with a disability when broken up into the following terms: (a) school year, (b) number of courses completed in school, (c) grade in specific courses and overall grade-point average, (d) inclusion status, (e) courses in which inclusion occurred, and (f) school completion status.

Measure a Broad Range of Transition Outcomes. Much of the early literature tracking the postschool status of youth with disabilities focused primarily on employment. Halpern (1985, 1993) discussed the problems associated with this practice by noting (a) that employment is only one indicator of a quality adult life, (b) that employment does not correlate highly with other important community adjustment variables, and (c) the importance of measuring a broad range of indicators of a quality adult life for a person with a disability. With this in mind, suggested postschool outcomes and related variables that Halpern (1990) recommended for follow-up or follow-along surveys were (a) employment status, such as full-time or part-time, history, salary, types of job, how job was found, and job satisfaction; (b) residential status, such as place of residence and satisfaction; (c) personal or social status, such as relationships and friendships, leisure activities, and overall quality of life; and (d) postschool education, such as admittance to college or university, community college, vocational or technical school, and apprenticeship program. In addition, we recommend surveying the degree of access and successful completion of general education coursework that was achieved by a youth with a disability while he or she was still in high school.

Summary of Transition Outcome Measurement Recommendations

Halpern (1990), in drawing on the insights gained from his extensive literature review of follow-up and follow-along studies, concluded that

> a useful strategy for tracking school leavers with disabilities should (1) be longitudinal in nature, (2) identify and use an appropriate subject sampling strategy, (3) use either personal or phone interviews as the primary source of information, (4) define its variables in a clear and concise manner, and (5) include content that represents the important dimensions of transition. (p. 19)

We thoroughly agree with these recommendations. Although limited time and resources may prevent school and transition services agency personnel from being able to fully and effectively implement all of them, we encourage inclusion of as many of these recommendations as possible when evaluating transition programs and services.

Sample Survey Questions for Tracking Between-School and Postschool Transition Outcomes of Youth and Adults with Disabilities

Regardless of whether transition personnel choose to conduct a follow-up, follow-along, telephone or personal interview, or mail survey to determine the postschool transition status of youth with disabilities, samples of potential questions for tracking between-school and postschool transition status of youth with disabilities are presented in Appendix 11–1. Transition personnel are encouraged to select questions that most appropriately serve their needs and purposes when designing a transition outcome survey or procedure.

A case study illustrating follow-up and follow-along procedures occurs next. This is followed by information on how to effectively conduct a transition program evaluation.

LET'S SEE IT IN ACTION! CASE EXAMPLE

Follow-Along Procedure

Maryville School District recently underwent a program quality review of its special education program. The school district was found out of compliance with federal law because, in several instances, agreed-upon transition services had not been provided by transition services agencies designated in the IEPs of several former special education students. In response to this situation, the school district decided to initiate a continuing series of follow-along studies to track the postschool status of special education students for up to 5 years after completing school. Program coordinators at the school district office designed a procedure that would select a random sample of names of 40% of students in special education who had completed school in the previous year. An hourly employee was hired to make copies of the transition portion of the IEPs for these students and to make initial telephone contact with these individuals to set up a date and time for a telephone interview regarding their quality of life

since completing school. Program specialists from the district office special education division subsequently conducted the telephone interviews, using a follow-along survey that determined the interviewee's postschool status across a variety of transition outcomes, such as postsecondary education and training, employment, independent living, residential satisfaction, marital status, recreation and leisure activities, and degree of access to and completion of general education courses while in high school. Of particular importance in the interview was checking whether agreed-upon transition services in the interviewee's IEP had been provided by designated transition services agencies. A data bank was kept at the district office and annual reports were written by the program specialists summarizing the results of the ongoing follow-along studies. Transition program services improvements were made by the school district annually in response to the follow-along study findings and reports.

HOW SHOULD TRANSITION SERVICES BE EVALUATED AFTER HIGH SCHOOL COMPLETION?

The final portion of this chapter discusses transition program evaluation. It is important for schools and adult services agencies to conduct periodic evaluations of their transition programs and services to determine if they are effectively meeting their students' or consumers' transition needs. We highly recommend a proactive approach to program evaluation, focused on anticipating, determining, and meeting the needs of consumers before an external agency program quality review. The following sections present and discuss major **transition program evaluation criteria** for schools and transition services agencies to consider:

1. Quality of transition services personnel
2. Quality of regional transition resources and services
3. Quality of IEP document and procedures
4. Quality of culmination and hand-off process
5. Quality of transition follow-up and follow-along procedures and data interpretation

Quality of Transition Personnel

Several qualities of the personnel who are responsible for providing transition services to youth with disabilities should be evaluated periodically. These include (a) knowledge of transition law and regulations, (b) transition resources and agency awareness, (c) inter- and intra-agency collaboration skills, (d) family empowerment skills, including the promotion of youth self-advocacy and self-determination, (e) IEP document preparation and procedure skills, (f) culmination and hand-off process skills, and (g) transition follow-up monitoring skills.

The specific knowledge needed by transition personnel in each of these areas has already been reviewed in previous portions of this text and chapter. This breadth and depth of transition personnel knowledge and skill should be evaluated periodically, at a minimum of once every 3 years. Suggested means include (a) personal interviews with transition inter- and intra-agency personnel, families, and youth with disabilities, focusing on the degree of collaboration and cooperation that exists between these individuals, as well as the transition services offered; (b) reviewing IEP documents prepared by transition personnel for quality and compliance with IDEA 2004; (c) evaluating the quality of the transition planning process and procedure implemented by transition personnel; and (d) monitoring follow-up data gathering procedures and findings of transition personnel. Information from these combined sources should be used to plan and provide updated training, support, and assistance as needed to personnel working with transition-age youth with disabilities.

Quality of Transition Resources and Agencies

This is the next area of focus for a transition program evaluation. A key indicator of an excellent transition program is the availability of quality resources and services in a variety of transition domains, such as education, employment, independent living, and recreation and leisure activities. Equally important is the availability of a variety of local transition services agencies providing needed transition services to families and youth with disabilities. Transition resources and services provided should be based on an assessment of the interests and abilities of a youth with a disability, rather than solely on what school districts and local transition services agencies are willing and able to offer. School transition personnel should know how to connect families with the most appropriate ones available.

As previously suggested, personal interviews with school and transition services agency personnel, as well as families and youth with disabilities, is a highly effective transition evaluation method. In addition, IEP documents should be reviewed to determine if quality transition resources and services are being provided. An evaluation of this type should focus on determining the degree of match that exists between the interests, preferences, and abilities of the youth with a disability and the transition resources and services written on the IEP. Degree of access and success in general education coursework in high school for the youth with a disability should be assessed as well.

Quality of IEP Documents, Process, and Procedure

A third important area of transition program evaluation is a review of IEP documents to determine the quality of required transition services language and the quality of the overall IEP transition planning process and procedure implemented by school personnel. The format and required transition services language contained on the IEP document should correspond to the recommendations presented and reviewed in chapter 9. With respect to evaluating the quality of the transition planning process and procedure, transition personnel should follow the recommended steps for organizing and conducting an IEP meeting in which transition planning is the focus (see Figure 9–12).

Several additional aspects of the IEP transition planning process and procedure should be evaluated as well. These include (a) the notification procedure for informing all parties to be present at the IEP meeting, (b) determining if all participants were provided ample opportunity to attend the IEP meeting or send a representative, (c) the degree to which family input and youth self-advocacy and self-determination was promoted before and during the IEP meeting, and (d) the degree of satisfaction the family and youth with a disability had with the outcome of the meeting. Personal interviews are perhaps the most effective means for obtaining this information.

Quality of Culmination and Hand-Off Process

The most valid way to evaluate the quality of the culmination and hand-off process is to interview families and youth with disabilities to determine the degree to which they experienced a smooth transition between the sending and receiving agency. Was there any truncation of services or were agreed-upon transition services provided after the youth with a disability completed or graduated from school? Equally important to evaluate is the length of time required before the agreed-upon transition services were provided by the receiving agency to the family and youth with a disability.

Finally, did the receiving agency attend the initial IEP meeting, as well as periodic annual review meetings prior to the time the youth with a disability completed or graduated high school? If meeting attendance was not possible, did periodic contact take place between the receiving agency and the school, family, and youth with a disability?

Quality of Follow-Up Data Gathering Procedures and Interpretation of Follow-Up Results

The quality of interpretation of obtained results from follow-up or follow-along studies is a key transition program evaluation component. It is important to determine if transition personnel are, in fact, conducting program evaluations and the specific methods being used. Transition **follow-along studies** have been highly recommended because they produce extremely valid information that can subsequently provide transition personnel with information regarding program strengths and areas of improvement. No matter the chosen method of program evaluation, the important question to ask is what data is being gathered by transition personnel, and how is it used for program improvement? Are written evaluation reports published periodically and program improvement efforts well documented? Can transition personnel demonstrate specific short-term and long-term program improvement efforts that have occurred in response to obtained recommendations?

Transition Program Evaluation Summary

Periodic evaluation activities to determine the quality of transition programs and services offered by schools and transition services agencies to families and youth with disabilities are extremely important. Valuable information can be gained that is useful for planning and implementing program improvements. Program evaluation should be multifaceted and focus on several key areas, including the quality of (a) transition personnel serving youth with disabilities and their families, (b) transition resources and services available in the local area, (c) IEP documents and procedures for meeting the letter and intent of IDEA, (d) the transition culmination hand-off process and procedure, and (e) program improvement efforts that occur as a result of follow-up or follow-along data-gathering procedures. These collective areas of transition program evaluation offer a breadth and depth of data, reflective of a comprehensive review of the overall quality of a transition services program. This type of program evaluation facilitates subsequent program improvement efforts. A case study illustrating transition program evaluation is presented next.

Case Study: Transition Program Evaluation

The special education department at Peterson High School decided to undergo a self-evaluation of their transition program and services. The evaluation would focus on the quality of the department's (a) IEP documents, (b) transition planning process and procedure, including culmination and hand-off process, and (c) knowledge and use of local transition services agency resources. Three teams were established to investigate each of these areas over a two-month period. The investigation focused on (a) the transition portion of the school district's IEP form for quality and compliance with federal law, (b) the degree to which the transition planning and procedure corresponded to the recommendations discussed in Chapter 9, and (c) the degree to which the locally published transition services agency resource guide was being used in the school district.

Results of the investigation showed that the IEP document for the district was using check boxes for transition goals rather than blank spaces on the IEP. The major shortcoming in the transition planning process was an apparent lack of student and family input into transition goals prior to the annual IEP meeting; this resulted in a much longer meeting than was necessary. Finally, the team concluded that greater collaboration was needed with local transition services agencies providing recreation and leisure assistance and integrated activities for youth with moderate to severe disabilities.

On the positive side, the transition program evaluation team found that there was a strong relationship between transition goals and annual IEP goals, objectives, and benchmarks for students in special education. Monitoring of the degree of access and successful completion of general education coursework for youth with disabilities was occurring as well. IEP meetings in which transition was discussed were well organized and well conducted, with the exception of the lack of student and family input prior to the meeting. Local transition services agencies were invited and were often in attendance at meetings when their services and input were needed. Finally, it was determined that agreed-upon transition services were being provided by transition services agencies according to stated timelines on the IEP and that a relatively smooth transition culmination and hand-off procedure was occurring at Peterson High School.

SUMMARY

Since its inception, special education has focused on providing individualized educational services and programs that result in the obtainment of specific and measurable annual goals and objectives for youth with disabilities. The achievement of long-term transition goals focused on postschool outcomes in a variety of domains for youth with disabilities is equally important. And yet, many special educators lack specific knowledge, training, methods, and procedures for writing the transition services language on an IEP, as well as how to effectively monitor the between-school and postschool status of their assigned caseload. This may be a potential explanation for the poor transition outcomes of youth with disabilities. The final phases of the transition process discussed in this chapter can potentially improve this situation.

This chapter began with a review of the culmination and hand-off process. Several culmination and hand-off process models were presented, along with the recommendation related to the best option for maximizing collaboration and cooperation between transition personnel and agencies. Implementation of either of these models by transition personnel and agencies increases the likelihood that agreed-upon transition services will be delivered without interruption in postschool environments for youth with disabilities.

Follow-up and follow-along procedures were subsequently discussed as effective means for improving and monitoring the long-term status of youth with disabilities. A number of important desired features recommended by Halpern (1990) were presented for designing transition tracking instruments, methods, and procedures. Transition personnel are encouraged to use follow-along strategies versus follow-up strategies because the former procedure produces more valid and reliable results. Regardless of the tracking procedures adopted, it is important to track transition outcomes in a variety of domains. sample survey instruments and questions for consideration by transition personnel interested in monitoring between-school and post-school transition status of youth with disabilities can be found in Appendix 11–1.

Finally, transition program evaluation procedures and recommendations were presented in this chapter. Periodic self-studies by local education agencies and adult services agencies are necessary to determine the quality of transition personnel, available regional transition resources and services, IEP documents and procedures, the culmination and hand-off process, and transition follow-up data gathered on youth with disabilities who have graduated or completed school. Transition program evaluation information is best obtained from personal interviews, reviews of IEP documents, and the transition planning process and procedure implemented by special education personnel. These combined sources of information can subsequently be used to validate transition program strengths and needed areas of improvement.

In closing, if the aim of transition personnel, programs, and agencies is to promote independence and a quality adult life for youth with disabilities, monitoring the transition status of these individuals is both logical and necessary. Engaging in the types of activities recommended in this chapter will draw important attention to the final phases of transition and provide better monitoring and support for youth with disabilities as they leave school to assume the role of an adult in society.

KEY TERMS AND PHRASES

follow-along studies

follow-up studies

guidelines for conducting follow-up
   and follow-along studies

models of interagency interaction

sending and receiving agencies

transition culmination and hand-off
   process

transition program evaluation criteria

QUESTIONS FOR REFLECTION, THINKING, AND SKILL BUILDING

1. What is involved in the transition culmination and hand-off process, and what steps should occur to promote a smooth transfer of responsibility from transition services sending agencies to receiving agencies?

2. What is a follow-along study versus a follow-up study, and why is the former procedure superior to the latter method for evaluating the quality of transition services and programs provided to youth with disabilities?

3. What postschool outcomes should be investigated by transition personnel when determining the transition status of youth with disabilities who have completed or graduated from school?

4. Which transition culmination and hand-off process model best describes the final phase of transition for youth with disabilities in your local school or district? Provide evidence to support your conclusion.

5. How can the transition culmination and hand-off process for youth with disabilities be improved in your school or district?

6. What type of transition outcome data is gathered on youth with and without disabilities in your school or district and how are these data used for program improvement? What improvements would you recommend for your school or district for determining the postschool transition outcome status of youth with disabilities?

7. How does your school or district evaluate transition programs and services for youth with disabilities, and what evaluation criteria does it use? What improvements would you recommend for your school or district for evaluating transition programs and services?

8. Create an interagency team in your school or district and implement the necessary steps to promote the adoption of Model B or C for the transition culmination and hand-off process.

9. Investigate the quality of the transition culmination and hand-off process in your school or district and make recommendations to key school or district administrative and special education personnel.

10. Conduct a pilot follow-up or follow-along study of youth with disabilities in your school or district and share your findings with key administrative and special education personnel.

11. Conduct a pilot transition program evaluation in your school or district and share your findings with key administrative and special education personnel.

Appendix 11–1

➡ BETWEEN-SCHOOL TRANSITION SURVEY

Youth name:_____

Date:_____

My child has permission to complete and return this survey.

Parent signature:_____   Date:_____

Place a check next to the appropriate item that accurately describes your current status in school.

1. Educational Placement:
   _____ Full Inclusion   _____ Partial Inclusion   _____ Full-Day Special Education

2. Educational setting and percentage of time in each setting:
   Setting (check all that apply)   %
   _____ General Education   _____
   _____ Resource Room   _____
   _____ Special Day Class   _____
   _____ Related Services_____   _____
   _____ Other:_____   _____

3. High school course of study you are currently pursuing (check all that apply):
   _____ College entrance/diploma/core curriculum
   _____ Community college entrance/diploma/core curriculum
   _____ Departmentalized special education/diploma/core curriculum
   _____ GED exam
   _____ Certificate of completion
   _____ Vocational emphasis
   _____ Functional/community-based instruction

4. Number of general education courses completed to date:_____

5. Number of units completed to date that apply toward graduation:_____

6. Cumulative grade-point average to date:_____

7. Participation in school extracurricular activities (list activities in which you are participating):

388

8. Participation in community-based activities (list activities in which you are involved):

9. List any paid work experience in which you have participated:
    Employer:
    Full time _____   Part time_____
    Hourly wage _____
    Length of employment _____

10. List any other information below about your life experiences since changing schools:

11. How satisfied are you with your high school experience?
    _____ Very satisfied
    _____ Somewhat satisfied
    _____ Somewhat dissatisfied
    _____ Very dissatisfied

12. Would you be willing to participate in a phone interview to discuss your transition to high school?
    _____ Yes   My phone number is:_____
    _____ No

→ POSTSCHOOL TRANSITION SURVEY

Name:_____

Date:_____

Please place a check next to the items below that best describe your life circumstances at the present time.

I. *Postschool Educational Status*
    _____ Four-year college or university
    _____ Community college
    _____ Vocational–technical school

_____ Adult school

_____ Military enlisted (branch of service):

_____ Army   _____ Navy   _____ Air Force   _____ Marines

_____ Not currently enrolled in school

Number of years in school: _____

Current college major (if declared): _____

Number of education courses completed to date: _____

Number of units completed to date that apply toward graduation: _____

Cumulative grade point average to date: _____

Participation in school extracurricular activities (list activities in which you are participating):

Are you receiving assistance from Disabled Student Services ? _____ Yes _____ No

What services are you receiving (check all that apply):

_____ Note-taking

_____ Subject-matter tutoring

_____ Study skills

_____ Test accommodations

_____ Adaptive technology

_____ Assistance with writing papers

_____ Other:_____

How satisfied are you with your postsecondary educational experience?

_____ Very satisfied

_____ Somewhat satisfied

_____ Somewhat dissatisfied

_____ Very dissatisfied

II. *Employment Status*

Place a check next to the items that best describe your employment status.

_____ Full-time employment (average of 40 hours per week)

_____ Part-time employment

_____ Currently unemployed

Employment setting

_____ Fully integrated/competitive employment

_____ Partially integrated/competitive employment

_____ Supported employment

Wages

_____ Salary: monthly income_____

_____ Hourly: wage per hour_____

Benefits (check all that apply):

_____ Medical _____ Dental _____ Vision _____ Vacation _____ Retirement

Employment history: number of jobs held since completing high school _____

How satisfied are you with your employment status?

_____ Very satisfied

_____ Somewhat satisfied

_____ Somewhat dissatisfied

_____ Very dissatisfied

III. *Residential Status*

Place a check next to the item that best describes your current living arrangements.

_____ Home purchased

_____ Home rental

_____ Apartment rental

_____ College youth housing

_____ Group home

_____ Room rental in a private home

_____ Living at home with parents

Independent living status (put a check next to the appropriate spaces)

_____ Married

_____ Single

_____ Divorced

_____ Fully independent

_____ Semi-independent

_____ Supported living

How satisfied are you with your living and independence status?

_____ Very satisfied

_____ Somewhat satisfied

_____ Somewhat dissatisfied

_____ Very dissatisfied

IV. *Community Access*

Place a check next to the space that best describes how you access your community.

_____ Drive my own car

_____ Drive motorcycle or moped

_____ Public transportation (bus)

_____ Drive with family or friend
_____ Walk
_____ Bicycle
_____ Other: _____

How satisfied are you with your ability to access your community?
_____ Very satisfied
_____ Somewhat satisfied
_____ Somewhat dissatisfied
_____ Very dissatisfied

V. *Recreation and Leisure Activities*

Please put a check next to any of the activities listed in which you regularly participate.
_____ Movies
_____ Concerts
_____ Plays
_____ Dancing
_____ Dining out
_____ Sporting events
_____ Clubs
_____ Gym or other form of exercise
_____ Church or synagogue
_____ Visit with friends
_____ Shopping
_____ Bowling
_____ Community recreation class
_____ Community sports league
_____ Other: _____

How satisfied are you with your recreation and leisure activities?
_____ Very satisfied
_____ Somewhat satisfied
_____ Somewhat dissatisfied
_____ Very dissatisfied

VI. *Social and Interpersonal Network*

Place a check next to the space that best describes your friendship status:
_____ I have 5–10 very close friends.
_____ I have 3–5 very close friends.
_____ I have 1–3 very close friends.
_____ I don't have any very close friends.

How satisfied are you with your friendships?
_____ Very satisfied
_____ Somewhat satisfied

_____ Somewhat dissatisfied
_____ Very dissatisfied

Would you be willing to participate in a phone interview to discuss your adult life experiences?

_____ Yes   My phone number is: _____
_____ No

Chapter 12

Planning for Postsecondary Transition

Carol A. Kochhar-Bryant

For most students, participation in postsecondary educa-
tion is not limited to being physically present in a lecture
hall. It is the possibility to ask questions, to discuss ideas
with classmates, to have a critical conversation with
professors about papers, to reflect upon readings, to explore
the library, to have access to information in accessible
formats at the same time as their non-disabled classmates,
to work on a research project, to have coffee with friends, to
participate at campus social and cultural events, and really
take part in the college experience

—*National Council on Disability, 2003*

Chapter Questions

- What postsecondary options are there?
- Who participates in postsecondary options?
- What changes as the student moves from the secondary to the postsecondary world?
- What strategies assist youth with transition to postsecondary education?
- What strategies assist youth with transition to employment?
- What can we learn from the voices of youth?

➡ INTRODUCTION

Americans throughout history have recognized the power of education to transform the lives of all people and strengthen their participation in their communities. Rapid changes in the employment market have made a postsecondary education essential for entry into careers and for career advancement. The past several decades have witnessed a growing national investment in youth development to increase access to education and employment preparation programs and to increase social and economic independence. Interest in career development and transition is greater than it has ever been in the past, both in the United States and in other nations. Successful transition from secondary school is becoming recognized as a *chief indicator of the effectiveness* of our educational system for preparing youth and young adults for employment, postsecondary education, and adult independence (Baer et al., 2003; Johnson, Sharpe, & Stodden, 2000; Wagner, Newman, Cameto, Garza, & Levine, 2005).

This chapter describes transition and system coordination strategies for students as they move from the secondary to postsecondary setting. This chapter explores how disability laws support young people in postsecondary institutions and the work setting and define responsibilities of professionals. A variety of coordination activities are described along with the professional roles in schools and communities that help young people at the crossroads of high school graduation.

LET'S SEE IT IN ACTION! CASE EXAMPLE

This case presents a central question for students with disabilities who plan to seek admission to postsecondary education after graduation from high school.

Question: I am a high school senior with a learning disability and I have just been admitted to the college of my choice. Will the accommodations that were provided to me in high school under my IEP automatically be provided to me in college?

Answer: First of all, no accommodations will be provided to you unless and until you identify yourself to be a student with a disability, and provide documentation of your disability. Once the proper administrator has been notified, under §504 of the Rehabilitation Act, and under the Americans with Disabilities Act, the college must provide reasonable and appropriate accommodations and academic adjustments that specifically address your known disability. By providing such accommodations, they afford you an equal opportunity to participate in the institution's programs, courses, and activities. The college, however, is not required to provide accommodations just because they appear in your IEP, though that information can certainly be very helpful to Disability Support Service (DSS) coordinators as they develop your personal accommodations plan. In fact, DSS personnel may determine that some accommodations you received in high school substantially alter aspects of the curriculum, and are therefore not reasonable. They were actually modifications to the curriculum. In short, it will be useful to refer to your IEP when discussing possible accommodations for college-level work, yet be prepared to consider alternative accommodations or adjustments in the event that some in the IEP are no longer available to you (HEATH Resource Center, 2005).

➡ WHAT POSTSECONDARY OPTIONS ARE THERE?

Postsecondary Options for Youth with Disabilities

The point of transition from high school to the postsecondary world is a challenging crossroad for all young people. They have to make choices about what college they will choose, what they will study, where they will live, whether they will work while they study, and how they will pay for their living expenses. If they choose to enter employment directly they may be concerned about the kind of job for which they should interview, whether they have the skills and the stamina to work the long hours, how they will save and budget their earnings, and how they will juggle all of life's demands.

There are many postsecondary options for youth with disabilities in the United States. *Four-year colleges and universities* offer Bachelor of Arts or Bachelor of Science degrees. Some also offer graduate and professional degrees. *Community colleges* are public, 2-year colleges that typically serve people in the surrounding communities and offer academic, technical, and continuing education courses. The programs often lead to a license, a certificate, or associate of arts or science degrees. Community colleges often operate under an *open admissions* policy and admissions requirements. Some community colleges offer programs for individuals with cognitive disabilities, autism, and other disabilities and are focused on developing functional and employment skills.

Career–Technical colleges offer a variety of options, including associate degrees, certificates, and work apprenticeships. Associate degree programs prepare students for technical occupations (e.g., accounting, dental hygienist, and computer programmer). Technical diploma programs meet the needs of businesses and industry and provide employees with required certification for employment (e.g., automotive maintenance, accounting assistant, information technology, carpenter's assistant, and pharmacy technician). Apprenticeships are typically geared toward those interested in working in industrial or service trades (e.g., carpentry, plumbing, and machining). *Military service* can also help young people achieve their career goals; however, the military branches are not required to accommodate individuals on the basis of disability (Brown 2000; HEATH Resource Center, 2005). Finally, *employment* in competitive jobs or supported work settings are common postsecondary goals for many youth, even if they plan eventually to enter into a 2- or 4-year college.

During the transition to college life, individuals with disabilities have the same choices to make as their nondisabled peers, and also face many additional considerations that add to the uncertainty and stress. These include

1. What colleges have the support services, accommodations, and assistive technology I need, and will the Disability Support Services (DSS) office need proof of my disability?
2. Will I get into a dormitory with my disability, and will I make friends in my classes?
3. Will professors help accommodate me if I cannot finish the tests on time due to my reading disability, or will they be suspicious of my motives?
4. Will there be counselors if I run into difficulty and need help?
5. Will the campus be accessible for my wheelchair?
6. Will people accept me as an equal in my new job?

Because these additional uncertainties place extraordinary demands on the young adult, supportive services are often (though not always) needed to help in the transition and adjustment to the college or work setting.

Table 12–1 shows the pathways introduced in chapter 1 and the postsecondary options described above. Box 12–1 describes a college program for individuals with significant disabilities.

Table 12–1   Transition Pathways and Levels of Support

Path/ Postsecondary Goal	Domains Emphasized	Coordinated Set of Activities (aligned with IDEA 2004 requirements)	Assessments Used	Postsecondary Option/Goal
Academic or postsecondary education	Academic	IEP or transition planning based on postsecondary goals Academic course of study designed to achieve postsecondary goals Self-determination and self-advocacy skill development Support services and accommodations VR and agency services as needed	Academic or Standardized	2- or 4-year college enrollment
Career-Technical Training	Career and social	IEP or transition planning based on postsecondary goals Blended academic and career-vocational courses (career pathway) designed to achieve postsecondary goals Self-determination and self-advocacy skill development Vocational evaluation Support services and accommodations VR and agency services as needed	Vocational and community-based authentic assessments	Vocational–technical school or career apprenticeship
Employment	Vocational and independent living	IEP or transition planning based on postsecondary goals Blended academic and career-vocational courses designed to achieve postsecondary goals Community-based employment experiences Self-determination and self-advocacy skill development Vocational evaluation Support services and accommodations VR and agency services as needed	Vocational Assessments in authentic or simulated settings	Competitive employment
Supported Setting	Social and independent living	IEP or transition planning based on postsecondary goals Functional academics and social and life skills designed to achieve postsecondary goals Community-based competitive or supported employment experiences Self-determination and self-advocacy skill development Vocational evaluation Support services and accommodations in the workplace VR and agency services as needed	Social, adaptive behavior, and independent living skills assessments	Competitive or supported employment and independent or supported living

> **Box 12–1**
>
> *LIFE Program Provides Postsecondary Education for Young Adults with Severe Challenges*
>
> Over the past few years, some 2- and 4-year colleges and universities are providing innovative independent living programs and courses to students with disabilities. For example, the Kellar Institute for Human disAbilities at the George Mason University, outside Washington DC, has launched a new program to prepare students with disabilities for careers and independent living. The program blends functional instruction with academics to prepare young adults with significant disabilities for employment and independent living in their communities. The Learning into Future Environments (LIFE) program, the first of its kind at a public 4-year university, allows these students to obtain a postsecondary education in a supportive, inclusive environment. At the same time, the program provides Mason students majoring in disciplines such as education, psychology, assistive technology, and social work with practical experience in working with individuals with disabilities (George Mason University, Kellar Institute for Human Disabilities, 2002, by permission).

Becoming Employed After High School

The next section takes a look at the types of employment opportunities available for young men and women with significant disabilities, including competitive, supported, and sheltered employment.

Competitive Employment.   **Competitive employment** means a mainstream full-time or part-time job with competitive wages and responsibilities. Typically, com-*petitive employment means that no long-term support is provided to the employee to help him or her learn the job or continue to perform the job. The absence of ongoing or long-term support distinguishes competitive employment from both* supported employment and sheltered employment (described below). All sorts of jobs are considered competitive employment—restaurant service worker, mechanic, teacher, secretary, factory worker, file clerk, or computer programmer. The amount of education or training a person needs *will vary depending on the type of* job.

Supported Employment.   **Supported employment** programs assist young people with the most significant disabilities to become and remain successfully employed in integrated workplace settings. Supported employment is designed for people who are not ready for competitive employment, or their competitive employment has been interrupted or is intermittent as a result of the disability. It is also designed for those who, because of the severity of their disability, need intensive or extended support services to work competitively (U.S. Department of Labor,

Office of Disability Employment Policy, 2005). Supported employment models include the following:

1. Individual placement: Consumers or employees obtain employment independently and then contact the supported employment providers to get assistance or support, as needed.
2. Agency supported: A rehabilitation or community services agency places the consumer in a job and provides or coordinates the ongoing support services needed to assist him or her to retain the job.
3. Entrepreneurial: The consumer or employee is supported by the rehabilitation or community services agency to get the services and supports needed to successfully run his or her own business.

Supportive services in an employment setting may include job development and placement; intensive job-site training; facilitation of natural supports; special skills training; supplementary assessment; contact with employers, parents, family members, and advocacy organizations; teaching compensatory workplace strategies. *Job development* means locating jobs for people with disabilities through networking with employers, businesses, and community leaders. The use of business advisory councils is an excellent way to develop contacts that lead to employment for people with disabilities. An *employment specialist* or *consultant (job coach)* is typically employed by a job-training and placement organization serving people with disabilities who matches clients with jobs, provides necessary supports during the initial employment period, and then facilitates the transition to natural workplace supports while reducing his or her role.

Sheltered Employment.   When employment is *sheltered,* individuals with significant and multiple disabilities work in a separate, self-contained center unit and are not integrated with non-disabled workers. This type of employment is generally supported by federal or state funds. The type of training that workers receive varies among programs, as does the type of work. Typical tasks include sewing, packing boxes, putting together packages or envelopes for mailing, or collating. In the past, segregated employment was thought to be the only option available for individuals with significant cognitive disabilities such as mental retardation or autism. Today, many individuals with significant disabilities are working in integrated settings when provided with adequate support.

➡ WHO PARTICIPATES IN POSTSECONDARY OPTIONS?

Participation and Outcomes of Postsecondary Education

Young adults with disabilities who complete a college degree are as likely to become employed as their peers without disabilities; however, they are much less prepared and likely to enroll or to complete college (National Center for Secondary Education and Transition, 2004a, 2004b; Wagner, Newman, Cameto, Garza, & Levine, 2005).

Preparation for Postsecondary Settings.   Many youth with disabilities are not adequately prepared to meet the entrance requirements and academic rigor of postsecondary institutions. There are several reasons for this. Students with disabilities are less likely than their peers without disabilities to complete a full secondary school academic curriculum, especially in math and science curriculum areas. Furthermore, many are not encouraged in high school to extend their education beyond secondary school. Many secondary students with disabilities still have minimal involvement in their IEP meetings and therefore are unprepared with a postsecondary transition plan or to self-advocate for their needs (Furney & Salembrier, 2000; Miller, Lombard, & Corbey, 2006; National Council on Disability, 2000b; Wagner, Newman, Cameto, & Levine, 2006). When ranked according to qualifications for college admission, students with disabilities were less likely than their peers to be minimally qualified, based on an index score of grades, class rank, National Education Longitudinal Study (NELS) composite test scores, and SAT or ACT scores (Brinckerhoff, McGuire, & Shaw, 2002; Jenkins & Boswell, 2002; National Center for Education Statistics, 1999; Rioux-Bailey, 2004).

Increased Number of Students in College Who Report Disabilities.   The number of postsecondary students (all types of institutions) reporting a disability has increased dramatically, climbing from 2.6% in 1978, to 9.2% in 1994, 19% in 1996 (Blackorby & Wagner, 1996), and 20% in 2002 (Blackorby & Wagner, 2002). This increase is partly due to changes in the Higher Education Act, §504 of the **Rehabilitation Act,** and **Americans with Disabilities Act** (ADA) that require institutions of higher education (2- and 4 -year colleges and universities, vocational and technical schools) to provide reasonable accommodations for students with disabilities. Since 1990, there has been a 90% increase in the number of colleges, universities, technical institutions, and career technical centers offering opportunities for persons with disabilities to continue education (Dare, 2006; National Center for the Study of Postsecondary Educational Supports & National Center on Secondary Education and Transition, 2001; Pierangelo & Crane, 1997; Sharpe, Bruininks, Blacklock, Benson, & Johnson, 2004; Skinner, 2004).

Long-Term Outcomes of Participation in College.   Although substantial federal and state investments in creating a seamless transition for students with disabilities have increased enrollment in postsecondary education programs, they have not had a significant impact on the completion of programs by students with disabilities (Blackorby & Wagner, 2002; Gilmore, Bose, & Hart, 2002). Large gaps remain in comparison to students without disabilities. Studies have found that only 27% of students with disabilities enroll in postsecondary education compared with 69% of students without disabilities (U.S. Department of Labor, 2005). More than 26% of freshmen with disabilities at 4-year colleges *do not return* for their sophomore year (Izzo, Hertzfeld, Simmons-Reed, & Aaron, 2001) compared with 73% of students without disabilities (ACT, 2006). Students with disabilities who enroll in postsecondary institutions are less likely than their non-disabled counterparts to complete a bachelor's degree (16% and 52%, respectively) (U.S. Government Accountability Office, 2003b). Students with disabilities who earn a bachelors degree do almost as well with employment as do individuals without a disability (67% of youth with disabilities with a bachelor degree were working full time compared with 73% for persons with disability holding the same degree) (National Center for Education Statistics, 2000a; U.S. Department of Education, Office of Special Education, 2002). Nonetheless, the enrollment of people with disabilities in postsecondary institutions is *still 50% lower than enrollment among the general population* (Getzel, Stodden, & Briel, 2001; Roessler & Rumrill, 1998; Sharpe & Johnson, 2001; Vreeburg-Izzo, Hertzfeld, Simmons-Reed, & Aaron, 2001, Winter). This gap in educational attainment affects long-term employment prospects.

What Are the Barriers to Participation in Postsecondary Education?

Many college students with and without disabilities are faced with challenging physical and social environments. These challenges are compounded for students with disabilities because they are faced with architectural barriers and attitudinal misperceptions about their skills and abilities by faculty, staff, and their non-disabled peers (Justesen & Justesen, 2000). Youth face several barriers as they prepare for and participate in postsecondary schools education.

Lack of Identification of the Disability in Early School Years. Many students with disabilities are not appropriately identified and provided needed special education and related services during childhood and adolescent years. For example, 31% of national survey respondents with specific learning disabilities (SLD) indicated that their disability was first identified at the postsecondary level (National Center for the Study of Postsecondary Educational Supports 2000b). When declaring a primary disability, 44% of participants with an attention deficit disorder (ADD) indicated that their disability was first identified at the postsecondary level (Vreeburg-Izzo, Hertzfeld, Simmons-Reed, & Aaron, 2001, Winter). Delayed identification prevents students from benefiting from years of needed services, and often requires that they seek support services on the college campus. Such students must pay for expert assessments to prove their disability and its impact on their learning. Early identification and intervention can prevent these difficulties.

Lack of Access to Guidance Counseling. As mentioned earlier, dropout rates and receipt of alternative diplomas are much higher for youth with disabilities than for their nondisabled peers. Few states have defined what it means to be college or career ready (Olson, 2007). Many high school youth with disabilities who are moved from content classes to special education classes may consequently not meet the entry requirements of many postsecondary schools (Johnson & Thurlow, 2003; Johnson, Thurlow, Casio, & Bremer, 2005). Others face barriers to tests and assessments, such as the SAT, which may require testing accommodations. Finally, many academic and career counselors lack the necessary skills to provide guidance to students with disabilities. Secondary students are often left with inadequate guidance due to poor coordination among teachers and counseling staff (Stodden, Galloway, & Stodden, 2003; Stodden, Jones, & Chang, 2002). Strengthening counselors' understanding of the needs of youth with disabilities can ameliorate these challenges.

Lack of Financial Support Through College. Individuals with disabilities are more likely to face financial barriers during postsecondary education. Individuals with disabilities are more than twice as likely to live below the poverty line as individuals without disabilities (Bush, 2004). At the same time, research has shown that few students with disabilities are accessing disability benefits that are available to them in postsecondary study. As one study shows, only 8.3% of postsecondary students with disabilities participate in SSI and SSDI disability programs. In general, postsecondary students with disabilities, when compared to non-disabled peers, receive less financial aid and are unable to participate in assistance programs due to lack of awareness about SSI or SSDI disability benefits and work incentive programs (Berry & Jones, 2000). Educating students about available benefits and resources while they are in high school can make the difference between independence and long-term dependence.

Attitudes and Stigma. Many youth who attend college experience negative self-concept, poor socialization skills, stress and anxiety, and professors who are reluctant to provide assistance or accommodations (Chadsey & Sheldon, 1998; Wolanin & Steele, 2004). Many students with disabilities choose to remain invisible because they are concerned about the *stigma of accommodations,* believing that "Teachers and other students think I'm getting away with something when I'm given accommodations" (National Center for the Study of Postsecondary Educational Supports, 2000b). Preparation for self-advocacy in high school, a welcoming attitude on the part of postsecondary institutions, and well informed faculty can reduce these stresses.

Barriers for Culturally and Linguistically Diverse Students. Entering postsecondary education from high school can be an overwhelming process for students with disabilities. These gaps are even greater for students with significant disabilities and who are culturally and linguistically diverse (CLD). Compared with their non-CLD peers, CLD students with disabilities are more likely to face language and social barriers, face the negative effects of having grown up in poverty, and have difficulty processing "standard English" oral and written information, all of which may contribute to their risk of school failure (Greene & Kochhar, 2003; Greene & Nefsky, 1999). Furthermore, students with disabilities who are from diverse cultures are less likely to disclose their disability and receive support services in postsecondary schools (Flowers, Edwards, & Pusch, 1996, July–September; Hart, Zafft, & Zimbrich, 2001; Hasnain, 2001; Stodden, Dowrick, Gilmore, & Galloway, 2003; Stodden et al., 2002). These conditions point to the need for greater assistance to CLD postsecondary students, as illustrated in Box 12–2.

Gap in Technology Access. Lack of access to technology impedes students' ability to achieve to their potential in high school and to use technology in the postsecondary environments. Only 28.4% of Americans with disabilities have access to the Internet at home or work, compared to 56.7% of those without disabilities. Almost 60% of Americans with disabilities have never even used a personal computer, compared to less than 25% of Americans without disabilities (Kaye, 2000; National Organization on Disability, 2000). When students with disabilities do have access to technology in high

Box 12–2

Circle of Support at the University of Hawaii

Fasy (pronounced as "Faz-ee") grew up in a small island country in the Pacific Ocean. He became paralyzed as a teenager when he fell from a cliff and suffered a serious spinal injury. Unable to walk, he learned to use a wheelchair. Neither the schools nor other government services provided much in special services for people like Fasy. However, with his determination and academic capabilities, he earned entry to the University of Hawaii at Manoa. A number of support services were available to him there. Due to the seriousness of his disability, Fasy required assistance to get around campus and take care of his basic needs, but extensive aide services were not available. Fortunately, in keeping with the family orientation of his Pacific Island culture, some of his family members were able to come to Hawaii specifically to support him to reach his postsecondary education goals. During much of his academic career, one or two of his brothers were always at his side, and when they were not available, other family members assisted him. With the support of his family, Fasy earned his bachelor's degree and then two master's degrees, one in history and the other in Pacific Islands Studies. The challenges presented by his disability as well as cultural and language differences resulted in his taking several extra years to complete his studies. However, his own efforts, the supports provided by his family, and supports provided by the university, were successful, and now, in his late 30s, he is the director of one of the four campuses of his country's national university.

This case study illustrates how a cultural strength (individuals giving priority to the success of the family as a whole) can be built upon to support a CLD student with disabilities to achieve postsecondary educational success. What is notable in this case is the ready and coordinated participation of the entire family? This *collectivist* orientation contrasts with the *individualistic* orientation of mainstream American society, and should be taken into account when addressing the support needs of persons with disabilities from collectivist cultural backgrounds (Leake & Cholymay, 2004, by permission).

school, it is more than likely that they will not be able to take the technology with them after graduation (Gaylord, Johnson, Lehr, Bremer, & Hazasi, 2004). Examples of technology-related supports in postsecondary settings include the following: accessible Web pages and instructional software, accessible telephones, scooters and wheelchairs, alternative automobile controls, environmental controls, prostheses, communication aids, hand splints, hearing aids, and alternative input and output devices for computers. Students must be prepared to advocate for their technological needs in the postsecondary setting.

Inadequate Preparation of College Faculty.   An important factor that affects students' persistence and retention is the lack of awareness of faculty members of the disability needs of students, available supports on campus, and their responsibility for making accommodations. Failure to make needed accommodations may lead to diminished student performance and invite misunderstanding or conflict that could lead to either dropping out or adversarial relationships with the institution (National Council on Disability, 2003c; Scott, Shaw, & McGuire, 2003). For example, a student who used a wheelchair and was partially visually impaired asked the professor if he could sit toward the front of class to see the board. The small classroom configuration allowed the wheelchair to be in the rear of the class only unless several chairs were moved at the beginning of each class. The professor persuaded the student not to inconvenience classmates by moving all the chairs and that he would send all of the notes and materials after class by e-mail. Of course, having the opportunity to see the board and follow along during the lesson is the student's need. Postsecondary institutions can promote student persistence and retention by educating faculty in accommodations for students with disabilities.

LET'S SEE IT IN ACTION! CASE EXAMPLE

A Miracle of Determination

Katherine's Story

Katherine defied all predictions for her medical prognosis. She is a survivor of a life-threatening traumatic brain injury suffered in her teens as a result of an auto accident. After weeks in a coma, she fought through a lengthy and difficult recovery, in spite of repeated warnings from medical professionals that she would never walk, talk, or have a normal life again.

Katherine's determination began when she first took stock of her recovery challenges and committed herself to defying all medical predications about her future. She continually replays that commitment, using cautions by others as one more reason to "prove them wrong." She went on to finish high school, complete undergraduate work, and then complete two masters' degrees in excellent standing; she is now a doctoral student in special education. Katherine still has residual physical and speech disabilities that she overcomes every day.

Her early dedication to constantly practicing and developing the skills she needed (speech, mobility, social, and cognitive) have made her a pillar of resilience. Her confidence, commitment to academic and personal goals, and natural leadership that she brings from her "place of experience" and her vision are witnessed by all who come in contact with her—her family, faculty, classmates, and many others. Katherine is now a doctoral student in special education and her research interests lie in the area of recovery of function related to brain injuries and how environments for recovery can accelerate the process.

A Professor's Story

Katherine was a graduate student who had survived a life threatening brain injury in high school.

Defying all her doctors' predictions, she fought hard to achieve a remarkable recovery. She finished high school and went on to complete an undergraduate degree with high honors.

She made it clear to her advisor from the beginning that she was a survivor. She spoke openly and honestly about her past and her struggles. She met frequently with me, her advisor, for counsel when she needed it. She spoke about her academic work, her struggles with relationships with peers, and about her long-range goals. Sometimes these meetings involved Kleenex, but that was a small price to pay if the time helped contribute to Katherine's persistence in her classes and to her success. Mostly, Katherine was very positive and dedicated to overcoming all of her struggles.

As her professor, I became very "invested" in this student's success, understanding her disability along the way, and gaining a great appreciation for her strength and her struggle.

This professor has become her strongest advocate.

What Do We Know About Youth Employment After High School?

Large gaps continue to exist between young people with disabilities and the remainder of the population with regard to education, transition, economic, and independent living outcomes. Despite decades of federal and state initiatives to improve employment outcomes for youth with disabilities, employment outcomes continue to reflect the widest gulf between youth with disabilities and the general population (Blanck, 2000). According to the Census Bureau (Simmons & O'Neill, 2000), only 3 in 10 working-aged people with disabilities are employed full- time, compared to 8 in 10 people in the rest of the population. Fabian, Lent, and Willis (1998) found that 2 years after high school only about 43% of young people with disabilities were employed, compared to 69% of their peers (Cameto, 2005). Currently, 20% of students in special education who complete high school are enrolled in postsecondary education compared to 68% of the general student population (Wagner, Newman, Cameto, Garza, & Levine, 2005; Wagner, Newman, Cameto, & Levine, 2005). And 3–5 years after high school, only a little more than half become employed compared to 69% of their peers.

What Are the Barriers to Employment for Youth with Disabilities?

Lack of Career-Related Course Work.   Although more than half (56%) of the students with disabilities had a goal of finding competitive employment after leaving high school, many who choose to enter directly into employment after completing high school are not adequately prepared to reach their goals (Wagner, Newman, Cameto, & Levine, 2006). Students with disabilities are less likely than students without disabilities to complete courses in high school that prepare them to succeed in skilled employment (Scholl & Mooney, 2005). Preparation must begin in the early school years to ensure that students participate in appropriate career development courses. *Schools can bridge the gap* by providing work experiences, career and academic counseling, job coaching and mentoring opportunities while encouraging students to enroll in the kinds of academic courses that will prepare them to succeed in work and college.

Work-Based Learning Experiences in School.   Over the past 15 years, work-based learning experiences have become more available to youth with disabilities (Wagner, Cadwallader, Newman, & Marder, 2003). According to parents' reports, almost 60% of youth with disabilities were employed during a 1-year period in high school, some at work–study jobs, but the vast majority at nonschool-related jobs (Cameto, Marder, Wagner, & Cardoso, 2003). Approximately 15% of youth with disabilities held work–study jobs in a given year (6 percentage points more than in 1987); increases of 14–18 percentage points were significant for youth with cognitive disabilities, emotional disturbance, or multiple disabilities. The most common work–study placements are at food service (19%), maintenance (16%), and clerical (15%) jobs.

More than 90% of youth in work–study jobs receive school credit and/or pay for their work. Older youth are more likely than younger youth to have work–study jobs.

Work–study employment rates are approximately 10% for youth 15 years of age or younger, 15% for 16-year-olds, and 19% for 17-year-olds. The percentage of youth with work–study jobs varies for youth in different disability categories. Youth with speech impairments or learning disabilities are the least likely to have work–study jobs (7% and 10%, respectively). In contrast, approximately 30% of youth with mental retardation, autism, multiple disabilities, or deaf-blindness hold work–study jobs (Wagener & Cameto, 2004). Participation in work-based learning is associated with successful outcomes for youth with disabilities. The IEP team can play a significant role in determining the appropriate contribution of work-based learning experiences in the student's education and transition plan.

➡ WHAT CHANGES AS THE STUDENT MOVES FROM THE SECONDARY TO THE POSTSECONDARY WORLD?

U.S. Department's Office for Civil Rights (U.S. Department of Education, Office for Civil Rights, 2007a) in a letter to parents advised that institutions of postsecondary education have no legal obligations under IDEA. OCR strongly encourages students with disabilities to know their rights and responsibilities, and those of postsecondary institutions, under §504 of the Rehabilitation Act and the ADA.

When students are in elementary and secondary school they are entitled to receive appropriate transition services and to expect school staff to coordinate with students, parents, and community agencies to provide appropriate transition services and resources. *Entitlements,* mandated under a variety of laws, are designed to ensure that students receive services for which they are eligible. When students with disabilities leave the school, they must rely on adult services agencies to continue providing supportive services that may be needed in employment or postsecondary education. *Services provided through adult agencies are not entitlements.* These agencies have various eligibility requirements and, because of limited funding, cannot always immediately offer services to eligible citizens. Applicants for services are placed on a waiting list. Planning for ongoing support before exiting school is key to accessing services. Awareness of agency eligibility criteria, meeting agency staff, gathering information from state and federal agencies about existing programs, and learning about community resources provides valuable information for students, families, and teachers to guide transition planning.

Students with disabilities and their parents are generally not well informed about the differences in the rights and responsibilities of schools and students as they move from high school to higher education. The result is that students are often harshly surprised rather than prepared for the disparity between the two levels of education (National Council on Disability, 2003; Office of Civil Rights, 2007a). In secondary school, teachers and other school professionals share the responsibility for the educational success with the student, but *in higher education it is up to the individual.* Student must gain the skills to advocate for their needs in college or on the job, skills they may not have learned in high school.

Self-Advocacy Skills Needed for Postsecondary Participation: It Is up to the Student

Every state is now emphasizing transition services and working to ensure that students with disabilities who need such services are provided with adequate planning and support. Only one half of secondary schools, however, have specific curriculum to teach secondary students *self-advocacy and self-determination skills* (Grigal, Neubert, & Moon, 2005; U.S. Department of Education, Office of Special Education, 2005a; U.S. Government Accountability Office, 2003a). Postsecondary school is different from secondary school in many ways. Class schedules are more flexible, class offerings are more varied, and class periods are shorter. Students are expected to take full responsibility for their progress and to spend much more time and effort on independent study. For students living on campus, there is a wide variety of social opportunities, and often a great sense of freedom from parental supervision. Postsecondary school is not free and books can be very costly. Financial planning is very important for students who need additional resources to attend postsecondary education.

Laws Governing Secondary and Postsecondary Settings Are Different

For students with disabilities, the laws governing special assistance in the postsecondary setting are different from those in secondary education and change students' experiences in several ways:

1. Although high school decision making is heavily parent- and professional-driven, in the postsecondary setting students are responsible for self-identifying their disabilities, providing documentation for the disability, and informing the institution of their need for accommodations (student-driven).
2. Students make decisions about the services available; there is no professional team to decide for them.
3. Disability services personnel make decisions about services based on the reasonable accommodations requirements of the ADA and Section 504 of the Rehabilitation Act, and not on services prescribed by the Individuals with Disabilities Education Act (IDEA).
4. Students with disabilities often have to repeat the process of requesting accommodations each new semester and often on a course-by-course basis, since different classes may require different accommodations (National Center on Secondary Education and Transition, 2002).

Postsecondary services under §504 of the Rehabilitation Act are not mandated for each individual by law as they are for students with IEPs in the secondary setting. Rather, they are based on whether (a) the individual is determined to be eligible for the services, and (b) whether the accommodation does not result in a change in content or standards expected for all students. In the postsecondary setting, supports are based on what is reasonable, rather than what is appropriate and least restrictive, as mandated by IDEA. Therefore, support services and accommodations are aimed at providing access to content and reduction of barriers to learning, rather than on promoting achievement. For example, a postsecondary school is more likely to provide a note taker than a tutor.

➡ WHAT STRATEGIES ASSIST YOUTH WITH TRANSITION TO POSTSECONDARY EDUCATION?

Despite the challenges of entering a "different world" of postsecondary education, recent laws have greatly improved access and support for youth with disabilities. Most postsecondary institutions are responding to the mandates and are developing greater capacity to recruit, retain, and support students with disabilities.

Postsecondary Planning in the Last Year of High School

IDEA legislation requires transition planning for youth preparing for graduation. An important part of transition planning is determining the student's postsecondary goal (e.g., enrolling in college or entering employment) and gathering information about the requirements for achieving it. Then, through *backward planning,* the student's transition plan incorporates the secondary course of study, support services, needed assessments, and appropriate community-based experiences. The classes that secondary students take in their final years—both academic and career-technical—should meet requirements not only for graduating from secondary school but also for entering postsecondary education or employment. The IEP team identifies and explores supports and accommodations that the student will need in postsecondary environments and plan for ways to prepare the student to transition to these supports (Baer & Kochhar-Bryant, in press; National Center on Secondary Education and Transition, 2002a).

In the final year of high school, the student, in consultation with parents and guidance counselors, should identify potential colleges that (a) they can qualify for, (b) have programs that match their interests and abilities, (c) have student support services available, and (d) have a strong record of welcoming and supporting students with disabilities. If the student is planning to enroll in a 2- or 4-year college or technical school, he or she can ask a guidance counselor to help them select colleges, apply and negotiate for support services, obtain appropriate documentation of their disability required by those colleges, find information on how to access campus resources, discuss interview techniques, discuss self-advocacy techniques and ways to promote one's strengths, and the advantages and disadvantages of self-disclosure of the disability. There are several important questions that youth with disabilities should ask when preparing to apply for DSS:

1. Who is responsible for coordinating services for students with disabilities?
2. What documentation of my disability will the college need? What should I make sure I take with me from high school?
3. Is there anyone to help me coordinate academic and other support services? Will I have an advocate or mentor?
4. How many students does the disability services office serve and what is the ratio of professionals to students?

5. Is a program representative available to answer all your questions clearly and thoroughly?
6. What do students pay for support services? Are these charges considered in the school's financial aid packet?

In the last year of high school, with the support and involvement of the family and transition team, each student should make sure the IEP includes transition plans and a **summary of academic and functional performance,** now required under IDEA 2004 (see a sample of the summary in Chapter 9). Finally, students should learn to discuss their disability and describe accommodations that are necessary or helpful. If appropriate, they should contact the vocational rehabilitation (VR) agency and/or the Social Security Administration at age 18 or earlier if there is a partnership between the school and VR, to provide early eligibility determination.

Responsibilities of Postsecondary Institutions and Students

It is important that students are aware of their responsibilities and those of institutions of higher education (IHE) before they enroll. IHE may ask whether a student applicant can meet the academic and technical standards required for admission, but may not ask about a prospective student's disabilities before they are admitted. Prospective students may voluntarily choose to provide an individual plan for employment (IPE) with information about their disability. Applicants can request changes in admissions requirements related to standardized entrance examinations (e.g., SAT and GRE) if they can provide documentation from a qualified professional who evaluates and verifies the existence of a disability. The IHE is not required to pay for such evaluations; however, they must inform students of their documentation requirements (U.S. Department of Education, Office of Civil Rights, 2007a). Generally, students' IEPs from elementary and secondary school are not sufficient documentation of a disability, but assessment reports and summary of students' academic achievement may meet some documentation requirements.

Unlike elementary and secondary schools, once a student is admitted to an IHE, the institution does not have a legal obligation to identify students with disabilities. To obtain accommodations, the students must identify themselves as having a disability and make a formal request for an academic adjustment. Unlike school districts under IDEA, IHE have no obligation to create individualized education programs. *In making accommodations or academic adjustments, the IHE does not have to eliminate or lower its essential requirements or standards for student performance, or make any modifications that would result in a fundamental change in the program or activities being offered* (U.S. Department of Education, Office of Civil Rights, 2007a, 2007b).

Coordination with Community Service Agencies in the Last Year of High School

Adult service agencies provide a comprehensive system of services responsive to the needs of individuals with disabilities. These services typically include mental heath, developmental disabilities, employment, and independent living services. Examples of employment services include supported and sheltered employment and competitive employment support for those who need minimal assistance. Examples of adult and independent living services include service coordination to access and obtain local services, therapeutic recreation, day activities, respite care, and residential services (group homes and supervised apartments).

IDEA 2004 requires school-linked human service agencies to support students' transition from school to postsecondary education and employment. Although the school system is required by law to provide the services that are written into the IEP or ITP, organizations that provide supportive services are expected to share the responsibility for transition support services. For example, if the student needs medical services, they can be sought and provided from Medicaid, public health agencies, private insurance, early periodic screening, or diagnosis and treatment programs. If transition support services are needed, they may be sought and provided from VR agencies, employment services, adult service agencies, job training programs, **Workforce Investment Act** programs, or supported employment projects.

The student's IEP should contain a *statement of interagency responsibilities* or any linkages required to ensure that the student has the transition services needed from outside agencies and that representatives from those agencies are invited to attend IEP meetings. This requirement for interagency services means that there must be formal interagency agreements between schools and cooperating agencies.

Concept of Supported Education

Early efforts to address the needs of individuals with psychiatric disabilities in postsecondary settings are know as *supported education,* a term that is based on the definition of supported employment in the Rehabilitation Act (Unger, 1998). According to Unger (1998), supported-education programs involve three prototypes: (a) a self-contained setting, where students are reintegrated into the postsecondary setting; (b) on-site support, where ongoing support is provided by the institution's disabilities support staff or a mental health professional; and (c) mobile support, where support is largely provided by community mental health service providers. Generally, accommodations and strategies that appear to be the most common and effective include the following:

1. Extra time and/or a private environment for examinations
2. Priority registration
3. Audio recording of lectures
4. Note takers for lectures
5. Modified deadlines for assignments
6. Reduced course load
7. Preferential classroom seating
8. Early availability of syllabus and/or textbooks (Sharpe et al., 2004; Sharpe, Johnson, Izzo, & Murray, 2005)
9. Peer or faculty mentoring relationship.

There is much more that needs to be learned about the growing population of students with psychiatric disabilities and their needs within the postsecondary setting.

For example, much more needs to be known about how many students exhibit severe and persistent mental illness in relation to those whose illness is considered *mild*.

What Professional Roles Support the Transition of Youth to Postsecondary Settings?

The following sections describe several service coordination roles that assist youth to successfully navigate a transition from high school to postsecondary settings.

Secondary Transition Coordinator: Bridge to the Postsecondary World.   Secondary transition specialists typically begin work with students when they reach the age at which they are eligible for services and planning (16 under IDEA 2004, with option to begin earlier if needed). The coordinator works with the student to identify preferences and goals. He or she collaborates with general educators to recommend a course of study through high school to prepare for careers and independent living in either college or employment settings. The coordinator arranges opportunities for the student (or a group of students) to learn about different careers through videos, job shadowing, visits to work environments, and hands-on work activities that allow the student(s) to try out a job. Finally, the coordinator makes connections with the adult service system, identifies the support services or accommodations the student may need in the postsecondary setting, assists students to assemble portfolios of academic records, job experiences, resumes, and postsecondary recommendations. **Transition coordinators** may follow-up with the student and continue their support services for a period of time after the student has graduated. Recent research on the role of transition coordinators shows that 94% of states employ one or more at the state level (Jackson, 2003; Schiller et al., 2003; U.S. Department of Education, Office of Special Education, 2003).

School Guidance Counselor.   At the high school level, guidance counselors are concerned with educational and career guidance while they also focus on the personal development of the students. High school counselors help students choose school courses and activities that relate to their interests and will prepare them for life after high school. They also show students how to apply for college or for job-training programs. At the postsecondary level, academic advisors provide information about college entrance requirements, financial-aid programs, and entry-level job opportunities in the areas where they might be attending school.

Disability Support Specialist.   The disability support specialist provides consultation and ongoing support to enable students to make full use of opportunities at the college or university. The DSS director often serves as liaison with college faculty, staff and administrators, VR counselors, and other social service agencies. Disability services offices serve as the central point of contact for information on physical and programmatic access, specific accommodations, resolution of complaints and problems, faculty and staff concerns, and identification of available services. In addition, the disability services office can provide training, consultation, and information regarding disability issues. Typically, the coordinator of the disability resource center also fulfills the role of 504 coordinator and helps provide for reasonable accommodations.

Vocational Rehabilitation Specialist (Counselor).   The VR specialist is often involved in a student's transition planning while the student is still in school. Upon graduation, the VR specialist works with the student to assist with access to and support in employment or postsecondary education. The rehabilitation specialist typically works for the state's VR agency, helping people with disabilities prepare for and find employment. For students who are eligible for VR, services may include evaluation of the person's interests, capabilities, and limitations; job training; transportation; aids and devices; job placement; support to begin postsecondary education; and job follow-up. Priority in services is given to individuals with the most significant disabilities. The term *specialist* is becoming more widely used today because, as one state VR director shared, the traditional term *counselor* connotes a person who sits behind a desk that separates him or her from the client and they just "talk." The new specialist is active, mobile, working with youth in schools, and meeting students where they are in a variety of contexts.

Job Development Specialist.   A job development specialist works for either a school system or an adult service agency such as the VR agency or a supported employment agency. As the job title suggests, the primary role is to find jobs for people with disabilities. The job development specialist identifies the need for and assists in the development of supportive services that can help the individual become job ready. He or she informs business, labor, and the public about training programs and may instruct applicants in resume writing, job search, and interviewing. The job developer visits employers to inquire about available positions and may offer the employer services such as placement of individuals into jobs; training the employee on job tasks and appropriate workplace behavior; talking with supervisors and coworkers about disability awareness; providing long-term support to the employee on the job; and helping to promote interaction between the employee and his or her coworkers. The job development specialist demonstrates to employers the effectiveness and profitability of employing individuals with disabilities by identifying the tasks that they can perform (Levinson & Palmer, 2005; Parent Advocacy Coalition for Educational Rights Center, 1999; Thuli & Hong, 1998; U.S. Department of Labor, 2007).

How Does IDEA 2004 Promote Collaboration for Postsecondary Participation?

Collaboration and the Summary of Performance.   The IDEA 2004 included a new requirement to assist students to make the transition from high school to postsecondary education or employment. Under IDEA 2004 local educational agencies must "provide students with a summary of the student's academic achievement and functional performance (Summary of Performance, SOP), which includes recommendations on how to assist the student in meeting their postsecondary goals" [IDEA, 2004, §300.305(e) (3)]. The SOP also provides documentation of the disability that is necessary under §504 of the Rehabilitation Act and the ADA to help establish a student's eligibility for reasonable accommodations and supports in postsecondary settings (Shaw, 2005). It is also helpful in the Vocational Rehabilitation Comprehensive Assessment process to determine eligibility for VR services. Developing the SOP may be the responsibility of the special educator or school psychologist, but coordination and participation of teachers, counselors, and related services professionals is essential to gathering all relevant information on the student (Vreeburg-Izzo & Kochhar-Bryant, 2006).

Postsecondary educational institutions do not typically accept an Individualized Education Program (IEP) from a high school as documentation of a disability or an academic accommodation (HEATH Resource Center, 2006). Colleges, however, may use high school testing results, documented in the SOP, if the information is current and disability specific (Madaus, Bigaj, Chafaleaus, & Simonsen, 2007). For example, after consultation with the college, a student with a learning disability might submit the psychoeducational evaluation from 11th grade as documentation of the learning disability. It is very important that students collect and maintain their high school records and summary of performance for the purposes of disability documentation in the future (Hart et al., 2001; Kochhar-Bryant & Vreeberg-Izzo, 2006a, 2006b, 2006c; Shaw, 2006; Shaw & Dukes, 2001).

Collaboration at the Age of Majority.   **Age of majority** refers to the age at which a young person acquires all the rights and responsibilities of being an adult. In most states the age is 18. IDEA outlined a procedure for the transfer of parental rights to the student when he or she reaches the age of majority. Collaboration and communication among school professionals and parents is essential. Schools must now notify the student and both parents about the student's rights when he or she reaches the age of majority. One year before the student reaches the age of majority under state law, the IEP must include a statement that he or she has been informed of the rights that transfer to the student once he or she reaches the age of majority. This **transfer of rights** is an enormous step toward the student's independence and participation in the decision making for further education and future planning (Bremer, Kachgal, & Schoeller, 2003; Eisenman & Chamberlin, 2001; Kupper, 1997).

Collaboration and §504 of the Rehabilitation Act

The 1998 Rehabilitation Amendments (Pub. L. No. 102-569) strengthened the collaboration and coordination among secondary schools, postsecondary schools, and rehabilitation agencies to support transition to employment or postsecondary settings. Interagency agreements were required in every state, which transferred responsibility for transitioning students from the state education agency to the state unit providing VR services. This provision *links the IEP and the individualized plan for employment (IPE) in accomplishing rehabilitation goals before high school graduation.* An individual is now viewed as a collaborating partner with the rehabilitation specialist in the development, implementation, and evaluation of the IPE.

Vocational rehabilitation provides funds for eligible students with disabilities to attend postsecondary education or technical education programs. VR assists persons with cognitive, sensory, physical, or emotional disabilities to attain employment, postsecondary education, and increased independence. Students with disabilities are entitled to accommodations to help them succeed in the postsecondary program, but students are responsible for disclosing their disabilities and asking for the accommodations they need. VR services typically last for a limited period of time and are based on an individual's rehabilitation plan.

The 1998 and 2003 Amendments to the Rehabilitation Act also required rehabilitation agencies to make information about services and providers available to students in their final 2 years of high school. Rehabilitation services such as early assessment for eligibility for services, vocational assessments, and counseling in work behaviors are now available to students in their final years of high school, and after graduation. Close collaboration between secondary personnel and rehabilitation counselors after the student reaches age 16 is vital to linking the student with VR services and engaging parents in planning. Many states are now specifically hiring VR specialists who will visit schools and begin the direct collaboration and planning with students, families, and professionals before high school graduation.

Collaboration and the Higher Education Act

The **Higher Education Act** Amendments of 2002 (HEA, Pub. L. No. 107-139) is designed to assist individuals to participate in postsecondary education, including students with disabilities. HEA encourages collaborative partnerships between IHEs and secondary schools, particularly those that serve low-income and disadvantaged students. HEA encourages collaboration among IHEs, businesses, labor organizations, community-based organizations, and private and civic organizations to improve accessibility and support in higher education. It also promotes collaboration between IHEs, schools, and other community agencies for outreach to students with disabilities and aims to reduce attitudinal barriers that prevent participation of individuals with disabilities within their community. The Higher Education Act aims to improve college retention and graduation rates for low-income and first-generation college students with disabilities and to encourage programs that counsel students about financial aid and support services.

Coordination and the ADA in Postsecondary Institutions and Employment

The ADA of 1990 promotes collaboration to provide accommodations in both public and private organizations, including public and private schools, colleges and universities, postsecondary vocational–technical schools, employer-based training programs, and other private training programs. Under ADA, transition activities can include preparation for college interviews, knowledge about reasonable accommodations provided in the programs, and assistance with applications and supporting documentation. ADA prohibits discrimination against individuals with disabilities in postsecondary applications, postsecondary education, job training, job application procedures, hiring, advancement, and employee compensation. According to ADA regulations, **reasonable accommodations** at the postsecondary level include modifications to a postsecondary education admission procedure to enable individuals to be considered for admission, modifications in classrooms, modifications in test taking, and instructional modifications that would help the student participate in and learn in the college setting. Through antidiscrimination provisions, the ADA encourages postsecondary institutions to consider applicants with disabilities in their recruitment of teachers, professors, and support personnel.

In most colleges and universities, students can expect to apply for and receive services from an office with a title such as "student support services" or "office of disability services." Although a student will not have an IEP or **504 plan** in college, postsecondary institutions are required under ADA and the HEA to provide a plan of reasonable accommodations to students with documented disabilities who require them (Brinckerhoff, McGuire, & Shaw, 2002; Ekpone & Bogucki, 2003; HEATH Resource Center, 2005; Shaw, 2006). Often, students have support service plans that are similar to 504 plans, because they specify the kinds of accommodations that the student is to receive in classrooms and in non-academic activities. Accommodations that can be requested in postsecondary education include testing accommodations, physical accommodations, adaptations of technology, special software for large print, note takers, supplemental online tutorials, extensions of time for papers and homework, tutors, and groups support sessions.

For example, Pamela, a gifted graduate student, has dyscalculia, a disorder affecting mathematical concepts or computations. Adults with dyscalculia often have difficulty moving on to more advanced math applications. Pamela had particular difficulty with math operations and confusion of symbols. She was very good with general math concepts, but was frustrated when specific computation and organization skills needed to be used. Pamela consulted with the campus disability services specialist who arranged for testing. An individualized plan for intervention was developed that involved testing accommodations, use of computer for testing, and tutorial services. The student successfully completed her statistics classes with these accommodations.

WHAT STRATEGIES ASSIST YOUTH WITH TRANSITION TO EMPLOYMENT?

The Vocational Rehabilitation Role

As the primary federal vehicle for assisting individuals with disabilities to obtain employment, the VR program is a critical link in assisting youths with disabilities to prepare for education, training, and employment opportunities beyond high school ("Special Demonstration Programs, Model Demonstration Projects," 2007). VR professionals bring to the table valuable knowledge and expertise about the world of work and disability, including career planning, occupational trends and local employment opportunities, job-related education, training and skills, job seeking and retention skills, and accommodations. They also are knowledgeable about adult service systems and the range of benefits and resources available to assist individuals with disabilities. There, however, remains a gap between transition service needs and VR professional involvement in assisting students with disabilities during the transition years (National Longitudinal Transition Study-2, 2005; Study Group, 2007).

Several provisions of the Rehabilitation Act address coordination with high schools to improve transition services for students who will be eligible for VR services after leaving school. Recognizing that some youth with disabilities leaving school will require assistance, state VR agencies are encouraged to supplement the cost of transition services for any student determined eligible to receive VR services (Horn, 2001, September). The state educational agency (SEA) is required to create plans that transfer the responsibility for transitioning students from the school to the VR agency for eligible students. This provision links the IEP and the IPE under the Rehabilitation Act to accomplish rehabilitation goals before high school graduation.

ADA in Employment

The ADA prohibits discrimination by employers against *qualified individuals with disabilities (visible or hidden)*—those who possess the skills, experience, education, and other job-related requirements of a position and who, with or without reasonable accommodations, can perform the essential functions of the job. This antidiscrimination provision covers all aspects of employment, including application, testing and medical examinations, promotion, hiring and layoffs, assignments and termination, evaluation and compensation, disciplinary actions and leave, and training and benefit. Examples of reasonable accommodations include job restructuring, modified work schedules, reassignments of position, modifications to equipment, modifications of examinations, training materials or policies, and provision of readers or interpreters (Dixon, Kruse, & Van Horn, 2003). Employers are not required to lower their standards to make such accommodations, nor are they required to provide accommodations if they impose 'undue hardships' on the business through actions that are very costly or disruptive of the work environment (National Information Center for Children and Youth With Disabilities, 1999a). Most accommodations, however, cost less than $500. Box 12-3 provides examples of accommodations worked out through discussions and negotiations between employees and employers, in consultation with the U.S. Department of Labor, Office of Disability Employment Policy (2005).

Social Security Administration

The Social Security Administration operates the federally funded program that provides benefits for people of any age who are unable to do substantial work and have a severe mental or physical disability. Several programs are offered for people with disabilities, including Social Security Disability Insurance (SSDI), Supplemental Security Income (SSI), Plans to Achieve Self-Support (PASS), Medicaid, and Medicare. Examples of employment services include cash benefits while working (e.g., student-earned income), Medicare or Medicaid while working, help with extra work expenses the individual has as a result of the disability, and assistance to start a new line of work. Postsecondary services generally include financial incentives for further education and training.

PASS Plan.   To provide incentives for young people to enter the workforce, the Social Security Administration developed the Plan for Achieving Self-Support (PASS) to help individuals make the transition without losing disability benefits (U. S. Department of Labor, Office of Disability Employment Policy, 2005). A **PASS plan** lets the young worker use his or her income or other assets to achieve work goals. For example, a young graduate could set aside money to go to school, to get specialized training for a job, or to start a business. The job that the individual wants should allow him or her to earn enough to reduce or eliminate the need for benefits provided under both the Social Security and Supplemental Security Income (SSI) programs. A plan is designed to help the individual to obtain services, items, or skills that are needed to reach their employment goals.

Box 12–3

Simple Accommodations for Workers with Disabilities

Situation: A bowling alley worker with mental retardation and finger dexterity problems in both hands was having difficulty wiping the bowling shoes that had been returned by customers. *Solution:* A local job coach service provider fabricated a device that allowed the individual to roll the shoes in front of a brush rather than run a brush over the shoes. Cost: no cost as scraps of wood that were left over from other projects were used to make the device.

Situation: A high school guidance counselor with attention deficit disorder was having difficulty concentrating due to the school noise. *Solution:* The school replaced the bell on his phone with an electric light bulb device that lights up when the phone rings, sound-proofed his office, and provided a floor fan for white noise. Cost: under $600.

Situation: A machine operator who developed arthritis had difficulty turning the machinery control switches. *Solution:* The employer replaced the small machine tabs with larger cushioned knobs and provided the employee with non-slip dot gripping gloves that enabled him to grasp and turn the knobs more effectively and with less force. Cost: approximately $130.

Situation: A 25-year veteran warehouse supervisor whose job involved managing and delivering company supplies was having difficulty with the physical demands of his job due to fatigue from cancer treatment. *Solution:* The employer provided the employee with a three-wheeled scooter to reduce walking and enable him to manage the warehouse. The employer also rearranged the layout of supplies in the warehouse to reduce climbing and reaching. Cost: $3,000.

Situation: A part-time college instructor had a learning disability, specifically, auditory discrimination difficulties. This was causing problems for her during meetings and in class and prevented her from meeting time lines for projects. *Solution:* The employee was permitted to take notes during staff meetings and to provide written responses to all attendees on the questions raised during the meeting within a time frame agreed upon by the meeting participants. The employee also received a copy of meeting agendas and project expectations in advance of the face-to-face meetings and was thereby able to ask questions or provide follow-up responses in writing. Cost: $0.

Three requirements are needed to qualify for a PASS plan: (1) has desire to work, (2) is currently receiving SSI (or can qualify for SSI by having this plan) because the person has a disability, and (3) has other income or resources to get a job or start a business (U. S. Department of Labor, Office of Disability Employment Policy, 2005). Under SSI rules, any income that the individual has reduces the SSI payment for disability. But, with an approved PASS plan, the individual can use that income to pay for the items needed to reach their work goal. Money that is set aside toward work-related goals is not counted under this plan when the SSI payment amount is determined. Money set aside can be used for transportation to and from work; tuition, books, fees, and supplies needed for school or training; child care; attendant care; employment services, such as job coaching and resume writing; supplies to start a business; equipment and tools to do the job; or uniforms, special clothing, and safety equipment. If the plan is approved, the coordinator or specialist will stay in contact to make sure that the plan is followed and

> **Box 12–4**
>
> *Go for It!: The PASS Plan for Self-Support*
>
> Dana Simpkins likes spending time in front of the computer. As an e-mail specialist for the Gap Inc. in Columbus, Ohio, that is his job. But Dana has spinal muscular atrophy and relies on a wheelchair. There was a time when he did not know the joy of job satisfaction. Supplemental Security Income (SSI) helped make ends meet, but he wanted to work. "My PASS [Plan for Achieving Self Support] was what allowed me to work," Dana remembers. The PASS let him keep his SSI while he went to work. He used his SSI to meet his basic needs, and his wages were saved in a special PASS account to help meet his goal of getting a van modified for wheelchair transportation. Now, with his modified van, Dana no longer needs the help of SSI. "My advice to those who are considering work is to simply go for it. Don't be afraid to try and fail. The feeling I got cashing that first paycheck was sweeter having overcome greater challenges than most." (*Working While Disabled—A Guide To Plans For Achieving Self-Support,* Social Security Administration, 2004).

the goals are being met. Box 12–4 illustrates how the PASS plan can open doors for individuals with disabilities transitioning to employment.

Ticket to Work and Work Incentive Improvement Act.   In late 1999, the Congress enacted the Ticket to Work and Work Incentive Improvement Act (TWWIIA, Pub. L. No. 106-170). The Social Security Administration (SSA) administers the act and the Department of Health and Human Services administers the health care component. Under the voluntary Ticket to Work Program, individuals with disabilities can obtain job-related training and placement assistance from an approved provider of their choice. For example, youth in transition to work can receive employment services, career-technical training, or other services to help them enter employment. *Employment networks* are private organizations or government agencies that have agreed to work with SSA to provide employment services to persons with disabilities at no cost. The second measure expands health care coverage so that individuals with disabilities will be able to become employed without fear of losing their health insurance (U.S. Department of Labor, Office of Disability Employment Policy, 2001b). The **ticket to work program** has helped many young people make the transition into employment.

➡ WHAT CAN WE LEARN FROM THE VOICES OF YOUTH?

The voices of students and parents are seldom heard in the professional conversation about transition and postsecondary outcomes (Akos, 2002; Akos & Galassi, 2004a; Franklin, Cranston, Perry, Purtle, & Robertson, 2002; Hitchings et al., 2001; Sharpe et al., 2004). It is important to understand the perspective of students and parents in order to understand what concerns youth about transition and what they find to be helpful? How do they view their participation planning for transition? Are there differences in how students and their parents view the transition process? How do professionals support transition for students? These questions, and how we come to understand what is actually effective with students, are important in light of recent data on the rising number of students who declare a disability in the postsecondary setting. For example, increases ranging from 30% to 10% in one year have been reported by major colleges and universities among students service with psychiatric disabilities in their first 2 years (Eudaly, 2002; Franklin et al., 2002; Measel, 1998; Sharpe et al., 2004).

What Do the Voices of Youth Tell Policy Makers?

The following reflections are synthesized from many conversations and interviews with students and professionals in post-secondary settings over the past 5 years.

1. "We need to start thinking very early on about what they want to do because it can take some students with learning disabilities longer to get the same requirements completed. Planning is important." (postsecondary sudent).
2. "Accommodations addressed in high school are so focused on the curriculum and individual assignments that they don't consider the whole career development picture for families or for a person with the disability" (Burghstahler & Whelley, 2001).
3. "More academic support services are needed to help first-year students, including writing centers, math labs, tutoring programs, technology support, counseling and other services" (Keeling, 2003; Schroeder, 2003).
4. "Faculty training resources are needed to educate faculty about the needs of students with disabilities and faculty responsibilities in advising and instruction." (postsecondary sudent).
5. "A peer or mentor or person who had made that transition to postsecondary is an important resource for high school students and their families." (postsecondary sudent).
6. "Provide competent and caring counselors who understand a student's individualized needs, have expertise in accommodations needed for successful transition into college, and can help students find a college that matches their needs" (Hitchings et al., 2001).

What Do the Voices of Youth Tell Parents?

1. "I had to prove myself above my parents' low expectations, and then after that, my family was very, very supportive of me. But initially it was difficult. I had to go of what they thought of me" (Burghstahler & Whelley, 2001).
2. "I was born with a disability but my family didn't see me as someone with a disability; they saw me as a family member" (Burghstahler & Whelley, 2001).
3. "It is important to keep the communication with the family during the postsecondary years." (postsecondary student).
4. "When looking for a college, consider smaller schools with smaller class sizes." (postsecondary student).
5. "I wanted to go to a small school close to home because I still needed a lot of support from my family. I just believed I could be more successful in a small school." (postsecondary student).

What Do the Voices of Youth Tell Postsecondary Personnel?

1. "It can be shocking when we come to the university and find out we are not going to get the same support services that we received when we were in high school. We need to be prepared for this as we enter college."

2. "SATs! I had a difficult time taking the SATs and really struggled with multiple-choice questions. The SAT was not a true reflection of what I knew or what I could do academically. But, colleges really rely on the SATs in the admissions process and I knew that I wouldn't be able to go to a great school because of my SAT scores. Once I got into college, I struggled with the placement tests at the school, which were also in multiple-choice format. I was placed in courses that were too low for my ability during my freshman year because I couldn't demonstrate my knowledge on the placement tests. I decided to go to a very small private school that provided a lot of supports in my first two years at college. I attended a three-week college preparation course at the college, which taught me about study skills, note taking, and different learning and teaching styles."

3. "We lack access and practice with empowering technology, including computers. We come to the university having used adaptive technology in computers but to such a minimal degree that we are really not proficient."

4. "It is really helpful to have something like an 'activities carnival' at the beginning of the freshman year that introduces new students to different campus organizations and activities and leaders."

5. "We often don't know how best to use our advisors and what to expect. We could benefit from an orientation to advisor roles and planning conferences with advisors."

6. "We could use help in some areas of weakness that we may have, such as math or writing, or computer or library skills."

7. "We could benefit from health education and information that makes us aware of health services offered on campus and how to access them" (Keeling 2003; Schroeder, 2003).

8. "I mainly face accessibility barriers like the absence of ramps or doors that are difficult to open. It is difficult to get around the large campus because the buildings are so far apart from each other. The elevators break down sometimes and some bathrooms are not big enough for wheelchairs, especially in older buildings. Students were willing to help me when I needed help.... I go to community college, so the class sizes are smaller. The campus has an ADA coordinator, who is very helpful. I can go to him when I have difficulties at the school.... My biggest supporters are my parents who taught me to speak up and make my needs known. My mother said the world is full of diverse people, and being a person with a hearing loss adds to that diversity. I remember this when I am embarrassed about needing help.... I sought out professors, making sure that I communicated any difficultites I was having. Smaller schools with smaller classes and more individualized attention can provide a more conducive environment during the first few years of college for a student with LD."

Recommendations for Postsecondary Personnel and Faculty

1. "Postsecondary personnel should remain open to their students' diverse learning styles."
2. "Faculty members should encourage students to advocate for themselves. Offer a course on how to self-advocate."
3. "When faculty change assignments or modify the syllabus, take time to highlight the changes and check for understanding."
4. "Teachers and parents need to tone down the pressure applied to students in their junior and senior years of high school."
5. "Consider alternatives to the SAT, which many students believe sets up a disadvantage for students with learning disabilities."
6. "Make technology available in the classroom for students because it really does level the playing field for those with learning disabilities."
7. "Encourage professors to use visual strategies along with lecture and that movement breaks are still important for adults."

LET'S SEE IT IN ACTION! CASE EXAMPLE

Reflection on My Cousin's Postsecondary Experience

My cousin Brian is a 21-year-old student at Cypress College, and he has a learning disability. He struggles with reading and writing, has difficulty understanding assignments, has very poor handwriting, and has difficulty with written expressive language skills. As a result, Brian has to use a computer for all of his assignments and note taking. Brian had to work extra hard in high school so he would be able to apply to the college of his choice. He knew early on in high school that he wanted to attend Cypress College, so he focused on his academics to ensure he would meet the admissions criteria. Although Brian did not believe that he faced special barriers to admission, once he enrolled in college he met many obstacles. Brian found that it was too difficult for him to take the college recommended full course load that freshmen typically take. It took him longer to complete assignments and grasp academic concepts, and so Brian had to reduce his load by dropping a class.

While Brian was in college, he struggled in English and sociology classes, which the university required him to take, but he excelled in math and business courses and found his areas of academic strength. Brian also had difficulty completing examinations in the required time period, so he did have to take advantage of student disability services and special test taking facilities which allowed him extended time on tests. The extended time permitted Brian to read and understand the questions without being pressured to turn in incomplete work due to time constraints. Brian reported that although it may take his peers one minute to answer a question it took him several minutes to just understand the question. After advice from Brian's parents, he decided to find out what additional services the college could provide. Brian took advantage of special testing services the college offered to students with disabilities. After doing this he saw a huge improvement in his grades and in his self-confidence.

At Cypress College, Brian has had a lot of support from his professors. This was very important to Brian because he often felt that he was not as smart as his peers. His teachers, however, supported him and made themselves available to assist with his academics outside of class. Some of Brian's professors would go over lessons again with him during office hours to make sure he understood the concepts being taught. At first, Brian was very hesitant to ask his professors for this extra help because he did not want them to think that he was incapable of learning the material. He was worried about what his teachers would think of him. However, after overcoming that fear and reaching out to his teachers for help he was very grateful he did. Brian said that his teacher's time and patience with him was a key component to assisting him through the sometimes difficult course material.

Brian attributes his success in college to his desire and motivation to achieve the goals he established for himself. His primary goal, however, was never to give up. There were many times during his college experience when he was tempted to give up because of the pressures and the frustration that he could not learn things that his classmates seemed to pick up so easily. Brian, however, was able to overcome these feelings and pushed himself to struggle through times that were very difficult.

Brian's support system of family and professors who encouraged and assisted and supported him has played an important role in Brian's achievements. When asked where Brian sees himself in 5 years, he hesitated and said that was a very diffi-cult question for him to answer. He is majoring in accounting and hopes to be as successful as he can in the field. Brian wants to use the skills he has learned in college to help him succeed in his career. He does not want his learning disability to interfere with his desire to succeed. Brian knows that just because he has been successful in college does not mean that his challenges will end when he graduates. He will face lifelong struggles in some areas, but he believes that college has prepared him to face these challenges.

As he was completing his final year, Brian was offered a job at a top level accounting firm. His friends and family and teachers were so very proud of him, but instead of feeling excitement, Brian felt overwhelmed. He was and is still worried that he will not be able to perform as well as his coworkers. But Brian is reminded about his primary goal of never giving up when things are tough. Brian has a difficult time realizing that he is just as qualified as the other candidates chosen to work with him.

Brian has several recommendations to postsecondary students. He believes that it is important not to waste time trying to push yourself beyond your limits. Seeking help and using the supports of the college will make the postsecondary experience much more pleasant if you are having difficulties. Brian believes that having open communication with professors is key, and when you need help you have to ask. Brian's most important lesson was that having a positive mindset will keep one focused to achieve the goals they have set for themselves (Susan Kauffman, *Special Educator,* by permission, 2007).

SUMMARY

This chapter explored transition and system coordination strategies for students as they move from the secondary to postsecondary (post–high school) settings, and discusses disability laws that affect young people in postsecondary institutions and the work settings.

Since 1990, there has been a 90% increase in the number of colleges, universities, technical institutions, and career-technical centers offering opportunities for persons with disabilities to continue their education. IDEA mandates transition services for youth preparing for graduation. Local interagency collaborative teams are effective in helping students with disabilities make the transition to postsecondary education and employment. Postsecondary services are not mandated by law as they are for students with disabilities in high school; college disability services personnel make decisions about services based on the 'reasonable accommodations' requirements of the ADA and §504 of the Rehabilitation Act, and not on services prescribed by IDEA. Although progress is clearly being made, employment outcomes continue to reflect the widest gulf between youth with disabilities and the general population.

Successful transition to postsecondary education and employment is a process that requires the active participation of the youth in their future planning. There is a growing national investment in youth development to increase access to education and employment preparation programs and to increase social and economic independence. Interest in career development and transition is greater than it has been in the past, both in the United States and in nations around the globe. Successful transition from secondary school is becoming recognized as a *chief indicator of the effectiveness* of our educational system for preparing youth and young adults for adult life.

KEY TERMS AND PHRASES

504 plan
age of majority
Americans with Disabilities Act
competitive employment
Disability Support Services
documentation of disability
Higher Education Act
PASS plan
postsecondary setting
reasonable accommodations

Rehabilitation Act
self-advocacy/self-determination
sheltered employment
summary of academic and functional
  performance
supported employment
ticket to work program
transfer of rights
transition coordinator
Workforce Investment Act

QUESTIONS FOR REFLECTION, THINKING, AND SKILL BUILDING

1. Discuss the key difference between the secondary and postsecondary environments for students with disabilities in terms of their rights and responsibilities.
2. How does the '"age of majority"' impact youth with disabilities as they prepare for transition from high school?
3. Why is documentation of the disability important in the postsecondary setting?
4. Discuss five barriers to access to postsecondary education and employment for youth with disabilities.
5. Have you met or had a friendship with someone with a disability while you were in college

or university? What do you remember about the special barriers that he or she had to overcome, if any?

6. Have you met or had a friendship with someone with a disability while you were in an employment setting? What do you remember about the special barriers that he or she had to overcome, if any?

7. Conduct research on the Internet for standards for accessibility on postsecondary campuses. On the basis of these standards, design a template or checklist to record your assessment. In a team of two or more, using your assessment checklist, take a tour of a local college or university campus and assess the accessibility of the campus in general for individuals with disabilities using the standards that you researched. Discuss your findings.

8. With prior permission and approval of the student with a disability, interview them and ask if they have encountered barriers to participation in their education in the following areas: physical accessibility, course taking, test taking, use of technology, communication with faculty, homework assignments or projects, or issues with peers. Ask about the particular supports or conditions that have helped make a positive difference in their lives and participation in postsecondary education. To what do they attribute their persistence and success in achieving access to and success in postsecondary education?

Chapter 13

Transition of Culturally and Linguistically Diverse Youth with Disabilities

Gary Greene and Carol A. Kochhar-Bryant

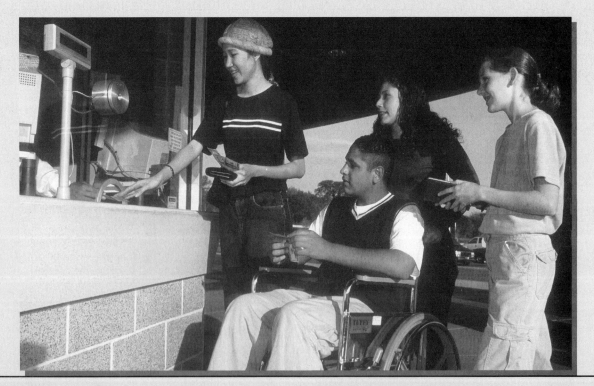

Chapter Questions

- How do transition outcomes of culturally and linguistically diverse (CLD) youth with disabilities compare with their non-CLD peers?
- What barriers to the transition process exist for CLD youth with disabilities and their families?
- What are best practices in transition for CLD youth with disabilities and their families?
- How should the quality of transition services to CLD youth with disabilities be evaluated?

INTRODUCTION

Children who are culturally and linguistically diverse (CLD) in the United States have historically been at greater risk for experiencing school problems and poorer postschool outcomes than non-CLD children. This is equally true for CLD youth with disabilities. Data from the National Longitudinal Transition Study-1 (NLTS-1) (Blackorby & Wagner, 1996) and National Longitudinal Transition Study-2 (NLTS-2) show that substantial gaps exist between the postschool outcomes achieved by these individuals compared with their nonminority peers with disabilities. This chapter explores potential explanations for this finding.

We begin with a review of NLTS-1 and NLTS-2 data comparing the transition outcomes of minority and nonminority youth with disabilities, followed by a discussion of barriers faced by CLD families of youth with disabilities when interacting with schools, transition services agencies, and transition personnel. Historical seminal and contemporary literature on effective cultural diversity special education practices is then explored, with an emphasis on transition planning for CLD youth with disabilities. This chapter concludes with recommended best practices in transition for CLD youth with disabilities and their families. Included in this section is an instrument designed to help transition personnel evaluate the quality of transition services and programs offered to CLD youth with disabilities and their families for use by school and transition services agency personnel. Case studies are presented throughout the chapter to illustrate key concepts.

HOW DO TRANSITION OUTCOMES OF CLD YOUTH WITH DISABILITIES COMPARE WITH THEIR NON-CLD PEERS?

In the face of NCLB accountability requirements for state testing of students, many school districts are struggling to address the needs of this population to achieve Annual Yearly Progress (AYP) (McLeod, 2005; Northwest Evaluation Association, 2005; Ruiz-de-Velasco, Fix, & Clewell, 2000). States must now provide data on how English language learners (ELL) are performing on state assessments and ELL students must participate in these assessments (U.S. Department of Education, 2005a). The research and education policy community is divided on whether bilingual education or English immersion is best for non-English speakers and more research is needed (Albus, Lieu, & Thurlow, 2002; Albus & Thurlow, 2005; Educational Policy Reform Research Institute, 2004).

The needs of culturally and linguistically diverse (CLD) students are currently largely unmet in today's schools, as reflected by two important statistics. First, a disproportionate percentage of Hispanic, black, and Native American students drop out or do not obtain a high school diploma (Garcia, 2005; National Center for Education Statistics, 2002; U.S. Department of Education, 2004). Second, and equally as important, is the disproportionate percentage of Hispanic, black, and Native American students placed in special education classes (Cummins, 2001; Northwest Evaluation Association, 2005; Obiakor & Wilder, 2003). Although special education may meet the needs of students with disabilities, it can be inappropriate for students *without* disabilities. Recent research has demonstrated that improperly placing CLD students in special education can negatively impact their educational outcomes and potential career possibilities (Artiles, 2003; Cummins, 2001; Greene & Kochhar, 2003; Obiakor & Wilder, 2003; Salend, Garrick-Duhaney, & Montgomery, 2002).

These conditions and the growth in diversity of the student population is driving many changes in curriculum and instruction, student assessment, school organizational structure, administration, personnel preparation, and transition services. CLD students demand a different lens on the educational environment and the needs of the students, particularly if they also have disabilities.

Children for whom English is not their primary language have numerous challenges to learning that require special responses on the part of teachers and administrators so that all students are given every opportunity to succeed in school and to make successful transitions to the postsecondary world. These challenges include (a) language differences that require teachers to understand how students learn to speak and read English when their primary language is different; (b) how student's immersion in the mainstream language affects academic progress and student assessment; (c) how student and family cultures affect students' learning and progress and curriculum and instruction; (d) how CLD students are evaluated and referred to special education, so as to avoid overrepresentation or underrepresentation; (e) implications of culture and language for accessing community services; (f) impacts of attitudes and practices that negatively affect ethnic and language diverse student groups; and (g) implications of culture for high school transition planning and employment preparation.

These challenges demand that educators appreciate the complex interaction of language, culture, and professional knowledge and attitudes in the education and transition of CLD students. According to many observers, the implications of this new reality are not being fully considered by those advocating or undertaking school reform and improvement (Mcleod, 2005; Zehler et al., 2003). So important are cultural factors in preparing educators that the Council for Exceptional Children (2002) developed specific content standards for teachers and administrators, which address diversity and the role of families in the educational process. Highly qualified educators, counselors, and administrators must be familiar with the special needs of CLD students with and without disabilities.

National Studies of Transition Outcomes

This section examines the findings from two national studies of transition outcomes: The NLTS-1 (1996) and NLTS-2, which began in 2002 and is ongoing. The NLTS-1 reported by Blackorby and Wagner (1996) tracked the long-term transition outcomes of youth with disabilities in several key areas at intervals of 2 or less years and again at 3-5 years (see Table 13-1). The data was aggregated by ethnicity and included transition outcomes for White, African American, and Hispanic youth with disabilities. The four major transition outcomes investigated and reported by the NLTS-1 were percentages of youth with disabilities who (a) obtained competitive employment, (b) obtained earnings more than $6 per hour, (c) attended postsecondary education, and (d) were living independently. A review of the NLTS-1 findings on the transition of minority versus nonminority youth with disabilities follows.

NLTS-1: Competitive Employment

Minority youth with disabilities, compared with their White counterparts, fared less well in competitive employment at both points in time according to the data. White percentages of competitive employment were 53.1 and 60.8 for less than or equal to 2 years and 3-5 years out of school, respectively, compared with percentages of 25.5 and 47.3 for African Americans and 49.4 and 50.5 for Hispanics at the same respective points in time. Overall, these differences were found to be significant ($p < .10$) and demonstrate that White youth with disabilities experienced greater success in employment than did their minority peers after completing secondary school.

Table 13-1 National Longitudinal Transition Study Data-1 on Transition Outcomes of Minority and Nonminority Youth with Disabilities

Transition Outcome	2 years or less	3-5 years
Competitive Employment (%)		
Whites	53.1	60.8
African Americans	25.5	47.3
Hispanics	49.4	50.5
Earnings > $6 per hour		
Whites	8.7	46.3
African Americans	14.2	13.7
Hispanics	0.1	25.0
Postsecondary School Attendance		
Whites	14.8	27.5
African Americans	12.7	23.2
Hispanics	9.9	27.7
Independent Living		
Whites	13.4	42.3
African Americans	5.1	25.5
Hispanics	15.2	31.1

Source: Data taken from "Longitudinal Postschool Outcomes of Youth with Disabilities: Findings from the National Longitudinal Transition Study," by J. Blackorby and M. Wagner, 1996, *Exceptional Children 62,* pp. 399–413.

NLTS-1: Earned Wages

For the initial 2 years out of secondary school, the percentage of African American youth with disabilities earning more than $6 per hour (14.2) exceeded both Whites and Hispanics (8.7 and 0.1, respectively). This pattern, however, drastically changed during the 3- to 5-year postschool period. Significant increases occurred for Whites (46.3, $p < .001$) and Hispanics (25.0, $p < .01$), but not for African Americans, who actually experienced a slight decrease in percentage of individuals with disabilities earning more than $6 per hour (13.7). These data show that, overall, Whites with disabilities were the most likely to be high wage earners compared with their minority peers, particularly when comparing Whites with disabilities with their African American peers (46% versus 14%, $p < .01$).

NLTS-1: Postsecondary School Enrollment

Rates of and increases over time in postsecondary school enrollment did not differ significantly by ethnic background. The percentage of Whites with disabilities enrolled in postsecondary school for up to 2 years after graduation was 14.8, compared with 12.7 for African American and 9.9 for Hispanic youth with disabilities. These percentages increased significantly for the period of 3–5 years following secondary school completion for Whites (27.5, $p < .001$), African Americans (23.2, $p < .10$), and Hispanics (27.7, $p < .10$). However, despite these significant gains in postsecondary school attendance, the data indicated that, overall, youth with disabilities and ethnically diverse youth with disabilities in particular were significantly less likely than youth in general (e.g., without disabilities) to have attended postsecondary school 3–5 years after high school completion.

NLTS-1: Independent-Living Status

Significant gains in independent living were experienced by youth with disabilities in all ethnic groups, although the increases were not as statistically strong for Hispanics. Percentages of Whites with disabilities living independently for up to 2 years and 3–5 years after secondary school completion were 13.4 and 42.3, respectively. This represented an overall percentage gain of 28.9, which was found to be highly significant ($p < .001$). Percentages for African American youth with disabilities living independently during the same time periods were 5.1 and 25.5, respectively, with an overall percentage gain of 20.4, a gain that was also found to be highly significant ($p < .001$). Finally, percentages of Hispanic youth with disabilities living independently for up to 2 years and 3–5 years after secondary school completion were 15.2 and 31.1, respectively. This represented an overall percentage gain of 15.9, which was found to be only slightly significant ($p < .10$). Despite the positive percentage gains of all ethnic groups with disabilities for independent living status, Whites still fared significantly better on this transition outcome compared with African Americans (42% versus 26%, $p < .01$) 3–5 years after secondary school completion. Furthermore, Whites made significantly greater percentage gains in independent living status during this time period compared with Hispanics (28.9% versus 15.9%, $p < .001$ versus $p < .10$, respectively).

Table 13–2   National Longitudinal Transition Study-2 Data on Transition Outcomes in Minority and Nonminority Youth with Disabilities

Transition Outcome	1 year or less
Competitive Employment (%)	
Whites	63
African Americans	42
Hispanics	36
Earned Minimum Wage or More	
Whites	54
African Americans	39
Hispanics	41

Source: Data taken from *Reports and Products, National Longitudinal Transition Study 2,* by SRI International, http://www.nlts2.org/contact/index.html

National Longitudinal Transition Study-2

The National Longitudinal Transition Study-2 (NLTS-2) began in December 2000 and involves a nationally representative sample of roughly 12,000 students in special education aged 13–16 years old. The NLTS-2 follows these students through 2010 and assesses a variety of outcomes as they transition from adolescence to early adulthood (e.g., educational, vocational, social, and personal experiences). Table 13–2 shows data from NLTS-2 published in 2003, which allows for a comparison of the data obtained from NLTS-1 published in 1996. Note, however, that outcome data for NLTS-2 (2003) are restricted to less than or equal to 1 year and, as yet, does not include postsecondary school attendance or independent living data.

The data from NLTS-2 demonstrate with respect to employment and earned minimum wage that African American and Hispanic youth with disabilities continue to lag behind their White peers with disabilities (42% and 36% compared to 63% respectively for employment; 39% and 41% compared to 54% respectively for earned minimum wage). When comparing NLTS-1 $\leq$ 2 year data and NLTS-2 $\leq$ 1 year data in these categories, African Americans have made percentage gains in competitive employment, whereas Hispanics have lower comparative employment rates. Specifically, African American employment is 42% on NLTS-2 compared to 25.5% on NLTS-1 and Hispanic employment is 36% on NLTS-2 compared to 49.4% on NLTS-1. With respect to earned minimum wage or more, African Americans and Hispanics have made substantial gains on NLTS-2 compared to NLTS-1 (39% compared to 14.2% for African Americans and 41% compared to 0.1% for Hispanics). Despite these encouraging gains, particularly for Hispanic youth with disabilities, minority youth with disabilities continue to lag behind their White peers with disabilities with respect to earned minimum wage or more (54% for White youth with disabilities). Hence, we see in NLTS-2 and from the comparison data with NLTS-1 that minority status continues to be associated with poorer transition outcomes for CLD youth with disabilities. In addition, CLD youth with disabilities are more likely to come from lower socioeconomic households and live with parents who lack postsecondary educations (Wagner, Newman, & Cameto, 2004).

Summary of NLTS Data on Transition of Minority Youth with Disabilities

Blackorby and Wagner (1996, p. 410) commented on NLTS-1 data that "the gap between white and minority youth with disabilities on measures of effective transition that was observed in the early years after high school was largely sustained in the subsequent three years." This pattern, though showing some improvement in the area of employment on NLTS-2, continues to exist, leading one to conclude that minority status presents obstacles to successful transition of youth with disabilities beyond that of disability alone (Wagner et al., 2004). A potential explanation for this lies in a variety of barriers that CLD youth with disabilities and their families face during the transition years. A comprehensive review of these barriers is the focus of the second portion of this chapter.

WHAT BARRIERS TO TRANSITION EXIST FOR CLD YOUTH WITH DISABILITIES AND THEIR FAMILIES?

Significant barriers exist to successful transition for CLD youth with disabilities and their families during the transition years. These are shown in Figure 13–1 and have been grouped into three categories: (a) professional insensitivity in transition personnel, (b) school-imposed barriers to transition, and (c) characteristics of particular CLD

Professional Insensitivity to Cultural Group Differences

1. Dimensions of culture and cultural diversity
2. Degrees of interaction and acculturation of CLD families
3. Differences in values between U.S. society and those of varying CLD groups

School-Imposed Barriers to Transition

1. Professional educator behavior that deters CLD parent participation:
   - Late notices and inflexible scheduling of conferences
   - Limited time for conferences
   - Emphasis on documents rather than participation
   - Use of jargon
   - Structure of power

Inherent Characteristics of CLD Groups

1. Lower socioeconomic status
2. Attitudes toward disability
3. Interpersonal communication style and native language
4. Knowledge and comfort with school infrastructure

Figure 13–1   Barriers to Transition of CLD Youth with Disabilities

groups. A discussion of research findings in each of these categories will subsequently be presented, along with several case studies, to illustrate these findings in an applied setting. Implications for transition personnel are also discussed.

Professional Insensitivity to Cultural Group Differences

Professional insensitivity to cultural group differences can lead to significant conflicts when members of IEP teams are discussing transition with CLD youth with disabilities and their families. Team members must possess a unique blend of cultural sensitivity, knowledge, and skills. Examples include knowledge and sensitivity to (a) dimensions of culture and cultural diversity, (b) degrees of interaction and acculturation of CLD families of youth with disabilities, and (c) differences in values between U.S. society and those of other cultures. A discussion of each of these follows.

Dimensions of Culture and Cultural Diversity. Smith (1992) defined **culture** as patterned behavior, learned by instruction or imitation of members of a social group. Cultural behavior includes, but is not limited to, institutions, language, values, religion, symbols, ideals, habits of thinking, artistic expressions, and patterns of social and interpersonal relationships. Culture is not a set of rigidly prescribed rules or behaviors but, rather, is an evolving framework of actions that are filtered and checked through daily life (Lynch & Hanson, 1998).

Cultural diversity is defined as the presence of individuals who are from a variety of cultural backgrounds. There are, however, many definitions of culture. Review the definitions listed below and identify themes that emerge:

1. Culture is a body of past human accomplishments that is inherited socially. It is a resource for the lives of current people who live in a specific country or area (Gallego & Cole, 2001).
2. Culture is the aggregate of morals, beliefs, customs, knowledge, laws, art, and any other skill that a person acquires by participating in a social community (Chanchani & Theivanathampillai, 2002; Dahl, 2003).
3. Culture is the combined effort of citizens to establish and develop meaning about collective and individual values, beliefs, and actions. Culture is used as a reference point from which people construct their perceptions and reactions to the environment (Dahl, 2003).

The multiple definitions of culture suggest several core themes: Culture is a resource; it embraces beliefs, morals, customs, and values; and it is usually inherited collectively, not individually. Each person's identity is unique, and culture is inexplicably tied to personal identity.

Within specific ethnic groups there is a wide variation of culture. As mentioned before, regional differences within the same nation can be significant. For example, imagine two European-American families with French heritage whose past five generations have lived in the United States. The only difference is that one has lived in Vermont their entire life and the other in Mississippi. Although surely they will have some elements of their culture that are similar, they also will differ on any number of beliefs, customs, and linguistic patterns. Similarly, differences are also found within the same ethnic groups who emigrate from other countries to the United States. Individuals who may be considered Hispanic or Latino are not all similar. People from El Salvador are very different from people who have emigrated from Honduras, Mexico, Peru, Argentina, or Bolivia. All of them differ from families who have emigrated from Spain.

In the United States, there are individuals from multiple cultures, but an overarching American culture exists, which is referred to as the *macroculture*. The macroculture is comprised of numerous *microcultures,* which are the specific cultural practices of individuals within the population (Banks, 2001). So, within specific families there may be various combinations of cultural practices. For example, many Latino or Asian families participate in a traditional 4th of July celebration with fireworks and a picnic. Others do not acknowledge the holiday and continue with routine activities. Many immigrant children create traditional Valentines Day cards, yet their parents and grandparents may not acknowledge the holiday. Obviously, the student or child may be more receptive to accepting new cultural values and norms than a parent or grandparent for whom these practices are unfamiliar. Because many cultures embrace an extended family that actively participates in the family structure, within one household there may be a blending of cultures, both native and American (Midobuche, 2001)

Culture, therefore, is a kaleidoscope of infinite combinations and variations of individual's native and American culture and language. This provides a challenge for collaboration and coordination of services for culturally and linguistically diverse populations (Soodac & Erwin, 1995), since no two families or individuals are the same, regardless of their ethnic heritage.

Gallimore and Goldenberg (2001), as cited in Rueda, Monzo, Shapiro, Gomez, and Blacher (2005, p. 403), use the term *cultural models* to mean a shared mental schema or normative set of understandings regarding "how the world works, ought to work, including what is valued and ideal, what settings should be enacted and avoided, who should participate, the rules of interaction, and the purpose of interactions."

Cultural beliefs and practices exist on a continuum. Rueda et al. (2005) point out that one problem when discussing culturally based beliefs and values is *the mistake of assuming that these are stable, context free, and pervasive among all members of a given cultural group*. Every family within a given culture is a unique blend of its own cultural heritage, acculturation, social status, and idiosyncratic style (Gallimore & Goldenberg, 2001; Harry et al., 1995). Therefore, *not all families within a specific cultural group can be considered alike*. For example, Rueda et al. summarized a number of studies containing evidence that demonstrate (a) cultural variation regarding normal childrearing or family practices for young adults without disabilities, (b) variation in the meaning attached to disability in various cultures, and (c) varying attitudes related to service delivery systems in special education and the values embedded in these systems. Rueda et al. caution professionals to *not assume universality of the values* of various cultural groups regarding "development, life outcomes, family structures and roles, parenting, independence, and individual achievement apart from one's nuclear family that may be implied in discussions of the concepts of normalization and least restrictive environment" (p. 402).

Although it is important that educators be very careful not to generalize about people from different regions of the world, it is also important that they understand that some families have left countries in deep poverty or in conflict. For example, educational systems in some regions of the world are weak, minimal, or nonexistent due to sustained conflict. Even if education is available, many children leave school because of lack of security or economic pressures to go to work to help support the family. Consequently, individuals who have left their countries due to war or poverty may not have experience with or exposure to traditional education. This can place the students and parents at a distinct disadvantage when attending schools in the United States, interacting with educators, and making educational decisions, particularly if they have special learning needs. These families, however, may also be very resilient and possess many other resources that enable them to adapt to requirements of the schools. It is the responsibility of the educator to identify these sources of resilience.

Theories About Cultural Difference

Three distinct theories influence perspectives on cultural difference—*ethnocentrism, assimilation,* and *the cultural model perspective.* They are presented here because of the enormous impact that these perspectives can have on collaborative relationships among professionals. As these theories are introduced, keep in mind the principles and concepts discussed previously about effective collaboration and system coordination. Remember that systems are complex, dynamic, and interdependent. They are composed of a network of flexible, mutual relationships.

Ethnocentrism

Ethnocentrism is the belief that one culture is superior to another, that culture and its accompanying actions, values, norms, traditions, and beliefs becomes the basis on which all other cultures are compared. Within this framework, differences between the dominant culture and other cultures are viewed as deficits.

Deficit Model. Within a deficit perspective, people who differ from the dominant cultural patterns are viewed as having deficits or deficiencies (Bernhard, Freire, Pacini-Ketchabaw, & Villanueva, 1998; Cummins, 2001; Gallego & Cole, 2001; Harry, 2002; Lee, 2003; Midobuche, 2001; Nieto, 2000; Valencia & Black, 2002). Deficit perspectives justify prejudice, stereotyping, stigmatizing, and distorting culturally different populations. This framework also allows learning difficulties to be located within the student (Nieto, 2000). Similarly, if parents do not participate in school activities in a traditional manner, they are perceived negatively as uninvolved. Lack of parental involvement is considered to be a deficit (Bernhard et al., 1998). According to Nieto (2000), placing the blame on the student or the parent relieves educators of the daunting task of creating an educational system that is equitable and meaningful to all students. Ethnocentrism can also lead to the belief that children are best taught by teachers of like ethnicity.

Assimilation

The second perspective that stands in contrast to ethnocentrism is based on the assumption that for culturally different individuals to be successful, they must *assimilate into the dominant culture.* The goal of *assimilation* is to replace the native culture with knowledge of and behaviors associated with American culture (Gallego & Cole, 2001; Nieto, 2000). Consequently, until those who are different assimilate into the dominant culture, members of the dominant group develop identities that characterize groups in terms of *us* and *them* (Apple, 1996; Cochran-Smith, 2000; Kumashiro, 2001; Valencia & Black, 2002).

Both the ethnocentric and assimilation models attach a stigma to culturally diverse individuals. As Artiles (1998) observed, "The deficit view of minority people might often mediate [the dominant group's] cognitive, emotional, and behavioral reactions to minority individual's phenotypes, interactive styles, language, professions, and world views" (p. 33). This stigma makes it difficult for professionals and educators to recognize the strengths and cultural capital within these populations (Dennis & Giangreco, 1996).

Acculturation, a concept related to assimilation, refers to the process of how individuals adjust, change, or modify their lives as a result of exposure to another culture or society (Fuligni, 2001). The process of acculturation can positively or negatively impact the individual. In the effort to achieve acculturation, individual cultural backgrounds can be viewed as either (a) mismatched with the mainstream culture and in need of modifying or (b) beneficial and complementary to the mainstream culture and viewed as additive.

The *cultural mismatch theory* posits that individuals who are culturally different from the majority population face challenges bridging the gap between the home and school cultures (Delpit, 1995). These individuals do not possess the same interaction styles, values, beliefs, and understandings to enable them to easily participate in an environment defined by a different culture. Because these cultural challenges impact learning, educators and related service personnel must help students bridge the gap between the native and new culture.

A *cultural model perspective* is similar to acculturation, but more positive. It predicts differences in home and school cultures and is based on the assumption that individuals change in response to exposure to new cultural processes, creating a *shared model* of culture (Gallimore & Goldenberg, 2001; Reese & Gallimore, 2000). Educators with this perspective view cultural changes as *additive and beneficial* to the educational setting. Cultural transformation or change is a result of a process that deepens meaning and understanding about cultural differences by students and teachers (Artiles, 2003).

Accommodation is a concept related to the cultural model perspective. Those who embrace an accommodation framework accept cultural differences and recognize different cultures as equal. Within this framework, poor school performance and relationships with parents are altered by making accommodations that try to narrow some of the differences between the home culture and the school culture (Gallego & Cole, 2001). Within the accommodation framework, various interventions or strategies are used to bridge the cultural gap, but all individuals are considered equally valued regardless of their ethnicity.

Although most people are not consciously aware of it, behavior is mostly a result of our cultural experiences. Children born and raised in the United States possess an understanding of interaction styles characteristic of American culture. Sometimes these characteristics are described as *scripts*. For example, in the United States, when students are spoken to they know to maintain eye contact, use courtesy markers, and respond (Obiakor & Wilder, 2003). In other cultures, the "script" may be very different. When addressed, it may be expected that students remain quiet and make no eye contact. What we consider *normal* student behavior may be unfamiliar to students of other cultures. Their behavior is different and therefore is sometimes perceived by educators as unacceptable. All behavior patterns and expectations are culturally relative.

Unfortunately, behaviors that are unfamiliar to teachers can sometimes be misinterpreted as challenging, oppositional, disrespectful, or even indicative of learning or emotional disabilities. Identifying nondisabled CLD students as having emotional disabilities because of behaviors that are rooted in their native culture can have a devastating impact on their education and self-concept. Explicit instruction on expectations and behaviors may be necessary to assist students in developing a repertoire of interaction skills necessary for them to be successful in American schools. Knowing the student is essential.

Degree of Integration and Acculturation.

Degree of integration and *acculturation* into mainstream U.S. society are two examples of ways in which people within a specific cultural group may differ. Degree of integration and acculturation of CLD individuals and their families into mainstream U.S. society is often determined by socioeconomic status, generational status, religion, age at immigration, language ability, education level, gender, cultural attitudes, geographical location, length of residence in the United States, ability, and personality (Grossman, 1995; Harry et al., 1995; Hyun & Fowler, 1995; Lynch & Hanson, 1998).

Several authors have identified a continuum of characteristics associated with degree of integration and acculturation in members of different cultural groups (Grossman, 1995; Harry, 1992; Lynch & Hanson, 1998). These characteristics include (a) *overacculturated,* (b) *mainstreamers,* (c) *bicultural,* and (d) *culturally marginal* individuals. **Overacculturated** individuals are those who show extreme rejection of their native culture in favor of the mainstream culture. This behavior is frequently found in young people born in the United States to first-generation immigrant parents. **Mainstreamers** are those who have assimilated or adopted the standard values of the mainstream culture. These individuals are comfortable in the mainstream but have not necessarily rejected all aspects of their native culture. For example, they may consider themselves American but still recognize and celebrate certain holidays from their native culture (e.g., Cinco de Mayo, Chinese New Year). **Bicultural** individuals demonstrate an efficient level of integration in both cultures. **Culturally marginal** individuals are at the juncture of two cultures; they accept neither the old nor the new cultural values, practices, and beliefs and may experience alienation from both as a result. Culturally different individuals, on the other hand, have been exposed to the mainstream culture but choose to remain in their native cultural enclave.

Other Views on Cultural Diversity.

Degree of integration and acculturation, along with several other important variables related to cultural diversity, are shown in Table 13-2. The table contrasts U.S. mainstream values with those of various culturally diverse groups. Note that one must be cautious not to overgeneralize the variables shown in Table 13–2. Many cultural observers are critical of these arbitrary dichotomies that categorize and generalize cultural values to all CLD groups. Such distinctions, however, can provide useful frameworks for identifying and becoming sensitive to differences between cultures.

Luft (1997) noted that mainstream U.S. society is represented by middle-class culture and values. Some of these culturally valued American traits include the following: being rational, being efficient in use of time and energy, controlling distracting impulses and delaying gratification, valuing work over play, being economically and socially successful and ambitious, being independent and self-reliant, being White and Native born, and being intellectually superior.

Likewise, Black, Mrasek, and Ballinger (2003) discussed values and goals in the United States that emphasize individualism. **Individualism** emphasizes separateness and the unique strengths of a person. Examples of this include (a) standing out from the crowd, (b) independent enterprise, (c) personal accomplishments, (d) individual rights and opportunities, (e) pursuing personal interests, (f) setting and achieving personal goals, (g) self-reliance based on people being true to their own values and beliefs.

In contrast, the views, values, and beliefs of various culturally and linguistically diverse groups may differ greatly from those held by the American majority. Examples include the following:

1. Family and group identity taking precedence over individual identity
2. The importance of family reputation, status, and cohesiveness
3. Group solidarity and collective responsibility as opposed to individual responsibility
4. Personal esteem and honor, trustworthiness, and the giving and earning of respect, rather than intellectual, social, and economic status
5. Interpersonal relationships and mutual caring as opposed to external measures of individual success

Black et al. (2003) and others (e.g., Luft 1997, 2001) refer to these as collectivist values and note that this difference has the potential to create cultural conflicts for CLD youth with disabilities and their families. Black et al. provide examples, such as (a) the extreme difficulty in conforming to a system in which school demands are expected to take precedence over family needs, (b) students having to compete with and outperform their peers, (c) the expectation that schoolwork and extra curricular activities are high priorities, and (d) independent living, employment, and assumption of substantial adult responsibilities being expected when the individual leaves school.

Rueda et al. (2005) investigated culturally based variation in attitudes, beliefs, and meanings of transition in Latina mothers of young adults with developmental disabilities. In contrast to values of individualism, findings from this study indicated that these mothers placed a high priority on their children's development of life skills (e.g., fixing light meals and bathing) not for the reason of gaining increased independence needed for independent living in the community. Rather, these mothers wanted their children to learn these skills to develop better hygiene and personal self-help in the context of living and staying at home. The home was seen as the most appropriate living setting and as a safe environment in case anything should happen to the mother. Independent living was seen as a *ludicrous and inappropriate concept* and the mother or another family member, if the mother was no longer able to care for the child, were deemed to be the primary individuals responsible for the child's long-term care. Furthermore, these mothers perceived themselves as more knowledgeable and able to make transition related decisions about their children compared to professionals. They felt that they, not the professionals, should make all of the final decisions about transition planning.

Contrasts between U.S. society and other cultures can also be seen in the respective groups' intrapersonal and interpersonal relationships. According to Luft (1997) "Despite social changes impacting American families, there remains a social value on the nuclear family as the centerpiece for primary relationships" (p. 3). Rationalism, efficiency, and independence are the values that govern the manner for establishing and maintaining relationships in U.S. society. In contrast, interpersonal and intrapersonal relationship characteristics of other cultures include the following:

1. A value on collectivism, harmony, and social order extending beyond the nuclear family
2. Relationships governed by prescribed roles regarding subordination, interdependence, reciprocity, obligation, propriety, and cooperation
3. Families and groups that function as strong supports with side and flexible kinship webs, including extended and nonfamily support relationships
4. Work ethics that include working mothers as evidence of strength and not need
5. Kinship obligations and fosterage of children as evidence of patterns to strengthen and maintain kinship bonds
6. Childrearing practices based on admonitions and advising of children rather than the use of punishment and rewards
7. A lack of confrontation in relationships, with an emphasis on saving face for the person in authority when conflicts occur
8. Respect for authority figures, including the school, with an unwillingness to argue or contradict (Luft, 1997)

Lack of awareness and sensitivity of IEP team members of the contrasting values shown in Table 11-2 during the transition planning process can result in

1. the formation of false assumptions about CLD youth with disabilities and their families;
2. transition personnel engaging in implicit or explicit discouragement of CLD parent participation;
3. feelings of isolation, helplessness, and exclusion in CLD parents (Artiles, 2003);
4. low self-confidence in CLD parents when interacting with transition personnel; and
5. dissonance and conflicts during IEP meetings (Harry, 1992; Luft, 1997).

Summary of Professional Insensitivity to Cultural Group Differences. The characteristics of people within and between particular cultural groups vary widely. Not all members of a given culture are the same with respect to their acculturation into U.S.

society, values, or beliefs. For this reason, transition personnel should not make assumptions that an individual will behave in a certain way or possess a set of values and beliefs related to their culture. Stereotypical behaviors of this type in IEP team members can result in barriers to effective communication with CLD youth with disabilities and their families during the transition years. Members of IEP teams need to become as knowledgeable as possible of the complexities of cultural groups. Ways to effectively accomplish this objective are presented in the concluding section of this chapter. Our discussion now turns to the second major category of barriers to successful transition for CLD youth with disabilities and their families, specifically, barriers that are school imposed.

LET'S SEE IT IN ACTION! CASE EXAMPLE

Professional Insensitivity to CLD Groups

Su-Lin Yee, a ninth-grade Asian student with a learning disability, was practicing a self-directed IEP meeting in the resource room. Transition planning was the topic of the discussion. The resource specialist was surprised to learn that Su-Lin was not interested in going to college because Su-Lin was Asian. Nevertheless, the specialist had Su-Lin rehearse stating she wanted to go to cosmetology school after graduation.

The annual IEP meeting was held and her parents were in attendance. They were highly educated professionals who had recently immigrated to the United States to give their children a better life. Su-Lin's disability was difficult for them to accept but they knew if she applied herself, she could be successful academically in high school and make their family proud. This was very important to them because she was the oldest of their children.

Su-Lin was hesitant and did not speak up in response to the psychologist's request to state her goals and dreams for the future. The resource specialist then said to her, "Come on Su-Lin, your parents need to hear what we've been practicing. Tell them what you want to do with your life in the future. Go ahead, dear." Su-Lin then shared her desire to pursue transition pathway 2 and hopes to go to cosmetology school. Her parents were very quiet and when asked what they thought of this plan, responded, "We will do what the school thinks is best for Su-Lin."

School-Imposed Barriers to Transition

IDEA 2004 strongly encourages **self-advocacy** and active participation of youth with disabilities and their families during the IEP transition planning process. In contrast to families from the mainstream U.S. culture, members of CLD groups frequently face school-imposed barriers that prevent them from engaging in effective self-advocacy and active participation during IEP meetings. For example, CLD parents of youth with disabilities may feel uncomfortable within the school setting if they have limited educational backgrounds and experience with schools. IEP team members, in turn, often falsely assume that these parents are not sophisticated enough to grasp the material discussed in an IEP meeting.

A study by Harry, Allen, and McLaughlin (1995) revealed the following five aspects of professional educator behavior that functioned as active deterrents to African

American parents' participation and advocacy for their children in special education conferences.

1. Late notices and inflexible scheduling of conferences: Problems included (a) parents receiving notices two to three days prior to a scheduled meeting despite the state's 10-day prior notice requirement, (b) administrator's reluctance to adjust meeting dates or attend meetings, and (c) scheduling of meetings at times that were impossible for parents to attend.

2. Limited time for conferences: Only 20–30 minutes were allowed for most conferences, regardless of the complexity or status of the deliberations. Parents who needed additional time were advised to continue their discussions with teachers after the meeting despite the fact that many of the teachers were not available because they had to cover classes and no assistant was available to release them from their teaching responsibilities.

3. Emphasis on documents rather than participation: It was common for parents to be advised not to worry about missing a conference they could not attend because the documents would be mailed to them to sign. Many parents said they had trouble understanding the terminology in the reports and perceived their main role to be a receiver of information about their child's progress and to sign documents rather than to provide input to school personnel.

4. The use of jargon: Parents were confused by unexplained educational jargon, classification codes, test results, and information contained in technical reports, resulting in parents generally feeling that the conference process was intimidating.

5. The structure of power: The interpersonal dynamics of the meetings placed parents at a distinct disadvantage and undermined their effort and ability to act as advocates for their children. Conferences were structured in a way that gave power and authority completely to professionals (e.g., professionals reported and parents listened), resulting in parents generally feeling that the conference process was intimidating.

A study by Geenan, Powers, and Lopez-Vasquez (2001) surveyed over 300 African American, Hispanic, Native American, and European–American parents to asses their involvement and experiences in transition planning. Results demonstrated a mismatch in school professionals' perception of CLD parent involvement compared to the perceptions of the parents themselves. School professionals reported significantly less involvement by CLD parents than did the reports by the parents on 8 of 10 transition activities (e.g., helping the child prepare for life after high school, finding work, finding out about adult services, teaching the child to care for their disability). CLD parents in the study actually placed significantly more importance than European Americans upon talking to their children about transition, helping their children prepare for post-secondary education, and teaching their child to care for their disability. And yet, despite these differences, school professionals reported a lack of involvement and perceived CLD parents as less involved in transition planning than their European–American counterparts. A potential explanation for this lies in the context in which CLD versus European Americans seek support and begin preparing their child for transition. "For many CLD families, the "launching" of a young person into adulthood stems from family and community rather than experiences provided by educational or other formal institutions" (Geenan et al., 2001, p. 279). The view of professionals regarding participation, or lack thereof, of CLD parents may be based upon only the context of the school. This misperception on the part of school professionals and lack of understanding of the importance placed by CLD families on family or community-based settings and supports for transition can lead professionals to quickly misjudge them as apathetic or uninterested. Geenen et al. go on to state:

> Rather, professionals may be most successful in promoting parent participation if they first examine their own behavior in terms of how it facilitates or discourages partnership with parents, particularly in light of enduring institutional barriers and the historical experiences of minorities with the educational system (p. 280).

The importance of the quality of the relationship between CLD parents and professionals is echoed by Kim and Morningstar (2005), who reviewed a study by deFur, Todd-Allen, and Getzel (2001). The primary themes of the deFur study were investigating barriers to parent participation and the professionals who make a difference. Professionals who made a difference in the lives of CLD families were ones who were characterized as "honest, clear, and knowledgeable" and encouraged and supported the child to reach his or her full potential.

In short, schools can be a foreign place for CLD families and youth with disabilities. This can lead to their feeling of not belonging when participating in a transition planning meeting. These feelings are exacerbated when IEP team members behave in ways that discourage active participation of CLD parents, such as allotting limited time for meetings, using lots of educational jargon, or using authority in an intimidating manner. Further complicating matters is the misguided perception of school professionals that CLD parents do not care or are apathetic to school-based approaches to transition planning, as well as a lack of understanding by school professionals of the cultural context in which CLD parents wish to address planning transition for their child. All of these things can result in CLD youth with disabilities and their families retreating into silence, offering few contributions to the transition plan because they feel their input is not valued.

Our discussion in this section concludes with inherent characteristics of CLD groups that act as barriers to transition.

LET'S SEE IT IN ACTION! CASE EXAMPLE

School-Imposed Barriers to Transition of CLD Groups

Marcus is a 17-year-old African American youth with an attention deficit disorder and low-average cognitive ability. He has been in special day classes receiving departmentalized instruction throughout high school and pursuing transition pathway 3. Marcus will graduate with a diploma, based on differential standards on his IEP. He lives in a two-bedroom apartment with his mother and three siblings. His mother works as a waitress in a neighborhood restaurant and cleans homes for extra income. She stopped attending IEP meetings after Marcus entered high school because the high school special education staff could only hold meetings before school from 7:30 to 8:15 a.m.

or after school from 3:15 to 4:00 p.m. Neither of these times fit her schedule. In response to this situation, the school psychologist calls her every year and tells her by phone what the IEP goals and objectives are for Marcus and asks if it would be all right if the papers were mailed home for her signature. She agreed to do this because no alternative time was offered to her to attend the IEP meeting. Moreover, she believed the elementary school had mislabeled Marcus as a child with low ability and she never understood the meaning of the test results. In her opinion, Marcus is a wonderful boy who is just shy in school.

This year, a representative from the Department of Rehabilitation is scheduled to attend the IEP meeting and explain how Marcus can become eligible to receive job development and placement services. Marcus is excited because he is interested in training to become a salesperson at an athletic shoe store in the local mall. Marcus told his special education teacher that his mother would not be able to attend the meeting due to her work schedule and having to take his sisters to school. Marcus is worried he would not be able to receive services from the Department of Rehabilitation because his mother cannot attend the meeting.

Barriers to Transition for CLD Groups

A number of environmental and cultural characteristics of CLD groups can act as barriers to the transition planning process, such as (a) socioeconomic status, (b) attitudes toward disabilities of particular CLD groups, (c) interpersonal communication style differences and language barriers, (d) knowledge and comfort with the infrastructure of schools, and (e) attitudes toward careers. A discussion of each of these follows.

Socioeconomic Status. **Socioeconomic status** (SES) is an important confounding variable that can create barriers to effective transition planning for CLD youth with disabilities and their families. **Culturally based attitudes toward disability,** career preparation, and school structures can create barriers to transition despite the socioeconomic status of the family. One must be cautious to avoid painting a broad picture associating cultural and linguistic diversity and lower SES. Nevertheless, data exist demonstrating greater socioeconomic class disparities in ethnically diverse groups in comparison to members of White middle- and upper-middle class U.S. society. For example, 68% of English language learners in pre-kindergarten through grade 5 are of low income and 60% in grades 6–12 (National Center for Education Statistics, 2006). It is also estimated that the number of language minority children is growing at a rate that is four times that of native English speaking students (McCloskey, 2002).

Socioeconomic status often affects the attitudes, perceptions, and receptiveness of school personnel toward CLD parents and their educational desires for their children (Lott & Rogers, 2005; Walker, Shafer, & Liams, 2004). In an analysis of studies on attitudes toward low-income and middle-income parents, conducted from 1985 to 2000, Lott and Rogers (2005) concludes that teachers and administrators hold many stereotypes about low-income parents. Other authors have concurred with Lott in their research with related services personnel (Roaches, Shore, Gouleta, & Burkevich, 2003). These findings further suggest that the exclusionary behavior that low-income parents face today has held true for several generations. Research occurring over the past two decades echoes these conclusions.

For example, in the late 1980s, Lareau (1989) found that upper-middle-class parents, compared with working-class parents, were better able to achieve a customized or individualized educational career for their child. The author believed this was a result of upper-middle-class parents' (a) greater educational competence, (b) social status, (c) income and material resources, (d) views of work, and (e) social networks. An additional advantage for upper-middle-class parents posited by Lareau was the more favorable perceptions of school personnel toward them, in comparison with low-SES parents. Also, Davies (1994, April) indicated that educators in low-income communities often viewed low-SES families as *deficient* and hard to reach because of personal characteristics or home and neighborhood condition. Ortiz and Yates (1986) listed several common stereotypes held by educators of parents and children living in poverty environments:

1. People from these environments are culturally disadvantaged and possess characteristics assumed to be part of their ethnic group as opposed to their economic status.
2. People on welfare are not responsible individuals.
3. People from poverty environments have violent dispositions.
4. Children who live in poverty are unteachable, cannot learn, and are unlikely to succeed in life.

Stereotypes of this nature might actually be the result of a conflict in values and perceptions of school personnel and those of low-SES parents. For families living in poverty, priorities such as providing adequate food, shelter, and clothing often take precedence over a child's education (Baca & Cervantes, 1986; Lott & Rogers, 2005).

In short, lower SES status can result in CLD parents and youth with disabilities feeling as though they are unequal partners in the transition planning process. Moreover, because of their lowered sense of societal status, these individuals may avoid attending transition planning meetings altogether. Family expectations for the future also help shape the achievements of youth with disabilities, particularly with regard to academic engagement and achievement (Newman, 2004). One reason for the continuing discrepancy in achievement outcomes between children with and without disabilities in all grade levels is the absence of approaches that promote the students' and families' involvement in developing educational and transition goals and services.

Attitudes Toward Disability of Particular CLD Groups.   The attitudes toward disability of a particular CLD group may affect the way these individuals behave in the educational and transition planning process. Members of diverse cultures may vary in child-rearing practices, in their views about disabilities, and in their responses to the authority of the school (Harry, 2002; Valle & Aponte, 2002). A family's cultural beliefs will impact the nature of their participation with professionals and schools and how they view disabilities.

Family responses to having a child with a disability differ greatly among cultures. In some nations, children with disabilities are hidden and not presented as part of the family. For example, in Russia, only since the early 1990s have education policies been developed to transfer children with disabilities from institutions into community schools.

Even today the special education program of the Moscow State Pedagogical University, ranked first among such institutions in Russia, is called defectology (Moscow State Pedagogical University, n.d.).

There are great differences in the way disability is regarded among societies, and the type and severity of a child's disability affect social attitudes toward the disability. Children with mild disabilities are often assimilated into the culture, whereas those with more severe disabilities are often socially isolated and cared for only within the immediate family. For instance, a learning disability or mild cognitive disability might go unnoticed in a developing nation or in a remote rural community that provides limited education and has low levels of literacy. The disability may only be acknowledged if it is readily apparent, either physically or behaviorally. It may be difficult for parents to comprehend the concept of a learning or cognitive disability in a child who functioned adequately within that cultural context of their home country.

Some cultures attribute disability to causes other than biomedical. For example, a study in Papua, New Guinea, showed that 32% of persons with disability and their families attributed disability to sorcery or supernatural causes (Byford & Veenstra, 2004). Some families may attribute their child's disability or developmental delay to something the mother did during her pregnancy or to a family transgression. Another may view an emotional disability in their young teen as the result of a supernatural cause (Harry, Kalyanpur, & Day, 1999). These attitudes breed shame about the child's disability and can hinder family participation in school activities.

Native Americans, on the other hand, share a common belief that the spirit chooses the body it will inhabit and a body with a disability is merely the outward casing of the spirit; the spirit within the body is whole and perfect and is distinguishable from the body itself (Clay, 2007; Locust, 1988, 1994). Most tribal languages do not have a word for handicap or disability, an idea that is familiar to Western culture but has no direct parallel in American Indian culture. The closest American Indian concept views disability as a disharmony of the spirit, although these beliefs vary greatly among tribes (Clay, 2007). For this reason, some Native Americans may have difficulty understanding or accepting the Western emphasis on a strictly medical or biological explanation for severe disabilities and may be inclined to avoid such services offered to them.

It has been observed that many African Americans have enduring and well-founded concerns about their children being misdiagnosed as having a mild disability and being inappropriately treated by mental health services (Bender, 2004; Feagin, Early, & McKinney, 2001; Harris, 2003; McNeil, Capage, & Bennett, 2002). Hence, African American families of youth with disabilities may avoid attempts in transition planning meetings to connect them with postschool mental health services.

Some cultures place great value on cooperation, cohesiveness, and interdependence—characteristics that differ from many school cultures that emphasize individual achievement and a competitive spirit. For these and other reasons, culturally and linguistically diverse families are sometimes only marginally involved in the education of their children. An understanding of cultural factors is fundamental to implementing educational and related services that are culturally sensitive. Such attitudes toward disabilities can cause family members to avoid seeking special education services or not actively participate in the transition planning process because of embarrassment.

Interpersonal Communication Style Differences and Language Barriers. Interpersonal communication style differences and language barriers affect the ability of CLD families and youth with disabilities to engage in self-advocacy during transition planning meetings. Studies of CLD parent involvement in schools have consistently shown that these parents tend to place their trust in the school system, exhibit respect and deference to school personnel, and withdraw from collaboration in matters where they do not wish to contradict authority figures and possibly lose face (Harry, 1992). Consequently, they will tend to agree or adhere to the counsel and directions of school personnel, even if it is at odds with their knowledge base, beliefs, or value systems. This pattern of interpersonal interaction and communication is observed in many CLD families.

A related communication style difference of many cultural groups noted by Lynch and Hanson (1998, 2004) is high context (versus low context) communication. In *high context communication,* words are less important than nonverbal cues, gestures, body language, and facial expressions. This type of communication style is common in Asian, Native American, Latino, and African American cultures and is in contrast to the *low context communication* style of mainstream U.S. culture, which relies much more heavily on precise, direct, and logical verbal communication. These communication style differences can lead to misunderstandings between transition personnel and CLD families and youth with disabilities during IEP meetings.

Finally, language barriers can cause similar problems. A common strategy of special educators engaged in meetings with non-English-speaking families is to use interpreters. However, the technical vocabulary of medical, educational, and other postschool transition services options for persons with disabilities places unfair responsibility on interpreters to translate complex information to CLD families and youth with disabilities. Further problems may arise if the interpreter is not familiar with many key aspects of cultural diversity reviewed earlier in this chapter, such as the degree of acculturation, generational status, religion, or social class of the CLD family.

In short, CLD families of youth with disabilities are unlikely to actively participate in the transition planning process if they lack the necessary spoken and written language skills to understand the proceedings in the IEP meeting. Many parents are uncomfortable expressing their lack of understanding and may not ask the questions necessary for them to comprehend and actively participate in a conference or conversation with teachers. It is important to be mindful of the technical language that is used to communicate with all parents, especially with culturally and linguistically diverse families. Moreover, cultural background differences in communication style and interpersonal interaction may cause certain CLD families (a) to miss many of the subtleties expressed by transition personnel during the meeting or (b) not to think it is their role to engage in self-advocacy. This, in turn, can lead them to play a less active role during planning meetings in comparison with non-CLD families.

Knowledge and Comfort with the School Infrastructure. Many CLD parents have difficulty accessing and making appropriate connections with the educational system and school personnel. Reasons cited for this in literature reviewed previously include (a) lack of parent education; (b) professional behavior by school personnel that reinforces parents' feelings of not belonging; (c) active deterrents to parent participation by school personnel, such as withholding of information, inflexible scheduling of conferences, and use of jargon; and (d) a general lack of understanding by parents of school practices and procedures (Harry, 1992, 2002; Harry et al., 1999; Hughes, 1995; Lynch & Hanson, 2004).

A further explanation for CLD family alienation from the educational system comes from both classic and contemporary findings from Ogbu (1978, 1991, 2003), Calebrese (1990), and Spring (2006). Ogbu, in a seminal discussion of cross-cultural issues in education, made a distinction between the psychological adaptations to the host society of *immigrant minorities,* such as Japanese and Koreans, versus *indigenous minorities,* such as African Americans and Native Americans. He noted that because immigrant minorities have moved to the host society more or less voluntarily, they tend to achieve their goals, such as economic success, within society without being deeply affected by the local hierarchical ideology. This makes them less likely to internalize experiences of rejection and discrimination. Moreover, their psychological frame of reference can be found within their traditional culture. Although often contested in the field of education for overgeneralizations regarding the academic performance of these students, Ogbu's work has been seminal as a framework for understanding the attitudes and behaviors of black students in public schools.

In contrast, Ogbu noted that indigenous minorities, defined as those who have grown up in or lived naturally in the host society for long periods of time, can be described as **caste-like,** operating from a position of low social status and disadvantage within a society that they consider their own. These minority groups tend to internalize the rejection they experience within the dominant society and potentially become psychologically predisposed toward failure. Blacks in the United States were offered by Ogbu (1987) as an example of a minority group that represented a prototypical caste-like minority. He argued that many blacks have developed an "oppositional" social identity or frame of reference and a "retreatist adaptation to school," resulting in their rejection of school values and, consequently, high rates of educational failure.

Summary of Barriers to Transition for CLD Youth with Disabilities and Their Families

Promoting the successful transition of youth with disabilities from school to a quality adult life is a very complex undertaking that is difficult and challenging to achieve, even in the most typical of circumstances. Cultural and linguistic differences in youth with disabilities further intensify the complexity of this task. Support for this statement can be found in a number of barriers faced by CLD youth with disabilities and their families during the transition years.

First, lack of knowledge in transition personnel of many aspects of cultural and linguistic diversity can prevent quality communication and interaction with members of various CLD groups. Important knowledge needed by IEP team members includes degree of integration and acculturation status of CLD individuals, as well as a number of important cultural value and trait differences of various CLD groups (see Table 13–3 based on the work of Nisbett, Peng, Choi, & Norenzayan, 2001; Weaver, 2000).

Second, CLD youth with disabilities and their families face a number of barriers during the transition planning process, some of which are school imposed and others

Table 13–3   Cross-Cultural Comparison of Values and Beliefs Related to Variables of CLD

Variables of CLD	Values and Beliefs of Various CLD Groups	U.S. Mainstream Values and Beliefs
Integration and acculturation status	Cultural pluralism; desire to maintain native cultural values, practices, and beliefs	Ethnocentrism; other cultures should fully assimilate U.S. mainstream values
Attitudes toward disability	Mind–body imbalance, retribution for past sins, shame, and evil spirit in child	Medical model; disability is a treatable condition
Interpersonal communication style	High-context communication; reliance on nonverbal cues, gestures, and body language	Low-context communication; reliance on precise, logical, and verbal communication
Individual's place in family, society, and world (ancestral world views)	Family extendedness; interdependence of individual, family, and society; cultural trust; cooperative behavior; holistic, collectivist orientation to life	Nuclear family; self-determination; independence; competitive behavior; individualism

that are associated with characteristics and environments of particular CLD groups. School-imposed barriers involve actions and behaviors by school personnel that make CLD families feel uncomfortable and unwelcome at IEP meetings. Examples presented include inconvenient and inflexible scheduling of meetings, limited time for conferences, emphasis on documents and overuse of educational jargon, and imbalances of power imposed during meetings. Barriers related to characteristics and environments of cultural and linguistic diversity involve (a) the effects of lower SES status, (b) attitudes toward disabilities of particular cultural groups, (c) interpersonal communication style differences, (d) language barriers of non-English-speaking families, and (e) a lack of knowledge and comfort with the infrastructure of schools in CLD families of youth with disabilities.

Several recommended best practices in transition for CLD youth with disabilities and their families emerge from the material that has been presented. These recommendations are the subject of the final portion of this chapter.

LET'S SEE IT IN ACTION! CASE EXAMPLE

Barriers to Transition for CLD Youth with Disabilities

Salvador received bilingual special education services throughout elementary school. He is currently in eighth grade, proficient in English, and enrolled in a resource specialist program for 50% of the day, receiving departmentalized instruction in social science, math, and language arts. He will begin high school next year. Course of study requirements

and the transition pathway to be pursued were discussed at his upcoming annual IEP meeting.

His parents and older sister, who is in 12th grade, attended the IEP meeting. His older sister was asked to serve as the interpreter at the meeting because his parents possess limited English skills. The family is not highly educated and the IEP team believes that college is not an important goal they have for their children. The IEP team recommends that Salvador continue to receive departmentalized special education instruction in the resource specialist program for three periods a day, similar to the program he received in middle school. They add that he should pursue pathway 2 for transition. They further recommend that Salvador participate in a work–study program in high school, eventually leading to paid, full-time employment after graduation. The IEP team assumes these goals are acceptable to Salvador's parents because they ask few questions during the meeting. They were subsequently asked to sign the papers designating their approval of the IEP for Salvador.

⇨ WHAT ARE BEST PRACTICES IN TRANSITION FOR CLD YOUTH WITH DISABILITIES AND THEIR FAMILIES?

The formation of effective partnerships among transition personnel, transition-age CLD youth with disabilities, and their families is facilitated by several best practices. These are outlined in Figure 13–2 and include (a) developing in transition personnel increased knowledge and sensitivity about the multiple dimensions of cultural groups, (b) using family-centered approaches and collaborative techniques with CLD families of youth with disabilities, (c) employment of effective communication practices with CLD groups, and (d) promoting in CLD families increased knowledge and comfort with school policy, practices, and procedures. A review of each of these best practices recommendations follows.

Increasing CLD Knowledge and Sensitivity in Transition Personnel

Transition personnel must possess knowledge beyond the superficial level about the multiple dimensions of cultural diversity if they are to respond and interact in a sensitive manner with members of various CLD groups. Harry et al. (1995) recommend direct, explicit, and intensive personnel preparation on multicultural issues for special educators, with an emphasis that "inculcates the understanding that cultures are fluid and are greatly influenced by acculturation, generational status, gender, social class, education, occupational group, and numerous other variables" (p. 106). Note the following

---

1. Develop increased knowledge and sensitivity about the multiple dimensions of cultural groups in IEP team members.

2. Use family-centered approaches and collaborative techniques when interacting with members of CLD groups.

3. Employ effective communication practices with members of CLD groups.

4. Promote increased knowledge and comfort with school policy, practices, and procedures in CLD families.

Figure 13–2   Best Practices in Transition for CLD Youth with Disabilities and Their Families

caution, however, regarding cultural sensitivity training programs: It may be unrealistic to expect transition personnel to become culturally competent in all aspects of the myriad cultures they may potentially encounter in today's public schools. Attempts to achieve this objective may run the risk of promoting in cultural sensitivity training participants stereotypical assumptions regarding various cultural groups.

Cultural sensitivity training begins with an understanding and respect for a CLD family's perspective on their youth with disabilities, along with their hopes and plans for the child's future. Answers to the following questions by CLD family members will help provide this transition-related information:

1. What language is spoken in the home and by which members? What is the literacy level of family members?
2. What are the family's norms for personal and social development for their youth with a disability, such as the degree of independence encouraged?
3. What residential and work-related goals for the youth with a disability are held by the family?
4. What are the family's views on disabilities and how does this affect their choice of treatment for their youth with a disability?
5. How is the family conceptualized? For example, does it represent the common mainstream U.S. concept of a nuclear unit, which views individual health as belonging to the individual, or does it represent the more extended family structure common in other cultures that conceptualize the health of an individual in terms of the family as a whole?
6. What are the family child-rearing practices? Are they authoritarian and hierarchical, with children having little decision-making power, or do children possess equal and individual rights, as practiced in many U.S. homes?
7. How much legal knowledge about parental rights and advocacy does the family possess? For example, is schooling viewed as a privilege or a right?

Many of these recommendations are echoed by Kim and Morningstar (2005) and Kyeong-Hwa and Morningstar (2007), who adapted and summarized the recommendations of Kalyanpur and Harry (1999) on how to enhance the cultural competence of professionals. These include professionals (a) knowing their own worldview and factors that shape their own cultural beliefs and traditions; (b) learning about the families they serve in the community, such as their customs, traditions, languages, communication styles, organizations, and structures; (c) acknowledging and respecting cultural differences; (d) reaching mutual goals between families and professionals by taking the time to understand them and work with them in a respectful and caring manner; (d) empowering families by increasing their knowledge about resources needed to achieve desired outcomes; (e) providing knowledge and information related to transition, such as informing them of their legal rights, the transition planning concept, and community resources; (f) encouraging the involvement of extended family members in the transition planning process; and (g) providing parent support programs to help them network with other veteran parents who can provide informational and emotional support in the transition planning process.

In summary, transition personnel must possess knowledge and sensitivity to the complex nature of cultural and linguistic diversity. Cultural diversity training programs are one vehicle for accomplishing this objective, provided they offer the necessary breadth and depth of understanding about various cultural groups and provide valid answers to the critical questions about a CLD family's unique characteristics.

A second recommended best practice in transition for CLD youth with disabilities and their families is the use of family-centered approaches and collaborative techniques. Information regarding this best practice is presented next.

Using Family-Centered Approaches and Collaborative Techniques

Much has been written in the past decade on the topic of family-centered approaches and collaborative communication with families of children with disabilities (see books by Kroth & Edge, 1997, and Singer & Powers, 1993, for summaries of such literature). A paradigm shift in family case management practices has occurred in response to problems associated with past, more traditional models of assisting families with special needs children. Traditional case management models and practices have been characterized as (a) providing families with a safety net of protection in response to their dire circumstances, (b) fraught with eligibility requirements for services and bureaucratic delivery of services in a paternalistic and punitive fashion, (c) heavily oriented toward professional control and the fitting of families to available programs and services, and (d) dominated by a medical orientation toward families, using language such as *pathology, treatment, cure,* and *prescription* when describing family needs and problems (Singer & Powers, 1993).

In contrast, newer models and principles of family support have emphasized (a) a recognition in practitioners of the unique strengths of each individual family and their capacity to change and grow when provided with the proper facilitating conditions; (b) the responsibility of practitioners to assist families in identifying available resources that meet their perceived needs rather than trying to fit families into rigid, existing programs and services; and (c) an equal relationship between family members and professionals, based on mutual respect, open communication, shared responsibility, and collaboration. In addition, Dunst, Trivette, Starnes, Hamby, and Gordon (1993) have noted that an effective family support program should aim to (a) enhance a sense of integration into the community in all family members, (b) mobilize resources and support, (c) strengthen and protect the integrity of the family unit, and (d) enhance and promote the competence of each family member.

It is essential for transition personnel to incorporate as many of these practices and principles as possible when interacting with CLD youth with disabilities and their families during the transition process. IEP team members should make a concerted effort to establish rapport with CLD families by building a mutual sense of trust, determining ground rules for how to get along, and developing a relationship that allows for more risk-taking behavior and mutual involvement. Harry et al. (1995) have suggested visiting the family in its home or in a community setting, identifying shared interests or family practices, or sharing a snack or meal with the family to help accomplish this task.

Establishing rapport and trust between transition personnel and CLD families is also facilitated through effective communication. This third best practice recommendation is covered next.

Using Effective Communication Practices with CLD Groups

Transition planning requires active participation of parents and their youth with a disability. A transition planning meeting is a much lengthier and complex process compared with an annual IEP meeting. Hence, effective communication with a CLD family is essential when discussing transition.

A number of helpful strategies for improving communication with CLD groups involved in the special education process have appeared in the literature in the past two decades. With regard to the use of interpreters, it has been suggested that special education personnel use persons who are familiar with the culture of the family to promote accurate, unbiased interpretation (Harry et al., 1995). Historic work by Condon, Peters, and Sueiro-Ross (1979), as well as Leung (1988) recommended involving other influential family members or qualified community members. Other children in the family should not be relied on to serve as interpreters because they may not possess adequate English skills to understand the technical vocabulary and terms involved in special education proceedings (Trueba, Jacobs, & Kirton, 1990). In addition, use of children as interpreters may place the child in an inappropriate power position in the parents' eyes, particularly in more hierarchical cultures (Harry et al., 1995).

A second suggested strategy for improving communication with CLD youth with disabilities and their families during the transition planning process is awareness by transition personnel of high context communication cultural groups. For example, extensive verbal directiveness may be perceived as mechanistic and insensitive by Asians, Native Americans, Hispanics, and African Americans. Lynch and Hanson (1998) recommended that special educators slow down, listen more, observe family communication patterns, be aware of nonverbal behavior or gestures, or consult cultural guides or mediators when interacting with members of these CLD groups.

It is equally important to help CLD families understand the complex nature of schools. Information on this fourth best practice recommendation is covered next.

Promoting Improved CLD Family Knowledge of School Policy, Practices, and Procedures

Schools must take a leadership role in developing and implementing practices that make appropriate connections with CLD families and enable them to become actively involved in their children's education (Harry, 1992; Hughes, 1995). Harry et al. (1995) note that CLD parents often know little about their legal rights and may come from backgrounds where schooling is seen as a privilege rather than a right. Transition personnel, therefore, must provide CLD parents with access to all sources of information about transition, such as legal mandates, postsecondary options and service agencies for their youth with disabilities, and parental advocacy organizations. In addition, transition personnel should consider creating transition support groups, mentor programs, and advocacy training programs for CLD families. A study by Trueba and Delgado-Gaitan (1988) found that the use of *academic mentors* (Hispanic parents whose children, regardless of social status, successfully completed school as opposed to dropping out) was an important strategy in creating parent empowerment in CLD families. Liontos (1991) pointed out that successful CLD parent support programs (a) emphasized the strengths of CLD parents and families, (b) let parents know that these strengths were valued, and (c) taught parents new techniques, what they were capable of doing, and how to overcome obstacles. Parent support programs with these characteristics have been shown to promote increased self-esteem and conscious acquisition of skills in dealing with schools in parent participants (Boone, 1992; Delgado-Gaitan, 1990).

Inger (1992) offered several recommendations for establishing successful parent outreach programs:

1. Make it as easy as possible for parents to participate, such as offering bilingual programs and materials, providing baby sitting, not charging fees, providing interpreters and transportation, and scheduling meetings at times and locations convenient for parents.
2. Establish personalized, face-to-face, individual contact with parents, such as meeting in their homes, if necessary.
3. Disseminate information and gain access to parents through traditional community supports, such as churches or ethnic organizations, as opposed to impersonal efforts such as letters and flyers.

These collective strategies, when implemented by transition personnel, will greatly enhance CLD family knowledge of the intricacies involved in schools and transition for CLD youth with disabilities.

Summary of Best Practices in Transition for CLD Youth with Disabilities and Their Families

Transition personnel must find ways to create positive, mutually beneficial relationships with CLD youth with disabilities and their families during the transition years. Several best practices in transition to accomplish this objective have been reviewed.

First, transition personnel must receive training to increase their knowledge and sensitivity about various cultural groups and the complex dimensions of culture. Transition personnel should also make concerted efforts to get to know the unique characteristics of each CLD family. This is best accomplished by establishing trust and rapport with the family, followed by asking them important key questions about their values, cultural characteristics, and family practices. Other family-centered approaches should be employed as well, such as promoting equal relationships with CLD families during meetings and offering them assistance in finding available resources that meet their unique needs.

Second, we discussed the importance of using effective communication practices with CLD families during the transition planning process. This includes being aware of **high- and low-context communication** differences of particular CLD groups, as well as effective use of interpreters during meetings. Children from the family should not serve as interpreters. Interpreters who are members of and familiar with the community of the CLD family should be sought.

Finally, strategies were presented to help CLD families better understand school policies, practices, and procedures. Suggestions included providing them with information about legal aspects of transition, creating CLD parent support groups and mentoring programs, and employment of parent outreach practices such as offering bilingual programs, services, and information.

We close this chapter with the presentation of an evaluation instrument for assessing the quality of transition services and programs for CLD youth with disabilities and their families. An accompanying case study for applying this instrument is presented as well.

LET'S SEE IT IN ACTION! CASE EXAMPLE

Best Practices in Transition for CLD Youth with Disabilities and Their Families

Magnolia School District has a very ethnically diverse population with high numbers of families whose primary language is not English. Teachers in the district have undergone extensive training to increase their knowledge, sensitivity, and skills for interacting with CLD youth and their families. This is evident at a recent IEP meeting for Maria, a 16-year-old Hispanic youth with multiple disabilities. The IEP meeting is held in her home on an evening when both her parents are able to attend. In addition, a bilingual, bicultural member of the school district parent mentor team participates in the meeting.

The meeting begins with introductions and time is spent getting to know the family, their child-rearing practices, and values in the home. Maria's parents are asked to share what they love about their daughter and their dreams for her in the future. Maria is asked the same question and uses a picture communication system to answer. Everyone agrees that Maria should participate in

an inclusive education in high school with the help of an inclusion facilitator so she can increase her ability to interact with nondisabled peers, develop appropriate social skills, and form friendships with others at the high school. Her parents would eventually like her to have a job in the community but are worried about her safety. The IEP team acknowledges this concern and suggests that Maria attend the community-based transition class after she turns age 18, where she will learn life skills and mobility training and participate in supported employment. This pleases Maria's parents because at this point, they do not think she is mature enough to be out in the community. Maria's mother has hopes that her daughter can help out in the family bakery someday but wants Maria to do something she likes best. A functional vocational evaluation is added to the IEP to help determine Maria's career interests, aptitude, and capability.

Maria's mother serves a traditional Mexican meal to the IEP team at the conclusion of the meeting.

How Should Transition Services to CLD Youth with Disabilities and Their Families Be Evaluated?

Table 13–4 contains a rating scale to be used by schools and transition services agencies for evaluating the quality of transition programs and services offered to CLD youth with disabilities and their families. The evaluation instrument contains three separate sections: (a) quality of transition services personnel, (b) quality of transition planning meetings, and (c) quality of practices designed to promote CLD family knowledge of school or agency transition policy, practices, and procedures. The authors acknowledge that some of the specific items contained on the evaluation instrument are generic in nature

Table 13–4   CLD Transition Services and Programs Evaluation Instrument

Use the following scale to evaluate the quality of transition services and programs provided within your school or agency to culturally and linguistically diverse youth with disabilities and their families.

1 = inadequate   2 = somewhat poor   3 = good   4 = excellent

I. Quality of CLD Knowledge and Skill in Transition Services Personnel
1. Overall sensitivity, knowledge, and skill related to CLD youth with disabilities and their families.   1   2   3   4
2. Transition services personnel knowledge, sensitivity, and skill related to the following specific dimensions of culture and cultural diversity:
    a. CLD family degree of integration and level of acculturation.   1   2   3   4
    b. CLD family attitudes and beliefs related to disabilities.   1   2   3   4
    c. CLD family interpersonal communication style (i.e., low versus high context).   1   2   3   4
    d. CLD family structure and norms (i.e., degree of interdependence, child-rearing practices).   1   2   3   4

II. Quality of Transition Planning Practices
1. Degree to which transition personnel and education professionals promote active involvement of all CLD family members during conference.   1   2   3   4
2. Specific conference practices that promote active involvement of all CLD family members:
    a. Advance notice of meetings provided.   1   2   3   4
    b. Meetings scheduled at a convenient time and location.   1   2   3   4
    c. Childcare provided if needed.   1   2   3   4
    d. Limited use of jargon during meeting.   1   2   3   4
    e. All family members viewed as equal partners with equal decision-making power during meeting.   1   2   3   4

III. Quality of Practices for Promoting CLD Family Knowledge of School/Agency Transition Policy, Practices, and Procedures
1. Degree to which transition legal mandates are adequately explained to CLD family members.   1   2   3   4
2. Degree to which eligibility requirements of postsecondary transition services agency and programs are adequately explained to CLD family members.   1   2   3   4
3. Existence and quality of CLD parent outreach programs and services (e.g., mentors and CLD parent outreach committees).   1   2   3   4
4. Degree of personalized, face-to-face communication with CLD parents which occurs in traditional CLD community organizations (e.g., churches, homes, ethnic organizations).   1   2   3   4

and are applicable to all youth with disabilities and their families, both CLD and non-CLD. These generic items, however, were included on the instrument because they represent concerns specifically related to barriers to active involvement of CLD families in special education and transition.

It is hoped that the use of this evaluation instrument will provide transition personnel, agencies, and schools with valuable feedback regarding the quality of transition programs and services offered to CLD youth with disabilities and their families. In addition, the instrument should be useful in assisting transition agencies and schools in identifying areas where they can improve in this regard. A case study of a transition-age CLD youth with a disability is presented at the end of this chapter. The evaluation instrument can be used to analyze the quality CLD transition best practices represented in the case study.

SUMMARY

The transition of youth with disabilities from school to a quality adult life is a complex task, involving multiple services, personnel, and agencies. Data clearly shows that the transition needs of CLD youth with disabilities and their families are not being met to an equal degree as are those of nonminority youth with disabilities (NLTS-1 and NLTS-2). Professional ignorance of cultural group differences is a potential explanation for these findings. Transition personnel must possess unique knowledge, sensitivity, and skill to promote successful movement from school to postsecondary education, community participation, employment, and independent living for CLD youth with disabilities. This includes knowing that not all members of a cultural group are the same with respect to heritage, acculturation, social status, or values. CLD youth with disabilities and their family members must be treated by transition specialists as unique individuals, possessing their own blend of cultural group characteristics. CLD training programs covering this breadth and depth of knowledge are suggested as a means for eliminating professional ignorance of cultural group differences.

Transition personnel must also make concerted efforts to reduce school-imposed barriers to active participation of CLD families of youth with disabilities during the transition years. Scheduling IEP meetings to accommodate a CLD family's life style, availability, and unique cultural characteristics is important. IEP meeting proceedings should take into consideration culturally related communication characteristics and differences of a CLD family when discussing transition. Adopting a family-centered approach and collaborative communication when discussing transition with CLD families will help accomplish this objective. This approach to communication is characterized by IEP team members attempting to determine the unique strengths and needs of a CLD family, along with identifying the transition resources and services available in the community that match. In addition, a family-centered approach to transition planning is based on mutual trust, respect, and sharing of responsibility and resources between the IEP team and CLD family members.

Finally, this chapter reviewed recommended best practices in transition for CLD youth with disabilities and their families. In addition to the best practices mentioned in the previous paragraph, we noted the importance of providing training to CLD families on school policies, practices, procedures, and the legal aspects of transition. The creation of CLD parent mentors and support groups have proven to be a successful strategy for improving CLD parent knowledge of school policy and procedures. Other transition best practices to facilitate outreach to CLD families include offering bilingual transition information, programs, and services, as well as bilingual or bicultural translators at IEP meetings involving transition planning.

LET'S SEE IT IN ACTION! CASE EXAMPLE

A Transition-Age CLD Youth with a Disability

Myoung-Hee Park is a 16-year-old Korean youth with mild to moderate disabilities and is the oldest of three children. She was born and raised in Los Angeles, California, and has attended neighborhood schools since kindergarten. Myoung-Hee's parents are first-generation immigrants to the United States and moved to Los Angeles from Seoul, Korea, six months before Myoung-Hee was born. As soon as they were financially able to do so, the Parks brought their parents from Korea to live with them in their home in Los Angeles, in a heavily populated Korean neighborhood known as Korea Town. Myoung-Hee was pleased to have her grandparents living with the family. Myoung-Hee and her friends have always embraced the mainstream U.S. culture and desired to act and be American in every way, rejecting most aspects of their native culture. This produced conflicts over the years with her parents and extended family, which can be appropriately labeled as culturally different.

Myoung-Hee was placed and educated in a segregated special day class from second through fourth grade and transitioned into a resource specialist program beginning in sixth grade. She participated in mainstream classes from sixth grade through high school, with resource specialist support and assistance on an average of one to two hours per day. Her current educational placement in high school remains the same, and she is pursuing transition pathway 3. Myoung-Hee's parents have always been somewhat embarrassed by their

daughter's school-related academic difficulties, as demonstrated by their continuing promises at annual IEP meetings that they will see to it that Myoung-Hee does not act lazy and works harder in school. Mr. and Mrs. Park contribute little else to the discussion during IEP meetings. They were pleased when the IEP team recommended in sixth grade that their daughter be placed in a resource room instead of continuing in a special day class.

Myoung-Hee is scheduled to graduate high school in 2 years but lacks the academic skills to be successful in a community college or university. This is acceptable to her parents, who own and operate a small neighborhood market in Korea Town. They would like for Myoung-Hee to live at home, help care for the family and extended family, and possibly work at the store once in a while.

Given this scenario, a number of problems and conflicts can potentially arise in the interactions among transition personnel, Myoung-Hee, and her parents in an IEP meeting discussing transition, particularly if members of the IEP team are ignorant of the multiple variables related to cultural diversity.

The IEP meeting begins with introductions, followed by a request by the case carrier for Myoung-Hee to identify her interests and preferences in a variety of transition areas. Mr. and Mrs. Park fail to maintain eye contact with their daughter or members of the IEP team after Myoung-Hee

(Continued)

begins talking. No one on the team notices this nonverbal behavior in Mr. and Mrs. Park. Myoung-Hee advocates several transition outcomes that are in direct conflict with her parents' wishes. Specifically, she states in the meeting that she wants to live outside the home and work independently in the community. Her parents continue to look down at the table during the conversation and fold their arms across their bodies. The IEP team asks Mr. and Mrs. Park how they feel about these transition goals, and the Parks respond that they will support the team's recommendations. The resource specialist subsequently writes transition services language into the IEP document reflecting Myoung-Hee's transition interests, preferences, and goals.

The meeting ends in the following manner: (a) the Parks sign the IEP document with little or no emotional expression, (b) the Parks nod their heads and say "yes" when asked by the specialist if they approve of the transition goals, (c) Myoung-Hee appears very happy and leaves the meeting excited about her future plans, and (d) members of the IEP team assume they have effectively completed their task and have met the transition requirements of IDEA 2004.

KEY TERMS AND PHRASES

acculturation

bicultural

caste-like

CLD parent mentor advisory committee

collectivism

culturally based attitudes toward disability

culturally marginal

culture

family-centered collaborative approaches

high- and low-context communication

immigrant and indigenous minorities

individualism

mainstreamers

National Longitudinal Transition Study

overacculturated

school infrastructure comfort

self-advocacy

self-determination

socioeconomic status

QUESTIONS FOR REFLECTION, THINKING, AND SKILL BUILDING

1. What barriers to transition of CLD youth with disabilities are caused by professional ignorance of cultural group differences?

2. How can transition personnel promote more active involvement of CLD youth with disabilities and their families in IEP transition planning meetings?

3. Use the CLD Transition Services and Programs Evaluation Instrument to evaluate the quality of transition services in a school or agency. Write a report of your findings and recommendations.

4. Create the ideal transition program at a school or agency serving the needs of CLD

youth with disabilities and their families. Specify the services to be provided and training needed for transition personnel.

5. Organize an interdisciplinary team, including parents of CLD youth with disabilities, to investigate the quality of transition services provided to CLD youth with disabilities and their families. Develop an action plan for improving the quality of transition services for this population and share the plan with supervisory or administrative personnel.

6. Organize a CLD parent advisory committee to develop family-centered collaborative practices for CLD youth with disabilities and their families. Include a parent-mentoring program in the practices to be developed.

Chapter 14

Teachers as Transition Leaders

Gary Greene

Chapter Questions

- How is teacher leadership defined, and why is it important?
- What knowledge and skills do special educators need to serve as effective transition leaders?
- How can special education teachers provide leadership to improve transition outcomes for youth with disabilities?

INTRODUCTION

This book has presented information on how to improve the quality of adult life for youth with disabilities. We have discussed the history and philosophy of transition, transition legislation, best practices in transition, systems coordination, interagency agreements, transition assessment, pathways, planning, and the final phases of transition. We also presented information on special considerations for transition planning, such as cultural and linguistic diversity. Common themes in all of the topics discussed is that transition from school to a quality adult life for youth with disabilities is a complex process that involves collaboration and coordination among multiple personnel and agencies and national and state policy mandates and incentives. The ability to facilitate this collaboration requires considerable leadership. Other than the youth with a disability and their parents, perhaps no one plays a more critical role in leading the transition process than special education teachers. These are the individuals who see the youth with a disability daily and shoulder the greatest responsibility for guiding and managing their students down a pathway to success into, through, and beyond school. With these thoughts in mind, this chapter addresses the topic of *teachers as transition leaders,* with hopes of empowering special education teachers to serve in this capacity.

HOW IS TEACHER LEADERSHIP DEFINED AND WHY IS IT IMPORTANT?

Wynne (2001, 2002), in a review of teacher leadership research, indicated that the majority of studies on the subject agree that teacher leaders

1. demonstrate expertise in their instruction and share that knowledge with other professionals;
2. are consistently on a professional learning curve;
3. frequently reflect on their work to stay on the cutting edge of what is best for children;
4. engage in continuous action research projects that examine their effectiveness;
5. collaborate with peers, parents, and communities, engaging them in dialogues of open inquiry, action, or assessment models of change;

6. become socially conscious and politically involved;
7. mentor new teachers;
8. become more involved at universities in the preparation of preservice teachers; and
9. are risk takers who participate in school decisions.

In addition to these skills, Wynne mentions the importance of teachers becoming active researchers in their classroom and schools, and for administrators, particularly school principals, to embrace the idea of teachers as equal partners in leadership.

When teachers are empowered as leaders, the focus of control for organizational change shifts from school principals to teachers (Terry, 2007) (see recommendations on promoting organizational change in the third section of this chapter). This requires trust on the principal's part and a paradigm shift in decision making from top-down to bottom-up. According to Wellins, Byham, and Wilson (1991), as reported by Terry (2007), empowerment occurs when power is given to employees who subsequently experience a sense of ownership and control over their jobs. This does not mean that principals relinquish their authority in school matters or that teachers should constantly challenge this authority. Rather, empowerment implies liberating teachers in such a way that they are free from experiencing "unwarranted control or unjustified beliefs" (Prawat, 1991, p. 749, as cited in Terry, 2007). Terry subsequently lists three strategies that outstanding principals utilize that go beyond simply involving teachers in decision making and ultimately promote teacher leadership: (a) provide a supportive environment that encourages teachers to examine and reflect upon their teaching and school practice; (b) use specific behaviors to facilitate reflective practice, and (c) make it possible for teachers to implement ideas that result from reflective practice.

Teacher leadership in the context of transition is critically important for a number of reasons, one of which is that school principals typically lack expertise and leadership ability in the area of special education, particularly related to transition. Given these circumstances, it is logical for special education teachers to serve in this leadership capacity for their staffs and for school principals to empower them to do so. A second reason for special education teachers to serve in a leadership capacity in the area of transition is that they have a history with the caseload of students and families they serve and are in the best position to coordinate services for these individuals. Whereas general education teachers, particularly those at the secondary level, have large numbers of students they serve and have frequent turnover of students (i.e., on a yearly basis), special education teachers have the luxury of a relatively much smaller caseload and see their students over multiple years. This promotes better opportunity for them to serve in a leadership capacity because they know their students well and the issues their students face when transitioning into, through, and beyond school. Finally, special education teachers should serve as transition leaders because they have a greater opportunity than general education teachers to influence and shape the educational program of their students by virtue of the individualized educational program (IEP) process and related services their students receive. In short, special education teachers are perhaps in the best position to serve in a transition leadership capacity and can effectively do so if empowered by their school principals or school districts to take on this role (see Case study 14-1).

CASE STUDY 14–1

Transition Leadership Empowerment

A secondary special education teacher at Marion High School was embarrassed by the lack of transition services options in the area of employment she was able to offer a parent in a recent IEP meeting. The parent was a strong advocate and wanted career assessment and employment development for their child within the next 2 years. The special education teacher said she recognized how important this was and would take a leadership role to make it happen at the school. She subsequently met with the rest of the special education staff, as well as the school principal and director of special education for the school district, to determine ways in which the school could develop better career and vocational training for students in special education. The district director of special education offered to place the special education teacher on special assignment for a year to investigate and develop better career and vocational options for

secondary level special education students in the district. He would hire a long-term substitute or additional special education teacher in her place during this time. The special education teacher subsequently enrolled in a local university course on career, vocational, and transition services and began collaborating with an individual at her local regional occupational program (ROP) in charge of special services. Together, with the help of their respective administrators, they were able to obtain funding and personnel to create a special needs employment development program at the ROP for secondary special education students in the school district. This resulted in the placement of eight students in local jobs in the community within the first year of the new program. Enrollment in the ROP class continued to grow and the possibility of offering two sections of the class in future years was being considered.

→ WHAT KNOWLEDGE AND SKILLS DO SPECIAL EDUCATION TEACHERS NEED TO SERVE AS EFFECTIVE TRANSITION LEADERS?

In answer to this question, we looked at a variety of sources, including (a) published transition specialist or coordinator roles and competencies, (b) a current graduate transition special education certificate program, and (c) existing transition literature. A review of each of these sources follows.

Transition Specialist Role and Competencies

The transition specialist role is a relatively new one for secondary special educators. Many high schools are focusing attention on helping students think about and plan their life beyond high school and on preparing them for the transition to postsecondary education, employment, and independent living. Some states have designated transition specialists to develop and improve transition services throughout the local districts. Where there is strong state-level leadership, each local school system has a designated lead transition specialist or coordinator who is responsible for providing information about local transition practices and services. The **transition specialist** or coordinator, who is often also a teacher, becomes an important link between the student and the post-high school world. Some of the many different roles that transition specialists perform include assessment specialist, information provider, problem solver, trainer and human resource developer, manager, service coordinator, evaluator, diplomat, and public relations agent (Kochhar, West, & Taymans, 2000).

Asselin, Todd-Allen, and DeFur (1998) conducted a state study of full-time-employed transition coordinators to describe their roles and competencies. The study yielded over 150 specific job duties that were then validated by transition specialists and coordinators. Although the study was validated within the state of Virginia, the findings have been validated by other states as well (Academy for Educational Development, 1999; Kochhar, 1995). Following are the nine categories and a sampling of the tasks under each category.

Intraschool Linkage

1. Disseminate transition information to teachers or administrators.
2. Provide preservice and in-service training.
3. Assist families, parents, and students to access transition services.
4. Serve as a liaison between the vocational-technical school and special education teachers to monitor student progress.
5. Facilitate appropriate referrals to school and community-based programs.
6. Assist school staff to interpret assessment results and recommend appropriate placements.
7. Assist vocational-technical teachers in adapting curricula.

Interagency or Business Linkages

1. Identify, establish, and maintain linkages with community agencies and businesses.
2. Write cooperative agreements.
3. Facilitate referrals to other agencies.
4. Lead interagency transition meetings.
5. Link students with postsecondary support services coordinators.

Assessment and Career Counseling

1. Identify and refer students for vocational assessment within the school.
2. Identify and refer students for vocational assessments at regional centers.
3. Coordinate the development of career awareness and explore activities as part of the career counseling process.

Transition Planning

1. Identify transition services provided by community agencies.
2. Attend or participate in team and IEP meetings.
3. Assist in planning and placement decisions.

4. Identify appropriate assistive technology.
5. Monitor adherence to federal laws.

Education and Community Training

1. Train special education teachers and employers to understand the need for self-advocacy.
2. Coordinate school and community work-based learning opportunities.
3. Identify job placements.
4. Develop community-based training and sites and school-based training.
5. Implement job support services for work adjustment and success.
6. Manage and coordinate job coaches.
7. Coordinate community-based instruction.
8. Coordinate teaching of daily living skills.
9. Examine or identify postsecondary training and education options.

Family Support and Resource

1. Develop and provide parent training.
2. Promote understanding of laws, eligibility requirements, and availability of services.
3. Assist students and families in understanding the system and accessing services.

Public Relations

1. Write newspaper articles, public service announcements, and presentations.
2. Develop business partnerships.
3. Promote work-based learning opportunities with businesses and recruit businesses.
4. Coordinate or sponsor transition fairs.

Program Development

1. Develop processes for transition planning.
2. Develop system guidelines and policies.
3. Develop transition curriculum.

Program Evaluation

1. Carry out school and community needs assessment.
2. Identify gaps in transition services.
3. Devise evaluation forms.
4. Analyze and use information gained from evaluations (Asselin, Todd-Allen, and DeFur, 1998).

The Council for Exceptional Children developed Performance-Based Standards for Transition Specialists that outline a set of competencies beyond those required of beginning teachers (Division on Career Development and Transition, Council for Exceptional Children, 2000a). These standards were based on several transition competency studies in the United States (Asselin & DeFur, 1998; Knott & Asselin, 1999; Kohler, 1995) and can be found in Figure 14–1.

Standard #1: Foundations

TS1K1 Theoretical and applied models of transition.
TS1K2 Transition-related laws and policies.
TS1K3 History of national transition initiatives.
TS1K4 Research on relationships between individual outcomes and transition practices.
TS1K5 Procedures and requirements for referring individuals to community service agencies.

Standard #2: Development and Characteristics of Learners

TS2K1 Implications of individual characteristics with respect to postschool outcomes and support needs.

Standard #3: Individual Learning Differences

None specified for this set of advanced standards.

Standard #4: Instructional Strategies

TS4K1 Methods for providing community-based education for individuals with exceptional learning needs.
TS4K2 Methods for linking academic content to transition goals.
TS4K3 Strategies for involving families and individuals with exceptional learning needs in transition planning and evaluation.
TS4S1 Arrange and evaluate instructional activities in relation to postschool goals.

Standard #5: Learning Environments and Social Interactions

TS5K1 School and postschool services available to specific populations of individuals with exceptional learning needs.
TS5S1 Identify and facilitate modifications within work and community environments.
TS5S2 Use support systems to facilitate self-advocacy in transition planning.

Standard #6: Language

None specified for this set of advanced standards.

Standard #7: Instructional Planning

TS7K1 Job seeking and job retention skills identified by employers as essential for successful employment.
TS7K2 Vocational education methods, models, and curricula.
TS7K3 Range of postschool options within specific outcome areas.
TS7S1 Identify outcomes and instructional options specific to the community and the individual.
TS7S2 Arrange and evaluate instructional activities in relation to postschool goals.
TS7S3 Ensure the inclusion of transition-related goals in the educational program plan.
TS7S4 Develop postschool goals and objectives, using interests and preferences of the individual.

Standard #8: Assessment

TS8K1 Formal and informal approaches for identifying students' interests and preferences related to educational experiences and postschool goals.
TS8S1 Match skills and interests of the individuals to skills and demands required by vocational and postschool settings.

TS8S2 Interpret results of career and vocational assessment for individuals, families, and professionals.

TS8S3 Use a variety of formal and informal career, transition, and vocational assessment procedures.

TS8S4 Evaluate and modify transition goals on an ongoing basis.

TS8S5 Assess and develop natural support systems to facilitate transition to postschool environments.

Standard #9: Professional and Ethical Practice

TS9K1 Scope and role of transition specialist.

TS9K2 Scope and role of agency personnel related to transition services.

TS9K3 Organizations and publications relevant to the field of transition.

TS9S1 Show positive regard for the capacity and operating constraints of community organizations involved in transition services.

TS9S2 Participate in activities of professional organizations in the field of transition.

Standard #10: Collaboration

TS10K1 Methods to increase transition service delivery through interagency agreements and collaborative funding.

TS10K2 Transition planning strategies that facilitate input from team members.

TS10S1 Design and use procedures to evaluate and improve transition education and services in collaboration with team members.

TS10S2 Provide information to families about transition education, services, support networks, and postschool options.

TS10S3 Involve team members in establishing transition policy.

TS10S4 Provide transition-focused technical assistance and professional development in collaboration with team members.

TS10S5 Collaborate with transition-focused agencies.

TS10S6 Develop interagency strategies to collect, share, and use student assessment data.

TS10S7 Use strategies for resolving differences in collaborative relationships and interagency agreements.

TS10S8 Assist teachers to identify educational program planning team members.

TS10S9 Assure individual, family, and agency participation in transition planning and implementation.

Figure 14–1 CEC Knowledge and Skill Base for Special Education Transition Specialists[1,2]

Notes:

"Individual with exceptional learning needs" is used throughout to include individuals with disabilities and individuals with exceptional gifts and talents.

"Exceptional condition" is used throughout to include both single and co-existing conditions. These may be two or more disabling conditions or exceptional gifts or talents co-existing with one or more disabling conditions.

"Special curricula" is used throughout to denote curricular areas not routinely emphasized or addressed in general curricula; e.g., social, communication, motor, independence, self-advocacy.

[1]*Note On Coding:* CC in the number code indicates a Common Core item; EC indicates an Early Childhood Special Education item; K indicates a Knowledge item; S indicates a Skill item.

[2]These standards were developed with the assumption that candidates would have had previous training in special education.

Source: Reprinted from *What Every Special Educator Must Know: Ethics, Standards, and Guidelines for Special Educators*, 5th ed., by Council for Exceptional Children, 2003, Arlington, VA: Council for Exceptional Children.

Combining Roles

Schools are experimenting with many new ways to build transition support services into instructional or related service roles in the schools. Strategies used in many schools today include the following:

1. Additional transition related responsibilities are added to the teacher's role. In many schools, the transition coordination responsibilities are attached to existing roles such as the special education teacher, the related services specialist, the vocational-technical education specialist, or the guidance counselor (Division on Career Development and Transition, Council for Exceptional Children, 2000a; Kohler, 1998; West, Taymans, Corbey, & Dodge, 1994).

2. Transition responsibilities are assigned to teams of teachers, including subject matter teachers and consulting special education teachers.

3. Separate transition coordinator roles are established that focus entirely on transition support and coordination for students and families.

The roles that these individuals play in linking the student and the community may vary in several ways:

1. The types of transition coordination and support functions that are performed

---

Qualifications: Bachelors degree in education, with teaching certification and 1 year of relevant teaching experience.

Role and Functions: The Teacher/Student Transition Service Coordinator position is both an instructional position and a direct support provider for students. The position is supervised by the faculty coordinator and director and is housed in the middle school.

1. **Maintains daily contact with students:** is assigned a caseload of students for which the teacher/coordinator is responsible. Meets daily with the student and provides supportive academic counseling and assistance when needed. Makes referrals for specialized services as needed and reviews student's weekly activities and assignments.

2. **Teaching responsibilities:** carries a modified class load in the academic subject area and provides academic evaluation of students, attends interdisciplinary team meetings, attends administrative and curriculum revision meetings, and attends staff development meetings and technology education seminars.

3 **Family contacts and follow-along:** makes contact with family as needed and arranges for parent visits and consultations, and provides information to families about available community services as appropriate. Makes home visits if needed to intervene when student is at risk of poor performance or dropout.

4. **Develops individual student guidance plans:** with the student, develops individual guidance plans for each semester, which includes measurable objectives for academic performance, vocational program participation, behavior, extracurricular activities, parent participation, at-home activities, future planning, and other appropriate activities.

5. **Develops and maintains student records:** maintains log of support meetings and activities on behalf of the student or family including record of student meetings and tutorials, family contacts, referrals, contact notes, changes in guidance plan, and any other relevant information.

Figure 14–2   Sample Position Description for a Transition Service Coordinator: Middle School (Pennsylvania)

2. The kind and amount of student and family contact that the transition specialist may have
3. The relationship of the specialist with the student and the family
4. Primary goals of the transition coordination activities
5. The size of the transition *caseload* or number of students participating in transition services
6. The scope of school and interagency responsibility and extent of authority of the specialist
7. The degree to which the transition coordination functions are attached to a primary role such as teacher, counselor, administrator, or specialist
8. The way that the role is evaluated

There is also considerable variation in how specialists and coordinators view the scope of their roles. There is no *right way* to craft the role of the transition specialist. What is important is that the coordination functions are appropriate for and responsive to the needs of students preparing for transition from secondary education. Figures 14-2 through 14-5 present sample position descriptions for transition service coordination roles. These descriptions are composites of many descriptions drawn from a variety of agency documents.

The districtwide transition coordinator coordinates the development and implementation of an area-wide transition process, used by area educational agency teams in developing IEPs for students with disabilities who will turn 16 within the current school year (and annually thereafter) and are preparing to enter into the world of employment, independent living, and postsecondary education. The coordinator promotes collaboration and coordination between local school districts and agencies outside of education that include: Department of Human Services, Division of Vocational Rehabilitation Services, Central Point of Coordination administrators (CPCs), case management and adult service agencies (vocational and residential), and postsecondary education facilities (Southern Prairie AEA, Oskaloosa, Iowa, 2000).

Figure 14–3 Districtwide Transition Coordinator (Iowa)

One of the crucial elements in the effectiveness of the Youth Transition Program (YTP) resulted from the decision to create new positions within the system to support students. In each participating school district, YTP services are provided by a team consisting of a school teacher who serves as the teacher coordinator, one or more transition specialists, and a vocational rehabilitation counselor from the local office. The leadership and guidance of the transition specialists and the teacher coordinator depart from traditional school practices and have allowed for both a wide array of opportunities for students and rich connections with the larger community.

In general, the transition specialist's role includes recruiting students, assessing students, developing individualized plans (both individualized education plans and individualized written rehabilitation plans), developing job placements, and supervising students on job sites. Individualized instruction is one of the keys to YTP's effectiveness. Each student completes an individualized assessment and receives an appropriately tailored instructional program. The local vocational rehabilitation counselor then establishes student eligibility for the program, develops individualized plans, provides or purchases support services not provided by the school, and provides postsecondary placements in employment or training.

Figure 14–4 Youth Transition Program (Oregon)

The New England Literacy Resource Center (NELRC) / World Education is seeking a half-time project coordinator for a new, comprehensive college transition program in partnership with six learning centers in New England (Connecticut, Maine, New Hampshire, and Rhode Island). The program goal is to prepare adult ESOL, GED, or diploma program graduates to enter and succeed in postsecondary education so as to help them improve and enrich their own and their families' lives. The six programs will provide instruction in academic reading, writing, math and computer skills, counseling, and posttransition mentoring. There are measurable goals related to program completion, college entry, and retention.

This is a program of NELRC funded by the Nellie Mae Foundation. NELRC is a six-state collaborative whose mission is to strengthen adult literacy services through sharing and collaborative projects among State Literacy Resource Centers (SLRCs), adult literacy practitioners, and policy makers in the region. NELRC is part of World Education, a Boston nonprofit organization that provides training and technical assistance in adult education.

Responsibilities

Coordinate and support the implementation of the ABE to college transition program at the six partner learning centers including:

1. Develop, in consultation with program staff, advisors, and existing materials, a course outline with suggested teaching materials and publications for three classes: algebra, college reading, writing, and study skills, including the integration of computer skills.
2. Organize two 2-day training institutes for project staff for February and June.
3. Review each program's plan for project activities, and if necessary, help refine it.
4. Provide ongoing support to program staff through monthly phone meetings, e-mail, mailings, and two visits to each site per year.
5. Facilitate online and offline sharing between programs regarding promising practices.
6. Develop project monitoring tools; monitor program implementation and attainment of goals.
7. Write quarterly progress updates and a longer final report on the project.
8. Ensure the implementation of the program evaluation.
9. Participate in the World Education Literacy Division staff meetings and activities as needed.

Qualifications

10. Demonstrated ability to organize and manage multifaceted projects, meet deadlines, and be self-directed.
11. Documented experience in college transition teaching and curriculum development.
12. Excellent communication and interpersonal skills; ability to work in a team.
13. Willingness to travel out of state; access to a car for work-related travel.

Figure 14–5   Transition to College: The New England ABE-to-College Transition Program Coordinator

Graduate Transition Specialist Training Program(s)

Since the mid-1980s, Congress has authorized funds to prepare personnel to educate children and youth with disabilities. Included in this funding are grants designed to prepare transition specialist personnel. A variety of programs of this nature have existed over the years, typically found in college or university programs in teacher education, vocational education, or vocational rehabilitation (see Greene & Albright, 1994, for a description of one of the first transition services personnel training programs). A recently established Transition Special Education Certificate program can be found at George Washington University (GWU, 2007) in Washington, DC (for information on

this program, go to http://gsehd.gwu.edu/Transition+Special+Education+Certificate).
According to recruitment documents, the GWU program is designed to meet the
expressed needs of educators and rehabilitation personnel by focusing on research
concerning youth with disabilities and the legislative requirements to provide transition services to this special population, such as ongoing assessment, curriculum planning, and collaboration with a variety of stakeholders involved in the transition
process (e.g., community agency personnel, school administration and faculty, and
parents). In addition, the program meets the CEC Advanced Knowledge and Skills
Base for Transition Specialists (CEC, 2003) recognized by most states, and the National
Standards and Quality Indicators of the National Alliance for Secondary Education and
Transition (2005).

Four courses make up the certificate program with content that includes career,
vocational, and transition services; vocational assessment; interagency collaboration;
and curriculum in transition special education (intended for school-based personnel)
or employment models for individuals with disabilities (intended for agency-based
personnel). The program can be completed through distance education, thereby
increasing the recruitment pool to persons interested in gaining transition leadership
skills in other states and regions outside of the Washington, DC area.

The program at GWU and others like it in states and regions around the country
provide an excellent opportunity for special educators, rehabilitation personnel, counselors, and related services personnel to improve their transition leadership skills. For
this reason, graduate transition services training programs are highly recommended.

Existing Transition Literature

Competencies for persons interested in transition leadership can be derived from
existing transition literature. Much has been written on best practices in transition
(see Chapter 6, on this subject, and Figure 6-2 and Table 6-1), and this information
can be translated into competencies needed by individuals who wish to act in a transition leadership capacity. For example, three major categories of transition best practice discussed in Chapter 6 were (a) transition services agency best practices, (b)
transition education programming best practices, and (c) transition planning best
practices. Transition leaders should be competent in interagency and interdisciplinary collaboration with a variety of school personnel, related service providers, and
business and industry personnel (i.e., transition services agency best practices). Second, transition leaders should be adept at promoting inclusion of youth with disabilities in school, employment, and community settings and be able to select appropriate
curriculum or be adept at modifying curriculum for youth with disabilities while they
are in school (i.e., transition education programming best practices). Equally important for transition leaders is to have knowledge about valid and reliable ways to promote social and interpersonal skill development in youth with disabilities, as well as
how to conduct career and vocational assessment for these individuals. Finally, transition specialist should be competent in the transition planning process, including
teaching self-determination skills to youth with disabilities and promoting active
involvement of parents and their child in the creation of the transition portion of the
IEP (i.e., transition planning best practices).

A second transition literature source for deriving transition leadership competencies is Kohler's (1995) *Taxonomy for Transition Programming* (see Figure 6–1). Kohler's model emphasized (a) student-focused planning, (b) student development, (c) family involvement, (d) interagency collaboration, and (e) program structures. The Division on Career Development and Transition (DCDT, 2000b) published a fact sheet that summarized competencies for secondary special educators in these major areas that emerged through research presented by Kohler. These are shown in Table 14–1.

Summary of Important Transition Leadership Knowledge and Skills

Special education teachers interested in serving as transition leaders must possess a unique combination of knowledge and skills. Much has been written on this subject, and we have attempted to review the various sources of this information, including research on the transition specialist role, competencies emphasized in graduate level training programs designed for transition specialists, and published literature on best practices in transition. Transition leaders may be hard pressed to master all of the knowledge, skills, or competencies we have discussed, but those presented certainly serve as an effective guideline for people interested in transition leadership. It may be appropriate to share the leadership role between several individuals within a school, school district, or transition services agency. A case study illustrating the process involved in determining transition leadership knowledge and skill is presented in Case study 14–2.

Possessing transition leadership knowledge and skills, though very important, does not necessarily guarantee positive results will occur when attempting to lead an organization in a different or improved direction. Equally important is knowledge of how to implement strategies that promote organizational change. This final transition leadership skill is reviewed in the next section.

➡ HOW CAN SPECIAL EDUCATION TEACHERS PROVIDE LEADERSHIP TO IMPROVE TRANSITION OUTCOMES FOR YOUTH WITH DISABILITIES?

The desire to lead an organization in a different direction does not necessarily translate into action and successful outcomes. Much has been written on the subject of organizational change and leadership in the context of management in business and industry. Little, however, has been published on promoting organizational change in the context of transition services for youth with disabilities. An article by Brault, Ashley, and Gallo (2001) describing a change process adapted from Ambrose (1987), which was applied to an early intervention program for families of infants and toddlers with special needs, contained information related to strategies for promoting organizational change in transition services. Ambrose, as reviewed by Brault and Ashley, highlight five key variables needed to ensure change. These include

1. having a clear vision of the desired outcomes,
2. providing incentives to participants to promote change,
3. developing skills in the people associated with the change process,

Table 14–1 Five Categories of Transition Competencies Found in the Taxonomy for Transition Programming

Student-Focused Planning

Identify and document students' postschool goals, learning, and need for accommodations

Use a variety of assessment information as a basis for the individual education program

Identify measurable transition-related goals and objectives that focus on postsecondary education or training, employment, independent living, and community and leisure activities

Develop educational experiences that correspond with postschool goals and objectives, such as participation in college preparatory curricula and/or in vocational and technical education

Through the IEP plan, specify responsibility for transition-focused instruction activities or services

Develop students' abilities to participate meaningfully in the development of their IEP

Utilize a planning process that is student-centered and facilitates students' self-determination, including student decision making

Provide appropriate accommodations to facilitate student and family involvement in the individual planning process and specifically in the IEP meeting

Evaluate the progress or attainment of student goals, including student evaluation of his or her progress, at least annually

Student Development

Teach academic skills in the context of real life experiences

Teach self-determination skills

Teach social skills for school, work, and community living

Teach learning strategies and study skills

Teach independent and family living skills

Develop students' career awareness

Develop accommodations and adaptations that meet student needs across a variety of settings, such as academic, vocational, home, and community

Use mentors to facilitate student learning

Interagency Collaboration

Interact effectively with community service providers to identify and address students' service and support needs

Collaborate with general and vocational educators regarding students' learning needs and instructional programs

Provide information about upcoming service needs of students for strategic planning purposes

With appropriate authorization from students and families, provide student assessment information to relevant service providers

Family Involvement

Provide pre-IEP planning activities for parents

Identify and provide information about transition services and program and/or curriculum options

Facilitate parent attendance at IEP planning meetings

Actively include parents and family members in planning and decision making

Program Structures and Policies

Develop outcome-based curricula

Provide flexible program and curricular options to meet student needs

Participate in program and curriculum development and evaluation

Teach students in integrated settings

Source: From *Transition-Related Planning, Instruction, and Service Responsibilities for Secondary Special Educators: Fact Sheet*, by Division on Career Development and Transition, March 2000. Reprinted with permission.

Reprinted from *A Taxonomy for Transition Programming: Linking Research and Practice*, by P. Kohler, 1995, Urbana-Champaign, IL: Transition Research Institute.

CASE STUDY 14–2

Transition Leadership Knowledge and Skill Determination

Secondary level special education teachers in the Greenville Unified School District had complained for years that they lacked the knowledge, skill, and training to effectively write the transition portion of the IEP. They felt inadequate in IEP meetings collaborating with parents on these matters and were concerned that either a compliance review or lawsuit by a strong parent advocate would ultimately expose their weaknesses. The director of special education decided to take action on the matter by creating a transition specialist position for the school district. She began the process by determining the competencies and skills of a transition coordinator or specialist, utilizing information available from the Council for Exceptional Children and the Division on Career Development and Transition. She verified these competencies by searching out positions of this nature that already existed in other school districts within her local region and state. She interviewed a few people who were currently serving in this capacity. She utilized this collective information to formulate a position description for a transition specialist. She was able to convince the school board that this position should not come from the current special education teacher ranks and obtained school board level approval for funding of a new and permanent transition services coordinator.

---

4. providing the resources needed to promote change, and
5. developing an action plan.

Ashley et al. reviewed a change process that was utilized by the HOPE Infant Family Support Program in San Diego, California. The vision of the HOPE program was to serve families of infants and toddlers with special needs in more natural environments rather than in a center-based program. The change process began by HOPE personnel examining their values, beliefs, guiding principles, and the mission of the organization. With respect to incentives, IDEA legislation was cited as *the most pressing incentive* because federal compliance reviews were placing increased attention on providing services in natural environments. The organization subsequently spent considerable time researching how other programs were accomplishing this objective and held forums with their staff to involve and inform them in the change process. A workgroup developed a philosophy of service in natural environments and gained staff feedback and final approval to move forward in this direction. The staff then identified and determined the skills and knowledge that would be needed by parents to support their child in a natural environment, trained their personnel in how to teach these skills to parents, and then shifted resources in such a way to support this change. All of this was guided by an action plan developed by HOPE personnel and supported by key administrative leaders in the organization. Finally, the organization engaged in ongoing evaluation of the changes by conducting consumer satisfaction surveys and holding parent focus groups. A statement by HOPE personnel appearing at the end of Brualt et al. article summarizes well an effective change process: "As a program, we don't have all the answers. Yet we are committed to moving forward and exploring new ideas to provide what we believe is quality early intervention for children and families" (p. 18).

Similar strategies and recommendations appeared in a paper by Greene (unpublished) entitled "Promoting Organizational Change." The author interviewed six successful school administrators who had a wide variety of leadership knowledge and expertise in the public schools (e.g., school superintendents, school principals, directors of special education, and program specialists) and were considered highly successful in their professions. Listed in Table 14–2 are the recommendations of these school leaders. Several key points should be seriously considered by those individuals interested in serving in a transition leadership capacity. First, one needs to assess and be aware of the needs of their school organization with respect to the quality of transition services being provided to youth with disabilities and their families and utilize this information to develop a vision and related action plan of the necessary steps to move forward. Two excellent resources for determining the quality of transition services offered in a school or school district presented in this textbook are the Transition Best Practices Evaluation Instrument (see Table 6–3) and the CLD Transition Services and Programs Evaluation Instrument (see Table 13–3). These instruments can be utilized to conduct a needs assessment of transition services quality in one's school or school district. Second, in developing a vision and action plan related to transition services, an effective transition leader will do several important things, including (a) sharing their agenda with personnel within the organization, (b) inviting key leadership (i.e., influential and highly respected employees) to participate in the development and implementation of the change process, (c) gaining the input of others following the change recommendations of key personnel, and (d) actively confronting people's fear of change by offering them the resources (e.g., time for meetings, financial incentives, mentors, or peer collaborators) and training needed to move forward in the change process. Third, an effective transition leader should recognize that once the action plan is developed, change should be initiated in small steps and carefully monitored by gathering informative, evaluative data that can be used to help guide the change process. Active involvement of key personnel should continue throughout the change process, not simply in the planning phase.

Table 14–2 Strategies for Promoting Organizational Change

Establish a trusting relationship prior to expecting change
Gain staff input into all aspects of change
Utilize the expertise of key leadership
Promote change initially in small steps
Recruit and hire growth oriented, enthusiastic employees who are likely to support change
Share the agenda, evidence, and expectations for change with employees
Provide employees with training to develop new skills
Actively confront employees' fear of change
Invite people to change rather than force them
Match the change strategy to your unique organization
Do not change for the sake of change
Change or pay the price
Influence the influencers
Provide the resources to support change
Promote personal development in employees to promote change

CASE STUDY 14–3

Promoting Organizational Change

Special education teachers of students with moderate to severe disabilities at Longview High School wanted their students to have the opportunity to participate in more academic general education classes, rather than simply be included in elective classes. They began the process by conducting a needs assessment, determining parent input on the matter, and gathering data on the current number of special education students enrolled in academic general education classes. All data pointed to the need to move forward with this vision. They formed a subcommittee that included a few strong parent advocates and met with the school administrative staff for input, support, and guidance. This subsequently led to a series of meetings with academic department chairs to explore resources and training that would be needed to make this vision a reality. Though it took time and commitment on the part of all persons involved, eventually the program developed and took shape. All students with moderate to severe disabilities were included in at least one academic class per semester; special education teachers were successfully collaborating with the teachers by offering curriculum modifications, accommodations, and coteaching; and the students were developing improved social and interpersonal skills.

Finally, effective transition leaders should recognize the importance of bringing on board new people who support the vision of the organization and who can contribute to translating this vision into action; hence, hiring growth-oriented, enthusiastic employees who possess the type of skills needed to move the organization forward is a critical change strategy. Likewise, recognizing that change cannot be forced upon those who are resistant to change is an important transition leadership skill. Inviting such individuals to get involved in the change process by seeking their input, providing them with incentives, training, or other resources can potentially promote their movement in the desired direction.

In summary, transition leadership involves more than simply knowing what needs to be done to promote better quality transition services for youth with disabilities. Equally important is knowing how to accomplish the task, including a multitude of organizational change strategies that can be used to help move an organization in a needed and desired direction. A case study illustrating promotion of organizational change can found at the end of this chapter (see Case study 14–3).

SUMMARY

Data continues to demonstrate that youth with disabilities are not exiting school prepared for the transition to a quality adult life. According to Murray, Goldstein, Nourse, and Edgar (2000) "Secondary special education programs appear to have little impact on students' adjustment to community life. More than 30% of the students enrolled in secondary special education programs drop out, and neither graduates nor dropouts find adequate employment opportunities" (p. 55). Lack of leadership was determined to be a major factor contributing to the underdevelopment of transition services across states in follow-up studies of transition outcomes and state educational improvement grants (Kochhar-Bryant, 2002a).

In our opinion, secondary level special education teachers are in the best position to lead their organization toward promoting better quality transition outcomes for youth with disabilities. In order to do so, it is critical for them to develop and refine their transition leadership skills. We have identified in this chapter specific **transition leadership competencies** for special education teachers, methods for acquiring training to achieve these leadership skills, and strategies for leading an organization in a new and improved direction. We recognize that many special education teachers already feel overwhelmed by the day-to-day demands of their jobs and may be unwilling to serve in a transition leadership capacity. We hope, however, that others are willing to do so because without teacher leadership in transition, outcomes for youth with disabilities are unlikely to change. Equally important is for school administrators to provide resources and incentives for special education teachers to serve in a transition leadership capacity. Many school districts and states have funded transition specialist positions and more need to do so.

An old saying exists: "Realize when pointing a finger at someone else for problems that exist, three fingers are pointing back at you." Change begins with one's willingness to make a change and putting forth the personal effort to make the change happen. We hope that the information presented in this chapter will inspire special education teachers to serve in a transition leadership capacity, resulting in better quality outcomes for youth with disabilities seeking a quality adult life.

KEY TERMS AND PHRASES

leadership
organizational change
organizational change strategies
top-down, bottom-up management

transition coordinator
transition leadership competencies
transition specialist

QUESTIONS FOR REFLECTION, THINKING, AND SKILL BUILDING

1. What are examples of transition leadership competencies and skills?
2. What are the essential elements needed to promote organizational change?
3. Why do you think transition outcomes for youth with disabilities continue to be poor, and what leadership role do you think special education teachers can potentially play in this regard?
4. What leadership role do you think you can play in your organization with respect to transition services, and how will this improve your organization?

5. Conduct a needs assessment within your school or organization, and create an action plan to improve the quality of transition services offered.
6. Organize a team of professionals and community members to evaluate the quality of transition services offered in your region and utilize three or more of the organizational change strategies discussed in this chapter to improve the transition outcomes for youth with disabilities.

References

Abrahams, D., Boyd, S., & Ginsburg, G. (2001). *Fair labor standards handbook for states, local governments and schools*. Washington, DC: Thompson Publishing Group.

Abrams, L. S. (2002). Rethinking girls "at-risk": Gender, race, class intersections and adolescent development. *Journal of Human Behavior in the Social Environment, 6*(2), 47-64.

Abrams, L. S., & Gibbs, J. T. (2002). Disrupting the logic of home–school relations: Parent participation and practices of inclusion and exclusion. *Urban Education, 37*(3), 384-407.

Academy for Educational Development. (1999). *Positive youth development: AED makes young people a priority*. Washington, DC: Author.

ACT. (2006). *Breaking barriers: Ensuring college and career success* (ACT Annual Report). Iowa City, IA: Author.

Adams, G., Gullotta, T., & Montemayor, R. (1992). *Adolescent identity formation*. Newbury Park, CA: Sage.

Addams, J. (1916). *The long road of woman's memory*. New York: Macmillan.

Adelman, H., & Taylor, L. (1997). Addressing barriers to learning: Beyond school-linked services and full service schools. *American Journal of Orthopsychiatry, 67*(3), 408-421.

Akos, P. (2002). Student perceptions of the transition from elementary to middle school. *Professional School Counseling, 5*, 339-345.

Akos, P., & Galassi, J. P. (2004a). Middle and high school transitions as viewed by students, parents, and teachers. *Professional School Counseling, 7*(4), 212-221.

Akos, P., & Galassi, J. P. (2004b). Gender and race as variables in psychosocial adjustment to middle and high school. *The Journal of Educational Research, 98*(2), 102-108.

Alaska Department of Education and Early Development. (2007). *2007-2008 neglected & delinquent annual application for schools in state operated facilities: Title I, part D, subpart 1*. Juneau: Author.

Albright, L. A., & Cobb, R. B. (1988). Curriculum-based vocational assessment: A concept whose time has come. *Journal for Vocational Special Needs Education, 10*(2), 13-16.

Albus, D., Lieu, K., & Thurlow, M. (2002, April). *Large scale assessment participation and performance of limited English proficient students with disabilities: What public data reports tell us*. Roundtable presentation at annual meeting of the American Educational Research Association, New Orleans, LA.

Albus, D., & Thurlow, M. (2005). *Beyond subgroup reporting: English language learners with disabilities in 2002-2003 online state assessment reports* (ELLs with Disabilities Report 10). Minneapolis: University of Minnesota, National Center on Educational Outcomes.

Algozzine, B., Browder, D., Karvonen, M., Test, D. W., & Wood, W. M. (2001). Effects of interventions to promote self-determination for individuals with disabilities. *Review of Educational Research, 71*(2), 219-277.

Alper, S., Ryndak, D., & Schloss, C. (2001). *Alternate assessment of students with disabilities in inclusive settings*. Boston: Allyn & Bacon.

Ambrose, D. (1987). *Managing complex change*. Pittsburgh, PA: Enterprise Group.

American Association of Colleges for Teacher Education. (2002). *Research-based literacy instruction: Implications for teacher education, a white paper of the focus council on literacy*. Washington, DC: Author.

American Association of Mental Retardation (AAMR). (2002). *Mental retardation: Definition, classification, and systems of support* (10th ed.). Washington, DC: Author.

American Psychiatric Association. (2000). *Diagnostic and statistical manual of mental disorders (DSM-IV-TR)*. Arlington, VA: Author.

American Vocational Association. (1998). *The official guide to the Perkins Act of 1998*. Alexandria, VA: Author.

Americans With Disabilities Act of 1990, P.L. 101-336, 42 U.S.C.A. §12101 et seq. (1990).

Ames, N., & Dickerson, A. (2004). Five barriers to parent involvement. *Middle Matters, 13*(1), 6-10.

Ames, N., & Miller, E. (1994). *Changing middle schools: How to make schools work*. San Francisco: Jossey-Bass.

Anderman, E. M., Maehr, M. L., & Midgley, C. (1999). Declining motivation after the transition to middle school: Schools can make a difference. *Journal of Research and Development in Education, 32*(3), 131-147.

Anderson, A. R., Christenson, S. L., & Lehr, C. A. (2004). Promoting student engagement to enhance school completion: Information and strategies for educators. In A. Canter, S. Carroll, L. Paige, & I. Romero (Eds.), *Helping children at home and school II: Handouts from your school psychologist* (pp. 65–68). Washington, DC: National Association of School Psychologists.

Anderson, D., Kleinhammer-Tramill, P. J., Morningstar, M. E., Lehmann, J., Bassett, D., Kohler, P., et al. (2003). What's happening in personnel preparation in transition? A national survey. *Career Development for Exceptional Individuals, 26*(2), 145–160.

Anderson, L. (1995). *An evaluation of state local efforts to serve the educational needs of homeless children and youth.* Washington, DC: U.S. Department of Education.

Andregg, M. L., & Vergason, G. A. (1996). Preserving the least restrictive environment: Revisited. In W. Stainback & S. Stainback (Eds.), *Controversial issues in special education* (2nd ed., pp. 44–54). Boston: Allyn & Bacon.

Apple, M. W. (1996). *Cultural politics and education.* New York: Teachers College Press.

Arnsten, A. F., & Shansky, R. M. (2004, June). Adolescence: Vulnerable period for stress-induced prefrontal cortical function? *Annals of the New York Academies of Science, 1021,* 143–147.

Aron, L. (2003). *Towards a typology of alternative education programs: A compilation of elements from the literature.* Washington, DC: The Urban Institute.

Artiles, A. J. (2003). Special education's changing identity: Paradoxes and dilemmas in views of culture and space. *Harvard Educational Review, 73*(2), 164–202.

Aspel, N., Bettis, G., Test, D. W., & Wood, W. M. (1998). An evaluation of a comprehensive system of transition services. *Career Development for Exceptional Individuals, 21* (2), 203–222.

Asselin, S. B., Hanley-Maxwell, C., & Szymanski, E. M. (1992). Transdisciplinary personnel preparation. In F. R. Rusch, L. DeStefano, J. Chadsey-Rusch, L. A. Phelps, & E. Syzmanski (Eds.), *Transition from school to adult life: Models, linkages, and policy* (pp. 265–283). Sycamore, IL: Sycamore.

Asselin, S. B., Todd-Allen, M., & DeFur, S. (1998). Transition coordinators. *Teaching Exceptional Children, 30*(3), 11–15.

Association for Career and Technical Education (ACTE). (2005a). *Summary of S. 250: Carl D. Perkins Career and Technical Education Improvement Act of 2005.* Alexandria, VA: Author.

Association for Career and Technical Education (ACTE). (2005b). *Conference priorities related to the Carl D. Perkins Vocational and Technical Education Act, H.R. 366, S. 250.* Alexandria, VA: Author.

Association of University Centers on Disability. (2007). *Developmental disabilities assistance and bill of rights act (DD Act).* Washington, DC: Author.

Aune, E. (1991). A transition model for postsecondary-bound students with learning disabilities. *Learning Disabilities Research and Practice, 6*(3), 177–187.

Autism Society of America. (2007). Defining autism. Retrieved January 21, 2008, from http://www.autism society.org

Avoke, S., & Wood-Garnett, S. (2001, March/April). Language minority children and youth in special education. *Teaching Exceptional Children, 33*(4), 24–31.

Baca, L., & Cervantes, H. (1986). *The bilingual special education interface* (3rd ed.). Upper Saddle River, NJ: Prentice Hall.

Bachrach, L. L. (1986). Deinstitutionalization: What do the numbers mean? *Hospital and Community Psychiatry, 37*(2), 118–122.

Baer, G., Quinn, M. M., & Burkholder, S. (2001). *Interim alternative educational settings.* Bethesda, MD: NASP.

Baer, R., Flexer, R., Beck, S., Amstutz, N., Hoffman, L., Brothers, J., et al. (2003). A collaborative follow-up study on transition. *Career Development for Exceptional Individuals, 26*(1), 7–25.

Baer, R., & Kochhar-Bryant, C. A. (in press). How can school collaboration and system coordination promote progress of high school students? In C. A. Kochhar-Bryant (Ed.), *Collaboration and system coordination for students with special needs: Early childhood to postsecondary.* Columbus, OH: Merrill/Prentice Hall.

Baer, R., Simmons, T., & Flexer, R. (1997). Transition practice and policy compliance in Ohio: A survey of secondary special educators. *Career Development for Exceptional Individuals, 20*(2).

Bailey, L., & Stadt, R. (1973). *Career education: New approaches to human development.* Bloomington, IL: McKnight.

Bailey, L. J. (2001). *Working: Learning a living* (3rd ed.). Cincinnati, OH: South-Western/ITP.

Balfanz, R., & Herzog, L. (2006, May). *Keeping middle grades students on track to graduation: Initial analysis and implications.* PowerPoint presentation at the meeting of the Philadelphia Education Fund and Johns Hopkins University with support from the William Penn Foundation, Philadelphia.

Bandura, A. (1977). *Social learning theory.* Upper Saddle River, NJ: Merrill/Prentice Hall.

Bandura, A. (1986). *Social foundations of thought and action.* Englewood Cliffs, NJ: Prentice Hall.

Bank-Mikkelson, N. (1980). A metropolitan area in Denmark: Copenhagen. In R. Kugel & W. Wolfensberger (Eds.), *Changing patterns in residential services for the mentally retarded.* Washington, DC: President's Committee on Mental Retardation.

Banks, J. A. (2001). Multicultural education: Historical development, dimensions, and practice. In J. A. Banks & C. A. M. Banks (Eds.), *Handbook of research on multicultural education* (pp. 3–24). San Francisco: Jossey-Bass.

Barr, R. D., & Parrett, W. H. (2001). *Hope fulfilled for at-risk and violent youth: k-12 programs that work.* Needham Heights, MA: Allyn & Bacon.

Bassett, D. S., & Kochhar-Bryant, C. A. (2006, October). Strategies for aligning standards-based education and transition. *Focus on Exceptional Children, 29*(2), 1–19.

Bates, P., Suter, C., & Poelvoorde, R. (1986). *Illinois transition plan: Final report.* Chicago: Governor's Planning Council on Developmental Disabilities.

Bates, P. E., Bronkema, J., Ames, T., & Hess, C. (1992). State-level interagency planning models. In F. R. Rusch, L. DeStefano, J. Chadsey-Rusch, L. A. Phelps, & E. Syzmanski (Eds.), *Transition from school to adult life: Models, linkages, and policy* (pp. 115–129). Sycamore, IL: Sycamore.

Bazelon Center for Mental Health Law. (2003). *Failing to qualify: The first step to failure in school?* Washington, DC: Author.

Beatty, A., Neisser, U., Trent, W., & Heubert, J. (Eds.). (2001). *Understanding dropouts: Statistics, strategies, and high-stakes testing.* Washington, DC: Committee on Educational Excellence and Testing Equity, National Research Council.

Bee, H., & Mitchell, S. (1980). *The developing person: A life-span approach.* San Francisco: Harper & Row.

Bender, E. (2004). Complex factors keep many blacks from MH system. *Psychiatric News, 39*(21), 14.

Benitez, D., Lattimore, J., & Wehmeyer, M. L. (2005). Promoting the involvement of students with emotional and behavioral disorders in career and vocational planning and decision-making: The Self-Determined Career Development Model. *Behavioral Disorders, 30,* 431–447.

Benz, M., Lindstrom, L., & Yovanoff, P. (2000). Improving graduation and employment outcomes of students with disabilities: Predictive factors and student perspectives. *Exceptional Children, 6*(4), 509–529.

Berman, P., McLaughlin, M., Bass-Golod, G., Pauley, E., & Zellman, G. (1977). *Federal programs supporting educational change, Vol. VII: Factors affecting implementation and continuation.* Santa Monica, CA: RAND.

Bernhard, J. K., Freire, M., Pacini-Ketchabaw, V., & Villanueva, V. (1998). A Latin-American parent's group participates in their children's schooling: Parent involvement reconsidered. *Canadian Ethnic Studies, 30*(3), 77–99.

Berry, H., Conway, M., & Chang, K. (2004, October). Social security and undergraduates with disabilities: An analysis of the National Postsecondary Student Aid Survey. *Information Brief, 3*(4). Retrieved February 11, 2008, from http://www.ncset.org/publications/viewdesc.asp?id=1747

Berry, H., & Jones, M. (2000). *Social security disability insurance and supplemental security income for undergraduates with disabilities: An analysis of the National Postsecondary Student Aid Survey (NPSAS 2000).* Honolulu, HI: National Center for the Study of Postsecondary Education Supports.

Bijou, S., & Baer, D. (1961). *Child development I: A systematic and empirical theory.* Upper Saddle River, NJ: Prentice Hall.

Billig, S. (2001). Meeting the challenges of family involvement in the middle grades. *Middle Matters, 10,* 3–4.

Birnbaum, W. (2003). *Introduction to strategic planning.* Costa Mesa, CA: Birnbaum Associates.

Black, R. S., Mrasek, K. D., & Ballinger, R. (2003). Individualist and collectivist values in transition planning for culturally diverse students with special needs. *Journal of Vocational Special Needs Education, 25*(3), 20–29.

Blackorby, J., & Wagner, M. (1996). Longitudinal postschool outcomes of youth with disabilities: Findings from the national longitudinal transition study. *Exceptional Children, 62*(5), 399–413.

Blackorby, J., & Wagner, M. (2002). *Special education elementary longitudinal study.* Menlo Park, CA: SRI International.

Blanck, P. D. (Ed.). (2000). *Employment, disability, and the Americans with Disabilities Act: Issues in law, public policy, and research.* Evanston, IL: Northwestern University Press.

Blasi, M. (2001). *Returning to the reservation: Experiences of a first year Native American teacher.* Washington, DC: Office of Educational Research and Improvement. (ERIC Document Reproduction Service No. ED456001)

Blechman, E., Fishman, D., & Fishman, D. (2004). *Caregiver alliances for at-risk and dangerous youth.* Champaigne, IL: Research Press.

Bloom, H. (1990). *Testing re-employment services for displaced workers.* Kalamazoo, MI: Upjohn Institute for Employment Research.

Blos, P. (1962). *On adolescence.* New York: Free Press.

Blos, P. (1979). *The adolescent passage.* New York: International University Press.

Blum, R. (2005). Adolescents with disabilities in transition to adulthood. In D. W. Osgood, E. M. Foster, C. Flanagan, & G. Ruth (Eds.), *On your own without a net: The transitions to adulthood for vulnerable populations.* Chicago: University of Chicago Press.

Blum, R., White, P., & Gallay, L. (2005). Moving into adulthood for youth with disabilities and serious health concerns. In D. Wayne Osgood, E. M. Foster, C. Flanagan, & G. Ruth (Eds.), *On your own without a net: The transitions to adulthood for vulnerable populations.* Chicago: University of Chicago Press.

Bonner-Thompkins, E. (2000, October). Well being and school achievement: Using coordinated services to improve outcomes among students. *Gaining Ground Newsletter.*

Boone, R. (1992). Involving culturally diverse parents in transition planning. *Career Development in Exceptional Individuals, 15*(2), 205–221.

Bosma, H., Graafsma, L., Grotevant, H., & De Levita, D. (Eds.). (1994). *Identity and development: An interdiscipli-nary approach*. Newbury Park, CA: Sage.

Brault, M. J., Ashley, B. S., & Gallo, M. S. (2001). One program's journey: Using the change process to implement service in natural environments. *Young Exceptional Children, 5*(1), 11-19.

Bremer, C., Kachgal, M., & Schoeller, K. (2003, April). Self-determination: Supporting successful transition. *Research to Practice Brief: Improving Secondary Education and Transition Services Through Research, 2*, 91.

Brendtro, L., & Shahbazian, M. (2003). *Troubled children and youth: Turning problems into opportunities*. Champaign, IL: Research Press.

Briar-Lawson, K., & Lawson, H. (2001). *Family-supportive policy practice: International perspectives*. New York: Columbia University Press.

Brinckerhoff, L. C., McGuire, J. M., & Shaw, S. F. (2002). *Postsecondary education and transition for students with learning disabilities*. Austin, TX: Pro-Ed.

Brindis, D. C., Driscoll, A. K., Biggs, M. A., & Valderrama, L. T. (2002). *Fact sheet on Latino youth: Health care access*. San Francisco: University of California, Center for Reproductive Health Research and Policy.

Brolin, D. (1973). *Life centered career education: A competency-based approach* (4th ed.). Reston, VA: Council for Exceptional Children.

Brolin, D., & Kokaska, C. (1995). *Career education: A functional life skills approach* (5th ed.). Reston, VA: Council for Exceptional Children.

Brolin, D. E. (1995). *Career education: A functional life skills approach*. Upper Saddle River, NJ: Merrill/Prentice Hall.

Brolin, D. E., & Loyd, R. J. (2004). *Career education: A functional life skills approach*. Upper Saddle River, NJ: Merrill/Prentice Hall.

Brown, D. S. (2000). *Learning a living: A guide to planning your career and finding a job for people with learning disabilities, attention deficit disorder, and dyslexia*. Bethesda, MD: Woodbine House.

Bruyere, S. (2000). *Disability employment policies and practices in private and federal sector organizations*. Ithaca, NY: Cornell University, Program on Employment and Disability, School of Industrial and Labor Relations, Extension Division. Retrieved August 18, 2005, from http://dsl.snet/features/issues/rticles/2001/07130101.shtml

Bryson, J. M. (1999). *Strategic management in public and voluntary services: A reader*. Minneapolis, MN: Pergamon Press.

Bullis, M., & Cheney, D. (1999). Vocational and transition interventions for adolescents and young adults with emotional or behavioral disorders. *Focus on Exceptional Children, 31*(7), 1-24.

Burgstahler, S., Crawford, M. S., & Acosta, J. (2001). Transition from two-year to four-year institutions for students with disabilities. *Disability Studies Quarterly, 21*(1), 25-38.

Burghstahler, S., & Whelley, T. (2001). *Parent involvement in postsecondary education*. University of Minnesota, Institute on Community Integration, National Center on Secondary Education and Transition Web site. Retrieved January 22, 2008, from http://www.ncset.org/teleconferences/transcripts/2001_08.asp

Busby, H. R., & Danek, M. M. (1998, May/June). Transition: Principles, policy and premises. *Perspectives in Education and Deafness, 16*(5), 8-11.

Bush, G. W. (2004). *The president's new freedom initiative for people with disabilities: The 2004 Progress Report*. Washington, DC: The White House.

Buss, A., Plomin, R. (1984). *Temperament: Early personality traits*. Hillsdale, NJ: Erlbaum.

Buss, A. H. (1991). The EDS theory of temperament. In J. Stroll & A. Angleitner (Eds.), *Explorations in temperament: International perspectives on theory and measurement* (pp. 43-60). New York: Plenum Press.

Butler, R., & Hodge, S. (2004). Social inclusion of students with disabilities in middle school physical education classes. *Research in Middle Level Education Online, 27*(1). Retrieved March 21, 2008, from http://www.nmsa.org/Publications/RMLEOnline/Articles/Vol27No1Article2/tabid/530/Default.aspx

Byford, J., & Veenstra, N. (2004). The importance of cultural factors in the planning of rehabilitation services in a remote area of Papua New Guinea. *Disability and Rehabilitation, 26*(3), 166-175.

Calebrese, R. L. (1990). The public school: A source of alienation for minority parents. *The Journal of Negro Education, 59*(2), 148-154.

California Department of Education. (2001). *Transition to adult living: A guide for secondary education*. Rohnert Park, CA: Sonoma State University.

California Department of Education. (2004). *Text from January 29th CAPA training of trainers*. Retrieved May 15, 2005, from http://www.cde.ca.gov/sp/se/sr/webcsto129.asp

Cameto, R. (2005). *Employment of youth with disabilities after high school*. National Longitudinal Transition Study-2 (NLTS-2). Menlo Park, CA: SRI International.

Cameto, R., & Levine, P. (2005). *Changes in the employment status and job characteristics of out-of-school youth with disabilities*. National Longitudinal Transition Study-2 (NLTS-2). Menlo Park, CA: SRI International.

Cameto, R., Marder, C., Wagner, M., & Cardoso, D. (2003). Youth employment: NLTS2 data brief. *Report from the National Longitudinal Transition Study, 2*(2), 1-3.

Campeau, P., & Wolman, J. (1993). *Research on self-determination in individuals with disabilities*. Palo Alto, CA: American Institutes for Research.

Caplow, T. (1954). *The sociology of work*. Minneapolis: University of Minnesota Press.

Capps, R., Fix, M. E., Murray, J., Ost, J., Passel, J. S., & Herwantoro, S. (2005).

The new demography of America's schools: Immigration and the No Child Left Behind Act. Washington, DC: Urban Institute.

Carl D. Perkins Career and Technical Education Improvement Act of 2006, 20 U.S.C. §2301 *et seq.* as amended by Pub. L. No. 109-270 (2006).

Casey, B. J., Giedd, J. N., & Thomas, K. M. (2000). Structural and functional brain development and its relation to cognitive development. *Biological Psychology, 54,* 241-257.

Cashman, J. (1998). *Design and plausibility in school-to-work systems developed to serve all students, with implications for individuals with disabilities.* Unpublished doctoral dissertation.

Casper, B., & Leuchovius, D. (2005). *Universal design for learning and the transition to a more challenging academic curriculum: Making it in middle school and beyond.* Minneapolis, MN: National Center for Secondary Education and Transition.

Catalano, R. F., Berglund, M. L., Ryan, J. A., Lonczak, H. S., & Hawkins, J. D. (2002). Positive youth development in the United States: Research findings on evaluations of positive youth development programs. *Prevention & Treatment, 5*(15). Retrieved January 15, 2008, from http://journals.apa.org/prevention/volume5/pre0050015a.html

Center for Applied Special Technology. (2004). *Universal design for learning.* Wakefield, MA: Author. Retrieved June 5, 2007, from http://www.cast.org/about/index.cfm?i=231

Center for Law and Social Policy. (2007). *Recommendation for reauthorization of title I of the Workforce Investment Act Adult and Youth Programs.* Washington, DC: Author.

Center on Education Policy. (2005). *Achievement gaps on high school exit exams largely unchanged despite major push by states to boost pass rates.* Washington, DC: Author.

Centers for Disease Control and Prevention. (2007). *Improving the health of adolescents and young adults: A guide for states and communities.* San Francisco: National Center for Chronic disease Prevention and Health Promotion, Division of Adolescent and School Health; Health Resources and Services Administration, Material and Child Health Bureau, Office of Adolescent Health; National Adolescent Health Information Center, University of California.

Centre for Educational Research and Innovation. (1998). *Coordinating services for children and youth at risk: A world view.* Paris: Organization for Economic Co-operation and Development.

Certo, N. J., Mautz, D., Pumpian, I., Sax, C., Smalley, K., Wade, H., et al. (2003). A review and discussion of a model for seamless transition to adulthood. *Education and Training in Developmental Disabilities, 38*(1), 3-17.

Certo, N. J., Pumpian, I., Fisher, D., Storey, K., & Smalley, K. (1997). Focusing on the point of transition. *Education and Treatment of Children, 20,* 68-84.

Chadsey, J., & Sheldon, D. (1998). Moving toward social inclusion in employment and postsecondary school settings. In F. R. Rusch & J. Chadsey (Eds.), *Beyond high school: Transition from school to work* (pp. 406-437). Belmont, CA: Wadsworth Publishing.

Chadsey-Rusch, J., & O'Reilly, M. (1992). Social integration in employment and postsecondary educational settings: Outcomes and process variables. In F. R. Rusch, L. DeStefano, J. Chadsey-Rusch, L. A. Phelps, & E. Syzmanski (Eds.), *Transition from school to adult life: Models, linkages, and policy* (pp. 244-263). Sycamore, IL: Sycamore.

Chambers, C., Hughes, C., & Carter, E. (2004). Parent and sibling perspectives on the transition to adulthood. *Education and Training in Developmental Disabilities, 39*(2), 79-94.

Chambers, C. R., Wehmeyer, M. L., Saito, Y., Lida, K. M., Lee, Y., & Singh, V. (2007). Self-determination: What do we know? Where do we go? *Exceptionality, 15,* 3-15.

Chanchani, S., & Theivanathampillai, P. (2002). *Typologies of culture.* Dundein, New Zealand: University of Otago.

Checkoway, B. (2005, Fall). Youth participation as social justice. *Community Youth Development Journal.* Retrieved January 22, 2008, from http://www.cydjournal.org/contents.html

Chess, S., & Thomas, A. (1991). Temperament and the concept of goodness of fit. In J. Stroll & A. Angleitner (Eds.), *Explorations in temperament: International perspectives on theory and measurement* (pp. 15-28). New York: Plenum Press.

Christenson, S. L., & Thurlow, M. L. (2004). School dropouts: Prevention, considerations, interventions, and challenges. *Current Directions in Psychological Science, 13*(1), 36-39.

Christie, K. (2005). Changing the nature of parent involvement. *Phi Delta Kappan, 86*(9), 645-646.

Christman, J. (2001). *Powerful ideas, modest gains: Five years of systemic reform in Philadelphia middle schools.* Philadelphia: Consortium for Policy Research in Education, University of Pennsylvania.

Clark, G., Carlson, B., Fisher, S., Cook, I., & D'Alonzo, B. (1991). Career development for students with disabilities in elementary schools: A position statement of the Division on Career Development. *Career Development for Exceptional Individuals, 14,* 109-120.

Clark, G., & Kolstoe, O. (1995). *Career development and transition education for adolescents with disabilities* (2nd ed.). Boston: Allyn & Bacon.

Clark, G. M. (1991). *Functional curriculum and its place in the regular educational initiative.* Paper presented at the seventh International Conference on the Division of Career Development, Kansas City, MO.

Clark, G. M. (1994). Is a functional curriculum approach compatible with an inclusive education model? *Teaching Exceptional Children, 26*(2), 36-39.

Clark, G. M. (1996). Transition planning assessment for secondary-level students with learning disabilities. *Journal of Learning Disabilities, 29*(1), 79–92.

Clark, G. M. (2007). *Assessment for transitions planning.* Austin, TX: Pro-Ed.

Clark, G. M., Field, S., Patton, J. R., Brolin, D. E., & Sitlington, P. A. (1994). Life skills instruction: A necessary component for all students with disabilities: A position statement of the division on career development and transition. *Career Development for Exceptional Individuals, 17*(2), 125–133.

Clark, G. M., & Kolstoe, O. P. (1990). *Career development and transition education for adolescents with disabilities.* Boston: Allyn & Bacon.

Clark, G. M., & Kolstoe, O. P. (1995). *Career development and transition education for adolescents with disabilities* (2nd ed.). Boston: Allyn & Bacon.

Clark, G. M., & Patton, J. R. (1997). *Transition planning inventory: Administration and resource guide.* Austin, TX: Pro-Ed.

Clark, G. M., Sitlington, P., & Kolstoe, O. P. (2000). *Transition education and services for adolescents with disabilities* (3rd ed.). Boston: Allyn & Bacon.

Clark, T. (2002). *Graduation exit exams.* Washington, DC: National Governors Association.

Clay, J. (2007). *American Indians and disability: Montana's AIDTAC program.* Missoula, MN: American Indian Disability Technical Assistance Center, University of Montana Rural Institute. Retrieved January 22, 2008, from http://usinfo.state.gov/journals/itsv/1106/ijse/aidtac.htm

Cobb, R. B., & Neubert, D. A. (1992). Vocational education models. In F. R. Rusch, L. DeStefano, J. Chadsey-Rusch, L. A. Phelps, & E. Syzmanski (Eds.), *Transition from school to adult life: Models, linkages, and policy* (pp. 93–113). Sycamore, IL: Sycamore.

Cobb, R. B., & Neubert, D. A. (1998). Vocational education: Emerging vocationalism. In F. R. Rusch & J. Chadsey (Eds.), *Beyond high school: Transition from school to work*

(pp. 101–126). Belmont, CA: Wadsworth Publishing.

Cochran-Smith, M. (2000). Blind vision: Unlearning racism in teacher education. *Harvard Educational Review, 70*(2), 157–190.

Cohen, J. H. (2005). *Succeeding with autism: Hear my voice.* Philadelphia: Jessica Kingsley Publishers.

Collins, K. D., Hedrick, B. N., & Stumbo, N. J. (2007, May 23). *Transitional support services to enhance the health, independence, and employment success of persons with severe physical and/or psychiatric disabilities: The University of Illinois approach.* Paper presented at the 2007 Enriching Academic Experience of College Science Students, University of Michigan's Science Learning Center, University of Illinois, Champagne.

Commission on Certification of Work Adjustment and Vocational Evaluation Specialists. (1996). *Standards and procedures manual for certification in vocational evaluation.* Washington, DC: Author.

Comprehensive Employment and Training Act of 1973, Pub. L. No. 93-203, Title VII, 87 Stat. 879 (December 28, 1973).

Condon, E. C., Peters, J. Y., & Sueiro-Ross, C. (1979). *Special education and the Hispanic child: Cultural perspectives.* New Brunswick, NJ: Teacher's Corp Mid-Atlantic Network.

Congressional Research Service. (2004a). *Summary of the Assistive Technology Act of 2004.* Washington, DC: Domestic Social Policy Division.

Congressional Research Service. (2004b). *Report for Congress: The Workforce Investment Act of 1998 (WIA): Reauthorization of job training programs.* Washington, DC: Ann Lordeman, Domestic Social Policy Division.

Conzemius, A., & O'Neill, J. (2001). *Building shared responsibility for student learning.* Alexandria, VA: Association for Supervision and Curriculum Development.

Cooperrider, D. L., & Whitney, D. (1998). When stories have wings: How "relational responsibility" opens new options for action. In S. McNamee & K. Gergen (Eds.), *Relational responsibility.* Thousand Oaks, CA: Sage.

Council for Exceptional Children. (1993). *CEC policy on inclusive schools and community settings.* Reston, VA: Author.

Council for Exceptional Children. (1997). *Life-centered career education: A competency-based approach* (4th ed.). Reston, VA: Author.

Council for Exceptional Children. (2002). *What every special educator must know: International standards for the preparation and licensure of special educators.* Arlington, VA: Author.

Council for Exceptional Children. (2003). *CEC advanced knowledge and skills base for transition specialists.* Arlington, VA: Author.

Council for Learning Disabilities. (2001, September). College opportunities for students with disabilities. Infosheet, Over land Park, KS: Author.

Council of State Administrators of Vocational Rehabilitation. (2005). *Comments on HR 27, Job Training Improvement Act of 2005, Housing Education and the Workforce, Committee.* Washington, DC: Author.

Council of State Administrators of Vocational Rehabilitation. (2006). *Public vocational rehabilitation: An investment in America.* Bethesda, MD: Author.

Covey, S. (2004). *The seven habits of highly effective people.* New York: The Free Press.

Crane, K., Gramlich, M., & Peterson, K. (2004, September). Putting interagency agreements into action. *Issue Brief, 3*(2). Minneapolis: University of Minnesota, National Center for Secondary Education and Transition.

Cremin, L. (1957). *The republic and the school: Horace Mann and the education of free men.* New York: Teachers College Press.

Crites, J. O. (1981). *Career counseling.* New York: McGraw-Hill.

Crites, S. A., & Dunn, C. (2004). Teaching social problem solving to individuals with mental retardation. *Education and Training in Developmental Disabilities, 39*(4), 301-309.

Cuban, L., & Usdan, M. (2002). *Powerful reforms with shallow roots: Getting good schools in 6 cities.* New York: Teachers College Press.

Cummins, J. (2001). Empowering minority students: A framework for intervention. *Harvard Educational Review, 71*(4), 656-676.

Dahl, R. E. (2004). Adolescent brain development: A period of vulnerabilities and opportunities (Keynote address). *Annals of the New York Academy of Sciences, 1021,* 1-22.

Dahl, S. (2003). *Communications and culture transformation: Cultural diversity, globalization and cultural convergence.* Luton, UK: University of Luton.

Damon, W. (2004). What is positive youth development? *The Annals of the American Academy of Political and Social Science, 591*(1), 13-24.

Dare, D. (2006, Fall). The role of career and technical education in facilitating student transitions to postsecondary education. *New Directions for Community Colleges, 135,* 73-80.

Davies, D. (1994, April). Attitudes toward low-income parents. In P. M. Landurand & P. Peterson (Eds.), *Developing cross-cultural skills to work with limited English proficient special education students.* Paper presented at the Council of Exceptional Children Annual Convention, Denver, CO.

De Leon, B. (1996). Career development of Hispanic adolescent girls. In B. Leadbeater & N. Way (Eds.), *Urban girls: Resisting stereotypes, creating identities* (pp. 380-398). New York: New York University Press.

Dearing, E., McCartney, K., Weiss, H. B., Kreider, H., & Simpkins, S. (2004). The promotive effects of family educational involvement for low-income children's literacy. *Journal of School Psychology, 42,* 445-460.

Deci, E. L., & Ryan, R. M. (1985). *Intrinsic motivation and self-determination in human behavior.* New York: Plenum.

Deci, E. L., & Ryan, R. M. (2000). The "what" and "why" of goal pursuits: Human needs and the self-determination of behavior. *Psychological Inquiry, 11,* 227-268.

Deci, E. L., & Ryan, R. M. (Eds.). (2006). *The handbook of self-determination research.* Rochester, NY: University of Rochester Press.

DeFur, S., Todd-Allen, M., & Getzel, E. E. (2001). Parent participation in the transition planning process. *Career Development for Exceptional Individuals, 24,* 19-36.

Delgado-Gaitan, C. (1990). *Literacy for empowerment.* New York: Falmer.

Delpit, L. (1995). *Other people's children: Cultural conflict in the classroom.* New York: The New Press.

Dennis, R. E., & Giangreco, M. F. (1996). Creating conversation: Reflections on cultural sensitivity in family interviewing. *Exceptional Children, 63*(1), 103-116.

Deshler, D. D., Ellis, E. S., & Lenz, B. K. (1996). *Teaching adolescents with learning disabilities* (2nd ed.). Denver, CO: Love.

Deshler, D. D., & Schumaker, J. B. (2006). *Teaching adolescents with disabilities: Accessing the general education curriculum.* Thousand Oaks, CA: Corwin Press.

Deshler, D. D., Schumaker, J. B., & Bui, Y. (2005). High schools and adolescents with disabilities: Challenges at every turn. In D. D. Deshler & J. B. Schumaker (Eds.), *Teaching adolescents with disabilities: Accessing the general education curriculum* (pp. 1-34). New York: Corwin Press.

DeStefano, L., Heck, D., Hasazi, S., & Furney, K. (1999). Enhancing the implementation of the transition requirements of IDEA: A report on the policy forum on transition. *Career Development for Exceptional Children, 22*(1), 85-100.

DeStefano, L., & Wermuth, T. (1992). IDEA (P.L. 101-4-76): Defining a sec-

ond generation of transition services. In F. Rusch, L. DeStefano, J. Chadsey-Rusch, L. Phelps, & E. Szymanski (Eds.), *Transition from school to adult life: Models, linkages, and policy* (pp. 537-549). Sycamore, IL: Sycamore.

Dewey, J. (1916). *Democracy and education.* New York: Macmillan.

Diamond, S. (1957). *Personality and temperament.* New York: Harper.

DiMatties, M. E., & Sammons, J. H. (2003). *Understanding sensory integration.* Arlington, VA: ERIC Clearinghouse. (ERIC Document Reproduction Service No. ED478564)

Division on Career Development and Transition, Council for Exceptional Children. (2000a). *CEC performance-based standards for transition specialist.* Arlington, VA: Author.

Division on Career Development and Transition, Council for Exceptional Children. (2000b). *Transition-related planning, instruction, and service responsibilities for secondary special educators: Fact sheet.* Austin, TX: Pro-Ed.

Dixon, K. A., Kruse, D., & Van Horn, C. E. (2003). *Restricted access: A survey of employers about people with disabilities and lowering barriers to work.* New Brunswick, NJ: John J. Heldrich Center for Workforce Development. Retrieved August 15, 2005, from http://www.heldrich.rutgers.edu

Dorn, S. (1993). Origins of the "dropout problem." *History of Education Quarterly, 33,* 353-373.

Dounay, J. (2006, August). *Involving families in high school and college expectations.* Denver, CO: Education Commission of the States. Retrieved January 22, 2008, from http://www.ecs.org/clearinghouse/70/37/7037.pdf

Doyle, A., & Moretti, M. (2000). *Attachment to parents and adjustment in adolescence: Literature review and policy implications.* Montreal, Canada: Center for Research in Human Development.

Dudley, G., & Tiedeman, D. (1977). *Career development: Exploration and commitment*. Muncie, IN: Accelerated Development Co.

Dunn, L. (1968). Special education for the mildly retarded: Is much of it justifiable? *Exceptional Children, 34,* 5–22.

Dunst, C., & Bruder, M. (2002). Valued outcomes of service coordination, early intervention, and natural environments. *Exceptional Children, 68*(3), 361–375.

Dunst, C. J., Trivette, C. M., Starnes, A. L., Hamby, D. W., & Gordon, N. J. (1993). *Building and evaluating family support initiatives: A national study of programs for persons with developmental disabilities.* Baltimore: Paul H. Brookes.

Edgar, E. (1991). Providing ongoing support and making appropriate placements: An alternative to transition planning for mildly handicapped students. *Preventing School Failure, 35*(2), 36–39.

Edgar, E., Levine, P., & Maddox, M. (1986). *Statewide follow-up studies of secondary special education students in transition.* Working Paper of the Networking and Evaluation Team. Seattle, WA: CDMRC, University of Washington.

Education Commission of the States. (2004). *Report to the nation: State implementation of the No Child Left Behind Act.* Retrieved August 15, 2005, from http://www.ecs.org/ecsmain.asp?page=/html/special/nclb/reporttothenation/reporttothenation.htm

Education for All Handicapped Children Act of 1975, Pub. L. No. 94-142, 20 U.S.C. §1401 *et seq.* (1975).

Education for All Handicapped Children Act of 1983, Amendments, 97 Stat. 1357, 20 U.S.C. §1400 (1983).

Education Policy Reform Research Institute. (2004). *Ensuring accountability for all children in an era of standards-based reform: Alternate achievement standards.* Arlington, VA: Author.

Ehran, B. J., & Nelson, N. W. (2005, April/June). Topics in language disorders: Responsiveness to intervention and the speech-language pathologist.

Speech-Language Pathologist, 25(2), 120–131.

Ehren, B. J., & Nelson, N. W. (2005). The responsiveness to intervention approach and language impairment. *Topics in Language Disorders, 2,* 120–131.

Eisenman, L. T. (2001). Conceptualizing the contribution of career-oriented schooling to self-determination. *Career Development for Exceptional Individuals, 24,* 3–17.

Eisenman, L. T., & Chamberlin, M. (2001). Implementing self-determination activities: Lessons from schools. *Remedial and Special Education, 22,* 138–147.

Ekpone, P. M., & Bogucki, R. (2003). *Students with psychiatric disabilities in postsecondary education.* Washington, DC: The George Washington University HEATH Resource Center.

Elders, J. (2002, March). *Keynote address.* Paper presented at the 57th Annual Conference of the Association for Supervision and Curriculum Development, San Antonio, TX.

Elias, M. (2001, Winter). Middle school transition: It's harder than you think. *Middle Matters,* 1–2.

Elksnin, N., & Elksnin, L. (2001). Adolescents with disabilities: The need for occupational social skills training. *Exceptionality, 9*(1 & 2), 91–105.

Enderle, J., & Severson, S. (2005). *Enderle-Severson transition rating scale.* Moorhead, MN: ESTR Publications.

Englert, C. S., Tarrant, K. L., & Mariage, T. V. (1992). Defining and redefining instructional practice in special education: Perspectives on good teaching. *Teacher Education and Special Education, 15*(2), 62–86.

Epstein, J. L. (2001). *School, family, and community partnerships: Preparing educators and improving schools.* Boulder, CO: Westview Press.

Epstein, M. H., Rudolph, S., & Epstein, A. A. (2000). Using strength-based assessment in transition planning. *Teaching Exceptional Children, 32*(6), 50–54.

ERIC/OSEP Special Project. (2000, Spring). New ideas for planning transitions

to the adult world. *Research Connections, 6.* Retrieved March 21, 2008, from http://www.eric.ed.gov/ERICDocs/data/ericdocs2sql/content_storage_01/0000019b/80/16/22/6c.pdf

Erikson, E. (1968). *Identity, youth, and crisis.* New York: Norton.

Etcheidt, S. (2006). Issues in transition planning: Legal decisions. *Career Development for Exceptional Individuals, 29*(1), 28–47.

Eudaly, J. (2002). A rising tide: Students with psychiatric disabilities seek services in record numbers. Retrieved October 10, 2007, from http://www.heath.gwu.edu/files/active/0/psychiatric_disabilities.pdf

Everson, J. M., & Reid, D. H. (1999). *Person-centered planning and outcome management: Maximizing organizational effectiveness in supporting quality lifestyles among people with disabilities.* Morganton, NC: Habilitative Management Consultants.

Fabian, E., Lent, R., & Willis, S. (1998). Predicting work transition outcomes for students with disabilities: Implications for counselors. *Journal of Counseling & Development, 76,* 311–316.

Fair Minimum Wage Act of 2007, 29 U.S.C. 202 *et seq.* (2007).

Feagin, J. R., Early, K. E., & McKinney, K. D. (2001). The many costs of discrimination: The case of middle-class African Americans. *Indiana Law Review, 34,* 1313–1360.

Ferguson, C. (2005). *Reaching out to diverse populations: What can schools do to foster family–school connections?* Austin, TX: Southwest Educational Development Laboratory, National Center for Family and Community Connections.

Field, S. (1996). Self-determination instructional strategies for youth with learning disabilities. In J. R. Patton & G. Blalock (Eds.), *Transition and students with learning disabilities: Facilitating the movement from school to adult life* (pp. 61–84). Austin, TX: Pro-Ed.

Field, S., & Hoffman, A. (1994). Development of a model for self-determination. *Career Development for Exceptional Individuals, 17*(2), 159-169.

Field, S., & Hoffman, A. (1996a). Increasing the ability of educators to promote youth self-determination. In L. E. Powers, G. H. S. Singer, & J. Sowers (Eds.), *Promoting self-competence among children and youth with disabilities: On the road to autonomy* (pp. 171-187). Baltimore: Paul H. Brookes.

Field, S., & Hoffman, A. (1996b). *Steps to self-determination.* Austin, TX: Pro-Ed.

Field, S., Hoffman, A., & Spezia, S. (1998). *Self-determination strategies for adolescents in transition.* Austin, TX: Pro-Ed.

Field, S., Martin, J., Miller, R., Ward, M., & Wehmeyer, M. (1998a). *A practical guide for teaching self-determination.* Arlington, VA: Council for Exceptional Children.

Field, S., Martin, J., Miller, R., Ward, M., & Wehmeyer, M. (1998b). *Self-determination for persons with disabilities: A position statement of the division on career development and transition.* Arlington, VA: Council for Exceptional Children.

Fix, M., & Passel, J. (2001). *U.S. immigration at the beginning of the 21st century: Testimony before the subcommittee on immigration and claims hearing on "the U.S. population and immigration" committee on the Judiciary U.S. House of Representatives.* Retrieved March 21, 2008, from http://www.urban.org/url.cfm?ID=900417&renderforprint=1&CFID=30018429&CFTOKEN=76260636

Flexer, R. W., Simmons, T. J., Luft, P., & Baer, R. M. (2005). *Transition planning for secondary students with disabilities* (2nd ed.). Upper Saddle River, NJ: Merrill/Prentice Hall.

Flowers, C. R., Edwards, D., & Pusch, B. (1996, July–September). Rehabilitation cultural diversity initiative: A regional survey of cultural diversity within CILs. *Journal of Rehabilitation, 62,* 22-27.

Fowler, S., Donegan, M., Lueke, B., Hadden, S., & Phillips, B. (2000). Evaluating community collaboration in writing interagency agreements on the age 3 transition. *Exceptional Children, 67*(1), 35-50.

Frank Porter Graham Child Development Institute. (2002). *Youth Risk Behavior Survey: Risk behaviors among middle school students with and without disabilities.* The North Carolina Middle School YRBS. Chapel Hill: University of North Carolina.

Franklin, K. K., Cranston, V., Perry, S. N., Purtle, D. K., & Robertson, B. E. (2002). Conversations with metropolitan university first-year students. *Journal of the First-Year Experience & Students in Transition, 14*(2), 57-88.

Freud, S. (1960). *The ego and the id.* New York: W. W. Norton & Company Inc.

Friedman, P. (2000). *Career opportunities and support services for low-income, post-high school young adults.* Retrieved April 9, 2008, from Welfare Information Network Web site: http://76.12.61.196/publications/issuenoteposthighschool.htm

Friesen, B., & Poertner, J. (Eds.). (1997). *From case management to service coordination for children with emotional, behavioral, or mental disorders: Building on family strengths.* Baltimore: Paul H. Brookes.

Fuligni, A. (2001). A comparative longitudinal approach to acculturation among children from immigrant families. *Harvard Educational Review, 71*(4), 566-578.

Furney, K., & Salembrier, G. (2000). Rhetoric and reality: A review of the literature on parent and student participation in the IEP and transition planning process. In D. R. Johnson & E. J. Emmanuel (Eds.), *Issues influencing the future of transition programs and services in the United States* (pp. 111-126). Minneapolis: University of Minnesota, Institute on Community Integration.

Furstenberg, F. F., Jr., Rumbaut, R. G., & Settersten, R. A., Jr. (2005). On the frontier of adulthood: Emerging themes and new directions. In R. A. Settersten Jr., F. F. Furstenberg Jr., & R. G. Rumbaut (Eds.), *On the frontier of adulthood: Theory, research, and public policy* (pp. 3-28). Chicago: University of Chicago Press.

Future Education Funding Council. (2002). *Strategic planning: Analysis of institutions' plans 1999-2000 to 2001-2002.* Cardiff, Wales: Author.

Gabriels, R. L., & Hill, D. E. (2007). *Growing up with autism: Working with school-age children and adolescents.* New York: Guilford Press.

Gajar, A., Goodman, L., & McAfee, J. (1993). *Secondary schools and beyond: Transition of individuals with mild disabilities.* Upper Saddle River, NJ: Merrill/Prentice Hall.

Gallagher, C. A. (1999, March). *Juvenile offenders in residential placement: OJJDP fact sheet.* Washington, DC: Office of Juvenile Justice and Delinquency Prevention, U.S. Department of Justice.

Gallagher, T. M., & Hedrick, B. (2004, February 9). *Comprehensive postsecondary transitional services that enhance the health, independence and employment success of persons with severe physical disabilities.* paper presented at The Emerging Workforce Conference, Weston Florida.

Gallego, M. A., & Cole, M. (2001). Classroom culture and culture in the classroom. In V. Richardson (Ed.), *Handbook of research on teaching* (4th ed., pp. 951-997). Washington, DC: American Educational Research Association.

Gallimore, R., & Goldenberg, C. (2001). Analyzing cultural models and settings to contact minority achievement and school improvement research. *Educational Psychologist, 36*(1), 45-56.

Gallivan-Fenlon, A. (1994). Their senior year: Family and service provider perspectives on the transition from school to adult life for young adults with disabilities. *Journal for the Association for Persons with Severe Handicaps, 19*(1), 11-23.

Gambone, M. A., & Arbreton, A. J. A. (1997). *Safe havens: The contributions of youth organizations to healthy adolescent development.* Philadelphia: Public/Private Ventures.

Garcia, E. (2005). *NCLR Escalera Project: Taking steps to success.* Washington, DC: Division of Workforce and Economic Development, National Council for La Raza.

Gaylord, V., Johnson, D. R., Lehr, C. A., Bremer, C. D., & Hazasi, S. (Eds.). (2004). Feature issue on achieving secondary education and transition results for students with disabilities. *Impact, 16*(3).

Geenan, S., Powers, L. E., & Lopez-Vasquez, A. (2001). Multicultural aspects of parent involvement in transition. *Exceptional Children, 67*(2), 265-282.

George Washington University. (2007). Transition special education (M.A. in Ed. & H.D.). Retrieved March 21, 2008, from http://gsehd.gwu.edu/Transition+Special+Education+(M.A.+in+Ed.+&+H.D.)

Gerhardt, P. F., & Holmes, D. L. (2005). Employment: Options and issues for adolescents and adults with autism. In F. Volkmar, R. Paul, A. Klin, & D. Cohen (Eds.), *Handbook of autism and pervasive developmental disorders* (3rd ed., pp. 1087-1101). New York: Wiley.

German, S., Martin, J., Marshall, L., & Sale, H. (2000, Spring). Promoting self-determination: Using "take action" to teach goal attainment. *Career Development for Exceptional Individuals, 23*(1), 27-38.

Gerry, M. H., & McWhorter, C. M. (1990). A comprehensive analysis of federal statutes and programs for persons with severe disabilities. In L. H. Meyer, C. A. Peck, & L. Brown (Eds.), *Critical issues in the lives of people with severe disabilities* (pp. 495-527). Baltimore: Paul H. Brookes.

Getzel, E., & Wehman, P. (2005). *Going to college: Expanding opportunities for people with disabilities.* Baltimore: Paul H. Brookes.

Getzel, L., Stodden, R. A., & Briel, L. (2001). Pursuing postsecondary education opportunities for individuals with disabilities. In P. Wehman (Ed.), *Life beyond the classroom: Transition strategies for young people with disabilities* (3rd ed.). Baltimore: Paul H. Brookes.

Gil-Kashiwabara, E., Hogansen, J. M., Geenen, S., Powers, K., & Powers, L. E. (2007). Improving transition for marginalized youth. *Career Development for Exceptional Individuals, 30*(2), 80-91.

Gilmore, D. S., Bose, J., & Hart, D. (2002). Postsecondary education as a critical step toward meaningful employment: Vocational rehabilitation's role. *Job Training & Placement Report, 26*(3), 1-3.

Ginzberg, E., Ginsburg, S., Axelrod, S., & Herman, H. (1951). *Occupational choice: An approach to a general theory.* New York: Columbia University.

Gladieux, L. E., & Swail, W. S. (2002, May). *Beyond access: Increasing the odds of college success.* Indianapolis, IN: Phi Delta Kappan.

Glatthorn, A., & Craft-Tripp, M. (2000). *Standards-based learning for students with disabilities.* Larchmont, NY: Eye on Education.

Goals 2000: Educate America Act of 1993, Pub. L. No. 103-227 (1993).

Gonzalez-DeHass, A. R., Willems, P. P., & Doan Holbein, M. F. (2005). Examining the relationship between parental involvement and student motivation. *Educational Psychology Review, 17*(2), 96-123.

Gordon, H. (1999). *History and growth of vocational education in America.* Boston: Allyn & Bacon.

Gottfredson, L. S. (1996). Gottfredson's theory of circumscription and compromise. In D. Brown, L. Brooks, & Associates (Eds.), *Career choice and development* (3rd ed., pp. 179-232). San Francisco: Jossey-Bass.

Grack, A. (2005). *What states either have, or plan to adopt, legislative or regulatory language requiring secondary transition.* Minneapolis, MN: North Central Regional Resource Center.

Greene, G. (unpublished). *Promoting organizational change.* Unpublished manuscript, California State University, Long Beach.

Greene, G., & Albright, L. (1994). Transition services personnel preparation: A collaborative program. *Career Development for Exceptional Individuals, 17*(1), 91-103.

Greene, G., & Albright, L. (1995). "Best practices" in transition services: Do they exist? *Career Development for Exceptional Individuals, 18*(2), 1-2.

Greene, G., & Kochhar, C. (2003). *Pathways to successful transition for youth with disabilities.* Upper Saddle River, NJ: Merrill/Prentice Hall.

Greene, G., & Nefsky, P. (1999). Transition for culturally and linguistically diverse youth with disabilities: Closing the gaps. *Multiple Voices for Ethnically Diverse Exceptional Learners, 3*(1), 15-24.

Griffin, C., & Targett, P. S. (2001). Finding jobs for young people with disabilities. In P. Wehman (Ed.), *Life beyond the classroom: Transition strategies for young people with people disabilities* (3rd ed.). Baltimore: Paul H. Brookes.

Grigal, M. E., Neubert, D. A., & Moon, M. S. (2005). *Transition services for students with significant disabilities in college and community setting* (Transition Series). Austin, TX: Pro-Ed.

Grossi, T. (2000). *Transition to adult life, a shared responsibility: Vocational rehabilitation services, policy to practice guidebook.* Bloomington: Indiana Institute on Disability and Community.

Grossman, H. (1995). *Special education in a diverse society.* Boston: Allyn & Bacon.

Gutman, L. M. (2005). How student and parent goal orientations and classroom goal structures influence the math achievement of African Americans during the high school transition. *Contemporary Educational Psychology, 31,* 44–63.

Guy, B., & Schriner, K. (1997). Systems in transition: Are we there yet? *Career Development for Exceptional Individuals, 20,* 141–163.

Hageback, B. (1992). *Getting local agencies to cooperate.* Baltimore: University Park Press.

Hale, L. F. (1998). *Dropout prevention: Information and strategies for parents.* Bethesda, MD: School Psychologists.

Hall, G., Yohalem, N., Tolman, J., & Wilson, A. (2002). *Promoting positive youth development as a support to academic achievement.* National Institute on Out-of-School Time. Boston: Boston's After School For All Partnership.

Hallahan, D. P., & Kauffman, J. M. (2003). *Exceptional learners, introduction to special education* (9th ed.). Needham Heights, MA: Allyn & Bacon.

Halloran, W., & Simon, M. (1995). The transition service requirement. A federal perspective on issues, implications and challenges. *Journal of Vocational Special Needs Education, 17*(3), 94–98.

Halloran, W. D. (1993). Transition services requirement: Issues, implications, challenge. In R. C. Eaves & P. J. McLaughlin (Eds.), *Recent advances in special education and rehabilitation* (pp. 210–224). Boston: Andover Medical.

Halpern, A. (1985). Transition: A look at the foundations. *Exceptional Children, 51,* 479–486.

Halpern, A. (1987). Characteristics of quality programs. In C. S. Warger & B. B. Weiner (Eds.), *Secondary special education: A guide to promising public school programs* (pp. 25–55). Arlington, VA: Council for Exceptional Children.

Halpern, A. (1990). A methodological review of follow-up and follow-along studies tracking school leavers from special education. *Career Development for Exceptional Individuals, 13*(1), 13–27.

Halpern, A. (1994). The transition of youth with disabilities to adult life: A position statement of the Division on Career Development and Transition, the Council for Exceptional Children. *Career Development for Exceptional Individuals, 17,* 115–124.

Halpern, A. (1999). *Transition: Is it time for another rebottling?* Paper presented at the 1999 Annual OSEP Project Directors' Meeting, Washington, DC.

Halpern, A. S. (1993). Quality of life as a conceptual framework for evaluating transition outcomes. *Exceptional Children, 59*(6), 486–498.

Halpern, A. S. (1996). *An instructional approach to facilitate the transition of high school students with disabilities into adult life.* Washington, DC: U.S. Office of Special Education.

Halpern, A. S., Herr, C. M., Wolf, N. K., Doren, B., Johnson, M. D., & Lawson, J. D. (1997). *Next S.T.E.P.: Student transition and educational planning.* Austin, TX: Pro-Ed.

Hamaguchi, P. M. (2001). *Childhood speech, language, & listening problems: What every parent should know* (2nd ed.). New York: Wiley.

Harley, D. A., Donnell, C., & Rainey, J. A. (2003). Interagency collaboration: Reinforcing professional bridges to serve aging populations with multiple service needs. *Journal of Rehabilitation, 69*(2), 32–37. Retrieved January 24, 2008, from http://findarticles.com/p/search?qt=Reinforcing+professional%20bridges%20to%20serve%20aging%20populations%20with%20multiple%20service%20needs&qf=all&qta=1&tb=art&x=0&y=0

Harmony, M. (1964). A vocational biography. *Vocational Guidance Quarterly, 13,* 37–40.

Harris, P. (2003, April 29). Barriers to the diagnosis and treatment of attention deficit disorder among African American and Hispanic children. *Health Care News, 3*(7). Retrieved January 22, 2008, from http://www.harrisinteractive.com/news/newsletters/healthnews/HI_HealthCareNews2003Vol3_Iss07.pdf

Harry, B. (1992). *Cultural diversity, families, and the special education system: Communication and empowerment.* New York: Teachers College Press.

Harry, B. (2002). Trends and issues in serving culturally diverse families of children with disabilities. *The Journal of Special Education, 36*(3), 131–138.

Harry, B., Allen, N., & McLaughlin, M. (1995). Communication versus compliance: African-American parents' involvement in special education. *Exceptional Children, 61,* 364–377.

Harry, B., Grenot-Scheyer, M., Smith-Lewis, M., Park, H. S., Xin, F., & Schwartz, I. (1995). Developing culturally inclusive services for individuals with severe disabilities. *Journal for the Association of Severe Handicaps, 20,* 99–109.

Harry, B., Kalyanpur, M., & Day, M. (1999). *Building cultural reciprocity with families.* Baltimore: Paul H. Brookes.

Hart, D., Zafft, C., & Zimbrich, K. (2001). Creating access to postsecondary education for all students. *The Journal for Vocational Special Needs Education, 23*(2), 19–30.

Hart, D., Zimbrich, K., & Whelley, T. (2002). Challenges in coordinating and managing services and supports in secondary and postsecondary options. *Issue Brief, 1*(6). Minneapolis, MN: University of Minnesota, National Center on Secondary Education and Transition.

Harvard Civil Rights Project. (2004). *No child left behind: A federal, state, and district-level look at the first year.* Retrieved August 10, 2005, from http://www.gse.harvard.edu/news/features/orfield02092004.html

Hasazi, S., Furney, K., & DeStefano, L. (1999). Implementing the IDEA transition mandates. *Exceptional Children, 65*(4), 555–566.

Hasazi, S., Gordon, L., & Roe, C. (1985). Factors associated with employment status of handicapped youth exiting high school from 1979–1983. *Exceptional Children, 51,* 455–469.

Hasnain, R. (2001). *Entering adulthood with a disability: Individual, family, and cultural challenges.* Unpublished doctoral dissertation, Boston University, Boston.

Hausslein, E. B., Kaufmann, R. K., & Hurth, J. (1992). From case management to service coordination: Families, policy making, and part H. *Zero to Three, XII*(3), 10–12.

Havinghurst, R. (1972). *Developmental tasks and education.* New York: McKay.

HEATH Resource Center. (2005). *Frequently asked questions.* Washington, DC: George Washington University. Retrieved July 21, 2006, from http://www.heath.gwu.edu/usefulanswers.htm

HEATH Resource Center. (2006). *The counselor's toolkit.* Washington, DC: George Washington University.

Henderson, A. T., Mapp, K., Jordan, C., Orozco, E., Averett, A., Donnelly, D., et al. (2003). *A new wave of evidence: The impact of school, family, and community connections on student achievement.* Austin, TX: Southwest Educational Development Laboratory.

Hendrick Hudson Central School District Board of Education v. Rowley, 458 U.S. 176, 200 (1982).

Herring, R. (1998). *Career counseling in schools: Multicultural and developmental perspectives.* Alexandria, VA: American Counseling Association.

Heubert, J., & Hauser, R. (1999). *High stakes: Testing for tracking, promotion and graduation.* Washington, DC: National Research Council, National Academy Press.

Hibbard, M., Gordon, W., Martin, T., Raskin, B., & Brown, M. (2001). *Students with traumatic brain injury: Identification, assessment and classroom accommodations.* New York: Research and Training Center on Community Integration of Individuals with Traumatic Brain Injury, Mt. Sinai School of Medicine.

Higher Education Act of 1965, Pub. L. No. 89-329, 79 Stat. 1219 (1965).

Hill, J. M. (1969). *The transition from school to work.* London: Tavistock Institute of Human Relations.

Hitchings, W., Lusso, D., Ristow, R., Horvath, M., Retish, P., & Tanners, A. (2001). The career development needs of college students with learning disabilities: In their own words. *Learning Disabilities Research and Practice, 16*(1), 8–17.

Hodgkinson, B. (2003). *Leaving too many children behind: A demographer's view on the tragic neglect of American's youngest children.* Washington, DC: Institute for Educational Leadership.

Holland, J. (1959). A theory of vocational choice. *Journal of Counseling Psychology, 6,* 35–45.

Hollingshead, A. (1949). *Elmtown's youth.* New York: Wiley.

Hong, S., & Ho, H. (2005). Direct and indirect longitudinal effects of parental involvement on student achievement: Second-order latent growth modeling across ethnic groups. *Journal of Educational Psychology, 97*(1), 32–42.

Hood, D., Todis, B., & Glang, A. (2005). *Life after high school.* McLean, VA: Brain Injury Association of America.

Horn, R. (2001, September). *The Workforce Investment Act (WIA): Creating opportunities for youth with disabilities.* Minneapolis, MN: Teleconference, National Center for Secondary Education and Transition.

Horne, R., & Morris, S. (1998, March). Transition of youth with disabilities. *Liaison Bulletin, 28*(4).

Horney, K (1945). *Our inner conflicts: A constructive theory of neurosis.* New York: W. W. Norton.

Horney, K. (1950). *Neurosis and human growth.* New York: W. W. Norton.

Hough, D. L. (2003). *Research, rhetoric, and reality: A study of studies addressing NMSA's 21st century research agenda.* Columbus, OH: National Middle School Association.

Howlin, P. (2000). Outcome in adult life for more able individuals with autism or Asperger syndrome. *Autism, 4*(1), 63–83.

Howlin, P., Goode, S., Hutton, J., & Rutter, M. (2004). Adult outcomes for children with autism. *Journal of Child Psychology and Psychiatry, 45,* 212–229.

Hoyt, K. (1975). *Career education: What it is and how to do it.* Indianapolis, IN: JIST Publishing.

Hoyt, K. B. (1993). Reaction to three solutions for transition from school to employment. *Youth Policy, 15*(6 & 7), 36.

HSC Foundation. (2006, November 28). Health issues impacting youth transitions roundtable. *Health Transitions Briefing.*

Hubbard, S., Bell, A., & Charner, I. (1998). *We need to be in it for all 9 innings: Lessons from employer participation in school-to-careers in Colorado.* Washington, DC: Academy for Educational Development, National Institute for Work and Learning.

Huffman, L. R., & Speer, P. W. (2000). Academic performance among at-risk children: The role of developmentally appropriate practices. *Early Childhood Research Quarterly, 15,* 167–184.

Hughes, M. T. (1995). Increasing involvement of Hispanic parents. *LD Forum, 21*(1), 16–19.

Hull, C. (1928). *Aptitude testing.* Yonkers-on-Hudson, NY: World.

Hyun, J. K., & Fowler, S. A. (1995). Respect, cultural sensitivity, and communication. *Teaching Exceptional Children, 28,* 25–28.

Ianacone, R. N., & Leconte, P. J. (1986). Curriculum-based vocational assessment: A viable response to a school-based service delivery issue. *Career Development for Exceptional Individuals, 9,* 113–120.

Illinois State Board of Education. (2003). *The status of transition services for secondary students with disabilities in Illinois: Interagency Coordinating Council's 2002 annual report on the status of transition services for secondary students with disabilities in Illinois.*

Individuals With Disabilities Education Act Amendments of 1997, Pub. L. No. 105-17, 20 U.S.C. §1400 *et seq.* (1997).

Individuals With Disabilities Education Act of 1990, Pub. L. No. 101-476 (October 30, 1990).

Individuals With Disabilities Education Act of 2004, Pub. L. No. 108-446, 20 U.S.C. §1400 *et seq.* (2004).

Individuals With Disabilities Education Act of 2004, Pub. L. No. 108-446, §602, Definition 3 (2004).

Ingels, S. J., Pratt, D. J., Wilson, D., Burns, L. J., Currivan, D., Rogers, J. E., et al. (2007). *Education longitudinal study of 2002/06.* Washington, DC: Institute for Educational Sciences, U.S. Department of Education.

Inger, M. (1992). Increasing the school involvement of Hispanic parents. *ERIC Clearinghouse on Urban Education Digest, 80,* 24-25.

Institute on Rehabilitation Issues. (2002). *Investing in the transition of youth with disabilities to productive careers.* Paper presented at the Twenty-Eighth University of Arkansas Region VI Rehabilitation Continuing Education Program.

Izzo, M., Cartledge, G., Miller, L., Growick, B., & Rutkowski, S. (2000). Increasing employment earnings: Extended transition services that make a difference. *Career Development for Exceptional Individuals, 23*(2), 139-156.

Izzo, M., Hertzfeld, J., Simmons-Reed, E., & Aaron, J. (2001, Winter). Promising practices: Improving the quality of higher education for students with disabilities. *Disability Studies Quarterly, 21*(1). Retrieved January 25, 2008, from http://www.dsq-sds.org/_articles_pdf/2001/Winter/dsq_2001_Winter_03.pdf

J. L. v. Mercer Island School District, No. C06-494P. United States District Court, Western District of Washington at Seattle (December 8, 2006).

Jackson, T. (2003). *Secondary transition coordinators at the state level* (Project Forum Brief). Alexandria, VA: National Association of State Directors of Special Education.

Jacobs, J. E., & Bleeker, M. M. (2004). Girls' and boys' developing interests in math and science: Do parents matter? *New Directions for Child and Adolescent Development, 106,* 5-21.

Jelicic, H., Bobek, D. L., Phelps, E., Lerner, R. M., & Lerner, J. V. (2007). Using positive youth development to predict contribution and risk behaviors in early adolescence: Findings from the first two waves of the 4-H Study of Positive Youth Development. *International Journal of Behavioral Development, 31*(3), 263-273.

Jenkins, D., & Boswell, K. (2002). *State policies on community college remedial education: Findings from a national survey.* Washington, DC: Education Commission of the States Policy Paper.

Jennings, J. (1995). *A brief history of the federal role in education: Why it began and why it is still needed.* Washington, DC: Center on Education Policy.

Jennings, J. (2000). *The future of the federal role in elementary and secondary education.* Washington, DC: Center on Education Policy.

Jerald, C. D. (2006, June). *Identifying potential dropouts: Key lessons for building an early warning system.* Washington, DC: American Diploma Project Network, Achieve, Inc.

Jeynes, W. H. (2005). Effects of parent involvement and family structure on the academic achievement of adolescents. *Marriage & Family Review, 37*(3), 99-116.

Job Training Partnership Act of 1982, Pub. L. No. 97-300, Title I, 96 Stat. 1357 (October 13, 1982).

Johnson, D., & Guy, B. (1997). Implications of the lessons learned from a state systems change initiative on transition for youth with disabilities. *Career Development for Exceptional Individuals, 20*(2).

Johnson, D., & Halloran, W. (1997). The federal legislative context and goals of the state systems change initiative on transition for youth with disabilities. *Career Development for Exceptional Individuals, 20*(2).

Johnson, D. R., & Sharpe, M. (2000). *Analysis of local education agency efforts to implement the transition services requirements of IDEA of 1990.* Minneapolis: University of

Minnesota, Institute on Community Integration.

Johnson, D. R., Sharpe, M. N., & Stodden, R. A. (2000). The transition to postsecondary education for students with disabilities. *Impact, 13*(1), 2-3, 26-27.

Johnson, D. R., Thurlow, M., Cosio, A., & Bremer, C. D. (2005). High school graduation requirements and students with disabilities. *Information Brief: Addressing Trends and Developments in Secondary Education and Transition, 4*(2).

Johnson, D. R., & Thurlow, M. L. (2003). *A national study on graduation requirements and diploma options* (Technical Report 36). Minneapolis: University of Minnesota, Institute on Community Integration, National Center on Secondary Education and Transition and National Center on Educational Outcomes.

Johnson, J. R., & Rusch, F. R. (1993). Secondary special education and transition services: Identification and recommendations for future research and demonstration. *Career Development for Exceptional Individuals, 17*(2), 1-18.

Joint Commission on Accreditation of Healthcare Organizations. (1979). *Principles of accreditation of community mental health service programs.* Oakbrook Terrace, IL: Joint Commission on Accreditation of Hospitals.

Jorgensen, C. (1998). *Restructuring high schools for all students: Taking inclusion to the next level.* Durham: University of New Hampshire.

Judd, B. (2006). *Incorporating youth development principles into adolescent health programs: A guide for state-level practitioners and policy makers.* Washington, DC: The Forum for Youth Investment, Impact.

Justesen, T. R., & Justesen, T. R. (2000). *Helping more students with disabilities prepare for college: A review of research literature and suggested steps GEAR UP grantees can take.* Washington, DC: U.S. Department of Education, Office of Postsecondary Education, Gaining Early Awareness and Readiness for Undergraduate Programs (GEAR UP).

Kalyanpur, M., & Harry, B. (1999). *Culture in special education: Building reciprocal family-professional relationships.* Baltimore: Paul H. Brookes.

Kauffman, J. M., & Brigham, F. J. (2000). Zero tolerance and bad judgment in working with students with emotional or behavioral disorders. *Behavioral Disorders, 25,* 277–279.

Kaye, H. S. (2000). *Computer and internet use among people with disabilities* (Disability Statistics Report 13). Washington, DC: U.S. Department of Education.

Keeling, S. (2003). Advising the millennial generation. *NACADA Journal, 23*(1 & 2), 30–36.

Kendziora, K., Bruns, E., Osher, D., Pacchiona, D., & Mejia, B. X. (2001). *Wraparound: Stories from the field. 2001 Series: Vol. 1.* Washington, DC: American Institutes for Research, Center for Effective Collaboration and Practice.

Kidscount. (2003). *Percent of families with children headed by a single parent.* Retrieved October 15, 2003, from http://www.aecf.org/kidscount/kc2002/summary.htm

Kim, K. H., & Morningstar, M. E. (2005). Transition planning involving culturally and linguistically diverse families. *Career Development for Exceptional Individuals, 28*(2), 92–103.

Kim-Rupnow, W. S., Dowrick, P. W., & Burke, L. S. (2001). Improving access and outcomes for individuals with disabilities in postsecondary distance education. *American Journal of Distance Education, 15*(1), 25–40.

King-Sears, M. E. (2001). Three steps for gaining access to the general education curriculum for learners with disabilities. *Intervention in School and Clinic, 37*(2), 67–76.

Kirchler, E., Palmonari, A., & Pombeni, M. L. (1993). Developmental tasks and adolescents' relationships with their peers and their family. In S. Jackson & H. Rodriques-Tome (Eds.), *Adolescence and its social worlds.* Hillsdale, NJ: Erlbaum.

Kirst, M., & Jehl, J. (1995). *Getting ready to provide school-linked, integrated services.* Oak Brook, IL: North Central Regional Educational Laboratory.

Kitson, H. (1925). *The psychology of vocational adjustment.* Philadelphia: Lippincott.

Knight, S. L., & Boudah, D. (2003). Using participatory research and development to impact student outcomes. In D. Wiseman & S. Knight (Eds.), *The impact of school–university collaboration on K–12 student outcomes.* Washington, DC: American Association of Colleges of Teacher Education.

Knott, L., & Asselin, S. B. (1999). Transition competencies: Perception of secondary special education teachers. *Teacher Education and Special Education, 22,* 55–65.

Kochhar, C. A. (1995). *Training for interagency, interdisciplinary service coordination: An instructional modules series.* Des Moines: Iowa State Department of Education and Drake University.

Kochhar, C. A. (1999). *Synthesis of state needs and barriers to systemic reform in the 1998 special education state improvement grants.* Washington, DC: Academy for Educational Development.

Kochhar, C. A., & Erickson, M. (1993). *Partnerships for the 21st century: Developing business-education partnerships for school improvement.* Rockville, MD: Aspen.

Kochhar, C. A., & Gopal, M. (1997). The concept of full participation in promoting sustainable educational development. In J. Lynch, C. Modgil, & S. Modgil, (Eds.), *Education and development: Concepts, approaches and assumptions.* London: Cassell Publishers.

Kochhar, C. A., West, L., & Taymans, J. (2000). *Successful inclusion: Practical strategies for a shared responsibility.* Upper Saddle River, NJ: Merrill/Prentice Hall.

Kochhar-Bryant, C. (2002a). Building transition capacity through personnel development: Analysis of 35 state improvement grants. *Career*

Development for Exceptional Individuals, 26(2), 161–184.

Kochhar-Bryant, C. (2002b). Coordinating systems and agencies for successful transition. In G. Greene & C. Kochhar-Bryant (Eds.), *Pathways to successful transition for youth with disabilities.* Columbus, OH: Prentice Hall/Merrill.

Kochhar-Bryant, C. (2006, July/August). New requirements for youth transition: What administrators should know. *CASE Newsletter.*

Kochhar-Bryant, C. (2007). *What every teacher should know about transition and IDEA 2004.* Boston: Allyn & Bacon.

Kochhar-Bryant, C. (2008). *Collaboration and system coordination for students with special needs: From early childhood to the postsecondary years.* Merrill/Prentice Hall.

Kochhar-Bryant, C., & Bassett, D. (2002). *Aligning transition and standards-based education.* Arlington, VA: Council for Exceptional Children.

Kochhar-Bryant, C., & Vreeburg-Izzo, M. (2006a, Fall). Transition assessment and the new summary of performance [Special issue]. *Career Development for Exceptional Individuals, 29*(2).

Kochhar-Bryant, C., & Vreeburg-Izzo, M. (2006b, Fall). Access to post-high school services: Transition assessment and the summary of performance. *Career Development for Exceptional Individuals, 29*(2), 70–89.

Kochhar-Bryant, C., & Vreeburg-Izzo, M. (2006c). The summary of performance as transition "passport" to employment and independent living. *Assessment for Effective Intervention, 32*(3).

Kochhar-Bryant, C. A. (2003). Leadership to promote transition services. In *Pathways to successful transition for youth with disabilities.* Upper Saddle River, NJ: Merrill/Prentice Hall.

Kochhar-Bryant, C. A., & Bassett, D. (2002). Challenge and promise in aligning transition and standards-based education. In C. A. Kochhar-Bryant & D. Bassett (Eds.), *Aligning transition and standards-based education: Issues and strategies.* Arlington, VA: Council for Exceptional Children.

Kochhar-Bryant, C. A., & White, D. L. (2007). *Evolving role of the educational administrator: Building capacity and connectivity for alternative education.* National Council for Professors of Educational Leadership.

Kohler, P. (1995). *A taxonomy for transition programming: Linking research and practice.* Urbana-Champaign, IL: Transition Research Institute.

Kohler, P. (1996). *A taxonomy for transition programming: Linking research and practice.* Urbana-Champaign, IL: Transition Research Institute.

Kohler, P. (1998). Implementing a transition perspective of education. In F. Rusch & J. Chadsey (Eds.), *Beyond high school: Transition from school to work* (pp. 179-205). Belmont, CA: Wadsworth Publishing.

Kohler, P. D. (1993). Best practices in transition: Substantiated or implied? *Career Development for Exceptional Individuals, 22*(1), 55-65.

Kohler, P. D. (2003). *Taxonomy for transition programming: Worksheet for interagency collaboration practices.* Kalamazoo: Department of Educational Studies, Western Michigan University.

Kohler, P. D., DeStefano, L., Wermuth, T. R., Grayson, T. E., & McGinity, S. (1994). An analysis of exemplary transition programs: How and why are they selected? *Career Development for Exceptional Individuals, 17*(2), 187-202.

Kohler, P. D., & Hood, L. K. (2000). *Improving student outcomes: Promising practices and programs for 1999-2000.* Urbana-Champaign, IL: Transition Research Institute.

Kokaska, C. J., & Brolin, D. E. (1985). *Career education for handicapped individuals* (2nd ed.). Columbus, OH: Merrill.

Kortering, L., Sitlington, P., & Braziel, P. (2004). The use of vocational assessment and planning as a strategic

intervention to help keep youths with emotional or behavioral disorders in school. In D. Cheney (Ed.), *Transition of students with emotional or behavior disorders: Current approaches for positive outcomes.* Arlington, VA: Council for Children with Behavior Disorders and Division on Career Development and Transition.

Kovaleski, J., & Prasse, D. (2004). Response to instruction in the identification of learning disabilities: A guide for school teams. In A. Canter, et al. (Eds.), *Helping children at home and school II: Handouts for families and educators.* Bethesda, MD: National Association of School Psychologists.

Kreider, H., Caspe, M., Kennedy, S., & Weiss, H. (2007, Spring). *Family involvement in middle and high school students' education* (Harvard Family Research Project, No. 3). Cambridge, MA.

Kroger, J. (1992). *Identity development: Adolescence through adulthood.* Thousand Oaks, CA: Sage.

Kroth, R. L., & Edge, D. (1997). *Strategies for communicating with parents and families of exceptional children.* Denver, CO: Love.

Krup, J. (1987). Counseling with an increased awareness of the transition process. *Counseling and Human Development, 19*(7), 2-15.

Kumashiro, K. (2001). Posts' perspectives on anti-oppressive education in social studies, English, mathematics, and science classrooms. *Educational Researcher, 30*(3), 3-12.

Kupper, L. (1997). *The Individuals with Disabilities Education Act Amendments of 1997.* Washington, DC: National Information Center for Children and Youth with Disabilities.

Kyeong-Hwa, K., & Morningstar, M. E. (2007). Enhancing secondary special education teachers' knowledge and competencies in working with culturally and linguistically diverse families through online training. *Career Development for Exceptional Individuals, 30*(2), 116-128.

Land, D., & Legters, N. (2002). The extent and consequences of risk in U.S. education. In S. Stringfield & D. Land (Eds.), *Educating at-risk students* (pp. 1-28). Chicago: National Society for the Study of Education.

Lareau, A. (1989). *Home advantage: Social class and parental intervention in elementary education.* New York: Falmer.

Leake, D., & Cholymay, M. (2004, February). Addressing the needs of culturally and linguistically diverse students with disabilities in postsecondary education. *Information Brief, 3*(1). Minneapolis: National Center on Secondary Education and Transition, University of Minnesota.

Leake, D., Kim-Rupnow, S., & Leung, P. (2003). *Issues of transition for youth with disabilities from culturally and linguistically diverse backgrounds.* Retrieved June 3, 2007, from http://ncset.org/teleconferences/transcripts/2003_08.asp

Leconte, P. J. (1994). Vocational appraisal services: Evolution from multidisciplinary origins and applications to interdisciplinary practices. *Vocational Evaluation and Work Adjustment Bulletin, 27*(4), 119-127.

Leconte, P. J., & Neubert, N. A. (1997). Vocational assessment: The kick-off point for transition. *Alliance, the Newsletter of the National Transition Alliance, 2*(2), 1, 3-4, 8.

Lee, M. Y. (2003). A solution-focused approach to cross-cultural clinical social work practice: Utilizing cultural strengths. *Families in Society, 84*(3), 385-398.

Lee, S. H., Palmer, S. B., Turnbull, A. P., & Wehmeyer, M. L. (2006). A model for parent-teacher collaboration to promote self-determination in young children with disabilities. *Teaching Exceptional Children, 38*(3), 36-41.

Lehman, J. P., Davies, T. G., & Laurin, L. M. (2000). Listening to student voices about postsecondary education. *Teaching Exceptional Children, 32*(3), 60-65.

Lehr, C. A. (2004). Alternative schools and students with disabilities: Identifying and understanding the issues.

Information Brief, 3(6). Minneapolis: National Center on Secondary Education and Transition, University of Minnesota.

Lehr, C. A., Moreau, R. A., Lange, C. M., & Lanners, E. J. (2004). *Alternative schools: Findings from a national survey of the states.* Minneapolis: Institute on Community Integration, University of Minnesota.

Leonard, P. Y., Mathews, B., & Bowes, J. (1987). Mid-life women: Research and implications (Conference Paper ED 295 074).

Leone, P., & Drakeford, W. (1999). Alternative education: From a "last chance" to a proactive model. *The Clearing House, 73*(2), 86–88.

Leone, P., & Meisel, S. (1997). Improving education services for students in detention and confinement facilities. *Children's Legal Rights Journal, 17*(1), 1–12.

Leone, P., Quinn, M., & Osher, D. (2002). *Collaboration in the juvenile justice system and youth serving agencies: Improving prevention, providing more efficient services, and reducing recidivism for youth with disabilities.* Washington, DC: American Institutes for Research. Retrieved December 10, 2005, from http://cecp.air.org/juvenilejustice/docs/Collaboration

Leung, E. K. (1988, October). *Cultural and acculturational commonalities and diversities among Asian Americans: Identification and programming considerations.* Paper presented at the Ethnic and Multicultural Symposia, Dallas, TX.

Levine, P., Marder, C., & Wagner, M. (2004). *Services and supports for secondary school students with disabilities.* Menlo Park, CA: SRI International.

Levinson, E. M. (2002). Best practices in school-based vocational assessment. In A. Thomas & J. Grimes (Eds.), *Best practices in school psychology IV* (pp. 1569–1584). Bethesda, MD: National Association of School Psychologists.

Levinson, E. M., & Palmer, E. J. (2005). *Preparing students with disabilities for school-to-work transition and post-school life.* Bethesda, MD: National Association of School Psychologists.

Lewis, R. A. (1999). Multifocal motor neuropathy and Lewis-Sumner syndrome: Two distinct entities. *Muscle Nerve, 22,* 1738–1739.

Lichtenstein, S. (1993). Transition from school to adulthood: Case studies of adults with learning disabilities who dropped out of school. *Exceptional Children, 59*(4), 336–347.

Lichtenstein, S., & Michaelides, N. (1993). Transition from school to adulthood: Four case studies of young adults labeled mentally retarded. *Career Development for Exceptional Individuals, 16*(2), 183–195.

Lightfoot, S. L. (2001). *Partnerships with families: The presence of parents can transform the culture of a school.* Portland, OR: Northwest Regional Educational Laboratory. Retrieved January 22, 2008, from http://www.nwrel.org/cfc/frc/beyus12.html

Lighthouse Youth Services, Inc. (2001). *Healthy and ready to work: Career connections for students.* Cincinnati, OH: Author.

Liontos, L. B. (1991). *Involving at-risk families in their children's education.* ERIC Clearinghouse on Educational Management.

Locust, C. (1988). Wounding the spirit: Discrimination and traditional American Indian belief systems. *Harvard Educational Review, 58*(3), 315–330.

Locust, C. (1994). *The Piki maker: Disabled American Indians, cultural beliefs, and traditional behaviors.* Tucson, AZ: Native American Research and Training Center.

Lofquist, W. L. (1989, Fall). The spectrum of attitudes: Building a theory of youth development. *New Designs for Youth Development.* Tucson, AZ: Associates for Youth Development, Inc.

Loprest, P., & Maag, E. (2001). *Barriers and supports for work among adults with disabilites: Results from the NHIS-D.* Washington, DC: The Urban Institute.

Lott, B. (2001). Low income parents and the public schools. *Journal of Social Issues, 57*(2), 247–259.

Lott, B. (2003). Diversity in consultation: Recognizing and welcoming the standpoint of low-income parents in the public schools. *Journal of Educational and Psychological Consultation, 14*(1), 91.

Lott, B., & Rogers, M. R. (2005). School consultants working for equity with families, teachers, and administrators. *Journal of Educational and Psychological Consultation, 16*(1 & 2), 1.

Luecking, R., & Certo, N. (2002). Integrating service systems at the point of transition for youth with significant disabilities: A model that works. *Addressing Trends and Developments in Secondary Education and Transition, 1*(4), 1–3. Retrieved December 12, 2007, from http://www.ncset.org/publications/viewdesc.asp?id=705

Luecking, R., & Fabian, E. (2000). Paid internships and employment success for youth in transition. *Career Development for Exceptional Individuals, 23,* 205–222.

Luecking, R. G., Fabian, E. S., & Tilson, G. P. (2004). *Working relationships: Creating career opportunities for job seekers with disabilities through employer partnerships.* Baltimore: Paul H. Brookes.

Luft, P. (1997, October). *Multicultural transition planning: "Individual" plans that are culturally inclusive.* Paper presented at Division for Career Development and Transition, "Creating Amazing Transitions," Scottsdale, AZ.

Luft, P. (2001). Multicultural competence in transition planning processes. In R. W. Flexer, T. J. Simmons, P. Luft, & R. M. Baer (Eds.), *Transition planning for secondary students with disabilities* (pp. 120–160). Upper Saddle River, NJ: Merrill/Prentice Hall.

Lynch, E. W., & Hanson, M. J. (1998). *Developing cross-cultural competencies: A guide for working with young children and their families* (2nd ed.). Baltimore: Paul H. Brookes.

Lynch, E. W., & Hanson, M. J. (2004). *Developing cross-cultural competencies: A guide for working with children and their families* (3rd ed.). Baltimore: Paul H. Brookes.

Lynch, J. (1994). *Provision for children with special education needs in the Asia region* (The World Bank Technical Paper No. 261). Asia Technical Department, Population and Human Resources Division.

Madaus, J. W., Bigaj, S., Chafaleaus, S., & Simonsen, B. (2007). Mining the files: What key information can be included in a comprehensive summary of performance? *Career Development for Exceptional Individuals.*

Madson-Ankeny, E. (2000). Open door or revolving door: Is the community college a viable option for students with disabilities? *Journal for Vocational Special Needs Education, 22*(3), 3-6.

Mager, R. (1975). *Preparing instructional objectives* (2nd ed.). Belmont, CA: Fearon-Pitman.

Mannix, D. (1998). *Life skills activities for secondary students with special needs.* Arlington, VA: Council for Exceptional Children.

Manpower Development and Training Act of 1965, Pub. L. No. 89-174, §2, 79 Stat. 667 (September 9, 1965).

Manzo, A. (1997). *Content area literacy: Interactive teaching for active learning* (2nd ed.). New York: Wiley.

Martin, J. (2002). The transition of students with disabilities from high school to post-secondary education. In C. A. Kochhar-Bryant & D. S. Bassett (Eds.), *Aligning transition and standards-based education: Issues and strategies.* Arlington, VA: Council for Exceptional Children.

Martin, J., Marshall, L., & DePry, R. (2002). Participatory decision-making: Innovative practices that increase student self-determination. In R. Flexer, T. Simmons, P. Luft, & R. Baer (Eds.), *Transition planning for secondary students with disabilities* (2nd ed., pp. 246-275). Columbus, OH: Merrill.

Martin, J. E., & Marshall, L. H. (1994). *Choicemaker self-determination transition curriculum matrix.* Colorado Springs: University of Colorado Center for Educational Research.

Martin, J. E., Marshall, L. H., Maxson, L. M., & Jerman, P. L. (1997). *The self-directed IEP.* Longmont, CO: Sopris West.

Martin, J. E., Van Dycke, W., Christensen, R. W., Greene, B. A., Gardner, J. E., & Lovett, D. L. (2006). Increasing student participation in IEP meetings: Establishing self-directed IEP as an evidenced-based practice. *Exceptional Children, 72*(3), 299.

Martinelli, F. (2002). *Strategic planning.* Madison, WI: Learning Institute for Nonprofit Organizations Collaboration, Center for Community Economic Development, University of Wisconsin Extension.

McCarney, S. B., & Anderson, P. D. (2000). *Transition behavior scale 2.* Columbia, MO: Hawthorne Educational Services.

McClamroch, J., Byrd, J. J., & Sowell, S. L. (2001). Strategic planning: Politics, leadership and learning. *Journal of Academic Librarianship, 27*(5), 372-378.

McCloskey, M. (2002). The president's message: No child left behind. *TESOL Matters, 12,* 4. Retrieved September 15, 2007, from http://www.tesol.org/s_tesol/sec_document.asp?CID=534&DID=964

McDonnel, L., McLaughlin, M., & Morison, P. (1997). *Educating one and all: Students with disabilities and standards-based reform.* Washington, DC: National Research Council, National Academy Press.

McGlashing-Johnson, J., Agran, M., Sitlington, P., Cavin, M., & Wehmeyer, M. L. (2003). Enhancing the job performance of youth with moderate to severe cognitive disabilities using the self-determined learning model of instruction. *Research and Practice for Persons with Severe Disabilities, 28*(4), 194-204.

McLanahan, S., Garfinkel, I., & Mincy, R. B. (2001). *Fragile families, welfare reform, and marriage* (Policy Brief No. 10). Washington, DC: Brookings Institution.

McLanahan, S., & Sandefur, G. D. 1994. *Growing up with a single parent: What hurts? What helps?* Cambridge, MA: Harvard University Press.

McLaughlin, M. W., & Talbert, J. E. (2001). *Professional communities and the work of high school teaching.* Chicago: University of Chicago Press.

McLeod, P. (2005). *Instructional strategies for English learners with disabilities.* Washington, DC: Council of Chief State School Officers.

McNair, J., & Rusch, F. R. (1991). Parental involvement in transition programs. *Mental Retardation, 29*(2), 93-101.

McNeil, C. B., Capage, L. C., & Bennett, G. M. (2002). Cultural issues in the treatment of young African American children diagnosed with disruptive behavior disorders. *Journal of Pediatric Psychology, 27*(4), 339-350.

Meers, G. (1980). *Introduction to special vocational needs education.* Rockville, MD: Aspen Publications.

Meisel, S., Henderson, K. Cohen, M., & Leone, P. (2000). *Collaborate to educate: Special education in juvenile correctional facilities.* College Park: University of Maryland, National Center on Education, Disability and Juvenile Justice. Retrieved December 30, 2003, from http://www.edjj.org/Publications/pub01_17_00.html

Michaels, C. (1994). *Transition strategies for persons with learning disabilities.* San Diego, CA: Singular.

Midobuche, E. (2001). More than empty footprints in the sand: Educating immigrant children. *Harvard Educational Review, 71*(3), 529-535.

Milano, M., & Ullius, D. (1998). *Designing powerful training: The sequential-iterative model.* San Francisco: Jossey-Bass, Pfeiffer.

Miller, J. (2002, May 6). *Investing in the transition of youth with disabilities to productive careers.* Paper presented at the Twenty-Eighth National Forum of the Institute on Rehabilitation Issues, Rehabilitation Services

Administration, U.S. Department of Education, Alexandria, VA.

Miller, J., Ross, T., & Sturgis, C. (2005, November). *Beyond the tunnel problem: Addressing cross-cutting issues that impact vulnerable youth. Briefing Paper #2: Redirecting youth from the school-to-prison pipeline: Addressing cross-cutting issues in youth services.* A Briefing Paper Series of Youth Transition Funders Group in partnership with the Annie E. Casey Foundation.

Miller, R. J., Lombard, R. C., & Corbey, S. A. (2006). *Transition assessment: Planning transition and IEP development for youth with mild to moderate disabilities.* Columbus, OH: Allyn & Bacon.

Miller, R. J., Lombard, R. C., & Corbey, S. A. (2007). *Transition assessment: Planning transition and IEP development for youth with mild to moderate disabilities.* Boston: Pearson/Allyn & Bacon.

Milou, E., & Bohlin, C. F. (2003, September). High school exit exams across the nation. *News Bulletin.*

Minnesota System of Interagency Coordination Communication Project. (2003, Fall). Service coordination: What's it all about? *Newsletter of the Minnesota System of Interagency Coordination.* Minneapolis: University of Minnesota, Institute on Community Integration.

Mithaug, D. E., & Horiuchi, C. N. (1983). *Colorado statewide followup survey of special education students.* Denver: Colorado Department of Education.

Mizelle, N. B., & Irvin, J. L. (2000). Transition from middle school to high school. *Middle School Journal, 31*(5), 57–61.

Mizelle, N. B., & Mullins, E. (1997). Transition into and out of middle school. In J. L. Irvin (Ed.), *What current research says to the middle level practitioner* (pp. 303–313). Columbus, OH: National Middle School Association.

Montiel-Overall, P. (2005). *Toward a theory of collaboration for teachers and librarians.* Chicago: American Library Association.

Morgan, L. P., & Hertzog, C. J. (2001). Designing comprehensive transition plans. *Principal Leadership, 1*(7), 10–18.

Morningstar, M. (2002). The role of families of adolescents with disabilities in standards-based reform and transition. In C. A. Kochhar-Bryant & D. Bassett (Eds.), *Aligning transition and standards-based education: Issues and strategies.* Arlington, VA: Council for Exceptional Children.

Morningstar, M., & Wehmeyer, M. (in press). The role of families in enhancing transition outcomes for youth with learning disabilities. In J. Patton & G. Blalock (Eds.), *Transition and students with learning disabilities: Facilitating the movement from school to adult life* (2nd ed.). Austin, TX: Pro-Ed.

Morningstar, M. E., & Benitez, D. (2004). *Critical issues facing youth with emotional and behavioral disabilities during the transition to adulthood.* Arlington, VA: Division of Children with Behavior Disorders, Council for Exceptional Children.

Morningstar, M. E., Kleinhammer-Tramill, P. J., & Lattin, D. L. (1999). Using successful models of student-centered transition planning and services for adolescents with disabilities. *Focus on Exceptional Children, 31*(9), 1–19.

Moscow State Pedagogical University. (n.d.). *Contemporary educational programmes.* Retrieved January 23, 2008, from http://www.cep.ru/mspu.shtml

Mount, B., & Zwernik, K. (1988). *It's never too early, it's never too late: An overview of personal futures planning.* St. Paul, MN: Governor's Planning Council on Developmental Disabilities.

Muller, E. (2004). *Autism: Challenges relating to secondary transition.* Project Forum, National Association of State Directors of Special Education.

Müller, E., Schuler, A., Burton, B., & Yates, G. B. (2003). Meeting the vocational support needs of individuals with Asperger syndrome and other autism spectrum disabilities. *Journal of Vocational Rehabilitation, 18*(3), 163–175.

Murray, C., Goldstein, D., Nourse, S., & Edgar, E. (2000). The postsecondary school attendance and completion rates of highschool graduates with learning disabilities. *Learning Disabilities Research & Practice, 15* (13), 199–227.

National Alliance for Secondary Education and Transition. (2005). *National standards and quality indicators: Transition toolkit for systems improvement.* Minneapolis: National Center on Secondary Education and Transition, University of Minnesota.

National Association of Elementary School Principals. (2004). *When schools and families work in partnership, students benefit: Strengthening the connection between school and home.* Alexandria, VA: Author.

National Association of Protection and Advocacy Systems. (2004). *FY 2004 annual report: Advancing values through protection & advocacy.* Washington, DC: Author.

National Center for Education Statistics. (1999). *Students with disabilities in postsecondary education: A profile of preparation, participation, and outcomes.* Washington, DC: U.S. Department of Education.

National Center for Education Statistics. (2000a). *Dropout rates in the United States: 1998.* Washington, DC: U.S. Department of Education.

National Center for Education Statistics. (2000b). *The condition of education 2000.* Washington, DC: U.S. Government Printing Office.

National Center for Education Statistics. (2001). *The condition of education.* Washington, DC: U.S. Department of Education.

National Center for Education Statistics. (2002). *Digest of education statistics, 2002.* Washington, DC: U.S. Department of Education.

National Center for Education Statistics. (2005). *The condition of education*. Washington, DC: U.S. Department of Education.

National Center for Education Statistics. (2006). *The condition of education*. Washington, DC: U.S. Department of Education.

National Center for Family Literacy. (2004). *Stories of impact: Improving parent involvement through family literacy in the elementary school*. Louisville, KY: Author.

National Center for the Study of Postsecondary Educational Supports. (2000). *Technical report: National survey of educational support provision to students with disabilities in postsecondary education settings*. Honolulu, HI: Author.

National Center for the Study of Postsecondary Educational Supports & National Center on Secondary Education and Transition. (2001). *Preparing youth with disabilities for successful participation in postsecondary education & employment*. National Capacity Building Institute Proceedings.

National Center on Education, Disability and Juvenile Justice. (2004). *Transition planning and services*. College Park: University of Maryland.

National Center on Outcomes Research. (2001). *Practice guidance for delivery outcomes in service coordination*. Towson, MD: Author.

National Center on Secondary Education and Transition. (2002a). Integrating services systems at the point of transition for youth with significant disabilities: A model that works. *NCSET Information Brief, 1*(4). Minneapolis, MN: Author.

National Center on Secondary Education and Transition. (2002b, May). Age of majority: Preparing your child for making good choices. *NCSET Parent Brief*. Minneapolis, MN: Author.

National Center on Secondary Education and Transition. (2002c, December). Youth with disabilities and the Workforce Investment Act of 1998.

NCSET Policy Update, 1(2). Minneapolis, MN: Author.

National Center on Secondary Education and Transition. (2004a). *Current challenges facing secondary education and transition services for youth with disabilities in the United States*. University of Minnesota, National Center on Secondary Education and Transition Web site. Retrieved May 26, 2005, from http://www.ncset.org/publications/discussionpaper/default.asp

National Center on Secondary Education and Transition. (2004b, November 17). Preparing for post-secondary education. *NCSET Topics*. Minneapolis, MN: Author.

National Clearinghouse for English Language Acquisition. (2005). *Biennial report to Congress on the implementation of title III, part A of ESEA*. Washington, DC: The George Washington University.

National Collaborative on Workforce and Disability. (2005, January). Youth development and youth leadership in programs. *Information Brief, 11*.

National Council for Research on Women. (1998). *Girls report*. New York: Author.

National Council for Research on Women. (2001). *Balancing the equation: Where are women & girls in science, engineering & technology?* New York: Author.

National Council on Disability. (2000a). *Back to school on civil rights: Advancing the federal commitment to leave no child behind*. Washington, DC: Author.

National Council on Disability. (2000b). *Transition and post-school outcomes for youth with disabilities: Closing the gaps to post-secondary education and employment*. Washington, DC: Author.

National Council on Disability. (2003a). *National disability policy: A progress report: December 2001–December 2002*. Retrieved September 4, 2007, from http://www.ncd.gov/newsroom/publications/2003/progressreport_final.htm

National Council on Disability. (2003b, September 15). *People with disabilities and post-secondary education* (Position Paper). Washington, DC: Author.

National Council on Disability. (2003c, January 24). *Youth advisory committee to the national council on disability*. Record of personal meeting, teleconference, Washington, DC.

National Council on Disability. (2004, May). *Improving educational outcomes for students with disabilities*. Retrieved February 11, 2008, from http://www.ncd.gov/newsroom/publications/2004/educationoutcomes.htm

National Dropout Prevention Center for Students with Disabilities. (2006, April). *An analysis of state performance plan data for Indicator 2 (dropout)*. Elson, SC: Author. Retrieved September 1, 2007, from http://www.ndpc-sd.org/assistance/docs/Indicator_2—Dropout.pdf

National Employer Leadership Council (NELC). (1996). *The employer participation model*. Washington, DC: Author.

National Governors Association, Center for Best Practices, (2001). Setting high educational standards in alternative education. *Issue Brief*. Washington, DC: Author.

National High School Center. (2007a). *State and district level support for successful transitions into high school*. Washington, DC: American Institutes for Research.

National High School Center. (2007b). *Dropout prevention for students with disabilities: A critical issue for state education agencies*. Washington, DC: American Institutes for Research.

National High School Center. (2007c). *Toward ensuring a smooth transition into high school*. (C. Herlihy, Author). Washington DC: American Institutes for Research.

National Information Center for Children and Youth with Disabilities. (1999). Helping students with cognitive disabilities find and keep a job. *Technical Assistance Guide 3 (TA3)*. Washington, DC: Author.

National Institute of Mental Health. (2003). *Attention deficit and hyperactivity disorder*. Washington, DC: Author.

National Longitudinal Transition Study-2. (2005). *Changes over time in post-school outcomes of youth with disabilities*. Retrieved January 23, 2008, from http://nlts2.org/pdfs/str6_completereport.pdf

National Middle School Association. (2006, September). *Transition from middle to high school*. Westerville, OH: Author.

National Organization on Disability. (2000, October). *Conflicting trends in employment of people with disabilities 1986-2000*. Washington, DC: Louis Harris & Associates.

National Organization on Disability. (2004). *N.O.D. Harris survey of Americans with disabilities*. Washington, DC: Louis Harris & Associates.

National Research Council and Institute of Medicine. (2002). *Community programs to promote youth development. Committee on Community-Level Programs for Youth*. (J. Eccles & J. A. Gootman, Eds.). Board on Children, Youth and Families, Division of Behavioral and Social Sciences and Education. Washington DC: National Academy Press.

National Research and Training Center. (2002). *Self-determination framework for people with psychiatric disabilities*. Chicago: University of Illinois. Retrieved March 17, 2008, from http://www.psych.uic.edu/UICNRTC/sdframework.pdf

National Youth Development Center. (1998). *What is youth development?* Washington, DC: National Collaboration for Youth Members.

National Youth Development Information Center. (2001). Talking about youth development: Helping campers grow into successful adults. *Camping Magazine, 74*(1), 24-27.

Neubert, D. A. (2000). Transition education and services guidelines. In G. M. Clark, P. Sitlington, & O. P. Kolstoe (Eds.), *Transition education and services for adolescents with disabilities* (3rd ed., pp. 39-69). Boston: Allyn & Bacon.

Neubert, D. A. (2003). The role of assessment in the transition to adult life process for individuals with disabilities. *Exceptionality, 11*, 63-71.

New Mexico Developmental Disabilities Planning Council. (2001, December). *Statewide transition participants and services project*. Albuquerque: NM Statewide Transition Coordinating Council.

New York State Department of Education. (2005). *Sample individualized education program (IEP) and guidance document*. Albany: The University of the State of New York, The State Education Department, Office of Vocational and Educational.

New York State Office of Mental Health. (2001). *2001-2005 statewide comprehensive plan for mental health services*. Rochester, NY: Author.

Newman, L. (2004). *Family involvement in the educational development of youth with disabilities*. Menlo Park, CA: SRI International.

Newman, L. (2005). *Family involvement in the educational development of youth with disabilities*. Menlo Park, CA: SRI International.

Nieto, S. (2000). *Affirming diversity: The sociopolitical context of multicultural education* (3rd ed.). Boston: Allyn & Bacon; Reading, MA: Longman.

Niogi, S. N., & McCandliss, B. D. (2006). Left lateralized white matter microstructure accounts for individual differences in reading ability and disability. *Neuropsychologia, 44*, 2178-2188.

Nirje, B. (1976). The normalization principle. In R. B. Kugel & A. Hearer (Eds.), *Changing patterns in residential services for the mentally retarded* (rev. ed.). Washington, DC: President's Committee on Mental Retardation.

Nisbett, R. E., Peng, K., Choi, I., & Norenzayan, A. (2001). Culture and systems of thought: Holistic versus analytic cognition. *Psychological Review, 108*, 291-310.

No Child Left Behind Act of 2001, Pub. L. No. 107-110, 20 U.S.C. §6301 *et seq.* (2001).

Northwest Evaluation Association. (2005, April). *Impact of NCLB on student achievement and growth: 2005 education research brief*. Lake Oswego, OR: Author.

Novick, R. (2001). *Family involvement and beyond: School-based child and family support programs*. Portland, OR: Northwest Regional Education Laboratory.

O'Leary, E., & Collision, W. (2002). *Transition services: Helping educators, parents and other stakeholders understand*. Mountain Plains Regional Resource Center. Retrieved June 8, 2007, from http://www.rrfcnetwork.org/content/view/156/245/

O'Leary, E., Lehman, M., & Doty, D. (2001). *The Individuals with Disabilities Education Act of 1997 transition requirements: A guide for states, districts, schools, universities and families*. Minneapolis: University of Minnesota, Institute on Community Integration.

Obiakor, F. E., & Wilder, L. K. (2003). Disproportionate representation in special education. *Principal Leadership, 4*(2), 16-22.

Ogbu, J. (1991). Immigrant and involuntary minorities in comparative perspective. In M. Gibson & J. Ogbu (Eds.), *Minority status and schooling: A comparative study of immigrant and involuntary minorities*. New York: Garland Press.

Ogbu, J. (2003). *Black American students in an affluent suburb: A study of academic disengagement*. Mahwah, NJ: Lawrence Erlbaum Associates.

Ogbu, J. U. (1978). *Minority education and caste: The American system in cross-cultural perspective*. San Francisco: Academic Press.

Ogbu, J. U. (1987). Variability in minority school performance: A problem in search of an explanation. *Anthropology and Education Quarterly, 18*, 312-336.

Olbrich, S. (2002). *Children in need of help for emotional problems: Children's mental health: Current challenges and a future direction.* Center for Health and Health Care in Schools.

Olson, L. (2007). Diplomas count: What does ready mean? *Education Week, 26*(40), 7–8, 10, 12.

Ontario Association for Families of Children with Communication Disorders. (2001). *Transition planning resource guide.* Tillsonberg: Ontario Ministry of Education. Retrieved May 15, 2007, from http://www.edu.gov.on.ca.http://www.edu.gov.on.ca

Orfield, G. (2004). *Dropouts in America: Confronting the graduation rate crisis.* Cambridge, MA: Harvard Education Press.

Ornstein, A., & Levine, D. (1997). *Foundations of education.* Boston: Houghton Mifflin.

Ortiz, A., & Yates, J. R. (1986). Staffing and the development of individualized educational program for bilingual exceptional students. In L. M. Baca & H. T. Cervantes (Eds.), *The bilingual special education interface* (pp. 187–212). Upper Saddle River, NJ: Merrill/Prentice Hall.

Osgood, D. W., Foster, E. M., Flanagan, C., & Ruth, G. R. (Eds.). (2005). *On your own without a net: The transition to adulthood for vulnerable populations.* Chicago: University of Chicago Press.

Osipow, S. (1983). *Theories of career development.* Upper Saddle River, NJ: Prentice Hall.

Osipow, S. H., & Fitzgerald, L. F. (1996). *Theories of career development* (4th ed.). Boston: Allyn & Bacon.

Pannabecker, J. R. (1996). Diderot, Rousseau, and the mechanical arts: Disciplines, systems, and social context. *Journal of Industrial Teacher Education, 33*(4), 6–22.

Parent Advocacy Coalition for Educational Rights Center. (1999). *Point of Departure, 4*(2), 1–22.

Parsons, F. (1909). *Choosing a vocation.* Boston: Houghton Mifflin.

Patrikakou, E. N. (2004). *Adolescence: Are parents relevant to students' high school achievement and postsecondary attainment?* Cambridge, MA: Harvard Family Research Project, Harvard University.

Patterson, G. R. (1975). *Families.* Champaign, IL: Research Press.

Patton, J., & Dunn, C. (1998). *Transition from school to young adulthood: Basic concepts and recommended practices.* Austin, TX: Pro-Ed.

Patton, J. R., & Blalock, G. (1996). *Transition and students with learning disabilities: Facilitating the movement from school to adult life.* Austin, TX: Pro-Ed.

Perez, M. A., & Pinzon, H. L. (1997). Latino families: Partners for success in school settings. *Journal of School Health, 67*(5), 182–185.

Perna, L. W., & Titus, M. A. (2005). The relationship between parental involvement as social capital and college enrollment: An examination of racial/ethnic group differences. *The Journal of Higher Education, 76,* 485–507.

Phelan, P., Davidson, A., & Yu, H. (1998). *Adolescents' worlds: Negotiating family, peers, and school.* New York: Teachers College Press.

Phelps, L. A., & Hanley-Maxwell, C. (1997). School-to-work transitions for youth with disabilities: A review of outcomes and practices. *Review of Educational Research, 67*(2), 197–226.

Piaget, J. (1929). *The child's conception of the world.* New York: Harcourt, Brace Jovanovich.

Piaget, J. (1970). *The science of education and the psychology of the child.* New York: Grossman.

Pierangelo, R., & Crane, R. (1997). *Complete guide to special education transition services.* West Nyack, NY: Center for Applied Research in Education.

Plank, S., DeLuca, S., & Estacion, A. (2005, October). *Dropping out of high school and the place of career and technical education: A survival analysis of surviving high school.* St. Paul: National Research Center for Career and Technical Education, University of Minnesota.

Polloway, E., Patton, J., Smith, J., & Rodrique, T. (1991). Issues in program design for elementary students with mental retardation: Emphasis on curriculum development. *Education and Training in Mental Retardation, 26,* 142–250.

Powers, K. M., Gil-Kashiwabara, E., Geenen, S. J., Powers, L. E., Balandran, J., & Palmer, C. (2005). Mandates and effective transition planning practices reflected in IEPs. *Career Development for Exceptional Individuals, 28*(1), 47–59.

Powers, L., Dinerstein, R., Holmes, S., Crowley, R., Decker, C., Frattarola-Saulino, M., et al. (2005). Self-advocacy, self-determination, and social freedom and opportunity. In K. C. Lakin & A. Turnbull (Eds.), *National goals and research for people with intellectual and developmental disabilities* (pp. 257–287). Washington, DC: American Association on Mental Retardation.

Powers, L. E., Ellison, R., Matuszewski, J., Wilson, R., & Turner, A. (1997). *Take charge for the future.* Portland, OR: Health Sciences University, Center on Self-Determination.

Prawat, R. S. (1991, Winter). Conversation with self and settings: A framework for thinking about teacher empowerment. *American Education Research Journal, 28,* 737–757.

President's Commission on Excellence in Special Education. (2002). *A new era: Revitalizing special education for children and their families.* Jessup, MD: Educational Publications.

Prokop, S. (2006, February 14). *The future of vocational rehabilitation.* Bethesda, MD: Council of State Administrators of Vocational Rehabilitation.

Racino, J. A. (1992). Living in the community: Independence, support, and transition. In F. R. Rusch, L. Destefano, J. Chadsey-Rusch, L. A. Phelps, & E. Szymanski (Eds.), *Transition from school to adult life* (pp. 131–145). Pacific Grove, CA: Brooks-Cole.

Raimondo, B., & Henderson, A. (2001). Unlocking parent potential. *Principal Leadership, 2*(1), 26–32.

Ralabate, P. (2007). *The relationship of students with disabilities performance on adequate yearly progress accountability measures to inclusion rates.* Unpublished doctoral dissertation, George Washington University, Washington, DC.

Rank, O. (1927). Psychoanalytic problems. *Psychoanalytic Review, 14,* 1-19.

Rank, O. (1958). *Beyond psychology.* New York: Dover.

Rapp, M. (1998). Adolescent development: An emotional roller coaster. In M. A. Nichols & C. A. Nichols (Eds.), *Young adults and public libraries* (pp. 1-10). Westport, CT: Greenwood.

Raywid, M. A. (1994). Synthesis of research: Alternative schools. The state of the art. *Educational Leadership, 52*(1), 26-32.

Raywid, M. A. (1998). The journey of the alternative schools movement: Where it's been and where it's going. *The High School Magazine, 6*(2), 12-15.

Reese, L., & Gallimore, R. (2000). Immigrant Latinos' cultural model of literacy development: An evolving perspective on home-school discontinuities. *American Journal of Education, 108,* 103-134.

Rehabilitation Act Amendments of 1998, §504, Pub. L. No. 102-569, 29 U.S.C. §794 (1998).

Repetto, J., Webb, K., Garvan, C., & Washington, T. (2002). Connecting student outcomes with transition practices in Florida. *Career Development for Exceptional Individuals, 25*(2), 123-139.

Repetto, J., Webb, K., Neubert, D. A., & Curran, C. (2006). *Succeeding with middle school learners: Using universal design to promote transition and self-determination.* Austin, TX: Pro-Ed.

Repetto, J. B., White, W., & Snauwaert, D. T. (1990). Individualized transition plans (ITP): A national perspective. *Career Development for Exceptional Individuals, 13*(2), 109-119.

Research and Training Center on Service Coordination. (2001). *Data report: Service coordination policies and models.* Farmington, CT: Author.

Reynolds, M., Wang, M. C., & Walberg, H. J. (1987). The necessary restructuring of special and regular education. *Exceptional Children, 53,* 391-398.

Rhode Island Department of Education. (2002). *Rhode Island transition council vision.* Providence, RI: Author: Retrieved March 21, 2008, from http://www.ridoe.net/Special_needs/transition.htm

Rhodes, J. E., Grossman, J. B., & Resch, N. L. (2000). Agents of change: Pathways through which mentoring relationships influence adolescents' academic adjustment. *Child Development, 71,* 1662-1671.

Riccomini, P. J., Bost, L. W., Katsiyannis, A., & Zhang, D. (2005, August). Cognitive behavioral interventions: An effective approach to help students with disabilities stay in school. *Effective interventions in dropout prevention: A practice brief for educators, 1*(1). Clemson, SC: National Dropout Prevention Center for Students with Disabilities, Clemson University.

Riehl, C. J. (2000). The principal's role in creating inclusive schools for diverse students: A review of normative, empirical, and critical literature on the practice of educational administration. *Review of Educational Research, 70*(1), 55-81.

Rioux-Bailey, C. (2004). *Students with disabilities and access to community college: Continuing issues and new directions.* Washington, DC: George Washington University, HEATH Resource Center.

Roaches, M., Shore, J., Gouleta, E., & Burkevich, E. (2003, Spring). An investigation of collaboration among school professionals in serving culturally and linguistically diverse students with exceptionalities. *Bilingual Research Journal,* 117-136.

Roe, A. (1957). Early determinants of vocational choice. *Journal of Counseling Psychology, 4,* 212-217.

Roeser, R. W., Eccles, J. S., & Sameroff, A. J. (2000). School as a context of early adolescents' academic and social-emotional development: A summary of research findings. *The Elementary School Journal, 100*(5), 443-471.

Roessler, R. T., & Rumrill, P. D. (1998). Self-advocacy training: Preparing students with disabilities to request classroom accommodations. *Journal of Postsecondary Education and Disability, 13*(3), 20-31.

Rogers, C. (1951). *Client-centered therapy.* Boston: Houghton Mifflin.

Rogers, E. L., & Rogers, D. C. (2001). Students with EB/D transition to college: Make a plan. *Beyond Behavior, 11*(1), 42-49.

Rosman, E., McCarthy, J., & Woolverton, M. (2001). *Interagency coordination.* Washington, DC: Georgetown Child Development Center.

Rossi, P., Lipsey, M., & Freeman, H. (2003). *Evaluation: A systematic approach* (6th ed.). Newbury Park, CA: Sage.

Roth, J. L., & Brooks-Gunn, J. (2003). Youth development programs: Risk, prevention, and policy. *Journal of Adolescent Health, 32,* 170-182.

Rubin, A. (1992). Is case management effective for people with serious mental illness? A research review. *Health and Social Work, 17*(2), 138-150.

Rueda, R., Monzo, L., Shapiro, J., Gomez, J., & Blacher, J. (2005). Cultural models of transition: Latina mothers of young adults with developmental disabilities. *Exceptional Children, 7*(4), 401-414.

Ruiz-de-Velasco, J., Fix, M., & Clewell, B. (2000). *Overlooked and underserved: Immigrant students in U.S. secondary schools.* Washington, DC: Urban Institute Press. Retrieved August 10, 2005, from http://www.urban.org/UploadedPDF/overlooked.pdf

Russell, L. H. (2001). A comprehensive approach to transition planning. In L. Brinkenhoff, J. McGuire, & S. Shaw (Eds.), *Postsecondary education and transition for students with learning disabilities*. Austin, TX: Pro-Ed.

Rutherford, D. (Ed.). (2006). *The Cambridge companion to early modern philosophy*. Cambridge: Cambridge University Press.

Rutherford, R. B. (1997). Why doesn't social skills training work? *CEC Today, 4*(1), 14.

Rutherford, R. B., Chipman, J., DiGangi, S., & Anderson, K. (1992). *Teaching social skills: A practical approach*. Arlington, VA: Council for Exceptional Children.

Rutherford, R. B., Jr., & Quinn, M. M. (1999). Special education in alternative education programs. *The Clearing House, 73*(2), 79-81.

Ryan, R. M., & Deci, E. L. (2000). Self-determination theory and the facilitation of intrinsic motivation, social development, and well-being. *American Psychologist, 55*, 68-78.

SABE USA. (2000). *The history of the developmental disabilities assistance and the bill of rights act*. New Fairfield, CT: Author. Retrieved January 23, 2008, from http://www.sabeusa.org/actdda.html

Sagawa, S. (2003). Service as a strategy for youth development. In A. Lewis (Ed.), *Shaping the future of American youth: Youth policy in the 21st century*. Washington, DC: American Youth Policy Forum.

Salembier, G., & Furney, K. S. (1997). Facilitating participation: Parents' perceptions of their involvement in the IEP/transition planning process. *Career Development for Exceptional Individuals, 20*(1), 29-42.

Salend, S. J., Garrick-Duhaney, L. M., & Montgomery, W. (2002). A comprehensive approach to identifying and addressing issues of disproportionate representation. *Remedial and Special Education, 23*(5), 289-300.

Sargent, L. (1998). *Social skills in the school and community: Systematic instruction for children and youth with cognitive delays*. Arlington, VA: Council for Exceptional Children.

Sarkees, M. D., & West, L. (1990). Roles and responsibilities of vocational

resource personnel in rural settings. *The Journal for Vocational Special Needs Education, 12,* 7-10.

Sarkees-Wircenski, M., & Scott, J. L. (2003). *Special populations in career and technical education*. Homewood, IL: American Technical Publishers, Inc.

Savage, R. (1991). Identification, classification, and placement issues for students with traumatic brain injuries. *Journal of Head Trauma Rehabilitation, 6*(1), 1-9.

Sax, C., & Thoma, C. (2002). *Transition assessment: Wise practice for quality lives*. Baltimore: Paul H. Brookes.

Schaffer, R. (1953). Job satisfaction as related to need satisfaction in work. *Psychological Monographs, 67*(14).

Schall, C., Cortijo-Doval, E., Targett, P. S., & Wehman, P. (2006). Applications for youth with autism spectrum disorders. In P. Wehman (Ed.), *Life beyond the classroom: Transition strategies for young people with disabilities* (4th ed., pp. 535-575). Baltimore: Paul H. Brookes.

Schalock, R. L., & Keith, K. D. (1993). *Quality of life questionnaire*. Worthington, OH: IDS.

Schalock, R. L., & Keith, K. D. (1995). *Quality of school life questionnaire*. Worthington, OH: IDS.

Scharff, D., & Hill, J. (1976). *Between two worlds: Aspects of transition from school to work*. London: Consultant Books.

Schargel, F. (2003). *Strategies to help solve our school dropout problem*. Larchmont, NY: Eye on Education.

Schiller, E., Burnaska, K., Cohen, G., Douglas, Z., Joseph, C., Johnston, P., et al. (2003). *Study of state and local implementation and impact of the Individuals with Disabilities Education Act—final report on selected findings*. Bethesda, MD: ABT Associates Inc.

Schloss, P., Schloss, M., & Schloss, C. (2006). *Instructional methods for secondary students with learning and behavior problems* (4th ed.). Upper Saddle River, NJ: Pearson.

Schlossberg, N. K. (1985). Adult development theories. In *Adult career*

development. Alexandria, VA: National Career Development Association.

Scholl, L., & Mooney, M. (2005, Spring). Students with learning disabilities in work-based learning programs: Factors that influence success. *The Journal for Vocational Special Needs Education*.

School to Work Opportunities Act of 1994, Pub. L. No. 103-239, 20 U.S.C. §6101 *et seq.* (1994).

Schriner, K. (2001). Disability and institutional change: A human variation perspective on overcoming oppression. *Journal of Disability Policy Studies, 12*(2), 100-106.

Schroeder, C. (2003). The first year and beyond. *About Campus, 8*(4), 9-16.

Schwarz, S. L., & Taymans, J. M. (1991). Urban vocational/technical program completers with learning disabilities. *Exceptional Children, 58*, 47-59.

Scott, S., Shaw, S., & McGuire, J. (2003). Universal design for instruction: A new paradigm for adult instruction in postsecondary education. *Remedial and Special Education, 24*(6), 369-379.

Sears, R. R. (1972). A theoretical framework for personality and social behavior. *American Psychologist, 6*, 476-483.

Settersten, R., Furstenberg, F., & Rumbaut, R. (Eds.). (2004). *On the frontier of adulthood: Theory, research and public policy*. Chicago: University of Chicago Press.

Shafer, M. S., & Rangasamy, R. (1995). Transition for youth with learning disabilities: A focus on developing independence. *Learning Disabilities Quarterly, 15,* 237-249.

Shapiro, I. (1980). *Social justice in the liberal state*. New Haven, CT: Yale University Press.

Sharpe, M., & Johnson, D. R. (2001). A 20/20 analysis of postsecondary support characteristics. *Journal of Vocational Rehabilitation, 16(3/4)*, 169-177.

Sharpe, M. N., Bruininks, B. D., Blacklock, B. A., Benson, B., & Johnson, D. M. (2004, September). The emergence of psychiatric disabilities in postsecondary education. *Issue Brief, 3*(1).

Sharpe, M. N., Johnson, D. R., Izzo, M., & Murray, A. (2005). An analysis of instructional accommodations and assistive technologies used by postsecondary graduates with disabilities. *Journal of Vocational Rehabilitation, 22*(1), 3-11.

Shaw, S., Kochhar-Bryant, C., Izzo, M., Benedict, K., & Parker, D. (2005). *Summary of performance under IDEA 2004.* National Documentation Summit.

Shaw, S. F. (2005). IDEA will change the face of postsecondary disability documentation. *Disability Compliance for Higher Education, 11*(1), 7-9.

Shaw, S. F. (2006, Fall). Legal and policy perspectives on transition assessment and documentation [Special issue]. *Career Development for Exceptional Individuals, 29*(2), 108-113.

Shaw, S. F., & Dukes, L. L. (2001). Program standards for disability services in higher education. *Journal of Postsecondary Education and Disability, 14*(2), 81-90.

Shogren, K., Wehmeyer, M. L., Reese, M., & O'Hara, D. (2006). Promoting self-determination in health and medical care: A critical component of addressing health disparities in people with intellectual disabilities. *Journal of Policy and Practice in Intellectual Disabilities, 3,* 105-113.

Siegel, L. M. (2007). *The complete IEP guide: How to advocate for your special ED child.* Berkeley, CA: NOLO.

Silverberg, M., Warner, E., Fong, M., & Goodwin, D. (2004, June). *National assessment of vocational education: Final report to Congress: Executive summary.* Washington, DC: U.S. Department of Education, Office of the Under Secretary, Policy and Program Studies Service.

Simeonsson, R. J., McMillen, B. J., McMillen, J. S., & Lollar, D. (2002). *Risk behaviors among middle school students with and without disabilities: The North Carolina Middle School YRBS.* Chapel Hill: University of North Carolina.

Simmons, T., & O'Neill, G. (2000). *Households and families 2000. Census 2000 brief.* Washington, DC: U.S. Census Bureau.

Simpson, R. L., Myles, B. S., Sasso, G. M., & Kamps, D. M. (1997). *Social skills for students with autism.* Arlington, VA: Council for Exceptional Children.

Sinclair, M. F., & Christenson, S. L. (1992). Home-school collaboration: A building block of empowerment. *IMPACT-Feature Issue on Family Empowerment, 5*(2), 12-13.

Singer, G. H. S., & Powers, L. C. (1993). Contributing to resilience in families: An overview. In G. H. S. Singer & L. C. Powers (Eds.), *Families, disability, and empowerment: Active coping skills and strategies for family interventions* (pp. 1-25). Baltimore: Paul H. Brookes.

Sitlington, P., & Clark, G. (2006). *Transition education and services for students with disabilities.* Boston: Allyn & Bacon.

Sitlington, P., Neubert, D., Begun, W., Lombard, R. C., & Leconte, P. (2007). *Assess for success: A practitioner's handbook on transition assessment* (2nd ed.). Thousand Oaks, CA: Corwin Press.

Sitlington, P. L. (1996). Transition to living: The neglected component of transition programming for individuals with learning disabilities. In J. R. Patton & G. Blalock (Eds.), *Transition and students with learning disabilities: Facilitating the movement from school to adult life* (pp. 43-59). Austin, TX: Pro-Ed.

Sitlington, P. L., & Clark, G. M. (2001). Career/vocational assessment: A critical component of transition planning. *Assessment for Effective Intervention, 26*(4), 5-22.

Sitlington, P. L., Clark, G. M., & Kolstoe, O. P. (2000). *Transition education and services for adolescents with disabilities* (3rd ed.). Boston: Allyn & Bacon.

Sitlington, P. L., & Neubert, D. A. (2004). Preparing youth with emotional and behavioral disorders for transition to adult life: Can this be done under No Child Left Behind and Individuals with Disabilities Education Act priorities? *Behavior Disorders, 9*(3), 279-288.

Sitlington, P. L., Neubert, D. A., Begun, W., Lombard, R. C., & Leconte, P. J. (1996). *Assess for success: Handbook on transition assessment.* Arlington, VA: Council for Exceptional Children.

Sitlington, P. L., Neubert, D. A., & Leconte, P. J. (1997). Transition assessment: The position of the division on career development and transition. *Career Development for Exceptional Individuals, 20*(1), 69-79.

Skinner, M. E. (2004). College students with learning disabilities speak out: What it takes to be successful in postsecondary education. *Journal on Postsecondary Education and Disability, 17*(2), 91-104.

Skrtic, T. (1991). *Behind special education: A critical analysis of professional knowledge and school organization.* Denver, CO: Love.

Small, K. (1953). Personality determinants of vocational choice. *Psychological Monographs, 67*(1).

Smink, J., & Schargel, F. P. (2004). *Helping students graduate: A strategic approach to dropout prevention.* Larchmont, NV: Eye on Education, Inc.

Smith, D. (1992). The dynamics of culture. *Treatment Today, 7,* 15.

Smith, F., & Leconte, P. (2004). Universal design for learning: Assuring access and success for all. *VSTE Journal, 19*(1), 25-29. Retrieved July 7, 2007, from http://www.vste.org/publications/journal/attach/vj_1901/vj_1901_05.pdf

Smith, F., & Leconte, P. (2005, Fall/Winter). Universal design for learning: Ensuring access and success for all. *Journal of the Virginia Society for Technology in Education, 19*(1), 25-29.

Smith, J. S. (2006, April). *Similarities and difference in stakeholder perceptions of the transition from middle school.* Paper presentation at the annual meeting of the American Educational Research Association, San Francisco.

Smith, T. (2007, May). Managing the transition to ninth grade in a comprehensive urban high school. *National High School Center*, 1-4.

Smith, T. E. C., Polloway, E., Patton, J. R., & Dowdy, C. A. (2001). *Teaching students with special needs in inclusive settings* (3rd ed.). Boston: Allyn & Bacon.

Smith, T. E. C., Polloway, E., Patton, J. R., & Dowdy, C. A. (2003). *Teaching students with special needs in inclusive settings* (4th ed.). Boston: Allyn & Bacon.

Smith-Davis, J. (1991). *Planned change for personnel development: Strategic planning and the CSPD*. Lexington: University of Kentucky, Mid-South Regional Resource Center.

Smull, M., & Harrison, B. (1992). *Supporting people with severe reputations in the community*. Alexandria, VA: National Association of State Mental Retardation Program Directors.

Smylie, M. A., & Crowson, R. L. (1996). Working within the scripts: Building institutional infrastructure for children's service coordination in schools. *Educational Policy, 10*(1), 3-21.

Snyder, H. N. (2000, November). Juvenile arrests 2000. *Juvenile Justice Bulletin*.

Social Security Administration. (2001). Children Receiving SSI—December 2000 (OP/ORES/DSSA). Baltimore: Author.

Soodac, L. C., & Erwin, E. J. (1995). Parents, professionals, and inclusive education: A call for collaboration. *Journal of Educational and Psychological Consultation, 6*(3), 257-276.

Southeastern Louisiana University. (2000). *The strategic planning process*. Hammond, LA: Office of Institutional Research.

Special demonstration programs, model demonstration projects: Improving the postsecondary and employment outcomes of youth with disabilities.

(2007). *Federal Register, 72*(31), 7427-7430.

Spera, C. (2006). Adolescents' perceptions of parental goals, practices and styles in relation to their motivation and achievement. *Journal of Early Adolescence, 26*(4), 456-490.

Spinks, S. (2002). *Adolescent brains are works in progress: Here's why*. Retrieved August 2, 2005, from http://www.pbs.org/wgbh/pages/frontline/shows/teenbrain/work/adolescsent.html

Spotsylvania County Schools. (2000). *Facilitating successful transition (FAST)*. Spotsylvania County, VA: Author.

Spring, J. (1988). *Conflicts of interest: Politics of American education*. White Plains, NY: Longman.

Spring, J. (2006). *Intersection of cultures: Multicultural education in the United State and the global economy* (3rd ed.). Mahwah, NJ: Lawrence Erlbaum Associates.

SRI International. (2006, November). *Facts from NLTS2: School behavior and disciplinary experiences of youth with disabilities*. Washington, DC: National Center for Special Education Research, Institute of Education Sciences, U.S. Department of Education.

Stainback, S., Stainback, W., & Ayers, B. (1996). Schools as inclusive communities. In W. Stainback & S. Stainback (Eds.), *Controversial issues in special education* (2nd ed., pp. 31-43). Boston: Allyn & Bacon.

Stedman, J. (2003). *The Higher Education Act: Reauthorization status and issues*. Congressional Research Service. Washington, DC: Library of Congress.

Steere, D. E., Rose, E., & Cavaiuolo, D. (2007). *Growing up: Transition to adult life for students with disabilities*. Boston: Pearson/Allyn & Bacon.

Steere, D. E., Wood, R., Pancsofar, E. L., & Butterworth, J. (1990). Outcome-based school-to-work transition planning for students with severe disabilities. *Career Development for Exceptional Individuals, 13*, 57-69.

Steinburg, P., & Baier, S. (2003). *Alderwood middle school makes a difference*. Seattle, WA: New Horizons for Learning.

Stephens, R. D., & Arnette, J. L. (2000). *From the courthouse to the schoolhouse: Making successful transitions*. Washington, DC: U.S. Department of Justice.

Stiker, H. J., & Sayers, W. (2000). *A history of disability*. Minnesota: University of Michigan Press.

Stodden, R. A. (2001). Postsecondary educational supports for students with disabilities: A review and response. *The Journal for Vocational Special Needs Education, 23*, 4-12.

Stodden, R. A., Brown, S. E., Galloway, L. M., Mrazek, S., & Noy, L. (2004). *Essential tools: Interagency transition team development and facilitation*. Minneapolis: University of Minnesota, Institute on Community Integration, National Center on Secondary Education and Transition.

Stodden, R. A., Dowrick, P. W., Gilmore, S., & Galloway, L. (2003). *A review of secondary school factors influencing postschool outcomes for youth with disabilities*. Manuscript submitted for publication.

Stodden, R. A., Galloway, L. M., & Stodden, N. J. (2003). Secondary school curricula issues: Impact on postsecondary students with disabilities. *Exceptional Children, 70*(1), 9-25.

Stodden, R. A., Jones, M. A., & Chang, K. (2002). *Services, supports and accommodations for individuals with disabilities: An analysis across secondary education, post-secondary education and employment*. Honolula: Center on Disability Studies, University of Hawaii at Manoa. Retrieved February 15, 2005, from http://www.rrtc.hawaii.edu/capacity/papers/StoddenJones_formatted.htm

Stoffner, M. F., & Williamson, R. D. (2000). Facilitating student transitions into middle school. *Middle School Journal, 31*(4), 47-51.

Storms, J., O'Leary, E., & Williams, J. (2000). *Transition requirements: A guide for states, districts, schools, universities, and families.* Minneapolis: Western Regional Resource Center, National Network Institute on Community Integration, University of Minnesota.

Story, K., Bates, P., & Hunter, D. (2002). *The road ahead: Transition to adult life for persons with disabilities.* St. Augustine, FL: Training Resource Network.

Strawn, J., & Duke, A. E. (2007). *Updating WIA Title II to help more adult education students gain postsecondary credentials and move up to better jobs.* Washington, DC: Center for Law and Social Policy.

Study Group, Inc. (2007). *An assessment of transition policies and practices in state vocational rehabilitation agencies* (Final draft report). Kill Devil Hills, NC: The Study Group.

Sullivan, H. S. (1953). *The interpersonal theory of psychiatry.* New York: W. W. Norton.

Sum, A., Harrington, P., Bartishevich, C., Fogg, N., Khatiwada, I., Motroni, J., et al. (2003, February). *The hidden crisis in the high school dropout problems of young adults in the U.S.: Recent trends in overall school dropout rates and gender differences in dropout behavior.* Boston: Center for Labor Market Studies, Northeastern University.

Super, D. (1957). *The psychology of careers.* New York: Harper & Row.

Sutherland, J. (1973). *A general systems philosophy for the social and behavioral sciences.* New York: George Braziller.

Sword, C., & Hill, K. (2002, December). Creating mentoring opportunities for youth with disabilities: Issues and suggested strategies. *Issue Brief, 1*(4), 1–5.

Sylwester, R. (2006). Seven areas of the brain that will shift the current behavioral orientation of teaching and learning. *The School Administrator.* Retrieved February 12, 2008 from http://www.aasa.org/publications/saarticledetail.cfm?ItemNumber=7814

Szymanski, E. M., & Hanley-Maxwell, C. (1996). Career development of people with developmental disabilities: An ecological model. *Journal of Rehabilitation, 62,* 48–55.

Szymanski, E. M., & Hershenson, D. B. (1998). Career development of people with disabilities: An ecological model. In R. M. Parker & E. M. Szymanski (Eds.), *Rehabilitation counseling: Basics and beyond* (3rd ed.). Austin, TX: Pro-Ed.

Szymanski, E. M., Hershenson, D. B., Enright, M. S., & Ettinger, J. (1997). Career development theories, constructs, and research: Implications for people with disabilities. In E. M. Szymanski & R. M. Parker (Eds.), *Work and disability: Issues and strategies in career development and job placement.* Austin, TX: Pro-Ed.

Tashie, C., & Jorgensen, C. (1998). *Transition in an era of education reform.* Institute on Disability, University of New Hampshire.

Technical Assistance Alliance for Parent Centers. (2001). *Developing parent leadership: A grant writing manual for community parent resource centers.* Minneapolis, MN: Author.

Technical Assistance on Transition and the Rehabilitation Act. (2007). *Helping families transition to the future: Rehabilitation services administration parent information and training programs outcome data 2005–2006.* Minneapolis, MN: Parent Advocacy Coalition for Educational Rights.

Tepas, J. J. (2004). The national pediatric trauma registry: A legacy of commitment to control of childhood injury. *Seminar on Pediatric Surgery, 13*(2), 126–132.

Terry, P. M. (2007). Empowering teachers as leaders. *National FORUM Journals.* Lake Charles, LA.

Test, D., Mason, C., Hughes, C., Konrad, M., Neale, M., & Wood, W. (2004). Student involvement in individualized education program meetings. *Exceptional Children, 70,* 391–412.

Test, D. W., Aspel, N. P., & Everson, J. M. (2006). *Transition methods for youth with disabilities.* Upper Saddle River, NJ: Pearson.

Test, D. W., Karvonen, M., Wood, W. M., Browder, D., & Algozzine, B. (2000, November/December). Choosing a self-determination curriculum. *Teaching Exceptional Children,* 48–54.

The Internet Nonprofit Center. (2000). *What is strategic planning.* Seattle, WA: Author.

Thoma, C. A. (1999). Supporting student voices in transition planning. *Teaching Exceptional Children, 31*(5), 4–9.

Thoma, C. A., & Wehmeyer, M. L. (2005). Self-determination and the transition to postsecondary education. In E. E. Getzel & P. Wehman (Eds.), *Going to college: Expanding opportunities for people with disabilities* (pp. 49–68). Baltimore: Paul H. Brookes.

Thompson, A. E., & Kaplan, C. A. (1999). Emotionally abused children presenting to child psychiatry clinics. *Child Abuse and Neglect, 23,* 191–196.

Thompson, J. E., & Wehmeyer, M. L. (in press). Historical and legal issues in developmental disabilities. In P. Parette, G. Peterson-Karlan, & R. Rignlaben (Eds.), *Research based and emerging practices in developmental disabilities.* Austin, TX: Pro-Ed.

Thompson, J. R., Fulk, B. M., & Piercy, S. W. (2000). Do individualized transition plans match the postschool projections of students and parents? *Career Development for Exceptional Individuals, 23,* 3–26.

Thuli, K. J., & Hong, E. (1998). *Employer toolkit.* Washington, DC: National Transition Alliance for Youth with Disabilities, Academy for Educational Development.

Thurlow, M. (2002). Accommodations for students with disabilities in high school. *Issue Brief, 1*(1). Minneapolis, MN: University of Minnesota, National Center on Secondary Education and Transition.

Thurlow, M. L., Elliot, J. L., & Ysseldyke, J. E. (1998). *Testing students with disabilities: Practical strategies for complying with district and state requirements.* Thousand Oaks, CA: Corwin Press.

Thurlow, M. L., Sinclair, M. F., & Johnson, D. R. (2002, July). Students with disabilities who drop out of school: Implications for policy and practice. *Issue Brief, 1*(2), 1-7. Minneapolis: University of Minnesota, Institute on Community Integration, National Center on Secondary Education and Transition.

Timmons, J. (2007). Models of collaboration and cost sharing in transition programming. *Information Brief, 6*(1). Minneapolis, MN: National Center on Secondary Education and Transition Institute on Community Integration. Retrieved January 23, 2008, from http://www.ncset.org/publications/viewdesc.asp?id=3447

Timmons, J., Podmostko, M., Bremer, C., Lavin, D., & Wills, J. (2004). *Career planning begins with assessment: A guide for professionals serving youth with educational and career development challenges.* Washington, DC: National Collaborative on Workforce and Disability for Youth, Institute for Educational Leadership. Retrieved January 23, 2008, from http://www.ncwd-youth.info/resources_&_Publications/assessment.html

Tindle, K., Leconte, P., Buchanan, L., & Taymans, J. M. (2005, April). Transition planning: Community mapping as a tool for teachers and students. *Research to Practice Brief, 4*(1).

Togerson, C. W., Miner, C. A., & Shen, H. (2004, January). Developing student competence in self-directed IEPs. *Intervention in School & Clinic, 39*(3), 162-167.

Trainor, A. A. (2005). Self-determination perceptions and behaviors of diverse students with LD during the transition planning process. *Journal of Learning Disabilities, 38*(3), 233-249.

Trueba, H., & Delgado-Gaitan, C. (1988). *Minority achievement and parental support: Academic resocialization through mentoring.* Santa Barbara: University of California.

Trueba, H., Jacobs, L., & Kirton, E. (1990). *Cultural conflict and adaptation: The case of Hmong children in American society.* New York: Falmer.

Turnbull, A., Turnbull, H. R., Erwin, E., & Soodak, L. (2006). *Families, professionals, and exceptionality: Positive outcomes through partnerships and trust* (5th ed.). Upper Saddle River, NJ: Merill/Prentice Hall.

Turnbull, A. P., & Turnbull, H. R. (1997). *Families, professionals, and exceptionality: A special partnership.* Upper Saddle River, NJ: Merrill/Prentice Hall.

Turnbull, H. R., Turnbull, A., & Wehmeyer, M. (2007). *Exceptional lives: Special education in today's schools* (5th ed.). Upper Saddle River, NJ: Merrill/Prentice Hall.

Tyack, D. (1992). Health and social services in public schools: Historical perspectives. *The Future of Children, 2*(1), 19-31.

U.S. Census Bureau. (2000). *Profile of selected social characteristics: 2000. Census 2000.* Retrieved August 10, 2005, from http://factfinder.census.gov/

U.S. Department of Commerce. (2007). *Personal income and outlays.* Washington, DC: Bureau of Economic Analysis. Retrieved January 23, 2008, from http://www.bea.gov/newsreleases/national/pi/pinewsrelease.htm

U.S. Department of Education. (1992). Assistance to states for the education of children with disabilities program and preschool grants for children with disabilities: Final rules. *Federal Register, 57*(208), 48694-48704.

U.S. Department of Education. (2002). *Strategic Plan for 2002-2007.* Washington, DC: Author.

U.S. Department of Education. (2003). *National symposium on learning disabilities in English language learners, October 14-15, 2003: Symposium summary.* Washington, DC: Office of Special Education and Rehabilitative Services.

U.S. Department of Education. (2004a). *Letter to chief state school officers regarding inclusion of students with disabilities in state accountability systems.* Washington, DC: Author.

U.S. Department of Education. (2004b). *2004 National Postsecondary Student Aid Study (NPSAS:04).* Washington, DC: Author.

U.S. Department of Education. (2005a). *Biennial evaluation report to Congress on the implementation of the State Formula Grant (2002-2004), English Language Acquisition, Language Enhancement and Academic Achievement Act (ESEA, title III, part A).* Washington, DC: Author.

U.S. Department of Education. (2005b). *Engagement, academics, social adjustment and independence: The achievements of elementary and middle school students with disabilities.* Washington, DC: Special Education Elementary Longitudinal Study (SEELS), Office of Special Education Programs.

U.S. Department of Education. (2006a). *Raising achievement: Alternative assessments for students with disabilities.* Washington, DC: Author.

U.S. Department of Education. (2006b). *Questions and answers regarding the implementation of the Carl D. Perkins Career and Technical Education Act of 2006.* Non-Regulatory Guidance. Washington, DC: Office of Vocational and Adult Education.

U.S. Department of Education, Office for Civil Rights. (2007a). *Dear parent letter: Transition of students with disabilities.* Washington, DC: Author.

U.S. Department of Education, Office for Civil Rights. (2007b). *Students with disabilities preparing for postsecondary education: Know your rights and responsibilities.* Washington, DC: Author.

U.S. Department of Education, Office of Special Education. (2001). *Twenty-third annual report to congress on the implementation of the Individuals with Disabilities Education Act.* Washington, DC: Author.

U.S. Department of Education, Office of Special Education. (2002). *Twenty-fourth annual report to Congress* on the implementation of the Individuals with Disabilities Education Act. Washington, DC: Author.

U.S. Department of Education, Office of Special Education. (2003). *Twenty-fifth annual report to Congress on the implementation of the Individuals with Disabilities Education Act.* Washington, DC: Author.

U.S. Department of Education, Office of Special Education. (2005a). *Final report on Focus Study IV: Providing access to the general curriculum (December).* Washington, DC: The Study of State and Local Implementation and Impact of the Individuals with Disabilities Education Act (SLI-IDEA).

U.S. Department of Education, Office of Special Education. (2005b). *Twenty-sixth annual report to Congress on the implementation of the Individuals with Disabilities Act.* Washington DC: Author.

U.S. Department of Education, Office of Special Education Programs. (2007). *Secondary transition brief.* Washington, DC: Author.

U.S. Department of Health and Human Services. (2001). *Report of the Surgeon General's conference on children's mental health: A national action agenda.* Rockville, MD: Author.

U.S. Department of Health and Human Services. (2003). *President's New Freedom Commission on Mental Health Final Report: Achieving the promise: Transforming mental health care in America* (DHHS Publication No. SMA-03-3832). Washington, DC: Author.

U.S. Department of Health and Human Services (HHS), Office for Human Research Protection (OHRP). (2001). *Basic definitions for determining when studies meet the definitions of human research, title 45, CFR part 46.* Washington, DC: Author.

U.S. Department of Health, Education, and Welfare. (1977). *Federal policy on education and work.* Washington, DC: U.S. Government Printing Office.

U.S. Department of Labor. (2002). *High school/high tech state grants, 2002 WL 1591618 (F.R.).* Washington, DC: Office of Disability Employment Policy.

U.S. Department of Labor. (2007). *Dictionary of occupational titles.* Retrieved January 23, 2008, from http://www.dol.gov/dol/findit.htm

U.S. Department of Labor, Office of Disability Employment Policy. (2001a). *Accommodating employers with hidden disabilities.* Washington, DC: Author.

U.S. Department of Labor, Office of Disability Employment Policy. (2001b). *Personal assistance services in the workplace.* Washington, DC: Author.

U.S. Department of Labor, Office of Disability Employment Policy. (2004). *Working while disabled: A guide to plans for achieving self-support* (SSA Publication No. 05-11017). Washington, DC: Author.

U.S. Department of Labor, Office of Disability Employment Policy. (2005). *Opening doors to job accommodations.* Washington, DC: Author. Retrieved July 22, 2005, from 7y7y//www.dol.gov/odep/pubs/ek98/jan.htm

U.S. General Accounting Office. (1993). *System-wide education reform: Federal leadership could facilitate district level efforts.* Washington, DC: U.S. Government Printing Office.

U.S. General Accounting Office. (2000, October 10). *At-risk youth: School-community collaborations focus on improving student outcomes* (GAO-01-66). Washington, DC: Author.

U.S. General Accounting Office. (2001, October 4). *Workforce Investment Act: New requirements create need for more guidance* (GAO-02-94T). Washington, DC: Author.

U.S. Government Accountability Office. (2003a). *Federal actions can assist states in improving postsecondary outcomes for youth* (GAO-03-773). Washington, DC: U.S. Government Printing Office.

U.S. Government Accountability Office. (2003b). *College completion: Additional efforts could help education with its completion goals* (GAO-03-568). Washington, DC: U.S. Government Printing Office.

U.S. Government Accountability Office. (2004). *Foster youth: HHS actions could improve coordination of services and monitoring of states' independent living programs* (GAO-05-25). Washington, DC: U.S. Government Printing Office.

U.S. Government Accountability Office. (2005). No Child Left Behind Act: *Education could do more to help states better define graduation rates and improve knowledge about intervention strategies* (GAO-05-879). Washington, DC: U.S. Government Printing Office.

U.S. Office of Special Education. (2005). 27th annual report to congress on the implementation of the Individuals with Disabilities Education Act (Vol.1). Washington, DC: Author.

U.S. Office of Special Education. (2006). *OSERS priorities.* Washington, DC: U.S. Department of Education.

U.S. Office of Special Education Programs. (2006). *Data* Analysis System (DANS), 2006. Washington, DC: U.S. Department of Education.

Unger, K. (1998). *Handbook on supported education: Providing services to students with psychiatric disabilities.* Baltimore: Paul H. Brookes.

Valencia, R. B., & Black, M. S. (2002). Mexican Americans don't value education!—On the basis of the myth, mythmaking, and debunking. *Journal of Latinos and Education, 1*(2), 81–103.

Valle, J., & Aponte, E. (2002). IDEA and collaboration: A Bakhtinian perspective on parent and professional discourse. *Journal of Learning Disabilities, 35*(5), 469–479.

Van Dycke, J., Martin, J., & David, L. (2006). Why is this cake on fire? Inviting students into the IEP process. *Teaching Exceptional Children, 38,* 42–47.

Vandercook, T., & York, J. (1989). The McGill Action Planning System (M.A.P.S.): A strategy for building vision. *Journal of the Association for the Severely Handicapped, 14,* 205-215.

Vaughn, S., Bos, C., & Schumm, J. S. (2003). *Teaching exceptional, diverse and at-risk students in the general education classroom.* Boston: Allyn & Bacon.

Villa, R., Thousand, J., Stainback, W., & Stainback, S. (Eds.). (1992). *Restructuring for caring and effective education: An administrative guide to creating heterogeneous schools.* Baltimore: Paul H. Brookes.

Vinson, N. B., Brannan, A. M., Baughman, L. N., Wilce, M., & Gawron, T. (2001). The system-of-care model: Implementation in twenty-seven communities. *Journal of Emotional and Behavioral Disorders, 9*(1), 30-42.

Virginia Department of Education. (2000). *Virginia state improvement grant.* Richmond, VA: Author.

Virginia Department of Education. (2005). *Guidance document on the implementation of IDEA 2004—part B requirements.* Division of Special Education and Student Services. Richmond, VA: Author.

Volkow, N. (2005). Confronting the rise in abuse of prescription drugs. *National Institute on Drug Abuse Notes, 19*(5), 3.

Von Bertalanffy, L. (1969). *General system theory: Foundations, development, applications.* New York: George Braziller.

Vreeburg-Izzo, M., Hertzfeld, J., Simmons-Reed, E., & Aaron, J. (2001, Winter). Promising practices: Improving the quality of higher education for students with disabilities. *Disability Studies Quarterly, 21* (1).

Vreeburg-Izzo, M., & Kochhar-Bryant, C. (2006, Fall). Implementing the SOP for effective transition: Two case studies. *Career Development for Exceptional Individuals, 29*(2), 100-107.

Wagener, M., & Cameto, R. (2004). The characteristics, experiences, and outcomes of youth with emotional disturbances. *NLTS2 Data Brief, 3*(2). Minneapolis: University of Minnesota, National Center on Secondary Education and Transition.

Wagner, M., Cadwallader, T. W., Newman, L., & Marder, C., with Levine, P., Garza, N., & Cardoso, D. (2003). *Life outside the classroom for youth with disabilities.* Menlo Park, CA: SRI International.

Wagner, M., Cameto, R., & Guzmán, A. M. (2003, June). Who are secondary students in special education today? *NLTS2 Data Brief, 2*(1).

Wagner, M., Cameto, R., & Newman, L. (2003). *Youth with disabilities: A changing population.* Menlo Park, CA: SRI International.

Wagner, M., D'Amico, R., Marder, C., Newman, L., & Blackorby, J. (1992, December). *What happens next? Trends in postschool outcomes of youth with disabilities.* Menlo Park, CA: SRI International.

Wagner, M., & Gomby, D. (2000). Evaluating a statewide school-linked services initiative: California's Healthy Start. In J. M. Marquart & E. Konrad (Eds.), *New directions in program evaluation: Evaluation of human services integration initiatives.* San Francisco: Jossey-Bass.

Wagner, M., Marder, C., & Cardoso, D. (2002). Characteristics of children's households. In M. Wagner, C. Marder, & J. Blackorby with D. Cardoso (Eds.), *The children we serve: The demographic characteristics of elementary and middle school students with disabilities and their households.* Menlo Park, CA: SRI International.

Wagner, M., Newman, L., & Cameto, R. (2004). *Changes over time in the secondary school experiences of students with disabilities.* Menlo Park, CA: SRI International. Retrieved March 21, 2008, http://www.nlts2.org/pdfs/achievement_execsum.pdf

Wagner, M., Newman, L., Cameto, R., Garza, N., & Levine, P. (2005, April). *After high school: A first look at the post-school experiences of youth with disabilities* (SRI Project P11182). Menlo Park, CA: SRI International.

Wagner, M., Newman, L., Cameto, R., & Levine, P. (2005, June). *Changes over time in the early post-school outcomes of youth with disabilities* (SRI Project P11182). Menlo Park, CA: SRI International.

Wagner, M., Newman, L., Cameto, R., & Levine, P. (2006). *The academic achievement and functional performance of youth with disabilities* (NCSER 2006-3000). Menlo Park, CA: SRI International.

Wagner, M., Newman, L., Cameto, R., Levine, P., & Garza, N. (2006, August). *An overview of findings from wave 2 of the National Longitudinal Transition Study-2 (NLTS2).* Menlo Park, CA: SRI International.

Walker, A., Shafer, J., & Liams, M. (2004, Winter). "Not in my classroom": Teacher attitudes toward English language learners in the mainstream classroom. *NABE Journal of Research and Practice, 2*(1), 130-160.

Walker, S. F. (2000, Winter). High-stakes testing: Too much? Too soon? Education Commission of the States. *State Education Leader, 18*(1), 1-22.

Walter, R. (1993). Development of vocational education. In C. S. Anderson & L. C. Ramp (Eds.), *Vocational education in the 1990s. Sourcebook for strategies, methods, and materials* (pp. 1-20). Ann Arbor, MI: Pakken Publications.

Ward, M., & Halloran, W. (1993). Transition issues for the 1990s. *OSERS News in Print, VI*(1), 4-5.

Ward, M. J., & Berry, H. G. (2005, Summer). *Students with disabilities and postsecondary education: A tale of two data sets.* Washington, DC: HEATH Center.

Warren, J., & Edwards, M. (2001, August). *The impact of high stakes graduation tests on school dropout.* Paper presented at the annual meeting of the American Sociological Association, Anaheim, CA.

Washington Department of Education. (2000). *Transition project.* Olympia, WA: Office of the Superintendent of Public Instruction.

Weaver, G. (Ed.). (2000). *Culture, communications and conflict: Readings in intercultural relations*. Boston: Pearson Technology Group.

Webster-Stratton, C. (2003). *The incredible years*. Toronto, Canada: Umbrella Press.

Wehman, P. (1992). Transition for young people with disabilities: Challenges for the 1990's. *Education and Training in Mental Retardation, 27*, 112–118.

Wehman, P. (1996). *Life beyond the classroom: Transition strategies for young people with disabilities* (2nd ed.). Baltimore: Paul H. Brookes.

Wehman, P. (2001). *Life beyond the classroom: Transition strategies for young people with disabilities* (3rd ed.). Baltimore: Paul H. Brookes.

Wehman, P. (2006). *Life beyond the classroom: Transition strategies for young people with disabilities* (4th ed.). Baltimore: Paul H. Brookes.

Wehman, P., Everson, J. M., & Reid, D. H. (2001). Beyond programs and placements: Using person-centered practices to individualize the transition process and outcomes. In P. Wehman (Ed.), *Life beyond the classroom: Transition strategies for young people with disabilities* (3rd ed.). Baltimore: Paul H. Brookes.

Wehman, P., Moon, M. S., Everson, J. M., & Barcus, J. M. (1988). *Transition from school to work: New challenges for youth with severe disabilities*. Baltimore: Paul H. Brookes.

Wehman, P. H., Kregel, J., Barcus, J. M., & Schalock, R. L. (1986). Vocational transition for students with developmental disabilities. In W. E. Kiernan & L. Stark (Eds.), *Pathways to employment for adults with developmental disabilities* (pp. 113–127). Baltimore: Paul H. Brookes.

Wehmeyer, M. (2003). Transition principles and access to the general education curriculum. In C. A. Kochhar-Bryant & D. S. Bassett (Eds.), *Aligning transition and standards-based education: Issues and strategies*. Arlington, VA: Council for Exceptional Children.

Wehmeyer, M. L. (2005). Self-determination and individuals with severe disabilities: Reexamining meanings and misinterpretations. *Research and Practice in Severe Disabilities, 30*, 113–120.

Wehmeyer, M. L. (2006). Universal design for learning, access to the general education curriculum, and students with mild mental retardation. *Exceptionality, 14*, 225–235.

Wehmeyer, M. L., Abery, B., Mithaug, D. E., Powers, L. E., & Stancliffe, R. J. (2003). *Theory in self-determination: Foundations for educational practice*. Springfield, IL: Charles C. Thomas.

Wehmeyer, M. L., & Agran, M. (2006). *Mental retardation and intellectual disabilities: Teaching students with innovative and research-based strategies*. Columbus, OH: Merrill/Prentice Hall.

Wehmeyer, M. L., Agran, M., & Hughes, C. (2000). A national survey of teachers' promotion of self-determination and student-directed learning. *Journal of Special Education, 34*(2), 58–68.

Wehmeyer, M. L., Agran, M., Hughes, C., Martin, J., Mithaug, D. E., & Palmer, S. (2007). *Promoting self-determination and self-determined learning for students with intellectual and developmental disabilities*. New York: Guilford Press.

Wehmeyer, M. L., & Kelchner, K. (1995). *Whose future is it anyway? Student-directed transition planning program*. Austin, TX: The Arc of the United States.

Wehmeyer, M. L., & Schwartz, M. (1998). The relationship between self-determination and quality of life for adults with mental retardation. *Education and Training in Mental Retardation and Developmental Disabilities, 33*(1), 3–11.

Weidenthal, C., & Kochhar-Bryant, C. (2007). An investigation of transition practices for middle school youth. *Career Development for Exceptional Individuals, 30*(3), 147–157.

Welch, M., & Brownell, K. (2002). Are professionals ready for educational partnerships? The evaluation of technology-enhanced course to prepare educators for collaboration. *Teacher Education and Special Education, 25*(2), 133–144.

Wellins, R. S., Byham, W. C., & Wilson, J. M. (1991). *Empowerment teams: Creating self-directed work groups that improve quality, productivity, and participation*. San Francisco: Jossey-Bass.

West, L., Taymans, J., Corbey, S., & Dodge, L. (1994). Summary of a national survey of transition specialists. *Capital connection policy newsletter*. Joint publication of the Division on Career Development. Washington, DC: The George Washington University and Mankato State University.

West, L., Taymans, J. M., & Gopal, M. I. (1997). The curriculum development process: Integrating transition and self-determination at last. *The Journal for Vocational Special Needs Education, 19*(3), 116–122.

What makes workability work? (2004, Summer). *The Special Edge*. Rohnert Park, CA: Sonoma State University, CalSTAT/CIHS.

Whelley, T., Hart, D., & Zafft, C. (2002). *Coordination and management of services and supports for individuals with disabilities from secondary to postsecondary education and employment*, Honolula: National Center for Research on Post-Secondary Education, University of Hawaii.

White, D. L., & Kochhar-Bryant, C. A. (2007, Spring). *Status and contemporary issues in alternative education*. Washington, DC: Hamilton Fish Institute, The George Washington University.

White, J., & Weiner, J. S. (2004). Influence of least restrictive environment and community based training on integrated employment outcomes for transitioning students with severe disabilities. *Journal of Vocational Rehabilitation, 21*, 149–156.

White, P., & Gallay, L. (2005). Youth with special health care needs and disabilities in transition to adulthood. In D. W. Osgood, E. M. Foster, C.

Flanagan, & G. Ruth (Eds.), *On your own without a net: The transitions to adulthood for vulnerable populations*. Chicago: University of Chicago Press.

Wiley, T. G. (2005). *Literacy and language diversity in the United States* (2nd ed.). Baltimore: Center for Applied Linguistics and Delta Systems Co., Inc.

Will, M. (1984). *Bridges from school to working life: Programs for the handicapped*. Washington, DC: The Office of Special Education and Rehabilitative Services, Office of Information and Resources for the Handicapped.

Williams, S. L., Walker, H. M., Todis, B., & Fabre, T. R. (1989). Social validation of adolescent social skills by teachers and students. *Remediation and Special Education, 10*, 18–27.

Wilms, W. W. (1979, Fall). New meanings for vocational education. *UCLA Educator, 21*(1), 5–11.

Wilson, L., & Horch, H. (2004, September). Implications of brain research for teaching young adolescents. *Middle School Journal, 34*(1), 57–61.

Winzer, M. A., & Mazurek, K. (1998). *Special education in multicultural contexts*. Upper Saddle River, NJ: Merrill/Prentice Hall.

Wirt, J., Choy, S. Provasnik, S., Rooney, P., Sen, A., & Tobin, R. (2003). *The conditions of education*. Washington, DC: U.S. Department of Education, Institute for Educational Sciences.

Wolanin, T., & Steele, P. (2004). *Higher education opportunities for students with disabilities*. Washington, DC: The Institute for Higher Education Policy.

Wolfensberger, W. (1972). *The principle of normalization in human services*. Downsview, Ontario, Canada: G. Allan Roeher Institute.

Wolfensberger, W. (1983). *Reflections on the status of citizen advocacy*.

Downsview, Ontario, Canada: National Institute on Mental Retardation.

Wolfensberger, W., & Thomas, S. (1983). *Program analysis of service systems' implementation of normalization goals*. Downsview, Ontario, Canada: National Institute on Mental Retardation.

Woodside, M. R., & McClam, T. (2002). *Generalist case management: A method of human service delivery*. Belmont, CA: Wadsworth Publishing.

Wright, P. W., & Wright, P. D. (2007). *Law is always changing*. Retrieved August 15, 2007, from http://www.wrightslaw.com/

Wynne, J. (2001). Teachers as leaders in education. *ERIC Digest*. Retrieved September 12, 2007, from http://www.eric.ed.gov/ERICDocs/data/ericdocs2sql/content_storage_01/0000019b/80/19/d9/d1.pdf

Wynne, J. (2002). Teachers as leaders in education reform. *ERIC Digest*. Retrieved March 18, 2008, from http://www.ericdigests.org/2002-4/teachers.html

Ylvisaker, M., Adelson, D., & Braga, L. (2005). Rehabilitation and ongoing support after pediatric TBI: Twenty years of progress. *Journal of Head Trauma Rehabilitation, 20*(1), 95–109.

Ysseldyke, J., & Erickson, R. (1997, Winter). *How are you doing?* Washington, DC: Academy for Educational Development.

Ysseldyke, J., Olsen, K., & Thurlow, M. (1997). *NCEO synthesis report 27: Issues and considerations in alternate assessments*. Minneapolis: University of Minnesota.

Ysseldyke, J. E., Thurlow, M. L., Kozleski, E., & Reschly, D. (1998). *Accountability for the results of education students with disabilities*. Minneapolis: National Center for Educational Outcomes, University of

Minnesota, College of Education and Human Development.

Zarrett, N., & Eccles, J. (2006). The passage to adulthood: Challenges of late adolescence. *New Directions for Youth Development, 111*, 13–28.

Zeedyk, M. S., Gallacher, J., Henderson, M., Hope, G., Husband, B., & Lindsay, K. (2003). Negotiating the transition from primary to secondary school: Perceptions of pupils, parents, and teachers. *School Psychology International, 24*(1), 67–79.

Zehler, A. M., Fleischman, H. L., Hopstock, P. J., Pendzick, M. L., & Stephenson, T. G. (2003). *Descriptive study of services to LEP students and LEP students with disabilities, 4, special topic report: Findings on special education LEP students*. Arlington, VA: Development Associates, Inc.

Zhang, D., Ivester, J. G., Chen, L., & Katsiyannis, A. (2005). Perspectives on transition practices. *Career Development for Exceptional Individuals, 28*(1), 15–25.

Zhang, D., Wehmeyer, M., & Chen, L. J. (2005). Parent and teacher engagement in fostering the self-determination of students with disabilities: A comparison between the U.S. and the Republic of China. *Remedial and Special Education, 26*, 55–64.

Zigmond, N., & Miller, S. E. (1992). Improving high school programs for students with learning disabilities: A matter of substance as well as form. In F. R. Rusch, L. DeStefano, J. Chadsey-Rusch, L. A. Phelps, & E. Syzmanski (Eds.), *Transition from school to adult life: Models, linkages, and policy* (pp. 265–283). Sycamore, IL: Sycamore.

Zuckerman, M. (2005). Land of opportunity. *U.S. News and World Report, 138*(23), 64.

Name Index

Subject Index